Additional Praise for *Liturgy as Revelation*

"This work admirably fills a gap in the needed intersection between fundamental and liturgical theology. Offering a profound understanding of four important twentieth-century Catholic theologians (as well as Catholic theology in general since the late nineteenth century), Caldwell makes a fine case that the fundamental truths of revelation, faith, and worship are one."

John F. Baldovin, SJ
Boston College

"Fr. Philip Caldwell's new study *Liturgy as Revelation* comes as a timely contribution to the Church's continuing celebration of the fiftieth anniversary of the Second Vatican Council. It offers fresh insights into the theological method of some of the most significant thinkers and writers to influence the development of the theology and ecclesiology of Vatican II, and it encourages us to a deeper appreciation of the gift of the liturgy in the life and mission of the Church. Informed by Fr. Caldwell's work as a teacher and formator, this book should also prove a useful tool in the context of ecumenical dialogue and reflection."

The Most Rev. Bernard Longley
Archbishop of Birmingham

Liturgy as Revelation

Liturgy as Revelation

Re-Sourcing a Theme in Catholic Theology

Philip Caldwell

Fortress Press
Minneapolis

LITURGY AS REVELATION

Re-Sourcing a Theme in Catholic Theology

Scripture quotations are from the New Revised Standard Version Bible, copyright (c) 1989 by the Division of Christian Education of the National Council of the Churches of Christ in the USA. Used by permission. All rights reserved.

Cover image: Priest at the altar, Francois Marius Granet, Bridgeman-Giraudaon/Art Resource, NY

Cover design: Laurie Ingram

Library of Congress Cataloging-in-Publication Data

Print ISBN: 978-1-4514-8038-2

eBook ISBN: 978-1-4514-8947-7

The paper used in this publication meets the minimum requirements of American National Standard for Information Sciences — Permanence of Paper for Printed Library Materials, ANSI Z329.48-1984.

Manufactured in the U.S.A.

This book was produced using PressBooks.com, and PDF rendering was done by PrinceXML.

To

my mother

Bernice Caldwell

13th September 1933–21st July 2013

Contents

Renewal: Conversations in Catholic Theology

Edited by Lewis Ayres and Medi Ann Volpe

"Continue your search without tiring and without ever despairing of the truth. Recall the words of one of your great friends, St. Augustine: 'Let us seek with the desire to find, and find with the desire to seek still more.' Happy are those who, while possessing the truth, search more earnestly for it in order to renew it, deepen it and transmit it to others. Happy also are those who, not having found it, are working toward it with a sincere heart. May they seek the light of tomorrow with the light of today until they reach the fullness of light. But do not forget that if thinking is something great, it is first a duty.

For this purpose, without troubling your efforts, without dazzling brilliance, we come to offer you the light of our mysterious lamp which is faith. He who entrusted this lamp to us is the sovereign Master of all thought, He whose humble disciples we are, the only one who said and could have said: 'I am the light of the world, I am the way, the truth and the life.'"

These words are from the Second Vatican Council's closing message to Thinkers and Scientists delivered on 8th December 1965. While they were addressed first to those beyond the Church, they can and should speak to us all. These words remind us well of the importance and the duty of thinking as a bringing toward the light of reason that which may be known and a showing to reason of the resources we have received in faith. In this call to those beyond the Church's boundaries is hidden one of Vatican II's great charges to those within the Church: the charge to think for renewal using all the resources we can appropriately bring to bear.

"Renewal" is a series of books offered in aid of contemporary Catholic conversation, although readers of theology across the ecumenical spectrum will find them stimulating and rewarding. The series will offer resources that seek to further the work of the Council, exploring, excavating, explaining aspects of the faith that we have inherited. Some volumes in the series will have a strongly historical focus, excavating old treasures in order to aid us now; these may concern figures from our Patristic or Medieval heritage, while others will focus on figures more proximate in time. Some books will be primarily in constructive mode, bringing forward treasures that are new. Theologians or themes well-known and under-studied, those who shaped the distinctive emphases of Vatican II as well as those whose theologies represent different modes of taking forward the Council's agenda: all will be welcome who seek to aid the flourishing of the Catholic conversation.

Acknowledgements

For the initial inspiration of this study and for encouragement in the early stages, my thanks must go to Dom. Jeremy Driscoll, OSB, of the Pontifical Institute of St Anselmo. The course he taught on Liturgy and the Theology of Revelation at the Gregorian University in the summer term of 1996 first engaged my interest in this topic.

Sustaining these initial ideas and shaping them into a coherent whole would never have been possible without the loving support and theological expertise of Fr. Philip J. Rosato, SJ, my doctoral supervisor. Likewise, without the assistance, advice and encouragement of Professor Lewis Ayers the work wouldn't have been reshaped and published.

Three different communities have helped to bring this book about: The Venerable English College, Rome; St Cuthbert's, Ushaw; and St. Mary's College, Oscott—now my own seminary in two senses. I thank the rectors, staff and seminarians who have worked with me in each place. Mgr. Mark Crisp, the previous Rector of Oscott, deserves my particular thanks, as do the present staff and seminarians here, for the patience and support they showed as this project came to completion. Specifically, I would like to express my appreciation to the Dean of Studies, Fr. John Flynn, and to the Dean of Philosophy, Fr. Paul Moss, for their friendship and encouragement.

I'm particularly grateful for the opportunity to state special appreciation to my ordinary, Bishop Terence J. Brain of Salford, who has been more than generous in releasing me to work outside the diocese and who has always encouraged me in the work of priestly formation. Similarly, I welcome the chance to thank Archbishop Bernard Longley for inviting me to work in his seminary and for the confidence he has placed in me as a teacher and formator.

In addition to the help of Michael Gibson, Lisa Gruenisen, and the team at Fortress, the sustained support of a wider network of friends and family was invaluable in the long journey to publication. Particular mention must be made of the Sisters of Mercy, Sunderland, especially Sr. M. Calasanctius, of my diocesan brother, Fr. Brendan Curley, Dr. Medi Ann Volpe, Miss Marjorie Wood, Ms. M. M. Bennett, Ms. Harriet Powney and Mr. and Mrs. Paul and Barbara Mason. Of course, the loving support of my brothers and sisters and their families cannot go without mention and has never been taken for granted. Above all others, I would like to thank my father, Gerard Caldwell, for his patience, love and quiet encouragement: he and my mother were, together, the first and best teachers of faith.

Since this work first began to take shape, a number of those most significant in its coming to light have gone to their eternal reward. At first, one is tempted to regret their not being here to see the finished article and to read how important they were to its generation. But it was one of these who, through a most moving passage of patristic literature, taught me that even the beatific vision itself will not quench the loving interest of our friends and family. Saint Augustine confidently states of his friend Nebridius,

> Nebridius now rests in Abraham's bosom. Whatever may be meant by this, there dwells my own Nebridius, my dear friend. There he lives on. … He no longer waits for words from my lips, but his own lips stoop to heavenly springs, to unending bliss. Yet I do not believe that this

will satiate him to the point of forgetting me, since you, Lord, at whose source he drinks, are mindful of us all.[1]

It's with such confidence in the resurrection that I am mindful of Fr. John J. O'Donnell, SJ, my friend Fr. Philip J. Rosato, SJ, and Bernice Caldwell, my mother. With love and gratitude, this book is dedicated to her.

Feast of the Presentation of the Lord 2014

* * *

The following texts are quoted at length in this book. I thank the publishers for their permission to reprint the material here.

© Réné Latourelle, 1966, *Theology of Revelation*, Alba House reproduced with permission of St Paul's Publications, Alba House, New York.

© Réné Latourelle, 1972, *Christ and the Church: Signs of Salvation*, Alba House reproduced with permission of St Paul's Publications, Alba House, new York.

© Réné Latourelle, 1988, *The Miracles of Jesus and the Theology of Miracles*, Reproduced with permission of Paulist Press, New York.

© Réné Latourelle, 1966, *Théologie de la Révélation*, Desclée Brouwer, reproduced with permission of Groupe Artège – DDB

© Réné Latourelle, 1986, *Miracles de Jésus et théologie du miracle*, reproduced with permission of Éditions du Cerf, Paris

Exerpts from *Models of the Church* by Avery Dulles, copyright © 1974 by Avery Dulles. Used by permission of Doubleday, an imprint of the Knopf Doubleday Publishing Group, a division of Random House LLC. All rights reserved.

---

1. St Augustine,*Confessions*, IX, 3.

Abbreviations

AAS	*Acta Apostolicae Sedis*, Città del Vaticano
AA. VV.	various authors
ASS	*Acta Sanctae Sedis*, Città del Vaticano
CCC	*Catechism of the Catholic Church*. London: Geoffrey Chapman, 1994.
DS	H. Denzinger and A. Schönmetzer. *Enchiridion Symbolorum Definitionum et Declarationum*.33rd ed. Freiburg im Breisgau, 1965
DV	*Dei Verbum*, Dogmatic Constitution of Vatican Council II on Divine Revelation
GS	*Gaudium et Spes*, Pastoral Constitution of Vatican Council II on the Church in the Modern World
LG	*Lumen Gentium*, Dogmatic Constitution of Vatican Council II on the Church
[21][23*]	Where the pagination of a Second Vatican Council document appears in square brackets, the version used is the parallel text of N. Tanner, ed. *Decrees of the Ecumenical Councils*. Vol. 2: *Trent–Vatican II*. London: Sheed and Ward, 1990. Asterisked numeration indicates the Latin text.
ND	J. Neuner and J. Dupuis, ed. *The Christian Faith in the Doctrinal Documents of the Catholic Church*. New York: Alba House, 1996.
PIL	Pontificio Istituto Liturgico, Rome
PUG	Pontificia Università Gregoriana, Rome
SC	*Sacrosanctum Concilium*, Dogmatic Constitution of Vatican Council II on the Sacred Liturgy
ST	St. Thomas Aquinas, *Summa Theologiae*. London: Blackfriars edition

Introduction

Sometimes where one "is at" can reveal an interesting and fruitful point of departure for reflection, and such proved true for this study. The thesis that eventually gave rise to the present book was finalized at Ushaw College,[1] the then-senior seminary for the Catholic dioceses of the north of England, founded in 1808. It was St. Cuthbert's College, Ushaw, that, if in nothing other than its annals, was responsible for the meeting of two men of very different sensibilities and perspectives: Rafael Merry Del Val, Cardinal Secretary of State to Pius X, and the poet Francis Thompson. Being at Ushaw, conscious of a rich heritage as well as of the acute pastoral situation for which the college trained priests, provided a constructive environment for the specific issue under examination. The juxtaposition of these two alumni does not merely offer a personal dimension to the nineteenth-century setting in which the parameters of our question first emerged with any clarity. To compare and contrast these characters provides both the limits of our problem and a hint at its resolution.

To explain why Pedro José de Zulueta, the maternal grandfather of the future Cardinal Del Val, had "joined the Church of England and married a Scottish lady" of rigid evangelical stock, F. A. Forbes cites

1. Cf. D. Milburn, *A History of Ushaw College* (Durham: Northumberland, 1964).

the influence of a rationalistic cousin and the freedom that England offered "to be a good Christian though not a Catholic."[2] Perhaps more to the point was the fact that England much preferred good Christians to Catholics. It was almost thirty years after his arrival in London that De Zulueta witnessed the restoration of the Catholic hierarchy in 1850, and some twenty-five years after that, John Henry Newman still had to plead insistently, against William Gladstone's suspicions of sedition, that it was possible to be a faithful citizen of both Britain and the Church of Rome. Less than a decade after this infamous *Letter to the Duke of Norfolk*,[3] Merry Del Val began his education at Ushaw.

The college stands six miles outside Durham on open moorland, and its position and design had the deliberate purpose of secluding a life that, so soon after emancipation, needed to be protected and remote from the outside world. On the development of Merry Del Val, Gary Lease makes much of the fact that "in short, the Catholic Church in England felt itself to be a distinct minority and one under implied, if not always open, attack from the anti-Roman Anglican majority."[4]

Such a formation as Del Val received instilled "the quasi-paranoia"[5] that permeated the English Catholic Church at the end of the nineteenth and beginning of the twentieth centuries.[6] Under

---

2. F. A. Forbes, *Rafael Cardinal Merry Del Val: A Character Sketch* (London: Longmans, Green and Co., 1932), 12.

3. J. H. Newman, *A Letter Addressed to His Grace the Duke of Norfolk, on Occasion of Mr Gladstone's Recent Expostulation, by John Henry Newman D.D., of the Oratory* (London 1875) reprinted in J. H. Newman, *Certain Difficulties Felt by Anglicans in Catholic Teaching Considered*, vol. 2 (London: Longmans, Green and Co., 1879), 171–378. See also F. Kerr, "Did Newman Answer Gladstone?" in *John Henry Newman: Reason, Rhetoric and Romanticism*, ed. D. Nicholls and F. Kerr (Bristol: Bristol, 1991), 135–52.

4. G. Lease, "Merry Del Val and Tyrrell: A Modernist Struggle," *The Downside Review* 102 (1984): 133.

5. Ibid.

6. For a fuller account of the state of English Catholicism at the turn of the century, see J. J. Hughes, *Absolutely Null and Utterly Void* (London: Sheed and Ward, 1968), 227–42.

suspicion, and self-consciously at odds with society, ultramontanism was a natural response: a siege survival shored up by fierce obedience to, and dependence upon, an unquestionable external authority. Though deeply influential, Merry Del Val's stay at Ushaw College was largely uneventful. Ironically, biographers attest to his widening of the playing courts,[7] when in fact what was being marked out was the beginning of an energetic defense of church teaching based on a penetrating but narrow formation. Surely, the theological parameters clearly and firmly set by this early education at Ushaw cannot be regarded as insignificant in any estimation of Del Val's part in the subsequent playing out of the Modernist crisis.

Once at the Vatican's Accademia dei Nobili Ecclesiastici, the propaedeutic work of the English seminary became a sure foundation for a thoroughly Roman schooling under the Jesuit neo-Scholastic Louis Billot.[8] Reacting against Modernism, this Gregorian University professor minimized the experiential component of assent, and dwelt predominantly on the transcendence of God, while accentuating, if not exaggerating, the role of the authoritative demand of revelation on the intellect and will in the act of faith. Such components were obviously conducive to an ultramontane mind, as was the appeal of a scholastic style to a sharp, perceptive, if unimaginative intellect.[9]

---

7. Cf. Forbes, *Rafael Cardinal Merry Del Val*, 22; M. C. Buehrle, *Rafael Cardinal Merry Del Val* (Milwaukee: Bruce, 1957), 15.

8. For a concise summary of Louis Billot's thought, see A. Dulles, *The Assurance of Things Hoped For: A Theology of Christian Faith* (Oxford: Oxford University Press, 1994), 104–7.

9. "Louis Billot, who came to the Gregorian in 1885, was a striking contrast to the drab background of mediocrity in Roman theology. Billot was a brilliant metaphysician who possessed an extensive and profound knowledge of St. Thomas. Billot could not only understand the principles of St. Thomas' metaphysical theology, but he could extend them to meet new problems through the deductive conclusions of his speculative theology. The influence which Billot exerted on Catholic theology through his published works and through the presence of his former students in seminaries and scholasticates throughout the world was enormous. Billot was the first of the great Thomistic speculative theologians." G. McCool, *Catholic Theology in the Nineteenth Century: The Quest for a Unitary Method* (New York: Seabury, 1977), 239. Interestingly, George Tyrrell was an enthusiastic champion of Billot during his early Thomistic period, impressed by his critical and independent treatment of

Yet perhaps most attractive in the thought of the professor later rumored to be coauthor of the theological sections of *Pascendi*,[10] and who sought to give the education of John Henry Newman a certain scholastic *romanità*, was an understanding of the fiduciary act as personal obedience to authority and the sense of faith as simple homage. Whether one chooses to paint Del Val as the rigid, intransigent, and uncompromising secretary of state; a convenient foil to a gentle, saintly pope; or as the unswervingly loyal executor of wise decrees that saved the Church from greater perils, he was appropriately formed to his task.[11]

Though Henry Gillow, professor of theology throughout the time of Thompson and Merry Del Val at Ushaw, remained a determined upholder of neo-scholasticism against later interpretations and those advocating a return to the primary sources, it was not the subtle technicalities of the syllogism that awed the young and future poet:[12]

> The boy who at home had demanded to wear a red and purple cassock now responded more fully than he knew at the time to the greater beauties of the Ushaw ceremonial. Here was poetry of the highest order complemented and completed by the movement and the colour of the rites themselves. And here, therefore, was nourishment for the poetry to come, drawing on his own inborn sense of pattern and order in arousing his awareness of the ordered pattern uniting the visual and verbal symbolism of the liturgy—which in turn is the formal expression of the cyclical rhythm uniting natural with human life in accordance with a supernatural pattern.[13]

Aquinas. See G. Daly, *Transcendence and Immanence: A Study in Catholic Modernism and Integralism* (Oxford: Clarendon, 1980), 15.

10. M. R. O'Connell, *Critics on Trial: An Introduction to the Catholic Modernist Crisis* (Washington, DC: Catholic University of America, 1994), 341.

11. Cf. Forbes, *Rafael Cardinal Merry Del Val*, 1–2.

12. For biographical background and some analysis of his work, see E. Meynell, *The Life of Francis Thompson* 2nd ed. (London: Burns Oates & Washbourne, 1925); J. C. Reed, *Francis Thompson: Man and Poet* (London: Routledge & Kegan Paul, 1959); P. van Kuykendall Thomson, *Francis Thompson: A Critical Biography* (Edinburgh: Thomas Nelson & Sons, 1961).

13. B. Boardman, *Between Heaven and Charing Cross: The Life of Francis Thompson* (London: Yale University Press, 1988), 27.

Though easily contrasted and perhaps somewhat caricatured, the response to the world and to faith that their alma mater shaped in these two men was most likely born of a common root—the skeptical preoccupation of the nineteenth century with discerning the self-revelation of God. Echoing Matthew Arnold, J. Hillis Miller gives a telling description of the time:

> The lines of connection between us and God have broken down, or God himself has slipped away from the places where he used to be. He no longer inheres in the world as the force binding together all men and all things. As a result the nineteenth and twentieth centuries seem to many writers a time when God is no more present and not yet again present, and can only be experienced negatively, as a terrifying absence. In this time of the no longer and the not yet, man is "Wandering between two worlds, one dead,/ The other powerless to be born."[14]

The ways in which these two tried to reestablish connection were very different, but, in discerning their particular paths, the extremes and limits of alternative routes can be acknowledged and a via media perhaps emerge. Those who Marvin O'Connell refers to as the "strong men in the papal entourage"[15] believed that the line of connection that clearly and irrefutably opened up the communication of God's self-revelation was neo-scholastic metaphysical philosophy, and their case should not be dismissed out of hand. As Austin Farrer makes clear in a most interesting series of sermons given as the Bampton Lectures of 1948, and later collected under the title of *The Glass of Vision*:

> To reject metaphysics is equivalent to saying that there are no serious questions for the human mind except those which fall under the special

14. J. Hillis Miller, *The Disappearance of God: Four Nineteenth-Century Writers* (London: Oxford University Press, 1963), 2.

15. "The strong men in the papal entourage—Merry Del Val, Gaetano de Lai (a cardinal in 1907), Louis Billot (a cardinal in 1911)—were all convinced that Modernism posed an imminent and mortal threat to the Church." O'Connell, *Critics on Trial*, 360.

sciences. We can ask historically why the crucifixion of Christ came about: physiologically, whether he died of heart-failure or of some other cause: psychologically what train of thoughts and feeling induced him to put his neck into the noose: morally, how his action squared with a copy-book of ethical imperatives. But we cannot consider what in itself, in its intensity and elevation of being, in its divinity, the voluntary passion of Christ was. We have a first interest in keeping this road unblocked, the road by which a serious and realistic wonder advances through the contemplation of Christ's manhood into the adoration of his deity, that it may lay hold upon the eternal Son, who, hanging on the Cross, is enthroned in Heaven; who, lying in the sepulchre, lies in the bosom of the Father; and standing in the upper room, breathes forth from the heart of all being the Paraclete, the Holy Ghost.[16]

Yet the important qualification to be made is that the metaphysics to which Farrer refers here and that which Merry Del Val learned from Billot are quite distinct. The system of this great and highly influential neo-Thomist was *exclusively* metaphysical, with Scripture, exegesis, and a sense of history lending almost nothing to his argumentation[17]—a logical appeal to the intellect reigning supreme. And yet, if it is of primary interest to keep this way unblocked, the means of progressing along it would seem to be another matter altogether. While it has already been suggested that the nineteenth-century mind struggled to assert belief in a positive revelation due to the perception of God's absence,[18] as underscored in the encyclical

---

16. A. Farrer, *The Glass of Vision* (Westminster: Dacre, 1948), 78.

17. "But the trouble was that Billot was an exclusively metaphysical and speculative theologian. He had no feel for history and showed little interest in it. Scripture, exegesis, and positive theology were played down in his teaching and in his writing." McCool, *Catholic Theology in the Nineteenth Century*, 239.

18. Here we might even call to mind the well-known passage of *An Essay in Aid of a Grammar of Assent* (1870) as a fitting example: "He has made this path of thought rugged and circuitous above other investigations, that the very discipline inflicted on our minds in finding Him may mould them in due devotion to Him when He is found. 'Verily, Thou art a hidden God, the God of Israel, the Saviour,' is the very law of his dealings with us. Certainly we need a clue into the labyrinth which is to lead us to Him; and who among us can hope to seize upon the true starting-points of thought for that enterprise." J. H. Newman, *An Essay in Aid of a Grammar of Assent* (New York: Doubleday, 1955), 276. And, for a useful reflection on this point, see A.

Pascendi dominici gregis,[19] the following assertion may seem strange: the excesses of a merely cognitive metaphysic, as of an indulgently immanentist method, are equally the product of agnosticism. As the great English Dominican Vincent McNabb makes clear in his essay on Francis Thompson,

> Now agnosticism, psychologically speaking, is the offspring of intelligence divorced from truth and conscience unacquainted with the commandment. Agnosticism is logic lacking emotion and logic is the antipodes of poetry. Therefore as a matter of history agnosticism has always made a good pleader and an indifferent poet: for the reason that it is rhetoric and logic rather than poetry. Between logic and poetry lies the great world of life, over against which the authentic poet sits, a spectator of all time and all existence.[20]

The privileged position of the poet allows a perspective on the great world of life that reveals "the ways of God to men."[21]

In choosing to "start further back," the new theologians of the late nineteenth and early twentieth centuries recognised that a historical consciousness would open up the riches of the whole tradition, so that metaphysics could be expanded and enriched by biblical and patristic

Nichols, "John Henry Newman and the Illative Sense," in *A Grammar of Consent: The Existence of God in Christian Tradition* (Edinburgh: T. & T. Clark, 1991), 19–38.

19. "Modernists place the foundation of religious philosophy in that doctrine which is commonly called *Agnosticism*. According to this teaching human reason is confined entirely within the field of *phenomena*, that is to say, to things that appear, and in the manner in which they appear: it has neither the right nor the power to overstep these limits" ("Philospiae religiosae fundamentum in doctrina illa modernistae ponunt, quam vulgo *agnosticismum* vocant. Vi huius humana ratio *phaenomenis* omnino includitur, rebus videlicet quae apparent eâque specie qua apparent: earumdem praetergredi terminus nec potestatem habet.") Pius X, *Pascendi Dominici Gregis*, in *ASS* 40 (1907): 597. English trans. in B. Reardon, *Roman Catholic Modernism* (London: Adam and Charles Black, 1970), 237–42.

20. V. McNabb, *Francis Thompson and Other Essays* (London: Blackfriars, 1955), 11.

21. "... while it pursues/ Things unattempted yet in prose or rhyme./ And chiefly thou, O Spirit, that dost prefer/ Before all temples th' upright heart and pure,/ Instruct me, for thou know'st; thou from the first/ Wast present, and with mighty wings outspread/ Dove-like sat'st brooding on the vast abyss/ And mad'st it pregnant: what in me is dark/ Illumine, what is low raise and support;/ That to the highth of this great argument/ I may assert Eternal Providence,/ And justify the ways of God to men." John Milton, "Paradise Lost, Book I," in *Milton: Poetical Works*, ed. D. Bush, 2nd ed. (Oxford: Oxford University Press, 1973), 212–13.

insights. In *The Glass of Vision*, Farrer is conscious of how Scripture, metaphysics, and poetry rub together in the mind and "seem to kindle one another,"[22] forming the light of revelation that ignites faith. The insight or "inscape"[23] of the poet is to see that the ascent to God, and more importantly his descent to us, occurs by means of symbol.[24] For the architects of the early Christian tradition, this fact was ever present and all pervasive, and nowhere was it expressed more clearly than in the celebration of the Eucharist:

> The Eucharist was the archetype of the divine analogy whereby created things participated in the supernatural reality they signified. Poetry in turn was, in one way or another, modelled on sacramental or scriptural language. The words of the poem incarnated the things they named, just as the words of the Mass shared in the transformation they evoked. The symbols and metaphors of poetry were no mere inventions of the poets. They were borrowed from the divine analogies of nature. Poetry was meaningful in the same way as nature itself—by a communion of the verbal symbols with the reality they named.[25]

22. Farrer, *The Glass of Vision*, ix.

23. This is a term particularly associated with the Scotist aesthetics expressed in the poetry of the nineteenth-century English Jesuit G. M. Hopkins. Christopher Devlin gives a useful definition of the concept: "In 'inscape' . . . there is a momentary contact between the Creative Agent who *causes* habitual knowing in me, and the created individual who terminates it in my actual insight. And the medium of this contact, if I am correct, is the *species specialissima*, the dynamic image of nature being created. In easier language: the poet, if the original motion of his mind is unimpeded, does perhaps see things for a moment as God sees them." Quoted in P. Ballinger, *The Poem as Sacrament: The Theological Aesthetic of Gerard Manley Hopkins* (Louvain: Peeters, 2000), 130.

24. "Man cannot conceive it [revelation] except in images; and these images must be divinely given to him, if he is to know a supernatural divine act. The images began to be given by Jesus Christ; the work was continued by the Spirit of Christ moving in the minds of the Apostles. It was possible for Christ and the Apostles to use the images meaningfully, because the old archetypes were there to hand, already half transformed under the leading of God in the expectant faith of Israel. Christ clothed himself in the archetypal images, and then began to do and to suffer. The images were further transformed by what Christ suffered and did when he put them on: they were transformed also by their all being combined in his one person. What sort of victorious David can it be, who is also the martyred Israel and the Lamb of sacrifice? What sort of new Adam can it be, who is also the temple of God? And what sort of living temple can it be, who is also the Word of God whereby the world was made?" Farrer, *The Glass of Vision*, 109.

25. Miller, *The Disappearance of God*, 3.

This was why witnessing the sacred mysteries in St. Cuthbert's Chapel, Ushaw, had such a deep effect on the young Francis Thompson. It was there that he first saw "shine the traffic of Jacob's ladder": symbols "pitched betwixt" that would eventually be the means of reconnecting "Heaven and Charing Cross."[26] And here it is to light upon the mode and means of meeting between transcendence and immanence for which many in the modern era have searched.[27] In fact, there could be no better example in modern poetry of the imperative of symbol in the communication of divine revelation than the man who fled the Hound of Heaven.[28] He surely is the nineteenth-century version of Farrer's Jeremiah:

> If we accept Jeremiah's own assumptions, all is plain. What constrains his images is the particular self-fulfiling will of God, perceptible in the external events of history and nature which God controls, perceptible also in the direct impact upon Jeremiah's inspired mind. If we are not prepared to believe in the perceptibly expressed particular divine will, we can still make some sense of Jeremiah's poetry, so long as we grant an eternal creative act from which the creature cannot escape. If we grant that the self-will of the creature can be experienced by the creature as a straining of its bond with the creative act, then we can say that the prophet dramatizes the ineluctable hold of the creator, and the self-punishment of our rebellions; he casts into personal and

---

26. "But (when so sad thou canst not sadder)/ Cry;- and upon thy so sore loss/ Shall shine the traffic of Jacob's ladder/ Pitched betwixt Heaven and Charing Cross." From "The Kingdom of God: In No Strange Land," in *The Works of Francis Thompson, Poems*, vol. 2, ed. W. Meynell (London: Burns Oates & Washbourne, 1913), 226.

27. One cannot but think here of the theological aesthetic of Hans Urs von Balthasar, who maintains without compromise that the means of reconnecting with the data of revelation is an acknowledgement of primal transcendent beauty, which directly reflects the glory of the Lord. "If theology ignores, banishes or excludes beauty from its method it deprives itself of an essential element of the Christian faith." Cf. J. Coulson, "Hans Urs von Balthasar: Bringing Beauty Back to Faith," in *The Critical Spirit and the Will to Believe: Essays in Nineteenth Century Literature and Religion*, ed. D. Jasper and T. R. Wright (London: Macmillan, 1989), 220.

28. "Adown Titanic glooms of chasmèd fears,/ From those strong feet that followed, followed after./ But with unhurrying chase,/ And unperturbèd pace,/ Deliberate speed, majestic instancy,/ They beat—and a Voice beat/ More instant than the Feet—/ 'All things betray thee, who betrayest Me.'" From "The Hound of Heaven," in *The Works of Francis Thompson, Poems*, vol. 1, ed. W. Meynell (London: Burns Oates & Washbourne, 1913), 107.

mythological form the ever varying revenges of eternal Truth upon our restless infidelities.[29]

And thus, by way of the broad brushstrokes of this introductory sketch, do we arrive at the core question of the book: the symbolic actualization of divine revelation in the liturgy of the church. For now we have centered on the straining bond by which the prophet dramatizes in symbol the hold of the Creator on his creation, which is at once his judgment on the world. Philosopher and poet have brought us to the prophet, who at last is fulfilled in Christ, whose unique repetition of the Jewish prophetic act or $\bar{o}t$ seals the union between his risen body and the sacramental symbols of the church.[30]

In following Gallagher's injunction[31] concerning our point of departure, we have in fact arrived at a point that allows the sacraments to be envisaged as symbols that have the credibility demanded by the people of today:

> Highlighting the parallel between the uses of $\bar{o}t$ by Jesus and by the Church can be of aid in presenting the commemorative, ethical and prognostic aspects of Christian ritual to modern persons who might be searching for some ultimate rationale of their attempts to be just and fraternal towards others. People usually perform such moral behavior spontaneously in particular acts throughout life, but occasionally they reflect on whether these apparently passing acts might enjoy an ontic and lasting character.[32]

---

29. Farrer, *The Glass of Vision*, 125.
30. "Exegetical, liturgical and systematic theologians have pointed out that, as at once commemorative and prognostic acts, the sacraments have their roots in Jesus' use not only of the *zikkaron*, or memorial, but also of the *ōt*, or prophetic act, two complex components of Jewish religious symbolism." See P. J. Rosato, "The Prophetic Acts of Jesus: The Sacraments and the Kingdom," in *Gottes Zukunft--Zukunft der Welt, Festschrift für Jürgen Moltmann zum 60. Geburtstag*, ed. H. Deuser, et al. (Munich: Chr. Kaiser, 1986), 59, 59–67.
31. "'Start further back' meant not jumping into doctrinal language too early, or more positively, paying attention to the soil of experience into which the Sower has to sow today." M. P. Gallagher, *Dive Deeper: The Human Poetry of Faith* (London: Darton, Longman and Todd, 2001), 3.
32. Rosato, "The Prophetic Acts of Jesus," 64.

10

Yet, in bringing together what is essentially fundamental theology and liturgy, this end is also a beginning. In settling on symbol as the key element of inquiry, we must now look to what insights the developments of the past might give to the scope and nature of our question, and what particular avenues might yield a fruitful response.

The first effort to start further back was the shift from neo-scholasticism and the search for a broader basis to the theological pursuit in biblical and patristic thought-patterns. This return to the sources was, in fact, a reappropriation of the whole *loci theologici*, yet within this a special appreciation of the role of the liturgy in shaping the symbols of faith was apparent. Thus the focus of the first chapter of this book will be a historicoalcritical examination of the pontificate of Leo XIII and its heritage for modern theology, especially as that is expressed in the liturgical movement and the *nouvelle théologie*.

In itself, this multifaceted movement was an effort to start further back with the natural, anthropological, and personal categories that are fundamental to human communication. Yet, inevitably, within the Christian memory all words begin and have their origin with the Word, who was, in the fullness of time, made flesh in Jesus Christ. In essence, then, the whole of the *ressourcement* is simply an effort to start with Christ. The second chapter of the book will therefore focus on the work of the French-Canadian Jesuit, René Latourelle, whose work as a fundamental theologian straddles the Second Vatican Council and focuses on the christological basis of the signs of revelation.

The third chapter will develop this line of inquiry from an ecclesiological perspective, while examining more thoroughly the notion of symbol and its significance within postcritical theology. Again, the focus will be the works of a Jesuit fundamental theologian, Avery Dulles, who, though roughly contemporary with and hailing from the same continent as Latourelle, uses the more fluid, open, and eclectic methods of the New World, thus offering a contrast to the largely European influences to which Latourelle is subject. Nevertheless, the affinity between the two writers is such as to form a natural development between the second and third sections of the work.

The works of the Italian Benedictine Salvatore Marsili allow chapter 4 to make a distinct and obvious contrast to preceding sections. Though writing in the European context roughly contemporary with and geographically proximate to Latourelle, Marsili offers a unique contribution from his particular liturgical stance. The monastic approach to theology, undoubtedly shaped by the rhythms of daily worship, does contribute an obvious foil to the cerebral, blackboard science of the Jesuits, and it opens up an entirely different perspective from which to examine the question.

Yet finally, it is to another member of the Society that we turn in chapter 5. A French dogmatician, Council *peritus* and teacher at the famous Jesuit house at Lyons-Fouvière, Gustave Martelet has both experiences in common and a privileged particularity in order to give contrast and depth to the study as a whole. That is, he provides a singular response to the circumstances and events that were common to each writer.

Thus, by way of four writers, the fundamental aspects of this study have been selected: a work of historical perspective that seeks to reinterpret the connections between the aboriginal revelation of the historical Jesus and its persistence in the sacraments of the church today according to the christological, symbolic, liturgical, and anthropological insights that have emerged from Vatican II. In this, René Latourelle, Avery Dulles, Salvatore Marsili, and Gustave Martelet will be our expository guides, so that a final chapter can both synthesize and speculate on the elements of the discussion entered into. Hence the volume will be divided into three parts. The first will comprise a historical overview, which will focus on the emergence of the major themes of the book in the period directly prior to that in which the chosen authors worked. The second part will be expository, concentrating on a presentation and analysis of selected texts by these theologians, and the final part will be evaluative, indicating the significant contributions made and pointing out certain prospectives that are likely to be significant in the further development of this question.

Finally, a note should be made as to translations. Wherever an English version of one of the selected texts is available, this has been used in conjunction with the original language edition. When unacknowledged translations are given in the main text and notes, they are to be understood as coming from the English translation referenced in the bibliography. Where an English edition is not available or significant changes have been deemed necessary, I acknowledge such translations as my own.

PART I

The Historical-Theological Background and Major Themes

1

Overtures for Change

In the nineteenth century, various themes arose to prominence within the mind of the church. Some surfaced from within, by the natural process of maturation and development, while others resulted from sharp reminders given by a rapidly changing secular world. Among these, perhaps the most significant, and that because its influence was so far-reaching, was the awakening to a sense of history.[1] This questioned fundamentally the prevailing certainties of knowledge, and had the potential to transform the intellectual disciplines completely. To become aware of historicity is to acknowledge a sense of contingency, pluralism, and the possibility of change. Much that had been considered absolute was opened up to question and reinterpretation, not least the Bible, the liturgy, and dogmatic truth.

---

1. For a specific analysis of this question, see O. Chadwick, *The Secularization of the European Mind in the Nineteenth Century* (Cambridge: Cambridge University Press, 1975), especially 189–228, and A. Dru, *The Church in the Nineteenth Century: Germany 1800–1918* (London: Burns and Oates, 1963). But for a general overview and useful bibliography, see T. Schoof, *A Survey of Catholic Theology 1800–1970* (London: Paulist Newman, 1970.)

The Question in Context

To face history and all it teaches of origins, development, and alteration is to accept a heavier responsibility than that required to maintain the status quo. Retreat always seems safest when the stakes are high. This opening chapter seeks to examine the contours of such a dilemma as it was played out in the church's turn-of-the-century reaction to a historical consciousness. Being an introduction to the whole book, here its major themes will be sounded out in overture as they arise in the decades that precede the focus of this study. More fully elaborated later, they first emerged with any clarity between the silences imposed during the reigns of Pius IX (1846–1878) and Pius X (1903–1914). The relatively relaxed atmosphere of the pontificate of Leo XIII (1878–1903) allowed for some encouragement of the "new things" that theology might discover in the awareness of historicity. And although, like the themes of all overtures, their introduction was initially subtle and ambiguous, they were stated with occasional clarity before being pushed into the background, yet to emerge more strongly.

It would seem that the triple repetition of a theme is pleasing to the ear, as its cadence carries a sense of increasing resolution and so as this chapter unfolds it will seek to exploit these triple sequences so as to give a better sense of both the interaction of discordant themes and the development of harmonious ones. Between the three caesuras of the *Syllabus*,[2] *Pascendi Dominici Gregis*,[3] and *Humani Generis*,[4] it might be said that the themes and variations central to the question in hand were played out in triplets of increasing harmony. *Aeterni*

---

2. Pius IX, *Syllabus Errorum*, *Acta Pii IX,* 3, 1864, 687–700 (*Quanta cura*), 701–11 (*Syllabus errorum*).
3. Pius X, *Pascendi Dominici Gregis*, *ASS* 40 (1907): 593–650. English translation in B. Reardon, *Roman Catholic Modernism* (London: Adam and Charles Black, 1970), 237–42.
4. Pius XII, *Humani Generis*, *AAS* 42 (1950), 561–78. English trans. R. Knox, *False Trends in Modern Teaching* (London: CTS, 1959).

Patris,[5] *Providentissimus Deus,*[6] and *Divinum Illud Munus*[7] begin to express the relationship between revelation and history in terms of credible theological method, biblical criticism, and liturgical practice. Yet, while these three novel themes gradually fade before the silence imposed by *Pascendi*, they are given fresh, if for some discordant, variation by the Modernists, for example, Alfred Loisy's (1857–1940) *L'Évangile et L'Église,*[8] and George Tyrrell's (1861–1909) three works *Lex Credendi: A Sequel to Lex Orandi,*[9] *Through Scylla and Charybdis: Or the Old Theology and the New,*[10] and *Christianity at the Cross-Roads.*[11] These rework the same liturgical, methodological, and biblical themes that were first heard under Pope Leo XIII. However, any emerging harmony was quietened by authority and swamped by the noise of war, only to return in its aftermath, having been kept alive by the liturgical movement, emerging biblical scholarship and the *nouvelle théologie*. These brought the triple theme to the fore again under the aegis of Pius XII (1876–1958) in *Divino Afflante Spiritu,*[12] *Mystici Corporis Christi,*[13] and *Mediator Dei.*[14] And though the crescendo was temporarily broken by *Humani Generis*, its energy

---

5. Leo XIII, *Aeterni Patris*, ASS 12 (1879): 97–115. English trans. in Claudia Carlen, *The Papal Encyclicals 1878–1903* (Raleigh: McGrath, 1981), 17–26.
6. Leo XIII, *Providentissimus Deus*, ASS 26 (1893): 269–92. English trans. in Carlen, *The Papal Encyclicals 1878–1903*, 325–38.
7. Leo XIII, *Divinum Illud Munus*, ASS 29 (1897): 644–58. English trans. in Carlen, *The Papal Encyclicals 1878–1903*, 409–17.
8. A. Loisy, *L'Évangile et L'Église* (Paris: Alphonse Picard et Fils, 1902).
9. G. Tyrrell, *Lex Credendi: A Sequel to Lex Orandi* (London: Longmans, Green and Co., 1906).
10. G. Tyrrell, *Through Scylla and Charybdis, or The Old Theology and the New* (London: Longmans, Green and Co., 1907).
11. G. Tyrrell, *Christianity at the Cross-Roads* (London: George Allen and Unwin, 1963; first published by Longmans, Green and Co., 1909).
12. Pius XII, *Divino Afflante Spiritu*, AAS 35 (1943): 297–325, English trans. G. Smith, *Biblical Studies and Opportune Means of Promoting Them* (London: CTS, 1943).
13. Pius XII, *Mystici Corporis Christi*, AAS 35 (1943): 193–248, English trans. G. Smith, *On The Mystical Body of Jesus Christ and Our Union with Christ Therein* (London: CTS, 1943).
14. Pius XII, *Mediator Dei*, ASS 39 (1947): 521–600, English trans. G. Smith, *Christian Worship*, (London: CTS, 1947).

built again until the overture ceased and the major work of the Council began. Hence a triple structure appears appropriate for this opening chapter, three sections emerging naturally.

First, the departures and developments of the pontificate of Leo XIII will be examined for the light that context sheds, for it was out of this period that the prevailing question this work tracks emerged. Having gained a sense of the historical roots of some of the abiding issues to be discussed, analysis will be made of the effects and contribution of Modernism to the development of questions that later become central to the four theologians of this study. Lastly, some evaluation of the importance of the liturgical movement and of the new theology in shaping the theological milieu of these writers must be made. Perhaps this can be achieved only by appreciating the significance of their contemporaneity and fundamental theological cohesion. It is in the depths of that relationship that the themes that bear fruit in the *aggiornamento* of the Second Vatican Council take root.

The Pontificate of Leo XIII: An Opportunity for Development?

If verification were needed for the conviction of Avery Dulles[15] that the question of revelation has been at the heart of every theological controversy or undertaking since the Enlightenment, the nineteenth century would provide adequate evidence. Catholic theologians were engaged throughout this period with the refutation of rationalism, skepticism, and their associated errors, and the unity of their enterprise is remarkable.[16] The implications of the challenge that these philosophers had made to the intellectual foundations of belief

---

15. A. Dulles, *Models of Revelation* (Maryknoll, NY: Orbis, 2013), ix.

in positive revelation were many, but the debate soon focused on the transmission of divine revelation, that is, the method of God's self-communication, and the cognate problems of the relationship of faith and reason, nature and grace.

While the Catholic theology of this period was unified in its response to the rationalist attack, it was bitterly divided as to the philosophical and theological method that would best serve its purpose. The quest for a single coherent system,[17] which would provide a united defense against antagonistic philosophies, molded the theology of the nineteenth century, and the outcome of the search has shaped theology since then. Some considered the methodological odyssey to be nearing its end when, toward the close of the century, the Apostolic Constitution *Dei Filius* was approved,[18] and to have reached its goal when, some nine years later, Leo XIII promulgated *Aeterni Patris*.[19] Whether the triumph of Thomism and the scholastic method be considered a victory force majeure[20] or the

16. G. McCool, *Catholic Theology in the Nineteenth Century: The Quest for a Unitary Method* (New York: Seabury, 1977), 17. Cf. E. Hocedez, *Histoire de la théologie au xixe siècle*, 3 vols. (Paris: Desclée, 1948), 1:8–9.

17. McCool, *Catholic Theology in the Nineteenth Century*, 18. Notice too the subtitle of McCool's work. The theology of the nineteenth century represents the search for a method.

18. Interestingly, James Hennesey points to this triplet of encyclicals as indicating the tenor of the pontificate of Pius IX: "Authoritative decrees became the criterion of truth, or, rather, certitude guaranteed by authority displaced the quest for truth. A new theological anthropology emerged, well illustrated in three major events of Pius IX's reign: the Immaculate Conception definition of 1854, the syllabus of errors of 1864, and the Vatican Council of 1869–70." Here the repeated theme was that "sin-weakened man was incapable of self-government. He needed the reign of God-given authority to control him. These were the conclusions immediately drawn by contemporary commentators." J. Hennesey, "Leo XIII's Thomistic Revival: A Political and Philosophical Event," *The Journal of Religion* 58 (1978) Supplement, S187. So R. Aubert insists, "To understand the grimness with which Pius IX fought liberalism (which he stigmatised as the delusion of our century) it is important to see this long drawn out battle as part and parcel of his own untiring effort to restore the fundamental data of revelation to their central place in Christian thinking—an effort of which the Vatican Council was intended in his own mind to be the fulfilment." R. Aubert, *The Christian Centuries*, vol. 5: *The Church in a Secularised Society* (London: Darton, Longman and Todd, 1978), 5.

19. McCool, *Catholic Theology in the Nineteenth Century*, 6.

20. "The conception of theological orthodoxy which triumphed over modernism by *force majeure* rather than by free and open debate was described appositely by some of its defenders as

discovery of the only method capable of addressing the questions that modernity posed, it cannot be denied that Leo's pontificate marks the beginning of a desire within Catholic theology to understand the significance of its own history.[21] Whatever the motives of its inception and however ambiguous its outcome, this is the period that determines "the method according to which Catholic positive and speculative theology endeavoured to retrieve the heritage of its own Catholic doctrinal tradition and to present that tradition to the modern world."[22]

It is with hindsight and the benefit of considerable scholarship[23] that such an understanding has been achieved. The ambiguity, some would say ambivalence,[24] that marked many of the attitudes of Leo XIII, especially his approach to scholarship, has not always been fully appreciated. Some perceive his pontificate as simply a bright opportunity for progress between the stifling and trenchant periods that came before and after.[25] Some have seen the reign as one characterised by the diplomatic relation of tradition with the modern spirit,[26] while still others see only the illusion of change:

What he wanted was to realize ultramontane goals unrealized under

'integralism.' In their minds it stood or fell *as a whole,* and a divinely guaranteed whole at that."
G. Daly, *Transcendence and Immanence: A Study in Catholic Modernism and Integralism* (Oxford: Clarendon, 1980), 7.

21. Perhaps the most reliable biography of Leo XIII is E. Soderini, *Il pontificato di Leone XIII*, 3 vols. (Milan: A. Mondadori, 1932–33), English trans. by Barbara Carter, *The Pontificate of Leo XIII*, vol. 1, and *Leo XIII, Italy and France*, vol. 2 (London: Burns, Oates and Washbourne, 1934).

22. McCool, *Catholic Theology in the Nineteenth Century*, 1.

23. Cf. ibid., 6.

24. J. D. Holmes, *The Triumph of the Holy See: A Short History of the Papacy in the Nineteenth Century* (London: Burns and Oates, 1978), 194.

25. See C. Falconi, *The Popes in the Twentieth Century from Pius X to John XXIII*, trans. Muriel Grindrod (Boston: Little, Brown and Co., 1967), xi–xiii. Italian orig., *I papi del ventesimo secolo* (Milan: Rusconi, 1967). See also E. Poulat, *Église contre bourgeoisie* (Tournai: Casterman, 1977), 175.

26. See G. Lease, "Vatican Foreign Policy and the Origins of Modernism," in *Catholicism Contending with Modernity: Roman Catholic Modernism and Anti-Modernism in Historical Context*, ed. D. Jodock (Cambridge: Cambridge University Press, 2000), 43–48.

Pius IX by intellectualizing the combat with modernity, by providing a theoretical underpinning for his policies. He would not come to terms with modern values; rather he would restore in the world an objective and immutable order with the church as its most effective guardian. Renewal of Thomistic philosophy was the tool essential to his purpose.[27]

All three positions hold their portion of truth, yet perhaps the stark judgement of the last has the potential to limit most an understanding of nascent theological change. Standing alone, it is an interpretation that does not fit the context. Unlike his predecessor, Leo XIII was no prisoner of the Vatican and therefore could not remain aloof from the intellectual and political problems of his age and retain a credible position for the Church.[28] Neither would merely cosmetic or superficial change convince a world facing monumental shifts with regard to society, government, economics, and culture. The extent to which the iron fist of the ancien régime remained hidden in Leo's new white velvet glove can be questioned. But to suggest that in the light of the recent past, he could harbor a restorationist agenda that defied innovation absolutely goes beyond cynicism and ignores what was unquestionably new and not mere diplomacy in his reign.[29] That

27. Hennesey, "Leo XIII's Thomistic Revival," S190. Bernard Reardon also adopts a similar line when he suggests, "Leo was much less a liberal intellectual than a *politique*, more solicitous than his predecessor for the enlightened image which the Catholic Church should now present the world. The substance of Vatican policy continued, that is to say, as before; it was only the means of effecting it were altered." B. Reardon, "Roman Catholic Modernism," in *Nineteenth Century Religious Thought in the West*, vol. 2, ed. N. Smart, J. Clayton, S. Katz and P. Sherry, (Cambridge: Cambridge University Press, 1985), 148.

28. Speaking of the new political departures, Bernard Reardon maintains, "Leo XIII, who succeeded Pius IX in 1878, outlined in his first encyclical letter, *Inscrutabile Deo consilio*, a programme for the reconciliation of the Catholic Church with modern civilization, thus evidently reversing the policy of his predecessor." Reardon, "Roman Catholic Modernism," 147. And of the impetus for theological change in Leo's pontificate, he suggests that "Towards the century's end, however, it was becoming only too obvious to Catholic scholars, awake now to the nature and extent of modern Protestant research in the field of the Bible and early Christianity, that the narrowly traditionalist stand-point upon these matters, upheld in the seminaries, was likely to involve all Catholic teaching and apologetic in increasing discredit." Reardon, *Roman Catholic Modernism* (London: Adam and Charles Black, 1970), 13.

29. See M. O'Connell, *Critics on Trial: An Introduction to the Catholic Modernist Crisis* (Washington, DC: Catholic University of America Press, 1994), 31–33.

the pontificate of Leo XIII is ambiguous must be conceded without doubt, but the heart of the question—as Derek Holmes suggests[30]—is why his ambivalence in matters of scholarship should be greater than that with which he met the social and economic concerns of his day.[31]

The Impact of *Aeterni Patris*

Many reasons could be suggested as to why Leo XIII promulgated *Aeterni Patris* in 1879. Undoubtedly, it was delivered as the foundation to his "grand design":[32] the unified philosophical basis of theological, social and political renewal.[33] As Paul Misner suggests, the encyclical forms the "operational plan" that flows naturally from the claims of the First Vatican Council. Thomistic philosophy would

30. "Leo XIII was less ambiguous in his approach to social or economic problems and in promoting the development of Social Catholicism." Holmes, *The Triumph of the Holy See*, 196.

31. G. McCool posits a clear distinction between the encyclicals that Leo XIII promulgated in the first half of his pontificate and those in the second. *Aeterni Patris*, appearing toward the beginning of his reign, signalled the restoration of a traditional and conservative rationale that alone could provide the secure basis from which later and more progressive social encyclicals might depart. See G. McCool, *From Unity to Pluralism: The Internal Evolution of Thomism* (New York: Fordham University Press, 1989), 6–7. However, some still also note a degree of ambiguity or at least inconsistency in the later encyclicals: "Among his pontifical directives there were decrees concerning duels. Duelling is not entirely dead in this generation but then neither is the duck-billed platypus. On the other hand, Leo's concern with the social problem and the functions of the State are altogether resonant with our worries in the second half of the twentieth century." G. Weigel, "Leo XIII and Contemporary Theology," in *Leo XIII and the Modern World*, ed. E. T. Gargan (New York: Sheed and Ward, 1961), 213.

32. See P. Misner, "Catholic Anti-Modernism: The Ecclesial Setting," in Jodock, *Catholicism Contending with Modernity*, 56–87, 79.

33. "Whoso turns his attention to the bitter strifes of these days and seeks a reason for the troubles that vex public and private life must come to the conclusion that a fruitful cause of the evils which now afflict, as well as those which threaten us, lies ·in this: that false conclusions concerning divine and human things, which originated in the schools of philosophy, have crept into all the orders of the state, and have been accepted by the common consent of the masses." (Si quis in acerbitatem nostrorum temporum animum intendat, earumque rerum rationem, quae publice et privatim geruntur, cogitatione complectatur, is profecto comperiet, fecundam malorum causam, cum eorum quae premunt, tum eorum quae pertimescimus, in eo consistere, quod prava de divines humanisque rebus scita, e scholis philosophorum iampridem profecta, in omnes civitatis ordines irrepserint, communi plurimorum suffragio recepta.) Leo XIII, *Aeterni Patris*, 98; Carlen, *The Papal Encyclicals 1878–1903*, 17.

provide a unified method for priestly formation throughout the world, and this unity would bring "force and light and aid"[34] to an ordering of the Church's much-weakened intellectual defenses. That Leo's Thomistic revival was as much political as philosophical is a truth argued by many,[35] but as a result, its impact on theology should not be overshadowed.

Aeterni Patris makes clear that philosophy is the handmaid of theology, and therefore any renewal within the philosophical disciplines will reach its fulfilment in a new apologetic:

> Whence it clearly follows that human reason finds the fullest faith and authority united in the word of God. In like manner reason declares that the doctrine of the Gospel has even from its very beginning been manifested by certain wonderful signs, the established proofs, as it were, of unshaken truth; and that all, therefore, who set faith in the Gospel do not believe rashly as though following cunningly devised fables, but, by a most reasonable consent, subject their intelligence and judgement to an authority which is divine.[36]

The close relationship between Vatican I and *Aeterni Patris* must be asserted if an accurate understanding of this period is to be gained. *Dei Filius* had reaffirmed, in the face of rationalist philosophers and the Reformers, the Church's teaching on revelation, faith, and reason. The existence of a free, omnipotent, and personal Creator could be known by natural reason, taught the Council, though knowledge beyond this was entirely dependent on the historical revelation contained in Scripture and the living tradition. The act of faith,

---

34. Ibid., 100; Carlen, *The Papal Encyclicals 1878-1903*, 18.

35. See especially J. Hennesey, "Leo XIII's Thomistic Revival," S185–97, but also P. Thibault, *Savoir et Pouvoir: Philosophie thomiste et politique cléricale au XIX siècle* (Québec: Les Presses de l'Université Laval, 1972).

36. "Simili modo ratio declarat, evangelicam doctrinam mirabilibus quibusdam signis, tamquam certis certae veritatis argumentis, vel ab ipsa origine emicuisse: atque ideo omnes, qui Evangelico fidem adiungunt, non temere adiungere, tamquam doctas fabulas secutos, sed rationabili prorsus obsequio intelligentiam et iudicium suum divinae subiicere auctoritati." Leo XIII, *Aeterni Patris*, 101; Carlen, *The Papal Encyclicals 1878–1903*, 19.

however, was no blind leap; it was supernatural but remained reasonable. In its fourth chapter, the Constitution on Faith distinguished the limits of the knowledge afforded by reason to faith. Though the two are related and complementary, beyond the truths available to natural reason were unknowable mysteries of God glimpsed only by faith through revelation. Whatever Leo XIII's political, philosophical, and theological intentions in promulgating *Aeterni Patris,* he certainly believed there to be a harmony between his teaching and that of *Dei Filius.*

The neo-scholastics,[37] among whom Leo XIII can be considered, held that Thomism offered the most perfect scientific expression of the scholastic method.[38] The grounds for such confidence might be roughly divided into philosophical, theological, and historical aspects, all of which are touched upon in *Aeterni Patris.* As a scientific discipline, the scholasticism of St. Thomas offered a seemingly simple objectivity. Against rationalist and skeptical assertions about the impossibility of supernatural revelation, Aquinas was thought to offer clear proofs of the existence of God and the divine attributes, logically deduced within a system of cause and effect, according to the principles of analogy, and through a pragmatic examination of signs and wonders. The clear formulas of an Aristotelian-inspired

37. For an excellent historical survey of scholasticism, discussion of its major features, and its specific relation to Thomism, see Elizabeth Gössmann, "Scholasticism," in *Sacramentum Mundi: An Encyclopedia of Theology,* ed. K. Rahner, C. Ernst, and K. Smyth, vol. 6 (New York: Herder and Herder, 1969), 19–38. For a specific analysis of the nineteenth-century scholastic revival, see J.-P. Golinas, *La restoration du Thomisme sous Léon XIII et les philiosophies nouvelles, Ètude de la pensée de M. Blondel et du Père Laberthonnière* (Washington, DC: Catholic University of America Press, 1959), and J. Perrier, *Revival of Scholastic Philosophy in the Nineteenth Century* (New York: AMS, 1967).

38. "Indeed . . . reason, borne on the wings of Thomas to its human height, can scarcely rise higher, while faith could scarcely expect more or stronger aids from reason than those which she had already obtained through Thomas." (Ita quidem ut ratio ad humanum fastigium Thomae pennis evecto, iam fere nequeat sublimius assurgere; neque fides a ratione fere possit plura aut validiora adiumenta praestolari, quam quae iam est per Thomam consecuta.) Leo XIII, *Aeterni Patris,* 109; Carlen, *The Papal Encyclicals 1878–1903,* 23.

philosophy provided a logical foundation for the truths of faith because, as *Aeterni Patris* maintained, the best philosophers are those who combine the pursuit of philosophy with dutiful obedience to the Christian faith.[39] Thus the philosophical gives way to the theological implications of Leo XIII's agenda: to establish scientifically the veracity of signs and miracles so as to both justify the credibility of the Christian revelation that they accompany, and to vindicate the church which, as the bearer of these truths, claims a divine origin.[40] Thus scholastic methodology showed itself to be naturally suited to apologetic aims.[41] Moreover, because systematically, Thomism held together as an integrated whole the various elements of the church's scriptural, patristic, and medieval theologies, it lent itself to easy transmission. Scholasticism, and more specifically Thomism, which had so consistently shaped Catholic theology, not least at the Council of Trent, offered a sound structure for the handing down of a secure tradition.[42] Gerald McCool usefully summarises these points:

39. "For in this, the most noble of studies, it is of the greatest necessity to bind together, as it were in one body the many and various parts of the heavenly doctrines, that, each being allotted to its own proper place and derived from its own proper principles, the whole may join together in a complete union; in order, in fine, that all and each part may be strengthened by its own and the others' invincible argument." (In hac enim nobilissima disciplinarum magnopere necesse est, ut multae ac diverse caelestium doctrinarum partes in unum veluti corpus colligantur, ut suis quaeque locis convenienter dispositae, et ex propriis principiis derivatae apto inter se nexu cohaereant; demum ut omnes et singulae suis iisque invictis argumentis confirmentur.) Ibid., 101; Carlen, *The Papal Encyclicals 1878–1903*, 19.
40. Cf. McCool, *From Unity to Pluralism*, 7.
41. "Philosophy also provides the organizing structure of a scientific dogmatic theology. Through the principles that philosophy supplies, revelation's scattered data 'may be joined together in an appropriate connexion. . . .' Finally, philosophy furnishes the Church with solid arguments to use in her controversies with her opponents." Ibid., 7.
42. "The ecumenical councils, also, where blossoms the flower of all earthly wisdom, have always been careful to hold Thomas Aquinas in singular honour. In the Councils of Lyons, Vienna, Florence, and the Vatican one might almost say that Thomas took part and presided over the deliberations and decrees of the fathers, contending against the errors of the Greeks, of heretics and rationalists, with invincible force and with the happiest results. But the chief and special glory of Thomas, one which he has shared with none of the Catholic Doctors, is that the Fathers of Trent made it part of the order of conclave to lay upon the altar, together with the Sacred Scriptures and the decrees of the supreme Pontiffs, the *Summa* of Thomas Aquinas, whence to seek counsel, reason, and inspiration." (Ipsa quoque Concilia Oecumenica, in quibus

The scholastic philosophy described in the encyclical was a highly objective discipline. Its realistic epistemology prepared the way for a vindication of God's existence and attributes through causal arguments grounded on Aristotle's metaphysics. Its Aristotelian metaphysics laid the groundwork for the impersonal apologetics of signs and miracles, which would become the object of Blondel's trenchant criticism before the end of the nineteenth century. As in Kleutgen's *Die Theologie der Vorzeit*, scholastic positive theology was credited with the ability to order and unify the scattered data of revelation and subsume them under its developed concepts; and scholastic speculative theology could acquire a fruitful understanding of the Christian mysteries through its Aristotelian science of God.[43]

Such then are the primary reasons for the preferred status that Leo XIII gives to Thomism in *Aeterni Patris*. Clearly, the foreseen and intended impact on theology is of particular pertinence, if only because the exact nature of that prognostication remains the abiding ambiguity of the Leonine heritage. From the three perspectives mentioned emerges a clearer understanding of the motives of Leo XIII in his encyclical on Christian philosophy. Only a scientifically unassailable philosophy, both unified and comprehensive, could give the footing necessary for the robust apologetic required to win back the haute bourgeoisie—the educated upper classes of Europe who had been lost to the wiles of the new philosophies. Likewise, a uniform and logical mode of catechesis, vital and accessible, was

eminet lectus ex toto orbe terrarum flos sapientiae, singularem Thomae Aquinati honorem habere perpetuo studuerunt. In Conciliis Lugdunensi, Viennensi, Florentino, Vaticano, deliberationibus et decretis Patrum interfuisse Thomam et pene praefuisse dixeris, adversus errore Graecorum, haereticorum et rationalistarum ineluctabili vi et faustissimo exitu decertantem.—Sed haec maxima est et Thomae propria, nec cum quopiam ex doctoribus catholicis communicata laus, quod Patres Tridentini, in ipso medio conclavi ordini habendo, una cum divinae Scripturae codicibus et Pontificum Maximorum decretis *Summam* Thomae Aquinatis super altari patere voluerunt, unde consilium, rationes, oracular peterentur.) Leo XIII, *Aeterni Patris*, 110; Carlen, *The Papal Encyclicals 1878–1903*, 24.

43. McCool, *Catholic Theology in the Nineteenth Century*, 232. For a commentary on Leonine Thomism and especially Joseph Kleutgen's influence on the development of *Aeterni Patris*, see F. Kerr, *After Aquinas: Versions of Thomism* (Oxford: Blackwell, 2002), 17–21.

needed for the working classes who, although less resistant and more ultramontane in regard to the Church, needed to be swayed from the antireligious but increasingly popular doctrines of socialism. Capable of countering the new philosophies, of establishing a secure Catholic apologetic, and of providing a teaching that would prove cohesive and sustainable in its uniformity, Thomism instilled the confidence of a panacea.

Philosophically speaking, unity was to be the overriding contribution of neo-scholasticism to the Church. By the end of the pontificate of Pius IX, the state of Catholic theology was desperate. Writing some time earlier, John Henry Newman, training for the priesthood in Rome, wrote to a former Oxford colleague,

> We . . . find very little theology here, and a talk we had yesterday with one of the Jesuit fathers here shows we shall find little philosophy. It arose from our talking of the Greek studies of the Propaganda and asking whether the youths learned Aristotle. "O no—he said—Aristotle is in no favour here—no, not in Rome:—not St. Thomas. I have read Aristotle and St. Thos., and owe a great deal to them, but they are out of favour here and throughout Italy. St. Thomas is a great saint—people don't dare to speak against him—they profess to reverence him, but put him aside." I asked what philosophy they did adopt. He said odds and ends—whatever seems to them best. . . . *Facts* are the great things and nothing else.[44]

Certainly, one assumption behind the restoration of Thomistic Christian philosophy by Leo XIII was the provision of a unified method, the disparate and piecemeal philosophies[45] of the day

44. Newman to Dalgairns, 22 November 1846, in *The Letters and Diaries of John Henry Newman*, vol. 11, ed. S. Dessain, et al., (Oxford: Clarendon, 1961), 279. Roger Aubert, in his study of Pius IX, also quotes the letter of a young priest studying in Rome to his friend in France: "Roman theology is altogether too careless of what happens around it. Generally speaking, rationalism is generally badly understood and is opposed with futility. History has not a single celebrated representative. Linguistics are neglected. The study of medicine is backward and of law is stagnant." Both quotations found in O'Connell, *Critics on Trial*, 27–28.

45. "In 1878 Thomism was one feeble philosophical approach among many in the Catholic armory. Eclecticism prevailed. Some eighteenth-century Catholics had flirted with Enlightenment.

seeming to provide only a weak and ineffectual defense, often because they were tainted by the methodology of their opponents. Moreover in judging the intention of the pope in *Aeterni Patris*, one should be careful not to underestimate the threat, real and perceived, that the Church felt at this time. As Kenneth Scott Latourette said of the late-nineteenth century,

> The threat was multiform. One of its most striking features was that it arose in historic Christendom. Indeed, much of it had at least part of its source in perversions of what had come from Christianity. It seemed that Christianity was giving rise to forces which were making it an anachronism—as though it was digging its own grave.[46]

The newer philosophies, such as the ontologism of Vincenzo Gioberti (1801–1852) and Antonio Rosmini (1797–1855), or the Idealism of Georg Hegel (1770–1831), Johann Fichte (1762–1814), and Friedrich Schelling (1775–1854), essentially have their roots in the *cogito* philosophies[47] of René Descartes (1596–1650) and Immanuel Kant (1724–1804).[48] Not only did these latter two seminal

John Locke's ideas were taught in French Jesuit schools and imbibed there by the likes of Charles Carroll of Carrollton. Cartesianism had a wide following, and so did traditionalism and fideism growing out of romanticism. Nineteenth-century *deutsche Theologen* were influenced by rationalism and historical method. Ontologism had a vogue at Louvain, in France, and in Italy, where Gioberti and Rosmini were philosophers to the national movement. Only in Spain and there principally among Dominicans, was more than lip service paid to the Angelic Doctor as the nineteenth century began." J. Hennesey, "Leo XIII's Thomistic Revival," S190–91.

46. K. Scott Latourette, "The Church and the World in the Nineteenth Century," in Gargan, *Leo XIII and the Modern World*, 51.

47. "[Modern philosophy's] use of the *cogito* as its starting point and its demand for apodictic reflex certitude in the name of philosophical rigor cut it off from our legitimate spontaneous certitudes and imprison the philosopher in his own mind. Some modern philosophers are content to remain there, as we can see from the empiricism of Hume and the idealism of Kant. The modern philosophers who have opted for realism are obliged to postulate an intuitive grasp of God or the divine ideas to ground the necessary principles of their metaphysics." McCool, *From Unity to Pluralism*, 29. For a useful analysis of the modern philosophers and their engagement with theology, see D. Brown, *Continental Philosophy and Modern Theology* (Oxford: Blackwell, 1987).

48. T. Harper gives a suggestion of this process when he says, "Descartes may be justly said to have bequeathed to us a Hume; Hume in turn, a Kant, a Fichte, a Hegel, a Schelling. So, again, the ontology of Gioberti under a modified form, found its way into Catholic universities and

writers build their systems on the individual, but they established them by complete separation from Christian revelation. Rightly, *Aeterni Patris* was anxious about such "separated philosophies" as a danger to faith, the church, and society. Fundamental, however, was the neo-scholastic conviction that the new philosophies could not support Catholic dogmatics.[49] Because Thomism alone preserved a distinction of sense and intellect within its epistemology, Thomism alone could "defend the substantial unity of spirit and matter within the human agent"[50] that was crucial to Catholic theology. Hence, the pragmatism of St. Thomas and his belief in universals, his setting of humanity within a causal system that leads from a contingent world toward God, his teaching on the natural and supernatural, his conviction as to the essential difference between the created and uncreated orders, between faith and reason, even philosophy and theology, all speak of careful distinction, but far more importantly, of the possible integration of these poles in the union of a higher truth. Herein is the attraction that the neo-scholastic system held for the vulnerable, fragmented, and changing Christian world of Leo XIII, and therein lies the reason why many saw *Aeterni Patris* as fundamental to his "grand design."

Yet it was not as if this task was simple. Just as postrevolutionary, democratic society had the Christian faith among its sources, so many of the new philosophies from René Descartes onward and, indeed, what would later become the "new" theology, had their origin and took their departure from scholastic philosophy and theology. It was difficult to know the enemy exactly, and there was a constant risk of jettisoning legitimate development along with incompatible

---

colleges." T. Harper, "The Encyclical," *The Month* 18, no. 37 (1879): 363. See also Kerr, *After Aquinas*, 19–30.

49. See McCool, *From Unity to Pluralism*, 100–2.
50. Ibid., 100.

novelties. In the face of such tension between old and new, it was difficult to know the best course. Though many have interpreted Leo XIII's response in *Aeterni Patris* as definitive and absolute, in fact it could be said to reflect the ambiguity of the age and of theology in particular. Some see it as a reactionary measure designed to arrest the development of theology according to novel principles,[51] while still others regard the promulgation as simply another aspect of the extreme ultramontanism that sought unity and isolation at all costs.[52] However, it remains possible to see within the decision to impose the scholastic system of St. Thomas on the Church a desire to end the disarray of Christian philosophy[53] and to seek an impulse toward the rediscovery of a philosophical heritage that would serve the progress of theology.[54] For in fact the choice as seen by the neo-scholastics was more nuanced than old or new:

The early nineteenth-century Neo-Scholastic synthesis, of which

---

51. Cf. a contemporary review by Archibald Alexander, "Thomas Aquinas and the Encyclical Letter," *The Princeton Review* 5 (1880): 249, where Alexander claims that "there are certain characteristics of the scholastic thought of St. Thomas that make it useless in modern times." J. D. Holmes, quoting from the liberal journal *Siècle,* suggests that the encyclical "was interpreted as a declaration of stagnation restricting the development of future thought." J. D. Holmes, "Some English Reactions to the Publication of *Aeterni Patris*," *The Downside Review* 93 (1975): 270. Also, W. Ward, writing in *The Fortnightly Review* of 1903, speaks of the "restrictive" nature of the encyclical: W. Ward, "Leo XIII," *The Fortnightly Review,* 80 (1903): 256.

52. "The development of scholasticism reflected the aims and the policies of the more conservative and extreme ultramontanes. . . . By 1864 the revival of Thomism *was* an ultramontane movement." Holmes, "Some English Reactions to the Publication of *Aeterni Patris*," 270.

53. Cf. J. C. Hedley, "Pope Leo XIII and Modern Studies," *The Dublin Review* 34, no. 1, 3rd series (1880): 273. "The Encyclical is rather a domestic warning than a plan of campaign. It is an order to the household to attend to its own health rather than a call to go forth and fight. The Catholic flock has been wasting its time with second rate teachers; it has been divided, outside the domain of Faith, into sets and parties; its best men have spent a lifetime in elaborating systems to which the last touch had scarcely been given when they were found to be worthy of condemnation."

54. J. Collins, "Leo XIII and the Philosophical Approach to Modernity," in Gargan, *Leo XIII and the Modern World,* 182. "This (the renewal of Christian philosophy) is the main theme of *Aeterni Patris,* the key encyclical which has served since 1879 as the guiding stimulus toward recovering the sources of Christian philosophical ideas." Cf. F. Ehrle, *Zur Enzyklika "Aeterni Patris": Text und Kommentar* (Rome: Edizioni di storia e letteratura, 1954), 110–13.

Liberatore and Kleutgen are forceful and influential advocates, established Neo-Thomism as a modern system into which the Thomists believed the best of modern thought could be absorbed. None of them denied that the modern world had made many discoveries. None of them condemned its progress in natural and historical sciences. Nevertheless only the philosophy and theology of the Scholastic Doctors possessed the principles required to interpret the results of modern progress correctly and to integrate them into a Christian wisdom.[55]

Again, whatever the Thomists believed about their system, the degree to which they remained suspicious of notions of contingency and history, either with regard to the works of Thomas or the church as a whole, remains debatable. And if for no other reason, it therefore remains difficult to dismiss absolutely a sense of reactionary conservatism from Leo XIII's motivations in the promulgation of *Aeterni Patris*. The ambiguity that remains and that emerges the stronger in the theological response to the neo-scholastic system is not perhaps peculiar to this question but inherent to the nature of theology itself. As Karl Rahner was to point out much later,

> It is the bitter grief of theology and its blessed task too, always to have to seek (because it does not clearly have present to it at the time) what, in a sense—in its historical memory it has always known. The history of theology is by no means just the history of the progress of doctrine, but also a history of forgetting. . . . What was once given in history and is ever made present anew does not primarily form a set of premises from which we can draw conclusions which have never been thought before. It is the object, which while it is always retained, must ever be acquired anew.[56]

Thus from a perspective not dissimilar to Rahner, Gerald McCool can conclude that "*Aeterni Patris* must now be considered an historical moment in the dialectical progress of theological development."[57]

---

55. McCool, *From Unity to Pluralism*, 31.
56. K. Rahner, "Current Problems in Christology," in *Theological Investigations*, trans. C. Ernst, vol. 1, (London: Darton, Longman and Todd, 1974), 151–52.

Yet, for the Church of the nineteenth century, this ambiguous process of ongoing discovery may in retrospect be seen mainly as "a history of forgetting," and perhaps because of that the period was one of particularly "bitter grief."

A Positive Influence on Positive Theology

Even as the strong and cumulative effect of *Dei Filius* and *Aeterni Patris* begins to be assessed and the advantages of neo-scholastic methods examined, the essential weaknesses of the movement become apparent. The fatal flaw, as many have acknowledged, is there from the beginning, when the system establishes a tension between efforts to come to an understanding of faith and efforts to develop a science of faith.[58] The possibility of separating knowledge of the mysteries themselves from knowledge that can be deduced from them was an ever-present danger that post–Vatican I studies did not always avoid. Consistently, the theology of this period up until the Second World War and beyond fell into what Gerald McCool refers to as a sterile "conclusion theology."[59] This evolved from the neo-scholastic stunting and objectivization of the revealed mysteries in an effort to contain them within a deductive and ahistorical scientific system. So the positive attributes of the methodological system of St. Thomas chosen by the neo-scholastics of the late nineteenth century begin to yield their counterpoint problems and thus inspire the theological movements of the early twentieth century. The conviction of the neo-scholastics that their method

---

57. McCool, *Catholic Theology in the Nineteenth Century*, 6.
58. McCool makes this point and cites the distinction that Johannes Beumer makes between *Glaubensverständnis* and *Glaubenswissenschaft* in his *Theologie als Glaubensverständnis* (Würzburg, Echter, 1953), 13–24. See also B. Lonergan, "Theology and Understanding," in *Collection* (New York: Herder and Herder, 1967), 121–41.
59. McCool, *Catholic Theology in the Nineteenth Century*, 225.

offered a single metaphysical system, unaltered through the centuries from St. Bonaventure (1217–74) to Cardinal Cajetan (1480–1547) and beyond, gave rise to charges of a lack of historical awareness or of ignorance of the possibilities of dogmatic development.[60] Undoubtedly, there were those who championed the objective universality of the method, and saw within it respect for the unalterable truths of revelation and the authoritative teachings of the Church:

> It is still agreed, of course, that Thomas is not to be regarded as having an explicitly historical approach, yet it has been shown by his use of the neo-Platonist scheme of *egressus* and *regressus* he advanced historical thinking far more than had previously been suspected, not only in the Third Part of his *Summa* but throughout his work. Creation, incarnation with grace already at work in history, the bringing home of the world, these are all conceived by Thomas in terms of the economy of salvation and therefore historically, and not merely as necessary modes of being.[61]

---

60. "Yet only on a superficial interpretation would one infer from the untroubled and unhurried serenity of the work that the author himself lived in freedom from outer or inner disturbances. On the other hand, it is certainly clear that the *Summa Theologica* can only be the work of a heart fundamentally at peace. St. Thomas did not discover and map out his majestic outline of Christian teaching in the 'silence of a monastic cell.' It was not in some idyllic sphere of retirement cut off from the happenings in the world that he lived out his life. Such presentations, as untrue to history as they are impermissibly simplified, not only color, or rather *dis*color in many particulars the conventional portraits of Thomas; they frequently have an effect on biographical studies which make higher claims to accuracy." J. Pieper, *The Silence of St. Thomas* (South Bend, IN: St. Augustine's Press, 1999), 3–4. See also Pieper's reflections on the "Timeliness of Thomism," for example, "The fullness of truth can never be grasped by a neutral and indifferent mind, but only by a mind seeking the answer to a serious and urgent existential problem. But this urgency can only be aroused by an immediately experienced, real situation, of the individual and the community. This means that the truth will be more profoundly known *as* truth, the more vigorously its timeliness comes to light; it also means that a man experiencing his own time with a richer intensity of heart and fuller spiritual awareness has a better chance of experiencing the illuminating force of truth. Together with its timeliness, by which the responsive power of truth is focused on the immediate present, the eternal validity of truth which, incomparably compelling, transcends the whole of time, would become manifest. This makes clear the twofold, never-ending task of the true teacher: to reflect the totality of truth *and*, in a constantly inquiring meditation, to discover and point out wherein lies the relevance of truth to his own time." Ibid., 75–107, 106.
61. Gössmann, "Scholasticism," 32.

Ambiguity has remained, to varying degrees, with regard to whether Thomism adopts a consciously historical approach. Yet the question remains as to whether Leo XIII consciously desired to exploit this ambiguity in his efforts to restore Christian philosophy and theology.

Gabriel Daly makes the important point that *Aeterni Patris* did not seek a "return to scholastic philosophy *in general*," but was an unambiguous summons "to the philosophy of Aquinas *simpliciter*."[62] However implicit, within this restoration was the impulse to historical, if not critical, study. The opening of the Vatican archive to scholars for the first time in 1880, the promulgation of *Providentissimus Deus* in 1893, and the setting up of the Biblical Commission in 1902 support this tendency of Leo's to return to the sources.[63] Granted, Daly is skeptical of the pope's appreciation of the diversity, pluralism, and contingency to which such a study could give rise, but that he "initiated the movement" cannot be denied.[64] Indeed, something of the methodology of *Aeterni Patris* itself speaks of the dynamism that theology draws for the future through an appreciation of the interaction of the present with the past. As Marvin O'Connell says,

> To this Christian philosophy, to this handmaiden of robust theology, Pope Leo gave a broad historical dimension. The doctors and Fathers of the early church, he argued, had themselves been philosophers, had themselves "well understood that, according to the divine plan, the restorer of human science is Christ, who is the power and the wisdom of God, and in whom are hid all the treasures of wisdom and knowledge." From Justin Martyr to Augustine of Hippo they had all appreciated that "in the case of such doctrines that the human intelligence may perceive, it is . . . just that philosophy makes use of its own method, principles and arguments." This tradition was brilliantly continued by the Scholastic masters who flourished in the medieval universities and who "addressed

62. Daly, *Transcendence and Immanence*, 9–10.
63. See Reardon, *Roman Catholic Modernism*, 13–15.
64. Daly, *Transcendence and Immanence*, 10.

themselves to a great work—that of diligently collecting, and sifting, and storing up, as it were, for the use and convenience of posterity the rich and fertile harvests of Christian learning scattered abroad in the voluminous works of the holy Fathers."[65]

Whether or not Leo XIII had ambiguous intentions in promulgating *Aeterni Patris,* and whether he realized that with his nascent notions of history he had brought a Trojan horse into the theological camp, the effect of his encyclical was certainly ambiguous and not without irony.[66] While the practical interpretation of *Dei Filius* that he provided in *Aeterni Patris* gave a particular direction to Catholic theology by orienting it according to a particular school, the emergent vicissitudes of that method could never have been anticipated, nor could the final results of the rediscovery of St. Thomas have ever been expected. Responses to the apparent inadequacies of the scholastic system guided the theology of the period between the two Vatican councils, and significant shifts can be charted in fundamental, liturgical, and dogmatic theology, each initiated by the dialogue between Thomism and the modern world that *Aeterni Patris* began. Scholasticism, as opposed to Thomism, came to be regarded as a denial of the individual and subjective element of faith and of the inevitable historicity of revelation as given in Scripture and tradition. Hence, ironically

> the Thomistic synthesis, which the nineteenth-century Neothomists were convinced was required to defend and explain *Dei Filius'* teaching on faith and reason, would change and evolve from within until its

---

65. O'Connell, *Critics on Trial,* 35.

66. "Since it was Leo who initiated the movement which only later issued in a truly critical study of medieval philosophy, he himself can hardly be expected to have appreciated the diversity, indeed pluralism, of that philosophy, and he may have supposed that the differences between Thomism and Augustinianism were less significant than they in fact were." Daly, *Transcendence and Immanence,* 10. Cf. R. Aubert, "Aspects divers du néo-thomisme sous le pontificat de Léon XIII," in *Aspetti della cultura cattolica nell' età di Leone XIII* (Rome: Edizioni 5 Lune, 1961), 148–49.

epistemology, metaphysics, and philosophical method had ceased to be the epistemology, metaphysics, and philosophical method which in the minds of the drafters of *Aeterni Patris* distinguished the timeless, universal, Aristotelian, science of the Angelic Doctor from the individual, subjective, and historical thought of the modern philosophers.[67]

Indeed the irony is more bitter. The philosophical errors from which the neo-Thomists had sought to free Catholic theology became the springboard for the new theology and the revised systems of twentieth-century transcendental Thomists.[68]

Providentissimus Deus and *Divinum Illud Munus*

In a study of theological method, Jared Wicks asserts that

Vatican II reflected the interconnectedness of the mysteries when it showed how biblical interpretation, by which divine wisdom takes on written form, resembles the mystery of the incarnation, by which the divine Word assumed a human nature by the work of the Holy Spirit. Such theological reflections on the teachings of faith assume and further set forth, the symphonic harmony of the different truths of revelation.[69]

In *Providentissimus Deus* and *Divinum Illud Munus* are the beginnings of that later harmony. Written in the latter half of Leo's pontificate, these two encyclicals focus on biblical criticism and the role of the Holy Spirit in salvation and express more explicitly the historical consciousness and openness to plurality at which *Aeterni Patris* had

---

67. McCool, *Catholic Theology in the Nineteenth Century*, 235.
68. "Thus, sixty years after *Aeterni Patris* the Jesuit descendants of the early Neothomists had welcomed into their revised Thomistic synthesis the epistemology and metaphysics of their ancestors' theological arch-enemies." Ibid., 3. See also R. Aubert, "L'enciclica *Aeterni Patris* e le alter prese di peozione della Santa Sede sulla filosofia cristiana," in *La filosofia cristiana nei secoli XIX e XX*, vol. 2: *Ritorno all'eredità scolastica*, ed. E. Coreth, W. Neidl, and G. Pligersdorffer (Rome: Città Nuova Editrice, 1994).
69. J. Wicks, *Introduction to Theological Method* (Rome: Piemme, 1994), 24.

hinted. Emerging here is a congruency between the word, flesh, and spirit phases of revelation that the Second Vatican Council later harmonizes within the overarching notion of sacrament.

Though written with the specific purpose of countering rationalist attack, the letter on the study of Holy Scripture sustains a predominantly positive tone.[70] The pope realizes that the best defense against pernicious liberal exegesis is the better and correct use of modern methodologies. And though he remains suspicious of higher criticism, the welcome of thorough analysis by Leo XIII is far more than a begrudging relaxation of the traditional defiance. It is the positive recognition of scientific, linguistic, and exegetical studies. To accept critical exegesis, in no matter how limited a way, is to accept that the Scriptures do not offer easily accessed, univocal, and ahistorical truth, but a unique and complex blend of the human and divine aspects of revelation.[71] Effective and fruitful study of the word of God demands emergence from the "single system" mentality that was the tragedy of nineteenth-century Catholic theology. Jan Walgrave describes the prevailing mentality as follows:

A mind educated in one single system has a strength of its own. On his own ground, playing according to the rules he is accustomed to, he is undefeatable. But beyond his own ground he feels distressed and forlorn. He simply does not understand what it is all about. As he identifies thought with the requirements of his own system—there is but one truth, one true method, one true philosophy—it seems to him that those who do not think within the same frame of concepts, principles and methods, are obscure, muddled and somehow perverted. He is not disposed to take them seriously. He scorns them from the heights of eternal truth. They are but adversaries and villains whose opinions can be set forth in a few lines of the introduction and briefly confuted in

70. Cf. Leo XIII, *Providentissimus Deus*, 270; Carlen, *The Papal Encyclicals 1878–1903*, 325–26.
71. See J. Fitzmyer, *The Biblical Commission's Document "The Interpretation of the Bible in the Church": Text and Commentary* (Rome: Editrice Pontificio Istituto Biblico, 1995), 19.

a *scholion*. All along there is no real interplay, no dialogue, no advance toward mutual understanding.[72]

In the light of *Aeterni Patris*, many saw Leo XIII as the pope of a single system, yet perhaps *Providentissimus Deus* sheds some light on the implicit intentions of that earlier encyclical. Certainly, in 1893 the pope remained alert to the dangers of the unbridled use of modern methods: "There has arisen to the great detriment of religion, an inept method, dignified by the name of 'higher criticism,' which pretends to judge of the origin, integrity and authority of each Book from internal indications alone."[73]

Moreover, he did maintain that biblical analysis should be grounded within Thomistic method, stating that

> the best preparation [for biblical study] will be a conscientious application of philosophy and theology under the guidance of St. Thomas of Aquin, and a thorough training therein—as We ourselves have elsewhere pointed out and directed. By this means, both in biblical studies and in that part of theology which is called *positive*, they will pursue the right path and make satisfactory progress.[74]

Nevertheless, while Leo exhorts scholars to show reverence for the scholastic framework, he indicates that this is not the only acceptable system. Insisting that for biblicists "the first means is the study of

---

72. J. Walgrave, *Unfolding Revelation* (Philadelphia: Westminster, 1972), 154.

73. "Perperam enim et cum religionis damno inductum est artificium, nomine honestatum criticae sublimioris, quo, ex solis internis, uti loquuntur, rationibus, cuiuspiam libri origo, integritas, auctoritas diiudicata emergant." Leo XIII, *Providentissimus Deus*, 285; Carlen, *The Papal Encyclicals 1878–1903*, 334.

74. "Erunt autem optime comparati, si, quâ Nosmetipsi monstravimus et praescripsimus via, philosophiae et theologiae institutionem, eodem S. Thoma duce, religiose coluerint penitusque perceperint. Ita recte incedent, quum in re biblica, tum in ea theologiae parte quam *positivam* nominant, in utraque laetissime progressuri." Ibid., 284; Carlen, *The Papal Encyclicals 1878–1903*, 333. For an example of how the scholastic system helped to shape Leo's understanding of the Scriptures, see teaching on inspiration (ibid., 288–89; Carlen, *The Papal Encyclicals 1878–1903*, 336). Jared Wicks provides a helpful insight into this in *Introduction to Theological Method*, 56.

the oriental languages and the art of criticism,"[75] the pope declares interplay with modern methods to be legitimate and indicates the beginnings of a tentative dialogue with other theological systems. For example, the encyclical shows a greater awareness of the Scriptures and the early fathers as sources of doctrine, and this in itself opens up a consciousness of history, without which revelation cannot be adequately understood. Another important, yet to some extent implicit, element in this perspective is the notion of experience. The truth and power of the word of God have been increasingly appreciated through the church's reflection on her experience down the ages:

> The Holy Fathers well knew all this by practical experience, and they never cease to extol the sacred Scripture and its fruits. In innumerable passages of their writings we find them applying to it such phrases as "an inexhaustible treasury of heavenly doctrine," or "an overflowing fountain of salvation," or putting it before us as fertile pastures and beautiful gardens in which the flock of the Lord is marvellously refreshed and delighted.[76]

Essential to the recognition of historical-critical exegesis, and the growing respect given to the role of experience in the church, is a conviction with regard to the realism of the incarnation.[77] The

---

75. "Est primum in studio linguarum veterum orientalium simulque in arte quam vocant criticam." Leo XIII, *Providentissimus Deus*, 285; Carlen, *The Papal Encyclicals 1878–1903*, 334.

76. "Quae omnia SS. Patres cognitione et usu quum exploratissima haberent, nunquam cessarunt in divinis Litteris earumque fructibus collaudandis. Eas enim vero crebris locis appellant vel thesaurum locupletissimum doctrinarum caelestium, vel perennes fontes salutis, vel ita proponunt quasi prata fertilia et amoenissimos hortos, in quibus grex dominicus admirabili modo reficiatur et delectetur." Ibid., 272–73; Carlen, *The Papal Encyclicals 1878–1903*, 327.

77. "The Church of Christ takes the realism of the incarnation seriously, and this is why she attaches great importance to the 'historico-critical' study of the Bible. Far from condemning it, as those who support 'mystical' exegesis would want, my Predecessors vigorously approved. 'Artis criticae disciplinam,' Leo XIII wrote, 'quippe percipiendae penitus hagiographorum sententiae perutilem, *Nobis vehementer probantibus*, nostri (exegetae, scilicet, catholici) excolant' (Apostolic Letter *Vigilantiae*, establishing the Biblical Commission, 30 October 1902). The same 'vehemence' in the approval and the same adverb ('vehementer') are found in *Divino Afflante Spiritu* regarding research in textual criticism." John Paul II, "Address on The Interpretation of

union of the divine and the human in the historical life of Jesus Christ is the principle that determines our understanding of the gracious self-manifestation of God. *Providentissimus Deus* thus affirms a rich parallelism of meaning between the scriptural and the incarnate Word, a parallel that *Divinum Illud Munus*[78] extends to the Word made flesh in the life of the church:

> Let it suffice to state that, as Christ is the Head of the Church, so is the Holy Ghost her soul. "What the soul is in our body, that is the Holy Ghost in Christ's body the Church" (St. Aug., *Serm.* 187, *de Temp.*) This being so, no further and fuller "manifestation and revelation of the Divine Spirit" may be imagined or expected; for that which now takes place in the Church is the most perfect possible, and will last until that day when the Church herself, having passed through her militant career, shall be taken up into the joy of the saints triumphing in heaven.[79]

In this encyclical on the Holy Spirit, Leo XIII makes very clear the revelatory status of the church. The Spirit who made the Christ flesh in the womb of Mary and inspired the word of God in the minds and hearts of the writers of sacred Scripture, is the Spirit who makes manifest and reveals the same incarnate Word in the church. There is, as will be seen later, a surprising novelty in Leo's conviction in the present and perfect actualization of revelation in the life of the church. Surprising too is the personal and somewhat immanent

---

the Bible in the Church," in Fitzmyer, *The Biblical Commission's Document "The Interpretation of the Bible in the Church,"* 5.

78. For a very useful general overview, see A. Huerga, "La enciclica de Leon XIII sobre el Espiritu Santo," in *Credo in Spiritum Sanctum*, vol. 1: *Atti del congresso teologico Internazionale di pneumatologia* (Vatican City: Libreria Editrice Vaticana, 1983), 507–16.

79. "Atque hoc affirmare sufficiat, quod quum Christus caput sit Ecclesiae, Spiritus Sanctus sit eius anima: *Quod est in corpore nostro anima, id est Spiritus Sanctus in corpore Christi, quod est Ecclesia.*—Quae ita quum sint, nequaquam comminisci et expectare licet aliam ullam ampliorem uberioremque *divini Spiritus manifestationem et ostensionem*; quae enim nunc in Ecclesia habetur; maxima sane est, eaque tamdiu manebit quoad Ecclesiae contingat ut, militiae emensa stadium, ad triumphantium in caelesti societate laetitiam educatur." Leo XIII, *Divinum Illud Munus*, 650; Carlen, *The Papal Encyclicals 1878–1903*, 412.

manner by which he understands that the Holy Spirit makes himself manifest in the lives of the just:

> Among these gifts [of the Holy Spirit] are those secret warnings and invitations, which from time to time are excited in our minds and hearts by the inspiration of the Holy Ghost. Without these there is no beginning of a good life, no progress, no arriving at eternal salvation. And since these words and admonitions are uttered in the soul in an exceedingly secret manner, they are sometimes compared in Holy Writ to the breathing of a coming breeze, and the Angelic Doctor likens them to the movements of the heart which are wholly hidden in the living body (*ST* 3a q vii., a. I ad. 3).[80]

While there is some sense in which Leo regards the sacraments as the formal objectification of this inner movement,[81] his treatment of the *signum demonstrativum* remains muted. However, this may be because sacramentology is not central to his purpose. Moreover, while in this encyclical, the pope does not make explicit links between the liturgical celebration of the sacraments and the actualization of revelation in the church, his stressing of the unificatory role of the Holy Spirit within the economy of salvation opens the way to later more direct parallels.[82] Certainly, throughout Leo XIII's long reign

---

80. "In his autem muneribus sunt arcanae illae admonitiones invitationesque, quae instinctu Sancti Spiritus identidem in mentibus animisque excitantur; quae si desint, neque initium viae bonae habetur, neque progressiones, neque exitus salutis aeternae. Et quoniam huiusmodi voces et motiones occulte admodum in animis fiunt, apte in sacris paginis similes nonnunquam habentur venientis aurae sibilo; easque Doctor Angelicus scite confert motibus cordis, cuius tota vis est in animante perabdita: *Cor habet quamdam influentiam occultam, et ideo cordi comparatur Spiritus Sanctus, qui invisibiliter Ecclesiam vivificat et unit.*" Ibid., 653–54; Carlen, *The Papal Encyclicals 1878–1903*, 414.

81. "The beginnings of this regeneration and renovation of man are by Baptism. In this sacrament, when the unclean spirit has been expelled from the soul, the Holy Ghost enters in and makes it like to himself. 'That which is born of the Spirit, is spirit' (John iii., 6). The same Spirit gives himself more abundantly in Confirmation, strengthening and confirming Christian life." (Huius regenerationis et renovationis initia sunt homini per baptisma: in quo sacramento, spiritu immundo ab anima depulso, illabitur primum Spiritus Sanctus, eamque similem sibi facit: *Quod natum est ex Spiritu, spiritus est.* Uberiusque per sacram confirmationem, ad constantiam et robur christianae vitae, sese dono dat idem Spiritus.) Ibid., 652; Carlen, *The Papal Encyclicals 1878–1903*, 413.

it is possible to chart a circumspect yet increasing openness to the insights that an understanding of historical development gives to the theological disciplines. This, coupled with the recognition of methodologies other than the scholastic, beg for a reconsideration of the pope's intentions in promulgating *Aeterni Patris*.

Earlier Responses to the Question of Historicity

The rise of a historical consciousness in Catholic theology, and an investigation of the internal, subjective dimensions of faith, as well as the way these two phenomena shape both Scripture and tradition, were not movements that began in the twentieth century. Nor did they result solely in response to Leo XIII's philosophical and theological prescriptions. Although it would be difficult to imagine twentieth-century theology developing as it did without the decisive direction that *Aeterni Patris* gave,[83] there were, nevertheless, traces of a new theology prior to Pope Leo XIII. As Yves Congar points out,

---

82. One might single out the encyclical *Mirae Caritatis* of 1902, in which Leo XIII states, "The Eucharist, according to the testimony of the Holy Fathers, should be regarded as in a manner a continuation and extension of the Incarnation. For in and by it the substance of the Incarnate Word is united with individual men, and the supreme sacrifice offered on Calvary is in a wondrous manner renewed." (Eucharistia, Patrum sanctorum testimonio, Incarnationis continuatio quaedam et amplificatio censenda est. Siquidem per ipsam incarnati Verbi substantia cum singulis hominibus copulatur; et supremum in Calvaria sacrificium admirabili modo renovatur.) Leo XIII, *Mirae Caritatis*, ASS 34 (1902): 645. English trans. in Carlen, *The Papal Encyclicals 1878–1903*, 502.

83. "Without the firm leadership of Leo XIII himself in the Thomistic revival, it is hardly likely that the vast historical scholarship and the remarkable systematic development that characterized the Thomistic movement in the century after the publication of *Aeterni Patris* would have taken place. Certainly the history of twentieth-century Catholic philosophy and theology would have followed an entirely different course. The twentieth century would not have been the age of Rousselot, Mercier, de Raeymaeker, Grabmann, Gilson, Maritain, Garrigou-Lagrange, Journet, de Lubac, Bouillard, Rahner, and Lonergan. Less than a decade after *Dei Filius*, the practical interpretation of its teaching by Leo XIII in *Aeterni Patris* gave a decisive and irreversible orientation to Catholic philosophy and theology." McCool, *Catholic Theology in the Nineteenth Century*, 236.

The romantic current in theology is the first factor to bring about reconstruction in the course of the years from 1810–1840. Its action promotes unity and the reintegration of the elements dissociated in the preceding period. It regains first of all a sense of the past, of the Fathers and even of Scholasticism through its interest in the Middle Ages. In this way it begins to recapture a sense of the contemplation of truths of the faith and of speculation about them. . . . In this very manner, Romanticism recaptures or discovers a sense of development and history.[84]

The liberal Protestant theologian, Friedrich Schleiermacher (1768–1834), along with the Catholic theologians of the Tübingen school, whom he influenced, especially Johann Adam Möhler (1796–1838), the English convert John Henry Newman (1801–1890), and the French Traditionalists Félicité de Lamennais (1782–1854) and Louis Bautain (1796–1867), were perhaps the most influential forerunners with regard to the themes that occupied twentieth-century Catholic theology. Here were the beginnings of the rebellion against a totally objective and scientifically deduced scholastic method in theology, a rebellion that *Aeterni Patris* was ironically to deepen and intensify.

Schleiermacher bases his understanding of faith on the sense of certainty that arises from feeling oneself dependent on a transcendent reality, which is God.[85] The Christian community is the place where this faith is strengthened by the testimonies of experience. Faith results from such testimonies and is passed through the community. Hence faith may be defined as "the inward condition of one who feels content and strong in fellowship with Christ."[86] This basing of the act of faith on the testimony of others in the Christian community is also

---

84. Y.-M. Congar, *A History of Theology* (New York: Doubleday, 1968), 183.
85. For a concise study of the major themes of his work, and a selection of his writings, see K. W. Clements, *Friedrich Schleiermacher, Pioneer of Modern Theology* (London: Collins, 1987), especially 35–66.
86. F. Schleiermacher, *Der christliche Glaube nach den Grundsätzen der evangelischen Kirche im Zusammenhange dargestellt,* 2nd. ed., 2 vols. (Berlin: G. Reimer, 1830–31). English trans. of 2nd

at the heart of the French doctrine of traditionalism. This doctrine was the preferred alternative to the skepticism that the Enlightenment had brought. In its more radical forms, it responded to the question of faith and reason by asserting that the knowledge of God, morality, and religion is not accessible to human reason, but must be accepted in faith, a faith that is engendered by the historical transmission of the truths of revelation.[87] Tradition is the locus of supernatural knowledge, and without it, individual reason can lead only to skepticism and despair. Félicité de Lamennais was, in his early writings, the most typical exponent of extreme traditionalism. In his comprehensive four-volume work, *Essai sur l'indifférence en matière de religion*,[88] the first volume of which had wide and significant effect, he identifies the universal consent of the human race, represented by the church as the criterion of truth and certitude. Though in some ways initially pleasing to the authorities at Rome, his works became increasingly liberal in character and politically contentious.[89]

Louis Bautain, a professional philosopher, was more conversant with the modern philosophies, and as a result his arguments were more nuanced than those of De Lamennais. However, Bautain was certainly a traditionalist and, though philosophically knowledgeable,

German edition, *The Christian Faith*, ed. H. R. Mackintosh and J. S. Stewart (New York: Harper and Row, 1963), 483.

87. Like most theologians of this period, Schleiermacher and the traditionalists were seeking to respond to the devastating effect that the philosophy of Immanuel Kant had had on Christian epistemology. "But, if Kant's vindication of objective certitude were correct, how could an act of faith in Christian revelation be valid rational knowledge? And how could Catholic theology be a science? The act of faith was a free assent to a contingent fact revealed by God. Catholic theology had contingent historical revelation as its object. Science and History were mutually exclusive according to Kant. Yet, ever since the Middle Ages, Catholic theology had defined itself as a scientific discipline which moved from its revealed first principles to its conclusions according to the norms of a scientific method." Cf. McCool, *Catholic Theology in the Nineteenth Century*, 59–63.

88. F. de Lamennais, *Essai sur l'indifférence en matière de religion*, 2nd ed. (Paris: Tournachon-Molin et Seguin, 1818).

89. For a fuller discussion of the contribution of De Lamennais, see Y.-M. Congar, *L'Église de saint Augustin à l'époque moderne* (Paris: Éditions du Cerf, 1970), 146ff.

thought no philosophy claiming to be independent of faith was capable of establishing God's existence. Faith was the means to reality and truth, and no rational system was necessary to underpin, explain, or introduce revelation. The credibility of Christian revelation, and therefore the act of faith, was dependent not on natural reason but on an act of primitive revelation, prior to which "no mind can think."[90] An interesting aspect of Bautain's thought is his opinion of scholasticism as simply another philosophical method that sought to subject faith to an individual's rational understanding. Interestingly, Bautain's philosophy was never condemned and, after following the lectures of Giovanni Perrone (1794-1876) at the Roman College, he revised his position substantially, and was to be informed amicably by Gregory XVI that "he had sinned by too much faith."[91]

Such cordiality was not to be the experience of De Lamennais. Though his early ultramontane doctrines had been well received by Pope Leo XII in 1824, he was, in later years, unremitting in his efforts to realise his Christian philosophy practically and politically, efforts that resulted in his doctrines being condemned by Gregory XVI. Indeed, the career of De Lamennais forms an interesting contrast to Bautain's, and might be said to map the rising politicization of the approach in the new philosophy to faith and reason. Here, perhaps, is the incipient disdain for the wedding of any philosophical methods other than the Thomistic to papal ultramontanism, an alliance that was to be strengthened by Vatican I and the pontificate of Pius IX, and which would reach its fullest expression in *Aeterni Patris*. Though by the standards of the subsequent teachings of Vatican I, De Lamennais is wrong to reject the part played by reason in the act of faith, it was his political liberalism that led to his condemnation.[92] By

---

90. McCool, *Catholic Theology in the Nineteenth Century*, 50.
91. Ibid.
92. "But Maréchal was quite correct in pointing out that during this period Lamennais thought more theocratically than monarchically. From this vantage point it becomes understandable

this is meant his linking of the knowledge of the truths of salvation to the universal consent of the human race at the expense of the papal prerogative. Gregory took an increasingly inflexible stance on papal authority, which he came to see as the only means of defeating the rationalist threat. As Herbert Jedin makes clear,

> Gregory XVI's battle against the excesses of rationalism, indifferentism and Kantian subjectivism helped to achieve a balance between the sense of the supernatural and the value of human reason, and thus laid firm foundations for the future development of the Catholic spirit and Catholic spirituality. By insisting inflexibly on the prerogatives of the Holy See and the independence of the Church, however, the Pope also prepared the way for the future successes of ultramontanism which ultimately stifled pluralism and endangered the collegial nature of ecclesial authority.[93]

Until the relatively recent research of Josef Rupert Geiselmann (1890–1970) established the theological credentials of the Tübingen School,[94] their work tended to be "dismissed as one more nineteenth-century method which had failed the crucial test of dealing successfully with the relations between faith and reason, grace and nature."[95] Geiselmann, however, uncovered a careful and scientific theology of revelation, and an understanding of the development of doctrine and the role of the Holy Spirit within the church. Johann Sebastian Drey (1777–1853) was the founder of the Catholic School at Tübingen and, responsive to philosophical currents and especially the Kantian critique, devised a theology centered on "revelation as God's action in history for the education of the human race."[96]

that once he grew disillusioned with monarchy—he found it easy to turn away from it. He associated the Church with the growing cause of the people and strove to achieve what Verucci has called a democratic theocracy." H. Jedin, ed., *History of the Church*, vol. 7: *The Church between Revolution and Restoration* (London: Burns and Oates, 1981), 273–79.

93. Ibid., 265.
94. Cf. J. R. Geiselmann, *Die katholische Tübinger Schule* (Freiburg: Herder, 1964).
95. McCool, *Catholic Theology in the Nineteenth Century*, 4.
96. A. Dulles, *The Assurance of Things Hoped For*, 83.

J. Adam Möhler, Drey's pupil, an associate of Schleiermacher and Friedrich Schelling and the most imaginative theologian of the Tübingen School, developed Drey's traditionalism into an understanding of faith as something personal, interior, and transcendent. However, by the time of his final work, *Symbolik*, Möhler's thought had been tempered considerably by the Roman theology, though he still resisted a propositional theory of faith.[97] The theological themes of the Tübingen School were those of John Henry Newman, whose famous *Essay on the Development of Christian Doctrine* begins, "Christianity has been long enough in the world to justify us in dealing with it as a fact in the world's history."[98] Yet Newman refines continental traditionalism by suggesting that revelation exists as an inner tradition, and not in the propositional formulations of Scripture and creeds. Such expressions were merely the response to external attack. As Aidan Nichols explains, "A sound understanding of Christian revelation, then, depends on growth in holiness, is not accessible to secular reasoning, and exists as an internal tradition within the Church taking the form of an articulated Creed only in some doctrinal emergency."[99]

Newman consciously rejects the extrinsicism of the neo-scholastics, and looks to the experience of the historical church to arrive at an understanding of humanity's coming to faith. As Rino Fisichella says, Newman "gave first place, with the Pascalian *raison du coeur*, to the psychology of experience,"[100] and it is this that makes him a modern[101] and a harbinger of the new theology. From the

---

97. For an exposition of Möhler's theology of faith, see Geiselmann, *Die Katholische Tübinger Schule*, 146–53.

98. J. H. Newman, *Essay on the Development of Christian Doctrine* 3rd ed. (London: 1878; reprinted Notre Dame, IN: University of Notre Dame Press, 1989), 3.

99. A. Nichols, *From Newman to Congar: The Idea of Doctrinal Development from the Victorians to the Second Vatican Council* (Edinburgh: T. & T. Clark, 1995), 28.

100. R. Fisichella, "John Henry Newman," in *Dictionary of Fundamental Theology*, ed. R. Latourelle and R. Fisichella (New York: Crossroads, 1995), 734.

perspective of experience, he establishes a fundamental theology of the act of faith, a doctrine that is most clearly set forth in his *Grammar of Assent* of 1870. Here, Newman concludes that the act of assent "is in itself the absolute acceptance of a proposition without any condition," yet the act is based on "sense sensations, instinct, intuition,"[102] all of which can supply us with facts that the intellect can use. Thus, though the reasons are of the heart, they nevertheless remain reasons, and so allow Newman to provide a rational exposition of the act of faith, to provide a grammar for assent.

Between Newman, Bautain, Möhler, Drey, and De Lamennais there is a certain similarity not merely in their preoccupying theological themes, but also in their disregard of, or at least ambivalence toward, scholasticism. The Tübingen School was a noted rival to Roman scholasticism in the nineteenth century, embracing as it did the many and new German philosophies. French traditionalism had, in general, "a low opinion of scholasticism,"[103] and a parallel can easily be drawn with the stance of Newman:

> Newman had displayed not so much a dislike of, as psychological and intellectual discomfort with, the scholastic method. His mind worked in a concrete, image-laden manner which was out of harmony with the deductive, logic-based, method of neo-scholasticism. His distinction between implicit and explicit reasoning is the heuristic key to much of his thought. The long reign of the syllogism in Roman Catholic

---

101. "I cannot but think that if Newman were studied and assimilated it would tend to unbarbarise us and enable us to pour Catholic truth from the scholastic to the modern mould without losing a drop in the transfer." *Letters from a "Modernist": The Letters of George Tyrrell to Wilfrid Ward 1893–1908*, ed. M. J. Weaver (Shepherdstown, WV: Patmos Press, 1981), 3. And, for a general discussion of the relationship of Newman and the Modernists, see M. J. Weaver, ed., *Newman and the Modernists* (Lanham, MD: University Press of America, 1985).

102. J. H. Newman, *An Essay in Aid of a Grammar of Assent,* ed. I. Ker (Oxford: Oxford University Press, 1985), 13.

103. "Bautain shared the low opinion of scholasticism prevalent in Catholic circles during the early years of the nineteenth century. To him scholasticism was another form of rationalism, it was simply another philosophy of discursive reason which endeavoured to subordinate Christian faith and Christian tradition to the judgement of the individual understanding." McCool, *Catholic Theology in the Nineteenth Century*, 47.

theology had created an intellectual climate antipathetic to the working of some distinguished Christian minds, including Newman's. At many points during the second millennium of the Christian Church, Aristotle appeared to have been enshrined among the Apostles as a source of faith; for, as Tyrrell never tired of pointing out, as long as revelation was in practice identified with its theological expression, uniformity of method would be judged necessary to unity of faith.[104]

And yet, in that final allusion to George Tyrrell, Gabriel Daly points to a defect from which the Tübingen school was not entirely free, a defect with which Newman struggled. Though the introduction of the Romantic strain in theology had brought vitality to a desiccated scholastic system, the prevailing context remained cognitive. To quote Yves Congar again:

> Certainly, theology had never been defined there [Tübingen], as in the liberal Protestantism sprung from Schleiermacher, as an analysis and a description of religious experience. The thought of the greatest among those at Tübingen is thoroughly orthodox. But their theology is conceived too much as an intellectual realization of what the Church (and the theologian in the Church) has received and by which it lives. It is not sufficiently the human construction of a faith rising up from a datum objectively established and from objective criteria. In a word, their theology is too much a science of faith and not enough a science of Revelation.[105]

Though the inadequacies of the scholastic system had been detailed by these and other theologians prior to *Aeterni Patris,* with the promulgation of the teaching of Leo XIII a reassessment of the suitability of scholasticism to deal with the theological problems of the day began from within the school itself. What *Aeterni Patris* initiated among some twentieth-century Thomists was a search among the resources of the scholastic tradition for answers to the

104. G. Daly, "Newman and Modernism: A Theological Reflection," in Weaver, *Newman and the Modernists,* 185–204, 186.

105. Congar, *A History of Theology,* 184.

problems that critics of scholasticism, Modernist or otherwise, had made in the late nineteenth and early twentieth century. Before turning to the particular criticisms of the Modernists, it is necessary to come to some appreciation of the state of Catholic theology prior to what came to be known as the *nouvelle théologie.*

The Neo-Thomist Movement

The Thomistic movement had its origins in the first half of the nineteenth century. As Drey, the Tübingen school, the traditionalists, ontologists, and those critical of scholasticism developed a response to post-Enlightenment rationalism and Kant's criticisms of Christian epistemology, those who sought a solution in the work of St. Thomas began to formulate their own response. The suppression of the Jesuits was lifted in 1814,[106] and ten years later Gregory XVI returned the Roman College to their direction. Luigi Taparelli (1793–1862) was made rector. A belligerent and unyielding Thomist, he had held no position of influence for long but, as a result of his brief term of office at the Roman College and subsequently as Jesuit Provincial to the Province of Naples, he influenced a nucleus of men who were to hold critical positions later, and who were to do everything in their power to further the Thomist cause. At Rome, he influenced Carlo Maria Curci (1810–1891), the Jesuit neo-scholastic who was to be the founder of *Civiltà Cattolica,* and Gioacchino Pecci, the future Leo XIII and author of *Aeterni Patris.* In Naples, he converted to

---

106. "The influential position which these Jesuit theologians and philosophers acquired during the pontificate of Pius IX placed remarkable power over the development of Catholic theology in the hands of an incredibly small body of men. They were perhaps the most influential advisers to the Roman curia at the very moment when the papacy was resolutely determined to shape the course of Catholic theology by an unprecedented use of the authority which the curia had acquired in the centralized nineteenth-century Church." McCool, *Catholic Theology in the Nineteenth Century,* 135.

Thomism Pecci's brother, Giuseppe, a scholastic who was to become bishop of Perugia and establish Dominican control in the diocesan seminary, creating a center for the Thomistic revival. He influenced also Matteo Liberatore (1810–1892), who was later to become an influential Thomist and collaborator on *Civiltà Cattolica*. Through these personal associations, the somewhat scattered neo-Thomist movement took on a certain unity, and, when the time was ripe and it sought to express its understanding of method in theology more militantly, it was able to do so with a gathering momentum. As G. McCool says,

> By 1850 the intellectual force of the Romantic movement had been spent and the influence of German Idealism was on the wane. The revolutions of 1848 had turned Pius IX against modern movements in social and religious thought. The climate was favourable for an aggressive attack on modern philosophy and upon theological systems structured by it.[107]

On the back of a militantly defensive papacy, which was intransigent toward the rising Italian nationalism and liberalism, the neo-scholastics took their opportunity. *Civiltà Cattolica* was founded in 1849 by a group of Thomist academics at the request of Pius IX. Essentially it was to provide the Church with an intellectually rigorous response to the social and cultural changes that Italy was experiencing. However, by 1853 the review was synonymous with the campaign to restore Thomism as the only system within Catholic theology. Taparelli was influential on the editorial team,[108] their main aim being the theoretical explanation of the merits of Thomism and the restoration of the system in Catholic institutions.

In the period between the year of *Civiltà Cattolica's* flourishing in 1853, and the promulgation of *Aeterni Patris* in 1879, the Jesuit

107. Ibid., 86.
108. Cf. P. Dezza, *Alle origini del neotomismo italiano* (Milan: Fratelli Bocca, 1940), 52–55.

neo-Thomists became increasingly powerful,[109] and their associations at the court of Pius IX are well-known.[110] Yet essentially it was the linking of this newfound influence in the increasingly powerful and centralized papacy to their concise and clear response to the theological issues of the day that established them as the dominant school within Catholic theology. The First Vatican Council had highlighted the role of the papacy as the premier teaching organ within the Church, and had focused on the questions of faith and reason, nature and grace. The neo-Thomists saw in these two issues the means of establishing their method.[111] Using the increased status of the post-Council papacy and appealing to its newly asserted power, the neo-scholastics put forward their argument to answer the question of the relationship between faith and reason. Manipulating the conviction that modern systems both confused the natural and supernatural orders, and compromised the gratuitous nature of the workings of grace by an overestimation of humanity's rational capacities in the act of faith,[112] the neo-scholastics created a theological problem to which the system of St. Thomas provided the only competent and complete answer. With *Aeterni Patris* for approbation in the last years of the century, the schoolmen merely consolidated and extended their position.

Though *Aeterni Patris* did not evoke an instant response,[113] by the turn of the century there was a considerable degree of uniformity within Catholic theological institutions. Effective in achieving the

109. "At least one historian has implied that the real explanation of neo-Thomism's triumph over its rivals in the nineteenth century was an unscrupulously brutal use of its authority by a clerical establishment." McCool, *Catholic Theology in the Nineteenth Century*, 135. Here McCool cites P. Thibault, *Savoir et Pouvoir*, 95–99, 151–58, 229–31.

110. R. Aubert, *Le Pontificat de Pie IX, (1846–1878)* (Paris: Bloud et Gay, 1952), 286.

111. Daly, *Transcendence and Immanence*, 9.

112. McCool, *Catholic Theology in the Nineteenth Century*, 139. Cf. R. Aubert, *Le Problème de l'acte de foi* (Louvain: Warny, 1950).

113. R. P. Lecanuet, *La Vie de l'Église sous Léon XIII* (Paris: Aubier, 1930), 472.

aims of *Aeterni Patris* and the neo-Thomists were the theological manuals of the Roman colleges, which brought the scholastic system and standardization to seminaries and Catholic universities in the city and across the world. As Gabriel Daly is aware,

> It is to the manuals which one must go if one is to determine the character, quality, and, particularly, the limitations of Catholic theology between the Vatican Councils. Given a propositional view of revelation, deductive method in theology, and an ever-increasing concern to identify and label doctrinal assertions according to the degree of their ecclesiastical authority, the method employed by the manuals was both theologically consistent and pedagogically effective.[114]

The works of Giovanni Perrone and Louis Billot (1846–1931) are perhaps the best examples of the theology of this period, their persistence until the eve of the Second Vatican Council being enough of a testimony to their effectiveness.[115] There was little development, however, between Perrone's *Praelectiones theologicae*[116] and the publication of the fifth edition of Ludwig Ott's *Fundamentals of Catholic Dogma*[117] in 1962. Pertinent to this study is the clear fact that the manualists' understanding of revelation shows no development whatever. The same forensic and logical definition was reiterated for nearly eighty years. Translation of the manuals into the vernacular served only to keep the definition similar throughout the world, and did not encourage a reexamination or redefinition of the concepts themselves. In this case, when Daly terms a theologian *Roman*, we

---

114. Daly, *Transcendence and Immanence*, 12. Cf.: "The degree of uniformity achieved in these manuals is striking and should not be neglected by anyone seeking to appreciate the nature and temper of Roman Catholic theology between the two Vatican Councils," ibid., 13.

115. "In 1962, the year in which the Second Vatican Council opened, there appeared the fifth English edition of Ludwig Ott's *Fundamentals of Catholic Dogma*, a book which may go down in history as the last of the widely used neo-scholastic 'manuals,'" ibid., 1.

116. G. Perrone, *Praelectiones theologicae*, vols. 1–4 (Paris: Gaume Fratres Bibliopolæ, 1883).

117. L. Ott, *Grundriss der Katholischen Dogmatik*, 1952; *Fundamentals of Catholic Dogma*, trans. P. Lynch (Cork: Paulist, 1962).

may interpret his epithet to refer to almost any geographical location: "No Roman theologian will qualify in any essential respect Perrone's definition of revelation as the manifestation of some truth or truths which is supernatural both in origin and in the mode of its communication."[118]

Not only was there no essential qualification of this definition, in fact the Thomistic revival of the late nineteenth century and the Modernist crisis of the early twentieth served to refine the argument and tightened it against any possible nuance. If Perrone set the foundations, it was the Jesuit and future Cardinal Louis Billot who was largely responsible for solidifying the teaching on revelation. Billot's work concentrated on a profound analysis of the act of faith. He sought to chart an unwavering course through the Scylla and Charybdis of rationalism and fideism.[119] In this Billot showed complete disregard for any method that based itself on the feelings,

---

118. Daly, *Transcendence and Immanence*, 14. See also G. Perrone, *Praelectiones theologicae*, vol.1: *De vera religione*. Further examples would be two typical Roman manuals: H. Dieckmann, *De Revelatione Christiana* (Freiburg: Herder & Co., 1930), 130–54; and R. Garrigou-Lagrange, *De Revelatione*, 2nd ed. (Rome: Libreria Editrice Religiosa, 1932), 56–71. However, perhaps the best example of the scope of the Roman manual's influence is afforded by looking at the definitions of revelation contained in some of the vernacular translations based on the textbooks. A good example would be the much translated J. Brunsmann, *A Handbook of Fundamental Theology*, vol. 2: *Revealed Religion,* adapted and edited by A. Preuss (London: Herder, 1929). Here the author suggests, "To reveal means to make known something which was unknown before, to unveil to the intellect a truth or fact of which it had no previous knowledge. The term *revelation* may designate both the act of communicating knowledge and the communicated knowledge itself. Here we are interested mainly in the former, i.e. the manner in which knowledge is communicated. Revelation in this sense, that is, as manifestation of the truth, primarily concerns the intellect." 11. Thus, between the Latin definition of Perrone in 1883 and the vernacular definition of Brunsmann-Preuss some fifty years later, there is little if any development.

119. George Tyrrell charted quite a different course in his *Through Scylla and Charybdis*. As Aidan Nichols points out, "In this brief study, Tyrrell points out that 'theology' may refer in a Catholic context to one of two things. More narrowly it is the Scholastic tradition currently in possession in institutes of academic and ministerial formation. More widely, it is the attempt to articulate revelation, an enterprise defined by Tyrrell in terms of the unification and elucidation of data provided by Christian experience in the concrete. The applying of philosophical concepts to revelation, as carried out in Scholastic theology, tends like all philosophising to 'excessive abstraction and vague unreality.' It needs to be facts: 'the facts here being the Christian religion as lived by its consistent professors.'" Nichols, *From Newman to Congar*, 117.

affectivity, or experience. The intuition of which the Modernists and others spoke, "Billot simply regarded as weak-mindedness."[120] He can be regarded and dismissed summarily as "the leading exponent of a theological perspective which saw revelation as assertion, faith as intellectual assent, and theology as a mainly deductive procedure."[121] Describing his method as "clinical" and "robotic," Gabriel Daly gives no merely personal attack, but exposes one who epitomized the neo-scholastic apologetic of his age and beyond. Essentially, we are speaking of a dry theological system that lacked any humanity or dynamism, took little, maybe no, regard of the internal, personal response of human faith, and no cognizance of the social structure of that faith.[122]

Alternative Roman Responses and The Modernist Movement

Perhaps the only "Roman" figure to counter this apologetic in any way was Archbishop Victor Dechamps of Malines (1810–1883).[123] His subjective apologetics or "apologetics of providence" differed from the scholastic method by asserting the importance of the subjective "internal facts" in an individual's coming to faith, in addition to the verifiable external facts of signs and miracles on which the scholastic method concentrated solely. Indeed, Dechamps himself

---

120. Daly, *Transcendence and Immanence*, 15

121. Ibid.

122. "The *facta externa* were there to be observed and registered by the senses just as any pikestaff might be. The interpretative element was given a minimal role as something 'subjective' and therefore by definition open to error and waywardness. The would-be believer had merely to observe, register, and respond with his mind and will. He brought nothing of his own to the process beyond the *tabula rasa* so conveniently underwritten by Aristotelian epistemology." Ibid., 19–20.

123. The contribution of the Jesuit, Pierre Rousselot (1878-1915) in distancing Catholic theology from merely objective and propositional notions of faith by embracing a sense of faith as a living and loving knowledge that allows us to perceive the connections in what is given so as to be able to make assent, though of great importance comes later. See Pierre Rousselot, *The Eyes of Faith*, trans. Joseph Donceel, (New York: Fordham University Press, 1990).

prevented *Dei Filius* from making a direct identification between its own understanding of faith and reason and the Aristotelian method of the schools.[124] The theology that Dechamps championed at the First Vatican Council remained largely hidden until the Second. The desire for apologetic argument was as much a function of the ultramontane politics of the Church, buoyed up by recent teachings on infallibility, as it was part of the neo-scholastic method.

Together the powerful and united forces of curial authority and clear schoolroom method effectively stemmed the call for a reasoning of the heart in apologetics. The call that Dechamps had made, and that can be traced back through Newman, the Tübingen School, and Pascal to St. Augustine, though frequently silenced by the louder Christian Aristotelianism[125] and papal authority, was to be heard again in the writings of the Modernists. This time, the efforts to restrain the resurgent theme were even stronger than before. Nevertheless, the work begun by Dechamps and the others was about to be reshaped by Maurice Blondel (1861–1949),[126] and those who drew inspiration from his immanentist teachings, into theological forms that would instill a sense of crisis in Catholic theology.

In more recent studies, the concept of a body of writers putting forward a cohesive theology that might be represented by the term *Modernism* has been largely rejected. As Darrell Jodock clearly states,

> If Modernism is defined as a coherent system of thought, no such thing existed prior to the encyclical [*Pascendi*]. Alfred Loisy, Friedrich von

---

124. As McCool points out: "The important position which Dechamps occupied on the conciliar deputation on faith enabled the archbishop of Malines to exert a constant and significant influence upon the drafting of the revised schema which the deputation submitted to the council fathers in 1870." *Catholic Theology in the Nineteenth Century*, 223. See also the letter of Cardinal Billot, the president of the preconciliar Dogmatic Commission, to Dechamps, cited in Aubert, *Le problème de l'acte de foi*, 142.

125. Daly, *Transcendence and Immanence*, 24.

126. As G. Daly points out: "Maurice Blondel was delighted to discover in Dechamps's work striking similarities to his own approach." Ibid., 21. For a concise account of the contribution of Blondel to nineteenth century theology, see "The Blondelian Challenge," in ibid., 26–50.

Hügel, and George Tyrrell, all among those regularly considered to be Modernists, each objected to the accuracy of the portrait drawn by the encyclical. As Bernard Reardon points out, "Loisy, himself the most distinguished of them, [the Modernists], refused to accept any description of the movement's adherents as 'a homogeneous and united group'" and called "the pope's exposition of their doctrines 'a fantasy of the theological imagination.'"[127]

Maurice Blondel and the *Méthode D'Immanence*

Maurice Blondel, a loyal Catholic layman, submissive to authority and never censured by the Church, is perhaps an unlikely candidate for the description of Modernist, however disparate that group may be deemed to be. Yet it is with him that our analysis will begin, because it was there that *Pascendi* began with a notion of an underlying philosophy:

> We begin, then, with the philosopher. Modernists place the foundation of religious philosophy in that doctrine which is commonly called *Agnosticism*. According to this teaching human reason is confined entirely within the field of *phenomena*, that is to say, to things that appear, and in the manner in which they appear: it has neither the right nor the power to overstep these limits.[128]

---

127. D. Jodock, "Introduction I: The Modernist Crisis," in Jodock, *Catholicism Contending with Modernity*, 2. A similar sentiment is evidenced by Daly's remark about the draughtsman of *Pascendi*: "He evinces a stronger urge than they to connect up the disparate elements in the case he is attacking and thus to confer on those elements a logical cohesion which is academically tenuous but pedagogically satisfying." *Transcendence and Immanence*, 180. See also N. Provencher, "Modernism," in Latourelle and Fisichella, *Dictionary of Fundamental Theology*, 720: "As historians look back from a later time, too many of them tend to attribute to Modernism a unity and cohesiveness it never had."

128. "Iam ut a philosopho exordiamur, philosophiae religiosae fundamentum in doctrina illa modernistae ponunt, quam vulgo *agnosticismum* vocant. Vi huius humana ratio *phaenomenis* omnino includitur, rebus videlicet quae apparent eâque specie qua apparent: earumdem praetergredi terminos nec ius nec potestatem habet." Pius X, *Pascendi Dominici Gregis*, 596; Reardon, *Roman Catholic Modernism*, 238.

The philosophical stance that *Pascendi* radicalizes and intemperately terms *Agnosticism*, is but the negative aspect of a system of *vital immanence*—the latter arising naturally out of the former.[129] And, though Bernard Reardon rejects Guiseppe de Ruggiero's description of Blondel as its "spiritual father" as an "assessment so exaggerated to be false,"[130] one can begin to see why Blondel's *méthode d'immanence*[131] was attractive to the Modernists and regarded with suspicion by those trained in a scholasticism marked by extrinsicism.

Blondel defended his doctoral thesis on "Action" in the Faculty of Philosophy at Paris in 1893. Shortly before beginning work on the thesis, he had written to a friend detailing his intentions, "Between Aristotelianism which devalues and subordinates practice to thought, and Kantianism which segregates them and exalts the practical order to the detriment of the other, there is something needing definition, and it is in a very concrete manner, by the analysis of action, that I should like to establish what that something is."[132]

Blondel was convinced that experience was the point of departure for philosophy, and that an analysis of how human beings experience action would reveal the "something" he sought to establish. In this way, he endeavors to prove the presence of signs of transcendence in the human dynamic.[133] In so doing, he rejects the scholastic method of external objective argument beginning from a priori facts. Blondel

---

129. "Hic tamen *agnosticismus,* in disciplina modernistarum, non nisi ut pars negans habenda est: positiva, ut aiunt, in *immanentia vitali* constituitur." Ibid., 597; Reardon, *Roman Catholic Modernism*, 239.

130. Reardon, "Roman Catholic Modernism," 166.

131. This is the description that Blondel himself gives of his philosophical procedure in the article, "Lettre sur les exigences de la pensée contemporaine en matière d'apologétique," in *Lettres philosophiques* (Paris: Aubier, 1961). English trans. in A. Dru and I. Trethowan, *Maurice Blondel: The Letter on Apologetics and History and Dogma* (London: Burns and Oates, 1964).

132. Blondel, *Lettres philosophiques*, 10, in Daly *Transcendence and Immanence*, 30.

133. For a concise but fuller exposition of Blondel's theory in *L'Action*, see the analysis of R. Latourelle in "Maurice Blondel," in Latourelle and Fisichella, *Dictionary of Fundamental Theology*, 78–84.

accepts the Kantian critique of scholastic method, but rejects Kant's attempt to isolate pure reason from practical reason. For Blondel, analysis of human action "points inexorably toward a transcendent term."[134] In his *Letter on Apologetics*, he makes explicit the consequences of his study of action for Christian fundamentals. Here he speaks of the "necessity" of adhering to the supernatural,[135] and rejects the notion that the possibility and actuality of the supernatural can be demonstrated separately. Philosophy can reveal that the makeup of human existence is radically open to supernatural revelation. Though philosophy cannot produce but only prepare for faith, at the same time "it can show that man is not morally free to reject with impunity the possibility of faith and a supernatural order."[136] Philosophy has no competence within the supernatural realm. Hence Blondel rejects the traditional concern of apologetics with miracles as a proof of the faith, and concludes, "If the [revelatory] fact is to be accepted by our minds and even imposed upon our reason, an interior need and, as it were, an ineluctable appetite must prepare us for it."[137]

Blondel had opened wide discussion on the act of faith, apologetics, and theological method, but of crucial interest to those seeking a revitalized theology in the Catholic schools were the repercussions of his work for the relationship between the natural

---

134. Daly, *Transcendence and Immanence*, 31.

135. "We must show *the necessity for us* of adhering to this reality of the supernatural," M. Blondel, "Lettre sur les exigences de la pensée contemporaine en matière de la philosophie dans l'étude du problème religieux," in *Les premièrs écrits de Maurice Blondel*, vol. 2 (Paris: Presses Universitaires de France, 1956), 13. English trans. in Daly, *Transcendence and Immanence*, 36 (Blondel's italics).

136. "Que l'homme ne peut se passer impunément." "Blondel's continual use of the verbs 'se passer' and 'se dépasser' manifests his central concern with the dynamism of man's relationship with God. Faith has 'a logic' which is not extrinsically imposed on it but is interiorly generated by the dynamism of action." Daly, *Transcendence and Immanence*, 37.

137. Blondel, "Lettre sur les exigences," 14, in Daly, *Transcendence and Immanence*, 37. Here, Daly cites F. Rodé, *Le miracle dans la controverse moderniste* (Paris: Desclée, 1965), 53–99 as giving full documentation of the debate on miracles in Blondel's *Letter on Apologetics*.

and supernatural orders and the question of divine revelation. Lucien Laberthonnière (1860–1932) was right to warn Blondel that he was most likely to be denounced by the neo-scholastics for suggesting a continuity between the natural and supernatural orders.[138] And for this reason, too, it is not surprising that René Latourelle can draw, if not directly, a line from *L'Action* to the *Hörer des Wortes* of Karl Rahner.[139] Blondel had done more than inspire the Modernists by redefining the relationship of philosophy and theology. He had given theology a new point of departure, and had thus implied possibilities for a Catholic treatment of revelation that Louis Billot and his disciples could hardly have imagined.[140]

Alfred Loisy, The Gospel and the Church

If Blondel could be said to have provided the philosophical inspiration of the *méthode d'immanence*, then *L'Évangile et L'Église* by Alfred Loisy (1857–1940) must be regarded as the next departure of significance—"the book that could be said to have precipitated the Modernist crisis."[141] Usefully, C. J. T. Talar sets this study within

138. C. Tresmontant, ed., *Maurice Blondel–Lucien Laberthonnière: Correspondance philosophique* (Paris: Seuil, 1961), 79.

139. "What Rahner tried to do on the basis of the dynamism of human knowledge (*Hörer des Wortes*) Blondel attempted on the basis of the dynamic being of the essential human person." R. Latourelle, "Maurice Blondel," in Latourelle and Fisichella, *Dictionary of Fundamental Theology*, 83.

140. "One can only regret that Blondel was so ready to acquiesce in his gratuitous and arrogant exclusion from the theological field of play. Since it was the theologians who wrote the script for the philosophers in the neo-scholastic system, one must resolutely point out that any attempt to re-define the role of philosophy in that system must of necessity have a theological dimension of crucial importance, no matter how one chooses to define theology. Blondel had not passed through a course in seminary theology; but he was (partly in consequence) a far better theologian than many of his critics who had. Today's Roman Catholic theology of revelation and tradition owes infinitely more to Blondel than to Billot and his disciples." Daly, *Transcendence and Immanence*, 29.

141. C. J. T. Talar, "Innovation and Biblical Interpretation," in Jodock, *Catholicism Contending with Modernity*, 191.

the complex of institutional and methodological change that biblical exegesis was facing at the turn of the century. History was shifting from a strongly literary basis and was developing as a critical discipline. At the same time, changes in educational institutions were encouraging this transition from the study of flexible genres to that of organized disciplines. Though the state of Catholic exegesis with regard to the historical-critical method was substantially impoverished, it was not totally lacking.[142] Yet biblical exegesis was about to play a significant part in what Émile Poulat memorably terms "the end of the universe consecrated to the Council of Trent."[143] The position of the Church within this worldview had been entirely clear. To quote Talar again,

> As a continuation of the Incarnation, the church united the divine and human on earth. This view lent a more than human character to its teaching authority and reinforced its hierarchical nature. The attempts to extend the church's authority into the political order, the socio-economic order, and the cultural order have been discussed earlier. . . . Moreover, Ralph Keifer has argued that the institutional, hierarchical, and juridical understanding of church was not simply promulgated by theologians, but the very experience of worship communicated it more pervasively to the faithful.[144]

Bolstered by the scholastic hegemony emerging from the Thomistic revival of *Aeterni Patris*, a certain arrogance could be perceived in the confidence with which the schools deduced their theology, and in particular their ecclesiology, from the first principles of revelation. Within such a system, which subordinated history, philosophy—and indeed all other disciplines—to the science of theology, biblical exegesis was assigned a role that went little beyond the proof texting

---

142. Ibid., 195–97.
143. Quoted in R. de Boyer de Sainte Suzanne, *Alfred Loisy, entre la foi et l'incroyance* (Paris: Éditions du Centurion, 1968), 36.
144. Talar, "Innovation and Biblical Interpretation," 196.

of scholastic premises.[145] Studying within this context in the later decades of the nineteenth century,[146] Loisy began to face the dilemma in which he would later become embroiled: while Catholic exegesis continued in its traditional stasis, it remained continually open to rationalist criticism and yet closed to the modern methods that might yield an appropriate defense. At least that would be one view. Before embarking on a brief analysis of the import of *L'Évangile et L'Église*, it is necessary to be reminded of the ambiguity that still surrounds the person of Alfred Loisy, particularly with regard to his intellectual sincerity.[147] Gabriel Daly provides a suitably composite and complex picture:

> There are two views of Loisy which go back to the modernists themselves. The first is Loisy's self-portrait supplemented by Henri Bremond. The second, and diametrically opposite, view is given by Albert Houtin and Félix Sartiaux, Loisy's erstwhile friends and disciples. The first portrait gives us a man tragically caught up in the events of his time, broken on the wheel of ecclesiastical obscurantism and left to live out his life in lonely isolation and proud integrity at Garnay and Ceffonds. The second portrait is of a supercilious egoist, vain, querulous

145. Such a notion is still present in the relatively progressive encyclical *Divino Afflante Spiritu*: "Commentators must have as their chief object to show what is the theological doctrine touching faith and morals of each book and text so that their commentary may . . . assist teachers of theology in expounding and corroborating the dogmas of faith." (Sed, illis quidem opportune allatis, quantum ad exegesin conferre possint ostendant potissimum quae sit singulorum librorum vel textuum theologica doctrina de rebus fidei et morum, ita ut haec eorum explanatio non modo theologos doctores adiuvet et fidei dogmata proponenda confirmandaque.) Pius XII, *Divino Afflante Spiritu*, 310; Smith, *Biblical Studies and Opportune Means of Promoting Them*, 19. Joseph Ratzinger gives an interesting reflection on the closed and circular nature of this very relationship when he says, "This [method] is then developed to the point at which the task of theology is described as that of showing how what the teaching office has established is contained in the sources—and that precisely in the sense in which it has been defined." J. Ratzinger, "The Transmission of Divine Revelation," in *Commentary on the Documents of Vatican II*, ed. H. Vorgrimler, vol. 3 (London: Burns and Oates, 1968), 197.

146. These are the years in which Loisy studied at the seminary in Châlons and at the Paris Institute. See A. Loisy, *Choses passées* (Paris: Nourry, 1913); English trans. R. Wilson Boynton, *My Duel with the Vatican* 2nd ed. (New York: Greenwood, 1968), 62.

147. Ronald Burke provides a useful overview of the scholarly debate with regard to this issue in "Loisy's Faith: Landshift in Catholic Thought," *Journal of Religion* 60 (1980): 138–64.

and—most damaging of all—a thoroughgoing sceptic who maintained a front of religious belief and practice, in short, a hypocritical tactician.[148]

Whatever Loisy's motives, his objective was clear:

> I had conceived [he afterwards wrote] a programme of very simple but vast and logical teaching, which would have filled my life had I been left to fulfil it. My fundamental thought, which I did not utter too clearly, was that there was no scientific study of the Bible in the Catholic Church, and that it had to be created by shifting . . . questions of biblical introduction and exegesis from the theological and dogmatic spheres into the sphere of history for rational and critical study.[149]

Hence Alfred Loisy wrote to Blondel, after the publication of his book *L'Évangile et L'Église* in 1902, that "my book contains only one thesis: development is not extrinsic or foreign to the gospel."[150] Yet it is not difficult to detect that there is "at least one *implicit* thesis"[151] underlying Loisy's interest in doctrinal development, and the most significant of these implicit theses is his understanding of revelation.[152] By suggesting a certain separation between Gospel and church, Loisy rejects the doctrine of an unbreakable historical line between Jesus and the church, which he felt to be accentuated in Roman Catholic teaching so as to assert a unity between the revelation of Christ and subsequent church theology. Loisy makes a clear distinction between the original revelatory event of Jesus Christ, which he describes in anything but intellectual or objective terms,

---

148. Daly, *Transcendence and Immanence*, 51.
149. A. Loisy, *Mémoires pour servir à l'histoire religieuse de notre temps* (Paris: Nourry), 1:172; English trans. in Reardon, *Roman Catholic Modernism*, 16.
150. R. Marlé, *Au coeur de la crise moderniste: le dossier inédit d'une controverse* (Paris: Aubier, 1960), 84.
151. Daly, *Transcendence and Immanence*, 56.
152. For a comparison of Loisy's teachings on development with Newman's, see R. Burke, "Was Loisy Newman's Modern Disciple?" in Weaver, *Newman and the Modernists*, 139–57.

and the subsequent expression of this experience by believers.[153] As C. J. T. Talar makes clear,

> In lieu of the church founded by Jesus Christ with its essential hierarchical structures in place, its sevenfold sacramental system operative, and its "deposit" of faith handed over in order to be faithfully handed on, Loisy accentuated the apocalyptic element in the gospel tradition. Jesus preached the kingdom, a future event very near at hand. Under the influence of this eschatological perspective Jesus could not consciously and intentionally have founded a church replete with hierarchy, worship, and doctrine. This element of discontinuity was resolved by recourse to a developmental perspective, couched in organic metaphors. The Church in its various aspects developed after the death of Jesus in response to the varied environments in which his followers found themselves.[154]

In the metaphor of organic development, of which the Romantics, Möhler, and the Tübingen School were so fond, the Modernists clearly express their central convictions: the implicit rejection of deductive scholastic method, the centrality of history in the interpretation of the deposit of faith, and the essential distinction (if not separation) of revelation and church.[155] To complete the Modernist menu, we might add implicit immanentism. And this is because it is the very distinction between the kingdom message of Jesus and the emergence of the church that accounts for Loisy's infamous and condemned remark in *Autour d'un petit livre*: "Revelation can only be the acquired consciousness which human beings have of their relationship with God."[156] Norman Provencher

---

153. "He [Loisy] describes the original revelatory event in terms of 'religious experience,' 'perception,' contact with the divine." See Provencher, "Modernism," 720

154. Talar, "Innovation and Biblical Interpretation," 203.

155. One should bear in mind that a significant element of the teaching of Loisy is here concerned with a defense of the Catholic understanding of the church and its organic connection to the gospel. And this was over and against the liberal Protestant position of Adolf von Harnack, who claimed a simple gospel was in opposition to an institutional church. Cf. D. Jodock, "Introduction II: The Modernists and the Anti-Modernists," in Jodock, *Catholicism Contending with Modernity*, 21.

maintains that this must be understood in the light of a distinction that Loisy makes between "living revelation" and "revelation formulated in human language." Living revelation is reducible to the embodiment in human beings of the divine mystery of which religion is the chief expression. The progressive human consciousness of the person's relationship with God is revelation in its human embodiment, which then takes the form of symbolic language and teaching. Revelation cannot exist unless human beings grasp and express it.[157]

What was apparent to Loisy is the fact that Jesus Christ had the most perfectly clear consciousness of his relationship with God, and is the historical witness to the fact that "God reveals himself to humanity in humanity, and humanity enters into a divine association with God."[158] It is interesting that when discussing, in separate chapters, Loisy and Tyrrell, Gabriel Daly uses the same image to explain the two men's understanding of revelation as it was born out of recently emerging doctrines of development. Of Loisy, he asserts,

> Harnack had diagnosed a moral discontinuity between the Gospel message and the Hellenised Church. Loisy, with Weiss and Schweitzer, diagnosed an historical and eschatological break between Jesus and the kerygma. Roman Catholic orthodoxy of the period accepted no break whatever, either between Jesus and the kerygma or between the kerygma and the later Church.[159]

In his chapter on Tyrrell, Daly has this to say: "He [Tyrrell] has excavated the ground around 'primitive revelation,' detaching it from all later intellectual development. Blondel found a ditch between

---

156. A. Loisy, *Autour d'un petit livre* (Paris: Alphonse Picard et Fils, 1903), 195, in Provencher, "Modernism," 720.
157. Provencher, "Modernism," 720.
158. Loisy, *L'Évangile et L'Église*, 268.
159. Daly, *Transcendence and Immanence*, 56.

faith and fact; von Hügel found one between the absolute and the contingent; Tyrrell dug one between revelation and theology."[160]

Revelation as Experience in the Thought of George Tyrrell

George Tyrrell[161] was conscious of his "French connections"[162] from the beginning of that period that marked his maturity as a writer. He wrote the preface to the English translation of *L'Évangile et l'Église*[163] in 1908, and some years previously had proclaimed,

> I have read several times Blondel's little brochure, and am much impressed with it, though I do not pretend to enter into all his ideas owing to my unclearness as to much of his meaning. Wherever I understand him I agree with him; especially, for example, in his criticism of the insufficiency of current forms of apologetic; and also in his wider view of saving faith. It has driven me back to reconsider views of my own which I have always felt were censurable theologically as rash, but which would not always be rash.[164]

In 1897, when Tyrrell wrote the above to Friedrich Von Hügel (1852–1925), he was entering a period of "mediating liberalism" that would form the bridge from what Maude Petre called his phase of "militant orthodoxy."[165] Tyrrell had entered the Church in the same year that *Aeterni Patris* was promulgated, and throughout his early years as a Catholic and a Jesuit, showed great devotion to St. Thomas and Pope Leo's program of philosophical restoration. Indeed, his enthusiasm led to accusations that he was turning young Jesuits into

---

160. Ibid., 143.
161. For an excellent biographical study, see N. Sagovsky, *"On God's Side": A Life of George Tyrrell* (Oxford: Clarendon, 1990).
162. See M. O'Connell, "A French Connection," chapter 9 of *Critics on Trial*, 155–76.
163. A. Loisy, *The Gospel and the Church*, new ed. with prefatory memoir by G. Tyrrell, trans. Christopher Home (London: Pitman and Sons, 1908).
164. Tyrrell to von Hügel, 6 December, 1897, quoted in O'Connell, *Critics on Trial*, 155.
165. Maude Petre, *Autobiography and Life*, vol. 2 (London: Arnold, 1912), 42.

Dominicans, and he was removed from St. Mary's Hall, Stonyhurst, where he taught philosophy to scholastics, and was sent to Farm Street to work on the periodical *The Month*. It was in this period, as he began his work as spiritual guide and apologist,[166] that he was "driven back" to reconsider his formative theological influences. At first glance, he would, at this point, seem far from the critical milieu of Loisy, upbraiding Von Hügel for undermining the delicate balance of his daughter's faith by discussing with her the finer points of biblical criticism,[167] and theologians for shaking the simple devotion of the pious. However, in "The Relation of Theology to Devotion," an essay published in *The Month* for November 1899, a new departure is signaled in Tyrrell's thought. Speaking of devotion to Our Lord in the Blessed Sacrament, he says, "I have more than once known all the joy and reality taken out of a life that fed on devotion to the Sacramental Presence, by such a flash of theological illumination; and have seen Magdalens left weeping at empty tombs and crying: 'They have taken away my Lord, and I know not where they have laid him.'"[168]

Here, Tyrrell begins his "excavation" of a "primitive revelation," for if, as he concludes in this article, devotion exists before theology,[169] he must then wonder wherein revelation lies. In no sense is a rejection of theology implied;[170] rather, his fervor for

---

166. See H. Bremond, "Father Tyrrell as an Apologist," *New York Review* 1 (June–July 1905): 762–70.

167. See Maude Petre, *Von Hügel and Tyrrell: The Story of a Friendship* (New York: E. P. Dutton and Co., 1937), 14–28.

168. G. Tyrrell, "The Relation of Theology to Devotion," *The Month* (November 1999): 423. *The Month* reprinted this essay on the hundredth anniversary of its original appearance in the November 1899 issue.

169. "Devotion and religion existed before theology, in the way that art existed before art criticism." Tyrrell, "The Relation of Theology to Devotion," 425.

170. "Tyrrell's quarrel was not with reason or theology, but with 'theologism,' that is, theology dominated by scholastic rationalism." D. Schultenover, "George Tyrrell: Devout Disciple of Newman," *The Heythrop Journal* 33, no. 1 (1992): 38.

philosophical scholasticism has been chastened by the truth of the statement *lex orandi, lex credendi.*

Lex Orandi as Source for the Lex Credendi

In 1899, it was Tyrrell's conviction that devotion existed "in the Christian religion as lived by its consistent professors."[171] This devotion was the first and hidden expression of the self-communication of God in the hearts of his faithful. In such a conviction, some have seen obvious links with Newman's thought—his notion of the illative sense, the consensus of the faithful, and the development of doctrine.[172] Yet it is a notion that Tyrrell develops distinctively[173] in two works that he entitles with the maxim attributed to Prosper of Aquitaine. In the preface of *Lex Credendi*, which links the two volumes, he makes the following assertion:

> If "the heart has its reasons" it has also its language, often at strife with that of the lips—eloquent when these are silent, dumb when they are busiest. No explicit utterance of the Christian Faith can ever hope to equal the implicit utterance it finds in that Prayer which burst forth from the depth of Christ's heart and which is the embodiment of the spiritual life in its concrete fullness. There in truth we have the supreme rule and criterion of Faith, the divinely sanctioned *Lex Credendi*—no ready solvent indeed for theological controversies, but a law that lifts the heart to a higher plane where it can abide in peace, unaffected by the alternations of intellectual light and obscurity.[174]

---

171. Tyrrell, "The Relation of Theology to Devotion," 425.
172. See Schultenover, "George Tyrrell: Devout Disciple of Newman," 37.
173. "In 1899, as Tyrrell composed 'The Relation of Theology to Devotion' and pondered the essence of religion, he began to have problems with Newman's conception. In defining revelation as 'not merely a symbol or a creed' but 'in some sense more directly a *lex orandi* than a *lex credendi*,' Tyrrell introduced a criterion—the spiritual experience of prayer—by which the *expression* of revelation is to be criticized. Newman saw the criterion of criticism the other way round: spiritual experience is always to be criticized by the record and its authentic elaborations in doctrine." Ibid., 39. Perhaps even as early as this, we can hear tones of Salvatore Marsili's argument with Cipriano Vagaggini about the primacy of the liturgy.

By the time this passage was published, Tyrrell knew the difficulties of "abiding in peace unaffected by the alterations of intellectual light and obscurity." As a result of an imprudent article on hell he had been sent to the Jesuit house in Richmond, Yorkshire, where he was forbidden to preach and teach.[175] In the next nine years, conscious of failing health, he wrote feverishly. By the time *Lex Credendi* was published, he had been dismissed from the Jesuits, and the year after, as a result of his public protestations against *Pascendi*, he was denied the sacraments. Tyrrell's temperament was not an insignificant factor in all this,[176] but neither was his isolation and spiritual anguish without importance in the shaping of his final works. In the foreword to *Christianity at the Cross-Roads*, Alec Vidler suggests that "many regretted . . . that his [Tyrrell's] involvement in ecclesiastical controversy deflected him from concentrating on the deepest things of the spirit," but maintains that his works must be considered against that background of crisis.[177] Albert Cock captures something of that context when "in company with Tyrrell wandering restlessly around Clapham Common through the small hours of the morning he witnessed the spiritual anguish of a priest without an altar."[178]

The question of where Christ could be encountered was now one of immediate importance. In *Lex Credendi*, Tyrrell's purpose had been

---

174. G. Tyrrell, "Preface," in *Lex Credendi: A Sequel to Lex Orandi* (London: Longmans, Green and Co., 1906), xiii.

175. G. Tyrrell, "A Perverted Devotion," *Weekly Register* 100 (1899): 797–800; reproduced in *Essays on Faith and Immortality*, ed. Maude Petre (London: Arnold, 1914), 158–71.

176. "He was convinced that his opponents were censuring his views from a standpoint which identified Roman theology with Catholic orthodoxy and, worse still, with Christian revelation. He made no effort to control his impatience with an assumption he regarded as arrogant and ultimately destructive of a living Catholic truth. Thus he matched arrogance with arrogance. He chose to fight where others compromised, capitulated, or retired hurt. He never left the Church—a fact that we today are in a better position to appreciate than his contemporaries. Always isolable by temperament, he was effectively isolated by events." G. Daly, "Some Reflections on the Character of George Tyrrell," *The Heythrop Journal* 10, no. 3 (1969): 268.

177. A. Vidler, "Foreword," in Tyrrell, *Christianity at the Cross-Roads*, 7.

178. A. Cock, quoted in T. M. Loome, "'Revelation as Experience': An Unpublished Lecture of George Tyrrell," *The Heythrop Journal* 12, no. 2 (1971): 123.

to make plain to his audience what participating in the Spirit of Christ, by praying as he did, could mean for them. To pray with a spirit of devotion would mean that the *credo* they would come to utter would come from the depths and be true. According to *Christianity at the Cross-Roads*,

> In us Christ, the Spirit, lives and utters Himself in the ever-changing forms of thought and language. In this sense St. Paul says that, if we have known Christ after the flesh, we shall know him so no longer, but only after the Spirit as the Heavenly Adam, the Son of Man, the Spirit of God. We have long since outgrown those apocalyptic forms of religious thought in which the Spirit of Jesus first uttered itself as the Son of man—the Jewish Messiah. But the spirit itself we have not outgrown, and in us it seeks ever new forms wherein to clothe the same revelation.[179]

If, by this, it is felt that the "ditch" that Tyrrell has dug around the primitive revelation of God in Christ, in order to establish "the distinction between truth in itself and truth as possessed by the human mind,"[180] has grown perilously deep, then the role he asserts for the church should be remembered:

> But the Church of St Paul is the mystical body of Christ—an extension of that human frame through which His spirit and personality communicated itself to His disciples, as it were sacramentally, i.e. in the way that a personality makes itself felt, as opposed to the way in which a teacher imparts doctrine. In both cases signs are necessary; but in the latter thought speaks to thought, in the former spirit to spirit; in the latter an idea, in the former a force is transmitted. Through the mystical body, animated by the Spirit, we are brought into immediate contact with the ever-present Christ. We hear him in its Gospel, we touch and handle Him in its sacraments. He lives on in the Church not metaphorically but actually. He finds a growing medium of self-utterance, ever complementing and correcting that of His mortal individuality. Thus it is through the instrumentality of the Church and

179. Tyrrell, *Christianity at the Cross-Roads*, 174.
180. Provencher, "Modernism," 721.

its sacraments that his personality is renewed and strengthened in us; that the force of His spirit is transmitted and felt. The Church is not merely a society or school, but a mystery and sacrament; like the humanity of Christ of which it is an extension.[181]

That an adequate evaluation of Tyrrell's thought could be given here is unthinkable. But neither is that the intention. Others have given scholarly analysis of his struggle "to formulate a theology of revelation which would accommodate without nullifying the apocalyptic perspective of the New Testament as he saw it."[182] The point is that when reading *Christianity at the Cross-Roads*, even if only the passage above, the preemptive echoes of later theology, especially that of Vatican II,[183] necessitate a constant reminder of the date of publication. In the crucible of crisis, Tyrrell brought together and went some way to resolving ideas and theological difficulties that would occupy the Church for decades to come. As he said himself, "My own work—which I regard as done—has been to raise a question which I have failed to answer. I am not so conceited as to conclude that it is therefore unanswerable."[184]

---

181. Tyrrell, *Christianity at the Cross-Roads*, 178.
182. Loome, "Revelation as Experience," in Daly, *Transcendence and Immanence*, 140–64, 141–42; J. Lewis May, *Father Tyrrell and the Modernist Movement* (London: Burns Oates and Washbourne, 1938); J. Ratté, *Three Modernists* (London: Sheed and Ward, 1968); N. Sagovsky, *On God's Side: A Life of George Tyrrell* (Oxford: Clarendon Press, 1990); T. M. Loome, *Liberal Catholicism, Reform Catholicism, Modernism: A Contribution to a New Orientation in Modernist Research* (Mainz: Grünewald, 1979).
183. See M. Hurley, "George Tyrrell: Some Post–Vatican II Impressions," *The Heythrop Journal* 10, no. 3 (1969): 243–55; F. M. O'Connor, "Notes and Comments: Tyrrell's Cross-Roads," *The Heythrop Journal* 5, no. 2 (1964): 188–91; C. J. Mehok, "Hans Küng and George Tyrrell on the Church," *Homiletic and Pastoral Review* 72 (1972): 57–66; T. Foudy, "George Tyrrell and Modernism," *Irish Theological Quarterly* 49, no. 1 (1982): 1–18. With regard to Loisy, see also Burke, "Was Loisy Newman's Modern Disciple?" 151.
184. G. Tyrrell to Boutwood, 13 January 1909, in *George Tyrrell's Letters*, 1920, quoted in Loome, "George Tyrrell: 'Revelation as Experience,'" 123.

Looking Forward to Vindication

The Modernists were doing "theology under the lash,"[185] and, once the strictures of *Lamentabili* were imposed, every effort was made to silence not only the questioners but the questions. Yet, before suppression engulfed imaginative thinking in the Church for a decade and more, overtures for change had been heard loud and clear, so much so that Roger Haight could say that Modernism "was one of the most important movements in Roman Catholic Theology between Trent and Vatican II."[186] Coming before the liturgical movement had taken root, and before the rise of the *nouvelle théologie* and the encouraging encyclicals of Pius XII, this was the first move to establish a theology of revelation and church that was credible to the modern mind. The spirit of their questions was kept alive in movements that matured through the war years, so that the theological themes that have been heard to echo from *Aeterni Patris* could come together with a new resonance. Hence Karl Rahner, at the beginning of his theological career and on the eve of the Second World War, could begin to posit an answer to the problem of immanence and transcendence with the help of a richer and more mature theological vocabulary.[187] In his book *Understanding Karl*

---

185. J. H. Newman, Letter to Miss Bowles 4 January 1863, quoted in J. Coulson, *Newman and the Common Tradition* (Oxford: Clarendon, 1970), 100.

186. R. Haight, "Unfolding of Modernism in France," *Theological Studies* 35 (1974): 632.

187. "The theologian Thomas is concerned with man as the place in which God shows himself in such a way that he can be heard in his word of revelation, *ex parte animae*. In order to be able to hear whether God is speaking we must know that he is; so that his word does not come to one who already knows, he must be hidden from us; for him to speak to human beings his word must reach us where we already are, in our earthly place, in our earthly time. In that man is in the world *convertendo se ad phantasma*, the disclosure of being generally and in it the knowledge of the existence of God has always already taken place, but at the same time this God is always already hidden from us as being beyond the world. *Abstractio* is the disclosure of being which places man before God, *conversio* is entering into the here and now of this finite world which God makes the distant unknown. *Abstractio* and *conversio* are the same thing for Thomas: man. If man is understood in this way he can hear whether God does not say something because he knows that God is; God can speak because he is the unknown. And if Christianity is not

Rahner: An Introduction to His Life and Thought, Herbert Vorgrimler indicates a shift not only in Rahner's intellectual development, but more generally in theology. Such a text identifies Rahner as the first of the "second generation theologians":

> The first generation, whose social, spiritual and ecclesial life-work came to a climax in the period between the two world wars introduced the new mentality into theology in a more general way with a good deal of courage and constant threats from church officials. This new spirit could not yet have an effect in coping with the content of particular theological problems. In Germany, theologians like Peter Lippert, Romano Guardini, Erich Przywara and others opened up this new period in the sphere of theology. They represented the new spirit, but hardly went into individual questions of dogma, so the theological textbooks of the time took no notice of them.[188]

This new spirit had arisen in different circumstances. "In its philosophical and theological youth this generation had experienced the intrigues and heresy hunts within the Church and the harsh official reactions, for example against the so-called Modernists."[189]

---

the idea of an eternal ever-present spirit but Jesus of Nazareth, then Thomas's metaphysics of knowledge is Christian if it calls a man back into the here and now of his finite world, as the eternal also entered into it, so that man finds it and himself again in it." K. Rahner, *Geist in Welt* (Innsbruck: Felizian Rauch, 1939), 407, in H. Vorgrimler, *Understanding Karl Rahner: An Introduction to His Life and Thought* (London: SCM, 1986), 60–61.

188. Vorgrimler, *Understanding Karl Rahner,* 55. Significantly, James F. White posits such a generational distinction of the liturgical movement: "Our position is that the two liturgical movements had different objectives and that quite different personnel were involved. For the first liturgical movement, the term 'restoration' is crucial. It looked back to restoring treasures lost or overlooked but not to changing the liturgy itself. For this reason we can call the first movement the romantic liturgical movement. . . . The second liturgical movement revolved around the word 'reformation' and planned significant changes in the liturgy. Its chief promoters were diocesan priests and a considerable number of lay people who dreamed of things that the first liturgical movement never dared. It could justly be labelled the reformist or parish liturgical movement. Obviously, both movements overlap at a number of points: participation is mentioned in the nineteenth century and restoration is championed after World War II. But there seems to be a clear shift as *Mediator Dei* marks the end of one era in 1947 and new ideas and leaders take over." J. F. White, *Roman Catholic Worship: Trent to Today* (New York: Paulist, 1995), 71.

189. Vorgrimler, *Understanding Karl Rahner,* 56.

This was the time from *Pascendi* to *Humani Generis*, ostensibly difficult and unproductive years for Catholic theology, but in fact years when the ingredients of "second-generation" theology were coming together. These are the years of a rising interest in historical criticism and biblical analysis, of a return to the sources,[190] and the awakening of a sense of mystery in theology. Such factors were the common inspiration and driving force of the liturgical movement and the *nouvelle théologie*, and in order to understand the theological fruits of the "second generation," it is necessary to appreciate their inception in the first.

Sources of Renewal: The Parallel Rise of the Liturgical Movement and the *Nouvelle Théologie*

The "paradigm shift" to which the post-war theologians and architects of the Second Vatican Council were heirs had its origin in the romantic movement. It was a change that touched liturgy and theology equally, as the modern understanding of these disciplines met at its source. "The romantic liturgical movement had a long pre-history in Germanic lands where theologians had been discussing the nature of the Church."[191] Tempered by a certain scientific rigor, the product of both a scholastic and a rationalist heritage, nineteenth-century theology welcomed feeling, dynamism, and imagination. While J. Adam Möhler and the Tübingen School advocated a Spirit-centred, charismatic, and organic understanding of the church,

---

190. The return to the sources was not entirely a positively motivated movement, but for some a safe haven in a difficult period for theologians. "In its own way scholastic theology, too, represented such an evasion. If a dogmatic theologian had no desire to converse with contemporary educated people within the Church or despisers of religion outside it, he concentrated on editing the texts of old theologians; he worked on a backward-looking history of dogma and left official scholastic theology as it had been before." Vorgrimler, *Understanding Karl Rahner*, 56.

191. White, *Roman Catholic Worship: Trent to Today*, 76.

typical of Romantic thought, Prosper Guéranger (1805–1875) was seeking to revive monasticism, to place the liturgy at its center, and to rediscover a medieval simplicity.[192] Around the same time, John Henry Newman left the church of his baptism after reflecting on notions of doctrinal development.[193] Yet these beginnings of renewal were shaky. Möhler was criticised for *Einheit in der Kirche* and himself came to think he had somewhat overstated his position,[194] Newman was dismayed at the theological inertia of the church he had embraced, and Guéranger was condemned by many for his "amateurish kind of scholarship" and his naïve belief that "to go back to the authentic liturgy meant to go back to medievalism."[195] While Möhler and Newman were men before their time, who to some extent made progress despite their context, it was partly to Guéranger's purpose to collude with the spirit of centralized uniformity and ultramontanism that marked the age.[196] Guéranger is somewhat too ambiguous a figure to be classed with Möhler and Newman. Without doubt, he and his followers stimulated a respect

192. For a fuller discussion of this relationship, see G.-M. Oury, "Le romanticisme de Dom Guéranger: un faux problème?" in *Collectanea Cisterciensia* 48 (1986): 311–23, and also T. F. O'Meara, "The Origins of the Liturgical Movement and German Romanticism," *Worship* 59 (1985): 326–42.

193. "The generally accepted launching of the liturgical movement was the formation of a new Benedictine community at Solesmes, France, by Prosper Guéranger in 1833. The timing was significant. John Henry Newman marked the beginning of the Oxford Movement in the Church of England as a sermon preached by John Keble on July 14, 1833, and for a dozen years Newman provided vigorous leadership before leaving the Anglican communion. In Bavaria, Wilhelm Loehe began a long pastorate in Neuendettelsau in 1837, devoted to making frequent confession and communion a reality among Lutherans. Nikolai F. S. Grundtvig led a sacramental revival in the Lutheran church of Denmark. Already on the American frontier, the Disciples of Christ had been formed in 1831 and had made the first success in making weekly communion for all the baptised a permanent norm for worship. Something dynamic was in the atmosphere worldwide in the 1830's. This was the truly liturgical decade exceeded only by the 1960's." White, *Roman Catholic Worship: Trent to Today*, 76. See also J. Leclerq, "Le renouveau solesmien et le renouveau religieux du XIX siècle," *Studia monastica* 18 (1976): 157–98.

194. Cf. M. Himes, "Introduction," in J. Möhler, *Symbolism* (New York: Crossroad, 1997), xii.

195. See L. Bouyer, *Liturgical Piety* (Notre Dame, IN: Notre Dame, 1966), 65.

196. Pius IX gave papal approbation to the suppression of neo-Gallican rites and strengthened the Solesmes programme with the encyclical *Inter Multiplices*. See *Acta Pii IX*, 1, 1853, 439–48.

for medieval liturgical texts that precipitated their sound scientific study, and, though they did instill a sense of the importance of the liturgical life of the church and work for its correct celebration, the early work of Solesmes was too much concerned with a rediscovery of the medieval period, and that always linked to an excessive ultramontanism that sought to smother alternatives to the Roman model. While Guéranger was an inspirational figure, who was responsible for "a community whose spiritual life was above all centred in experienced contact with the prayer of the Church"[197]—an experience that encouraged a renewal of fervor that went beyond monastic circles—one must nevertheless agree that Lambert Beauduin (1873–1960) is the true father of the liturgical movement.[198] For only with him was a true alliance made between the nascent new theology and the liturgical movement: an alliance founded on a pastorally motivated fervor for renewal, and a spirit of *ressourcement* that reached its consummation at Vatican II.

Beauduin tried to bring the renewal out of its monastic setting and adapt it so as to achieve the active participation of the people in liturgical celebration, an aim that was to mark the movement thereafter. The approach he took was theologically more robust than

197. O. Rousseau, "The Liturgical Movement from Dom Guéranger to Pius XII," in *The Church at Prayer*, vol. 1: *Introduction to the Liturgy*, ed. A. G. Martimort (Shannon: Irish University Press, 1968), 51. See also J. D. Crichton, *Lights in the Darkness: Forerunners to the Liturgical Movement* (Dublin: Columba, 1996).

198. John Fenwick and Bryan Spinks wonder if the publication of Lambert Beauduin's *La Piété de l'Église* might not mark the beginning of the liturgical movement and claim for its author the title *Father*, and whether the title rightly belongs to Guéranger. See Fenwick and Spinks, *Worship in Transition: The Twentieth Century Liturgical Movement* (Edinburgh: T. & T. Clark, 1995), 13, 17, 23. Cf. B. Botte, "Birth of the Movement," in *From Silence to Participation* (Washington, DC: Pastoral, 1988), 9–17. For a more detailed and comprehensive account of Dom Guéranger's involvement in the liturgical movement, see O. Rousseau, *Histoire du mouvement liturgique, Esquisse historique depuis le début du XIX siècle jusqu'au pontificat de Pie X* (Paris: Édition du Cerf, 1945), 3. English trans. by the Benedictines of Westminster Priory, *The Progress of the Liturgy: An Historical Sketch from the Beginning of the Nineteenth Century to the Pontificate of Pius X*, (Westminster, MD: Newman, 1951).

his predecessor's with *Piété de L'Église* clearly identifying his desire to find an underlying fundamental theology that would give shape to his enterprise. Essentially, it was this search that marked the difference between the Tridentine liturgical reforms and the reforms and the aims of the twentieth-century liturgical movement.[199] The dogmatic decrees of Trent, especially those concerning the sacraments, never intended to establish a theology of the liturgy. For this reason they remained rubrical and superficial. As Kevin Irwin says,

> It was especially after the Council of Trent (1545–63) that a clear separation developed between the liturgy and sacramental theology. In the wake of the Tridentine concern for rubrical precision in the doing of liturgy—demonstrated by the printing of rubrics in the Roman Missal and Ritual—liturgy became equated with the external performance of the Church's rites. Sacramental theology was incorporated into manuals of dogmatic theology, which paid little attention to the rites themselves as a theological source. The sacramental discussions in such manuals focused on the Reformation debates about causality, the number of the sacraments, and their institution. The divorce between the *lex orandi* and *lex credendi* was exemplified in the division of what had been a single area of study into two: liturgy and sacramental theology. It was only somewhat later that the study of liturgy in the West began to focus on the historical evolution of the rites and the theological interpretation of these rites.[200]

Fundamentally, the liturgical movement in its later stage was working to reunite the two aspects of the Latin tag ascribed to Prosper of Aquitaine and more fully rendered: *legem credendi lex*

---

199. P. Jounel expresses this difference in an alternative way when he asserts, "The half-century of liturgical renewal preceding the Second Vatican Council developed in a direction quite the opposite of that following the Council of Trent. In the sixteenth century liturgical reformers began by revising their books, in order to instil a new liturgical life into the clergy and Christian people. In the twentieth century, the first step was a pastoral effort which would result in a revision of rubrics and liturgical books. The influence of Popes Pius X and Pius XII, essentially pastoral popes, was certainly not without effect on this orientation." Jounel, "From the Council of Trent to Vatican II," in Martimort, *The Church at Prayer*, 47.

200. K. Irwin, *Liturgical Theology: A Primer* (Collegeville, MN: Liturgical Press, 1990), 13.

statuat supplicandi.[201] By concentrating attention on the role and purpose of the liturgy, those interested in the pastoral renewal of worship were bound to discover foundational theological principles that would serve to refresh their efforts. This rationale showed obvious parallels with the emerging new theology. In the first place, those involved in the liturgical renewal were all too aware of the increasing separation between the faithful and the liturgy in the post-Tridentine Church. The root cause of this separation was quickly identified as the theological estrangement of word and sacrament. Ritual accretions, the (often polemical) regulations of dogmatic theology, allegorical parallels, and an increasing clericalism all threatened to push the directly evocative value of the sacraments as human events into the background.[202] Thus the sacramental symbol, the defining and constituent medium of the divine manifestation, was seemingly severed from its content. The event that raises the word of God beyond the merely cognitive or notional to the "psychosomatic substrata of human knowledge, experience, and meeting"[203] had been reduced to ritual ceremonial. Hence the aim to reunite the faithful in active participation with the sacramental symbols is in itself an effort to rediscover the ways of God's personal self-communication to humanity. As Beauduin maintained, "The active participation in the liturgical life of the Church is a capital factor in the super-natural life of the Christian."[204] The modern liturgical renewal cannot therefore be regarded as a movement apart, one that was concerned merely with the aesthetics of worship. Its solid theological basis is the revaluation of the relationship between word and sacrament in

---

201. For a useful analysis of the history and meaning of this phrase see: P. De Clerk, "'Lex orandi, lex credendi,' sens original et avatars historiques d'un adage equivoque," in *Questions Liturgiques*, 59 (1978), 193-212.

202. See L. G. M. Alting von Geusau, "Word and Sacrament," in *Liturgy in Development*, ed. L. G. M. Alting von Geusau (London: Sheed and Ward, 1965), 13–14.

203. Ibid., 18.

204. L. Beauduin, *Liturgy: The Life of the Church* (Collegeville, MN: Liturgical Press, 1926), 8.

the transmission of revelation. This was to be the ultimate source of liturgical renewal, and the notion most effective in securing it would be the concept of mystery theology, an idea that was simultaneously emerging in the ecclesiological developments of this period.[205] Here again, Lambert Beauduin might be seen as an originator, his *Piété de L'Église* identifying an understanding of the church as mystical body and the priesthood of all believers as the basis of renewal.[206]

Mystici Corporis, Mediator Dei, and the Liturgical Movement

Gregory XVI had made Guéranger abbot of Solesmes and head of the French Benedictine Congregation in 1837. Maurus and Placid Wolter visited there and refounded the German Abbey of Beuron in its likeness. From Beuron were founded the daughter houses of Maredsous in Belgium and Maria Laach in Germany. Physically and spiritually, there was close connection between the revived Benedictine monasteries of Europe, and this encouraged a uniformity that some consider to be a negative aspect of Guéranger's reform. Yet at least this situation made possible the cross-fertilization of ideas, most importantly between Mont César (a foundation of Maredsous) and Maria Laach. If the liturgical movement really did begin with the address that Lambert Beauduin gave at Malines, Belgium in

---

205. As with hindsight, Raymond Vaillancourt could succinctly say, "We must add that this sacramental renewal, both liturgical and theological, is far from being the result of a spontaneous generation. It goes back to Dom Guéranger in the last century and has continued to sink its roots with the help of numerous theologians like Dom Odo Casel. These theologians gave the impetus to a theological movement that went beyond the juridical and canonical aspects of the liturgy and located the liturgy in the very heart of the mysteries of Christ. The two theologians I have named also laid heavy emphasis on the theology of the mysteries. In short, their desire was to move beyond juridicism and place themselves on a level of meaning that lay within the mystery of man in Christ. It is against this background that the liturgical and theological renewal of Vatican II is to be understood." Vaillancourt, *Toward a Renewal of Sacramental Theology* (Collegeville, MN: Liturgical Press, 1979), 33.

206. See Crichton, *Lights in the Darkness*, 152–53.

1909, then it came to full strength when Odo Casel (1886–1948) solemnized the relationship between liturgy and theology with his notions of liturgical mystery. By way of his *Kultmysterion*, Casel brought a liturgical consciousness to a then-contemporary development in theology, one in which a number of recent religious trends had crystallized, such as a renewed interest in the Bible, a growing awareness of communion in the church, and new ideas on the transmission of God's self-communication. In the light of mystery theology, Pius XII was to take up each of these questions in the papal encyclicals *Divino Afflante Spiritu*, *Mystici Corporis*, *Mediator Dei*, and *Humani Generis*, and one way or another bring these themes to full consciousness in the post-war era.[207]

Even at the time of the First Vatican Council, theologians had sought to introduce an understanding of the church as the mystical body of Christ into the document *De Ecclesia*.[208] Rejected as too romantic at this point, its absence, along with other elements, meant that the Council's teaching suffered from an imbalance that theologians throughout the late nineteenth and early twentieth centuries worked to redress.[209] As noted above, prior to the First Vatican Council the origins of this ecclesiological movement can be traced in the Tübingen School of Drey, Möhler, and Kühn. Their aim was to develop the notion of the body of Christ as a

---

207. Cf. G. Philips, "Dogmatic Constitution on the Church: History of the Constitution," in *Commentary on the Documents of Vatican II*, ed. H. Vorgrimler, vol. 1 (London: Burns and Oates, 1967), 105–37, 105.

208. "Through the efforts of Passaglia, who was much influenced by these ideas, and of his disciples, Franzelin and Schrader, the theology of the mystical body found new vigour. It was introduced into the first schema of *De Ecclesia* at Vatican I, but to most of the fathers it appeared too romantic a notion." Cf. M.-J. le Guillon, "Church 1. History of Ecclesiology," in *Encyclopedia of Theology: The Concise Sacramentum Mundi*, ed. K. Rahner (New York: Crossroad, 1991), 208.

209. When the Second Vatican Council made the theme of the mystery of the church its primary interest, "it went back explicitly to the programme of the Council of 1870 and determined to take it further. That programme had remained incomplete, and to give it a proper dogmatic balance, it needed to be supplemented." G. Philips, "Dogmatic Constitution on the Church," 105.

people animated by the Spirit. Seeking to shift the emphasis away from a visible and hierarchical institution that possessed the gift of magisterium, Möhler and the Tübingen School stressed the idea of the people of God and their organic life together. In the twentieth century, these ideas gained strength in the Church, both as a reaction to a period of extreme institutionalism, and as the result of the life's work of the Belgian Jesuit Émile Mersch (1890–1940). In 1933, after intense study and much revision, Mersch published *Le corps mystique du Christ*,[210] in which he detailed the historical development of the doctrine of the mystical body in Scripture and tradition. Essentially, this was a prelude to his major work, *La théologie du corps mystique*,[211] which was published posthumously in 1944, though completed by 1939. Effectively, Mersch's work provides an extensive commentary on *Mystici Corporis,* the encyclical of Pope Pius XII that he never read. Like Pope Pius, Mersch recognised in the mystical body a concept key to modern theology. As Marie-Joseph le Guillon points out,

> The encyclical *Mystici Corporis* which saw in the Church—with Christ as its Head, constituting it in existence, sustaining and ruling it—a social, visible and living reality whose ultimate principle of action is the Holy Spirit, gave the stamp of official approval to the fundamental rediscovery of the vision of the Church. From then on theological studies developed in complementary directions: the Church as Sacrament, the Church as fellowship, the Church as Mystery. And this development of ecclesiology took place under the combined influence of the biblical and liturgical revivals.[212]

What is of pertinence here is Pius XII's recognition of the unity that exists between a number of theological themes, and his assertion that

---

210. É. Mersch, *Le Corps mystique du Christ* (Louvain: Museum Lessianum, 1936); English trans. J. R. Kelly, *The Whole Christ* (London: Dennis Dobson, 1938).

211. Mersch, *La Théologie du corps mystique* (Louvain: Museum Lessianum, 1944); English trans. C. Vollert, *The Theology of the Mystical Body* (New York: Herder, 1952).

212. Le Guillon, "Church 1. History of Ecclesiology," 209.

the means of their confluence is the overarching concept of mystery or sacrament. It is this meeting that went some way to shaping a consistent theology between *Sacrosanctum Concilium, Lumen Gentium,* and *Dei Verbum,* but which also was to mark postconciliar theology even more significantly.

The christological focus, which resulted from a mystical-body ecclesiology, had obvious consequences for sacramental and liturgical theology. No longer, for instance, could the church be regarded as the arbitrary distributor of the sacraments, for actions of the mystical body were actions of Christ—the church being the permanent and active presence of the risen Lord. Such a fundamental shift in principle demanded a rethinking of the relationship between the faithful believer and Christ encountered in the sacramental mysteries of the church, that is to say, a deepening of the theology of grace according to the categories of historicity and subjectivity. If the liturgy was to be the locus of the active participation of the faithful in the very life of God, then grace, the self-communication of that life, could no longer be regarded as a scarce and distant gift reserved for the privileged few. The encyclicals *Mystici Corporis* and *Mediator Dei* are significant in giving expression to the theological adjustment that the various strains of twentieth-century scholarship demanded.

If the two encyclicals are compared, some idea of the effect of the doctrine of the mystical body on developing notions of ecclesiology, liturgy, and grace will become immediately obvious. Because in *Mystici Corporis* Pius XII had identified the church as a unity with Jesus Christ as its head, and because he regarded this living body as empowered and sustained by the Holy Spirit, it followed naturally that he could say of the liturgy in *Mediator Dei,*

> The liturgical year, animated throughout by the devotion of the Church, is no cold and lifeless representation of past events, no mere historical record. It is Christ himself, living on in his Church, and

still pursuing that path of boundless mercy which "going about and doing good" (Acts 10:38), he began to tread during his life on earth. This he did in order that the souls of men might come into contact with his mysteries and, so to speak, live by them. And these mysteries are still now constantly present and active, not in the vague and incomprehensible way which certain writers describe, but as Catholic doctrine teaches us. The Doctors of the Church tell us that the mysteries of Christ's life are at the same time most excellent models of virtue for us to imitate and also sources of divine grace for us by reason of the merits and intercession of the Redeemer. They live on in their effects in us, since each of them is, according to its nature and in its own way, the cause of our salvation.[213]

Though the sources for this text are not solely to be found in the ecclesiological movement, and any examination of its background would involve some comment on Odo Casel's theory of mystery theology, the passage does reveal the convergence of themes and something of the gradual theological clarification that was taking place directly before the Second Vatican Council. While Émile Mersch had been laboring over his work on the theology of the mystical body, Dom Odo Casel, had begun a study of *Das christliche Kultmysterium* that was first published in 1932. Tracing this theme through Scripture and tradition, most notably in St. Paul and St. Leo the Great, Casel expounds a theology of the biblical notion of μυστήριον and of Christ as the revelation of God.[214] Transposing this theology into a liturgical key, he had concluded that Christ, having

213. "Quapropter liturgicus annus, quem Ecclesiae pietas alit ac comitatur, non frigida atque iners earum rerum repraesentatio est, quae ad praeterita tempora pertinent, vel simplex ac nuda superioris aetatis rerum recordatio. Sed potius est Christus ipse, qui in sua Ecclesia perseverat, quique immensae misericordiae suae iter pergit, quod quidem in hac mortali vita, cum pertransiit benefaciendo, ipse pientissimo eo consilio incepit, ut hominum animi mysteria sua attingerent ac per eadem quodammodo viverent; quae profecto mysteria, non incerto ac subobscuro eo modo, quo recentiores quidam scriptores effutiunt, sed quo modo catholica doctrina nos docet, praesentia continenter adsunt atque operantur; quandoquidem, ex Ecclesiae Doctorum sententia, et eximia sunt christianae perfectionis exempla, et divinae gratiae sunt fontes ob merita deprecationesque Christi, et effectu suo in nobis perdurant, cum singula secundum indolem cuiusque suam salutis nostrae causa suo modo exsistant." Pius XII, *Mediator Dei*, 580; Smith, *Christian Worship* (London: CTS, 1954), 65.

returned to the Father, has left to his church the mysteries of worship as the means of revelation and grace that in this present time allow immediate contact with God's saving acts. Though other aspects of Casel's work proved problematic, his central doctrine was taken up by *Mediator Dei*,[215] which in turn influenced *Sacrosanctum Concilium*.

Despite what is at times an unhelpful and unfair comparison with *Sacrosanctum Concilium*, Aidan Nichols identifies three important theoretical contributions in the evaluation of the liturgical movement that Pius XII offers in *Mediator Dei*. They are "the false antimony between 'objective' and 'personal' devotion, the honouring of the whole history of development in the appreciation of a sound liturgical tradition, and a consciousness of the realised and future eschatological dimensions of the liturgy."[216] Obvious parallels can be made between the issues that Pius XII recognizes as central to the liturgical movement and themes that other theologians had been seeking to emphasize from the 1930s onwards that were collectively being termed *nouvelle théologie*: that is to say, the active engagement of the Christian subject in the historical reality of the world, a rejection of a disconnected and overly objective theology, a return to the biblical sources and the whole doctrinal tradition, and the

214. "The Christian thing, therefore, in its full and primitive meaning of God's good word, or Christ's, is not, as it were, a philosophy of life with religious background music, nor a moral or theological training; it is a *mysterium* as St Paul means the word, a revelation made by God to man through acts of God-manhood, full of life and power; it is mankind's way to God made possible by this revelation and the grace of it communicating the solemn entry of the redeemed Church into the presence of the everlasting Father." O. Casel, *Das christliche Kultmysterium*, first ed., 1932; fourth ed., 1960, enlarged by various texts chosen by B. Neunheuser; English trans. *The Mystery of Christian Worship*, (London: Darton, Longman and Todd, 1962), 12–13.

215. For a brief but accurate summary of Casel's theology and its reiteration in *Mediator Dei*, cf. I. H. Dalmais, "Liturgy and the Mystery of Salvation," in *Introduction to the Liturgy* (Baltimore: Helicon, 1961), 190–211, especially 203. Also see C. E. O'Neill, *Meeting Christ in the Sacraments* (Cork: Mercier, 1964), 67–69. The preface of Neunheuser's edition of *The Mystery of Christian Worship* is also relevant here.

216. See A. Nichols, *A Pope and a Council on the Sacred Liturgy* (Farnborough, UK: St Michael's Abbey, 2002), 15–25.

development of an anthropology that was determined as much by a supernatural as by a natural end.[217] Borrowing a passage from Stephen J. Duffy is helpful in explaining the grounds for this association:

> These then are the . . . factors that loomed large in reawakening interest in the relationship between God's grace and the human being. However, it ought to be noted that all three factors are themselves permeated by and function within the context of a certain contemporary spirit which itself was a stimulus in this direction. The desire today is for a synthetic understanding of humanity, a holistic picture that integrates the many aspects of human being made known to us by "regional" fields of study. Further, perhaps due to a more existential and/or empirical approach to life, people today want to experience grace in experiencing themselves and their communities, ecclesial and non-ecclesial. Such a mentality obviously influenced theologians. Hence the effort of some theologians to show that in concrete existence and experience grace cannot be neatly sealed off from the so-called "natural" levels in a person, but that it must penetrate all activities, both conscious and unconscious.[218]

While liturgy needed to shed ceremonial accretions and a spirit of rubricism in order better to appreciate the very mystery it contains, so

---

217. "There was a common interest in what was called Kerygmatic theology, the theology that must be taught to non-theologians and must therefore begin with the mood and convictions actually obtaining in the milieu. The scene was the France of the 30's and 40's, when French thought was in confusion, and when the famed French rationalism was being attacked by the French as irrelevant and harmful. It was the time of French existentialism, and the 'new' theologians experienced existentialism as a fact, though they were cold to it as a theory. They knew that existentialism was a deep reaction to a kind of thinking which they found prominent in Catholic theology, and which for two reasons they wished to drop. First, they themselves were the sons of their time, and the prevailing discontent with the tactic of solving problems by reducing the terms of the problems to logical constructions worked in them no less than in the non-Catholics. Second, if theology was necessarily and exclusively a matter of rationalistic formulation, there would be no way to establish contact with the new generation which heartily despised such an approach." G. Weigel, "The Historical Background of the Encyclical *Humani Generis*," *Theological Studies* 12 (1951): 220–21. See also J. Komonchak, "Returning From Exile: Catholic Theology in the 1930s," in *The Twentieth Century A Theological Overview*, ed. G. Baum (New York: Orbis, 1999), 35–48.

218. S. J. Duffy, *The Graced Horizon: Nature and Grace in Modern Catholic Thought* (Collegeville, MN: Liturgical Press, 1992), 53. An example of this can be seen in M.-D. Chenu's desire to "incarnate the life of grace in the social milieux"; see C. Potworowski, "Dechristianization, Socialization and Incarnation in Marie-Dominique Chenu," *Science et Esprit* 43 (1991): 17–54.

the theology of grace needed to shed its disdain for the mundane and the cold objectivism of scholastic theology. If the objectives of the liturgical movement and the *nouvelle théologie* can be seen as distinct, the means of their accomplishment remain the same, and for this reason their contribution to the Council was as one.[219] It is time to pay attention to what were still seen as the theological disciplines proper and the innovations that were happening there.

Nouvelle Théologie and Humani Generis

The necessity of dialogue with modern society and its philosophies, made more immediate by the conflicts of the World Wars,[220] an increasing consciousness of the importance of the Scriptures in theology, the movement of *ressourcement*, patristic and medieval, and its concomitant rejection of scholasticism,[221] were factors that, emerging in the first half of the twentieth century, remained unsystematized. Speaking of Henri de Lubac, the inspiration of the *nouvelle théologie,* Hans Urs von Balthasar gives us an insight into the limitations that reawakening Catholic theology still experienced in this period:

> Together with some good friends—such as B. De Solages, Father Congar, Father Chenu, Moureux, Chavasse, and others—he [de Lubac] conceived the plan of a comprehensive theological work "that would have been less systematic than the manuals but more saturated with tradition, integrating the valid elements in the results of modern exegesis, of patristics, liturgy, history, philosophical reflection. . . . The lightening bolt of *Humani Generis* killed the project."[222]

219. See R. W. Franklin, "Humanism and Transcendence in the Nineteenth-Century Liturgical Movement," *Worship* 59 (1985): 342–53.

220. For an excellent summary, see T. M. Schoof, "The Challenge of the World in France," in *A Survey of Catholic Theology 1800–1970* (New York: Paulist Newman, 1970), 93–102.

221. See A. Nichols, "Thomism and the *Nouvelle Théologie*," *The Thomist* 64 (2000): 1–19.

Important to notice here is not only the frustrating influence of the Roman authorities with regard to the crystallizing of a new theology, but the frustration experienced by its innovators in their efforts to offer a system pertinent to their times.[223] Von Balthasar quotes from a letter sent to de Lubac by Étienne Gilson soon after he had read de Lubac's *Surnaturel*:

> You are a theologian of great stature but likewise a humanist in the great tradition of humanist theologians. Humanist theologians usually do not love scholastics, and they are almost always hated by the scholastics. Why? In part, it seems to me, because the latter understand only univocal propositions and those that seem to be univocal. The former, by contrast, are more interested in the truth that the proposition attempts to formulate and that always partly escapes it. Then the latter no longer understand; they become restless, and because they cannot be certain that what escapes them is not false, they condemn it as a matter of principle, because that is more secure.[224]

222. Balthasar quoting de Lubac directly in H. U. von Balthasar, *The Theology of Henri de Lubac* (San Francisco: Ignatius, 1991), 10–11.

223. Emerging from prolonged isolation, Catholic theology had to come to terms with the many disparate aspects that dialogue with the world demanded (cf. Komonchak's comments on M.-D. Chenu, in "Returning From Exile," 39–42). Yet neither did the content and method of the new theology yield to easy description or systematization; as Gustave Weigel says, "Like many historical things, the 'new theology' was a casually gradual realization of an idea, but the idea was never grasped clearly or totally by one man, nor did any one man proceed step by step in order to achieve the whole." Weigel, "The Historical Background of the Encyclical *Humani Generis*," 220.

224. Balthasar, *The Theology of Henri de Lubac*, 14.

In *Humani Generis*, Pius XII sought this security for the Church,[225] a security de Lubac was willing to forego while pursuing a larger truth. The Jesuit teacher was concerned that theology "allow the self-revealing God his freedom to disclose his truth in the way which pleases him."[226] He pursued a broader understanding of revelation than the narrow logic of the neo-scholastics, allowing for imaginative sensibility, abstraction, and religious exigence as means of understanding revelation and as tools that can be used in its articulation. As a result de Lubac was charged, in a similar way to Newman,[227] with suggesting an ongoing revelation that did not cease with the death of the last apostle but is actualized in the present.

Catholicisme and *Surnaturel*

In the thought of Henri de Lubac, the question of the relationship between grace and nature was inextricably linked to the question of the relationship between theology and apologetics. Hence, de

225. "The contempt for terms and notions habitually used by scholastic theologians leads of itself to the weakening of what they call speculative theology, a discipline which these men consider devoid of true certitude because it is based on theological reasoning." (Despectus autem vocabulorum ac notionum quibus theologi scholastici uti solent, sponte ducit ad enervandam theologiam, ut aiunt speculativam, quam, cum ratione theologica innitatur, vera certitudine carere existimant.) Pius XII, *Humani Generis*, 567; Knox, *False Trends in Modern Teaching*, 9. Cf. also *Humani Generis* paragraph 21, where Pius XII says, "It is also true that theologians must always return to the sources of Divine Revelation for it belongs to them to point out how the doctrine of the living Teaching Authority is to be found either explicitly or implicitly in the Scriptures and Tradition." (Verum quoque est, theologis semper redeundum esse ad divinae revelationis fontes: eorum enim est indicare qua ratione ea quae a vivo Magisterio docentur, in Sacris Litteris et in divina traditione.) The primary movement of theology for Pius is backward—only armed with the truths of the deposit is speculative theology fruitful. However, the power to explain what is contained in the deposit of faith, obscurely and implicitly, belongs "not even to theologians but only to the Teaching Authority of the Church." See *Humani Generis*, 568; Knox, *False Trends in Modern Teaching*, 11–12. For an insightful overview of the reaction of *Humani Generis* to the themes of the new theology see, Duffy, *The Graced Horizon*, 59–65.

226. Nichols, *From Newman to Congar*, 208.

227. Cf. I. Ker, "Newman's Theory—Development or Continuing Revelation," in *Newman and Gladstone: Centennial Essays*, ed. J. D. Bastable (Dublin: Veritas, 1978), 145–59.

Lubac's first book, *Catholicisme*,[228] attempts to give a credible vision of the church by refreshing ecclesiology with the "social aspects of dogma." The Christian gospel, working for the complete restoration of creation and history that has been wrought in Christ, takes objective shape in the communal and historical framework of the church. There the alienating and disassociating effects of sin are overcome, and all things are united in Christ. After the war, however, de Lubac became more and more concerned with what he would later term "a sort of unconscious conspiracy"[229] between forces that led to secularism and a shabby theology that placed the supernatural beyond the reach of nature. The ecclesial vision he had set forth in *Catholicisme* needed to be underpinned with an anthropology that, on the grounds of solid tradition, vigorously rejected attempts to confine humanity to a fulfillment restricted to its natural powers. In *Surnaturel*,[230] De Lubac sketched out such an anthropology. As T. M. Schoof says of the book, "In it de Lubac adopted a new position in an historical debate, but at the same time laid down the foundation of a Christian humanism—by virtue of creation, that is on the basis of his being, man is effectively called to community with God, the transcendent fulfilment of his longing for happiness."[231]

Immediately, and to varying degrees, this new position was attacked as a limitation of the sovereignty of God and the gratuity of grace, in some circles primarily because it was believed to be

228. H. de Lubac, *Catholicisme: Les aspects sociaux du dogme* (Paris: Cerf, 1938); English trans. by Lancelot C. Sheppard, *Catholicism: A Study of Dogma in Relation to the Corporate Destiny of Mankind*, (New York: Sheed and Ward, 1958). For a useful summary and analysis of this book, see P. McPartlan, *The Eucharist Makes the Church: Henri de Lubac and John Zizioulas in Dialogue* (Edinburgh: T. & T. Clark, 1993), 3–14.

229. H. de Lubac, "Internal Causes of the Weakening and Disappearance of the Sense of the Sacred," in *Theology in History* (San Francisco: Ignatius, 1996), 232, quoted in Komonchak, "Returning From Exile," 44.

230. H. de Lubac, *Surnaturel: Études historiques* (Paris: Aubier, 1946). New edition with preface by Michel Sales, H. de Lubac, *Surnaturel: Études historiques* (Paris: Desclée de Brouwer, 1991).

231. Schoof, *A Survey of Catholic Theology 1800–1970*, 113.

an attempt to discredit St. Thomas.[232] To many the specter of Modernism seemed to have returned and, though de Lubac maintained an impressive, scholarly, and Christian courtesy throughout, and though he was not and could never have been styled a rebellious leader, the misunderstanding from which he suffered was not insignificant.[233]

De Lubac recognised a difficulty in his own system, but nevertheless preferred his approximations to the secure arguments of the neo-scholastics. As Aidan Nichols suggests,

> Our problem admits no resolution until such time as we re-formulate—so de Lubac contends—our very idea of revelation itself. Here too we may discern the hand of Rousselot, who had suggested exactly the same thing. To call the original content of revelation a "series of propositions" is not, de Lubac complains, to designate it "exactly or sufficiently." The content of revelation is that divine redemptive action which is summed up in God's gift of his Son. The mystery of Christ is the "*Objet globale*" of revelation. The mystery of Christ is "*le Tout de dogme*," dogma in its unified entirety.[234]

The problem that exercised the minds of the exponents of *nouvelle théologie* was not a distinct question about the theology of grace. For them there could be no such thing. Fundamentally, it was a matter concerned with the idea of revelation itself. The heart of the theological question at issue was the manner of God's self-

---

232. For a detailed discussion of the position of de Lubac, largely from the negative perspective of his various opponents, see articles by P. Donnelly: "On the Development of Dogma and the Supernatural," *Theological Studies* 8 (1947): 471–91; "The Surnaturel of Henri de Lubac," *Theological Studies* 9 (1948): 554–60; "The Gratuity of the Beatific Vision and the Possibility of a Natural Destiny," *Theological Studies* 11 (1950): 374–404. A more positive appraisal can be gained from S. Moore, "The Desire of God," *Downside Review* 45 (1947): 246–59.

233. Cf. the personal address of Pope John Paul II that was read at de Lubac's funeral in 1991. There the pope explained that the honor of the cardinalate had been granted de Lubac "to acknowledge the merits of a tireless scholar, a spiritual master and a Jesuit who was faithful during the various difficult moments of his life." *L'Osservatore Romano* (English edition), 16 September 1991, 12.

234. Nichols, *From Newman to Congar*, 210.

communication in Christ and its present significance for believers. For de Lubac, the problem was one of apologetics as much as it was one of grace, and that is why his contribution is crucial to an understanding of the actualization of revelation in the mystery of Christ's body, the church. Rather than reducing the question of grace to the domestic level of church and believer, he raised it to a dramatic one within the economy of salvation. And rather than offering an answer, he, "together with some good friends," returned to the position of the Master many saw him as opposing: *Sed quia de Deo scire non possumus quid sit sed quid non sit.*[235] Hence von Balthasar could say of his contribution, "De Lubac is not only the great author who understood and experienced all his completed works as an approximation to an ever-unattained centre. This form gives the reader the chance of seeing how seemingly disparate elements converge upon a centre and thus of grasping them in their secret intention."[236]

At a more mundane level, the work of Henri de Lubac was significant on two counts. It gave inspiration and a vocabulary[237] to the further development and systematization of the then-prominent themes in theology, especially as they featured in the Council, and more particularly it presented an opportunity and a challenge to de Lubac's fellow Jesuit, Karl Rahner.

---

235. "Now we cannot know what God is, but only what he is not." Thomas Aquinas, *ST* 1a. 3, pref., English trans. T. McDermott, *Summa Theologiae*, vol. 2: *Existence and Nature of God* (London: Blackfriars, 1963), 18.
236. Balthasar, *The Theology of Henri de Lubac*, 12.
237. "There [in *DV*] we read that, through divine revelation, the most profound truth about God as well as about human salvation shines out for us *in Christo . . . qui mediator simul et plenitudo totius revelationis existit*: Christ . . . who is at one and the same time the mediator and the plenitude of the whole of revelation. And, in his 1968 commentary on *Dei Verbum*, *La Révélation divine*, de Lubac remarks, with surely a degree of personal satisfaction, 'The Council could say no better than this.'" Nichols, *From Newman to Congar*, 212.

Karl Rahner and Transcendental Thomism

If Karl Rahner is representative of the "second generation" of theologians, his direct forebears were Jacques Maritain (1882–1973), Étienne Gilson (1884–1978), and Joseph Maréchal (1878–1944). In the wake of Blondel, the Modernist Crisis, and the new theology, when the return to the Fathers was at its height, these three took advantage of the weakening of the political right in Rome, brought about as much by the excesses of the anti-Modernists as by the changed climate of post-War Europe,[238] and in quite different ways put new life into the flagging Thomist cause. G. McCool is correct in saying,

> Their contribution to scholasticism can be summarised as follows: the enrichment and development of the commentators' traditional Thomism, the historical recovery of St. Thomas' own philosophy, and the establishment of transcendental Thomism. Although many distinguished scholastics worked at these tasks, a single name has become associated with each one of them. Maritain's name is associated with the first, Gilson's with the second, and Maréchal's with the third.[239]

Maritain remained an old-fashioned Thomist, traditional in his conviction that the strength of St. Thomas lay in objectivity and abstraction. However, he shed the narrowness and rigidity of his ilk by embracing the notion that the metaphysics and epistemology of Thomism was singular in the clarification and integration that it could offer human experience. Maritain extended his philosophy to the imagination, art, poetry, and mystical experience. Though approaching his study from a differing angle, Gilson also endeavored to set Thomism in a much wider context. He brought to Thomism

---

238. G. McCool sees Pius XI's condemnation of Action Française and Don Luigi Sturzo's development of Christian Democracy as other influential factors in changing the Roman political climate. See McCool, *Catholic Theology in the Nineteenth Century*, 251.
239. Ibid., 252.

the historian's skills of textual analysis and synthesis, and enlarged significantly knowledge of St. Thomas by exploring medieval history and culture. In yet a different way, Joseph Maréchal sought to reinterpret St. Thomas within the wider vision that the modern world affords, achieving this specifically through dialogue with the philosophy of Kant.[240] In this Maréchal followed Blondel and Pierre Rousselot, but differed from them in his desire to establish a Kantian realistic metaphysics that would be identical to the metaphysics of St. Thomas. McCool gives a succinct summary of the position Maréchal adopts:

> The *a priori* condition of possibility for every speculative judgement is the existence of the Infinite Pure Act of *esse* as the term of the mind's dynamism. And in every judgement a universal form is united to a sensible singular and then placed in existence by the objective affirmation. Consequently, the extra-mental correlate of the objective judgement must be matter, form and existence. But matter, form, and existence are the metaphysical constituents of the sensible singular in the philosophy of St. Thomas.[241]

By the end of the Second World War, Thomism had certainly been revitalized by these three men, but in three distinct and differing directions. The unified method for Catholic theology envisaged by Leo XIII in *Aeterni Patris* was already yielding to the forces of the philosophical pluralism that was to mark later twentieth-century theology. Historical research, higher biblical criticism and the newly rediscovered method of patristics brought to crisis point the need for scholasticism to shed its traditional approach. The Modernists had failed in their methods, and the *nouvelle théologie* had been embarrassed by *Humani Generis,* yet Karl Rahner was to inherit many

---

240. See the famous *Cahier cinq,* the fifth volume of *Le Point de départ de la métaphysique* (Paris: Aclan, 1922–26), where Maréchal, having set Thomas within the history of philosophy, establishes a dialogue between him and Kant.
241. McCool, *Catholic Theology in the Nineteenth Century,* 256–57.

of its most valuable insights and achieve a theological synthesis of St. Thomas that "was receptive to a theological pluralism based on a plurality of conceptual frameworks."[242]

The transcendental Thomism of Karl Rahner is adequately explained elsewhere.[243] Of more significance here is the effect such a method had on Rahner's fundamental theology, especially his understanding of revelation. As Aidan Nichols points out at the beginning of the section on Rahner in his book *From Newman to Congar*,

> Much of the intrinsic interest, as also the problematic quality, of Rahner's work lies in the interplay between these two very different sides of his inheritance—the philosophical element, itself not only Scholastic and, to a degree, as with all "Transcendental Thomists," Kantian, but also Heideggerian, and the mystical-contemplative element, which is not only patristic but also Ignatian. As to the former, it is worth recalling that Heidegger himself considered any philosophical reflection worthy of the name to issue from *alêtheia*, the unveiling of the truth of being—the self-same metaphor, of course, that the term "revelation" also contains.[244]

As has been seen, the idea of the mystical element was having great effect generally on the wider background of theology. Such an influence can be seen in the details of Rahner's work. Mystery is an essential element within his system, because it constitutes the furthest pole from the human being, and as such is the reality that establishes

242. Ibid., 260. For a full discussion of the background and development of Rahner's ideas, see G. McCool, "Twentieth Century Scholasticism," *The Journal of Religion* 58 Supplement (1978): S198–21.

243. See G. McCool, "Karl Rahner and the Christian Philosophy of St. Thomas Aquinas," in *Theology and Discovery: Essays in Honour of Karl Rahner, SJ*, ed. W. J. Kelly (Milwaukee, Marquette University Press, 1980), 63–93. Cf. also the relevant sections of McCool, *Catholic Theology in the Nineteenth Century*, 241–67. An interesting alternative view that Rahner did not really remain within the Thomist tradition is offered by C. Fabro, *La svolta antropologica di Karl Rahner* (Milan: Rusconi, 1974).

244. Nichols, *From Newman to Congar*, 215.

a tension with world history. This tension is fundamental to Rahner's theology and, as John O'Donnell says,

> Perhaps the key term in Rahner's philosophical anthropology is transcendence. This term indicates that the human being is a dynamic propulsion beyond himself toward the Infinite. Like St Thomas Aquinas, Rahner understands the human subject according to the two faculties of intellect and will. . . . Hence knowledge is a dynamic process, a process in principle without a terminus. For Rahner this implies that knowledge is essentially ordered to Infinite Mystery.[245]

Revelation then, by virtue of its constantly transcendent goal, always remains a problematic concept. The mysterious horizon of the infinite, though permanently present, is always beyond. Natural revelation always brings an individual to a point of questioning, of awesome wonder as to whether God is seeking communion with the creatures he made. The Christian believer deems the incarnation of Jesus to be the definitive answer to this question.

For Karl Rahner the incarnation is the crux of supernatural revelation: to begin to understand God's disclosure of himself to human beings, we must begin with the hypostatic union.[246] The mystery of the unity of the divine and human natures in Christ lies at the heart of the problem of how God relates to the world.[247] As Rahner himself says, "The difference between God and the world is

---

245. J. O'Donnell, *The Mystery of the Triune God* (London: Sheed and Ward, 1988), 27–28. Or as Rahner himself puts it, "If God creates something other than himself and thereby creates it as something finite, if God creates spirit which recognises the other as finite through its transcendence and hence in view of its ground, and if therefore, at the same time it differentiates this ground as qualitatively and wholly other from what is merely finite, and as the ineffable and holy Mystery, this already implies a certain disclosure of God as the Infinite Mystery." Rahner, *Foundations of Christian Faith* (London: Darton, Longman and Todd, 1978), 170.

246. This Rahner sees as foundational as early as his "Current Problems in Christology," in *Theological Investigations*, vol. 1, 149–200.

247. "Rahner perceived that at the heart of this problem is the conundrum of how we are to understand the unity of Christ, or in the language of Chalcedon, the unity of the divine and human natures in Christ. Rahner also sees that this problem is not unique to Christology. It also underlies the problem of the doctrine of creation and God's relation to the world." O'Donnell, *The Mystery of the Triune God*, 30.

of such a nature that God establishes and is the difference of the world from himself, and for this reason he establishes the closest unity, precisely in the differentiation."[248] On the basis of the hypostatic union, the humanity can be understood as something distinct from the divine Logos only when it is thought of in unity with the Logos. The unity must always constitute the diversity. In the incarnation, God did not give to the world something distinct from himself, but his very self. Just as the humanity of Jesus is the revelation of the divinity, so in the incarnation of Jesus the giver and the gift are one. Later in his theology, this interplay of philosophical and mystical concepts takes its fullest expression in the language of symbol.[249] The idea of unity and distinction that underpins the theology of revelation, ecclesiology, grace, and the sacraments, and that is most perfectly expressed in the christological doctrine of the hypostatic union, is effectively explained through the concept of symbol:[250]

> Jesus . . . is the absolute symbol of God in the world, filled as nothing else can be with what is symbolised. He is not merely the presence and revelation of what God is in himself. He is also the expressive presence of what—or rather, who—God wished to be, in free grace, to the world, in such a way, that this divine attitude once expressed, can never be reversed but is and remains final and irreversible.[251]

It is by means of his understanding of revelation as symbolic communication that Rahner avoids the accusation, leveled at Tyrrell, Newman, and others who "dug a ditch" between revelation in Jesus Christ and its subsequent revealing in the church, suggesting that

---

248. Rahner, *Foundations of Christian Faith*, 62.

249. See Rahner, "The Theology of Symbol," in *Theological Investigations*, trans. K. Smyth, vol. 4 (London: Darton, Longman and Todd, 1966), 221–52.

250. The notion of symbol and the part it plays within Rahner's system is complex and will be discussed more thoroughly as the book develops. An article useful in providing a general overview and orientation can be found in G. Vandervelde, "The Grammar of Grace: Karl Rahner as a Watershed in Contemporary Theology," *Theological Studies* 49 (1988): 445–59.

251. O'Donnell, *The Mystery of the Triune God*, 31–32.

there is an ever-new revelation in the church subsequent to that of Christ. Christ is the symbol of the Father and the church of Christ. The church continually shows forth the word—nothing new but a speaking of the completed revelation of Christ through history.[252]

This revelation of the word is not merely propositional. It is the word proclaimed by the church, most typically in the sacraments. In seeking to express the plenitude of this revelation, Rahner finds in the church, the mystical body of Christ, the fullness of mystical vitality that allows it to equal the revelation of the living word:

> Revelation is not the communication of a definite number of propositions . . . to which additions may conceivably be made at will, or which can suddenly and arbitrarily be limited. Rather is revelation an historical dialogue between God and man in which something happens, and in which the communication (*Mitteilung*) is related to the happening, the divine action (*das Geschehen, das Handeln Gottes*). . . . Revelation is a saving happening, and only then in relation to this a communication of truths.[253]

Rahner differs from Tyrrell and the Modernists by rejecting the idea that the church can enjoy the saving reality of revelation in the present moment by somehow transcending, experientially, the original divine message: "The believing Church possesses what she believes: Christ, his Spirit, the earnest of eternal life and its vital

---

252. Peter Knauer, a German Jesuit cited by O'Donnell, provides an effective gloss on Rahner's theology. Speaking of revelation as a Word-event, he draws together the Rahnerian themes of unity and diversity, symbol and the fullness of revelation being in Christ. Knauer writes, "This being addressed by God in a human word is itself the event of community with God. Therefore the concept 'Word of God' in its genuine sense is so to be understood, that it comprehends the entirety of God's saving act and concerns the entire reality of man. Therefore, it is not to be completed through any further divine action, but it itself accomplishes what it says. In fact, salvation consists in being spoken to (Heb 2:3). Therefore the 'Word of God' is not speech *about* the love of God to man but it is itself the completion of this love; i.e. a Word-event." Knauer, *Der Glaube kommt vom Hören* (Frankfurt am Main, 1982), 75, in O'Donnell, *The Mystery of the Triune God*, 24–25.

253. Rahner, "The Development of Dogma," *Theological Investigations*, vol. 1, 48, in Nichols, *From Newman to Congar*, 221–22.

powers. She cannot leave the Word behind in order to grasp this reality. But no more does she possess a word about the thing instead of the thing itself."[254]

This is an extremely difficult concept to comprehend, if it can be grasped at all. The reality of revelation in the church is hidden and present, and it is a reality that takes part in its own understanding.[255] As Aidan Nichols rightly insists, this aspect of Rahner's thought is rooted in the mystical theology he had studied so closely. This is a strong theme in his work both pre- and post–Council, and, associated as it is with ecclesiological and liturgical themes, it witnesses to a confluence of ideas that would occupy theology for some years to come. Indeed, more than any other dogmatic theologian, Rahner promotes the paradigm shift that effected the change in the doctrine of revelation that can be seen in a simple comparison between *Dei Filius* and *Dei Verbum*. The understanding of revelation as an extrinsic, propositional, and purely intellectual body of evidence has, by the end of the Second Vatican Council, given way to a far more nuanced and profound concept. Revelation is the self-disclosure of God made to the community, to the human person as a whole, in view of their salvation. Revelation is understood no longer as the simple process of the communication of supernatural knowledge, but as a complex theological nexus that incorporates anthropology, ecclesiology, sacramentology, and soteriology. Only such a combination could begin to help unfold the mysterious relationship that exists between God and his people. With the help of the many and varied theological contributions from the late nineteenth and the twentieth century, such was the conviction reached by the eve of Vatican II. To extend, at the risk of cliché, the metaphor with which this chapter opened, the overtures for change were now to be taken

---

254. Rahner, "The Development of Dogma," 50.
255. Ibid. See also Nichols, *From Newman to Congar*, 223–24.

up by the symphonic movements of the four Constitutions. There the theological themes of renewal are played out and interconnected within the particular foci of *worship*, *word*, *church*, and *world*.

The Council, Revelation, and the Sacraments

As Thomas O'Meara points out in a useful summary of recent trends in revelation theology, "In short, during the years leading up to Vatican II, revelation was a field which exemplified the theological changes for which this period would become famous, and so it was no chance of the agenda that the crucial debates of the Council's first session centred around *De fontibus revelationis*."[256]

Indeed, revelation was a topic that remained central beyond the First Session. *Dei Verbum* was not promulgated until 18 November 1965, only twenty days before the close of the Council, which meant that the self-communication of God was, to varying degrees, the focus of debate throughout Vatican II.[257] And, while through this "long odyssey" of reformulation a significantly new theology of revelation was defined,[258] so too was the hermeneutical key[259] to the whole Council. Hence, in introducing his *relatio* on 30 September 1964, Archbishop Florit declared, "Because of its inner importance, as well as the many vicissitudes that it has undergone, the history of the draft of the Constitution on Divine Revelation has fused with the history of the Council into a kind of unity."[260]

---

256. T. F. O'Meara, "Toward a Subjective Theology of Revelation," *Theological Studies* 36 (1975): 401–27, 401.

257. Cf. Rino Fisichella's article on the history of the document, Fisichella, "Dei Verbum," in Latourelle and Fisichella, *Dictionary of Fundamental Theology*, 214–18.

258. Latourelle summarises the principal novelties of the Constitution in *Comment Dieu se révèle au monde: Lecture commentée de la Constitution de Vatican II sur la Parole de Dieu* (Québec: Éditions Fides, 1998), 93–99.

259. "Malheureusement, la constitution *Dei verbum*, clé herméneutique de tout le Concile, et probablement son plus beau texte, reste trop peu connue." Ibid., 8.

René Latourelle indicates clearly the nature of the methodological shifts that *Dei Verbum* has engendered, and describes the blue print of theological categories around which the main ideas of the Council are structured:

> After the period of panic, deceleration, and stagnation resulting from the Modernist crisis, the Constitution *Dei Verbum* seems like a breath of fresh sea air dispersing a heavy fog. The transition to a personalist, historical and christocentric conception of revelation amounts to a kind of Copernican revolution, compared with the extrinsicist, atemporal, and notional approach which prevailed until the 1950's.[261]

Later in the same article, Latourelle spells out the concrete expression of these changes in understanding. Clearly, the Fathers regard the object and nature of the self-manifestation of God as communion.[262] The object is the Blessed Trinity,[263] whose being is reflected in the nature of an economy of personal encounter through word, dialogue, and gesture. This essentially personalist dimension to God's self-disclosure is determined by his Trinitarian life—especially as that is expressed through Jesus Christ. Aptly quoting the First Letter of St. John, the bishops assert their motive: "That you may also have fellowship with us, and that our fellowship may be with the Father and with his son Jesus Christ."[264] The Son of God is the last word in God's self-communication. He is its fulfilment and completion,

---

260. Quoted in J. Ratzinger, "Dogmatic Constitution on Divine Revelation: Origin and Background," in Vorgrimler, *Commentary on the Documents of Vatican II*, vol. 3, 155.

261. R. Latourelle, "Dei Verbum," 218. Avery Dulles claims something similar when he says, "Revelation, I would say, is regarded as a real and efficacious self communication of God, the transcendent mystery, to the believing community. The deeper insights of revelatory knowledge are imparted, not in the first instance through propositional discourse, but through participation in the life and worship of the Church." Dulles, *The Craft of Theology*, 2nd ed. (New York: Crossroad, 1995), 18.

262. *DV*, 2, [*972].

263. "This revelation appears in its trinitarian dimension. The description of the object of revelation in its threefold personalist, trinitarian, and christocentric nature gives the text a richness and resonance that contrast with the formulation of Vatican I which spoke of revelation without any explicit and direct mention of Christ." Latourelle, "Dei Verbum," 219.

definitively expressed in the *gesta-verba* of history and the incarnation. Such an invitation to communion is, in itself, an invitation to conversation and friendship, the beginning of an intimate dialogue between the wise and good God and human beings who respond in faith.[265] Because of its fundamentally anthropological form, this saving action[266] is indescribable outside the human experiences which Scripture and tradition have verified, and this explains the preference given to biblical categories over scholastic formulations.[267]

These elements, which Latourelle has emphasized as the major points of departure in the understanding of revelation in *Dei Verbum*, are likewise apparent in the other dogmatic constitutions, where they underpin the particular endeavor of each. By drawing out these same issues with reference to the liturgy and to the church, the Council not only showed a congruency and consistency in its teaching, but intimated the need to integrate more successfully the various theological disciplines in order that the truths of salvation be understood in a more nuanced and holistic way.[268] To this end, it

264. *DV*, 1. Cf. 1 John 1:3 [*971–72]. "God revealed himself, then, in order to invite human beings to a communion of divine life and with God "to share in the divine nature." Latourelle, "Dei Verbum," 220.

265. "This is the first time that a document of the extraordinary magisterium has described the actual expression of the economy of revelation—God addresses human beings, creatures of flesh and mind located in time, and communicates with them by means of history and the Incarnation. This is the importance of the *gesta-verba* pairing within the text. Events and interpretation, works and words, form and organic indissoluble whole—an economy which reaches its fullness in Christ." Latourelle, "Dei Verbum," 220.

266. "In contradistinction to Vatican I, which spoke first of God's revelation through creation, then of the historical revelation, Vatican II reversed the perspective and began with the personal revelation of God and salvation in Jesus Christ. . . . Having affirmed the fact of revelation, the Council stated that it was essentially a divine initiative and a pure act of grace like all the rest of the work of salvation: 'We announce to you the eternal life which was with the Father, and has appeared to us.' (*Dei Verbum* 1)." Ibid., 218–19.

267. "To define the object of revelation, the Council makes generous use of biblical categories, especially those of Paul. Instead of speaking like Vatican I, of the decrees of the divine will, it uses the Pauline term 'mystery' (*sacramentum*). 'God chose to reveal himself and to make known to us the hidden purpose (*sacramentum*) of his will. (*Dei Verbum*, 2; Eph. 1:9).'" Ibid., 220.

268. This, in essence, is behind the prescription of *SC*, 16 [*824–*25]: "The study of sacred liturgy is to be ranked among the compulsory and major courses in seminaries and religious houses of

is helpful to map out in the other documents some implications of the theological categories that Latourelle recognized as somewhat novel in *Dei Verbum*. In essence, the values of the liturgical renewal evidenced by *Sacrosanctum Concilium* echo the shifts in revelation theology that *Dei Verbum* was gradually defining.

The Constitution on the Sacred Liturgy had "several aims in view,"[269] yet the primary objective was to foster that communion in Christ, the sharing of which is a participation in the divine life.[270] If increased vigor for the Christian life and the adaptation of reformable aspects of the liturgy to modern times seem a priority, these too are undertaken to effect a deeper sense of communion in the church.[271] Exactly for this reason, the reform gave a privileged place to an understanding of participation.[272] Of paramount importance for a correct understanding of the liturgy was the personalist and anthropological categories that reflection on the nature of revelation had engendered. These dimensions, particularly pertinent to

study; in theological faculties it is to rank among the principal courses. It is to be taught under its theological, historical, spiritual, pastoral, and juridical aspects. Moreover, other professors, while striving to expound the mystery of Christ and the history of salvation from the angle proper to each of their own subjects, must nevertheless do so in a way which will clearly bring out the connection between their subjects and the liturgy." (Disciplina de sacra liturgia in seminariis et studiorum domibus religiosis inter disciplinas necessarias et potiores, in facultatibus autem theologicis inter disciplinas principales est habenda, et sub aspectu cum theologico et historico, tum spirituali, pastorali et iuridico tradenda. Curent insuper aliarum disciplinarum magistri, imprimis theologiae dogmaticae, sacrae scripturae, theologiae spiritualis et pastoralis ita, ex intrinsecis exigentiis proprii uniuscuiusque obiecti, mysterium Christi et historiam salutis excolere, ut exinde earum connexio cum liturgia et unitas sacerdotalis institutionis aperte clarescant.)

269. Remarks here are based on the excellent and concise overview of the liturgical reform of *SC* given in Vaillancourt, *Toward a Renewal of Sacramental Theology*, especially 1–35. This is an English trans. of *Vers un Renouveau de la théologie sacramentaire* (Montreal: La Corporation des Éditions Fides, 1977).

270. *SC*, 1 [*820].

271. The liturgy is to be that which "daily builds up those who are within into a holy temple of the Lord, into a dwelling place for God in the Spirit, to the measure and fullness of Christ" (Unde, cum liturgia eos qui intus sunt cotidie aedificet in templum sanctum in Domino, in habitaculum Dei in Spiritu, usque ad mensuram aetatis plenitudinis Christi). *SC*, 2 [*820].

272. Ibid., 14, 48 [*824, *830].

liturgical celebration, are fundamental to an understanding of its renewal. Adopting the same quotation from the Letter to the Hebrews as *Dei Verbum*, the Constitution on the Sacred Liturgy identifies as its first general principle of restoration and reform the rooting of every aspect of God's self-communication in the words and actions of Jesus Christ.[273] Hence the fundamental premise of the liturgical reform is the restoration of an understanding of the liturgy as that event that effects the fulfillment of the human person through encounter with, and communion in, Christ.[274] As with revelation,[275] so the ultimate object of the liturgy is communion with God.

An interesting example may be given of how notions of revelation founded on a christological anthropology are fundamental to the reshaping of liturgy. Paul Post points to the significance of *Dei Verbum*, 13 (with footnote 11)[276] in a "diagnosis of the ritual-liturgical

---

273. Ibid., 5 [*821]; *DV*, 4 [*972].

274. "Thus by baptism men are plunged into the paschal mystery of Christ: they die with Him, and are buried with him, and rise with Him; they receive the spirit of adoption as sons 'in which we cry Abba, Father' (Rom 8;15), and thus become true adorers whom the Father seeks. In like manner, as often as they eat the supper of the Lord they proclaim the death of the Lord until he comes." (Sic per baptismum homines paschali Christi mysterio inseruntur: commortui, consepulti, conresuscitati; spiritum accipiunt adoptionis filiorum, "in quo clamamus: abba, Pater" (Rm 8, 15), et ita fiunt veri adoratores, quos Pater quaerit.) *SC*, 6 [*821].

275. *DV*, 2 [*972].

276. "Hence, in sacred Scripture, without prejudice to God's truth and holiness, the marvellous 'condescension' of eternal wisdom is plain to be seen 'that we may come to know the ineffable loving-kindness of God and see for ourselves how far he has gone in adapting his language with thoughtful concern for our nature.' (St. John Chrysostom, *In Gen.* 3, 8 [hom.17, 1]: *PG* 53, 134. *Attemperatio* corresponds to the Greek *synkatábasis*.) Indeed the words of God, expressed in the words of men, are in every way like human language, just as the Word of the eternal Father, when he took on himself the flesh of human weakness, became like men." (In sacra scriptura ergo manifestatur, salva semper Dei veritate et sanctitate, aeternae sapientiae admirabilis *condescensio* "ut discamus ineffabilem Dei benignitatem, et quanta sermonis attemperatione usus sit, nostrae naturae providentiam et curam habens." Dei enim verba, humanis linguis expressa, humano sermoni assimilia facta sunt, sicut olim aeterni Patris Verbum, humanae infirmitatis assumpta carne, hominibus simile factum est.) The English translation of *DV*, 13, used here is in A. Flannery, ed., *Vatican Council II: The Conciliar and Post-Conciliar Documents*, vol. 1 (Dublin: Dominican, 1987), 758. Latin orig. in N. Tanner, ed., *Decrees of the Ecumenical Councils,* vol. 2: *Trent–Vatican II* (London: Sheed and Ward, 1990), 977.

environment" as an anthropological movement between God and humanity centred on Christ:

> Here we touch on the double movement of *katabasis* and *anabasis* for which we can use the principle of the *synkatabasis*, a telling, though little known patristic term from the Vatican II documents. The term was coined by John Chrysostom and is really untranslatable. It is therefore, the only time that the Vatican II documents do not instantly have a Latin translation of Greek heritage, but leave the Greek term unchanged. Literally, the term can be translated as "go down with someone to the place where he or she is staying." This attitude is attributed to God and may therefore be referred to as "God's humaneness." Liturgy is inextricably linked to the anthropological, ritual and cultural environment. It is not that a divine matter is geared to or handed over to purely human matters or categories. . . . No, it is cherishing the "gentle kindness of God": God turns to his people by using means that are accessible and suitable. The diagnosis of that environment now puts the sacramentality of our environment on the line.[277]

It is the economy of revelation that determines the way in which the Council understands both the essence and action of the church. Three separate references in both *Sacrosanctum Concilium* and *Lumen Gentium* describe the revealing of God, and the salvation inherent in that disclosure, in terms of sacrament. Fundamentally, the three differently nuanced references in the Constitution on the Church make clear that the salvation that consists in union with God cannot exist apart from unity revealed in humanity. Articles 1, 9, and 48 comment in some way on the intimate communion that God brings about by his self-manifestation.[278] The same must be said of the three

---

277. P. Post, "Life Cycle Rituals: A Ritual-Liturgical Perspective," *Questions Liturgiques/Studies in Liturgy* 83, no. 1 (2002): 25.

278. "And since the Church is in Christ as a sacrament or instrumental sign of intimate union with God and of the unity of all humanity, the council, continuing the teaching of previous councils, intends to declare with greater clarity to the faithful and the entire human race the nature of the Church and its universal mission." (Cum autem ecclesia sit in Christo veluti sacramentum seu signum et instrumentum intimae cum Deo unionis totiusque generis humani unitatis, naturam missionemque suam universalem, praecedentium conciliorum argumento

occasions on which *Sacrosanctum Concilium* uses this description.[279] These texts plainly teach that "the human element becomes the manifestation and revelation of the divine."[280] That is to say, sacrament is to be understood as the instrument of *synkatabasis*.

What this notion of miraculous condescension achieves for sacramentology is an effective restoration of a sense of the intrinsic relation between God, the cosmos, liturgy, and human persons. In this way, the seven sacraments are seen "as uniquely revelatory of the immanent and transcendent God we believe in."[281] Therefore, the Fathers note, "the liturgy, 'through which the work of our redemption is accomplished,' most of all in the divine sacrifice of the eucharist, is the outstanding means whereby the faithful may express in their lives, and manifest to others, the mystery of Christ and the real nature of the Church."[282] The bishops show great solicitude that the liturgy be an authentic human expression related to life, and that it be fully and actively participatory and effect communion with God: "For all too many, liturgy can still be regarded as a cult of fixed forms, as impenetrable because it is derived from arcane sources and as hard to decipher given its terse phrasings and (often regrettably in

instans, pressius fidelibus suis et mundo universo declarare intendit.) *LG*, 1 [*849]. "God has called together the assembly of those who look to Jesus in faith as the author of salvation and the principle of unity and peace, and has constituted his body which is the Church as the universal sacrament of salvation." (Deus congregationem eorum qui in Iesum, salutis auctorem et unitatis pacisque principium, credentes aspiciunt, convocavit et constituit ecclesiam, ut sit universis et singulis sacramentum visibile huius salutiferae unitatis.) *LG*, 9 [*856]. "Christ, when he was lifted up from the earth, drew all people to himself; rising from the dead, he sent his life-giving Spirit down on his disciples and through him he constituted his body which is the Church as the universal sacrament of salvation." (Christus quidem exaltatus a terra omnes traxit ad seipsum; resurgens ex mortuis Spiritum suum vivificantem in discipulos immisit et per eum corpus suum quod est ecclesia ut universale salutis sacramentum constituit.) *LG*, 48 [*887].

279. *SC*, 2, 5, 26 [*820, *821, *826]. See Y.-M. Congar, *Un peuple messianique: L'Église sacrement du salut et libération* (Paris: Éditions du Cerf, 1975), 31.

280. Susan Wood, *Sacramental Orders* (Collegeville, MN: Liturgical Press, 2000), 21.

281. K. Irwin, "Liturgical Actio: Sacramentology, Eschatology and Ecology," *Questions Liturgiques/Studies in Liturgy* 81, nos. 3–4 (2000): 174.

282. *SC*, 2 [*820].

celebration) its minimalism in human expressiveness and in symbolic engagement."[283]

For the liturgy to achieve its aim, which is above all else the fostering of "full, conscious and active participation," it requires of sacramental celebrations a dynamism and creativity that express the human desire for self-realization in the divine. This desire comes gradually to completion when the individual comes into communion with Christ through the symbolic *synaxis* of the paschal mystery. In the invitatory dialogue of the *gesta-verba* of Christ, the liturgy actualizes revelation and encourages a response. "For in the liturgy God speaks to His people and Christ is still proclaiming His Gospel. And the people reply to God both by song and prayer."[284] Yet this is no private conversation, as through the mystical communication of the Holy Spirit, Christ "constitutes as his own body those brothers of his who are called together."[285] Hence, the dynamism and creativity that exist between the proclamation of the word of God and its fulfillment as the sacramental expression of the church in the lives of men and women. As Avery Dulles maintains,

> Sacrament, as we have been saying, is a sign of grace realising itself. Sacrament has an event character; it is dynamic. The Church becomes Church insofar as the grace of Christ, operative within it, achieves historical tangibility through the actions of the Church as such. The Church becomes an actual event of grace when it appears most concretely as a sacrament—that is, in the actions of the Church as such whereby men are bound together in grace by a visible expression.[286]

283. Irwin, "Liturgical Actio: Sacramentology, Eschatology and Ecology," 173.
284. *SC*, 33 [*827].
285. "The same idea reappears in the chapter on eschatology in the *Constitution on the Church*, where we are reminded that the deepest vocation of the Church is fulfilled when her children come together as one family and partake, by way of anticipation, in the liturgy of heavenly glory (LG 51). The implication of these passages is that the Church is neither a mere token nor a mere means; it already possesses in itself, in seminal form, the reality that it signifies and seeks to bring it to maturity." A. Dulles, "Vatican II and the Church's Purpose," *Theology Digest* 32, no. 4 (Winter 1985): 341–52, 346.
286. A. Dulles, *Models of the Church* 2nd ed. (London: Doubleday, 1987), 64.

Even in this brief exposition of the three Dogmatic Constitutions, a consonance in the underlying major themes can be discerned, and, though each document has its particular emphasis, the Council's rediscovery of the meaning and significance of revelation is fundamental to each of them. In the words of Dulles, "These variations notwithstanding, one may distil from the Council documents as a whole a rather unified body of doctrine which addresses our question."[287]

The question is one of a liturgy that arises from the unification of the realities of revelation and salvation and that can be recognised as their theological source.

The Postconciliar Period

In his article "A New Image of Fundamental Theology," René Latourelle provides a concise and interesting summary of the nature of the discipline and of the church's understanding of revelation at the end of the Second Vatican Council. For him, this point marks the completion of the "phase of expansion"[288] that the nascent subject, freed from its manualistic and apologetic past, had experienced. Fundamental theology at the close of the Council was a vibrant but somewhat unwieldy subject that lacked consolidation and internal organization, and had not yet achieved universal recognition.[289] Having traced the development of many of the themes that made up the new interests of this topic, it is possible to see how they came to a confluence in the years just after the Council, and how this became

287. A. Dulles, "Vatican II and the Church's Purpose," 350.
288. R. Latourelle, "A New Image of Fundamental Theology," in *Problems and Perspectives of Fundamental Theology*, ed. R. Latourelle and G. O'Collins (New York: Paulist, 1982), 37–58, 42.
289. R. Latourelle, "Absence and Presence of Fundamental Theology at Vatican II," in *Vatican II Assessment and Perspectives*, ed. R. Latourelle, vol. 3 (New York: Paulist, 1989), 378–415.

a critical time for the discipline. The meeting of these themes at and around the Council accounts for the relatively sudden emergence of fundamental theology as a distinct discipline. However, this coming to birth in the climate of theological buoyancy that Vatican II had engendered meant that, in the years that immediately followed, the subject was additionally vulnerable.[290] The great convergence of theological themes that has been seen as a feature of the Council bordered dangerously on a "sacred pantology,"[291] in which the specificity of the individual theological discipline was no longer respected. Another and simultaneous tendency that affected the security of the subject was the compartmentalization of the study of revelation into other disciplines such as Christology, biblical exegesis, and hermeneutics. Both these movements contributed to the theologians' need to search for the focal point of revelation studies, which explains why Latourelle aptly names the postconciliar period the "Phase of Focusing."

Such a period of sustained centering, however, was not a task peculiar to fundamental theology. Developments in understanding the foundations of revelation and faith had their consequences for dogmatics too. As Raymond Vaillancourt says of the sacramental theology of this period,

> We have been seeing how the realities—Christ, the Church, and man—which form the basis of the sacramental system are the ones that have profited most from the conciliar renewal. So true is this that the coherence with the rest of Christian thought which sacramental theology had earlier acquired has now been extensively undermined, and this at the level both of vocabulary and of approach and content.

290. That is additional to the vulnerability that Latourelle points out when he discribes the "insecurity" that is the very nature of the subject. Cf. R. Latourelle, "A New Image for Fundamental Theology," in R. Latourelle and G. O'Collins, eds., *Problems and Perspectives of Fundamental Theology*, 37.

291. R. Latourelle, "A New Image for Fundamental Theology," in Latourelle and O'Collins, *Problems and Perspectives of Fundamental Theology*, 51.

The present task of the theologians is to give sacramental theology a new coherence in relation to and as part of the Christian mystery.[292]

The postconciliar period is one in which the fruits of the previous theological expansion have to be appropriated. New discoveries have to be systematized and made intelligible, and, when a degree of focus has been achieved, the way in which these new insights affect the relationship between one theological discipline and another can be discussed. It is to such a discussion that this book is oriented.

In subsequent chapters, and by way of an examination of the work of four theologians, the effects of a transformed understanding of revelation on the liturgical celebration of the sacraments will be discussed. To this end, it was thought appropriate to examine authors who, while all postconciliar, vary both chronologically and in theological discipline. In his article "Liturgy and Fundamental Theology: Frameworks for a Dialogue," Jeremy Driscoll describes his particular enterprise when he says,

> In many ways much of the work which can make a dialogue between the two disciplines fruitful has already been done. In part what I want to do here is draw the attention of liturgists to Fundamental Theology and of fundamental theologians to Liturgical Theology. I would like to develop suggestions for both disciplines from work that has already been done. The importance of the dialogue presents a challenge in two directions.[293]

By examining the work of René Latourelle, Avery Dulles, Salvatore Marsili, and Gustave Martelet, it is hoped that this study will respond to the two-way challenge that Driscoll mentions.

---

292. Vaillancourt, *Toward a Renewal of Sacramental Theology*, 67.
293. J. Driscoll, *Theology at the Eucharistic Table* (Leominster, UK: Gracewing, 2003), 100.

PART II

The Exposition and Analysis of Selected Authors

2

René Latourelle

Establishing the Christological Foundations of Revelation

René Latourelle is a theologian typical of the focus phase[1] in the history of fundamental theology. Born in Montreal in 1918, he entered the Society of Jesus in 1938 and, after completing doctoral studies in both history and theology, he began in 1959 to teach theology at the Gregorian University, where he subsequently became dean of the faculty of theology.[2] Latourelle's career as a student, theologian, and teacher spans the era of the development of fundamental theology through phases that he later calls "Reaction," "Expansion," and "Focusing." Educated within the era of classical apologetics, he was involved with the development of his subject

---

1. See R. Latourelle, "Fundamental Theology I: History," in *Dictionary of Fundamental Theology*, ed. R. Latourelle and R. Fisichella (New York: Crossroads, 1995), 327–328. Here Latourelle distinguishes fundamental theologians whose work was marked by a search for the discipline's "identity" its "centre of unity" and "basic structure."
2. For a brief biographical survey see the chapter "Jalons biographiques," in R. Latourelle, *L'Infini du sens: Jésus-Christ* (Québec: Bellarmin, 2000), 15–66.

according to the methods and content that the Second Vatican Council promulgated.[3] Indeed, as dean, he was responsible for the completion of the restructuring of courses and for the introduction of new themes into this system in subsequent years.[4]

Laying the Foundations:
Théologie de la Révélation

Latourelle's major early work was *Théologie de la Révélation*. First published in 1963, it quickly became the most widely used work on revelation in Catholic teaching circles, and, through many augmentations, translations, and editions, has remained such up to the present day. The work gives a concise and comprehensive history of revelation studies from their biblical basis right up to a commentary on *Dei Verbum* that was added in a later edition of 1966. With this study, Latourelle achieved a certain amount of the systematization and focus that postconciliar fundamental theology was seeking. Even a brief analysis of his treatment of the major themes provides a valuable insight into the understanding of revelation that was prevalent immediately after the Council.

Various later works provide an excellent insight into the development of fundamental theology in the postconciliar period. They are useful in establishing essential shifts in the understanding of revelation theology, and the effects that these changes subsequently

3. "Mon intérêt pour la théologie fondamentale a commencé avec mon allergie à l'apologétique traditionnelle absorbée durant mes années de collège et mes études théologiques. Mon premier intérêt est allé au thème de la Révélation, particulièrement maltraité. Je ne blâme pas mes professeurs: ils ne faisaient que transmettre l'enseignement des manuels de l'époque. On nous disait alors avec beaucoup de sérieux que *révéler* signifiait enlever le voile sur des vérités cachés aux hommes et proposés à notre foi." Ibid., 179.
4. For Latourelle's account of this period, see ibid., 155–77; and for an accurate and independent appraisal of the details, see M. Chappin, "Dalla Difesa al Dialogo: L'insegnamento della teologia fondamentale alla PUG, 1930–1988," in *Gesù Rivelatore: Teologia Fondamentale*, ed. R. Fisichella (Casale Monferrato: Edizione Piemme, 1988), 33–45.

had on dogmatics as a whole. Basic to the contribution of René Latourelle is the provision of a theological system and vocabulary that provided the possibility of interdisciplinary coordination, while at the same time marking out the unique role of fundamentals in the restructuring of theology.

In 1959, René Latourelle succeeded Sebastian Tromp in teaching the course *De Revelatione in genere* at the Gregorian University. Tromp stopped teaching altogether in 1961 because of his commitments at the Vatican, where he was busy preparing for the Council. His involvement in the prehistory of the *Constitution on Divine Revelation*, particularly in the production of the *Schema Constitutionis dogmaticae de fontibus Revelationis*, is well-known,[5] but of interest here is the convenience with which Latourelle was able to follow the proceedings of the Council through his Jesuit colleagues Édoardo Dhanis and Tromp, and also the possibilities of a positive contribution on his part. Gerald O'Collins singles out Latourelle as one who, though not an official *peritus*, was able to study deliberations of the Council "closely and intelligently,"[6] and yet, even if only implicitly, as a Gregorian faculty member his influence would seem to be more far-reaching than this. During the second year of his teaching (1960–1961), and at a time when his work on *Théologie de la Révélation* was intensifying, Latourelle assiduously revised his lecture course and *dispensae*, adding a general introduction to the concept of revelation and, more significantly, extensive sections on the notion and reality of signs.[7] That *Théologie de la Révélation* would be consonant with much of the future teaching of *Dei Verbum* should

5. J. Ratzinger, "Dogmatic Constitution on Divine Revelation: Origin and Background," in *Commentary on the Documents of Vatican II*, ed. H. Vorgrimler, vol. 3 (London: Burns and Oates, 1969), 155–66.

6. G. O'Collins, *Retrieving Fundamental Theology* (New York: Paulist, 1993), 179.

7. Cf. R. Latourelle, *De Revelatione* (Rome: PUG, 1959). Also, Chappin discusses the significance of these developmental changes in "Dalla Difesa al Dialogo," 33–45.

come as no surprise, for it was written in the crucible of the Council, in a place where talk of Tromp, Alfredo Ottaviani, Pieter Smulders,[8] and Alfredo Sherer abounded, where drafts and documents were accessible, and the protagonists of the many sessions could be consulted. A relationship of reciprocal and mutual affinity would seem to have existed between the Council and the classroom.[9]

It may also be said that Latourelle's *Théologie de la Révélation* is indicative of that period in the history of fundamental theology that he was subsequently to call the "phase of expansion."[10] This was a crucial time, and one in which the construction of a sound and credible notion of revelation was an urgent task.[11] The majority of preceding studies had been preoccupied with establishing the existence of divine revelation, an enterprise in which supernatural signs played no insignificant part. In structuring a new image, Latourelle shifts the theological emphasis of the discipline away from extrinsic apologetic proofs, and seeks to offer a dogmatic that begins to penetrate both the content and means of divine self-manifestation. It is this restructuring and the relocation of revelation to the center

8. For an interesting analysis of Smulders's involvement in the Council's understanding of self-revelation or manifestation, see O'Collins, *Retrieving Fundamental Theology*, 52–62.

9. "Mon ouvrage *Théologie de la Révélation* est paru en 1963 mais, dès 1959, soit quatre ans avant le Concile, je publiais en latin, à Rome, pour mes étudiants, un *De revelatione* de 350 pages: ces notes représentaient la substance de mon ouvrage, dans sa partie biblique, ce qui correspondait au chapitre premier de *Dei Verbum*. Le père S. Tromp, rédacteur du premier schema sur la Révélation et mon voisin de chambre, connaissait bien mes notes latines et mon ouvrage sur la Révélation. Le père de Lubac, dans son commentaire sur le premier chapitre de *Dei Verbum*, souligne les affinités qu'il perçoit, non seulement au niveau du contenu mais aussi de la formulation, entre le texte conciliaire et *Théologie de la Révélation*. Je parle d'affinités, et non de paternité, car il serait futile, voire prétentieux, d'utiliser ce mot. Les instances, en effet, qui entrent en jeu dans un processus rédactionnel qui s'étend du premier schéma jusqu'au texte définitif, sont si nombreuses et si complexes, qu'il est impossible, sauf en certain cas rarissimes, de parler de paternité solidement attestée. Il s'agit plutôt d'une pluralité de voix et de témoignages appartenant au patrimoine conciliaire. C'est pourquoi je parle d'*affinités*, sans plus." Latourelle, *L'Infini du sens*, 35–36.

10. R. Latourelle, "A New Image of Fundamental Theology," in *Problems and Perspectives of Fundamental Theology*, ed. R. Latourelle and G. O'Collins (New York: Paulist, 1982), 42.

11. A. Dulles, "The Theology of Revelation," *Theological Studies* 25 (1964): 44.

of the theological enterprise that Latourelle sees as determining the unique status of fundamental theology.[12] As Rino Fisichella recognizes, such a centrality emerges from the articulation of the subject's constitutive elements expressing, as they do, the threefold, hermeneutic, semiological, and anthropological aspects of revelation.[13] A theology that examines the nature of the sources of revelation, the credibility of the signs that accompany this revelation, and the effect of this revealing on humanity is, without doubt, a fundamental pursuit.

The theological oeuvre of Latourelle is shaped in direct response to this threefold structure. After providing a history and analysis of the theological treatment of revelation in *Théologie de la Révélation*, in subsequent years he concentrated on the particular constitutive aspects of this topic. In 1978, he published *L'Accès à Jésus par les Évangiles*,[14] in which he dwelt on the methodological significance of hermeneutics to the discipline. Seven years previously, he had published *Le Christ et l'Église: Signes du salut*,[15] a semiological analysis of revelation, and, in 1981, *L'Homme et ses problèmes dans la lumière du Christ*[16] which focused on anthropological aspects. Fisichella is correct

---

12. Cf. his most recent description of this in R. Latourelle, *L'Infini du sens*, 197–204.

13. "Per comprendere a pieno il pensiero e la produzione teologica del p. Latourelle è necessario vedere l'articolazione su cui egli ha strutturato la nuova immagine della teologia Fondamentale e questa, è bene osservarlo subito, non è vista come realtà a se stante, ma pienamente inserita in un organico piano di studi teologici. All'apriori costitutivo della centralità e basilarità della Rivelazione per ogni studio teologico.subentra una triplice suddivisione della Fondamentale che viene espressa come momento *ermeneutico, antropologico e semiologico*." R. Fisichella, "Il Contributo di René Latourelle alla Teologia Fondamentale," in Fisichella, *Gesù Rivelatore*, 12.

14. R. Latourelle, *L'accès à Jésus par les Évangiles. Histoire et herméneutique* (Tournai: Desclée et Cie; and Montréal: Éditions Bellarmin, 1978); English trans., A. Owen, *Finding Jesus through the Gospels: History and Hermeneutics* (New York: Alba House, 1983).

15. R. Latourelle, *Le Christ et l'Église: Signes du salut* (Tournai: Desclée et Cie; and Montréal: Éditions Bellarmin, 1971); English trans., Dominic Parker, *Christ and the Church: Signs of Salvation* (New York: Alba House, 1972).

16. R. Latourelle, *L'homme et ses problèmes dans la lumière du Christ* (Tournai: Desclée et Cie; and Montréal: Éditions Bellarmin, 1981); English trans., M. O'Connell, *Man and His Problems in the Light of Jesus Christ* (New York: Alba House, 1983).

when he states of Latourelle, "Every year from Vatican II onward, without exception he has put forward one of the constitutive aspects of the subject [fundamental theology] and come out in favor of its exact position in the theological curriculum as the center, heart, and essential category of theology."[17]

This chapter aims to provide a fair and representative exposition of the revelation theology of Latourelle. Three major works from differing stages of his career will be examined so as both to provide a general background to his overall aim, and at the same time highlight material more specific to the semiological interests of this study. To this end, *Théologie de la Révélation*[18] (1963) will be used to explore Latourelle's core convictions concerning revelation, and to show the orientation that fundamental theology was receiving at the time of the Council. Having reflected upon this text, it will be used to situate the later works, *Le Christ et l'Église: Signes du salut* (1971), and *Miracles de Jésus et théologie du miracle*[19] (1987). These studies will be used to focus more clearly upon Latourelle's specific interest in the anthropological and semiological aspects of revelation.

Théologie de la Révélation systematically analyzes divine revelation according to the threefold structure Latourelle recognised as fundamental to the discipline. Taking a historical approach, the author examines how this structure has been variously articulated

17. "A partire dal Vaticano II ogni anno, in modo ininterrotto, ha proposto un aspetto costituivo di questa materia favorendo il suo esatto collocamento nell'organigramma teologico come 'centro,' 'cuore,' 'categoria essenziale' della teologia." R. Fisichella, "Il Contributo di René Latourelle alla Teologia Fondamentale," in Fisichella, *Gesù Rivelatore*, 12.

18. Quotations that appear from the original French will be taken from R. Latourelle, *Théologie de la Révélation: Deuxième édition revue et augmentée* (Bruges: Desclée Brouwer, 1966). The page numbers of the English translation by Sr. Dominic Parker, *Theology of Revelation: Including a Commentary on the Constitution "Dei Verbum" of Vatican II* (New York: Alba House, 1966), will appear in square brackets.

19. R. Latourelle, *Miracles de Jésus et théologie du miracle* (Paris: Éditions du Cerf, 1986); English trans., M. O'Connell, *The Miracles of Jesus and the Theology of Miracles* (New York: Paulist, 1988).

down the ages, beginning with scriptural formulations and progressing through the work of the Fathers and magisterial teaching to the present day. To quote Fisichella:

> The history of the reflection of the Fathers, the great masters of the Middle Ages, further theological research, are all brought in by Latourelle to explain the mystery of revelation. If, therefore, on the one hand this is presented to us as the source of faith, it also constitutes the central, necessary nucleus of critical reflection that the believer makes on faith.[20]

Hence it is out of a thoroughgoing and comprehensive theology that Latourelle draws an "apologetic" in its threefold aspects of hermeneutics, semiotics, and anthropology. In the final and longest part of the book, this pattern is used to facilitate the author's own reflections.[21] Latourelle reexamines the sources of revelation according to the hermeneutic of word, testimony, and encounter, proceeding to examine creation and history as sources of this revelation. He then offers a semiological analysis of revelation, discussing successively the incarnation, miracles, and the church, and finally the book concludes with anthropological reflections on revelation as the source of grace and the means to glory. In *Théologie de la Révélation*, Latourelle traces the emergence of those fundamental principles that will facilitate a rejuvenated theology of revelation appropriate to the modern era.

---

20. "La storia della riflessione dei Padri, i grandi Maestri del Medio Evo, le successive ricerche teologiche, vengono assunte del Latourelle per esplicitare il mistero della Rivelazione. Se da una parte quindi essa ci viene presentata come il sorgere della fede, dall'altra essa costituisce pure il nucleo centrale e obbligatorio della riflessione critica che il credente compie sulla fede stessa." Fisichella, "Il Contributo di René Latourelle," 14 (my translation).

21. "Le but de cette cinquième partie est précisément d'instituer une réflexion qui jaillisse de la contemplation même de l'objet de foi, recueilli et systématisé; une réflexion fidèle au donné révélé, tenant compte de l'apport théologique des siècles passés, dans ses éléments les meilleurs, tenant compte également des souhaits et des orientations de la recherche actuelle, le Magistère de l'Église fournissant une norme qui permette d'engager la recherche dans la bonne direction." Latourelle, *Théologie de la Révélation*, 385 [313].

Word as the Basic Category of Revelation

Like St. Thomas, Latourelle recognises word as the concept most basic to revelation, speaking being the unveiling of thought through a system of signs. However, he eschews quickly the "rather static conception"[22] of word that the scholastics held, enriching it with the insights that both philosophy and psychology have brought to language, making of it a category more suitably analogous to the self-revelation of God:[23]

> In revelation, it is God Himself who addresses man: not the God of philosophic abstraction, but the living God, all-powerful, thrice-holy. He wants to be a Me addressing You, in an interpersonal and living relationship, with a view towards communication, dialogue, sharing. This word springs up from the transcendent world of divine life, *calls* to man and invites him to the obedience of faith, with a view toward communion of life. It is teeming with the unheard-of news of salvation offered to humanity: man is saved, the Kingdom of heaven is among us, the plan of love pursued by God from all eternity is accomplished. For the word of God does more than speak and inform: it effects what it signifies, it changes the situation of humanity, it gives life. The word of God is an active, efficacious, creative word.[24]

22. "Conception plutôt statique." Ibid.
23. In this, Latourelle is fulfilling the mission of fundamental theology that he is to set out more clearly later: "As a boundary discipline that keeps an eye on the human sciences (history, philosophy, linguistics, psychology, sociology, ethnology), [fundamental theology] shares the eventful life of these sciences. If it is to give an account of Christianity in response to the demands of the human spirit it must respond to the sciences which that spirit is constantly developing or renewing." Latourelle and O'Collins, *Problems and Perspectives of Fundamental Theology*, 37.
24. "Dans la révélation, celui qui s'adresse à l'homme, c'est Dieu lui-même: non pas le Dieu de l'abstraction philosophique, mais le Dieu vivant, le Tout-puissant, le trois fois Saint. Il veut être, pour l'homme, un Moi qui s'adresse à un Toi, dans un rapport interpersonnel et vital, dans un dessein de communication, de dialogue, de partage. Cette parole qui surgit du monde transcendant de la vie divine, *interpelle* l'homme et l'invite à l'obéissance de la foi, en vue d'une communion de vie. Elle est lourde de la nouvelle inouïe du salut offert à l'humanité: l'homme est sauvé, le Royaume des cieux est parmi nous, le dessein d'amour poursuivi par Dieu de toute éternité s'accomplit. Car la parole de Dieu ne fait pas que dire et informer: elle opère ce qu'elle signifie, elle change la situation de l'humanité, elle donne la Vie. La parole de Dieu est une parole active, efficace, créatrice." Latourelle, *Théologie de la Révélation*, 391 [318].

Speaking is first and foremost a personal activity by which a person "addresses" and "expresses" himself or herself to another. It is a concept that does not permit of philosophical abstraction, because language is always revealing a particular person, manifesting a unique nature and attitudes. Language is an act of self-revelation. Revelation as the communication of a deposit of immutable teachings that are somehow extrinsic[25] to the speaker is a notion confounded by an understanding of word as self-communication.[26] In interpreting the language of speech in such a way, Latourelle directs the understanding of revelation away from the static concepts of nineteenth-century theology and toward the personalist categories later embraced by Vatican II.[27] Revelation is the self-manifestation of the divine, it is the expression of a "thrice-holy" God who communicates within himself and, in speaking *ad extra*, draws others into this communion. As a manifestation of his will, the *locutio Dei* reveals God as a being of wisdom, who generously shares his goodness and life by addressing those to whom he intends to extend communion as friends. It is in this sense that "every word is a call, a demand for reaction. By its dynamic character, it tends to establish a

---

25. Here Latourelle orientes revelation away from the progressive conceptualization of truth and the propositional approach that had dominated the theology of the nineteenth century, laboring as it did under philosophical rationalism. As Ignace de la Potterie says of this period, "The connection of Christian truth with Jesus Christ and the history of salvation is hardly perceived any longer; reference is made rather to the 'divine,' in a quite vague sense: 'truth divinely revealed.' The name 'extrinsicism' aptly describes this tendency, since both the relation of history to truth and the relation of the saving events to the Christian faith are extrinsic ones. This is one of the two types of thinking which M. Blondel criticized so severely back in the time of Modernism." See I. De La Potterie, "History and Truth," in Latourelle and O'Collins, *Problems and Perspectives of Fundamental Theology*, 90.

26. "C'est dans la mésure où nous nous exprimons dans notre parole, où nous nous *mettons en elle*, et c'est dans la mésure où nous communiquons vraiment avec autrui, où nous le *visons en lui-même* comme personne, que la parole trouve sa plénitude de sens." R. Latourelle, *Théologie de la Révélation*, 390. Cf. also G. Martelet, "Christology and Anthropology," in Latourelle and O'Collins, *Problems and Perspectives of Fundamental Theology*, 154.

27. Latourelle, *Miracles de Jésus et théologie du miracle*, 14 [2]. Also G. O'Collins, *Retrieving Fundamental Theology*, 46.

circle of address and response, to become conversation, dialogue."[28] So the word of God does more than speak and inform; rather it effects what it signifies. It signifies the life of God and, by its nature as language and dialogue, draws the human person into that life.

For the theological enhancement of the notion of the *locutio Dei*, Latourelle was in part dependent on the work of Louis-Marie Dewailly, who in 1945 had produced his work *Jésus Christ, Parole de Dieu*. Here, by means of a theology of incarnation, Dewailly explores the human word as the vehicle of divine revelation.[29] However, Latourelle's relationship with Édouardo Dhanis, the director of his doctoral thesis and composer of the draft submission *Constitutio De Revelatione et Fidei*, was probably more directly inspirational.[30] Latourelle develops his understanding of the revelatory word both in the light of, and in contradistinction to, the position of Dhanis. They shared the belief that the analogy of human speech allows a better appreciation of the means of revelation, and more especially of the eternal consequences that result from this self-communication of God for human beings. Yet there were differences between them with regard to the understanding of how the "content" of revelation related to the person of Christ. For Latourelle, precisely because of the nature of revelation as word, there could be no distinction between the revealer and that which is revealed. In the thought of Dhanis, a sense of the communication of religious truths, made comprehensible, accessible, and therefore definitive in their

28. "Toute parole est un appel, une demande de réaction. De par sa dynamique, elle tend à établir un circuit d'interpellation et de réponse, pour devenir un colloque, un dialogue." Latourelle, *Théologie de la Révélation*, 389 [316].

29. See L.-M. Dewailly, *Jésus Christ, Parole de Dieu* (Paris: Desclée, 1945); and, for a fuller commentary of his influence on Latourelle's *Théologie de la Révélation*, see A. Sierra, *La Revelación Según René Latourelle*, Serie Teologica, 60 (Rome: Tesi Gregoriana, 2000), 39–46.

30. For a detailed analysis of the submission *De Revelatione et Fide*, and therefore of the major elements of the revelation theology of E. Dhanis, see B. Cahill, *The Renewal of Revelation Theology (1960–1962)*, Serie Teologica, 51 (Rome: Tesi Gregoriana, 1999), 28–48; 223–30.

expression through the incarnate Word, predominated.[31] Seemingly, such emphasis on the inextricable connection between truths and the mysteries of salvation revealed in Christ, which can be seen in the submission schema of Dhanis, stemmed from an effort to counter those who, like Tyrrell, maintained that the truths of revelation were a later conceptual expression of an earlier experience.[32]

The Testimony of Witness

Latourelle identifies word as the sacramental mode in which God's saving and revealing self-communication appears. In doing so he is a harbinger of *Dei Verbum*, the document that from its prologue to its conclusion sees the word of God as revealing the dynamic coincidence of the nature and will of God. Understood as a strictly verbal communication, revelation would lack the capacity necessary to make manifest the full density of God's self-expression. Therefore Latourelle is right to expand the category of word so as to incorporate every dimension of interpersonal relations. Because the message of God to humanity is not "purely utilitarian"[33] but a communication of friendship and love, God necessarily chooses to speak in "action,

31. "J'ai eu comme directeur de thèse, à la Grégorienne, le père Édouard Dhanis. J'ai connu, dans cette période de recherche, des moments de joie, mais aussi des moments pénibles. J'insistais, dans ma thèse, sur la centralité du Christ, révélateur par toute sa personne, par toute la présence et la manifestation de lui-même, parce que Verbe fait chair, et donc Plénitude de la Révélation. Or, sur ce point, il y avait conflit entre Dhanis et de Lubac, à cause d'un article de celui-ci sur le développement du dogme, paru en 1948. Pour de Lubac, le Christ était à la fois automanifestation et autodonation de Dieu. 'En Jésus Christ, tout nous a été à la fois donné et révélé.' À partir de cette affirmation, de Lubac proposait sa théorie du développement du dogme: une perception d'abord globale du Christ trouve à se détailler peu à peu en vérités particulières, mais toujours en référence au mystère total du Christ, atteint selon un mode de connaissance supérieur. Tout en reconnaissant des ambiguïtés dans la théorie du père de Lubac, je me sentais en plein accord avec lui sur la notion de Révélation. De fait, Dhanis concevait la Révélation beaucoup plus comme une communication de vérités religieuses que comme une manifestation et une donation de personne." Latourelle, *L'Infini du sens*, 25–26.

32. See Cahill, *The Renewal of Revelation Theology*, 37–40.

33. "Une intention purement utilitaire," Latourelle, *Théologie de la Révélation*, 391 [318].

gesture, conduct and primarily word,"[34] that is, exploiting every resource of human "language."[35] As Latourelle points out, "Sometimes, a series of words and actions culminates in a gesture which, in some way, plastically sums up the fundamental intention of the person speaking: for example, in martyrdom, where the sacrifice of one's life is a seal upon what he professes in his words."[36] Thus Latourelle establishes the relationship between word and testimony that is fundamental to his understanding of revelation:

> Divine testimony is unique in species, as distinct from human testimony, on the objective plane as well as on the subjective plane. It has one particular characteristic about it first of all; not only does it affirm the truth of what it proposes for belief, but at the same time it affirms the absolute infallibility of its own testimony. When God testifies to a thing, He testifies at the same time to His own infallibility, for He is subsistent Testimony, pure Testimony, whose activity as witness is identified with pure Being. God who attests is in Himself the absolute and ultimate foundation of the infallible truth of His testimony. He is in Himself His own guarantee. In Christian revelation, the signs which accompany it are intended to assure the identification of the witness, to make known in the human voice and in the human words of Christ the testimony

---

34. "L'action, le geste, le comportement, et surtout la parole"; ibid., 392 [319].

35. In a roughly contemporary book, H. U. von Balthasar expresses this same point with some eloquence: "The free spiritual speech of man emerges from the deep-lying interconnection of all parts of nature, revealed for the first time by modern biology and palaeontology, which makes man the summit of the whole material and organic creation and its mouthpiece before God. Man as spirit dwells in being in its totality and likewise through his body he dwells in the whole of nature and can never detach himself from it. He speaks a corporeal, organic language, one of natural sounds and gestures. Hence there comes about the marvellous and multifarious interplay of nature and spirit in our speech, the gradual transition from natural images to half-emancipated symbols and then to freely chosen signs. These stages of transition from the speech of the whole body to that of the tongue and distinct syllables, from physiognomy to abstract logic and grammar, all this wealth of resources gives us some idea of what sort of being man is, a being of inexhaustible potentialities." Balthasar, *Word and Revelation: Essays in Theology 1* (New York: Herder and Herder, 1964), 104–5; first published as *Verbum Caro, Skizzen zur Theologie 1.*

36. "Parfois, une série de paroles et d'actions culminent dans un geste qui synthétise en quelque sorte plastiquement l'intention fondamentale de la personne: par exemple, dans le martyre où le sacrifice de la vie vient sceller la profession de la parole." Latourelle, *Théologie de la Révélation*, 390 [318].

of the living God and in the deposition of the apostles, the authentic message of God.[37]

As in the case of word, Latourelle recognises the essentially sacramental nature of Christian witness. Testimony is the process by which "word must become the substitute for the experience itself."[38] It is not merely the recounting of a deposition by witnesses, but the expression of a message that gains its authority from experience, and that is authenticated by the life of the individual. Testimony describes a unity between word and life from which an individual can inspire faith in another. It is not reducible to a function of reason,[39] but, like word, testimony appeals beyond the bluntly factual to the intersubjective relationship that exists between persons who are mystery.[40] Essentially, testimony is the only way of access to the personal mystery of another, because it is a self-revelation that comes only "under the inspiration of love."[41]

---

37. "Le témoignage divin est d'une espèce unique, qui le distingue du témoignage humain, sur le plan objectif comme sur le plan subjectif. Il a ceci de particulier, tout d'abord, que non seulement il affirme la vérité de ce qu'il propose à croire, mais du même coup il affirme l'infaillibilité absolue de son témoignage. Quand Dieu atteste une chose, il atteste en même temps sa propre infaillibilité, car il est le Témoignage subsistant, le Témoignage pur, dont l'action d'attester s'identifie avec l'Être pur. Dieu qui atteste est en lui-même le fondement absolu et ultime de la vérité infaillible de son témoignage. Il est à lui-même sa propre garantie. Dans la révélation chrétienne, les signes ont pour but d'assurer l'identification du Témoin, de faire reconnaître dans la voix et la parole humaines du Christ le témoignage du Dieu vivant et, dans la déposition des apôtres, l'authentique message de Dieu." Ibid., 397–98 [323–24].

38. "Sa parole doit devenir, pour celui qui n'a pas vu, substitut de l'expérience même." Ibid., 395 [322].

39. "La foi au témoignage réclame donc une certaine démission de la raison; démission légitime, toutefois, car elle a pour motif la santé mentale (science, perspicacité, esprit critique) et surtout morale du témoin." Ibid., 395 [322].

40. Ibid., 397 [323]. Later Latourelle will give this useful and succinct definition: "When witnesses fully commit themselves through word or action, they express themselves to the full extent of their existential freedom. At this point, testimony acquires an exceptional depth and dignity, since it has for its object the innermost mystery of personal being." Latourelle, "Testimony," in Latourelle and Fisichella, *Dictionary of Fundamental Theology*, 1046.

41. "Et les personnes ne témoignent d'elles-mêmes que sous l'inspiration de l'amour." Latourelle, *Théologie de la Révélation*, 396 [322].

The revelation of God has its source in the life of the immanent Trinity, where, in constant and dynamic communication, the three persons reveal themselves to each other in love.[42] This is the basis for Latourelle's description of God as subsistent Testimony. Through an act of witness, the persons of the Trinity identify their being. Fundamentally, Christianity is a religion of testimony, because it is through witness that the truth of the divine persons is communicated and made manifest.[43] Jesus Christ true man and true God is the perfect witness. He speaks of his experience of the Father and testifies to his knowledge by his life, death, and resurrection. The apostles' experience of this testimony in turn makes them founding witnesses, inviting all people to the truth they have experienced.

In focusing on the intimate relationship between the revelatory categories of word and testimony, Latourelle works for the rediscovery of the centrality of the person of Jesus Christ in fundamental theology. In the years prior to the Council, the manuals sought to establish the credibility of revelation by proving the truth of its accompanying signs. The centrality of Jesus Christ, revealer and revelation, was lost. In renewing the prevailing methodology, Latourelle makes a significant contribution to the shift away from an ecclesiocentric apologetic, where the notion of testimony had first emerged,[44] and that had dominated theology since the Council

---

42. "L'Écriture, en effet, nous décrit l'activité révélatrice de la Trinité sous forme de témoignages mutuels. Le Fils nous apparaît comme le Témoin du Père, et c'est ainsi qu'il se fait connaître aux apôtres. Mais le Père, à son tour, témoigne que le Christ est le Fils, par l'attraction qu'il produit dans les âmes, par les œuvres qu'il donne au Fils d'accomplir et surtout par la résurrection, qui est le témoignage décisif du Père en faveur du Fils. Le Fils témoigne de l'Esprit, car il promet de l'envoyer comme éducateur, consolateur, sanctificateur. Et l'Esprit vient, qui témoigne du Fils, car il le rappelle, le fait connaître, découvre la plénitude de ses paroles, l'insinue dans les âmes. Ainsi, dans le commerce des trois personnes divines avec les hommes, nous voyons un échange de témoignages qui a pour but de proposer la révélation et de nourrir la foi." Ibid., 394 [320].

43. Ibid.

44. "Over the course of about a century now, the category of testimony has gradually entered the vocabulary of the Church. The term made a modest appearance at Vatican I, where it described the Church in so far as the latter is, by its existence and whole presence in the world, 'a great

of Trent. The manuals, concentrating on the *demonstratio religiosa, Christiana et catholica*, attempted to prove the veracity of their assertions on the strength of incontestable supernatural signs that were further authenticated by copious scriptural quotations.[45] Much store was put by the truth of magisterial teaching, and this developed "an unpardonable dualism between the 'fact' of Revelation and its content."[46]

A brief comparison of the manuals, Latourelle's early teaching *dispensae*,[47] and *Théologie de la Révélation* shows a clear progression from a notion of testimony as a motive of credibility that is substantially independent of its object, to an understanding of testimony as a phenomenon inextricably linked to, and revealing of, Jesus Christ. Essentially, this movement is a passage from ecclesiocentrism to Christocentrism. Because of the ecclesiastical authoritarianism that marked post-Tridentine apologetics, and as a result of a further sanction by Vatican I, the church as a perennial sign of credibility did not find its terminus in Christ, nor did it appear to be ultimately subordinate to him. As Tullio Cirtiri makes clear,

> Paradoxically, the emphasis on the Church as sign could of itself have led in a quite different direction than ecclesiocentrism. It would in fact have done so if the originality of the "new" way proposed to Catholic apologetics had meant proceeding not from the credibility of Christ to

and perpetual motive of credibility and irrefutable *testimony* of her divine mission (DS 3013; ND 123).'" Latourelle, "Testimony," 1044–45.

45. Cf. A. Dulles, *A History of Apologetics* (New York: Hutchinson, 1971), 112–57.

46. R. Fisichella, *Introduction to Fundamental Theology* (Rome: Edizioni Piemme, 1996), 24. Cf. also T. Citrini, who maintains, "The excessive separation between proposition and *res*, a heritage from nominalism that passed not only into theology but, under Descartes' leadership, into the whole modern way of thinking, has permitted the development of an intellectualist and atomistic conception of revelation. This could only have the effect of lessening interest in a unified view of Christianity and therefore in finding a possible centre for the whole." Citrini, "The Principle of 'Christocentrism' and Its Role in Fundamental Theology," in Latourelle and O'Collins, *Problems and Perspectives of Fundamental Theology*, 171.

47. For a useful commentary on Latourelle's novel treatment of word and testimony in *De Revelatione*, see Cahill, *The Renewal of Revelation Theology*, 223–26.

that of the Church but from the credibility of the Church to that of Christ. For then the essentially mediatorial role of the church would have been clear, and there would have been justification for emphasizing the importance of immediate access to the sign which the church is.[48]

Although in large part, Latourelle's *dispensa De Revelatione* of 1959, follows the form and structure of the earlier manuals, already he has made a distinct move forward in methodology. By introducing a sense of the reciprocity that is an essential element of the word-testimony encounter,[49] Latourelle opens up the route by which the signs of revelation can be reattached to their source in the person of Christ. That is to say, he begins to effect a return from ecclesiocentrism to Christocentrism. Hence he concludes his section on the *Revelatio Stricte Dicta Definitur Locutio Dei Attestans* with the observation,

---

48. Citrini, "The Principle of 'Christocentrism,'" 172. Clear examples of this methodology can be given from the manuals. In his section on "The Testimony of Christ," R. Garrigou-Lagrange makes clear his way of proceeding: "Historica auctoritate quatuor Evangeliorum probata, ex eis et praesertim ex Synopticis, quorum historicitas facilius admittitur ab adversariis, determinandum est quodnam fuit testimonium Iesu Christi 1o *de sua divina legatione*, 2o *de credendis mysteriis et praeceptis servandis*, 3o *de institutione Ecclesiae* ad Revelationem infallibiliter servandam usque ad finem mundi. Hoc triplex testimonium pertinet ad tractatum de Revelatione, nam in primo assignatur huiusce Revelationis origo, in secundo eius obiectum, in tertio conditio eius perpetuae conservationis et propositionis." (Using the proof of the historical authenticity of the four Gospel writers, and especially the Synoptic Gospel writers whose historicity is readily accepted by (our) opponents, the original testimony of Jesus Christ must be determined regarding (1) his divine mission, (2) belief in the mysteries and the keeping of his commandments, (3) the instituting of the church for the purpose of sustaining revelation until the end of the world. This threefold testimony relates to our interpretation of revelation: first, how we explain the origin of this revelation; second, its purpose; and third, how we preserve and explain it) R. Garrigou-Lagrange, *De Revelatione*, vol. 2 (Rome: Libreria Editrice Religiosa, 1929), 158 (the translation is mine). Similarly, see also T. Zapelena, *De Ecclesia Christi—Pars Apologetica* (Rome: Typis Pontificiae Universitatis Gregorianae, 1946).

49. "Notandum est quod locutio, ubi fit expressio personae ut personae, non potest esse nisi *testimonium*. Si aliqua persona mysterium sui aperit alteri personae, *testificatur* et *petit fidem*. In ordine intersubiectivitatis personalis, relationes habent formam testimonii." (It should be noted that speech, when it involves one person talking to another, must be reckoned as *testimony*. If one person communicates the mystery of himself to another person, *he bears witness and looks for belief in that testimony*. In the area of personal intersubjectivity, relationships have the form of testimony.) R. Latourelle, *De Revelatione* (Rome: PUG, 1959), 152 (my translation).

Ut verificetur notio revelationis sensu stricto, *tria* requiruntur: (a) expressio distincta cogitati divini; (b) invitatio distincta ad credendum illud cogitatum; (c) cogitatum Dei et invitatio ad credendum debent apprehendi ut a Deo, scilicet debent comitari signis internis vel externis quae confirmant originem divinam cogitati et invitationis ad fidem.[50]

The development of the concept of testimony and the idea of Jesus as the personal testament of the Father that is evidenced by *Théologie de la Révélation*, does much to restore Christ to the position of sole guarantor of revelation.[51] It is a shift that, in a later work, Latourelle regards as fundamental to the Council. As he says,

> Vatican II resolutely adopts a personalist rather than an objectivist perspective. Just as it links revelation to persons, so it links the signs with the persons. Signs are not detached entities accompanying Christ's message after the manner of an ambassadorial seal that guarantees the authenticity of a letter. On the contrary, Christ Himself is the fullness or completion of revelation; He is God revealing Himself.[52]

---

50. "In order to verify the idea of revelation in the strict sense, *three* requirements are necessary. (a) a clear statement of divine thought; (b) a clear invitation to accept that thought; (c) the thought of God and the invitation to accept that thought should be understood as coming from God, in that they ought to be accompanied by internal or external signs that confirm the divine origin of the thought and the invitation to faith." Ibid., 155 (my translation).

51. In this way, as T. Citrini again points out, "The treatise *De Christo legato* continues to be part of Catholic apologetics as found in the manuals of theology. But while playing a decisive part in the argument as a whole, this treatise does not become the keystone and the methodological hinge of fundamental theology in its entirety. And until it does we cannot speak of christocentrism in a proper sense." T. Citrini, "The Principle of 'Christocentrism,'" 170–71.

52. Latourelle, *The Miracles of Jesus and the Theology of Miracles*, 2. Interestingly, an example of this shift is something that Rino Fisichella identifies as taking place in the genesis of *DV* 4: "The first draft, which still has a strong sense of fragmentation and functionality, dwells on the fact that Christ 'attests his divinity not only with words, but confirms it also with the outstanding holiness of his life, with miracles, prophesies and, above all, with his glorious resurrection from the dead.' This same passage is completely reformulated in the definitive version: 'As a result, he himself,—to see whom is to see the Father, completed and perfected Revelation and confirmed it with divine guarantees. He did this by the total fact of his presence and self-manifestation—by words and works, signs and miracles, but above all by [t]his death and glorious resurrection from the dead.' The first draft speaks of '*Revelatio in Christo ultima et completa*,' while in the final version the title given is '*De Christo Revelationis consumatore*.' It is clear that the change in terminology is not only a formal question. It indicates much more, it signals the taking up of categories of personalistic thought which are better equipped to highlight the person of

The principal element of revelation as word and testimony is its interpersonal nature. Word and testimony are the means by which God addresses human beings with his message of salvation, but this communication is complete only when they respond in faith "and this encounter develops into a communion of life."[53] Both word and testimony have this impulse to community, and, though this may appear a mundane assertion, it is one of crucial importance within the thought of Latourelle. This is because fundamentally the inherent relationship between word and testimony is descriptive of the "manner in which relations between the theory of faith and the practice of it are unified."[54] Hence the "unpardonable dualism" between the fact of revelation and its Revealer is overcome because the human words of Christ, which are the testimony of the living God, invite humanity to life in him.[55] It is this dynamic of mutual attestation existing between word and testimony that ultimately leads to the delineation of a specific subject matter and method that can be termed fundamental theology:[56] the formal object of this particular pursuit is the self-manifestation of the Word of God and the simultaneous attestation of its intrinsic credibility. Hence the word-testimony dynamic ultimately reveals the incarnation as its center and focus.[57]

the revealer without reducing it solely to the content of Revelation." Fisichella, *Introduction to Fundamental Theology*, 28–29.

53. "Dieu et l'homme *se rencontrent* et cette rencontre se développe en communion de vie." Latourelle, *Théologie de la Révélation*, 399 [325]. On this point see also Latourelle, "Église et parole," *Sciences ecclésiastiques* 15 (1962): 195–211.

54. Citrini, "The Principle of 'Christocentrism,'" 169. Here the influence of J. Guitton (1901–1999) on Latourelle can be seen clearly. His work *Le problème de Jésus et les fondements du témoignage chrétien* (Paris: Desclée, 1950), 53, contains the line, "On ne témoignage pas d'un fait, qui est physique, mais on témoignage d'un acte, qui est humain." For a fuller discussion of his influence on Latourelle, see, A. Sierra, *La Revelación Según René Latourelle*, Serie Teologia, 60 (Rome: Tesi Gregoriana, 2000), 46–52.

55. "Par suite de leur union au Christ et de l'union du Fils au Père, les croyants sont unis entre eux et unis au Père, comme le Père est uni au Fils. L'Esprit d'amour, qui unit le Père et le Fils, les fait vivre de la vie même des personnes divines." Latourelle, *Théologie de la Révélation*, 402 [327].

56. R. Latourelle, "Fundamental Theology I: History," 328.

The Word Takes Flesh

God's word, in seeking to communicate fully the message of his love, is continually condescending and taking on the mesh of action, gesture, conduct, sign, and expression that is human intercourse. Word by its nature is always becoming flesh, always seeking to optimize the resources that personal communication enjoys. For this reason, God's word can be fully expressed only in the incarnation, a movement preserved in the church:

> The Incarnation offers a solution to the most serious and apparently the only real difficulty posed by revelation, namely, that of the authentic communication of God's plan to the human mind. Actually, Christ is the qualified witness of the divine mysteries, for His revelation derives from the very vision with which the Son sees the Father. What is more, He who sees is at once God and man, connaturalized both to human discourse and divine thought. As the Word of God, He does not speak our human language, He speaks only to the Father; but as Word Incarnate, He speaks to us. And it is the same Person, living in the bosom of the Father, who expresses what He knows in human terms. The union of natures and the unity of person authorizes the transfer from the divine milieu, in all its inaccessibility, to the human milieu, and at the same time assures the fidelity of the transmission. Christ is the perfect seer of God, and He expresses what He sees in human language. The passage is thus effected from divine vision to human expression.[58]

57. "If I combine *self*-manifestation and *intrinsic* credibility, it is in order to emphasise the point that the sign, given in Jesus Christ, is inseparable from the person. By becoming incarnate, God manifests himself as both revealer and revealed, and at the same time bears witness to himself as such. Jesus Christ is simultaneously mediator, fullness of revelation, and sign of revelation." Ibid., 329.

58. "L'Incarnation semble bien résoudre la plus grave, et apparemment la seule vraie difficulté que pose la révélation, à savoir celle d'une communication authentique du dessein de Dieu à l'esprit humain. En effet, le Christ est le Témoin qualifié des mystères divins, car sa révélation, dérive de la vision même dont le Fils voit le Père. De plus, Celui qui voit est à la fois Dieu et homme, connaturalisé au discours humain comme à la pensée divine. Verbe de Dieu, il ne parle pas notre langage, il ne parle qu'au Père; mais Verbe incarné, il nous parle. Et c'est la même Personne, vivant au sein du Père, qui exprime en termes humains ce qu'elle sait. L'union des natures dans l'unité de la personne autorise le passage du milieu divin, inaccessible, au milieu humain, et en même temps assure la fidélité de la transmission. Le Christ est le parfait Voyant-Dieu, et il

What the concepts of word and testimony achieve within the natural order "the Incarnation accomplishes in the supernatural order of revelation."[59] Quoting St. Thomas, Latourelle explains this dynamic economy of revelation: "Just as man, in order to communicate his thought, clothes it in some way with letters and sounds, 'even so, God, wanting to manifest Himself to men, clothes with human flesh, in time, His Word conceived from all eternity'."[60] Christ is the completion of a process of revelation that God began with the patriarchs and prophets. The word and psyche of the prophets were the initial means of God's verbal revelation, the beginning of a continuum that came to fullness and completion in the incarnation.[61]

In discussing the revelation economy of the incarnation, Latourelle concentrates on the aspects of fullness and realism.[62] These two ideas are for him related—revelation at its most real is the fullest manifestation. In the person of Jesus, the message of God is most real, and in taking flesh that revelation has reached a fullness long awaited. So at the end of various times and methods, God in these last days has spoken to us through his Son (Heb. 1:2). That "Christ is God in a human manner, and Man in a divine manner,"[63] means that in his own person, there is a marvelous exchange that makes revelation

---

exprime en langage d'homme ce qu'il voit. Le passage est donc effectué de la vision divine à l'expression humaine." Latourelle, *Théologie de la Révélation*, 442–43 [365].

59. "Ce que le geste et la parole accomplissent dans la présence ordinaire, l'Incarnation l'accomplit dans l'ordre surnaturel de la révélation." Ibid., 437 [361].

60. "De même que l'homme, pour communiquer sa pensée, la revêt en quelque sorte de lettres et de dons, de même Dieu, voulant se manifester aux hommes, revêtit de chair, dans le temps, son Verbe conçu de toute éternité." Ibid., 436 [360].

61. "Le mystère de Dieu qui utilise la bouche et les paroles des prophètes, c'est le mystère de Dieu qui commence parmi les hommes son apprentissage de Verbe incarné. L'incarnation achève ainsi l'économie révélatrice de l'Ancien Testament." Ibid., 438 [361].

62. These are themes that had been addressed in the earlier article: R. Latourelle, "Révélation, histoire et Incarnation," *Gregorianum* 44 (1963): 225–62. An abridged English translation can be found in R. Latourelle, "Revelation, History and the Incarnation," *Theology Digest* 13 (1965): 29–34.

63. "Le Christ est Dieu d'une manière humaine, et homme d'une manière divine." Latourelle, *Théologie de la Révélation*, 438 [361].

possible. As Latourelle says, "The union of natures and the unity of person authorizes the transfer from the divine milieu." The fact of the incarnation is not in itself revelation; it is the "way"[64] God has chosen to communicate, the means by which revelation and history are united. The economy of the incarnation is fundamental to the self-manifestation of God in the world.

This revealing takes place through all the means open to Christ in the flesh. Within this economy, revelation takes on "a double line of manifestation: through words and gesture,"[65] a combined activity in which word is primary. Words explain actions and are the privileged expression of people; they allow judgment and are the means by which testimony to intangible experience may be given. Activity and gesture, or way of life, are the matrix and corroboration of these words. Word and action in the person of Christ become the formal elements of a sacramental economy through which God is revealed.

This immediately raises the further question of whether any human system is capable of containing the eternal divine truth. Revelation, even in the fullness and reality of the incarnation, remains beyond the grasp of humanity, and "is unthinkable apart from its basis in analogy, with its process of negation and pre-eminence."[66] It is analogy that allows the use of human notions when divine truth is expressed, a procedure that is legitimized absolutely by the incarnation and allows a certain conformity between the human and divine realities. The latter, however, remains unfathomable mystery.[67]

---

64. "Plus justement, l'Incarnation est la *voie* choisie par Dieu pour révéler et se révéler." Ibid., 440 [363].

65. "La révélation s'accomplit donc suivant une double ligne de manifestation: par paroles et par actions, par paroles et par gestes, les paroles explicitant les gestes, les actions, et en découvrant la mystérieuse profondeur; les gestes et les actions, à leur tour, incarnant les paroles et leur donnant valeur de vie." Ibid., 444 [364].

66. "La révélation, même par le Christ, n'est pensable que sur la base de l'analogie, avec son processus de négation et d'éminence." Ibid., 444 [366].

67. Ghislain Lafont explains the philosophical background to this point in the chapter of *God, Time and Being* entitled "God Without Analogy," 261–296, and especially where he devotes himself

The fact of the incarnation places Christ in a particular position with regard to God's self-manifestation, because he is at once revealer, revelation, sign of revelation, and perfect response to revelation. As the image of God in himself, he is the revelation of the Father and also the means by which this revealing is accomplished. As the perfect witness, Christ shows through his activity and in his Person the nature of God, and in so doing is the sign of revelation. As Son he conducts a harmonious dialogue with the Father,[68] a dialogue that reveals him to be the perfect expression of the response of humanity to God. In this sense Christ is the fullness of revelation, the living testament of God's love that is passed to the apostles and the church.

The Dynamic of Incarnation Persists in the Church

Just as Latourelle described a dynamic process of revelation up to the incarnation, so he insists on the continuation of this process when Christ is no longer visible in the flesh. Without losing a sense of the unique, new, complete, and perfect revelation that was given in the person of Jesus, Latourelle presents the revelation received by the apostles and preserved by the church not as a static deposit, but as an ever-developing economy through which God is revealed.[69] In

---

to the mystery of God: "God is Mystery, not in the sense of a plenitude at once inaccessible and omnipresent, or an insoluble puzzle. He comes to the heart of the world, acting in it, identifying himself continually with the crucified and bringing about a history which is always open to the faith of man who lives in the world. And man perceives God as Mystery of the world and responds to this God, not when he seeks him as the remedy for his limitations or the fulfilment of his desires, but on the contrary, when he opens himself up to a true autonomy and remains turned toward the future by stripping himself of self through an attitude of faith." G. Lafont, *God, Time and Being* (Petersham, MA: Saint Bede's, 1992), 274.

68. Latourelle, *Théologie de la Révélation*, 448 [369].

69. "Personne ne peut rivaliser avec les apôtres dans la connaissance du Christ. Moment unique dans l'histoire de la révélation. Plénitude et fraîcheur du premier matin sur la création nouvelle. Sans doute les apôtres n'ont-ils pas eu la connaissance *explicite* que possède l'Église actuelle; mais en revanche, par son intensité, sa profondeur, sa richesse d'intuitions, son caractère de totalité,

effecting the passage from divine vision to human expression, Christ opens the possibility of revelation being communicated by a human sign instituted by Christ, that is, the church.

> Not only does the Church make revelation constantly present by her preaching: not only does she propose and interpret it authentically for each generation, but she also constitutes, in herself, a great and perpetual motive for credibility on behalf of revelation. God, in making known His word, has never separated His word from the signs which authorize it as divine. From the very beginning, the proclamation of the Gospel was bound up with the signs of the kingdom, primarily miracles and prophecies. These signs lose nothing of their force to establish the fact of revelation, but normally, contemporary faith is based less upon miracles and the Scriptures as such than on the ever present sign of the Church. The Church is thus at once the instrument which receives and actualizes the ancient signs and the instrument which, by her always contemporary presence in the world, is herself a sign that her mission and doctrine are from God.[70]

Latourelle points out that the "word of God already possesses an objective intrinsic efficacy, which makes it analogous to sacrament."[71] Recognizing this analogous structure within the same economy, he applies the same circle of causality that had allowed Henri de Lubac

---

leur connaissance du Christ et de la révélation a pu surpasser toute connaissance actuelle ou à venir. Ils ont eu, affirme C. Journet, une 'connaissance suprême, exceptionnelle, qui assumait, mais dans une intuition supérieure, le sens explicite immédiatement saisissable du dépôt livré par eux à l'Église primitive' et qui 'dépassait en outre tout ce que l'Église, assistée de l'Esprit, pourrait découvrir au cours des siècles, en explicitant et développant ce premier dépôt'." Ibid., 450 [371].

70. "Non seulement l'Église rend la révélation toujours présente par sa prédication; non seulement elle la propose et l'interprète authentiquement pour chaque génération, mais encore elle constitue *par elle-même* un grand et perpétuel motif de crédibilité en faveur de la révélation. Dieu, pour faire reconnaître sa parole, n'a jamais disjoint la parole des signes qui l'autorisent comme divine. Dès le début, la proclamation de l'Évangile fut liée aux signes du Royaume, notamment les miracles et les prophéties. Ces signes gardent toute leur valeur pour établir le fait de la révélation, mais normalement la foi contemporaine s'appuie, encore plus que sur les miracles de l'Écriture, sur le signe toujours actuel de l'Église. L'Église est donc à la fois celle qui recueille et actualise les signes anciens, et celle qui fait signe, par sa présence toujours contemporaine, que sa mission et doctrine sont de Dieu." Ibid., 498–99 [417].

71. "Sans doute, la parole de Dieu possède déjà une efficacité intrinsèque objective, qui en fait l'analogue du sacrement." Ibid., 491 [410].

to proclaim in 1953 that "the Church makes the Eucharist" and "the Eucharist makes the Church."[72] The church incarnates the word in every age. Founded by this word, the church is dependent on it for her life, but the word is also dependent on the church for its preservation and actualization. In examining this relationship, Latourelle shows how the revelation of God, received through an economy of word and testimony, and having its most perfect expression in the incarnation, persists by the means of the same sacramental economy within the church.

Latourelle has shown that words as a phenomenon establish relationship and communion,[73] and, as human testimony accompanied by certain signs, become a motive for credibility. In this sense he understands the church. The church, in communicating the word through her preaching, establishes herself as a communion of people brought into relationship by the word. Together this community offer a testimony to its hearers[74] that imparts credibility, and so the church becomes in herself a sacramental sign that gives credibility to the word she speaks.

72. Cf. P. McPartlan, *The Eucharist Makes the Church: Henri de Lubac and John Zizioulas in Dialogue* (Edinburgh: T. &T. Clark, 1993), xv: "His [de Lubac's] conclusions and even his words have become theological currency, often without attribution. B. Sesboüé says that he saw the celebrated double principle coined by de Lubac, that 'the Church makes the Eucharist' and 'the Eucharist makes the Church,' quoted here and there as a patristic formula. In fact this double principle appeared for the first time only in de Lubac's *Méditation sur L'Église* in 1953. There . . . he says that the Church and the Eucharist stand 'as Cause to each other.'"

73. "En un sens, on peut donc affirmer que l'Église est convoquée et engendrée par la parole." Latourelle, *Théologie de la Révélation*, 485 [407].

74. Ghislain Lafont, in his study *God, Time and Being*, elaborates this point with some merit: "If it is a question of hearing a narrative, we should expect that the first thing one will want to know is *who* can make this narrative, *where* can it be heard and responded to, *what* community can stand between those who witnessed and those who hear the story today. The decisive question is one of *testimony*, since it is a question of a *dated* testimony, we must also reflect on the signification of the written documents to which this testimony is consigned. . . . This point is very important at this founding level, it is a question of *hearing* and of *commitment*, and not one of *reading* and *commentary*. In this sense, we must simply concede to Derrida that, when God is involved, the primacy goes to the phone (the voice), and not to the written word: the written word, in fact, when preached and proclaimed, becomes spoken word, word in this very act." Lafont, *God, Time and Being*, 135–36.

Revelation is "made present" in the church through the act of preaching. In proclaiming the word, the church represents the message of Christ, so that the time of the church is the time of salvation, the acceptable time of the gospel. In her preaching, the church actualizes the word of God so that "through the Church, revelation is always present and always active."[75] The word of the preacher must be one "springing from a commitment, with holiness of life for its credentials."[76] Receiving his ministry from Christ, the preacher must echo the words and commitment of his master. The preacher does not pass on a system of thought, but incarnates the revelation of God fully realized in Jesus Christ into his own life. The church is established by this testimony, because such testimony of life is the gospel in action, and "such a spectacle moves the man who hears him to desire a share in his universe of values which the word opens up before him."[77]

"From the very beginning," asserts Latourelle, "the proclamation of the Gospel was bound up with signs of the Kingdom." To the contemporary mind, the credibility that these signs afford to the

---

75. R. Latourelle, *Théologie de la Révélation*, 489 [409]. Though Latourelle is here concentrating on the actualization of the Word of God in the church, we should keep in mind his earlier comments on the relationship between word and sacrament: "D'une façon générale, révélation et sacrements peuvent être considérés comme des formes *diverses et analogues* de cette vaste économie divine par laquelle le salut nous est donné à travers les signes. Dans cette économie, la sacramentalité dessine comme des cercles concentriques, suivant un ordre d'efficacité décroissante: *a)* incarnation du Verbe, source de toute grâce; *b)* sacrements proprement dits; *c)* parole révélée. La révélation, en tant que parole divine, possède son efficacité propre, supérieure à celle de la parole humaine, inférieure à celle des sacrements." Ibid., 465 [385].

76. "Par suite, la vraie prédication doit être à la fois un *service* et un *témoignage*, c'est-à-dire une parole jaillie d'un engagement, accréditée par la sainteté de la vie." Ibid., 491 [411].

77. Ibid. It is for this reason that Latourelle makes the distinction between revelation and the sacraments: "Révélation et sacrements sont ordonnés au salut, mais chacun à sa manière. La révélation *tend* à l'obéissance de la foi, qui est le 'commencement du salut, le fondement et la racine de toute justification' (D 801), mais elle ne produit pas la foi *ex opere operato*, à la manière du sacrement. Elle est efficace, en ce sens que le secours actuel qui en constitue la dimension intérieure, excite, appelle, attire *vraiment* à recevoir le message, et développe *vraiment* dans l'âme une force de saisie capable de s'achever en adhésion de foi, si l'homme se rend *librement* aux prévenances et aux invites de la grâce." Ibid., 465–66 [385].

words of the message lies more in the sign of the church itself, a unified, stable, holy, and fruitful institution, than in the traditional proofs of miracles and prophecies. The church "receives and actualises" these ancient signs from God, and in themselves they become testament to the fact of the divine origin of the church. It is the will of the Father that all people enter the "society of love" that is his life, and be saved. God effected the transition of humanity from a state of disunity, finitude, sinfulness, and impotence by the death of his Son, which made possible the gathering of God's people into one to experience the beatitude of his kingdom forever. Of this, the unity, stability, holiness, and fruitfulness of the church are a sign and foretaste.

The Purpose of Revelation Is Salvation

The church is a credible sign that calls people to faith because she makes the kingdom historically present and invites individuals to a present experience of its future glorious realization. As such a sign of credibility, the church brings together the categories of miracle and prophecy, long the basis of Catholic apologetics. According to such a tradition, Latourelle can speak of the "*observable* facts, which make the Church, among human societies, a *miraculous* society whose very existence cannot be explained without appealing to an extraordinary intervention on the part of God."[78] These facts are at the same time

---

78. "Dans la société ecclésiale, telle qu'elle se manifeste au–dehors, quels sont ces faits, *observables*, qui font de l'Église, parmi les sociétés humaines, une société *miraculeuse* dont l'existence ne peut s'expliquer sans faire appel à une intervention extraordinaire de Dieu?" Ibid., 502, [419]. Cf. G. Martelet, "De la sacramentalité propre à l'Église," *Nouvelle Revue Théologique*, 95 (1973): 25–42: "Sans doute on peut analyser humainement l'Église et même estimer, comme on dit de nos jours, la *réduire* à des composantes politiques, culturelles et sociales que la chimie actuelle des groupes et des mœurs permet de détecter. Cependant le chrétien se définit ici par un refus don't l'arbitraire n'est qu'apparent, car ce refus, nous allons le montrer, s'appuie tout entier sur la Résurrection qui seul peut expliquer vraiment l'Église." 31.

"figurative": a prophecy of the new creation announced by revelation.[79]

> Revelation is ordered toward faith, and faith itself is in view of salvation. The goal of revelation, envisaged from the point of view of man, is the salvation of man; or, in more positive terms, it is vision, participation in divine life. Revelation, we must insist, is an essentially salvific operation. God does not reveal Himself in order to satistfy our curiosity or to increase the total sum of our human knowledge, but rather to snatch man away from the death of sin and give him the gift of eternal life. Stirred up by the living God, the revealed word, preached and received in faith, begets living souls, sons of God, sharing the glory of the Three Divine Persons. To deprive revelation of its salvific character would be to deprive it of one of its fundamental dimensions.[80]

Just as word and testimony elicit response and commitment, so the preaching and witness of the church elicits a response and a commitment specifically termed *faith*. Revelation of the word of God is an invitation to the life of God, which is salvation for man and woman: "We take God's word that he Himself is Father, Son, and Spirit; but the vision of Father, Son, and Spirit remains the object of hope."[81] Faith, the earthly beginning of vision, bridges these two degrees of experience. Through the word and testimony of the church, we enter the sacramental economy of sign and reality, which of its nature has both a present and a future reality. Sign incorporates the suggestion of a complete future, as yet only partially unveiled in

---

79. R. Latourelle, *Théologie de la Révélation*, 505 [422].

80. "La révélation est ordonnée à la foi, et la foi elle-même est en vue du salut. Le but de la révélation, envisagé du point de vue de l'homme, c'est le salut de l'homme; ou, en termes plus positifs, c'est la vision, la participation à la vie divine. La révélation, il faut y insister, est une opération essentiellement salvifique. Dieu ne révèle pas pour satisfaire notre curiosité ou pour accroître la somme de nos connaissances, mais pour arracher l'homme à la mort du péché et pour le faire vivre d'une vie éternelle. Suscitée par le Dieu vivant, la parole révélée, prêchée et reçue dans la foi, engendre des vivants, des fils de Dieu, participant à la vie des trois personnes divines. Priver la révélation de son caractère salvifique, ce serait la priver d'une de ses dimensions fondamentales." Ibid., 516, [435].

81. "Nous croyons sur parole que Dieu est Père, Fils et Esprit; mais la vision du Père, du Fils et de L'Esprit demeure objet d'espérance." Ibid., 506 [425].

its present reality. In the context of revelation, Latourelle expresses this as the vision and goal of salvation: "Revelation being essentially a word of friendship, it has real meaning only if God's plan is to consummate this friendship with man by a more complete gift of himself in presence and vision."[82] The word of God, which invites us to this life of communion and which is made a credible call by concrete signs, contains the assurance that the invitation will be honored completely. If the invitation is to life, then revelation cannot be separated from salvation—the present from the future, or sign from reality: "Revelation and vision are thus only two 'moments' of one and the same manifestation and communication of God to man."[83] That is to say, revelation and salvation are concurrent realities in the same process.

Again, Latourelle effects the shift from an understanding of revelation as a body of factual evidence, part of "the sum total of our human knowledge," to the experience of the gift of eternal life. This is not a static event, but part of the process of salvation that extends from the act of faith inspired by the word to the unambiguous experience of the life that it promises. Revelation is the constant narrowing of the distance between Revealer and recipient, between the present and its eschatological fulfilment. A fundamental dimension of revelation is the experience of salvation: the salvation that is expressed within the sacramental economy of revelation as an ecclesial feast achieving fulfillment in heaven.

---

82. "La révélation étant essentiellement parole d'amitié n'a sa place que si Dieu a dessein de consommer cette amitié avec l'homme par un don plus complet de lui-même dans la présence et la vision." Ibid., 507 [426].
83. "Révélation et vision ne sont donc que deux moments d'une seule manifestation et communication de Dieu à l'homme. La vision consomme ce que la révélation inaugure." Ibid.

The Revelation of Future Glory Invites the Response of Faith

Both the act of faith and its fulfillment in the beatific vision have an ecclesial dimension.[84] The eschatological vision of the blessed is expressed in the terms of a banquet at which everyone is united with the Lord. This, however, is not the only image given. As Latourelle points out, "The Apocalypse represents the heavenly Jerusalem as the society of the elect 'gathered' about the Lamb (Rev. 14:1-4) and reigning with Him (Rev. 22:5)."[85] The ultimate goal of the saving revelation of God is his own glory. "Salvation to our God" is the song of the blessed as they praise God in the sanctuary of the heavenly Jerusalem. Between the Synoptics and the book of Revelation, there is a strange juxtaposition of festive banquet and cultic celebration, both of which are ordered to God's glory.

> The glory of God, envisaged from the point of view of spiritual creation, means creation's recognition of the excellence of God and His gifts. Men are invited to glorify God who is manifest through the medium of creation, and make their thanks to him (Wis. 13:1-9, Rom. 1:18-21). More than that, they are invited to glorify God in His work of grace, that is, in the plan of salvation which He has from all eternity. The Letter to the Ephesians lists all these gifts of salvation, in succeeding strophes, in tones of gratitude and admiration: predestination, sonship, redemption, revelation, election of Israel, vocation of the Gentiles. All these gifts of God, including that of revelation, are ordered, Saint Paul repeats over and over again, "toward the praise and glory of his grace" (Eph. 1:6. 12. 14).[86]

84. "Tout comme la révélation première s'adresse à l'humanité comme telle, en vue de constituer ce corps du Christ qu'est l'Église, ainsi la révélation eschatologique se présente comme une expérience collective, comme une joie participée." Ibid., 511 [429].

85. "L'Apocalypse représente la Jérusalem céleste comme la société des élus 'rassemblés' autour de l'Agneau (*Apoc.* 14, 1–4) et régnant avec lui (*Apoc.* 22, 5;1, 6.9)." Ibid., 512 [430].

86. "La gloire de Dieu, envisagée du côté de la créature spirituelle, signifie la reconnaissance par celle-ci de l'excellence de Dieu et de ses dons. Les hommes sont invités à glorifier Dieu qui se manifeste à travers la création et à lui rendre grâces (*Sap.* 13, 1–9; *Rom.* 1, 18–21). Bien davantage encore, ils sont invités à glorifier Dieu dans son œuvre de grâce, c'est-à-dire dans le dessein de salut qu'il a arrêté de toute éternité. L'épître aux Éphésiens énumère, en strophes très denses, gonflées par la gratitude et l'admiration, tous les dons du salut: prédestination, filiation,

The purpose of revelation is, in the final analysis, the glory of God. Revelation is the process by which humanity comes to recognise the goodness of God and his purposes through experience and knowledge of him. If revelation might be said to have an eschatological perspective, so too does it display a protological one. Revelation brings the recipient to a knowledge of the whole of creation as gift. "It is not our mind that rises up toward God; it is God who, through creation, descends toward us."[87] The beauty of the physical world, and humanity as the apex of creation, reflect God and his will.[88] This is a revelation that demands homage and thanksgiving. However, while creation refers humanity to God as its cause, "it speaks of God, but God Himself does not speak."[89] The economy of word and testimony that is fundamental to the economy of supernatural revelation, that is to God's plan of salvation, is not a part of natural revelation. God intervenes as a person within history so that human beings can experience the call to friendship and communion that is his salvation. Fundamentally, it is for this revelation of grace that God commands the glory of all creation. "The glory of God means, in the first place, God Himself, in the perfection of His being and in the radiance of His perfection. This perfection spreads first of all throughout the inner life of the Trinity; it is then communicated to creatures, in various degrees and orders of participation."[90]

---

rédemption, révélation, élection d'Israël, vocation des Gentils. Tous ces dons de Dieu, y compris celui de la révélation, sont ordonnés, répète saint Paul avec insistance, 'à la louange de gloire de sa grâce' (*Eph.* 1, 6. 12. 14)." Ibid., 522–23 [440].

87. "Encore plus que notre esprit qui s'élève vers Dieu, c'est Dieu qui, par la création, descend jusqu'à nous." Ibid., 413 [337].

88. Ibid., 414 [338].

89. "Elle parle de Dieu, mais Dieu lui-même ne parle pas, n'entre pas en dialogue." Ibid., 415 [339].

90. "La gloire de Dieu désigne, au premier chef, Dieu lui-même, dans la perfection de son Être et dans le rayonnement de sa perfection. Cette perfection se répand d'abord à l'intérieur de la Trinité, puis se communique aux créatures, suivant des degrés et des ordres de participation différents." Ibid., 522 [440].

So, the processes of revelation, salvation and glorification can be said to be coterminous aspects of the same phenomenon. In an ascending paean of the praise of the glory of God, revelation moves through creation, election, salvation, predestination, and sonship to fulfillment in the beatific vision. Thus the movement of the Word of God can be traced from his leaving the Father's side, through the self-emptying mystery of his life and death, to the glorious return of his resurrection, by which he gathered all people to himself, so as to return all creation to the praise and glory of God. This is the perfect testimony of the Word made flesh, which persisting in the church, reveals the love of God still.

In *Théologie de la Révélation*, Latourelle presented the "first organic study of revelation."[91] Wide and comprehensive in scope, the work had no pretentions to be exhaustive;[92] rather the author saw his efforts as a foundation for the work of others. Without doubt, this work puts into place the essential categories that Vatican II envisaged for a fundamental theology of revelation. The ease with which a commentary on *Dei Verbum* could be appended, and the consonance this shows with the book as a whole, is witness to the conciliar nature of the work.[93] Dogmatic rather than apologetic, Latourelle succeeds in articulating a sound foundational theology of revelation. He presents us with something organic, vital and christocentric—a revelation rooted in the historical reality of the incarnation, and one that reflects its sacramental economy. The person of Jesus is the centre of Latourelle's reflection, for in him is the perfection and completion of revelation. Such a reorientation, which the Council was to confirm, would obviously have consequences for the more

91. Fisichella, *Gesù Rivelatore*, 12.
92. Cf. Dulles, "The Theology of Revelation," 52.
93. For corroboration of this fact, compare the central points of *Théologie de la Révélation* with the later commentary: R. Latourelle, *Comment Dieu se révèle au monde: Lecture commentée de la Constitution de Vatican II sur la parole de Dieu* (Québec: Fides, 1998).

traditional arguments of Catholic apologetics, and it was to a more thorough reworking of these that Latourelle was to turn in the years after the Council.

Establishing Credible Signs:
Le Christ et l'Église: Signes du Salut

Though from as early as 1961 Latourelle had begun to divide his course into two distinct sections,[94] one a general dogmatic treatment of revelation and the other a more apologetic study of the signs that accompany revelation, by 1964 that division had taken a more definite theological and pedagogical shape.[95] By the start of the academic year of 1967–1968, the second section of the tract had been expanded considerably to contain an examination of the fundamental signs of Christ and the church. In an effort to integrate the fruits of the Council ever more substantially, these class notes show constant revision up to 1971. As Marcel Chappin points out, "To the change in the description corresponds a change in teaching, visible in the *Subsidia*, published in the same year and partially reused in *Le Christ et l'Église: signes du salut*."[96] What becomes increasingly evident is a more existential approach, and a shift in focus away from an emphasis on miracle and prophecy, which are now incorporated into the overall scheme of revelation, where Christ and the church are the central lucidities.[97]

---

94. Cf. R. Latourelle, *De Revelatione, Pars dogmatica*, Schemata lectionum ad usum privatum auditorum (Rome: PUG, 1961); and R. Latourelle, *De signis divinis, Pars apologetica*, Schemata lectionum ad usum privatum auditorum (Rome: PUG, 1961).

95. Cf. R. Latourelle, *Theologia Revelationis*, Pars prima: *De ipsa Revelatione*, Schemata lectionum ad usum privatum auditorum (Rome: PUG, 1963), and R. Latourelle, *Theologia Revelationis*, Pars altera: *De signis Revelationis*, Schemata lectionum ad usum privatum auditorum (Rome: PUG, 1964).

96. "Al cambiamento nella descrizione corrisponde un cambiamento nell' insegnamento, visibile nei *Subsidia* pubblicate nello stesso anno e parzialmente riprese in *Cristo e la Chiesa. Segni di Salvezza*." Chappin, "Dalla Difesa al Dialogo," 42.

These changes in Latourelle's course mirror the larger scale restructuring of first-cycle theology that was taking place at the Gregorian University. Latourelle had worked for an organic inclusion of fundamental theology into the first cycle,[98] and this he achieved from 1969 onward, when the first year of studies is given "a format and articulation inspired by *Dei Verbum*."[99] It is during the years in which this restructuring was planned and executed that Latourelle reworked earlier articles that form some of the chapters of *Le Christ et l'Église: signes du salut,* and in which he published the book as a whole.[100]

Vatican II was the Council of signs, the concept returning as a leitmotif throughout various documents, and yet these were merely the expressions of a more profound renewal.[101] Such a concentration

97. Ibid.

98. Cf. R. Latourelle, *Nuova immagine della Facoltà di teologia* (Rome: Editionis Universitatis Gregorianae, 1974), and R. Latourelle, "Assenza e presenza della Fondamentale al Vaticano II," in *Vaticano II: Bilancio e Prospettive. Venticinque anni dopo, (1962–1987),* ed. R. Latourelle, vol. 2 (Assisi: Cittadella Editrice, 1987), 1331–415; English. trans., "Absence and Presence of Fundamental Theology at Vatican II," in *Vatican II: Assessment and Perspectives, Twenty-Five Years After (1962-1987),* ed. R. Latourelle, 3 vols. (New York: Paulist, 1988), 3:378–415. Also J. Alfaro et al., "La théologie fondamentale à la recherche de son identité," *Gregorianum* 50 (1969): 757–76.

99. "Inserita organicamente nel programma del primo ciclo e precisamente nel primo anno, che porta il titolo *Christus plenitudo Revelationis,* la Teologia Fondamentale conosce adesso un'impostazione ed articolazione ispirate alla *Dei Verbum.* La prima parte, affidata al P. Latourelle è *De ipsa Revelatione,* dove, dopo la *pars positiva seu historica,* segue una riflessione sistematica, con i seguenti temi: l'uomo come uditore della rivelazione; la rivelazione, l'iniziativa amorosa del Dio trascendente; il mistero rivelato; la rivelazione come dialogo di Dio; il carattere sacramentale della rivelazione; le diverse forme di comunicazione; Cristo, pienezza della rivelazione; la rivelazione di Dio come rivelazione dell'uomo a se stesso tematica veramente nuova; sul ruolo della Chiesa (popolo e magistero), coerenza tra rivelazione e la sua transmissione; rivelazione e fede, coloro che conoscono Cristo; storia umana, storia della salvezza, storia della rivelazione." Chappin, "Dalla Difesa al Dialogo," 43.

100. Cf. R. Latourelle, "La sainteté, signe de la Révélation," *Gregorianum* 46 (1965): 36–65; Latourelle, "Le Christ, Signe de la Révélation selon la Constitution *Dei Verbum*," *Gregorianum* 47 (1966): 685–709; Latourelle, "L'économie des signes de la Révélation," *Sciences ecclésiastiques* 19 (1967): 7–31; and Latourelle, "Vatican II et les signes de la Révélation," *Gregorianum* 49 (1968): 225–52.

101. Gustave Martelet, in a work that had obvious influence on Latourelle, expresses this point beautifully: " Au Concile, le renouveau des signes est de l'ordre bien plus prosaïque des textes et des écrits. Il est pensé, voulu, intellectuellement défini plus que réalisé encore ou simplement

was obviously an invitation to reexamine the classical tracts on signs and to explore their deeper significance within fundamental theology. As Latourelle points out himself, *Le Christ et l'Église: signes du salut* "set out only to illustrate a perspective, proposed by the Second Vatican Council, and a method for treating the problem of the signs of revelation in the right way."[102] As such it may be said that this work flows out of *La Théologie de la Révélation* and the teachings of the Council, because "a better understanding of the sacramental structure of revelation and the economy of the transmission . . . has made us grasp all the importance of the Christian life as a sign that salvation has come into the world."[103]

The findings of fundamental theology and the teaching of the Council concerning revelation necessitated a complete reexamination of the signs that accompany revelation and that traditional apologetics had interpreted as its proof. Here, adopting an essentially conciliar approach, and reflecting the way in which he had structured his own teaching, Latourelle concentrates on the person of Christ and on the church as fundamental signs, seeing prophecy and miracle only in relation to these fundamental signs and leaving more careful study of them to a later work.[104]

---

vécu, mais enfin il existe. Nous l'avons déjà vu, les écrits conciliaires surabondent d'aveux, de décisions, d'ouvertures en tout genre, de sympathie profonde, d'amour intelligent, d'amitié généreuse pour l'homme. C'est un vrai renouveau de cette divine *philanthropie* en laquelle les Pères grecs voyaient le trait le plus profond de Dieu. 'L'amour de Dieu pour l'homme, écrivait Clément d'Alexandrie, passe toute parole et sa haine du mal est sans limite.' 'Le mot Amour, disait à la fin de ses jours Valéry, le mot Amour ne s'est trouvé associé au nom de Dieu que depuis le Christ.' Le renouveau spirituel des signes depend de cet amour." G. Martelet, *Les idées maîtresses de Vatican II* (Paris: Desclée, 1966), 137.

102. "Nous n'avons voulu ici qu'illustrer une *perspective*, proposée par Vatican II, et une *méthode* pour traiter correctement le problème des signes de la révélation." R. Latourelle, *Le Christ et l'Église*, 10 [7].

103. "Une meilleure intelligence de la structure sacramentelle de la révélation (œuvres et paroles) et de l'économie de sa transmission à travers les siècles (par la *vie* de l'Église aussi bien que par son enseignement) a fait comprendre toute l'importance du témoignage de la vie chrétienne comme signe de l'avènement du salut dans le monde." Ibid., 11 [9].

Latourelle begins *Le Christ et L'Église: signes du salut* with a chapter on the Second Vatican Council and the signs of revelation, thus founding the whole enterprise on the "profound change" that had taken place since Vatican I. In subsequent chapters, he examines the effect that the new teaching has had on the understanding of the economy of revelation signs, and then focuses on Christ and the church. He discusses Christ with particular reference to *Dei Verbum*, and the church is examined according to the traditional notes of credibility, though these also are radically restructured so as to reflect the Council's teachings.[105]

In studying this work, the aim is to evaluate the fruit that a period of reflection on the Second Vatican Council yielded for fundamental theology. At the same time, any development of the themes of *Théologie de la Révélation* will obviously become apparent, as should the way in which this text forms a theological basis for a similar and later restructuring of the theology of miracles.

The Church—A Community of Credible Witnesses

Fundamental to the renewal of revelation theology that took place at Vatican II is the adoption of personalist and christocentric categories. The fundamental assumption is, "If Christ is God among us, 'signs' are not exterior to Christ and his revelation: they emanate from this personal centre which is Christ, and their purpose is to lead men to

---

104. "Suit logiquement le problème de la crédibilité de la Révélation. Sur ce point, comme sur bien d'autres, je me démarque de l'apologétique traditionnelle qui, à la suite de Vatican I, s'en tient aux signes des miracles, des prophéties et de la présence glorieuse de l'Église dans le monde. Je passe résolument d'une perspective d'objet à une perspective de personne. Les signes de crédibilité du christianisme ne sont pas des pièces détachés accompagnant la doctrine chrétienne à la manière d'un passeport ou d'un sceau d'ambassade sur une lettre, pour en garantir l'authenticité. Les signes, au contraire, sont le rayonnement multiforme de la personne du Christ." R. Latourelle, *L'Infini du sens*, 57.

105. For a fuller analysis of the ways in which Latourelle responds to the Constitutions of Vatican II in *Le Christ et l'Église*, see A. Sierra, *La Revelación Según René Latourelle*, 153–97.

identify this personal centre as divine."[106] The signs of revelation are not proofs of some abstract concept but aspects of a personal reality.[107] In the incarnation of Christ, revelation comes in person and cannot be separated from the individual who is both Revealer and revelation.

This personalist and christocentric approach, already apparent in *Théologie de la Révélation*, is also used specifically when the Council speaks of the church. *Lumen Gentium* makes it clear that the church is in the form of a sacrament, because as a social body she is the visible realization of the salvation of Christ. As Latourelle maintains, "It is her theandric structure which lies at the basis of her capacity to become a motive of credibility."[108] According to the Council, it is the personal life of grace as manifest by Christ and the individuals who make up the church in him that forms the primary motive of credibility for Christian claims.[109] So Latourelle can declare the perspective of the Council to be such that

> If the Church were to preach an abstract ideal, never lived and never to be met with, she would destroy the gospel and destroy herself. The more she talks about salvation the more she is bound to produce witnesses to salvation. In this respect we should give to the sign of the Church and the sign of holiness of life a very much greater importance than we have done in the past. There is room in fact, in the theology of signs, for methodical reflection on the action of the Spirit in human souls and in the concrete life of the Church.[110]

---

106. "Si le Christ est Dieu parmi nous, les signes ne sont pas extérieurs au Christ et à sa révélation: ils eminent de ce centre personnel qu'est le Christ et ils ont pour but d'amener les hommes à identifier ce centre personnel et divin." R. Latourelle, *Le Christ et l'Église*, 12 [11].

107. "Les signes on le voit. Sont inseparables de la Personne qu'ils visent à faire reconnaître et identifier à partir des traits observés. Le Christ est par lui-même Signe de *l'authenticité* de la révélation qu'il est en *Personne.*" Ibid., 14 [12].

108. "C'est la structure théandrique de l'Église qui fonde son aptitude à devenir motif de crédibilité." Ibid., 17 [15].

109. Cf. the work published in the same year as *Le Christ et l'Église*: R. Latourelle, *Le témoignage chrétien* (Montreal: Bellarmin, 1971); and also the article published previously: R. Latourelle, "La testimonianza della vita, segno di salvezza" in *Laici sulle vie del Concilio* (Assisi: Cittadella Editrice, 1966), 377–95.

110. "Si l'Église ne faisait que prêcher un ideal abstrait, jamais vécu et jamais rencontré, elle détruirait

In this passage, Latourelle identifies personal witness of life as the most potent aspect of the church's mission to be a sign to the nations. This witness is grounded on the person of Christ, the perfect witness, and it persists in the church inasmuch as individuals live a holiness of life founded on him. The church preaches no abstract ideal, but one lived and met with in the life and gospel of Jesus Christ. To be able to speak credibly of the salvation found in this gospel, the church must produce living witnesses in every age.[111]

Interestingly, in the "inventory of texts"[112] that Latourelle provides as an example of the changes in motive and perspective that the Council has inspired, he singles out *Sacrosanctum Concilium* for special attention.[113] Here, Latourelle amplifies the point he made in *Théologie de la Révélation* that there is a certain correlation between the revelatory nature of the sign of the church and the seven sacraments of which she is the custodian. To suggest that within a theology of signs there is room "for methodological reflection on the action

l'Évangile et se détruirait elle-même. Plus l'Église parle du salut, plus aussi elle doit produire des témoins du salut. A cet égard, il convient d'accorder au signe de l'Église et de la sainteté une importance beaucoup plus grande que dans le passé. Il y a place, en effet, dans la théologie des signes, pour une réflexion méthodique sur l'action de l'Esprit dans les âmes et dans la vie concrète de l'Église." R. Latourelle, *Le Christ et l'Église*, 35 [34–35].

111. Indeed, Latourelle would suggest that such a requirement is even more necessary for our own age: "L'homme contemporain écoute plus volontiers les témoins que les maîtres; ou, s'il écoute les maîtres, c'est parce qu'il découvre en eux des témoins. Seule compte, à ses yeux, la vérité incarnée dans une decision, dans toute une vie. Ce qu'il exige, pour se 'rendre,' c'est un engagement total, sans arrière-pensée, incluant tous les risques." R. Latourelle, *Le Christ et l'Église*, 255 [285]. See also R. Latourelle, "La Sainteté, signe de la Révélation," 36–65 [English trans., "Sanctity, a Sign of Revelation," *Theology Digest* 15 (1967): 41–46].

112. "L'inventaire des texts," R. Latourelle, *Le Christ et l'Église*, 11 [10].

113. "La *Constitution sur la Liturgie*, par example, declare: 'Puisque la liturgie édifie chaque jour ceux qui sont au-dedans pour en faire un Temple saint dans le Seigneur, une habitation de Dieu dans l'Esprit (*Eph.* 2, 21–22), jusqu'à la taille qui convient à la Plénitude du Christ (*Eph.* 4, 13), c'est d'une façon étonnante qu'elle fortifie leurs énergies pour leur faire proclamer le Christ, et ainsi elle montre l'Église à ceux qui sont au-dehors comme un signal levé devant les nations (*Is.* 11, 12), sous lequel les enfants de Dieu dispersés se rassemblent dans l'unité (*Jo.* 11, 52), jusqu'à ce qu'il y ait une seule bergerie et un seul Pasteur.' Ainsi, la vie liturgique, et notamment la vie sacramentaire, sanctifie les fidèles. Cette sainteté, lorsqu'elle rayonne, fait de la communauté des chrétiens unis dans la charité un signe qui attire ceux qui en sont témoins." R. Latourelle, *Le Christ et l'Église*, 17–18 [16].

of the Spirit in human souls," is to suggest that a perspective of the Council, waiting to be pursued, is the relationship between revelation and its actualization in the liturgy of the church. Latourelle indicates a possible point of departure for this when he identifies the witness of Christian lives expressed in a unity of charity as the most credible sign of the church, while relating this directly to her sacraments: "When the inner life of the Church, and especially her sacramental life and the life of the theological virtues, becomes intense, then she draws men's eyes toward her and becomes for the world the sign of the setting up of the kingdom of God, the sign of the coming of salvation in Jesus Christ."[114]

A process of christocentric personalization has turned the church from "the poor relation among signs,"[115] overshadowed as it was by miracle and prophecy, into the central motive for faith; it being the prolongation, in time, of the life and gospel of Jesus, the Sacrament of the Father. Such a shift is matched by a change in terminology. *Witness* becomes the new and preponderant term of the Council.[116] It is the calling of the Christian to be a witness to Christ, himself the perfect witness, and, through a transformation of life by grace, to be a sign of salvation.

114. "Lorsque la vie intérieure de l'Église, notamment sa vie sacramentaire et sa vie théologale, devient fervente, alors elle attire les regards et devient pour le monde le signe de l'établissement du Royaume de Dieu, le signe de l'avènement du salut en Jésus-Christ." Ibid., 18 [17].
115. "Le parent pauvre parmi les signes," Ibid., 20 [19].
116. "Le thème du témoignage est en effet l'un des thèmes majeurs et privilégiés de Vatican II. Comme un leitmotiv, il revient dans toutes les Constitutions et dans tous les Décrets. De même que les disciples du Christ sont appelés par Dieu, chacun suivant son état, à une sainteté dont la perfection est celle du Père (*LG*. §39–42), tous également sont appelés à *témoigner*, par la transformation de leur vie, de la réalité du salut donné en Jésus-Christ (*LG*. §35; §12, *GE* §2)." Ibid., 20 [19].

Grace Prepares for Perception

While considering the sign of salvation that comes from the testimony of the life of Christians, Latourelle juxtaposes the concepts of witness, sign, grace, and salvation, telescoping the witness of Christ, the church, and the individual into the same sacramental economy of revelation. Such a movement inevitably raises questions about the liturgical celebration of the sacraments themselves, and especially the Eucharist. Before discussing this in a later chapter, Latourelle turns first, in a chapter on the economy of signs, to the exact relationship between gospel, grace, and sign.

> Faith is the one and indivisible fruit of this threefold help: of the *gospel*, which proclaims salvation, of *grace*, which interiorly enlightens and strengthens us, and of the *signs* which accompany the message. So completely is the life of grace made for the gospel and its signs, that to speak of one without the other would be impossible. It is grace which, by the connaturality which infuses into us, opens our minds to an understanding of the gospel, and it is grace which makes us sensitive to the reality and the dynamism of the signs. On the other hand, without the gospel and the signs, we should not be able to know that salvation were offered to us, and offered to us by God.[117]

In chapter two of *Le Christ et l'Église: signes du salut*, Latourelle discusses the economy of the signs of revelation in the light of the Second Vatican Council's understanding of sign, a concept he had focused on during the first chapter. Here again he picks up the perspective of christocentric personalization that is such a mark of the Council's discussion of sign, and uses this as an assimilating force,

---

117. "La foi est le fruit unique et indivisible de ce triple secours de l'*Évangile* qui proclame le salut, de la *grâce* qui éclaire et fortifie intérieurement, et des *signes* qui accompagnent le message. La lumière de la grâce est si bien faite pour l'Évangile et les signes qu'on ne saurait parler de l'une sans parler des autres. C'est la grace, par la connaturalité qu'elle infuse, qui ouvre nos esprits à l'intelligence de l'Évangile, et c'est la grâce qui nous sensibilise à la réalité et au dynamisme des signes. Et, d'autre part, sans l'Évangile et les signes, nous ne pourrions savoir que le salut vient à nous et qu'il nous est adressé de la part de Dieu." Ibid., 43 [44].

in the light of which he can display the inherent consistency that exists in the sacramental economy. The signs of revelation radiate from Christ and the church, and are organically related to him as their foundation. They are not miraculous or unexplained inconsistencies within the natural order that perversely attest to the veracity of supernatural revelation, "but organic elements of an admirable economy of wisdom and goodness through which God, as it were, lays siege to man in order to make him understand that salvation is at hand."[118] Coherence is the first aspect of the economy to which Latourelle draws attention.[119]

The second aspect is compatability and suitability. The economy is "marvellously adapted"[120] to its function, which is to reveal personally the nature of God to humanity, and this visibly through history and the incarnation, and secretly to the hearts of individuals. It is in this enterprise that the "threefold help" of gospel, grace, and sign collaborate to effect a revelation both suitable to and compatible with the nature of humanity. In founding all revelation on Christ, the full and complete sign of revelation, Vatican II better expressed the unity of the gospel, grace, and sign which together flow from Christ their origin. As such they are extensions of the sacramental structure of his incarnation.[121] In addressing himself to the threefold structure of grace, gospel, and sign, Latourelle is seeking to clarify the coherence of the sacramental structure of revelation at every stage

---

118. "Mais les éléments organiques d'une économie admirable de sagesse et de bonté, par laquelle Dieu en quelque sorte investit l'homme pour lui faire entendre que le salut est parmi nous." Ibid., 40 [40].

119. Cf. R. Latourelle, "L'économie des signes de la Révélation," 7–31.

120. "Merveilleusement adaptée;" Latourelle, Le Christ et l'Église, 40 [40].

121. Here, as he says, Latourelle follows St. Thomas, who "observe justement que Dieu invite l'homme à croire par un triple secours: par un appel intérieur, par la prédication de l'Évangile et par les signes extérieurs. Le premier concile du Vatican, dans la description de la foi, rapproche les trois termes de révélation, de secours intérieurs de l'Esprit-Saint et de signes divins. Dans la perspective de Vatican II, la révélation et les signes sont liés au don du Christ, par lui-même Plénitude et Signe de la révélation, tandis que la foi est liée au don de l'Esprit, qui éclaire l'intelligence et meut le cœur de l'homme." Ibid., 41–42 [42].

of its development. The same interplay of exterior objective sign and interior attraction that is the revelatory dynamic of the incarnation persists so that all subsequent signs "are to be situated in a context of salvation and grace, and are not intelligible except in this context."[122]

Revelation:
A Dynamic between Inner Disposition and External Sign

Grace is the entity that supports and facilitates the whole process of revelation, effecting the necessary connection between the interior and exterior calls. Grace helps the individual to discern the signs in the first instance; it assists in the interpretation of the signs and provides the courage to respond to the challenge of these signs. Thus the persistent call of grace facilitates the appropriation of the truth of the signs without which "we should not be able to know that salvation were offered us." This economy exploits "all the means of expression accessible to man in his condition as a spatio-temporal, individual and social being, composed of body and spirit."[123] Latourelle regards miracle as a transformation of the natural world, of the space humanity inhabits, and prophecy he sees as the transfiguration of history, the time in which humanity lives. Holiness of life, however, is the sign of a changed individual or society.[124] Gospel, grace, and sign together "exhaust the significative virtualities provided by the human condition."[125]

Not only does revelation address the human person in a particular space-time reality, it also, by virtue of its economy, addresses the

---

122. "Sont à situer dans un contexte de salut et de grâce et ne se comprennent que dans ce contexte." Ibid., 42 [42].

123. "Toutes les formes d'expression accessibles à l'homme, dans sa condition d'être spatio-temporel, individuel et social, composé de corps et d'esprit." Ibid., 44 [44].

124. Ibid., 45 [45].

125. "Il épuise en quelque sorte les virtualités significatives offertes par la condition humaine." Ibid., 44 [45].

individual as a psychosomatic unity. Through the incarnation, the fullness of revelation, the human body has become "a mirror in which the divine is reflected."[126] It is by means of corporality that God communicates the divine truths of his plan for salvation. By the physical reality of his body, Christ makes God present in the world. Prolonging the same economy in sign preserves this reality, made manifest in the flesh. "Just as Christ was at once the Revealer and the sign of revelation, so the Church is at once the presence of revelation through the centuries and the sign of that revelation. The relationship between the signs of the Church and the signs of Christ is the same as that between the mystical Body of Christ and his glorious risen body."[127]

In this chapter on the economy of signs, Latourelle has detailed the aspects of the threefold help to faith and has clarified the relationship between them, but the question of the "mechanics" of the sacramental system remains in the background. How the passage from sign to reality is effected is a mystery in need of further exploration. How does the dialectic of sacramental revelation work? How does one move from church to Christ, from mystery to glory?

A Single Economy of Diverse Signs

Though Latourelle states that "the Constitution *Dei Verbum* does not say explicitly by what dialectic we pass from the signifier to the signified,"[128] he is confident that the choice of expression and terminology of the Council fathers gives sufficient indication of the

---

126. "Le miroir où le devin se réflète dans l'humain." Ibid., 46 [45].
127. "Et de même que le Christ était à la fois Révélateur et Signe de la révélation, ainsi l'Église est à la fois Présence de la révélation à travers les siècles et Signe de la révélation. Il existe, entre les signes de l'Église et les signes du Christ, le même rapport qui existe entre le corps mystique du Christ et son corps glorieux et ressuscité." Ibid., 68 [71].
128. "La Constitution *Dei verbum* ne dit pas explicitement par quelle dialectique nous passons du significant au signifié" Ibid., 83 [89].

nature and function of this dialectic. Consonant with the orientation of the whole Constitution is a desire to see the person of Jesus as the only hermeneutic by which this shift can be explained. In the entirety of the Word event, men and women experienced a "presence," "manifestation," or "epiphany" of "that eternal life which was with the Father" (1 John 1:2; *DV* 1), in such a way that the experience effected a meeting of signifier and signified, of sign and revelation.[129] The manifestation of Christ in the flesh is the hermeneutical key to the sacramental dialectic.[130] Through the sacrament of his humanity, Christ reveals both God and himself as God. Still it is necessary to examine this "epiphany" further, and indeed how it effects the mental shift required of the sacramental dialectic.

> But by what mental process do we pass from what we observe to the truth of what it is? How does this *unique sign* which is Christ operate on the mind? What we begin by observing is a *radiance*, a splendour (or casting back of light), emanating from a personal centre. This radiance is not simple, but complex. It is a radiance of *power*, manifesting itself in Christ's sovereignty, over the cosmos, over sickness and over death itself. It is a radiance of *truth*, manifesting itself in the gospel which Christ brings to the world, a message which has illumined and sanctified millions of human beings to whom it has been the inspiration of their lives. It is a radiance of *holiness*, manifesting itself in Christ's acts of charity and forgiveness and consummated in the silent giving of his life for the salvation of all men. It is a radiance which reaches its zenith in the miracle, unique in history, of a spontaneous and *glorious resurrection.* And yet this radiance is not confined to the past; for Christ is prolonged in time in his *Church*, marked century after century by the charisms which are his work.[131]

---

129. "A Cana, les disciples du Christ ont soupçonné que Dieu était là, présent en Personne. Ils ont eu une première intuition, confuse, mais exacte, de la gloire divine du Christ révélée à travers son humanité." Ibid., 85 [91].

130. "Dans ce qu'elle a de plus profond, l'économie chrétienne est une économie *sacramentelle*, puisqu'elle est manifestation et communication de l'invisible au moyen du visible. L'humanité du Christ est le Sacrement ou le Signe de Dieu par excellence." Ibid., 84[90].

The unique sign that is Christ operates on the mind by presenting it with a complex radiance. Within this complexity, Latourelle discerns aspects of power, truth, and holiness. This, then, is a sacramental complexity composed of the truth of the gospel and the sanctification of grace, both of which effect a power over matter and creation that might be called incarnation. Power, truth, and holiness are manifested in the doing, being, and saying of Christ, and the cumulative effect is enough to cause the transition from sign to reality. The overall effect of the incarnate signs conveys a "completeness of meaning"[132] that makes the sign itself intelligible. Witnessing the power of Jesus over creation, people are led to reflect on the nature of his own person—that is, the nature of the sign. "Who can this be?" ask the disciples when even the wind and the sea obey him (Mark 4:39-41). The same question had been asked when he had been declared "the Holy One of God" earlier in the gospel (Mark 1:24-28) and it would be asked again later when the people are amazed by the truth of his teaching (Mark 6:2-4).[133]

Essentially, Latourelle sees these aspects as "coalescing" or "casting back" to a personal presence that is at once a plenitude of love and meaning. To reveal the power, holiness, and truth of God is to reveal his love. Still, however, the process "which leads the mind from the

---

131. "Mais par quel processus mental passons-nous de ce que nous observons à la vérité de ce qui est? Comment opère sur l'esprit ce *Signe singulier* qu'est le Christ? Ce que nous observons au départ, c'est un *rayonnement*, une splendeur, émanant d'un centre personnel. Ce rayonnement n'est pas simple, mais multiforme. C'est un rayonnement de *puissance*, se manifestant par la souveraineté du Christ sur le cosmos, sur la maladie et sur la mort elle-même. C'est un rayonnement de *vérité*, se manifestant dans l'Évangile que le Christ apporte au monde: un message qui a éclairé et sanctifié les millions d'êtres qui en ont fait l'inspiration de leur vie. C'est un rayonnement de *sainteté*, se manifestant dans les gestes de pardon et de charité du Christ, et se consommant par le don silencieux de sa vie pour le salut de tous. C'est un rayonnement qui culmine dans le miracle, unique dans l'histoire, d'une *résurrection glorieuse* et spontanée. Enfin, ce rayonnement n'est pas sans lendemain, car le Christ se prolonge dans l'*Église*, son œuvre, avec les charismas qui rythment sa marche à travers les siècles." Ibid., 87 [93].
132. "D'une plénitude de sens et d'une plénitude d'amour," ibid., 87 [93].
133. Cf. ibid., 89–90 [96].

sign to the reality" requires more explicit analysis.[134] What, beyond the spontaneous reaction of people to the radiant manifestation of Christ, provides intelligibility and allows the believer to accept the sign as reality? Here Latourelle returns to the concept of "admirable proportion," that is, a "harmony" or correspondence between the radiance of a person and his testimony. Intelligibility is only possible:

> If we recognise as true the explanation he offered of the Mystery of his person, everything lights up and becomes intelligible: the synthesis which he makes of apparently contradictory figures (especially those of the suffering servant and the glorious Son of man), *and* the paradoxes of his own personality (its combination of simplicity and authority, humility and unheard of claims, a sense of sin in others and of absolute purity in himself), *and* the complex radiance of power and wisdom and holiness which is manifest in him, *and* the presence in the Church of the same paradoxes and the same charisms.[135]

This sign of Jesus Christ is twofold: expressing himself as God, Jesus is at once an expression of the Father through the Spirit. The sign is the gateway to a personal Mystery.

Latourelle points out that the paschal mystery is the "zenith" of this miraculous and spontaneous expression, and that this manifestation of radiance is prolonged in the church. The obvious conclusion here is that the radiance of power, truth, and holiness that flows from the personal center of Christ is shown in the sign of the church, which orders creation, preaches the true gospel, and is the sign and means of holiness. These aspects inhere in the church and make it an

---

134. "Le processus qui conduit l'esprit du Signe à la Réalité," ibid., 90 [96].

135. "Si nous reconnaissons comme vraie l'explication que le Christ a proposée du Mystère de sa personne, tout s'éclaire et tout devient intelligible: *et* la synthèse qu'il opère en lui de figures apparemment irréductibles entre elles (notamment celles de serviteur souffrant et de Fils de l'homme glorieux), *et* les paradoxes de sa personnalité (faite de simplicité et d'autorité, d'humilité et de prétentions inouïes, de sentiment du péché chez les autres et de pureté pour lui-même), *et* le rayonnement complexe de puissance, de sagesse et de sainteté qui se manifeste en lui, *et* la présence dans l'Église des mêmes paradoxes et des mêmes charismes." Ibid., 97–98 [104].

intelligible sign of salvation. Such a conclusion, however, has further implications. The celebration of the Eucharist persists in the church as source and summit, the liturgical "zenith" of the spontaneous expression of the person of Christ in history. Here Christ's power over creation and matter, the truth of his gospel way, and the holiness of his presence are communicated "in the time of the Church." Also present is the admirable proportion between person and testimony: the priest *in persona Christi* makes present the words and gestures of Christ and witnesses to this with his life, so that their persons coalesce and the sign becomes a reality: "Accipite et bibite ex eo omnes: Hic est enim calix Sanguinis mei novi et aeterni testamenti."[136]

The Church as Sacramental Paradox

In his subsequent chapter, "The Church, the Sign of the Coming of Salvation in Jesus Christ," Latourelle concentrates completely on the dialectic of the sign of the church by seeking to explain how the church is the sign and actualization of God's salvation in the world. In analyzing the church as sign, a threefold meaning can be recognised: The church is the sign, the sacrament of salvation, because "she is the place where Christ the saviour acts,"[137] where salvation is realized. Secondly, the church is the sign of salvation because "she both represents and images"[138] union between God and humanity, and among individuals one with another. In this sense, the church "is already the mystery of communion in practice."[139] And lastly, there is a sense in which the actualization of salvation and communion in each person gives a radiance to the church that makes

---

136. *Missale Romanum* (Rome: Typis Polyglottis Vaticanis, 1975), 452.
137. "Elle est le lieu où agit le Christ Sauveur par l'opération de l'Espirit." Latourelle, *Le Christ et l'Église*, 99 [105].
138. "Car elle *figure*, elle *représent*," ibid., 99 [106].
139. "Elle est déjà mystère de communion en exercise." Ibid., 100 [106].

of it a sign to the nations and a motive of credibility. In the same way in which the radiance of Christ "cast back" light on the reality and credibility of his person, so "the life of the members of Christ in unity and charity" casts back light on the essence and credibility of the church, locus of salvation and source of unity.[140]

> When the life of the members of Christ in unity and charity is in accord with the gospel, and when this accord is deeply lived, this life becomes a sign, not merely an allusive but an *expressive* sign, of the reality signified: it manifests visibly, even to the eyes of nonbelievers, that the Church is really the *locus* of salvation in Jesus Christ as she proclaims, and that the Spirit of Christ, which is the Spirit of love, really does live among men. The Church then becomes the visible and historical sign of the Spirit of Christ, who is the invisible source and principle of unity in the Church. Seen in this perspective, the economy of sacramental signs and the economy of the signs of revelation are obviously not parallel and independent economies. On the contrary, they are reunited, and each articulates the other. For it is insofar as the ecclesial community draws its life from the source in which the sacraments arise, that it becomes a "sign lifted up before the nations."[141]

The visible unity and charity of the faithful is a witness, by its very presence, that salvation is a fact and is active in the church. The church is testimony to a force for unity and sanctification within itself, and this sign, in conjunction with the gospel it preaches, gives

140. "De même que le Christ *faisait signe* aux hommes de son temps par le rayonnement de tout lui-même (doctrine, sagesse, sainteté, miracles, passion, mort, résurrection), ainsi l'Église, par le rayonnement de tout son être (expansion, unité, stabilité, sainteté, fécondité), *fait signe* aux hommes de tous les temps qu'elle tient son message et sa mission de Dieu. Elle participe à la gloire du Christ." Ibid., 102–3 [109].

141. "Lorsque la vie d'unité et de charité des membres du Christ est en accord avec l'Évangile, et que cet accord est vécu avec intensité, cette vie devient un signe, non seulement allusif, mais *expressif* de la réalité signifiée: elle manifeste dans la visibilité, même aux yeux des non-croyants, que l'Église est vraiment le lieu du salut en Jésus-Christ, ainsi qu'elle le proclame, et que l'Esprit du Christ, qui est Esprit d'amour, habite vraiment parmi les hommes. L'Église devient alors le signe visible et historique de l'Esprit du Christ, principe invisible de l'unité de l'Église. Dans cette perspective, on le voit, économie des signes de la révélation ne sont pas des économies parallèles et indépendantes. Tout au contraire, elles se rejoignent et s'articulent l'une à l'autre. Car c'est dans la mesure où la communauté ecclésiale puise à la source qui jaillit des sacrements qu'elle devient 'signe dressé à la vue des nations'." Ibid., 101 [107–8].

credibility to the church's claim that Christ is present and active within her, and that it is by his Spirit that people are made one and sanctified.[142] It is for this reason that Latourelle can say that "the process by which we pass directly from the Church to her divine origin takes its bearings from phenomenology rather than history."[143] The dialectical shift of the sacrament that leads the mind from sign to reality is founded on the congruence between what the sign displays and the witness of the message. The argument is that of the "admirable proportion" that exists within the economy of salvation between sign and witness, sacrament and reality—an argument that Latourelle projects beyond the signs of revelation to the sacramental signs of the church. In acknowledging the role of the seven sacraments in effecting the unity and sanctity of her members, Latourelle recognises a certain unity of function between the sign of the church and the sign of the sacraments. The shape of the ecomomy of both is identical and, in the same way in which a unity can be established between Christ and the church through the sacramental economy, so a unity between the church and the sacraments can be likewise defined.[144] Hence "the economy of sacramental signs and the economy of the signs of revelation are obviously not parallel and independent economies."

142. "L'Église annonce qu'elle a une mission de salut et que cette mission est divine. D'autre part, l'ensemble des traits miraculeux qu'elle manifeste, induit légitimement à penser que cette prétention est fondée. Si donc l'Église est de Dieu, et si elle atteste qu'elle a été fondée par le Christ, Fils du Dieu vivant, pour proposer aux hommes l'Évangile du salut, il faut accueillir son témoignage comme véridique et y ajouter foi. Dans cette démarche, nous reconnaissons directement l'Église comme Église de Dieu, et donc comme croyable." Ibid., 103, [110].

143. "La démarche par laquelle nous passons directement de l'Église à son origine divine, relève de la phénoménologie autant que de l'histoire." Ibid.

144. "The same relation which existed between the signs of revelation and Christ himself also exists between the signs and the Church. In the body of the Church, Christ prolongs his presence and activity on earth. The same things that revealed God in Christ now reveal God in the Church." R. Latourelle, "The Internal Coherence of the Signs of Revelation," *Theology Digest* 16 (1968): 226.

The movement from Christ to the church to the liturgical life of the individual is the process of the sacramental economy whereby Christ is projected and persists in history as a result of his resurrection. Yet, as an economy of sacramental re-presentation, it is just as easily concertinaed so that "the ecclesial community draws its life from the source in which the sacraments arise." To insist that the signs of revelation and the sacraments of the church are not parallel or independent economies is to insist on a single linear progression capable of extending forward or back, a dynamic that allows the liturgical celebration of the sacraments of the church to be understood as the contemporary actualization of divine revelation.[145]

While Latourelle is keen to assert that the relationship between the economy of the signs of revelation and the sacramental economy is neither parallel nor independent, he refrains from the positive suggestion that the two are identical. The two economies are united and articulate each other, but they are not here regarded as the same. As shall be seen later, the sacraments, and particularly the Eucharist, are the place where the sign of the church is best expressed, but, as Latourelle reminds us, "We have not the assurance of Cardinal Dechamps at the time of the First Vatican Council, who saw in the Church a sign which was efficacious and easy to recognise."[146] These

---

145. Importantly, Latourelle does not use the word *actualization* specifically of the sacraments, and, when he speaks of the actualization of the word of God in the church, it is concerned with theology's making current the content of the tradition: "Ce travail d'*actualisation* de l'unique et immutable parole du Christ s'articule à une tradition commencée aux origines de l'Église et jamais interrompue. . . . Si cette *actualisation* est l'œuvre du Magistère, elle est encore plus l'œuvre de la prédication et de la théologie. Celle-ci représente l'effort constant de l'Église pour demeurer en contact avec le monde, ses problèmes, ses doutes, ses projets. C'est par la théologie que s'opère la rencontre de la foi et du monde contemporain." R. Latourelle, *Le Christ et l'Église*, 126–27 [137]. Even in his article "Faith: Personal Encounter with God," there is no reflection on the sacraments as a source of faith and therefore of personal encounter. The categories of word and witness as elaborated by theology predominate. See Latourelle, "Faith: Personal Encounter with God," *Theology Digest* 10 (1962): 233–38.

146. "En tout cas, nous n'avons plus l'assurance du cardinal Dechamps, à l'époque de Vatican I, qui voyait dans l'Église un signe efficace et facile à reconnaître." R. Latourelle, *Le Christ et l'Église*, 113 [122–23].

days, it is the paradoxical nature of the sign that allows the mystery to be further fathomed and the reality discovered. The equivalence on which the sacramental economy depends is, in these modern times, more than ever an equivalence of paradox rather than of simple correspondence.[147]

> In the *Church,* a new type of society appears, where, as well as indications of her human and earthly condition, there is, as it were, a transparency, through which shine *incunabula* of the heavenly Jerusalem. There is already to be seen in her, in outline, the face of mankind assembled in unity and charity, in the image of the Trinity's communion of life. From this consistency between the gospel of Christ and the paradoxical characteristics of the Church, we may legitimately infer that the Church is really, as she declares, the sign of the advent of God among men, the place where the Presence of salvation in Jesus Christ is to be found. The *paradox* cloaks the *Mystery.*[148]

Essentially, the consistent correspondence that Latourelle recognizes between the gospel of Christ and the church is one of paradox. It is, however, at once this very paradox that "cloaks" and is "transparent" to the realities beneath. The inner reality illumines the veiling paradox and allows the onlooker to perceive in outline the concealed truth. The paradox is both the barrier from and the means to the mystery. In three successive chapters, Latourelle examines the paradoxes of unity, temporality, and sanctity, and, concentrating on the third of these, uses this method to gain a deeper insight into the sacramental mystery of the church. By means of their paradoxical

---

147. Cf. Martelet, *Les idées maîtresses de Vatican II,* 65–129.

148. "Dans l'*Église,* un type nouveau de société apparaît, laissant transparaître, avec des indices de sa condition humaine et terrestre, des traits plus lumineux, qui sont comme l'esquisse de la Jérusalem céleste. En elle s'ébauche la figure d'une humanité enfin rassemblée dans l'unité et la charité, à l'image de la communion trinitaire. Cette cohérence entre l'Évangile du Christ et les traits paradoxaux de l'Église, induit légitimement à conclure que l'Église est vraiment, parmi les hommes, comme elle le déclare, le signe de la venue de Dieu, le lieu de la Présence du salut en Jésus-Christ. Le *paradoxe* est le revêtement du *Mystère.*" Latourelle, *Le Christ et l'Église,* 242 [271].

structure, he is able to establish the link between the hypostatic union of the God-man and a church that is both scattered and one. The paradox of the eternal Son born in time can be traced in a church that is both timeless and rooted historically, and the paradox of the sinless one made sin seen in a church that is at once spotless bride and made up of sinners. Temporality, unity, and sanctity are three *incunabula* of the heavenly Jerusalem: three paradoxical characteristics of the church that point to her authenticity. In the case of temporality, Latourelle examines the enduring nature of the church and, on the basis of data that span almost two thousand years, builds a theological argument that asserts that beyond and behind the church as a phenomenon lies the mysterious action of the Spirit.[149] In the same way, the unity of the church is examined, the paradox being that:

> the Church seeks both *unity* and *catholicity*. Not only is she called together, assembled (internal unity) but—as witness the history of the missions—she calls together and assembles all the peoples of the earth. Catholic unity tries to triumph over the divisions of the spirit and the flesh. It transcends the biological community, with the all-powerful bonds which unite the family.[150]

Hence here on earth, is a glimpse of the heavenly city where God dwells among humankind.

Particularly interesting is the way in which Latourelle discusses the question of the sanctity of the church. This he regards as "the greatest paradox," the one "which gives rise to the most questioning."[151] Examples are quickly put forward that revolve around the fact that

---

149. Ibid., 121 [132].

150. "Le paradoxe est que l'Église poursuive à la fois *l'unité* et la *catholicité*. Non seulement elle est convoquée, rassemblée (unité interne), mais encore, comme en témoigne l'histoire des missions, elle convoque et rassemble tous les hommes de la terre. L'unité catholique s'efforce de triompher des divisions de l'esprit et du sang. Elle transcende la communauté biologique, aux liens si puissants, de la famille." Ibid., 140 [153].

151. "Le troisième et plus grand paradoxe de l'Église est celui de la coexistence en elle du péché et de la sainteté. C'est aussi celui qui suscite le plus de questions, même chez les croyants, car pour beaucoup il est Pierre d'achoppement, scandale, pur non-sens." Ibid., 189 [211].

the church displays a history of both holiness and sin.[152] The paradox of holiness is a sign that reveals the veracity of the claims of the church. Such holiness is a revelation of the sanctity of Christ, the foundation and life of the church. Yet this revelation, this sacrament of salvation, is made by way of sinful people. In seeking to explain the paradoxical nature of the holiness of the church and how it functions as a sign, Latourelle looks to the seven sacraments by way of example.[153] This would seem to be more than a convenient analogy. Latourelle's own theological reflection draws a similar conclusion to that of the majority of the theologians he examines by way of background.[154] The *how* of the paradox of holiness in the church is the *how* of the seven sacraments. Evidently, here is a development

---

152. "Comment, en effet, dans un monde sécularisé, qui se suffit à lui-même, l'Église peut-elle être signe d'une réalité transcendante et nécessaire à l'accomplissement de l'existence humaine? Comment surtout une Église ternie par le péché peut-elle encore être *signe expressif* du salut qu'elle annonce? Comment peut-elle se dire signe élevé à la vue des nations? N'est-elle pas plutôt un antisigne et un contre-témoignage?" Ibid., 193 [216].

153. In the section, "L'Église, Peuple de Dieu 'appelé' à la sainteté par l'Évangile, consacré et sanctifié par le baptême," of chapter 8, Latourelle alludes to baptism, Eucharist, and sacramental ordination in order to explain how the church can be the "chaste prostitute" she has been termed. Cf. ibid., 218–19 [244–45].

154. By way of example, here is Latourelle's summary of a number of theologians: A. de Bovis: "Cette sainteté de ressemblance consiste à exprimer l'Esprit du Christ, à laisser le Christ envahir notre existence, modeler nos pensées, nos actes, nos désirs: à vivre et à mourir comme le Christ. Cette sainteté de ressemblance ne saurait manquer totalement à l'Église, car le caractère sacramental 'constitué pour l'Église verra se lever en elle des saints au sens le plus fort du terme, c'est-à-dire des hommes configurés à l'image du Fils de Dieu, vivant pour Dieu en Jésus-Christ." Ibid., 207 [232]. Y.-M. Congar: "Comme institution, elle précède la communauté des fidèles et depend de Dieu: dans son libre décret et dans le Christ qui précontient l'Église, comme aussi dans les moyens établis par le Christ pour réunir et sanctifier les hommes. L'Église est sainte en vertu des *dons* qu'elle a reçus de Dieu: dépôt de la foi, sacrements, ministères. 'Ces réalités sont saintes en elle-mêmes, venant de Dieu, et elles visent à la sainteté. Elles sont, de soi, des instruments par lesquels Dieu sanctifie. On parle parfois à leur sujet de sainteté objective.'" Ibid., 208–9 [234–35]. K. Rahner: "Le péché est la contradiction de l'Église, et le pécheur, s'il reste membre de l'Église, prive son appartenance à l'Église de son sens et de son efficacité, à la manière d'un sacrement valide, mais infructueux." Ibid., 211 [237–38]. G. Martelet: "De plus, l'Église n'est jamais subjuguée totalement par le péché; elle ne cesse jamais d'être instrument du salut du monde. Même au sein de ses misères, elle demeure signe de sainteté et, en ce sens, elle participe à la *sacramentalité*. Il en est de l'Église comme des sacrements dont la valeur de sainteté ne se ramène pas à la valeur des hommes qui les reçoivent ou qui les donnent, mais à celle du Christ qui les fonde et qui ne cesse de s'offrir par eux." Ibid., 212–13 [239].

of Latourelle's position in *Théologie de la Révélation*, where he had distinguished revelation and sacrament "as different and analogous forms of this vast divine economy through which salvation is given to us by means of signs."[155] As has been discussed, the grounds for this distinction are the following: "Revelation *tends* to the obedience of faith, which is 'the beginning of salvation, the foundation and root of all justification' (*DS* 801), but it does not produce faith *ex opere operato*."[156] Yet it is this *ex opere operato* quality, this sense of infallible guarantee that can be recognised in the seven sacraments, that Latourelle invokes to explain the revelatory nature of holiness in the church. Though the distinction established in the earlier work may still exist, in *Le Christ et l'Église: signes du salut*, the tendency of revelation to produce the obedience of faith is now regarded as falling little short of the *ex opere operato* function of the sacraments. At the same time, and conversely, Latourelle is brought closer to the assertion that the liturgical celebration of the sacraments is revelation.

The final aspect highlighted in this passage is the way in which it alludes to the liturgical nature of the heavenly assembly that we glimpse in outline in the church. The allusion is to the liturgy of the just that is described in the book of Revelation, where all are gathered about the altar of the Lamb. Surely the conclusion can be made that the church is at her most transparent when celebrating the sacred mysteries of the Eucharist?

---

155. "D'une façon générale, révélation et sacrements peuvent être considérés comme des formes *divers et analogues* de cette vaste économie divine par laquelle le salut nous est donné à travers les signes." Latourelle, *Théologie de la Révélation*, 465 [385].
156. "La révélation *tend* à l'obéissance de la foi, qui est le 'commencement du salut, le fondement et la racine de toute justification' (D 801) mais elle ne produit pas la foi *ex opere operato*, à la manière du sacrement." Ibid., 466 [385].

Eucharist:
External Sign of Inner Reality

It is in the Eucharist that the church attains the greatest degree of actuality, visibility, and intensity. In essence, the church is the presence through the centuries of the Word made flesh. She is the concretization throughout history of the saving will of God that became a fact in Christ. Hence, she reaches the maximum of her palpability when Christ himself, in the consecration of the Mass, is present within the community of his faithful people, dispensing to them his salvation. The celebration of the Eucharist is the most intense way for the church to make herself present at a particular point in time and space. It makes visible and tangible the unity of Christians with Christ and their unity in charity with one another. The eucharistic celebration is therefore an *epiphany* of the mystery of the church in its deepest sense.[157]

After dwelling on the church as a sign expressed particularly by her constitutive paradoxes, Latourelle endeavors to return to an appreciation of the whole. Aware that theological dissection results in a mechanical and artificial picture of the passage from sign to signified, he recognizes that the coalescing of individual details happens as part of the everyday experience of life. This is a unified action that precedes synthetic or conceptual analysis: "In this experiential and intuitive awareness, it is not necessary to represent the sign conceptually, or to analyze the process by which the mind is led from the sign to the reality: in a single operation, in a sort of direct vision, the mind penetrates through the sign to the reality it signifies."[158]

---

157. "L'eucharistie est le lieu où l'Église atteint son maximum d'actualité, et de visibilité et d'intensité. Dans son essence, l'Église est la présence à travers les siècles du Verbe fait chair. Elle est la concrétisation historique de la volonté salvifique de Dieu qui s'est faite événement dans le Christ. Dès lors, l'Église atteint son maximum de palpabilité et d'intensité là où le Christ, par la consécration, est lui-même présent dans la communauté de ses fidèles en y dispensant le salut. La célébration de l'eucharistie constitue la façon la plus intense pour l'Église de se rendre présente en un point du temps et de l'espace. Elle rend visible et palpable l'unité des fidèles avec le Christ et leur unité entre eux, dans la charité. La célébration eucharistique est donc une *épiphanie* du mystère de l'Église dans ce qu'il a de plus profond." Latourelle, *Le Christ et l'Église*, 231 [259].

In the passage above, Latourelle identifies the Eucharist as the event in which the paradoxes of the church can be experienced as a single, unified sign. A moment "actual," "visible," and intense, it is an holistic experience of the saving will of God in history. The celebration of Mass reconciles intelligibly but mysteriously the paradoxes of time, unity, and holiness. By means of a sacramental structure, it unites the commemorative, demonstrative, and prognostic aspects into a single revelatory now.[159] The celebration is also the visible realization of the unity of those who live in Christ: "Not only the real and actual unity of members of the same Body, but also the actuating dynamism of union which is orientated toward bringing together mankind as such, in order to constitute the mystical Body of Christ."[160] So drawn together, these sinful people constitute the spotless bride of Christ.[161]

Here Latourelle begins to recognize the revelatory role of the liturgy, albeit in an implicit fashion. The church as sign of revelation has tended to be discussed as a monumental and overarching reality, but the church as she is constituted and understood liturgically gives an actuality and edge to Latourelle's understanding of the revelation transmitted through her. It also affords clarity to the way in which he perceives the relationship between the sacraments and the signs of revelation, because the church now has a definite and specific shape.

158. "Dans cette connaissance de type expérimental et intuitif, il n'est pas nécessaire de se représenter le signe conceptuellement et de décomposer le processus qui conduit du signe à la réalité: dans un acte unique, dans une sorte de plongée directe, l'esprit pénètre, à travers le signe, jusqu'à la réalité qu'il désigne." Ibid., 279 [313].

159. "L'eucharistie recueille aussi tous les moments de la *vie de l'Église*. Elle est le repas du souvenir, le mémorial de la passion et de la mort salvifique du Christ, qui a donné naissance à son Église. Dans le présent, elle est communion de tous les fidèles au Christ vivant et glorifié, et communion des fidèles entre eux dans la charité. Enfin, repas d'espérance, elle figure et anticipe le repas eschatologique où tous les élus seront réunis à la table du Seigneur." Ibid., 251 [282].

160. "Car la célébration eucharistique ne représente pas seulement l'unité réelle et actuelle des membres du même corps: elle est aussi animée d'un dynamisme unificateur, qui tend à rassembler les hommes pour constituer le Corps mystique du Christ." Ibid., 251 [282].

161. "Enfin, elle reproduit par la présence réelle du Christ dans le sacrement où il se donne en nourriture, la synthèse de la Présence personnelle et spirituelle du Christ glorieux avec le Christ, Verbe incarné dans l'histoire." Ibid.

The church is most fully and recognizably herself when she celebrates the Eucharist. Then she is most clearly a sign of revelation and then she is sacrament in the fullest sense. Therefore, Latourelle can afford to say, "It is precisely in the measure in which the Church lives to the full her reality as a sacrament, an efficacious sign, that she will become at the same time for those outside her the sign of the coming of salvation into the world. At this point, the sacramental economy and the economy of the signs of revelation meet and tend to coincide."[162]

The purpose of *Le Christ et l'Église: signes du salut* was to examine the general and foundational signs of revelation so as to establish the sacramental paradigm for all subsequent and related signs. Essentially, this is to question the nature of the relationship between the signs of revelation and sacramental signs. To clarify the economy whereby revelation takes place in Christ and his church is to discern a pattern that can be recognized within the economy of the seven sacraments. However, without taking into account the entirety of the signs and wonders that accompany revelation in Christ, the picture is incomplete.[163] To complete the examination of the economy of revelation is the task of *Miracles de Jésus et théologie du miracle*. This

---

162. "C'est précisément dans la mesure où l'Église vit en plénitude sa réalité de sacrement, de signe efficace, qu'elle devient en même temps, pour les hommes du dehors, signe de l'avènement du salut dans le monde. A ce moment, économie sacramentaire et économie des signes de la révélation se rencontrent et tendent à coïncider." Ibid., 252 [283–84]. A reflection in a more recent spiritual book would suggest that Latourelle is willing to go beyond the reserve he shows in the phrase "tend to coincide." He states, "Dans la révélation, il y a compénétration et soutien mutuel des œuvres et de la parole. Que serait, en effet, une économie d'incarnation réduite à un pur enseignement doctrinal? Une gnose, une philosophie, sans véritable impact sur la vie. La parole du Christ *opère* ce qu'elle *dit*. Quand le Christ *dit*: 'Sois guéri,' il *opère la guérison*. Dans l'eucharistie, les paroles du Christ *opèrent* ce qu'elles dissent. Par la parole du Christ, la réalité de sa présence substantielle *advient*: ce qui est dit se produit. Le Christ se donne réellement, tout entier." Latourelle, *Seigneur Jésus, montre-nous ton visage* (Québec: Bellarmin, 2001), 209–10.

163. "The book seems written for professors and practitioners of apologetics who may be at a bit of a loss since Vatican II. . . . I wish Latourelle had extended his insights on the role of signs back to the case of miracles (which, with prophesies, were one of the mainstays of the older apologetics)." P. Misner, review of R. Latourelle, *Christ and the Church: Signs of Salvation*, *Theological Studies* 34 (1973): 185–86.

book concludes Latourelle's investigation into the signs of revelation, and in turn provides a summary appraisal of his understanding of the relationship between revelation and the seven sacraments.

Completing the Christological Miracle:
Miracles de Jésus et Théologie du Miracle

In a review of *Miracles de Jésus et théologie du miracle* in the *Toronto Journal of Theology*, Wendy Cotter bemoans Latourelle's protracted examination of the historicity of the miracle stories. She wonders, "Who are the opponents against whom he crusades? The biblical experts in miracle narrative today (eg. Achtemeier, Theissen, Kee) are received favourably. And it is not the case that responsible biblical critics are denouncing the historicity of Jesus' miracles."[164] Latourelle was to make his position clear a year later in the article "Absence and Presence of Fundamental Theology at Vatican II," part of the three-volume *Vatican II: Assessment and Perspectives Twenty-Five Years After (1962–1987)*, which he edited. Here he suggests "a real conspiracy against the miracles of Jesus and their historical truth. The ground seems to be shaky and full of pitfalls even among exegetes and dogmaticians. It is considered bad form to speak of miracles."[165] Latourelle regarded the lack of status that miracle narratives had in the world of biblical exegesis and fundamental theology as symptomatic of a greater problem: the crisis of credibility that beset the postconciliar Church. In the years following the Council, faith in the historical truth of the gospels, the person of Jesus, and the authenticity

---

164. Wendy J. Cotter, review of R. Latourelle, *The Miracles of Jesus and the Theology of Miracles*, in *Toronto Journal of Theology* 6, no. 1 (1990): 118–19. In fact, Latourelle had clarified both the culture and the critics that had given rise to his anxieties in an earlier and carefully detailed essay: See R. Latourelle, "Authenticité historique des miracles de Jésus: Essai de critériologie," *Gregorianum* 54 (1973): 225–62.

165. Latourelle, "Absence and Presence of Fundamental Theology at Vatican II," 390–91.

of a supernatural order of revelation was sorely tested. Years before, Rudolf Bultmann had poisoned the theological waters, and many found in him "the expression of their own skepticism disguised as science."[166] The church shied away from predicating of Jesus and herself anything that would upset the sensibilities of a modern person, who constantly measured Christ "with a human yardstick."[167] Inertia seemed also to hamper the implementation of the principles of the Council's reform. As Latourelle said in 1988, "The Church has moved from a past not completely vanished to a future that is only just beginning."[168] Twenty-five years after the Council, he remained convinced that fundamental theology would be the principal agent of this movement. And if his work as a whole is considered as drawing out, reinforcing, and communicating the fundamental theology of the conciliar and postconciliar period, then *Miracles de Jésus et théologie du miracle* constitutes the apex of his work. Here Latourelle seeks to answer the crucial question, "Is Jesus identifiable as God-among-us?".[169]

Situating Miracles in the Economy of Salvation

Having examined the authenticity and credibility of the Gospels, and having dwelt on the revelation of Christ and his church in the light of modern society, Latourelle now seeks to explain how the "sovereign lordship of the Almighty, the holiness of the Thrice Holy, and the wisdom of the Logos. . . somehow 'swoop down' upon us, shatter our categories, and make us see and understand what is wholly other."[170] Essentially, Latourelle is keen to clarify the role

---

166. Ibid., 389.
167. Ibid., 391.
168. R. Latourelle, "Introduction," in Latourelle, *Vatican II: Assessment and Perspectives*, 1:xv.
169. "Jésus est-il identifiable comme Dieu-parmi-nous?" R. Latourelle, *Miracles de Jésus et théologie du miracle*, 13 [1].

of miracles in revelation, so that, "better situated"[171] by twentieth-century conciliar theology, their crucial apologetic function can be recaptured and renewed for the modern world. *Le Christ et l'Église: signes du salut,* faithful to the spirit of the Second Vatican Council, established the fact that all signs of revelation have their origin and meaning in Christ. The function of *Miracles de Jésus et théologie du miracle* is to make the connection between the basic signs of Christ and the church and the particular signs of revelation, specifically miracles. From the beginning, the sacramental structure of revelation is crucial to Latourelle's argument.

> Sacramental theology has likewise been renewed due to a better approach to the mystery of Christ and the Church. Contemporary thought indissolubly connects Christ as the sign of God, the Church as the sign of Christ, and the sacraments as actions of Christ done in and through the Church. The encounter of human beings with God takes place under the appearances of the primordial sacrament, that is, Christ, who is the saving presence of God in humanity, and through the mediation of the sacraments, which are earthly prolongations of the glorified Christ. The Eucharist is the high point in this encounter with Christ; it is "the source and summit of Christian life," the sacrament that signifies and effects the unity of God's people in love (*LG* 11). The Eucharist is therefore the ecclesial sacrament par excellence and the one which is being given an increasingly privileged place in instruction. For in fact the Eucharist gathers up all the phases of the life of Christ and the life of the Church.[172]

170. "La souveraineté du Tout-puissant, la sainteté du trois fois Saint, la sagesse du Logos doivent en quelque sorte 'fondre' sur nous, faire éclater nos catégories, nous faire voir et entendre du *Tout-autre*." Ibid., 15 [3].

171. "Mieux *situé*," ibid., 15 [2].

172. "La théologie sacramentaire s'est également renouvelée par une meilleure approche du mystère du Christ et de l'Église. La réflexion contemporaine relie indissolublement le Christ Signe de Dieu, l'Église Signe du Christ, et les sacrements, gestes du Christ accomplis dans l'Église et par l'Église. La rencontre de l'homme avec Dieu s'opère sous les espèces du sacrement primordial qu'est le Christ, présence salvifique de Dieu parmi les hommes, et par la médiation des sacrements qui sont les prolongements terrestres du Christ glorifié. L'Eucharistie, est le point culminant de cette rencontre du Christ: 'la source et le sommet de la vie chrétienne,' le sacrement qui signifie et réalise l'unité de charité de tout le Peuple de Dieu (LG 11). L'Eucharistie, par suite, est le sacrement ecclésial par excellence, celui que la présentation

In his opening chapter, which outlines "Problems of Approach and Preunderstanding," Latourelle indicates the point from which his theology will depart and the methodology he will employ. Indicating the Copernican change that theology has undergone since Vatican II,[173] Latourelle adopts its anthropological and christological approach. The human person is the central point of reference for theology and Jesus Christ is its only explanatory key. "In giving this approach a privileged place," he says, "theology is simply being faithful once more to the very movement of revelation itself and to the spirit of the liturgy which is entirely centred on Christ and the paschal mystery."[174] It may be said that here, implicitly and for the first time, Latourelle recognises the liturgy as a source of revelation that theology can explore profitably. The liturgy, centered on Christ, is faithful to the movement of revelation, and the Eucharist is "the place where the faithful express by their lives and manifest to others 'the mystery of Christ and the real nature of the true Church' (*SC* 2)."[175]

The liturgy is the place where the fundamental signs of revelation are encountered, those of Christ and the church. It is also the place where the particular signs of the sacraments and prophecy are encountered. In the church is manifest the pattern of the relationship that exists between the general and particular signs of revelation,

pédagogique elle-même tend à privilégier de plus en plus. L'Eucharistie, en effet, recueille tous les moments de la vie du Christ et de la vie de l'Église." Ibid., 25 [12].

173. Rahner speaks of this transformation of sacramentology as a result of "certain faith insights" as a Copernican change, and one which allowed a new and more vigorous theology of the sacraments to develop. See Rahner, *Meditations on the Sacraments* (London: Burns and Oates, 1979; originally published as *Die Siebenfältige Gabe* Munich: Ars Sacra, 1974), quoted in G. B. Kelly, ed., *Karl Rahner: Theologian of the Graced Search for Meaning* (Minneapolis: Augsburg, 1992), 282.

174. "En privilégiant cette approche, la théologie, à vrai dire, ne fait que retrouver sa fidélité au mouvement même de la révélation et à l'esprit de la liturgie, toute centrée sur le Christ et sur le mystère pascal." Latourelle, *Miracles de Jésus et théologie du miracle*, 22 [10].

175. Iibd.,

which will be the index for understanding the relationship between Jesus and his miracles.

Latourelle parallels the shift in understanding that has taken place in sacramental theology with the shift necessary to establish a credible theology of miracles. Both have "been renewed due to a better approach to the mystery of Christ and the Church," and a right understanding of both is based on the "indissoluble connection" of Christ, church, and sacrament. This is because all the encounters of human beings with God take "place under the appearance of the primordial sacrament that is Christ." It was only in the first half of the twentieth century that this concept began to be grasped with any depth. Previously, theology had been marked by the extrinsicism symptomatic of the scholastic approach. The function of miracles, as understood by the majority of pre-Council teachings, was to be testatory signs that "enable us to establish with certainty the divine origin of the teaching on salvation."[176]

Significantly, as Latourelle points out, Vatican I regarded the church as the only sign that fell "outside this extrinsicist perspective."[177] However, this in itself was to become problematic for theology, for "when Vatican I spoke of the sign of the Church in terms of a transcendence in the moral order that is analogous to the transcendence of physical forces in a miracle, it led apologetics into an impasse from which it had no way out."[178] As *Le Christ et L'Église: signes du salut* made quite apparent, the ambiguity of a

---

176. "Dans tous ces textes, les signes ont un rôle d'*attestation*: ils permettent d'établir avec certitude l'origine divine de la doctrine du salut." Ibid., 27, [14]. Such a function can be clearly contrasted with that laid out in an article written just prior to *Miracles de Jésus et théologie du miracle*. See R. Latourelle, "Originalité et Fonctions des Miracles de Jésus," *Gregorianum* 66 (1985): 641–53.

177. "Échappe à cette perspective extrinséciste." Latourelle, *Miracles de Jésus et théologie du miracle*, 27 [14].

178. "Vatican I, toutefois, en proposant le signe de l'Église en des termes de dépassement des forces physiques, dans le cas du miracle, a engagé l'apologétique dans une impasse dont elle n'a pu sortir." Ibid.

church composed of sinners and with a history of sin did, for future generations, make an uneasy analogy with the transcendence of the physical in miracles. This was experienced in much the same way as the humble church of Vatican II, always in need of purification, was felt to bear scant resemblance to the church triumphant of previous ages. The key to theology is christological, and the analogies that theological discourse develop, must, for coherence, be rooted in Christ. This is because "the signs flow from a personal centre: Christ himself; they are the many forms of the Son's epiphany in the midst of humanity."[179] The only analogies that were to be coherent and fruitful in the context of a post–Vatican II theology were those grounded in the person of Christ.

Miracles Make Manifest the Word of Salvation

In emphasizing Christ as at once the fullness of the divine self-manifestation and the supreme sign of that revelation, Vatican II points to a unity between signifier and signified that exists in all the signs of revelation because of their unique and personal source. It is because of this common origin that an analogy can be drawn between the diverse signs of the divine economy. As the focus and completion of the divine self-disclosure, Christ is the hermeneutical key to all the signs of God's self-manifestation. For this reason, each revelatory sign is made intelligible only by reference to its origin in the life and ministry of Jesus, and that as ultimately defined by the paschal mystery. As the Constitution on Divine Revelation makes clear, Christ "completed and perfected revelation and confirmed it with guarantees, [and] he did this by the total fact of his presence and self-manifestation—by words and works, signs and miracles, but

179. "Les signes éminent de ce Centre personnel qu'est le Christ lui-même: ils sont le rayonnement multiforme de l'épiphanie du Fils parmi les hommes." Ibid., 28 [15].

above all by his death and glorious resurrection from the dead, and finally by sending the Spirit of truth."[180]

This then is why, when defining a method of approach at the beginning of his study, Latourelle seeks a liturgical element to his argument and draws the parallel with sacramental theology. Analogously, sacraments and miracles are faithful "to the very movement of revelation" that is "entirely centred on Christ and the paschal mystery," and on which both miracles and the liturgical celebration of the sacraments are founded. The two have a common source and revelatory shape.

> Miracles are, in fact, always connected with the event of the word of salvation or with revelation. This word may be that of the Old Testament, announcing and promising salvation yet to come; it may be the word of God that was made flesh and became an event in Jesus Christ; it may be the word of the Church, which renders present and efficacious until the end of time the saving message uttered once for all. Miracles are always in the service of the word, either as an element in revelation or as an attestation of that revelation's authenticity.[181]

It may seem strange to suggest a similarity between the revelatory shape of sacraments and that of miracles. However, by stressing the relationship between miracle and word, Latourelle makes this comparison easier. He describes miracles as interpersonal signs that communicate a salvific message "like a divine utterance."[182] The word of God, as has been emphasized throughout the work of Latourelle, is more than propositional words—it has an event character. Miracles are connected with the event of revelation and, to varying degrees,

---

180. Ibid.
181. "Le miracle, en effet, est toujours en relation avec l'événement de la Parole du salut ou Révélation: qu'il s'agisse de la Parole de l'Ancien Testament qui annonce et promet le salut à venir, ou de la Parole de Dieu faite chair et devenue Événement en Jésus Christ, ou de la Parole de l'Église, qui présentialise et actualise jusqu'à la fin des temps la parole de salut donnée une fois pour toutes. Le miracle est toujours au service de la Parole, soit comme élément de la Révélation, soit comme attestation de son authenticité et de son efficacité." Ibid., 322–23 [280].
182. "Un langage divin." Ibid., 322 [280].

they embody the message of salvation. Here again, Latourelle establishes the sacramental sequence of revelation: Christ, church, and sacraments. Miracles have accompanied this chain of events not only as corroborative signs, but as elements of the revelatory message.[183] Miracles are part of the incarnational movement of revelation: "They are saving words that find expression in intelligible, meaningful actions."[184] In turn, these awesome actions give credibility to the word they embody. By such a theology, Latourelle points to the enrichment of the conceptual understanding of miracles that occurred between the First and Second Vatican Councils.[185] Such a shift is at the inception of Latourelle's understanding of miracles as polyvalent signs.[186]

Miracles as Vehicles of Revelation

Miracles are, at once, communications of God's power and love; they are signs of the divine mission and reveal the kingdom; they are actions that speak of Christ's glory, reveal the mystery of the Trinity, and symbolize the whole of the sacramental economy, as they prefigure the ultimate transformation that will come about in Christ. Each of these aspects "both interpret[s] and represent[s] the mysterious reality."[187] In describing their multifunctional nature, Latourelle gives to miracles a definition well known of the sacraments: "Expressive images of the spiritual gifts offered to human

---

183. Cf. R. Latourelle, "Miracle et Révélation," *Gregorianum* 43 (1962): 496–501.

184. "Ils sont parole de salut, s'exprimant en gestes intelligibles, signifiants." R. Latourelle, *Miracles de Jésus et théologie du miracle*, 325 [281].

185. Ibid., 325–26, [281–82].

186. Latourelle details the elements of this "polyvalence" as a manifestation of God's *agape*, a sign of the coming of the Redeemer's reign, a sign of the divine mission, a sign of the glory of Christ, a symbol of the sacramental economy, a sign of the ultimate transformation of the world. Such a complexity is detailed in Latourelle, "Miracle et Révélation,".

187. "Il déchiffre et en même temps figure la réalité du mystère." Latourelle, *Miracles de Jésus et théologie du miracle*, 336 [289].

beings in the person of Christ. The wonders accomplished in the corporeal order are symbolic representations of the wonders of grace and the splendor and variety of its gifts."[188] Such is not far from the Catechism's definition of the sacraments,[189] and, just as speaking of them earlier Latourelle described them as the "earthly prolongation of the glorified Christ," here miracles are seen as the embodiment of the word of the church, "which renders present and efficacious until the end of time the saving message uttered once and for all." This analogy Latourelle seeks to examine further:

> Because they so paradoxically transcend the order of nature, miracles are already marvellously apt for suggesting the mystery of our elevation to the supernatural order, being sensible analogues of the revealed mystery. For as a result of revelation the universe has become the setting for an unprecedented encounter between God and human beings; and God gives the universe the mission of "signifying" this mystery that is infinitely greater than the mystery to which the determinisms of nature bear witness. Furthermore, by their number and manifested forms miracles are fitted for suggesting the wealth of aspects to be found in the economy of grace and the sacraments. Thus the significatory aspect of the analogy between miracles and the world of grace becomes coherent and specific and is enriched. Miracles are then seen as themselves elements in revelation, as vehicles of revelation.[190]

---

188. "Il est l'image expressive des dons spirituels offerts aux hommes en la personne du Christ. Les merveilles accomplies dans l'ordre physique sont les figures, les symboles des merveilles de la grâce, de la splendeur et de la diversité de ses dons." Ibid., 336 [289].

189. *Catechism of the Catholic Church*, English trans. (London: Geoffrey Chapman, 1994), 259, § 1130.

190. "Déjà, par sa paradoxale transcendance dans l'ordre de la nature, le miracle est merveilleusement apte à suggérer le mystère de notre élévation dans l'ordre surnaturel, car il est l'analogue sensible du mystère révélé. Par la révélation, en effet, l'univers est devenu le milieu de la rencontre inouïe entre Dieu et l'homme; et Dieu lui donne la mission de 'signifier' ce mystère, infiniment plus grand que celui dont témoigne le déterminisme de la nature. Bien plus, par la multiplicité et la diversité de ses formes, le miracle est apte à suggérer la richesse des aspects de l'économie de la grâce et des sacrements. Ainsi, la portée significative de l'analogie du miracle avec le monde de la grâce prend consistance, se précise et s'enrichit. Le miracle apparaît lui-même comme élément de la révélation, comme porteur de la révélation." Latourelle, *Miracles de Jésus et théologie du miracle*, 342–43 [295].

Invitations to the Fullness of Easter Faith

Because it pleased God to reveal himself and his will to humanity, the whole of creation has become the theater of this self-manifestation. Miracles are a point of intersection where nature is transcended, and the palpable reality of creation signifies and reveals a supernatural reality. Latourelle recognises five equivalent terms that could be used to describe this function: "Declarative, expressive, figurative, symbolic, revelatory."[191] He wants to stress that, "*in one sense*, there is more in miracles than discourses."[192] Miracles are significative actions that provide an alternative dimension: "For revelation has an element of the ineffable which a discourse cannot capture."[193] The miracles of the Gospel of St. John are seen as the primary example of this "power of suggestion."[194] It is here, above all, that "by their number and manifold forms" they show themselves "fitted for suggesting the wealth of aspects to be found in the economy of grace and the sacraments." Here Latourelle is not making a naïve reference to the seven *semeia* of John as basis for the sacraments; rather, he is referring to the crystallization of properties that the gospel displays as a whole. Throughout, the text is composed of various interactive levels that seek to reveal the mysterious depths of its subject, Jesus Christ. The evangelist particularly associates action and discourse, event and interpretation, the actual and the symbolic.[195] In this sense it could be said that John's Gospel is the most "sacramental" of the four. As C. H. Dodd writes, "Thus the very nature of symbolism employed by the evangelist reflects his fundamental *Weltanschauung*. He writes in terms of a world in which phenomena—things and

---

191. "Declarative, expressive, figurative, symbolique, révélatrice." Ibid., 343 [295].
192. "*En un sens*, il y a plus dans le miracle que dans le discours." Ibid.
193. "Il y a, en effet, dans la révélation, une part d'ineffable que le discours n'arrive pas à traduire." Ibid.
194. "Force de suggestion," ibid.
195. Ibid., 233–34 [204–5].

events—are a living and moving image of the eternal, and not a veil of illusion to hide it, a World in which the Word is made flesh."[196] This symbolic sign function is of particular importance with regard to the miracle narratives of the Gospel.[197] As Latourelle remarks,

> In a miracle it is the shock and the qualitative leap produced by the event that direct the mind toward the super-abundant meaning and reality that dwell in Jesus. . . . Because, then, recognition of the miracles of Jesus is inseparable from the identification of Christ as Son of the Father, it pre-supposes that grace exerts its action not only in the confession of faith but all along the journey that leads through signs to the recognition of Jesus of Nazareth as Messiah and Son of the Father. In short: since the end to which the miracles of Jesus point is the personal mystery of Christ and since the signs are an invitation to faith in this mystery, the human beings involved must have, from the outset, an attitude of faith and therefore the grace to be open to the supernatural. It follows that even though miracles, as signs given by Christ, are numerous and striking, they leave room for freedom and meritorious faith. Above all they wait upon the light shed by Easter.[198]

---

196. Cf. some of the writers Latourelle cites at this point, especially C. H. Dodd, *The Interpretation of the Fourth Gospel* (Cambridge: Cambridge University Press, 1955), 133–43, particularly 138. The text here quoted is from 143.

197. "A healthy moderation ought to prevent us from pushing John's symbolism too far. But any exegesis which stopped at the external facts and at the most obvious meaning of the words would fail to understand the theological profundity of the 'pneumatic' Gospel. The first part is a 'book of signs' and John's conception of the *semeia* reveals the deep christological and soteriological meaning of the great miracles." R. Schnackenburg, *New Testament Theology Today* (London: Geoffrey Chapman, 1963), 102. See also R. Schnackenburg, *Die Sakramente im Johannesevangelium*, in Sacra Pagina, 2 (Gembloux: Duculot, 1959), and C. K. Barrett, *The Gospel according to John* (London: SPCK, 1958).

198. "Dans le miracle, c'est le choc et le saut qualitatif produits par l'événement qui orientent l'esprit vers l'excès de sens et de réalité qui résident en Jésus–. . . . Le discernement des miracles de Jésus, parce qu'il coincide avec l'identification du Christ comme Fils du Père, suppose que l'action de la grâce s'exerce, non seulement dans la confession de foi, mais tout au long de l'itinéraire qui, par les signes, amène l'homme à reconnaître en Jésus de Nazareth le Messie et le Fils du Père. En un mot, le terme que désignent les miracles de Jésus, étant le Mystère personnel du Christ, et les signes étant une invitation à la foi en ce Mystère, il faut qu'il y ait, dans l'homme, dès le depart, une attitude de foi, c'est-à-dire une grâce d'ouverture au surnaturel. Il s'ensuit que les miracles, comme signes addressés par le Christ, bien que nombreux et éclatants, laissent place à la liberté et au mérite de la foi. Et surtout ils attendent la lumière de Pâques." Latourelle, *Miracles de Jésus et théologie du miracle*, 236–37 [207], 367–68 [318].

To interpret the sign of the miracle is to recognize Christ as the key to its meaning. However, the question remains of how someone comes to this point of recognition. Latourelle dismisses the suggestion that this is a process of the intellect that responds to scientific observations about the created order. The intellect is only a contributor to a process of interior judgement that is religious rather than scientific. It is a judgment passed on whether a person considers him- or herself self-sufficient or whether the person has become aware of his or her poverty and need for salvation.[199] This is why recognition of the miracles of Jesus is inseparable from recognition of him as Savior. It is nowhere suggested that this process is an unaided action that is brought about simply by the wonder of the event. The inescapable wonder is a challenge that begins a process of recognition or rejection. Latourelle examines this in the case of the man born blind in chapter 9 of the Gospel of John.[200]

The Sacramental Structure of Miracles

Initially, the observing crowd suggest that the "cured" man is, in fact, a different man who has never been blind. Then both he and his parents verify his identity, and those who watch are confronted absolutely with the inexplicable. Immediately, the identity of Jesus must be faced, and the fact that Jesus cured on the Sabbath means the Pharisees are faced with a clear alternative. Either they reject their own truth and accept the Truth, or they remain self-sufficient and in control. Jesus is condemned as a sinner and the cured man cast out.

At first, the spontaneous wonder of the event is all-consuming, but slowly this factual, observable element fades and the miracle is begun to be understood as a "signifying totality."[201] It is the sign

199. Ibid., 347 [299].
200. Ibid., 349–52 [301–4].

value of the miracle that leads the witness through different stages of apprehension, but the point of departure is the totality of a composite but unified sign. This progressively acquires a "greater stability"[202] until the observer is prepared to acknowledge the divine nature of the intervention and its protagonist. "In a true miracle there is an unbroken correspondence of signifier and signified."[203]

It is not the case, then, that the process of recognition is unintelligible. The observed facts do not remain meaningless, but are gradually synthesized into a logical, credible process. As Latourelle is aware, "the signs which Christ gives are the signs of *the mystery of his person* and have for their purpose to lead human beings to this mystery."[204] As the reality to which the miracles point is a divine one, the human person cannot achieve it unaided. Hence Latourelle is sure that the process of recognition "pre-supposes grace."[205]

It is this faith that allows the sign value of the miracle to be appreciated fully. Faith in conjunction with the miraculous sign brings the person to decision, urging people, within the limits of their freedom, "to base their lives not on the security given by physical determinisms but by the mystery of God and his sovereign freedom."[206] Latourelle does also indicate that these signs are best interpreted within the wider faith context of the community, it being here that the miracle is verified as being of God.[207] Miracles do, then, have an ecclesiological significance, focused as they are on the paschal

---

201. "Totalité signifiante," ibid., 357 [308].

202. "Les traits de la 'figure' se précisent peu à peu, gagnent en fermeté," ibid., 358 [309].

203. "Là où il y a vrai miracle, le signifiant et le signifié se répondent sans faille," ibid., 357 [309].

204. "Les signes addressés par le Christ sont les signes de son *Mystère personnel* et ont pour but de conduire l'homme jusqu'à ce mystère." Ibid., 367 [317].

205. Ibid., 367 [318].

206. "L'homme est invité à fonder sa vie non sur la sécurité des déterminismes physiques, mais sur le mystère de Dieu et de sa liberté souveraine." Ibid., 380 [329].

207. This point is enhanced and developed by Latourelle's disciple, Rino Fisichella. In his definition of sign, he recognizes one function as "creating the conditions of interpersonal communication." Cf. R. Fisichella, "Semeiology," in Latourelle and Fisichella, *Dictionary of Fundamental Theology*, 988.

mystery, the central miracle that is source and summit of the faith of the church. It is in this context that the relationship between holiness and miracles is established:

> This connection of miracles and holiness appears most clearly in Christ himself. His miracles allow salvation to manifest itself in the elevated and transformed cosmos. This transformation is closely connected with his own glory as the risen Lord, whose glorified body is a permanent miracle. In the risen Christ the work of salvation is brought to completion, the renewal of humanity is a reality, and consequently, the very cosmos experiences the happy effects. Invisible salvation and the visible transformation of the cosmos are brought together in the risen Christ.[208]

There is an analogy between miracles and holiness—what is achieved by holiness in the human person is achieved by the miraculous throughout the whole order of creation. Here Latourelle is speaking of miracles as revelation in themselves. As a holy person makes visible the glorious destiny of humanity by their particular way of life, so miracles point to the future restoration of the whole of creation. Both are revelations of the will of God that the whole of creation comes to salvation. Miracles are also signs that point to this future unambiguous state—just as a life of holiness points to a future condition to which everyone is called. On both counts, miracles and holiness anticipate the permanent bodily glory which Christ has achieved through his death and resurrection.

---

208. "C'est dans le Christ qu'apparaît au mieux cette liaison du miracle et de la sainteté. Ses miracles sont la transparence du salut à travers le cosmos élevé et transformé. Cette transformation est en étroite liaison avec sa gloire de ressuscité, dont le corps glorifié est un miracle permanent. Dans le Christ ressuscité, l'œuvre du salut est accomplie, la rénovation de l'homme est opérée et, par suite, le cosmos lui-même en reçoit les bienheureux effets. Dans le Christ ressuscité, coincident les deux réalités du salut invisible et de la transformation visible du monde." Latourelle, *Miracles de Jésus et théologie du miracle*, 382–83 [331–32].

Moments in an Uninterrupted Dialogue

Latourelle returns to the basic principle that underlies his theology of signs—that of the necessity of an "unbroken correspondence of signifier and signified."[209] Analogies can be drawn between the signs of revelation because of the correspondence that exists between the particular sign, whether it be miracle, holiness, prophecy, or sacrament, and the basic sign of the resurrected Christ. The reality of the renewal of creation is to be found in the risen One. Through him, with him, and in him, the whole of creation will come to its unambiguous state of glory, and the appropriation of this reality to the whole of creation will be the work of the Holy Spirit.

It is interesting that Latourelle stresses the role of the Holy Spirit in the communication of the life of the risen Christ.[210] Christ mediates the life of the divine being through his transfigured human body, and it is the same Spirit who raised Jesus from the dead that will transform other mortal bodies into glory. The Spirit appropriates all that is present in the primordial sign of Christ to the individual believer through the church. As the divine life was mediated through the resurrected body of Jesus, so now it is mediated through his body, the church. The work of sanctification is a work of revelation accompanied by miraculous and sacramental signs, and both of these are founded on the paschal mystery. In this sense it is possible for Latourelle to conclude that

> miracles are works that involve the entire Trinity: Father, Son, and Spirit, and that tend to make ever more intimate the uninterrupted dialogue of the Father with his children whom Christ has redeemed. As signs of the great presence of God among human beings, miracles give a deeper and broader understanding of that presence, even more today than in the time of Jesus.[211]

209. Ibid., 357 [309].
210. Ibid., 383 [332].

This final quotation from *Miracles de Jésus et théologie du miracle* forms an apt conclusion not only to this particular work but to the whole of Latourelle's theological enterprise. Miracles can be understood properly only in the context of the Holy Trinity and the love that God seeks to reveal. Miracles are an integral part of that self-disclosure that it pleased God to undertake for the salvation of the world. This revelation is a dialogue between friends, and here Latourelle looks back to the foundational principles that he laid down in *Théologie de la Révélation*, and that have underpinned all his subsequent reflections. For Latourelle, revelation is an active, dynamic, personal dialogue, a conversation that became full and complete when the Word of God was made flesh in Jesus Christ. Such a theology implies a rejection of the static categories that revolved around the communication of extrinsic truths to the human mind. To make an option for the dynamic dialogue opens many new vistas for the theology of revelation, but one that is surely fundamental is the question of how revelation continues. This is a particular problem or perspective that Latourelle adopts at the end of this book, when he speaks of miracles giving a broader understanding of the presence of Jesus "today." "The miracles of Jesus, like those that line the course of the Church's history, make the continuous activity of the trinitarian God vividly present to human beings of every age."[212] The sacramental structure of this representation is fundamental to the question of how this revelation is communicated now. The cessation of revelation with the death of the last apostle is perhaps a teaching that sat more comfortably with the pre–Vatican

211. "Le miracle est une œuvre qui engage toute la Trinité: Père, Fils et Esprit, et qui tend à resserrer toujours davantage le dialogue ininterrompu du Père et de ses enfants, rachetés par le Christ. Aujourd'hui, plus encore qu'au temps de Jésus, le miracle, comme signe de la grande Présence de Dieu parmi les hommes, approfondit et amplifie sa signification." Ibid., 384 [333].

212. "Les miracles de Jésus, comme ceux qui jalonnent dans l'histoire de l'Église, présentialisent pour les hommes de tous les siècles l'activité continue du Dieu trinitaire." Ibid., 383 [332].

II notions of the content and processes of revelation.[213] To speak of a "continuous uninterrupted dialogue" happening now through the signs of revelation that persist in the church is perhaps to recognize that, if an answer can be found for such a question, it lies in the theology of sacramental re-presentation and the "today" of the liturgical celebration.[214]

213. "Of course, if one persists in thinking that revelation entails *primarily* the communication of revealed truths, it becomes easier to relegate revelation to the past. As soon as the whole set of revealed doctrines is complete, revelation ends or is 'closed.' For this way of thinking, later believers cannot immediately and directly experience revelation. All they can do is remember, interpret, and apply truths revealed long ago to the apostolic Church." See G. O'Collins, "Revelation Past and Present," in Latourelle, *Vatican II: Assessment and Perspectives*, 1:129. Also of interest on this topic is I. Ker, "Newman's Theory: Development or Continuing Revelation?" in *Newman and Gladstone: Centennial Essays*, ed. J. Bastable (Dublin: Veritas, 1978), 145–59.

214. Cf. K. Rahner, "The Death of Jesus and the Closure of Revelation," in *Theological Investigations*, trans. E. Quinn, vol. 18 (London: Darton, Longman and Todd, 1975), 132–42.

3

Avery Dulles

Diversifying the Models of Approach

Avery Dulles wrote one of the first and best critical appraisals of René Latourelle's *Théologie de la Révélation*. Not only did he recognise the work as an "enormous step forward,"[1] but he recognized in it "a number of major questions . . . which would seem to call for concentrated labour on the part of Catholic theologians."[2] Whether his extensive writings in fundamental theology are a conscious response to the invitation he recognized in Latourelle's work remains uncertain, but the points of issue that he identifies in his 1964 article "The Theology of Revelation" are ones that remain central to his subsequent studies. Indeed, it might be said that the particular aspects of the work of Latourelle that Dulles recognized as requiring elaboration or development themselves spring from the specific experience of his own conversion, his theological formation, and individual interests.

---

1. A. Dulles, "The Theology of Revelation," *Theological Studies* 25 (1964): 52.
2. Ibid., 52.

Opening up Methodology:
Models of the Church

Born in 1918 to a patrician American family, Avery Dulles had a largely secular upbringing and education. He entered Harvard in the autumn of 1936 and, to paraphrase his words, the tenor of his intellectual life was set amid the skepticism, materialism, and liberalism that held almost unchallenged sway in the secular universities.[3] It was there, however, "through an unmerited dispensation of Providence,"[4] that Dulles was slowly converted to Catholicism. Initially, and largely throughout, the process was intellectual.[5] Such an approach led him to full communion in the Church and, in 1946, Dulles entered the Society of Jesus, an order marked from its beginnings by conversion, intellectual honesty, and dedication to the person of Jesus and the church. Though the philosophical training that Latourelle and Dulles received[6] in the pre–Vatican II era would have been remarkably similar, their backgrounds and cultures were somewhat different.

A Departure Point for Something New

While Dulles recognizes the strength of Latourelle's sound dogmatic presentation of Judeo-Christian revelation, he is immediately captivated by two fundamental questions that arise at the interface

---

3. A. Dulles, "Foreword," *A Testimonial to Grace* (New York: Sheed and Ward, 1946), 31.
4. Ibid., 34.
5. "I was determined not to let sentiment draw reason in its wake. Whether in choosing reason I chose the better guide I am not certain. Man's natural religious inclinations often bring him more readily to the truth than his intelligence that is easily ensnared. There are many approaches by which God can lead souls to the Catholic faith. Mine was only one and perhaps not the best." Ibid., 85.
6. For Dulles's own autobiographical reflections, see *The Craft of Theology,* 2nd ed. (New York: Crossroad, 1995), 41–52. This can be compared with Latourelle's account in R. Latourelle, *L'infini du sens: Jésus Christ* (Québec: Bellarmin, 2000), 19–29; 179–80.

of this dogmatic and his own experience of the world. He seeks to widen the theological arena by dwelling on these questions. The first concerns the constitutive role of the interior illumination of grace in the process by which the unevangelized come to faith.[7] Essentially, this question displays a desire to clarify the theology of revelation itself by an analysis of the act of faith. Pertaining to it is the role of the preconceptual in the assent of faith, and the theology of symbol in the expression of that faith. That this particular question should occupy Dulles so keenly is not surprising. It is the central issue in the drama of his own conversion, which he had expressed almost twenty years earlier in *A Testimonial to Grace*:

> Trained as I was in the habits of scepticism, the act of faith was for me a terrible stumbling block. In a sense it seemed to be the surrender of that which I valued more than anything else: intellectual honesty. To make a subjective certainty out of an objective probability was a sacrifice of reason itself. Yet paradoxically, it was a reasonable sacrifice: for how else could one consent to follow Christ with that singleness of devotion which He, as God, could rightly exact? That I did eventually make this act of faith is attributable solely to the grace of God.[8]

The man who had identified grace as the cause of his coming to faith quite reasonably seeks to examine its processes within the economy of God's revelation and within the movement of faith response.

Perhaps, as a result, it should only be expected that the second most significant question that arose from *Théologie de la Révélation* for Dulles was the question of the ongoing nature of revelation, and the role of the church in actualizing God's message "in new forms, adapted to new situations."[9] As Dulles expresses in his *Testimonial*, he had sought a church that "could still sustain and nourish the unfeigned charity and the burning conviction of the first Apostles."[10]

7. Dulles, "The Theology of Revelation," 52.
8. Dulles, *A Testimonial to Grace*, 79–80.
9. Dulles, "The Theology of Revelation," 53.

Conversion and ecclesiology are the two abiding aspects of the fundamental theology of Avery Dulles. Significantly, the only two entries he made in the *Dictionary of Fundamental Theology* were an article on the history of apologetics and one on conversion. Taken together, these articles summarize the particular approach of Dulles. Conversion is the element central to fundamental theology, and the "attractive" sacramental symbols of the church are essential to its gracious facilitation.[11] Indeed, the role of the church is crucial to the process of faith assent: "To accept the revelation of God in Jesus Christ, as the Church presents him to us, is critically justified to the extent that it assists one to integrate the data of experience, to interpret the course of history, and to cope with what Vatican II referred to as 'the riddles of sorrow and death.'"[12]

The primary way in which the church effects this "integration" is by "sacramental incorporation" into the body of Christ.[13] It is as the sacrament of Christ that the church brings people to accept the truths of revelation. By making present the mysteries by means of symbol, the gathered assembly communicates a reality that provokes response:

10. Dulles, *A Testimonial to Grace*, 90.

11. In his article on conversion, Dulles asserts, "From one point of view fundamental theology may be understood as a systematic reflection on the structures of conversion and, more specifically, on conversion to the Christian faith. The genesis of faith cannot be adequately grasped unless account is taken of the workings of grace as known through revelation." A. Dulles, "Conversion," in *Dictionary of Fundamental Theology*, ed. R. Latourelle and R. Fisichella (New York: Crossroads, 1995), 192–93. In his article on apologetics, Dulles speaks of the ecclesial nature of the act of faith: "In contemporary theology apologetics is increasingly seen as an articulation of the intelligibility that is inherent in faith itself, and thus as inseparable from good theology. The intelligibility in question is not that of pure deductive reason but that of actual men and women, tempted to sin, but impelled by grace and attracted toward the God who is dimly known in the yearning he implants in the human heart. A. Dulles, "Apologetics," in Latourelle and Fisichella, *Dictionary of Fundamental Theology*, 35. Because of the particular insight Dulles displays, any reader of his work on John Henry Newman cannot fail to draw some interesting and enlightening parallels with the author's own story. This is especially true of the chapters on Newman's pilgrimage of faith and the church as organ of revelation. See: A. Dulles, *John Henry Newman* (London: Continuum, 2002).

12. A. Dulles, "The Church: Sacrament and Ground of Faith," in *Problems and Perspectives in Fundamental Theology*, ed. R. Latourelle and G. O'Collins (New York: Paulist, 1982), 264.

13. Ibid., 264.

"To accept a symbol is to take the risk that in following out the line of action and consideration suggested by the symbol one will achieve a richer and more authentic presentation of the real."[14]

If René Latourelle was influential in constructing a new image for fundamental theology in the "expansion" years that flank the Second Vatican Council, then Avery Dulles is responsible for developing the significance of the sacramental vision of the church that such a theology implied. It might be said that Dulles belongs to the phase of "focusing and of hierarchical organization of the tasks of fundamental theology."[15] The purpose of this chapter is to see, by means of three works by Dulles, how a sacramental understanding of revelation theology, developed in the post–Vatican II Church. *Models of the Church*, first published in 1978 and later revised and expanded in 1987, though an ecclesiological work, offers Dulles's basic thesis on the relationship between the church and revelation. In addition, a study of this text will avail some insight into the theological method of models, an approach also used, and further developed, in his subsequent study *Models of Revelation*, published in 1983. Here Dulles offers his mature convictions on revelation, describing symbolic communication as the most apt theological interpretation of the self-manifestation of God. Through an analysis of this work, and especially by way of reflection on the enhanced methodology employed, an assessment of the significance of the sacramental in postconciliar theologies of revelation can be achieved.

In both of these books, methodology is central to the understanding of the revelation theology that Dulles unfolds. Within this approach the liturgy as a theological source and method is a closely related, yet largely underdeveloped theme. However, within

---

14. Ibid., 266.
15. R. Latourelle, "A New Image of Fundamental Theology," in Latourelle and O'Collins, *Problems and Perspectives in Fundamental Theology*, 37.

a climate of its growing significance, Dulles does begin to articulate more systematically this very aspect of his method in later essays. To appreciate at least the beginnings of such a development, the last work to be studied here is the 1992 collection of essays, *The Craft of Theology: From Symbol to System.* Discussing his theology of sacramental communication within the perspective of the problems of contemporary theological method, Dulles makes an effort at the concrete contextualization of his ideas and this, in turn, causes reflection on the growing significance of the liturgy in the resolution of these problems.

Models of the Church

Aspects of the enterprises of René Latourelle and Avery Dulles show great similarity. As Jesuit members of theological faculties, both are self-conscious teachers and shape their material with pedagogical clarity. *Models of the Church* is as much a core text for ecclesiology[16] as *Théologie de la Révélation* is for students of fundamental theology. However, another common feature, perhaps not unrelated to the first, is the historical approach that both authors adopt.[17] Certainly, it is the intention of Dulles in *Models of the Church* to put to use a methodology that allows a balanced, holistic description of the mystery in question, one that could accommodate complexity and yet present the reality as a unity. And though, at first glance, the text seems to offer merely a sequence of well-described, static types

16. See most of the fly-leaf leaders that appear in the expanded paperback edition of 1987. Many applaud the arrival of a new study text and comment on Dulles's typical clarity of style and comprehensive analysis.

17. Notice such an approach in two earlier works by Dulles: *Revelation Theology: A History* (New York: Seabury Press, 1965), where Dulles offers "a brief history of Christian views of revelation;" and especially *A History of Apologetics* (London: Hutchinson & Co., 1971), where, after a historical overview, Dulles first shapes his material according to particular theological perspectives, perspectives that he later develops as models.

that contribute to a composite picture, it is the underlying historical development that effects an even deeper coherence in the material.[18]

> The mysterious character of the Church has important implications for methodology. It rules out the possibility of proceeding from clear and univocal concepts, or from definitions in the usual sense of the word. The concepts abstracted from the realities we observe in the objective world about us are not applicable, at least directly, to the mystery of man's communion with God.[19]

The Necessity of Dynamism

What becomes clear is that, for Dulles, models are not a succession of particular perspectives on a static phenomenon. Given a historical dimension, models can become the methodological expression of the development of dogma. This is not merely in the sense that one model succeeds or gives rise to another. Each model contains within itself two aspects: the explanatory and the exploratory.[20] In the first sense, models have a "functional correspondence"[21] and illustrate a reality not wholly accessible to direct experience. In the second,

---

18. For further reflection on the relationship between models and historical description, see D. Tracy, *Blessed Rage for Order* (New York: Seabury, 1975), 23: "The basic need for the development of models is perhaps best expressed by Paul Tillich when he states that, in matters of historical description, contemporary theologians cannot be content with the usual alternatives of either trying to say everything or of saying nothing at all. If we wish to locate our own enterprise historically, we must try to develop certain characteristic ideal types or models for interpreting the basic factors present in concrete historical realities." Notice here too how Dulles considers Tracy's understanding of model to differ from his: "For Tracy models represent mutually incompatible options. Every theologian is in consistency bound to choose one model and reject all the others. Tracy's concept of model thus differs from the generally inclusivist concept urged, e.g. in my *Models of the Church*. Tracy's models would be, in my terminology, methodological types. I have employed the notion of model to establish the sense in which pluralism is up to a point legitimate. Tracy uses the notion to clarify the limits of pluralism." A. Dulles, "Method in Fundamental Theology: Reflections on David Tracy's *Blessed Rage for Order*," *Theological Studies* 37 (1976): 305.
19. A. Dulles, *Models of the Church*, 2nd ed. (London: Doubleday, 1987), 18.
20. Ibid., 24.
21. Ibid., 23.

models have a capacity to facilitate advance into previously unchartered theological ground. Within an individual model therefore there can be a "movement" between established and speculative theology. By this, Dulles achieves an internal dynamism that effects a unity of both method and subject.[22] But one should not think that this methodology is restricted to ecclesiology in its suitability.[23] The organic and multifaceted approach that the method of models allows in an analysis of the church is necessitated by the fact that the church is part of the mystery of communion that exists between God and humanity. There is, then, a certain congruence between the church and revelation, and, though not expressed explicitly until chapter 11 of *Models of the Church*, this relationship should be kept in mind from the beginning. As Dulles asserts,

> My thesis will be that revelation, like the Church itself, is mystery—it is an aspect of the mysterious self-communication of God himself to man. The most adequate approach to revelation is through a plurality of models, and for present purposes these models may be matched with the ecclesiological types developed in previous chapters. In developing this line of thought, I shall be able to indicate in passing the types of Christology that go with the various models of the Church.[24]

22. "As we contemplate the theological history of the Catholic Church over the past thirty years, we cannot but be impressed by the rapidity with which, after a period of stability, new paradigms have begun to succeed one another. From 1600 to 1940 the juridical and societal model was in peaceful possession, but it was then displaced by that of the Mystical Body, which has been subsequently dislodged by three other models in rapid succession: those of People of God, Sacrament, and Servant. These paradigm shifts closely resemble what Thomas Kuhn has described as 'scientific revolutions.'" Ibid., 30.

23. See ibid., 12.

24. Ibid., 177. See also the following: "The method of models is applicable to the whole of theology, and not simply to ecclesiology. To a great extent, the five basic types discussed in these pages reflect distinctive mindsets that become manifest in a given theologian's way of handling all the problems to which he addresses himself, including the doctrine of God, Christ, grace, sacraments, and the like. At various points in this work, especially in the chapter 'The Church and Revelation,' I touch briefly on the connection between the types used in ecclesiology and the other treatises." Ibid., 12. Though Dulles alludes to the relationship between "Christ, the Church, and the seven ritual sacraments," and makes reference to the failure of the Council to "give a theological explanation" of this relationship," he nowhere makes reference to the liturgy as a comparable treatise or significant element in this argument.

If matching ecclesiological types with their equivalents in revelation theology is to be the reader's subconscious activity throughout this book, then it is appropriate for a historical study to begin with the institutionalized form of the mystery:

> Operating in terms of a world view in which everything remains essentially the same as it was when it began, and in which origins are therefore all-important, the institutionalist ecclesiology attaches crucial importance to the action of Christ in establishing the offices and sacraments that presently exist in the Church. Thus the Council of Trent taught that the seven sacraments, and a hierarchy consisting of bishops, priests, and ministers, were instituted by Christ. Vatican I affirmed the same of the papal office. By the same logic, the dogmas of the modern Church were affirmed to be part of the original deposit of faith, complete with the apostles.[25]

Dulles equates historically a period of triumphant ecclesiology with one in which the church "disclaimed any power of innovation in its teaching of revelation."[26] Yet this is not regarded as mere coincidence. It is precisely in a closed, complete, and unchanging deposit of revelation that a definite, summative and unchanging theology of the church can be found.[27] By means of the regressive method, present institutional structures can be traced back to the founding action and words of Christ.[28] Certainly, the institutional

---

25. Ibid., 39-40.
26. Ibid., 40.
27. "In Roman Catholic theology since the Counter Reformation the prevalent view of Revelation has been strongly coloured by the institutional view of the Church. The Church is understood as the guardian and conserver of revelation. . . . According to the official Roman documents of this period, the revelation authoritatively taught by the Church is a body of doctrine that derives from the Apostles, who received it 'from the mouth of Christ himself,' or 'by the dictation of the Holy Spirit.'" Ibid., 177.
28. Ibid., 40. For instance Pius IX, in the letter *Gravissimas inter* to Frohschammer (*Acta Pii IX*, 1/3, 548–56), had affirmed that "scientia catholica, ad cuius munus nobilissimum pertinet ostendere quomodo doctrina eo sensu quo definite est, in fontibus revelationis contineatur." For an exposition of the historical background to the point that Dulles is making here, see G. Alberigo, "The Authority of the Church in the Documents of Vatican I and Vatican II," in *Authority in the Church and the Schillebeeckx Case*, ed. L. Swidler and P. Fransen (New York: Crossroad, 1982), 119–45.

element was here treated as primary.[29] Plotting the historical succession of visible structures, powers, and offices was the theologian's major task, as authenticity was dependent on a pedigree of divine institution.[30] The interrelationship between this type of ecclesiology and a similar theology of revelation is not difficult to see.[31] Perhaps the example most revealing of their interdependence is the emergence of the doctrine of papal infallibility. Not only was this doctrine established during a period of ecclesiological triumphalism, such ultramontane self-assurance extended to apologetics, and the theology of revelation too: "The conception of infallibility that emerged in this period of Church history corresponds to its highly juridical, authoritarian, and propositional understanding of revelation."[32] Within this model, then, the death of the last apostle not only marks the closure and completion of revelation, but with it the definitive establishment of a church fully developed in all institutional aspects that need only perdure through the ages.

The Inner Life of Communion

Dulles does not suggest that the institutional model has nothing to offer to contemporary ecclesiology. Rather, he remarks on a paradigm shift that results from the resolution of theological tensions that exist between the model and its context: "By setting the juridical organization of the Church in the context of a fuller and broader theological consideration of the inner nature of the Church, Vatican II . . . avoided the pitfalls of juridicism."[33] That is to say, within the context of conciliar theology, other models such as *People of God,*

29. Dulles, *Models of the Church*, 35.
30. See A. Dulles, "A Half Century of Ecclesiology," *Theological Studies* 50 (1989): 419–42.
31. Dulles, *Models of the Church*, 177–78.
32. Ibid., 178.
33. Ibid., 35.

Sacrament, and *Mystery* take on increasing significance so as to hold the institutional elements more effectively in balance and reduce their dominance. In this way, theology endeavors to meet the limitations that result from the emergence of an overbearing model by holding it in tension with alternative models. Thus the shift in revelation studies, which René Latourelle notes in *Théologie de la Révélation* as resulting from the Council's insistence on personalist, subjective, and organic categories, is also basic to the changes that can be seen in ecclesiology. Hence the second chapter of *Models of the Church*, on the mystical communion that exists between members of the baptized faithful, grows out of the first.

> The bonds of union in these theories would be primarily the interior graces and gifts of the Holy Spirit, though the external bonds are recognised as important in a subsidiary way. The resulting union would surpass anything known to pure sociology; it would be a transforming mystical union, deeper and more intimate than anything describable in moral or juridical terms. The term "member" may still be used, but in this ecclesiology it is no longer a juridical term. Rather it is used in an organic, spiritual, or mystical sense, referring to the Church as a communion of grace. The primary factor that binds the members of the Church to each other is the reconciling grace of Christ.[34]

Historically speaking, the above quotation reflects the paradigm shift in theology that the Second Vatican Council both responded to and furthered.[35] These are the years in which the theology of the mystical body was developed and promulgated, years in which the pressing realities of the modern world questioned the old order in a search for more abiding answers. The movement was many faceted, but two aspects dominated: an increasing dissatisfaction with what

---

34. Ibid., 57.
35. For a clear description of this theological shift, see A. Anton, "Lo sviluppo della dottrina sulla Chiesa nella teologia dal Vaticano I al Vaticano II," in *L'Ecclesiologia Dal Vaticano I al Vaticano II* (Milan: Editrice La Scuola, 1973), 27–98, especially 64ff. See also Dulles's own article, "A Half Century of Ecclesiology," 421–23.

were quickly becoming inadequate institutional categories, and a deepening of the theological understanding of the church. Both these elements were intensified by a growing self-consciousness among the laity. The rise of Catholic Action was testament to such reflection on the significance of the baptized faithful in the apostolic life of the church, and the emphasis that the liturgical movement placed on the active participation of all in the liturgy provided a spirituality that endorsed their distinct and indispensable vocation within the body of Christ.[36] This renewed "presence" of the laity demanded a reinterpretation of what Congar describes as a certain "onesidedness"[37] in post-Tridentine ecclesiology. Raised consciousness of the laity itself was enough to point out the inadequacy of the institutional model, in which the faithful are virtually invisible and of no apparent consequence.[38] Of itself, church

36. See Y.-M. Congar, *Jalons pour une théologie du laicat* (Paris: Les Éditions du Cerf, 1953); English trans. by Donald Attwater, *Lay People in the Church* (London: Geoffrey Chapman, 1957), 48–49. Also, in conversation with Bernard Laurent, commenting on the major developments that had taken place in Catholic theology in the last fifty years, Congar had this to say on the shift from Tridentinism: "Tridentinism represented a kind of conditioning (though I do not mean that in the pejorative sense of the word), I mean a kind of enveloping, the provision of a framework into which one entered and in which one stayed. Whereas today . . . given that we live in a secularised world (and one which is particularly influenced by the media), I think that it is impossible to presume a Christian life-style without a degree of inner life. In this connection I would like to quote a rather strange remark by Fr. Émile Mersch, the Belgian Jesuit, who made such a contribution to the theology of the Mystical Body. He said: 'Some animals are surrounded by a shell because they have no skeleton.' I think that today the shell—ie. the Tridentine system, Tridentinism—has largely dissolved, been sloughed off in some way, and that the need for some kind of inner framework has become all the more imperative." See: B. Lauret, ed., *Fifty Years of Catholic Theology: Conversations with Yves Congar* (London: SCM, 1988), 5–6. See also Monika Hellwig, "Twenty Five Years of an Awakening Church: Liturgy and Ecclesiology," in *The Awakening Church, 25 Years of Liturgical Renewal,* ed. L. J. Madden (Collegeville, MN: Liturgical Press, 1992), 55–68, especially 60–61.

37. Congar, *Lay People in the Church*, 36.

38. "If the Church were to be considered solely from the point of institution, of her formal hierarchical cause, she would in fact exist without laity; a faithful people would be required only as *materia circa quam, materia cui*, object and beneficiary of her hierarchical actions. The faithful would not form, organically united with their clergy, one single active subject of the work of God's kingdom—that union of the people with their bishop which, on the testimony of St. Cyprian, constitutes the Church. They would be rather those who are ministered to, the matter on which clerical action is exercised, a sort of *homo religiosus* analogous to the much-criticised

as institution can never be an adequate description of the relationships that exist between those who make up that ecclesial reality. Such an insight led to a theology that more effectively described bonds deeper than those of a visible structure: those of mystical communion within the body of Christ.[39] This description of the church had the obvious advantage of being able to incorporate many of the biblical images and metaphors that the contemporaneous "return to the sources" revealed as such a significant aspect of patristic studies.

An Outward Sign of Inward Grace

From the beginning, however, a fundamental question was how this mystical communion was related to the perfect, visible society envisaged by Robert Bellarmine.[40] Pius XII's *Mystici Corporis* taught that a simple identity exists between the two. Yet it would seem that, for Dulles, even Pius XII's powers of synthesis failed to achieve an integration of theologies that facilitated further development.[41]

homo oeconomicus or the *homo politicus* under a totalitarian regime. They would have nothing to do but to receive, and as Father de Montcheuil wrote, they would be in the Church solely for their own good and not for the Church's good as well." Congar, *Lay People in the Church*, 46.

39. "In her ultimate reality the Church is man's fellowship with God and with one another in Christ. She is also the totality of the means to this fellowship. From this fellowship aspect, her ultimate reality, the Church is the aggregate of those who are 'in Christ Jesus.' This aggregate is quite a different thing from a simple juxtaposition of individuals in a group: it is a people, the People of God. Better still, it is the Body of Christ, and people of God precisely because body of Christ, as we shall see in our treatise on the Church. Here we are interested, not so much in the nature of the bond of fellowship in Christ, as in this simple fact: the Church in her ultimate reality is a fellowship of persons. And she is made up of these persons as a nation is made up of its citizens or a body of its members." Ibid., 22.

40. Cf. the discussion of Henri de Lubac in *Méditation sur L'Église* 3rd ed. (Paris: Aubier, 1954), especially chapter 3, "Les Deux Aspects de L'Église Une," 71–106, which gives a historical overview of the relationship between the mystical and the hierarchical aspects of the church. For a discussion of Bellarmine's ecclesiology, see J. Hardon, "Robert Bellarmine's Concept of the Church," in *Studies in Medieval Culture*, ed. J. Sommerfeldt, vol. 2 (Kalamazoo, MI: Western Mitchigan, 1966), 120–27.

41. "This encyclical attempts to harmonise the 'Mystical Body' concept with the societal concept of Bellarmine. It points to the pope and the bishops as the joints and ligaments of the body, and asserts that 'those who exercise sacred power in the Body are its first and chief

Indeed, the contrary theologies that resulted from an overemphasis on the church *semper idem* or *semper reformanda* led only "to the contrary errors of sociologism and biologism,"[42] both hampering a "unilateral progression" in ecclesiology.[43]

As *Models of the Church* proceeds, it becomes evident that it was through the development of another model born, or at least reborn,[44] out of the tension between the institutional and mystical types that further resolution was achieved. The theologian responsible for initiating such a theology of the church, which again took up the category of sacrament, rejected any "Monophysism in ecclesiology,"[45] and made an "effective union"[46] between the mystical and hierarchical, was Henri de Lubac.[47] In his chapter on *Church as Mystical Communion*, Dulles notes that in *Lumen Gentium*, the Council fathers "retrenched" from two positions taken by *Mystici Corporis.*[48] The fathers nuance the assertion of Pius XII that a simple

---

members.' The laity are said to 'assist the ecclesiastical hierarchy in spreading the kingdom of the divine Redeemer' and thus to occupy an honourable, even though often lowly, place in the Christian community." Dulles, *Models of the Church*, 52. See also A. Dulles, "A Half Century in Ecclesiology," 422–29.

42. Dulles, *Models of the Church*, 56.

43. "Il fantasma di un progresso unilaterale nella nuova tendenza ecclesiologica della Chiesa-mistero apparve più tardi all'orizzonte. . . . Nel campo della vita liturgico-sacramentale e pastorale della Chiesa si hanno interpretazioni unilaterali della forma di unione della Chiesa con Cristo in un orientamento prettamente misticistico, di cui danno testimonianza le opere di L. Deimel e K. Pelz. La *Mystici Corporis* tentò di correggere queste deviazioni teoriche e pratiche, orientate a un *biologismo spirituale* e un *falso misticismo,* dell'ecclesiologia del Corpo mystico, accentuando troppo a sua volta l'aspettto sociologico e visibile di questo Corpo mistico, ritardando così l'evoluzione della dottrina sulla Chiesa verso un'integrazione delle due correnti ecclesiologiche." Anton, "Lo sviluppo della dottrina sulla Chiesa nella teologia dal Vaticano I al Vaticano II," 75–76.

44. "In order to bring together the external and internal aspects into some intelligible synthesis, many twentieth-century Catholic theologians have appealed to the concept of the Church as Sacrament. Anticipated by Cyprian, Augustine, Aquinas, and Scheeben, this type of ecclesiology emerged in full clarity in our own century." Dulles, *Models of the Church*, 63.

45. H. de Lubac, *Catholicism* (London: Burns, Oates, and Washbourne, 1950), 29.

46. Ibid., 29.

47. As Dulles points out, this concept was further developed in "several important essays by Karl Rahner. After Otto Semmelroth's classic exposition, *The Church as Primordial Sacrament,* 1953, many theologians subsequently worked on this theme." Dulles, *Models of the Church*, 64.

identity exists between the mystical body of Christ and the Roman Catholic Church with the comparison that the two are related to each other as the human and divine natures relate in Christ.[49] De Lubac had adopted this position as early as 1937, as can be seen from *Catholicisme*,[50]which was first published that year. It was a stance he developed further in his *Méditation sur l'Église* of 1952, one that was to be influential on the Dogmatic Constitution itself.[51] A theology of sacrament, seeking as it did to respond to a great variety of problems in ecclesiology, took on "the status of a paradigm"[52] at the Council, so that Dulles could later say with confidence:

> Christ, as the sacrament of God, contains the grace that he signifies. Conversely, he signifies and confers the grace he contains. In him the invisible grace of God takes on visible form. But the sacrament of redemption is not complete in Jesus as a single individual. In order to become the kind of sign he must be, he must appear as the sign of God's redemptive love extended toward all mankind, and as the response of all mankind to that redemptive love. The Church therefore is in the first instance a sign. It must signify in a historically tangible form the redeeming grace of Christ. It signifies that grace as relevantly given to men of every age, race, kind and condition. Hence the Church must incarnate itself in every human culture.[53]

---

48. Ibid., 52.

49. Ibid., and *LG* articles 8 and 9.

50. "But the Church, the only real Church, the Church which is the Body of Christ, is not merely that strongly hierarchical and disciplined society whose divine origin has to be maintained, whose organization has to be upheld against all denial and revolt. That is an incomplete notion and but a partial cure because it works only from without by way of authority, instead of effective union. If Christ is the sacrament of God, the Church is for us the sacrament of Christ; she represents him, in the full and ancient meaning of the term, she really makes him present." De Lubac, *Catholicism*, 29.

51. See A. Acerbi, *Due ecclesiologie: Ecclesiologia giuridica e ecclesiologia di communione nella Lumen Gentium* (Bologna: Ed. Dehoniane, 1975). Also, K. Neufeld, "In the Service of the Council. Bishops and Theologians at the Second Vatican Council," in *Vatican II: Assessment and Perspectives*, ed. R. Latourelle, 3 vols. (New York: Paulist Press, 1988), 1:74–105, 94, and G. Philips, *L'Église et son Mystère au IIe Concile du Vatican* (Paris: Desclée, 1967), 1.

52. Dulles, *Models of the Church*, 29.

53. Ibid., 68.

In his commentary on *Lumen Gentium*, Aloys Grillmeier asserts that an ecclesiology of sacrament was fundamental to the aims of the Council. The way in which the church could be a light to the nations was best explained by such a theology.[54] Though an exact analysis of the relationship between sacramentology and ecclesiology is nowhere spelled out in the Constitution, in returning to biblical and patristic categories, the Council fathers offer a concept wider than the then-current definitions of the seven sacraments of the church. This is not to suggest, however, that the theology of the individual sacraments, as signs instituted by Christ that symbolize and effect grace, is not essential to this model of church. Not surprisingly, it is in the Constitution on the Liturgy that this concept is most widely employed.[55] In describing the church as the universal sacrament of salvation, and ascribing the two effects of intimate union with God and fellowship among people to this sacred sign, *Lumen Gentium* conflates into a single model aspects normally studied in diverse disciplines. The theology of the church as sacrament brings together theses on revelation, ecclesiology, and sacramentology, and juxtaposes them in a fresh way.[56]

54. "This explains the reform envisaged by the Council, namely, 'that the sign of Christ may shine more brightly over the face of the Church (LG, Article 15, *ad fin.*). This vocation, to be in Christ the light of the nations is then stated in a proposition which is basic for the ecclesiology of the Constitution: 'In Christ the Church is so to speak the sacrament . . .' The notion of the Church as sacrament (in a sense to be defined later more exactly) recurs often in the Constitution and in other documents of the Council." A. Grillmeier, "The Mystery of the Church," in *Commentary on the Documents of Vatican II*, ed. H. Vorgrimler, vol. 1 (London: Burns & Oates, 1967), 138–52, 139.

55. Dulles, *Models of the Church*, 64–65.

56. De Lubac expresses this point with characteristic lucidity: "Just as redemption and revelation, even though they reach every individual soul, are none the less fundamentally not individual but social, so grace which is produced and maintained by the sacraments does not set up a purely individual relationship between the soul and God or Christ; rather does each individual receive such grace in proportion as he is joined, socially, to that body whence flows this saving life-stream. Thus it has been said that the causality of the sacraments is to be found not so much 'in a paradoxical efficacy, in the supernatural order, of a rite or perceptible action, as in the existence of a society, which under the appearances of a human institution hides a divine reality.' All the sacraments are essentially sacraments of the Church; in her alone do they

Possibilities for a Sacramental Synthesis

The import of the connections that the sacramental model effects is hardly worked out by the documents of the Council, and, as demonstrated by Dulles's later reflections, this remains a disputed question in contemporary theology. The theological intersection that arises from the use of this specific notion of sacrament results in a point of great significance for this particular study, and one to which Dulles alludes in the above quotation. If the church is the universal sacrament of salvation, an effective sign of God's redemptive love, then this salvation is being actualized in the church now, precisely because of its sacramental shape. The sacrament effects intimate union between God and humanity and fellowship among people, a process that "is not complete in Jesus as a single individual" but that will come to fullness in his body, the church. The sacraments, and particularly the Eucharist, are essential in achieving the unity and communion of the body of Christ. As Dulles makes clear in his chapter on the community of disciples,

> The Eucharist is the climactic sacrament, signifying the deepest and most intimate union with Christ, who makes himself the life-sustaining food and drink of his spiritual family. The Eucharistic liturgy is structured in such a way that Christ addresses the community by word, as he spoke to the disciples at the Last Supper, and then gives himself in sacramental form under the invocation of the Holy Spirit. The Eucharist differs from the community meals of Jesus with his disciples insofar as the community now encounters him under symbolic forms as the crucified and risen Lord, and thus as the sacrifice that reconciles sinners to God.[57]

produce their full effect, for in her alone, 'the society of the Spirit,' is there, normally speaking, participation in the gift of the Spirit." De Lubac, *Catholicism*, 35.

57. Dulles, *Models of the Church*, 216.

In 1980, Dulles wrote an article discussing the ecclesial aspects of fundamental theology. There he maintained that the discipline had "only begun to ponder the sacramental vision of the Church."[58] This was consonant with the views he had expressed in the final chapter of the first edition of *Models of the Church*. A theology of the Church as sacrament, he believed, had potential to be "the basis for a systematic ecclesiology."[59] By the time he published what became chapter 13 of the expanded edition of the same work, Dulles had deviated somewhat from this approach. He had settled on the model *Community of Disciples*, recognising in it potentialities for the beginnings of a "comprehensive ecclesiology."[60] This new type of the church was "a wide and flexible concept,"[61] and one accommodating of the best aspects of the five models previously discussed. Dulles saw strong similarities between it and the sacramental model, and claimed that "in the perspectives of Scripture and theology, the same characteristics that make the Church the sacrament of Christ qualify it to be called the community of disciples."[62] Indeed, Dulles quotes Raymond Brown's summary of Johannine theology to stress how, scripturally speaking, the incorporation of the individual into the community of disciples is a fundamental aspect of the Fourth

---

58. Dulles, "The Church: Sacrament and Ground of Faith," 267.
59. Dulles, *Models of the Church*, 206.
60. Ibid., 207.
61. Ibid., 214.
62. Ibid., 223.

Gospel.[63] The notion of community of disciples is also basic, Dulles asserts, to any theology of the Eucharist or of the other sacraments.

The advantages found in this model are pastorally motivated and respond to the requirements of the church in the modern world. The church as community of disciples is close to people's experience; it implies personal commitment to Jesus, it is tangible and visible and yet accommodating of change, and it lacks the forbidding technical characteristics of the sacramental model.[64] In addition, a strongly beneficial aspect of the model is its ability to express the "ongoing relationship of the Church to Christ its Lord."[65] Dulles marshals scriptural and dogmatic arguments effectively to convince the reader of the comprehensive and systematizing qualities of this model. Though he discusses the relationship between the community model and the sacramental life,[66] and regards community as a reality achieved by faith, worship, and inward transformation[67] in widening or restructuring the model of church from sacrament to community of disciples, Dulles inevitably weakens the relationship of the model

---

63. In a summary reflection on John, the last of the canonical Gospels to be written, Raymond Brown observes, "Instead of writing of the rule or kingdom of God, John centres all imagery on Jesus as the one in whom the reign of God has been perfectly realised, so that inhering in him replaces entrance into the kingdom. Sacraments are signs through which Jesus gives and nourishes life. Church offices and even apostleship are of lesser importance when compared to discipleship, which is literally a question of (eternal) life and death." R. Brown, *The Churches the Apostles Left Behind* (New York: Paulist, 1984), 95, quoted in Dulles, *Models of the Church*, 211. Interestingly, in a passage just beyond this one quoted by Dulles, Brown emphasises the importance of sacraments as the means to community: "Johannine readers were told of a Jesus who during his lifetime fed the hungry and gave sight to the blind by marvelous deeds that were, in turn, signs of a heavenly reality. At the same time, by the inclusion of ecclesiastical, sacramental language in these chapters, the Johannine writer was teaching that Jesus continues to give the enlightenment of faith and the food of eternal life through the signs of baptism and the Eucharist. Jesus is not simply the one who instituted the sacraments of the Church; he is the life-giver who remains active in and through these sacraments. Thus the unique importance that John places on the relationship of the Christian to Jesus is being underlined through sacramental imagery." Brown, *The Churches the Apostles Left Behind*, 90.
64. A. Dulles, *Models of the Church*, 222–23.
65. Ibid., 206.
66. Ibid., 214–17.
67. Ibid., 217.

to the sacramental celebrations of the liturgy.[68] Somehow, this model does not carry forward the impetus and expectation that Catholic theology of the church had shown both prior to and during the Second Vatican Council. Not only is the promise of an integral and interdisciplinary theology deriving from the concept of sacrament muted by this change, but, as even Dulles himself concedes, "The more traditional images of People of God, Body of Christ, and Temple of the Holy Spirit retain their validity [and] in some respects . . . surpass the discipleship model in expressing the theological basis of the Church in the self-communication of the divine Trinitarian life."[69]

It would seem that the opportunity for fruitful dialogue between fundamental theology, understood as the theology of the self-communication of the divine Trinitarian life, and sacramentology is also somewhat curbed by this model.

---

68. As Dulles has alluded to, the writings of Henri de Lubac to some extent chart the development and flowering of sacramental themes in ecclesiology. Paul McPartlan's study gives an interesting insight into the remolding of the link between church and sacraments, and how this eventually shaped the ecclesiology of the Council. In his model of the church as community of disciples, Dulles prescinds slightly from this movement: "De Lubac's efforts in the 1940's to repair this inversion of the traditional terminology, with the exclusion of the Church from the eucharistic mystery which follows from it, may be seen as preparing the ground theologically for the more specifically *liturgical* research of others in the 1950's. To locate the Church once more *within* the Eucharist is implicitly to recognise the bishop's care of the former as something primarily exercised by celebration of the latter. Summarising the background of *Lumen Gentium*, Ratzinger says that '[f]or modern theology it is again clear that the *corpus verum* and the *corpus mysticum* are ordained one to another' and that service of one cannot be separated from service of the other: 'they constitute a unity of service to the one body of the Lord.' Giving credit to de Lubac, Ratzinger recalls not only *Corpus Mysticum*, but also the programmatic *Catholicism:* 'in everything that it [Vatican II] said on the Church it follows exactly the line of de Lubac's thought.'" P. McPartlan, *The Eucharist Makes the Church: Henri de Lubac and John Zizioulas in Dialogue* (Edinburgh: T. & T. Clark, 1993), 102. Perhaps also noteworthy is the fact that, in his article "A Half Century of Ecclesiology" of 1989, two years after his settling on the model "Community of Disciples," Dulles gives scant coverage of de Lubac and makes almost no mention of the church as sacrament. Conversely, he devotes considerable space to the theology of Yves Congar and the growth of the communion and people of God models. Though Dulles admits at the beginning of his article that "it will not be possible, in a single, brief article, to avoid arbitrary selectivity," inevitably his omissions are as interesting as his inclusions.

69. Dulles, *Models of the Church*, 222.

Though Dulles, within the section quoted from chapter 13 of *Models of the Church*, highlights the difference between a community meal and the Eucharist, he leaves largely undeveloped the relationship between the symbolic actualization of the community in the liturgical celebration and the concrete reality of the community of disciples in the world. This is, however, a question to which Dulles returns in *Models of Revelation*. His insistence, consonant with the Council, that the Eucharist is "source and summit," that it is "the climactic sacrament, signifying the deepest and most intimate union with Christ" and the place where the church is most typically expressed, sits somewhat uneasily with a model that is not explicitly liturgico-sacramental. Rather, these phrases resonate more deeply with the chapter, "The Church and Revelation," that appeared in the earlier edition of *Models of the Church*. There he had maintained: "If Christ as sacrament is the culminating self-revelation of God, it follows that the Church, to the extent that it is the sacrament of Christ, is also a kind of concrete revelation of the divine. All the Vatican II texts on the Church as sacrament thus become available for the theory of revelation."[70]

Essentially, it is the enterprise of Dulles in *Models of Revelation* to test theories of God's self-manifestation against each other and in the light of symbolic mediation. Dulles's thesis, as Leo O'Donovan said in a review, is that "the qualities of revelation thus correspond to those of genuine symbolism, which can then be seen as the most apt

---

70. Ibid., 182. A sense that the model of community of disciples is insufficient to the function of holding together the diverse elements of the sacramental economy expressed in revelation, church, and sacraments, can be gained from Dulles' reflection that "the liturgy reaches its high point in those actions we call sacraments. It can greatly help our understanding of the sacraments if we study them in relationship. They are the privileged moments in the life of the Church and its members when the crucified and risen Lord can be counted upon to be present and active, according to his promise. Every sacrament is a transaction between the living Lord and the community of the disciples. It is a social and ecclesial dimension that is often forgotten." Ibid., 215.

medium for God's communication with the world."[71] The question of the relationship between symbol, liturgy, and revelation is one that remains pertinent in the later works of Avery Dulles.

Recognizing the Value of Symbols:
Models of Revelation

While there are obvious similarities of method and style between *Models of the Church* and *Models of Revelation*, commentators have recognized something of a postcritical turn in the latter work.[72] The format of the book itself gives some indication of its being divided into two distinct parts: the first, an analysis of the contemporary state of revelation studies through a presentation of five models; and the second, a response to these models from "the lived context of the interpreting critic."[73] Symbolic mediation is fundamental to Dulles's experience and is the dialectical tool that he uses to appraise the individual models of revelation. *Models of the Church* allowed for a certain clarification not only of method, but of subject—a search for that which is essential to the great sign of salvation, the church. While refining his methodology here, Dulles sets his ecclesiological conclusions within the context of a broader theology of sign. In a sense, Dulles is now occupied with the question of whether what is essential to the church as sign and sacrament of salvation is also essential to the self-communication of God as a whole.[74]

---

71. L. O'Donovan, review of A. Dulles, *Models of Revelation, America* 153 (May 28, 1983): 423–24.
72. See L. O'Donovan, "For the Salvation of All Who Believe," in *Faithful Witness: Foundations of Theology for Today's Church*, ed. L. O'Donovan and T. Howland Sanks (London: Geoffrey Chapman, 1989), 33. See also the previously mentioned review by O'Donovan in *America*.
73. L. O'Donovan, review of *Models of Revelation*," 424.
74. See Dulles, "Preface," *Models of Revelation* (Maryknoll, NY: Orbis, 1992), x.

Symbolic Communication

Approaching *Models of Revelation*, it is perhaps best to begin in medias res, that is, with the very question that is central to the study:

> According to this approach [symbolic mediation], revelation never occurs in a purely interior experience or an unmediated encounter with God. It is always mediated through symbol—that is to say, through an externally perceived sign that works mysteriously on the human consciousness so as to suggest more than it can clearly describe or define. Revelatory symbols are those which express and mediate God's self-communication.[75]

The definition of symbol or symbolism that Dulles formulates in chapter 9, and that provides the central hypothesis of *Models of Revelation*, is a general one.[76] Symbols provide a medium through which another reality is passed or communicated. They act mysteriously on the perceiver, inviting participation in an expression that exceeds the literal or univocal. More specific types of symbol, such as the revelatory, function within this general system.

Accordingly, Dulles would rule out signs or indicators based on similitude that make a simple or correlative comparison from this definition. In this, he would seem to be in agreement with Philip Wheelwright's "tensive symbols,"[77] Michael Polanyi's distinction between "indicators" and symbols,[78] Karl Rahner's rejection of "derivative" symbols that function "precisely by reason of their agreement,"[79] and the efforts of Paul Ricoeur to extend the concept

---

75. Dulles, *Models of Revelation*, 131.

76. For a general but full survey of the theology of symbol, see A. Bernard, "Panorama des études symboliques," *Gregorianum* 55 (1974): 379–92.

77. Dulles, *Models of Revelation*, 132, where Dulles makes reference to P. H. Wheelwright, *Metaphor and Reality* (Bloomington, IN: Indiana University Press, 1962), 94.

78. Dulles, *Models of Revelation*, where Dulles cites M. Polanyi and H. Prosch, *Meaning* (Chicago: University of Chicago Press, 1975), 69–75.

79. K. Rahner, "The Theology of Symbol," in *Theological Investigations*, trans. Kevin Smyth, vol. 4 (London: Darton, Longman and Todd, 1966), 221–52, 225.

of symbol beyond analogy.[80] Dulles agrees that symbolic communication is a multivalent communication of "clues"[81] that requires of the perceiver participation of a "deeper degree"[82] than the detached recognition that a sign demands. "Thanks to symbols, we can bring an indefinite number of diffuse memories and experiences into a kind of focus."[83] This focus results from the complex relationships that symbols employ as part of the process of recognition that they engender of the very "thing" they mediate. Such a nexus may involve "other forms such as analogy, myth, metaphor, allegory, parable, and ritual,"[84] all of which participate to varying degrees in symbolic mediation. Biblical literature, as Dulles points out, is a choice example of such a symbolic network, and, as a result "of this symbolic dimension, the revelatory language of Scripture is capable of grasping and transforming the responsive reader."[85]

Toward a Definition of Symbol

The wide and somewhat fluid sense that Dulles affords to the concept of symbol does not result from a lack of specificity or failed systematization on his part. Rather, it would appear to stem from a positive option he has taken.[86] For Dulles, to state that revelation

80. P. Ricoeur, *The Conflict of Interpretations* (Evanston, IL: Northwestern University Press, 1974), 12.
81. Dulles, *Models of Revelation*, 132.
82. Ibid., 133.
83. Ibid., 132.
84. Ibid., 133.
85. Ibid., 136.
86. As Rahner states at the beginning of his exposition in "The Theology of Symbol," "An enquiry into the general sense of the word 'symbol' will show, however, that the concept is much more obscure, difficult and ambiguous than is usually thought, so that one of the tasks of these considerations must be to show that it is wrong to take the concept as an obvious one." Rahner, "The Theology of Symbol," 222. Neither seeking to present an "ontology of symbolism" nor "to look for the highest and most primordial manner in which one reality can present another,"

is always communicated through symbol necessitates a generality of category that can accommodate both broad-based and specific notions of the self-communication of God, while still responding to certain presuppositions about the created order and human consciousness. The search for such an interpretive category is surely the goal of the book's methodology: establishing a model that has enough scope and synthesis to facilitate an understanding of revelation. Though Dulles does not select the philosopher Ernst Cassirer as one of the "esteemed thinkers"[87] of the twentieth century who have popularized study of the role of symbol, Dulles would concur with the breadth of category that Cassirer gives to the mode of symbolic communication:

> Man lives is a symbolic universe. Language, myth, art and religion are parts of this universe. They are the varied threads which weave the symbolic net, the tangled web of human experience. All human progress in thought and experience refines upon and strengthens this net . . . . Instead of dealing with the things themselves man is in a sense constantly conversing with himself. He has so enveloped himself in linguistic forms, in artistic images, in mythical symbols or religious rites that he cannot see or know anything except by the interposition of this artificial medium.[88]

Moreover, and without hint of contradiction, Dulles would agree with the position of Paul Ricoeur, who defines his understanding of symbol in contradistinction to the universal definition of Cassirer. For, though Dulles would doubtless be in agreement with the limitations that Ricoeur imposes[89] on the description above, he would

as was Rahner, Dulles is happier to stay with a more ambiguous definition appropriate to a wider understanding of revelation and its communication.

87. Dulles, *Models of Revelation*, 131.

88. E. Cassirer, *An Essay on Man* (New Haven: Yale University Press, 1944), 25, in F. W. Dillistone, *The Power of Symbols* (London: SCM, 1986), 120.

89. "I give a narrower sense to the word 'symbol' than authors who, like Cassirer, call symbolic any apprehension of reality by means of signs, from perception, myth and art to science, but I give a broader sense than those who, starting from rhetoric or the neo-Platonic tradition, reduce

not want to lose the richness of Cassirer's fundamental vision, if only as source for more objective formulations. The theologian's particular understanding of symbol functions from within this far wider and related concept category. It is as theologians that both Dulles and Ricoeur "refine" this broad definition.

Indeed, it is the fact of this large-scope concept that allows Dulles to make an enlightening comparison between the common properties of symbolism and revelation. First of all, symbolism is the appropriate medium for revelation, because it shares a participatory property. Symbolism, like revelation, is an invitation to inhabit an environment.[90] Neither form of communication is specific, closed, nor definite. Rather, they initiate "an open-ended action, not a closed-off object."[91] Equally, another common property is that of transformation. Participation presumes an effect, as active involvement in a different context must involve change. Dulles illustrates this point by alluding to the healing effect of symbolism when employed within psychotherapy. A third and related common property of revelation and symbolic communication is the evocation of response. A sense of solidarity, strength, confidence, and security can result from the definition that a symbolic network provides. Finally, Dulles refers to the "sixth-sense" properties that both symbolism and revelation can encourage. Both these means of communication reach beyond that which is "normally accessible to discursive thought,"[92] and are consonant with the idea of mystery. Hence, while holding these two concepts together, Dulles would

the symbol to analogy. I define 'symbol' as any structure of significance in which a direct, primary, literal meaning designates, in addition, another meaning which is indirect, secondary and figurative and which is apprehended only through the first." P. Ricoeur, "Existence and Hermeneutics," quoted in Dillistone, *The Power of Symbols*, 128.

90. Cf. Nathan Mitchell's understanding, which Dulles alludes to here, in N. Mitchell, "Symbols Are Actions, Not Objects," *Living Worship* 13, no. 2 (1977): 1–2.

91. Dulles, *Models of Revelation*, 136.

92. Ibid., 137.

conclude that "the meaning of the symbol, therefore, cannot be precisely nailed down in terms of categorical thought and language. Yet the symbol is not without value for the serious quest of truth. It 'gives rise to thought,' according to Ricoeur's famous phrase. By putting us in touch with deeper aspects of reality symbolism can generate an indefinite series of particular insights."[93]

Christian Symbols

While Dulles would recognise and defend the importance of a general appreciation of symbol and symbolism for a correct appreciation of their role within revelation, he is also aware of the role of the particular. To speak of the particular revelation of God that came to fullness in the person of Jesus Christ demands a similar specificity in the definition of the symbols that pertain to that very self-manifestation. In this, Dulles recognizes the "important nuance"[94] that Karl Rahner has given to the symbols of Christian revelation.

Toward the end of chapter 9 of *Models of Revelation*, Dulles returns to the five models of revelation that he presented in the first half of the book and reexamines them in the context of symbolic mediation. His purpose is twofold: to allow the symbolic approach to correct inherent difficulties and absorb valid contributions from the models, but also to recognize that "these models in turn can contribute to the symbolic theory by further explicating what is required for symbol to be truly revelatory."[95] The models examined in this opening expository section are the following: firstly, revelation as *doctrine*, an understanding in which the propositional element of the divine

93. Ibid.
94. Ibid., 131.
95. Ibid., 141.

self-manifestation is regarded as of uppermost significance. Secondly, revelation as *history*, a model that focuses attention on the event character of revelation and sees the great acts of God in history as the primary mode of his self-disclosure. *Inner experience* is the third model that Dulles elaborates, and with it he shifts the focus of attention from the objective manifestation of revelation to its subjective realization in the experience of believers. The fourth model, that of *dialectical presence*, has the transcendence of God as its main focus, and though from this perspective the discovery of God in the language, history, and experience of humanity must be denied, paradoxically, these loci remain places of mysterious and salvific encounter. Finally Dulles looks at a model of revelation described as the *new awareness* or *consciousness model*. Here the focus is not on an extrinsic communication, but rather some sort of internal stimulation or enrichment from within is regarded as a better description of the mode of God's revelation. From these differing approaches, and in the light of a series of comparisons and contrasts, a common element is pursued by the process of dialectical retrieval.

Recognizing that theologians representative of all five models agree that Jesus Christ is the supreme mediator of revelation, it is possible to say that, in essence, each model requires of symbolic mediation an answer to the same question: "Does the symbolic approach lead to a doctrine of revelation in which Christ is no longer uniquely normative, but is reduced to 'one symbol among others'?"[96] That is to say, can something that is symbolic and therefore by its nature has a fluid and wide-ranging meaning also have objective validity?

Dulles would suggest that each model affirms, and is affirmed by, the recognition of Christ as the uniquely normative symbol

96. Ibid., 151.

of revelation. Hence, he suggests that it is only through a specific understanding of Jesus Christ as symbol that the fears of the propositionalists can be allayed. Christ is a symbol who communicates a surplus rather than an absence of meaning,[97] and from this fullness the specific truths of revelation are manifest. Likewise, in the historical figure of Jesus Christ, the seemingly antithetical positions of symbol and history are united. In Christ, the metahistorical symbol, are grounded the events of history, and the divine meaning that truly belongs to a particular event is opened to the symbolic interpretation of the religious inquirer. The demands made by the mystics of the experiential model for a "mediated immediacy" are met in Jesus Christ, a symbol who is, in himself, the self-communication of the divine. Dulles recognises that the Christ of symbolic mediation shares many features in common with the Word of God as described by dialectical theologians, even in their Barthian extremes.[98] Christ is the ever-transcendent Word who is, at the same time, the self-expression of the revealing God.

Finally, though, one might say that the understanding of symbolic mediation belonging to the new awareness model cannot allow for a Christ who can be regarded as a uniquely normative symbol. Yet Dulles would not agree. For him, the consciousness model only poses the question made by the dialectical theologians, but in reverse perspective. In recognizing symbol, as this school does, "as the prime bearer of revelation,"[99] because of its flexibility, the model must concede that as a result of that very pliability, "symbol can have an objective density"[100] that compels the subject to pursue a meaning in the permanent structures of being.

---

97. Ibid., 142.
98. Cf. ibid., 150–52.
99. Ibid., 153.
100. Ibid., 153.

Symbols and Sacraments

It is, however, the definition given to symbol from the permanent structures of being that allows Dulles, Rahner, and others to see Jesus Christ as someone normative for all revelatory symbols. Hence Dulles can refine his definition as follows:

> The terminology of sacrament generally has reference not so much to revelation as to the communication of grace and sanctification. For the communication of revelation, symbol is perhaps a better term than sacrament. If we take the term symbol in a strongly realistic sense, meaning a sign in which the thing signified is really present, Christ may be called the symbol of God par excellence. Such is in fact the teaching of Karl Rahner, who writes: "The Logos, the Son of the Father, is truly, in his humanity as such, the revelatory symbol in which the Father enunciates himself, in this Son, to the world—revelatory because the symbol renders present what is revealed."[101]

Dulles contends that *symbol* is the more appropriate term for that which mediates revelation. Then, with Rahner's theology as a background, he forms a particular understanding of symbol that justifies his initial contention. In his article "The Theology of Symbol," Rahner makes the specific nature of his enterprise clear. From an ontological point of view, he is "to look for the highest and most primordial manner in which one reality can represent another."[102] This, as Dulles recognises, is to search for a real symbol "in which the thing signified is really present." Both these requirements guard against an ambiguity of term, about which Rahner makes the reader well aware in the opening sections of his essay. They also allow him to assert that symbolism belongs to the fundamental reality that is God: "All beings are by their nature symbolic, because they necessarily 'express' themselves in order to

---

101. Ibid., 158.
102. Rahner, "The Theology of Symbol," 225.

attain their own nature."[103] The supreme example of this type of symbolism is that of the Father's expression of the Word, and it is in this sense that Rahner teaches that "the Logos is the symbol of the Father."[104] For Rahner, the normative and most perfect example of symbolic mediation is the life of the Blessed Trinity. Here are worked out the ontological principles[105] that allow him to suggest that "the whole of theology is incomprehensible if it is not essentially a theology of symbols."[106]

Because a being can realize itself only through the expression of its essential otherness in symbol, it is by means of this self-realization alone that a being can make itself known.[107] Hence, for Rahner, symbol is inherent to both God and his self-revelation. It is, presumably, for this reason that Dulles regards "symbol," rather than sacrament, as a more appropriate expression of that which is revelatory. However, essential to the christological and ecclesiological systems that Rahner develops from his understanding of symbol is the fact that these realities can never be regarded as something separate from, or extrinsic to, the object they symbolize. A real symbol affects a real presence. Thus, speaking of the commonly

---

103. Ibid., 224.
104. Ibid., 239.
105. "Being *as* such, and hence *as* one (*ens* as *unum*), for the fulfilment of its being and its unity, emerges into a plurality—of which the supreme mode is the Trinity. The distinct moments deriving from the 'one' which make for the perfection of its unity stem essentially, i.e. by their origin in and from another, from this most primary unity: they have therefore a more primary and basic 'agreement' with it than anything produced by efficient causality." Ibid., 228.
106. Ibid., 235.
107. "What then is the primordial meaning of symbol and symbolic, according to which each being is in itself and for itself symbolic, and hence (and to this extent) symbolic for another? It is this: as a being realizes itself in its own intrinsic 'otherness' (which is constitutive of its being), retentive of its intrinsic plurality (which is contained in its self-realization) as its derivative and hence congruous expression, it makes itself known. This derivative and congruous expression, constitutive of each being, is the symbol which comes in addition from the object of knowledge to the knower—in addition only, because already initially present in the depths of the grounds of each one's being. The being is known in this symbol, without which it cannot be known at all: thus it is symbol in the original (transcendental) sense of the word." Ibid., 231.

misconceived relationship that exists between the church and the sacraments, Rahner has this to say:

> In this way the relationship between the two remains so superficial and external that in the average view it would not be at all inconceivable that God might just as well have entrusted the administration of those means of grace to some other person or institution. The Church as Church, and the Church as dispenser of the mysteries of God, are almost only *per accidens* one and the same.[108]

Neither are the sacraments *per accidens* symbols of the church that reveal the presence of Christ to the world. Therefore, Rahner is clear that "the teaching on the sacraments is the classic place in which a theology of the symbol is put forward in general Catholic theology."[109] While the distinction that Dulles makes between symbol and sacrament may be an incidental aside, an argument that was thoroughgoing in its attention to Rahner's theology of symbol would, perhaps, not have found such a distinction possible.[110] The

---

108. K. Rahner, *The Church and the Sacraments* (London: Burns and Oates, 1974), 10. First published as *Kirche und Sakramente* (Freiburg: Herder, 1963). But such an assertion is obviously not without its problems, especially with regard to the salvific elements of other religions. Jacques Dupuis touches on something of this inherent difficulty with regard to Rahner's system when he seeks to explain his doctrine of "Anonymous Christianity": "Anonymous Christianity and explicit Christianity entail distinct regimes of salvation and distinct modalities of mediation of the mystery of Jesus Christ. Such mediation in explicit Christianity implies becoming 'conscious of itself explicitly in faith and in hearing the word of the gospel, in the Church's profession of faith, in sacrament, and in living an explicit Christian life which knows that it is related to Jesus of Nazareth.' Thus anonymous Christianity remains a fragmentary, incomplete, radically deficient reality. It harbours dynamics which impel it to become part of explicit Christianity. Nevertheless, the same mystery of salvation is present on both sides, through different mediations." J. Dupuis, *Christianity and the Religions: From Confrontation to Dialogue* (Maryknoll, NY: Orbis, 2002), 55.

109. Rahner, "The Theology of Symbol," 241.

110. To this ontological study, Joseph Wong provides the background of the "Religious Origin of Rahner's Symbol Concept," in the first chapter of his doctoral thesis. Basing his argument on the Ignatian spirituality that underlies all Rahner's theology, Wong concludes that "Rahner finds the term 'sacrament' most suitable to describe the mediating function of the world. For him the world is the 'effective sacrament of God,' through which God gives himself to us." As Wong also recognises, Rahner gives support to this position in his later *Meditations on Priestly Life*, when he states, "Their position between God and us can ultimately be described somehow only dialectically through the concept of sacrament, the Chalcedonian concept of *asynchytos kai*

relationship between a theology of symbol and a theology of revelation is a fundamental one,[111] and later, with Rahner's help, Dulles seeks to clarify the relationship further.

In the chapter entitled "Revelation and the Religions," Dulles seeks to show how, in the face of a common experience of "plural shock,"[112] each of the five models, to varying degrees, needs to invoke an understanding of symbol in order to establish a theology of revelation that is credible within the context of nonbiblical religions. In a pluralistic setting, distinctions become necessary, and they, not separations, make for happier resolutions. The separations that are inherent to the system of the dialectical school,[113] and that exist in

---

adiairetos." Hence Wong concludes, "The sacramental function of reality is explained by the 'unity in distinction' of the Chalcedonian formula. He [Rahner] also describes the sacramental mediatorship of reality as 'mediation in immediacy' to God." See J. H. P. Wong, *Logos-Symbol in the Christology of Karl Rahner* (Rome: LAS, 1984), 49.

111. Gerald O'Collins makes an interesting comment on this distinction: "Finally, salvation and revelation are too intimately connected to permit the thesis that Christ is universal Saviour but not the universal agent of revelation. The experience of salvation affects the entire existence of the subject receiving it. It is implausible to throw a *cordon sanitaire* around human cognition, as if Christ's saving grace could be 'invisibly active' (*Gaudium et Spes*, n. 22) in the hearts and lives of some people without *in any sense* affecting their knowledge. The divine self-communication, which is offered to the whole person, entails revelation and grace. One could put the point this way: Revelation is, as it were, salvation and grace for the mind and intellect. (As we have noted, this cognitive aura holds true even for contemporary theologies of revelation as interpersonal encounter). Where the process of salvation affects human knowing and thinking, this means something in the order of revelation. In these terms Christ cannot be the agent of saving grace for all without also being the agent of revelation for all. His unique mediatorship between God and human being (1Tim 2:5) involves both roles." G. O'Collins, *Fundamental Theology* (London: Darton, Longman and Todd, 1981), 117–18. As has been seen, one of the fundamental criticisms that Dulles made of Latourelle's *Théologie de la Révélation* is that it is "almost exclusively concerned with the historical Judeo-Christian revelation." And yet, at the same time, Dulles states, "It must be possible for men to receive supernatural revelation prior to any instruction about the facts of redemptive history and their doctrinal interpretation. In such a perspective, the interior illumination of grace seems to take on a greater constitutive role in the process of revelation than Latourelle is inclined to allow it." Dulles, "The Theology of Revelation," 52–53.

112. Cf. G. Fackre, "The Scandals of Particularity and Universality," *Mid-Stream: An Ecumenical Journal* 22 (1983), as quoted in Dulles, *Models of Revelation*, 191.

113. "For these theologians Christ as the word of God stands in judgement against all human achievements including religion itself insofar as it proceeds from man." Dulles, *Models of Revelation*, 185.

the revelation theologies of both the propositionalist and historical schools, Dulles shows to be largely untenable. The separation of the natural and supernatural orders,[114] or of universal and salvific history,[115] does not ultimately resolve the Christian's problem of Christ as universal and unique Revealer.[116] Neither, however, is this problem adequately addressed by the lack of distinction in the other models. In recognising a common, underlying, revelatory experience, the experiential school came to "regard the differences among the religions as accidental rather than essential."[117] Similarly, the elements that establish the distinction of the Christian faith are, for the new consciousness model, primarily "myth-symbols" whose fundamental historical data are largely irrelevant for salvation.[118]

The Symbolic Coincidence of Salvation and Revelation

By way of the insufficiencies that Dulles points out in the five models of his study, he brings the reader to the point of acknowledging symbolic mediation as an understanding of revelation that allows

114. "If one gives more exact theological thought to this matter, then one cannot regard nature and grace as two phases in the life of the individual which follow each other in time. It is furthermore impossible to think that this offer of supernatural, divinising grace made to all men on account of the universal salvific purpose of God, should in general remain ineffective." Cf. K. Rahner, "Christianity and the Non-Christian Religions," *Theological Investigations*, trans. K.-H. Kruger, vol. 5 (London: Darton, Longman and Todd, 1966), 123.

115. "This concession would seem to exclude all revelation within history were it not for the fact, recognised by Christians alone, that the end of universal history has already occurred proleptically in the Resurrection of Jesus from the dead. Pannenberg therefore agrees with Barth that revelation, as the disclosure of the one God, occurs only in Christ, in whom the divine breaks into the historical continuum." Dulles, *Models of Revelation*, 181.

116. "This pluralism is a greater threat and a reason for greater unrest for Christianity than for any other religion. For no other religion—not even Islam—maintains so absolutely that it is *the* religion, the one and only valid revelation of the living God." Rahner, "Christianity and the Non-Christian Religions," 116. For a valuable discussion of how Jacques Dupuis seeks to address this problem see: Gerald O'Collins, "Jacques Dupuis's Contribution to Interreligious Dialogue," Theological Studies, 64 (2003), 388-397.

117. Dulles, *Models of Revelation*, 183.

118. Ibid., 189.

Christianity to maintain its unique and universal role amid the world's religions. Crucial to this concept of revelation is Christ as the sacrament of salvation. It would seem that for Dulles, Rahner's symbol Christology gives the best, if necessarily approximate, explanation of this mystery:

> In holding the salvific and revelatory character of the religions in general, Rahner does not relativize biblical revelation and Christianity. In his terminology, the religion of the Old and New Testaments constitutes the "special" history of revelation and salvation, inerrantly directed toward Christ, in whom God and the world enter into "absolute and unsurpassable unity." Christ, the incarnate Word, is the absolute religious symbol in whom the aspirations of humanity for a definitive and irrevocable self-communication of God are fulfilled. The religions can be interpreted as expressions of a "searching memory" which somehow anticipates God's culminating gift in Jesus Christ.[119]

To hold together the salvific and revelatory aspects of the religions, Rahner must address the polarities that exist between the universal significance for salvation of the Christ event and its unique nature. This is, in fact, the polarity that can be found in the relationship of anthropology to Christology. Rahner establishes a deeper unity of the apparently unbridgeable separation of the human and divine by means of the symbol. The "absolute and unsurpassable unity" that God and humanity enter into is the unity of the Chalcedon definition, a reality that is itself to be understood symbolically. Christ is the absolute and unique symbol of God, his perfect self-expression. But Christ is also, and simultaneously, the universal symbol of perfect humanity.[120] It is the modern world that necessitates this correlation between the general religious impulse of humanity and its cultures,

119. Ibid., 182.
120. E. Schillebeeckx expresses the same concept of Christ as the unique interrelation of poles in *Jesus: An Experiment in Christology* (New York: Seabury, 1979), 603. See also J. Galot, *Who is Christ?* (Rome: Gregorian University Press, 1980), 31.

and the message of Christ in particular.[121] Hence, in his transcendental-anthropological method,[122] Rahner consciously seeks to combine fundamental and dogmatic theology.[123]

The concept of symbolic communication is central to Rahner's transcendental method. As Joseph Wong makes clear, it is because of his symbol Christology that Rahner can claim the absolute unity of God and humanity in the natural order: "Man as *potentia oboedientialis* for a possible word of God in history becomes *potentia oboedientialis*

121. It would be partisan not to make any reference to the significant criticism that von Balthasar made of this system: "My main argument . . . is this: It might be true that from the very beginning man was created to be disposed towards God's revelation. . . . *Gratia supponit naturam.* But when God's grace sends his own living Word to his creatures, he does not do so . . . primarily to fulfil their deepest needs and yearnings. Rather he communicates and actively demonstrates such unheard-of things that man feels not so much satisfied as awestruck by a love that he could never have hoped to experience. For who would dare to have described God as love, without having first received the revelation of the Trinity in the acceptance of the Cross by the Son?" H. U. von Balthasar, "Current Trends in Catholic Theology and the Responsibility of the Christian," *Communio* 5 (1978): 79. Whatever the merits of this criticism (for an analysis, see A. Nichols, "Rahner and Balthasar: The Anonymous Christianity Debate Revisited," in *Beyond the Blue Glass* [London: Saint Austin, 2002], 107–28), such a focus on the paschal mystery is not without significance in regard to the overall topic of this book.

122. To come to a better understanding of the centrality of this method and its consequences within the major areas of Rahner's theology, it is necessary to draw a composite picture from the following articles: K. Rahner, "Concerning the Relationship Between Nature and Grace," *Theological Investigations*, trans. C. Ernst, vol. 1 (London: Darton, Longman and Todd, 1961), 297–317; Rahner, "Current Problems in Christology," *Theological Investigations*, 1:149–200; Rahner, "Some Implications of the Scholastic Concept of Uncreated Grace," *Theological Investigations*, 1:319–46; Rahner, "Theology and Anthropology," *Theological Investigations*, trans. G. Harrison, vol. 9 (London: Darton, Longman and Todd, 1972), 28–45; Rahner, "Reflections on Methodology in Theology," *Theological Investigations*, trans. D. Bourke, vol. 11 (London: Darton, Longman and Todd, 1974), 68–114. See also his definition of the supernatural existential in K. Rahner and H. Vorgrimler, *Theological Dictionary* (New York: Seabury, 1965), 161. For a clear analysis of Rahner's transcendental Christology and its major critics, see W. Kasper, *Jesus The Christ* (London: Burns and Oates, 1976), 49ff. Also A. Amato, "Dall'uomo al Cristo, Salvatore assoluto, nella teologia di K. Rahner," *Salesianum* 41 (1979): 3–35.

123. See Gustave Martelet's discussion of this point. Conscious of Rahner's efforts in this area, he declares, "It follows that adherence to Christ by faith and the discovery of the full reality of the human person should be one and the same process, since Christ, the historical Messiah, is also the Truth, Foundation, Reason for being, and supreme Crown of the human person and all that is human." Cf. G. Martelet, "Christology and Anthropology: Toward a Christian Genealogy of the Human," in Latourelle and O'Collins, *Problems and Perspectives of Fundamental Theology*, 152. An interesting discussion of the issue can also be found in R. Latourelle, "L'uomo 'decifrato' da Cristo," in *Annunciare Cristo ai Giovani*, ed. A. Amato and G. Zevini (Rome: LAS, 1980), 265–80.

for the hypostatic union itself. Rahner describes the primary definition of man as 'the possible otherness (*Anderssein*) of the self-emptying of God and the possible brother of Christ.' Thus it is only in the mystery of Christ that man fully discovers his true destiny."[124] This is to say that, because Christ is at once the self-expression or *Realsymbol* of God and perfectly human, humanity finds itself able, in him, to be the "cypher" or "grammar" for God's symbolic expression.[125]

Symbolic Realism

Having acknowledged the predisposition of Dulles toward the Rahnerian symbol Christology as a basis for understanding symbolic mediation, it becomes possible to assess how this system accords with Dulles's own theology of revelation. In an article particularly pertinent to this point, and published two years before *Models of Revelation*, Dulles sets Rahner's transcendental method within the context of his own particular theological perspectives. Dulles describes the act of faith, or conversion, in Rahnerian terms: "The dynamics of conversion would be thrown into confusion if the enquirer focused on anything other than the divine transcendent as the goal of the search. In the light of this orientation to the 'unknown God' Jesus Christ can appear as the form in which God is to be found. The Christian is one who believes that God is to be found pre-eminently in Jesus Christ."[126] In speaking of humanity's yearning for a supernatural horizon and that restlessness being met by an

---

124. Wong, *Logos-Symbol in the Theology of Karl Rahner*, 232.
125. Ibid., 232: Here Wong makes use of Rahner's work in *Foundations of Christian Faith*, trans. W. V. Dych (London: Darton, Longman and Todd, 1978), 223ff. See also W. Kasper's explanation of this point in "Neuansätze gegenwartiger Christologie," in *Christologische Schwerpunkte*, ed. W. Kasper (Düsseldorf: Patmos, 1980), 22.
126. Dulles, "The Church: Sacrament and Ground of Faith," 263.

experience of the incarnate Son, Dulles approaches the question of the act of faith conscious not only of the transcendent categories of Rahner,[127] but also of his own conversion. For what particularly interests Dulles in this article is the role of symbol in the search for the divine transcendent—more specifically, that is to say, the part played by the church in the process of conversion. The role that Dulles describes is that of a sacrament, and this in turn, as already discussed, presupposes a particular theology of symbol.

> Looking upon the Church as the symbolic presence of Christ, who is himself the symbolic presence of the Word in human flesh, this vision preserves the realism of revelation. It safeguards the social character of revelation and yet makes room for the responsible participation of the individual believer, led by the grace of the Holy Spirit. It supplies a living, objective norm and at the same time assures an immediate, personal relationship to God on the part of every Christian. For all these values to be secure, it is essential that the Church be understood neither as a merely human construction nor as a merely invisible communion, but as a sacrament; that is to say, as a visible presence of the invisible Christ, who communicates his life by means of it. The symbolic words

127. Two sections from Rahner's article "Considerations on the Active Role of the Person in the Sacramental Event," serve to provide the background to Dulles's thought here. First, "It is true that we can speak of God as the nameless and incomprehensible mystery only in very abstract terms. And for this reason too the reference of man to God, the fact that his existence is open to and orientated towards the mystery of God has of its very nature something unnameable in it. How could it be so easy to describe the path, seeing that it leads into the pathlessness of the inconceivable God? How could we find it easy to describe in words the ultimate act of man in which, surrendering himself, hoping, loving, adoring—in a word believing, he allows himself to fall into this ineffable mystery which constitutes the innermost basis, *and at the same time* the infinite remoteness of his existence that draws him out of himself? And if grace constitutes precisely that power which enabled him to achieve this making over of himself to the absolute mystery and that most special quality given by God enabling him to achieve this, how then can it be easy to speak about it in "intelligible terms"? K. Rahner, "Considerations on the Active Role of the Person in the Sacramental Event" *Theological Investigations*, trans. D. Bourke, vol. 14 (London: Darton, Longman and Todd, 1976), 167. Second, "And precisely here one further point must be made concerning this grace which constitutes the innermost depths and the mystery of human life at its average and everyday level: this innermost dynamism of the normal 'secular' life of man as it exists always and everywhere has found in Jesus of Nazareth its clearest manifestation, and in him has proved itself as real, victorious and attaining to God." Ibid., 168. Cf. also Rahner's definition of "supernatural existential" in Rahner and Vorgrimler, *Theological Dictionary*, 161.

and actions of the Church, perceived in faith, are signs and sacraments of the encounter with God.[128]

The original definition of symbolic mediation that Dulles gave suggested that "revelation never occurs in a purely interior experience or unmediated encounter with God. It is always mediated through symbol."[129] Hence Dulles can begin his chapter on the church as bearer of revelation with the blunt assertion: "Jesus Christ, the great symbol of revelation, is not accessible except insofar as there are signs that point to him in the world today."[130] So Dulles singles out the church. While not pretending that the relationship between the Scriptures and the church is anything other than complex, he stresses the essentially ecclesial character of the Bible, and hence the fact that its contents remain only part of the revelation that is the church. It is in this sense that Dulles recognizes the church as fundamental to revelation and its mediation. Again, by means of his five models he analyzes how this can be so. The stiff extrinsicism of the propositional model, where the church is merely a channel to a supernaturally deposited scripture and tradition, is more than slightly softened by the historical model, which fleshes out this "giving" in the words and deeds of salvation history.[131] Yet both schools see the church as simply handing on something remembered, and have a restricted sense of either actualization in the present or the future possibilities of the original deposit. Thus the important question of the complete and yet ongoing nature of revelation forms a backdrop

128. Dulles, *Models of Revelation*, 227.
129. Ibid., 131.
130. Ibid., 211.
131. In distinguishing two main methods within the historical model, Dulles takes Oscar Cullmann as representative of a salvation history approach and Wolfhart Pannenberg of a universal history approach. For Cullmann, revelation was concluded in biblical times as both event and interpretation. And while Pannenberg writes in contradistinction to those who understand revelation as something occurring in the present as a sort of timeless kerygma, he does allow for an ongoing, Spirit-led manifestation of revelation, though he is keen to emphasize that this is not "an independent occurrence." Dulles, *Models of Revelation*, 214.

to the issues discussed here.[132] The experiential and dialectical models serve only to intensify these questions, the debate shifting between those who subordinate the historical "facts" of revelation to the present inner experience of the believer, and those who seek to maintain some sort of external objectivity. To some extent, Dulles's fifth model, the consciousness or new awareness model, struggles with the question of stasis and development. This "school" concentrates on the dynamics of the universal fulfillment of the revelation that came in Jesus Christ. God is "redemptively present in human history as a whole," and the communication of his revelation cannot be restricted to the life of the incarnate Word of God, but concerns the ongoing dissemination of this message to the cosmos.

What Dulles presents by way of these five models is a series of contradictory positions that he summarizes in a list of questions[133] before seeking a resolution to them in the concept of symbolic communication. Essentially, these are questions that have remained part of the theological discussion of revelation ever since it was regarded as a distinct topic, and even before. Fundamentally, the issue remains whether revelation is better understood as a body of intellectual truths extrinsically communicated in the past and preserved in the church, or as a living, organic revelation by way

---

132. For further discussion of this point, see K. Rahner, "The Death of Jesus and the Closure of Revelation," in *Theological Investigations*, trans. E. Quinn, vol. 13 (London: Darton, Longman and Todd, 1984), 132–42. See also the article by G. O'Collins, "Revelation Past and Present," in Latourelle, *Vatican II: Assessment and Perspectives*, 1:125–37.

133. "As this survey of propositions indicates, disagreements remain about the Church's relationship to revelation. Does it receive new revelation or only transmit a revelation given in the remote past? If the latter, is the revelation totally contained in the Bible alone? Does the Church transmit revelation by formal teaching or by incarnating it in its corporate life and worship? Does revelation continue to occur in the proclamation and worship of the Church? Does the individual believer receive revelation immediately from God or only mediately through the ministry of the Church? Is the Church maintained in the gospel by a 'charism of unfailing truth' or does it sometimes stray and have to be brought back again by prophetic protest, by biblical exegesis, or by historical research? On questions such as these there is as yet no general consensus among Christian theologians." Dulles, *Models of Revelation*, 217.

of which the truths of salvation are constantly made incarnate in the church. And if the latter is the preferable option, the question remains as to how this may be spoken of in relation to the former.

The church as sacrament is, for Dulles, an understanding of symbolic communication that reconciles some of the difficulties in the relationship between the church and the primordial revelation. The ability of the sacramental model to reconcile seemingly conflicting aspects has already been seen in an ecclesiological context, and Dulles exploits this potential again here. Being the sacrament of Christ, the church is a real symbol that communicates the life, veracity, and immediacy of her founder and sustainer. The corporate nature of the church is an essential aspect of her role as sacrament. The revelation that achieved fulfillment in Jesus Christ is a complex communication, which establishes a network of relationships ultimately rooted in the life of the Blessed Trinity. The church is the sacrament of the Trinitarian life that Christ came to reveal, and as such draws to univocal expression the many and varied aspects of God's self-communication.[134] It is in this sense that the church "safeguards the social character of revelation and yet makes room for the responsible participation of the individual." It is by means of the participation of the individual in the sacramental celebration, the coming together as one by the grace of the Holy Spirit, that the church can be constituted as the sacrament of salvation.

---

134. "The Church, rather than its individual members, is the prime recipient of revelation. In its history of salvation and perdition, of grace and sin, humanity exists and acts socially—that is to say, as a network of people in relationships. A sacrament and hence the Church as sacrament, is a socially constituted and communal symbol of grace as present and transforming individuals into a people. Sacraments have a dialogic structure insofar as they are administered in mutual interaction, so that individuals can achieve together, in their interrelatedness, new levels of life and meaning that they could not achieve in isolation. Every sacrament binds the individual in new ways to the Church, which is the great sacrament. Only in connection with the Church, the community of believers, does the individual have access to the revelation of God in Christ." Ibid., 220.

In a passage that appears almost directly after the previous excerpt in the chapter "Revelation and Eschatology," Dulles attempts to explain how the Holy Spirit constitutes the church in immediate unity with Christ. The paradigm he gives is inevitably sacramental:

> The time of the Church, therefore, is a sacramental, eucharistic time, in which the Lord is present in mystery through the Holy Spirit who has been given. Does this mean that God continues to reveal himself in the Church? Some distinctions seem to be necessary. The Constitution on Divine Revelation, after stressing the completeness of revelation in the career of the Incarnate Word, including his death and resurrection and the "sending of the Spirit of truth," added: "The Christian dispensation, therefore, as the new and definitive covenant, will never pass away, and now we await no further new public revelation before the glorious manifestation of our Lord Jesus Christ."[135]

Basing his thought on Hans Urs von Balthasar's *A Theology of History*,[136] Dulles here offers an explanation of how the church actualizes the revelation of Christ. In doing so, Dulles to some extent resolves the question of how revelation might be complete and yet ongoing. It is necessary, then, to establish the main lines of von Balthasar's thought if sense is to be made of the conclusions that Dulles draws from it in his own work.

For von Balthasar, the work of universalizing Christ's revelation is the function of the Holy Spirit. By exposing the full depth of the meaning of the life, death, and resurrection of Christ, the Holy Spirit establishes the life of the risen Lord as the norm of all history. Von Balthasar examines the nature of the Spirit's work of application in three steps: the forty days, the sacraments, and the missions.[137] Having

---

135. Ibid., 234.
136. H. U. von Balthasar, *A Theology of History* (San Francisco: Ignatius, 1994); German orig. *Theologie der Geschichte* (Einsiedeln: Johannes, 1959).
137. "This carving out of a section of history in order to make it relevant to the whole of history is a process involving several factors, all interconnected in their dependence on the Holy Spirit, but nevertheless distinguishable. The first involves the working of the Spirit in the Incarnate Son himself, as this becomes manifest archetypally, in the Forty Days after the Resurrection. A

distinguished these three steps, he is keen to point out that they are in fact a single, unified action. With this unity in mind, it is perhaps most helpful to see how a theology of the forty days underlies Von Balthasar's theology here.

The forty days, during which Christ showed himself after the Resurrection, is the first action of the Holy Spirit in applying the mysteries of the redemption to the world. In the resurrection, a transformation is worked on the corpse of Jesus of Nazareth, a fundamental metamorphosis takes place in time, and the individual historical existence of Jesus is changed. Jesus succumbs absolutely to history, and in his death his history is ended. The Holy Spirit works to transform this dead historical existence, and the forty days are the first testament to the Spirit's work. These days belong both to earthly and eternal time; Jesus comes into earthly time, and he is dead, risen, glorified. It is because of the work of the Holy Spirit that the risen Christ and his apostles can exist in the same time, that Jesus can walk and talk and eat with people in the time in which he died.[138]

The relationship of Christ to his disciples continues after death, though it should have ended, and this manifestation of Jesus in two times contemporaneously during the forty days is a clear indication of how Christ is related to humanity. Christ is with humanity in its time. Humanity is in the world, and, because Christ is present with

second factor is the working of the Spirit as he relates Christ, thus transformed to the historical Church of every age, which is expressed typically in the sacraments and most fully in the Eucharist. A third completes this relation by creating the missions of Church and individual as applications of the life of Christ to every Christian life and the whole of the life of the Church." Ibid., 82.

138. "All these events are so many unmistakable testimonies to the fact that the risen Christ and the apostolic witness exist contemporaneously in the same time. If Jesus is not a spirit but tangible flesh and blood, if he eats the same fish and honey and bread as the disciples, then his time too is not ghost time, not some fictitious appearance of duration, but time in the most genuine and real sense possible. The fact that it is simultaneously in eternal time makes no difference. That would only be a contradiction if one postulated that time and eternity could not be united, and consequently, that time could not be redeemed and preserved within eternity; in the most positive sense taken up into it." Ibid., 84.

human beings, all the fullness of eternity is manifested in time. The earthly life of the Lord, as far as he is concerned, is not past, and this is why his relationships persist. Jesus in his earthly life became someone in relationship, and this whole historical network that he had formed is risen with him and is part of him. "And since it is not possible that the mode of time belonging to the risen Christ should have altered with his Ascension (this being rather in the nature of a signing off gesture, purely for our benefit),"[139] the mode of time revealed during the forty days remains the foundation of every other mode of his presence in time, in the church and in the world. What is revealed in the forty days represents the ultimate form of Christ's relationship with humanity for "all days even until the consummation of the world" (Mt. 28:20). But the forty days have a more specific purpose, too: they serve to create a bond between the earthly life of the Lord Jesus and the time of the church. It is this specific purpose that is of such interest to Dulles, and that holds the key to reconciling the fact that revelation both ceased with the death of the last apostle and is yet still actualized and available in the church.

The church is a community completely bound to the earthly existence of Jesus, and that at the same time manifests his glorious body. This is because all of history meets in him and rises in him—the past is recapitulated in him, and, appearing in the present, the future of the world is always and also revealed through him. As has been seen repeatedly, creation and history are the two basic categories of the self-manifestation of God. By means of his resurrection, Jesus takes up the whole of history and creation into his own new life. The resurrection means that time comes backwards, as it were, and takes up all that was "behind" to save it and make it what it is meant to be. The same is true of the future, because Jesus the risen Lord is already living in the future, and his death and resurrection are shot through

139. Ibid., 87.

with this future time and therefore bring it back to the point of the paschal mystery. What is being described here is the dynamic of the sacraments. The way in which the risen Lord relates to the world is, at one and the same time, *memoria* and *eschaton*, the concentration of eternity in time.[140]

It is at this point, having established the principal and fundamental method of the universalizing of the redemptive action of Christ by the Holy Spirit, that von Balthasar passes to an examination of the second level of this work of application: the sacramental stage.[141] As von Balthasar himself points out, the transition should not be a difficult one: "Having got as far as this, we should not find any impenetrable obscurity in the second level of universalization, the sacramental level. We shall take as our first principle that Christ's existence, and hence his mode of duration, in the Eucharist and the sacraments is, as far as concerns himself, no different from that which belongs to the Forty Days."[142] The existence of Christ in the sacraments is the same as his existence in the forty days. He is the risen Lord present in earthly time. Present in majesty and glory, he accompanies his disciples, but now he does this in sacramental form. It is the full life of Jesus Christ that is present to us in the sacraments—the earthly life is equally present alongside the heavenly life. Christ brings these moments of time not as from the past or future, but in his being—Jesus Christ is present by virtue of the

---

140. Cf. ibid., 88–90. J. Driscoll expresses this idea of von Balthasar well when he says, "Just as the past is completely recapitualted in the personal existence of the risen Jesus, so the future of the human race, manifested progressively in the Church, is already present in him and revealed in the extension of the reality of his risen body to the Church. '. . .for as the end of history, the eschaton, he is present at its centre, revealing in this one particular *kairos*, this historical moment, the meaning of every *kairos* that can ever be. He does not do this from some point outside and above history, he does it in an actual historical moment." Driscoll, *Theology at the Eucharistic Table* (Leominster, UK: Gracewing, 2003), 120–21. Notice too Driscoll's n210, which refers the reader to an interesting parallel with Ghislain Lafont's understanding of narrative.

141. What follows here is essentially a summary of von Balthasar's *A Theology of History*, 90–97.

142. Ibid., 94.

resurrection and the participant's faith. The entire particular history that he lived in his own person is present sacramentally.[143]

It is necessary to examine more closely this concept of the contemporaneous interaction of Christ and the faith-disposed believer, which von Balthasar regards as essential to a correct understanding of the church's sacraments. He affirms that, as far as the Lord is concerned, the sacramental form of his existence does not differ from that of the forty days. "We imply," he says, "that he appears therein as interpreting, revealing and bestowing his earthly life."[144] Importantly, however, von Balthasar insists that it is within the dimension of faith that Christ encounters his people. Encountering them in the sacraments, Christ elicits a faith "as steadfast as Revelation"[145] and comparable to that evoked by the revelation of the forty days. In the same way as this apostolic faith response consisted in the establishment of the church, of her life, teaching, and dogma, so does the faith elicited now by the sacraments so cooperate. Therefore von Balthasar is able to conclude, "By becoming contemporaneous with the believer in the sacrament, the Lord bestows upon him the possibility, given him in faith, of becoming like him who became man. The grace he communicates is inseparable from his Incarnation, his relationship to the Church, his historicity."[146]

Though this sacramentology can be acknowledged as the logical and correct extrapolation of the role of Christ within a theology of the forty days, the density or concentration of thought in the

---

143. "Here, again, he is the risen Lord, living in the eternity of the Father, his earthly time transfigured into his eternal duration, the eternal Christ accompanying 'his own' throughout time. The new element of difference is only that whereas during the Forty Days he lets his companionship appear openly as fulfilment, in the time of the Church it happens in concealment under the sacramental forms." Ibid., 94.

144. Ibid., 95.

145. Ibid.

146. Ibid., 97.

argument is also apparent; this can make full appreciation difficult. That is to say, at this point the reader is more aware than ever that von Balthasar has sought only to give "indications" and not a comprehensive study in this work. As, by his own admission, he maintains, "If on every page the questions introduced cry out for more thorough discussion, the author would like to reserve the right to return at some later date to individual aspects of the theme."[147] One such aspect might surely have been the nature of the sacramental encounter between Christ and his people, an encounter that, von Balthasar maintains, holds the possibility of deification. The unfortunate fact of his never having returned to these questions specifically has meant that help in amplifying and clarifying his thought has to be found elsewhere. So it may be said that Dulles's inclusion of this particular section of von Balthasar in a chapter that concentrates on the eschatological time of revelation is a mutually enlightening coincidence. While a study of the forty days provides the fundamental basis of a theology of the sacraments, the analysis that Dulles provides of the role of symbol in the sacramental exchange and of the participation in the divine life that such a transaction may effect contributes a necessary development to this foundation. Indeed, participation is a concept crucial to the overall theology that Dulles establishes:

> By evoking participation, the revelatory symbols mediate a lived, personal communion with God, which is, in its way, immediate. This may be described as an experience of God or of grace, provided that God or grace is not depicted as an object to be encountered but as a horizon within which inner-worldly objects are encountered.[148]

147. Ibid., 8.
148. Dulles, *Models of Revelation*, 269.

Symbolic Participation in the Life of God

The concluding chapter of *Models of Revelation* is more than a resumé of its major points. In it, Dulles expresses succinctly the theology of symbol that has dialectically retrieved[149] the positive values of each of his five models. Then, as a consequence, he gives a conclusive shape to a theology of revelation, stating both what it is and what it is not. An understanding of participation is crucial to the new proposal which "sublates" the previous theories.[150] In claiming that revelatory symbols "evoke participation," Dulles points to the function of symbols that determines their revelatory nature, but, in choosing this particular term, he cannot be unaware of its theological resonance.[151] Participation, in the specific sense that Dulles employs, is the theological concept that arises from reflection on the process of symbolic communication,[152] and as such is crucial to his understanding of revelation. In his article on participation in Rahner's *Sacramentum Mundi*, Laurentio Bruno Puntel states that "these seemingly abstract considerations are the key to a possible understanding and rethinking of the classical notion of participation

---

149. Ibid., 127.
150. "I would use this notion [sublation] in Karl Rahner's sense rather than Hegel's to mean that what sublates goes beyond what is sublated, introduces something new and distinct, puts everything on a new basis, yet so far from interfering with the sublated or destroying it, on the contrary needs it, includes it, preserves all its proper features and properties, and carries them forward to a fuller realisation within a richer context." So Dulles quotes from Bernard Lonergan and gives his own understanding of "sublation." Ibid.
151. "Like such terms as being, unity and analogy, participation has had a major role in the metaphysical and theological thinking of the West, where it has been used to reflect on the Greek and biblico–Christian experience of reality. Hence the understanding and critical assessment of the notion of participation, with the possibility of rethinking it on one's own behalf, involves an interpretation of Western metaphysics which is particularly concerned with its origin and the fateful encounter between the Greek and the Christian experience of existence." L. B. Puntel, "Participation," in *Encyclopedia of Theology: The Concise Sacramentum Mundi*, ed. K. Rahner (New York: Seabury, 1975), 1160.
152. Interesting background to this process may be gained from Paul Ricoeur's discussion of conceptualization as a function of symbols in P. Ricoeur, *Interpretation Theory* (Fort Worth, TX: Texas Christian University, 1976), 65. A concise summary of Ricoeur's analysis can be found also in W. M. Thompson, *The Jesus Debate* (New York: Paulist, 1985), 80–84.

which might be used to expound Christian revelation in terms of present-day awareness of problems."[153]

Unwittingly, Puntel here provides a schema for *Models of Revelation* that neatly summarizes the work as a whole. Through a theology of symbol, Dulles has given concrete form to the abstract considerations of participation, and, recognizing it as the key to a present-day understanding of revelation, has tested it against five contemporary models. However, while symbolic communication is a criterion effective in allowing Dulles to set out the major aspects of his theology of revelation, he fails to elaborate the obvious relationship that exists between that communication and the liturgical celebration of the sacraments. The claim that the work is "pre-dogmatic" is hardly a defense here.[154] As Gerald O'Collins points out, Dulles makes scant acknowledgement of the liturgy throughout this work,[155] and in no sense could it be claimed that sacramental celebrations were seen as the epitome of symbolic communication.[156] At best, the liturgy remains a model among other models, and one struggling to compete with the primarily cognitive types that, in conclusion, must be said to dominate Dulles's enterprise.[157]

---

153. Puntel, "Participation," 162.
154. Cf. E. TeSelle, review of A. Dulles, *Models of Revelation, Religious Studies Review* 10, no. 3 (1984): 38.
155. G. O'Collins, review of A. Dulles, *Models of Revelation, Gregorianum* 65 (1984): 181.
156. One need only examine here the difference between the use Dulles makes of von Balthasar's theology of the forty days and the essentially liturgical dimension that J. Driscoll elaborates from the same sections. Cf. Dulles, *Models of Revelation*, 233–35 and J. Driscoll, *Theology at the Eucharistic Table*, ch. 5.
157. TeSelle, review of *Models of Revelation*," 38.

Postcritical Opportunities:
The Craft of Theology

Avery Dulles leaves us to wonder why, after considering *Models of Theology* as a title for this book, he decides against so naming it.[158] Nevertheless, it is possible to glean from this unified collection of essays that a certain progressive shift has taken place between the publication of *Models of Revelation* in 1983, the reworking and expansion of *Models of the Church* in 1987, and the publication of the expanded edition of *The Craft of Theology* in 1996. If those two earlier publications described a methodological advance from scholasticism to models, then this work, as its subtitle affirms, describes the shift "from symbol to system." Analysis of this study will be considerably enlightened by reflection on the development that can be traced through the works discussed to this point.

Methodology Revisited

When Dulles came to evaluate the five ecclesial types he had presented in *Models of the Church*, he discovered that therein lay the difficulty.[159] While skeptical of the possibility of finding an overarching supermodel,[160] Dulles did find it necessary to introduce criteria for assessing the suitability of each model's contribution to a harmonized whole. Yet neither was this convergent construction designed to suggest that "the essence of the Church somehow exists, like a dark continent, ready-made and only waiting to be mapped."[161] Such would be to fall back into the essential categories of a decadent scholasticism, out of which models were supposed to lead theology so

---

158. Dulles, *The Craft of Theology*, 41.
159. Dulles, *Models of the Church*, 179.
160. Ibid., 184.
161. Ibid., 187.

that it could reflect better the myriad possibilities of a modern church marked by pluralism, ecumenism, provisionality, and voluntariness.[162] Indeed, the problem that Dulles experienced here was a consequence of the mystery he was contemplating and the method he employed to do so. In the words of Sallie McFague, Dulles had met with an essential consequence of his method: "The tension of metaphorical thinking, its insistence on relativity and partiality while still supporting the possibility that some models 'fit' reality better than others, appears to be at the heart of science, as it should also be at the heart of theology."[163]

While Dulles recognized the ability of models to open theology up to variety and development, by the time he came to write *Models of Revelation*, he had become more aware of the need for a commensurate coherence and systemization.[164] Though it is true to say that these factors were obviously not missing in *Models of the Church*, it is interesting that, when publishing *Models of Revelation* some nine years later, Dulles reflected that "the method of models was excellent for identifying the basic questions at issue, but it did not greatly help to solve the questions."[165] Hence after presenting the five models that form the basis of this work, Dulles discusses the "theological options" available for the introduction of a further degree of system to his method.[166] His use of the terms *constellation*,

---

162. Ibid., 199–203.

163. Sallie McFague, *Metaphorical Theology* (Philadelphia: Fortress Press, 1982), 101. See also Dulles's quotation from Ewart Cousins's article, "Models and the Future of Theology," *Continuum* 7 (1969): 78–91 in Dulles, *Models of the Church*, 22 which expands on this point.

164. For a fuller discussion of this problem, see McFague, *Metaphorical Theology*, 106, where she asserts, "That enrichment, however, could result in chaos unless some structure were introduced into the panorama of images."

165. Dulles, *Models of Revelation*, viii–ix.

166. From choice of a single model, eclecticism, harmonization, innovation, or dialectical retrieval, he chooses the final option and employs symbolic mediation as his particular dialectical tool. See Dulles, *Models of Revelation*, 124–28.

root metaphor, *dialectical tool*, and the greater incidence of the word *system*, also support this desire for a structuring principle.

This move away from a method of models that is entirely metaphorical can be seen also in Dulles's expanding *Models of the Church* to include the chapter "The Church: Community of Disciples." The five models of the 1974 edition had each discussed the church *as* a particular image or metaphor. By 1987, Dulles feels the need to introduce a new model that goes further than providing a comparison complementary to other comparisons. Chapter 13 of the new edition is not entitled "The Church *as* Community of Disciples,"[167] because, "without being adequate to the full reality of the Church,"[168] this model has "potentiality as a basis for a comprehensive ecclesiology."[169] What Dulles recognizes in this model is the "guiding vision" that is discussed in the opening chapter of *A Church to Believe In*.[170] This reflects a maturing in Dulles's theological method. The recognition that there comes a point when, despite the particular aspect that individual models provide, and despite the coherence they offer when viewed collectively, it is necessary to face how the metaphorical language of models relates

167. Here Dulles is open to criticisms similar to those that David Tracy levels at Sallie McFague's *Models of God*: "Granted McFague's reluctance to follow the deconstructionists' dissolution of the hermeneutical 'as' into endless metaphoricity I think she should say more on how her use of 'as' is not equivalent (as I presume it is not) to her use of 'as if' language. Without that further clarification, I fear that other readers will be left puzzled, as I was, with questions about the exact nature of the claim for the new metaphors and models for God that McFague develops and, therefore, with questions about what kind of criteria are appropriate here." Tracy, "*Models of God*: Three Observations," in *Readings in Modern Theology*, ed. R. Gill (London: SPCK, 1995), 82–86, 84. While Dulles certainly shows resistance to the deconstructionists' dissolution that would result from the endless addition of "as" models, the exact nature of his claim for the model "Community of Disciples" remains unclear.

168. Dulles, *Models of the Church,* 207.

169. Ibid.

170. "To participate effectively in the Church's life, one needs a guiding vision. Such a vision, I submit, should suggest a rationale for the Church's existence; it should tally with one's experience of association with fellow believers; it should indicate a set of values and priorities; and it should clarify the proper relationship between the Church and the contemporary world." A. Dulles, *A Church to Believe In* (New York: Crossroads, 1982), 1.

to the reality that it seeks to describe. This is the issue that Dulles seeks to address in *Models of Revelation*. Here, even more than in his expanded edition of *Models of the Church*, Dulles is looking for a root metaphor that will provide a guiding vision for a theology of revelation. Hence, he maintains that the purpose of each model "is not the imagery but the structural relationships represented as obtaining between the revealer, the recipient, and the means of revelation."[171] The root metaphor or "pervasive category" that Dulles elects is symbolic mediation, and, as has been seen, this is the dialectical tool that he uses to integrate these models into a "larger context": that of a theology of revelation. However, in his article "Revelation as Metaphoric Process,"[172] Michael L. Cook challenges the success of Dulles's efforts. Cook wonders whether symbolic communication is, in fact, a category that effectively retrieves the best of all Dulles's chosen models, and asks, "What are the implications of the *primacy* of symbol for the interrelationships *among* the five models?."[173] Cook is essentially questioning whether symbolic communication is effective as a root metaphor that supports these five subsidiary models. As he explains,

> All models are metaphors with comprehensive, organizational potential, i.e., they mediate between primary, imagistic language and secondary, conceptual language; but root metaphors are even more fundamental and pervasive in that they express the most basic assumptions about reality. Root metaphors are constitutive of religious sensibility in such wise that to change the root metaphor would involve a radical shift in one's paradigm of religious understanding.[174]

Though Cook recognises symbol as a root metaphor, he does not regard it as pervasive of Dulles's five models, because three of those

---

171. Dulles, *Models of the Church*, 33.
172. M. L. Cook, "Revelation as Metaphoric Process," *Theological Studies* 47 (1986): 388–411.
173. Ibid., 390.
174. Ibid., see footnote on 389.

models he regards as subsequent to symbolic communication rather than part of it.[175] Symbolic experience is primary because it is the "primordial way of being human, because it touches upon and seeks to give expression to that which is rooted in the deepest mysteries of life, including our relationship to God, to self, to others in society, to our bodies, and to the whole of nature."[176] It is Cook's thesis that symbols are the beginnings of a metaphoric process that only in its totality becomes an adequate model of revelation—hence the title of his article. He insists that the propositional, historical, and experiential paradigmatic models of revelation are of a more conceptual order, and are therefore secondary to the fundamental, imagistic order of symbols. In this domain, he places Dulles's fourth and fifth models, the dialectical presence and new awareness models, and he sees them in tensive relationship to each other.[177] "The other three models (Propositional, Historical and Experiential) are thus seen to be subordinate models which move further in the direction of secondary conceptual language but which must always be funded by the primary images. The logical sequence is from metaphor to analogy (models) to concept."[178]

Having accepted Cook's thesis that the five models of Dulles are in fact divided into primary and secondary models, and that therefore symbolic mediation is not, in fact, the root metaphor of all five, it is possible to return to the models and offer an alternative root metaphor. When Sallie McFague discusses the relationship of primary metaphorical language to secondary conceptual language in her book *Metaphorical Theology*, she makes two interesting points. First, she

---

175. Ibid., 400–1.
176. Ibid., 392.
177. "At this point it is important to emphasize what has been done to Dulles' fourth and fifth models of revelation. We have placed the key image in each of them into a tensive interrelationship to elicit the root metaphor (i.e., the basic paradigmatic model) of Christian revelation." Ibid., 399.
178. Ibid.

insists that the two modes are so intimately related that any clear separation of the two is impossible.[179] Second, using insights of Paul Ricoeur, she stresses that symbols somehow contain these two levels of language within themselves. Out of the nonlinguistic bonds of symbols flow metaphorical linguistic bonds, which redescribe the reality that the symbol presents.[180] Hence McFague says, "These insights can be summed up in the following sentence: within the *continuity* of primary and secondary language there must be a genuine *separation*, for the purpose of secondary language is *interpretation* in order to return us to the *event* that primary language seeks to express."[181] This is why, as McFague points out, "The beginnings of religious language are in worship."[182] The liturgy is the locus where primary and secondary language mutually express and interpret each other, and as such the liturgy would be the better root metaphor for the five models in Dulles's *Models of Revelation.* Just as Michael Cook concludes from his theory of revelation as metaphoric process that the resurrection is an "absolute metaphor,"[183] so it is possible, taking the liturgy as root metaphor, to claim the Eucharist as its absolute expression. Cook asserts that

> in the *strict* sense, which can occur only at the end of history because it embraces the whole of creation, God is revealed in that which is contrary to what we "know," i.e., in the paradox of absolute reversal (in death, life), which includes but transcends our normal experience and can only be known through a specific meaning from God alone.

179. "It is important to notice at the outset that any attempt to make a hard and fast division between primary and secondary language in religion will fail because of their *intrinsic interdependence.*" Sallie McFague, *Metaphorical Theology*, 118–19.

180. "This living within the symbol—symbols for Ricouer being non-linguistic bonds uniting us to the cosmos—results in linguistic (e.g. metaphorical) interpretations, re-describing the reality that the symbols embody but do not themselves interpret. Symbols need metaphors for without them they are dumb; metaphors need symbols, for without them they lose their rootedness in life." Ibid., 120.

181. Ibid., 119 (her emphasis).

182. Ibid., 119.

183. Cook, "Revelation as Metaphoric Process," 401.

> Such revelation, which is once-for-all, can be called eschatological or apostolic. It is the revelation given to Peter and Paul and all those alluded to in 1Cor 15:5-8.[184]

Basing itself on 1 Cor. 15:23-28, a similar argument can be made for the Eucharist. Dulles claimed in *Models of Revelation* that "a theory of revelation is sound and acceptable to the extent that it measures up to, and illuminates, the reality of revelation."[185] It is the claim of that book that his chosen five models, dialectically retrieved by symbolic communication, provide such a theory. In claiming that Dulles's first three models are, in fact, secondary to the communication of symbols, Cook provides the opportunity for the root metaphor of communication to be widened from symbolic to liturgical, thus incorporating all five of the original models.

Undoubtedly, as can be seen from the previous analysis of *Models of Revelation*, Dulles is aware of the integral relationship that exists between the revelation that came to fullness in Jesus Christ and the sacramental life of the church. While he chooses symbolic communication as the best expression of that relationship, and while the theology of symbol Dulles offers goes a long way toward clarifying the revelatory processes that are common and fundamental to both expressions, he nevertheless consistently resists using the liturgy as root metaphor for his thesis. Again and again, he offers the liturgy as an example, even the best example of symbolic communication, but again and again he draws back from letting the liturgy become paradigmatic of his whole theory.

By the time Dulles comes to write *The Craft of Theology*, he has obviously reflected on much that was of issue in previous works. The postcritical turn that takes place in this work allows Dulles a reappraisal of the place of the liturgy and the role of models in

---

184. Ibid., 402–3.
185. Dulles, *Models of Revelation*, 127.

theological method. It would seem that here he has reached a new stage in his theology.[186]

A Model for Contemporary Method

After a brief and somewhat autobiographical introduction to his book *The Craft of Theology*, in which Dulles comments on "the pluralistic context of contemporary theology," he locates himself within that radically diverse scene in an opening chapter entitled "Toward a Post-Critical Theology."[187] And, though he would shy away from a label as "manipulative"[188] as "post-liberal" or "post-critical," in approaching theological study, conscious of a certain pluralism, and with an agenda of methodological revision, Dulles would recognize himself as typically postmodern, if anything can be typical of that amorphous category.[189] Describing the revisionist, postcritical theologian, David Tracy includes the following three interests as

186. "The process of interpretation as a creative engagement or conversation between the text of a tradition and contemporary experience involves a threefold movement for Ricoeur. First, there must be an initial openness to what the text might say or the questions it might raise in the light of the interpreter's own experience. This is a pre-critical and unreflective experience of symbol. The second step seeks to move from the vagueness of a merely subjective sense of the symbol or text to a critical explanation of it by employing various methods. Such methods are those employed, for example, in biblical criticism: historical, psychosocial, philosophical, comparative religions, literary, etc. All of these methods involve the move to some form of conceptualization: either definitions that are abstract and propositional, or descriptions that are experiential and historical. Here is where I would locate Dulles' first three models: propositional, historical and experiential. As indispensable, they are intrinsic to revelation as metaphoric process; but as subordinate, they can be perceived to be revelatory only in relation to the primacy of symbol. There is a natural and necessary move of the human mind toward definitions and descriptions, but the danger is to think that our human conceptualizations and systems have grasped or exhausted the content of the mystery. Thus Ricoeur's third step is a return to the symbol as primary. Once we have gone through the process of critical appropriation and have been transformed by a new comprehension, we experience the symbol ever anew with a second, post-critical naïveté." Cook, "Revelation as Metaphorical Process," 400–1.

187. For an excellent discussion of the pluralist context of theology to which Dulles refers, and of the revisionist, postcritical response to it, see the opening chapter of David Tracy's *Blessed Rage for Order*, 3–14.

188. Dulles, *The Craft of Theology*, 3.

fundamental to his enterprise: a concern for social praxis and participation, a desire for symbolic reinterpretation, and commitment to a new critical method.[190] Though Dulles claims only that the first three chapters of *The Craft of Theology* "deal rather generally with contemporary problems of theological method,"[191] he nevertheless deals subsequently with the major aspects of the postcritical agenda: praxis, symbol, and method.[192] And, despite the fact that the chapters are so divided, cumulatively they evoke the contemporary theological climate and direct the whole book toward a postcritical examination of theology.

Setting the postmodern scene in his opening chapter, Dulles identifies the antidote to the symptoms of modernism not in a return to the orthodoxy of the old order, but in a new orthopraxy. The cure of the fragmentation of belief consequent on the critical agenda is to be found partly in the social praxis of the believing community.

189. For a general background to the eclectic term, *postmodernism*, see E. Gellner, *Postmodernism, Reason, and Religion* (London: Routledge, 1992), and M. Sarup, *Post-Structuralism and Postmodernism* (London: Harvester Wheatsheaf, 1993), especially chapter 6. For a specifically theological inquiry pertinent to this study, see T. Guarinos, "Postmodernity and Five Fundamental Theological Issues," *Theological Studies* 57 (1996): 654–89.

190. Tracy describes the theologian of the revisionist model as follows: "The revisionist Christian theologian joins his secular colleague in refusing to allow the fact of his own existential disenchantment with the reifying and oppressive results of the Enlightenment to become the occasion for a return to mystification, Christian or otherwise. Rather he believes that only a radical continuation of critical theory, symbolic reinterpretation, and responsible social and personal *praxis* can provide the hope for a fundamental revision of both the modern and the traditional self-understandings. Revisionist theology, then, is intrinsically indebted to and derived from the formulations of the liberal task in theology classically formulated in the nineteenth century. It is post-liberal in the straightforward sense that it recognises and attempts to articulate not a new ideal for the theological task, but new methodological and substantive resources for fulfilling that ideal." Tracy, *Blessed Rage for Order*, 33.

191. Dulles, *The Craft of Theology*, "Introduction," xi.

192. The first three chapters of *The Craft of Theology* are entitled, "Towards a Postcritical Theology," "Theology and Symbolic Communication," and "The Problem of Method: From Scholasticism to Models." This, however, is not to suggest agreement between Tracy and Dulles in their description of either a postcritical theologian or his methodology. On this, see A. Dulles, "Method in Fundamental Theology: Reflections on David Tracy's Blessed Rage for Order," *Theological Studies* 37 (1976): 304–16. Here Dulles states, "In the remainder of this review I shall explain why I do not feel completely at home with revisionism as Tracy explains it. This does not mean that I can situate myself comfortably in any of his other models." Ibid., 306.

In some sense for Dulles, recognising the importance of the liturgy as a theological source is part of the movement toward a postcritical understanding. Theologically speaking, the paradigm change that allowed revelation to be considered not as a static deposit of propositions appropriated individually, but as active participation in a living reality with social consequences, is as much a function of postcriticism as the philosophical shift away from the "certainty, clarity and distinctiveness"[193] of Descartes's methodological "turn to the subject." Conscious of this climate, Dulles defines theology as follows:

> Theology, then, is a methodical effort to articulate the truth implied in Christian faith, the faith of the Church. The method cannot be pursued by the techniques of mathematics or syllogistic logic, but it depends on a kind of connoisseurship derived from personal appropriation of the living faith of the Church. The correct articulation of the meaning of the Christian symbols is not a science learned out of books alone but rather an art acquired through familiarity by being at home in the community in which the symbols function. To apprehend the meaning of the symbols, it is not enough to gaze at them in a detached manner as objects and dissect them under a logical microscope. The joint meaning of the symbols cannot be discerned unless one relies confidently on the symbols as clues, and attends to the realities to which they point. From within this stance of faith the theologian seeks to formulate in explicit terms what the Christian symbols have to say to the questions that call for solution.[194]

In paragraphs prior to this quotation, Dulles sets out the "presuppositions" of the postcritical theologian.[195] In contrast to the critical agenda of the Modernists, here there is a "prejudice in favour of faith" and a "hermeneutic of trust." The enterprise of postcritical

---

193. See the opening pages of D. Tracy, "Theology and the Many Faces of Postmodernity," in Gill, *Readings in Modern Theology*, 225–35. Also Y. Labbé, "Réceptions théologiques de la 'Postmodernité'" *Revue des sciences philosophiques et théologiques* 72 (1988): 397–426.
194. Dulles, *The Craft of Theology*, 8.
195. See ibid., 7–8.

theology can be executed only from "within a religious commitment," and therefore theology is here regarded as an ecclesial discipline. For this reason, theology cannot be equated solely with the detached observations proper to science, but is marked by the pursuit of a knowledge gained through participation.[196] It is this climate of study that determines postcritical theology and explains why the interrelation of method, symbol, and praxis is characteristic of this approach. Theology in this particular mode demands a method that bridges the objective and subjective aspects of the theological pursuit, and one that recognizes experience as a locus for knowledge. As a result symbols are highly significant for postcritical theology. They admit to knowledge not solely by the intellect, but allow the whole person to participate in that which is held and experienced by a community. Hence, the practical living out of the truths of revelation by the community creates the place of encounter.[197] So Dulles asserts immediately after this text that "liturgy has regularly been recognised as a prime theological source and it is securely established in this role by post-critical theology."[198]

196. Dulles's position may be interestingly contrasted with René Latourelle's, a comparison which is perhaps indicative of the postmodern shift. Latourelle defines theology in the strict sense (notice his differentiation of objective and subjective theology) as follows: "Supernatural theology, or theology proper, is the science of God, but a science which sets out from revelation. It speaks of God, but of God as he is known to us through his revelation and insofar as his revelation can introduce us to a deeper knowledge of his inner mystery. Theology's point of departure then is the living God, in the free witness which he gives of himself. To put it in another way, since faith and revelation are correlative notions it could be said that theology is the *science of the object of faith*, that is to say the science of what is revealed by God and believed by man. While the natural sciences are built on the *données* (data) of experience, theology is built upon the *données* of revelation received by faith." R. Latourelle, *Theology: Science of Salvation* (New York: Alba House, 1969), 7. For further discussion of the relationship of science to theology in systematic method, see G. Pozzo "Method I: Systematic Theology," in Latourelle and Fisichella, *Dictionary of Fundamental Theology*, 670–84.

197. In this regard, see Ghislain Lafont's description of a situated narrative as the means to the fundamental theology of a community: G. Lafont, *God, Time, and Being* (Petersham, MA: Saint Bede's, 1992), 134–41. This work is one of those discussed in Labbé's article, "Réceptions théologique de la 'Postmodernité'."

198. Dulles, *The Craft of Theology*, 8.

Symbolizing the Word

Liturgy is critical to the theological task as Dulles understands it. To make the move from wonder and unanswered questions, theology utilizes the clues that Scripture, tradition, and praxis offer.[199] The liturgy is a privileged locus because it affords a theological synthesis of these distinct sources. The celebration of the sacraments is the place where, to borrow Michael Polanyi's phraseology, the gradient of coherence deepens.[200] The main reason for this is its symbolic nature. As Dulles insists, the full apprehension of symbols requires participation on a level beyond that which is objectively apparent. This is the vision of faith, where answers to the problems of life can be appreciated in the light of the gospel that the community transmits.[201] Recognizing the importance of symbols in the transmission of revelation, Dulles identifies an interpretation of the symbolic that is specific to the postcritical approach to theology. The second chapter of *The Craft of Theology* is dedicated to an examination of the role of symbol according to the ecclesial-transformative type of theology.[202]

Revelation, understood as a real and efficacious self-communication, demands a theology of symbol different from that required by a transmission that is regarded as merely propositional, or indeed from a self-communication described as "non-informative

---

199. Ibid., 11.
200. Ibid.
201. This is the topic of Latourelle's *Man and His Problems in the Light of Jesus Christ* (New York: Alba House, 1982). Notice the more experienced-based and anthropological starting point of this work, in contrast to the previously quoted *Theology: Science of Salvation*, which, published some thirteen years previously, followed a much more objective and propositional model.
202. According to the ecclesial-transformative school, which (as Dulles explains) corresponds to the postcritical turn in theology, "Revelation . . . is regarded as a real and efficacious self-communication of God, the transcendent mystery, to the believing community. The deeper insights of revelatory knowledge are imparted, not in the first instance through propositional discourse, but through participation in the life and worship of the Church." Dulles, *The Craft of Theology*, 18.

and non-discursive."[203] The first type presumes revelatory symbols that display "a plenitude or depth of meaning that surpasses the capacities of conceptual thinking."[204] Dulles regards these symbols as belonging to Sacred Scripture and the tradition of the Christian community, and, because both these sources are re-presented and actualized in the celebration of the sacraments, the liturgy comes to be of primary significance in their discerning.

> The proclamation of the word, theologically considered, is not simply a communication of the gospel message, though it is obviously that too. The word of God is a revelatory, actualizing event, bringing with it that new life in God that it announces. The sacraments themselves are instances of Christian proclamation, for in them the word achieves its fullest efficacy. Seeking account for the salvific efficacy of the word, Otto Semmelroth contends that the proclamation is symbolic. The mission of the Church to preach the word of God, he declares, is a symbolic continuation of the divine mission whereby the Word of God, through the incarnation, entered human history. In this way "the Church's preaching of God's word becomes a portrayal and symbolic manifestation of the incarnation of God's Son in Jesus Christ."[205]

Once Dulles has set out the particular understanding of symbol that he associates with the ecclesial-transformative model of theology,[206] he explains how these symbols are an integral part of the ecclesial community, and how their communication effects the transformation of individuals. Symbols, as Dulles learned well from Rahner, are "the self realization of a being in the other."[207] Hence, of their nature, Christian symbols invite a participation that results in change: at once they reveal and redeem.[208] To this end Dulles quotes from Geoffrey

---

203. Ibid.
204. Ibid.
205. Ibid., 34.
206. "Ecclesial-transformative theology, in a form that I can personally accept, rests on a kind of symbolic realism in which reality is held to have a symbolic structure. Karl Rahner, among others has set forth an impressive ontology of the symbol, which will be the basis for some of the reflections that follow." Ibid., 20.
207. Ibid.

Wainwright's book *Doxology*, where he asserts that communion with God is symbolically focused in the liturgy.[209] The theological explanation that Dulles provides for this fact is that a combination of Karl Rahner's concept of self-communication, his theology of symbol, and his anthropology means that revelation is something of a connatural dialogue between God and humanity.[210] The liturgy is the natural locus for this dialogue.

In the quotation above, Dulles reevaluates the effect that a Rahnerian understanding of symbolic communication can have on the traditionally held elements of sacramental theology. One of the first consequences of viewing things from this perspective is the realization that word and sacrament display great similarities and are intimately related.[211] The developing fundamental theology created a systematic space for reflection on this aspect of revelation in the tract *De Verbo divino*. A shift from propositional to biblical categories

208. Notice that Dulles no longer seems to find it necessary to distinguish these two aspects as carefully as he had in *Models of Revelation*, cf. 158. In this regard, see the discussion above of Dulles's distinction between symbol and sacrament with regard to revelation. It is interesting also to compare this position with that of Latourelle in his *Theology of Revelation*.

209. G. Wainwright, *Doxology: The Praise of God in Worship, Doctrine and Life; A Systematic Theology* (London: Epworth, 1980), 20–21.

210. "But when Rahner's concept of self-communication is linked up with his anthropology and his doctrine of symbol, as previously set forth, the implications for our subject become evident. God's revelation, if it is to come home to human beings as embodied spirits, must come to expression through tangible, social, and historically transmitted symbols. The divine self-communication therefore, has a social and symbolic dimension." Dulles, *The Craft of Theology*, 22. Though Dulles enhances this description of social communication with allusion to Kilmartin and Ganoczy (see 34ff), Dulles does not make an explicit link between this connaturality and the liturgy. Such a link, however, is made quite clearly in Wainwright's *Doxology*: "A Barthian emphasis would fall on the fact that the *true God*, of whom we now have the image in Jesus Christ, is the proper recipient of human worship. A Bultmannian accent would stress that it is *within the human situation* that God is addressed as well as expressed. Rahner holds that the movement of humanity into the divine mystery is a movement of adoration." Wainwright, *Doxology*, 15–16.

211. "And this is the real reason for enquiring into the relationship of word and sacrament. They are so like each other that one cannot but ask what is the reason for their similarity and what is the possibility of making a distinction between them in spite of, or indeed because of, their similarity and its cause." K. Rahner, "The Word and the Eucharist," *Theological Investigations*, 4:254.

when discussing the word, and its relocation within an understanding of grace that is relational, have meant that word and sacrament have become closer, mutually enriching categories.[212] Rahner examines six points at which word and sacrament might be said to display a coextensive theology: they are communications made contemporary by their ecclesial nature. They represent "inner moments of God's salvific action"[213] that cause one to participate in the divine nature. Both word and sacrament establish an "essential connexion between the inner word of grace and the external word of revelation."[214] Both are signs under which "the reality itself draws nigh and announces itself and constitutes itself present."[215] In the church, the word of God realizes its presence "only in an historical process."[216] The sacraments, and ultimately the Eucharist, are part of this intensifying "dialogue between God-Christ and the Church."[217] Interestingly, Rahner determines these six aspects within a discussion of word and Eucharist—that is, he chose the most expressive liturgical celebration of a specific sacrament to establish a comparison with the word of God and not the sacramental category *in genere*.[218] Dulles has, as a background to his thought, expressed in the above quotation the relationship that Rahner has worked out between word and sacrament, but he goes further in realizing these aspects by setting them within a liturgical context. To this end, he makes an explicit

212. See ibid., 255–57.
213. Ibid., 257.
214. Ibid., 259.
215. Ibid., 255.
216. Ibid., 264.
217. Ibid., 265.
218. Edward Kilmartin makes this liturgical aspect more explicit in his *Christian Liturgy*, which Dulles alludes to here: "Through the experience of the liturgy, believers are led to the conclusion that the fixed forms of expression of faith, as well as the personal faith expressed by the assembly, are supported by Christ himself: the High Priest of the worship of the Church. In the language of the science of communication, Christ can be described as the chief speaker and actor of the event of communication." E. J. Kilmartin, *Christian Liturgy: Theology and Practice I; Systematic Theology of Liturgy* (Kansas City: Sheed and Ward, 1988), 46.

link with the liturgical theologies of Kilmartin and Ganoczy, and discusses the word of God only according to the above-mentioned category of Otto Semmelroth, that of proclamation within the liturgical assembly. Hence, by means of symbolic communication, Dulles effects a unity of word and sacrament to which Karl Rahner had looked forward in Catholic theology.[219] In this, however, Dulles shows an increasing awareness of the role that the liturgy has in providing a theological locus where the diverse aspects of sacramentology can be integrated. This leads Dulles back to the question of method and the role of models in theology, which can help "facilitate dialogue and reconciliation."

It has already been noted that Dulles decided not to call this book *Models of Theology*,[220] and that this decision perhaps reflects a desire for greater systemization in his theological method.[221] Autobiographically speaking, Dulles locates his option to pursue the method of models in an ambiguous reaction toward the scholasticism of the manual tradition.[222] That the title that he did choose for this work suggests a methodological journey from symbol to system, combined with the fact that there are aspects of the scholastic method that Dulles feels certain modern theologies neglect,[223] implies that, in his opinion, models have a necessary but inconclusive role in postcritical theological method.

---

219. See "The Word and The Eucharist," where Rahner says his thesis of the enriching symbiosis of word and sacrament may appear "strange or unusual" because "in Catholic theology it is mostly dealt with under other headings and in other perspectives." Rahner, "Word and Eucharist," 262; see also the final paragraph of 286.

220. See above and Dulles, *The Craft of Theology*, 41.

221. "Fifth and last, the method is impugned on the ground that it stops short of being truly systematic. This may or may not be the case." Ibid., 51.

222. See ibid., 41. Interestingly, an advantage that Dulles recognized in the Scholastic system was "the necessity of taking a definite position and supporting it by explicit arguments." This, he notes, is "in contrast with some contemporary authors, who often leave their own positions to be gathered from the way in which they speak about other authors." Ibid., 43.

223. See the previous footnote and also, "The systematization cannot rest with an unresolved contradiction, but it may be that in theology, as in micro- or macrophysics, one must sometimes confess one's inability to overcome certain apparent contradictions." Ibid., 51

Shifting to the Postcritical

By the time Dulles wrote many of the articles that came to make up *The Craft of Theology*, his attitude to theological method had solidified. In the brief history of the use of models that Dulles's own theology provides, it is possible to trace what can retrospectively be termed a gradual shift toward the postcritical. Though he declares that his intention in *Models of the Church* "was not to support or deepen the existing divisions but to facilitate dialogue and reconciliation," the critical element remained a prominent and integral part of his enterprise.[224] The agenda had changed somewhat when he came to write *Models of Revelation*. Though Dulles saw that his purpose in selecting five models was "to harmonize them critically,"[225] the emphasis was, undoubtedly, on synchronization rather than criticism. Here, far more than in *Models of the Church*, Dulles used the method to create a less compromised and more coherent, integrated theology of revelation. His use of "dialectical retrieval" to draw forth positive and complementary aspects from each model indicates a lull in the critical elements of the theological task.

An historical overview of the theological development evident in Dulles's use of models itself articulates answers to the first three objections that are most readily levelled against the method.[226] Between *Models of the Church* and *The Craft of Theology*, Dulles

---

224. In the introduction to the expanded edition, he declared, "I take a deliberately critical stance toward those ecclesiologies that are primarily or exclusively institutional." Dulles, *Models of the Church*, 10. And looking back years later, he reflected more mildly, "I hoped to make my readers more appreciative of the values of ecclesiologies other than their own, and at the same time conscious that their own preferred vision of the Church had its limitations and weaknesses." Dulles, *The Craft of Theology*, 49.
225. Ibid., 50.
226. Ibid., 50–52.

has clarified his position with regard to this method in response to suggestions that models are not appropriate for theology. Some would suggest that they categorize theologians excessively and unnecessarily, and that they can result in a certain relativism or agnosticism. However, it is in responding to the fourth objection against models, listed in *The Craft of Theology*, that Dulles's "postcritical turn" is most apparent:

> It is objected that the method of models is bookish and uncreative. To this I would reply that, like the old scholasticism, the method is ecclesial rather than individualistic. The theologian practicing the method does not try to rely upon merely private religious experience but seeks to integrate his or her experience into that of the Christian tradition, as represented by other believers. But the method makes ample room for the theologian to reflect on his or her own experience as a believer, participating in the prayer and worship of the Church.[227]

David Tracy, in his previously mentioned *Blessed Rage for Order*, takes the discussion of models in theology "a step further"[228] by suggesting that a distinguishing element of the major theological types is the relationship that exists between the subject and object referents of theology. As Tracy says: "To express my own hypothesis, the most basic of such terms and relations is, in fact, those references to the self of the theologian and to the objects within that self's horizon which any given model discloses."[229] Out of the five theological methods that Tracy offers,[230] his "revisionist" model comes closest to the "ecclesial transformative" type of Dulles.[231] It

---

227. Ibid., 51.
228. Tracy, *Blessed Rage for Order*, 22.
229. Ibid., 23.
230. Ibid., 24–34.
231. This of course is a generalization, as Tracy gives a very technical sense to his term—and one with which Dulles would not be wholly comfortable. See Dulles, "Method in Fundamental Theology," 304–16.

is no surprise, then, that Tracy should describe the subject–object referent relationship within this model as follows:

> The object referent of the revisionist model can perhaps be best described as a critical reformulation of both the meanings manifested by an interpretation of the central motifs of the Christian tradition. More exactly, the revisionist model for Christian theology ordinarily bears some such formulation as the following: contemporary Christian theology is best understood as philosophical reflection upon the meanings present in common human experience and the meanings present in the Christian tradition.[232]

In the quotation chosen from *The Craft of Theology* above, and according to Tracy's analysis, Dulles defines himself as an essentially postcritical or revisionist theologian. Characteristically, he displays the telling subject–object referent relationship of this type. The theologian practices the method of models by seeking to integrate personal experience with the public experience of the Christian tradition in the liturgy of the church.[233] The liturgy, or, as Tracy says, the tradition, in this sense becomes the place where the enterprise of fundamental theology[234] occurs, just as it is the locus of sacramental

---

232. Tracy, *Blessed Rage for Order*, 34.

233. "This general and familiar set of questions may take the more specific form of seeking ways to express anew the authentically *public* character of *all* good theology, whether fundamental theology, systematic theology or practical theology; whether 'traditional' or 'contemporary.' In initially general terms, a public discourse discloses meanings and truths which in principle can transform all human beings in some recognizable, personal, social, political, ethical, cultural, or religious manner. The key marks of 'publicness,' therefore, will prove to be disclosure and transformation. For example, Christian theological discourse—here understood as a second-order, reflective discourse upon the originating Christian religious discourse—serves an authentically public function, precisely when it renders explicit the public character of the meaning and truth for our actual existence embedded in the Christian classical texts, events, images, symbols, doctrines, and persons." D. Tracy, "The Necessity and Insufficiency of Fundamental Theology," in Latourelle and O'Collins, *Problems and Perspectives of Fundamental Theology*, 23.

234. Notice how Tracy describes fundamental theology in terms reminiscent of Dulles's description of the subject–object meeting that a theologian may experience in worship: "To describe the enterprise of fundamental theology as philosophical reflection upon the meanings present in our common human experience and the meanings present in the Christian fact obviously

celebration. Significantly, in the two chapters to be studied subsequently, Dulles returns to the question of fundamental theology and tradition.

The Fundamental Question of Experience

In chapter 4 of *The Craft of Theology*, Dulles discusses fundamental theology as a grace-filled process of conversion. Early in the text, he asserts that "Christian faith . . . cannot be justified by public criteria offered in common human experience."[235] This might initially be taken as a contradiction of his statement, studied above, that theology cannot be a private activity, but must be undertaken in dialogue with a community's expression of the Christian tradition. In fact, it would seem Dulles means that a theologian who adopts categories "apart from revelation and faith"[236] cannot hope to find "public criteria"[237] in common experience through which to establish the truths of the Gospel. Though Dulles recognizes the absolute importance of a rational and intellectual approach to Christian faith, this alone "cannot establish the truth of the Christian dogmas by proofs convincing to persons who have no experience of the power of the gospel."[238] For Dulles, reason can play its part effectively only when working within a person's "fiduciary framework"[239] that is established by participating in the faith experience of the community. Hence he can conclude,

implies that there are two main 'sources' of fundamental theological reflection." Tracy, *Blessed Rage for Order*, 64.

235. Dulles, *The Craft of Theology*, 54.
236. "The theologian practicing the method (of models in theology) does not try to rely upon merely private religious experience but seeks to integrate his or her experience into that of the Christian tradition." Dulles, *The Craft of Theology*, 51.
237. Ibid., 54.
238. Ibid., 68.
239. Ibid., 55.

Fundamental theology necessarily operates within the circle of faith, for the Christian believer cannot conceive of authentic religious conversion apart from the gracious self-communication of God and the gift of faith which is known only from within the faith commitment. To attempt an explanation of Christian faith that draws only upon the data derivable from universal experience is to foreclose the very possibility of a satisfactory account of faith. To persons untouched by a grace-filled Christian experience, I submit, Christian faith can only appear as exorbitant and irrational. At best, it would be dismissed as an over-commitment.[240]

So Dulles aligns himself with Bernard Lonergan's assertion that theology must shift its foundations from deductions resting on premises taken from Scripture and the magisterium, so as to embrace the subjective reality of a person's experience of religious conversion.[241] Within this reality can be distinguished a twofold movement: that of the individual and that of God mediated through the community. Dulles speaks of these two actions as "concurrent and mutually interdependent,"[242] but recognizes that, in theology, much effort has been spent on an examination of the subject's approach to faith, but little on the involvement of the object of faith: "Fundamental theology, I suggest, must ask not only how we get to God but how God gets to us."[243]

---

240. Ibid., 68.

241. Interestingly, when Lonergan defines what he means by *conversion*, he alludes to its communal orientation or ecclesial dimension. In asserting that an objectification of conversion is what provides theology with its foundations, he says, "Conversion is existential, intensely personal, utterly intimate. But it is not so private as to be solitary. It can happen to many, and they can form a community to sustain one another in their self-transformation and to help one another in working out the implications and fulfilling the promise of their new life. Finally what can become communal can become historical." B. Lonergan, *Method in Theology* (London: Darton, Longman and Todd, 1972), 130. Here Lonergan also speaks of conversion objectified in the community releasing "the symbols that penetrate to the depths" (cf. 131). This forms an interesting parallel with Dulles's own comments on the church and conversion and the particular role of the concept of sacrament in that process. Cf. A. Dulles, "The Church: Sacrament and Ground of Faith," 259–73, especially 263–65.

242. Dulles, *The Craft of Theology*, 56.

In seeking to examine the process of conversion and the resulting act of faith, Dulles steers a course through two more extreme understandings: one that relies almost exclusively on transcendent action, and one that concentrates (solely) on "demonstrative reasoning from historically accessible facts."[244] While aspects of both these approaches are necessarily important for the act of faith, "the chief criterion for a viable religious faith is the ability, or apparent ability, to satisfy those hungers of the human spirit which cannot be satisfied apart from faith."[245] Thus there is a return to this dialogue between the meaning of human experience and the meaning of Christian revelation, which is the ground of fundamental theology. A faith that in its living out establishes a credible and satisfactory dialogue between the human situation and Christian revelation, offers a "provisional glimpse"[246] of ultimate meaning and is experienced as credible. This is, by its nature, a communal or ecclesial activity,[247] because that is where Christian revelation is experienced with certainty. It is communicated most effectively through the medium of personal testimony, and "symbolic embodiment."[248] In elucidating the category of testimony Dulles is careful to express its nature of being beyond word or concept: the fact that the criterion of credibility is essentially located not in the content, but in the subject of the revelation.[249] The veracity of an act of testimony originates in

---

243. "To study faith as though it were a purely individual decision, uninfluenced by the impact of the community of faith, would be as foolish as to try to account for marriage by an investigation of a solitary individual." See Dulles, *The Craft of Theology*, 56–57, 56.

244. Ibid., 58.

245. Ibid., 61.

246. Ibid.

247. "The concrete experience of these hungers will vary from person to person and from culture to culture; but there seems to be a generic human drive to be known, valued and loved; to be drawn into communion with others; to be delivered from death and the threat of final absurdity." Ibid., 61.

248. Ibid., 62.

249. To clarify this point, Dulles draws on the example of miracles in the life of Jesus. This forms an interesting parallel with observations already noted in the work of Latourelle. Ibid., 64–65.

the degree of conformity between that which is proclaimed and its practical expression in the network of relationships that make up the life of a witness.

This "enfleshing in actual life"[250] is in itself a symbolic process. It is also a process of ecclesiogenesis, whereby in symbolizing the truth they confess, a community effects the sacrament of the church.[251] What Dulles is here speaking of is the incarnation of the gospel word in the lives of Christians, that is, the movement from word to sacrament. This is the process of conversion, whereby the individual takes on "a new self" in "the corporate identity of the Christian community."[252] As Dulles implies in his conclusion to this chapter, this process of conversion, symbolized in the making flesh of the word in the Christian community, has a liturgical expression in the celebration of the sacraments.[253]

Actively Participating in the Tradition

It might be said by way of conclusion that, in chapter 4 of *The Craft of Theology*, Dulles advocates that fundamental theology examine the act of faith from an ecclesial as well as a personal perspective.[254] He does this by delineating a communal dimension to the categories of testimony and symbol through which people come to a knowledge of

250. Ibid., 65.
251. "The successful proclamation of Christianity does not require, in the first instance, a better theory of apologetics. It does require that Christians be seriously committed to their faith, so as to make their communities living and corporate signs of the presence of Christ in the world. According to many contemporary ecclesiologists, with whom I align myself, the Church, in its basic reality, is a symbol or sacrament of Christ." Ibid.
252. Ibid., 66.
253. "Christian initiation, therefore, is initiation into Christ, whose Body is the Church. Baptism sacramentally symbolises both a death to one's former self (the self of the estranged individual) and a rebirth to new life in Christ, the life of the People of God." Ibid. This theme is examined explicitly and with great merit by Driscoll, *Theology at the Eucharistic Table*, ch. 6.
254. Dulles, *The Craft of Theology*, 56–57.

revealed truth. That symbol and testimony are the means of a living community's mediation means that historical process is a necessary part of the communication of revelation,[255] and leads Dulles, inevitably, to the discussions of Scripture and tradition that make up the next two chapters. In trying to determine further Dulles's postcritical reappraisal of the processes of revelation within the church, and in particular his recognition of any sacramental or liturgical aspect to this process, an examination of his discussion of tradition should be fruitful.

In concluding his chapter "Tradition as a Theological Source," Dulles asserts,

> In historical faiths such as Christianity tradition has still another function. It binds the contemporary believer to the founding events on which the community rests. Traditional feast days, readings, and rituals re-actualize in a powerful way the experience of the Exodus, Sinai, the conquest of the Holy Land, the return from the Babylonian Exile, and for Christians, the redemptive deeds of Jesus Christ. Communal actions such as the blessing and pouring of water, or the consecration of the bread and wine, do more than build on the symbolic potentialities of nature. They enable us to participate in the saving events that lie at the very sources of our religious existence.[256]

Participation in the source of religious existence, namely revelation, is the function of tradition. But, as Dulles details through a typically historical overview, the nature of the sources and their expression, as well as the mode in which they are experienced, have been interpreted theologically in very varied ways. In rehearsing the historical progress of the three main "schools" of interpretation, "classical," "*partim . . . partim,*" and "curial,"[257] Dulles is able to contextualize the dogmatic decrees of Trent and Vatican II and

255. Ibid., 58.
256. Ibid., 102.
257. Ibid., 87–89.

demonstrate points of continuity and development.[258] What a historical survey shows is that, in working out the relationship between Scripture, tradition, and magisterium, the church's motive was never solely theological, but variously polemical, political, juridical, and latterly, pastoral and ecumenical. Nevertheless, through this manifold process, Dulles recognizes two defining moments in the development of the contemporary understanding of tradition. The first is the teaching of Maurice Blondel, and the second is the shaping of the theology of tradition in the Dogmatic Constitution, *Dei Verbum*, by Yves Congar. Blondel, Dulles maintains, by means of his philosophy of action, taught that "tradition . . . sustains in the community a vital sense of the realities to which Christians are committed in faith. The primary vehicle of tradition is not word but faithful action including the liturgy of the Church."[259] Though misunderstood amid the polemics of the Modernist crisis and the prevailing "two source" theories, which the neo-scholastics inherited from the Counter-Reformation, Blondel's opinions persisted.[260]

It was, however, the vital debates of the Second Vatican Council and Yves Congar's influence on the alternative draft and what was to become chapter 2 of *Dei Verbum* that crystallized the modern concept of tradition.[261] The shift is from an objective body of propositions,

---

258. "The final text of the chapter on tradition in *Dei Verbum* reaffirms the basic positions of Trent but draws likewise on the dynamic, developmental concept of tradition defended by Congar. Whereas Trent had emphasised the objective elements in tradition, its continuity from the apostles, and the verbal element in transmission, the themes of subjectivity, progress, and action are more prominent in the utterances of Vatican II." Ibid., 94.

259. Ibid., 92.

260. For a general overview of the thought of Maurice Blondel and an analysis of his contribution to Vatican II, see R. Latourelle, "Blondel," in Latourelle and Fisichella, *Dictionary of Fundamental Theology*, 78–84; Latourelle, *Man and His Problems in the Light of Christ*, 195–214; J. Lacroix, *Maurice Blondel: An Introduction to the Man and His Philosophy* (New York: Seabury, 1968); A. Dulles, "Vatican II and the Recovery of Tradition," in *The Reshaping of Catholicism* (San Francisco, Harper and Row, 1988), especially 90–92.

261. Dulles, "Vatican II and the Recovery of Tradition," 75–92; J. Ratzinger, in *Commentary on the Documents of Vatican II*, ed. H. Vorgrimler, vol. 3 (London: Burns and Oates, 1968), 181–98.

contained in a static deposit, to a subjectively experienced, dynamic entity: "an organ of apprehension and transmission."[262] This the Council combines with an insistence on the "non verbal elements in tradition,"[263] so facilitating the formulation of the definition of tradition given in *Dei Verbum*, 8: "In its preaching, life and worship . . . [the Church] hands on to every generation all that it is and all that it believes."[264] Commenting on this passage, Dulles maintains that the Council has identified tradition with the "total life and praxis of the Church."[265]

A Question of Priorities

It must be said, however, that Dulles's discussion of the role of liturgy as locus or medium of tradition is somewhat muted, especially when one considers the raised awareness of worship that *The Craft of Theology* generally shows. Yet, while this might be a legitimate expectation of a theology seeking to be postcritical, it fails to take into account that the theology of Dulles is fundamentally and self-consciously ecumenical.[266] This is not to suggest that Dulles has restricted himself to a "confessionally neutral historical method"[267]

---

262. Dulles, *The Craft of Theology*, 94.
263. Ibid., *The Craft of Theology*, 95.
264. "Quod vero ab apostolis traditum est, ea omnia complectitur quae ad populi Dei vitam sancta ducendam fidemque augendam conferunt, sicque ecclesia, in sua doctrina, vita et cultu, perpetuat cunctisque generationibus transmittit omne quod ipsa est, omne quod credit." *DV*, 8.
265. Dulles, *The Craft of Theology*, 95.
266. In a general way this is borne out in Dulles's method of models. Moreover, each of his works studied in this chapter has ecumenism as a basic concern. See Dulles, "Introduction," *Models of the Church*, 12; Dulles, *Models of Revelation*, 14–17; Dulles, "Introduction," *The Craft of Theology*, xii; and, most importantly, chapter 12 of this work, entitled "Method in Ecumenical Theology," 179–96. For examples of Dulles's involvement in specifically ecumenical issues, see Dulles, "Paths to Doctrinal Agreement: Ten Theses," *Theological Studies* 47 (1986): 32–47; Dulles, "Dogma as an Ecumenical Problem," *Theological Studies* 29 (1968): 397–416, especially 410–16.
267. Dulles, *The Craft of Theology*, 187.

with regard to the liturgy, but he has certainly adopted a broader theological base in order to facilitate dialogue.[268] In the final analysis, the ecumenical motive is not a complete explanation for the ambivalence that Dulles shows toward the liturgy as *locus theologicus*. Hence, at the beginning of chapter 13, which is entitled "Theology and Worship," he resolves,

> If theology relies on symbolic communication as heavily as I have maintained . . . situations of worship in which the word of God is reverently heard, and in which the faithful participate in sacramental worship, deserve fuller treatment than I have given them thus far. In the present chapter I propose to look more closely into this theme, retaining, as I do so, the ecumenical perspective.[269]

In returning to the liturgy in the penultimate essay of this collection, Dulles not only returns to a question that he regards as "insufficiently developed"[270] in his own work, but to one that has been topical throughout the twentieth century. However, in seeking to situate and clarify the *lex orandi, lex credendi* principle within his own theological enterprise, Dulles prescinds somewhat from the debate on

---

268. Dulles asserts, "All who find themselves caught up in the quest for transcendence could profitably meditate together on what is implied in phenomena such as petitionary prayer, worship, thanksgiving, repentance, atonement, self-sacrifice for ideals, altruistic love, obedience to conscience, and hope in the face of inevitable death. Thus far Christian theologians have generally addressed these questions within the relatively narrow confines of their own traditions. If we wish to take advantage of the theological resources that are available in our day, we shall be well advised to widen our horizons so as to approach universal human questions within horizons that are equally universal." *The Craft of Theology*, 180.

269. Ibid., 197. It is interesting to note that in a collection of essays in honour of the ecumenist George H. Tavard to which Dulles contributed, the Methodist theologian Geoffrey Wainwright, a source for chapter 2 of *The Craft of Theology*, submitted an article entitled "Tradition as a Liturgical Act." Wainwright describes his enterprise thus: "My method and purpose here are systematic, offering a theological interpretation of Scripture and Christian history for the sake of a constructive understanding and practice of liturgy and tradition in the ecumenical present." In this article, he also addresses clearly the ecumenical issues surrounding the adoption of a stance that declares that "Tradition is liturgy." G. Wainwright, "Tradition as a Liturgical Act," in *The Quadrilog: Tradition and the Future of Ecumenism; Essays in Honour of George H. Tavard*, ed. K. Hagen (Collegeville, MN: Liturgical Press, 1994), 129–46, 129.

270. Dulles, *The Craft of Theology*, vii.

liturgical theology that has occupied a number of theologians in the postconciliar period. And, although the classical approach of Dulles to this question through Scripture, tradition, and contemporary questions is customary, in this instance it seems to afford an unwanted distance of objectivity in regard to his subject. Such criticism is consonant with observations that Bernard Cooke made in a review concerning Dulles's chapter on "The Use of Scripture in Theology." To paraphrase Cooke[271]: Dulles stands outside liturgy and, though he draws from it in theological argument, he does not enter into liturgical ways of thinking as he does into theology. Though his detailing of other thinkers' approaches is instructive, in practice there is much more overlap of the methods than he indicates. It is probably for this reason that the chapter "Theology and Worship" concentrates on a dispassionate historical survey of how liturgy has influenced theology and the formulation of dogma. It is perhaps also why, in conclusion, Dulles can make the following, somewhat ambivalent statement:

> Whether the law of prayer governs the law of believing or vice versa, it appears from all the cases here surveyed that the two finally coalesce and support one another. As the Church prays, so it believes; as it believes so it prays. It would be too simple, however, to imagine that the language of prayer and that of dogma totally coincide. In worship, the Church appeals more to the imagination and the emotions; it has more ready recourse to metaphor. Dogma tends to be formed in a more conceptually precise, and frequently philosophical, vocabulary. Hence a certain bridge has to be crossed from the figurative language of devotion to the prose of dogmatic statement.[272]

271. "My impression is that Dulles stands outside Scripture, draws from it as a theologian, but does not enter into the biblical ways of thinking as he does theology. This is reflected in his detailing various thinkers' approaches to handling the biblical texts; the distinctions he makes are instructive, but in practice there is much more overlap of the methods than he indicates. Besides, he does not bring together the use of the Scripture in the Church, especially in liturgy, with the explanation of how theology draws from the ongoing process of communal faith life that is the Christian tradition. Perhaps this is because Dulles does little with Christian ritual." B. Cooke, review of A. Dulles, *Models of Revelation*, *America* 168 (January 23, 1993): 21.

Whatever one makes of Dulles's reluctance and his ambiguity, in the end it can be said that he recognizes a certain priority in the liturgy. If the craft of theology involves a movement from symbol to system, then it must be concerned with the building of bridges between liturgy and systematics. And, if this conclusion leaves the point of departure for the theological endeavor suggestively discreet, it would seem logical to conclude that liturgy is first theology. It was the lifetime's craft of Salvatore Marsili to formulate a liturgical theology that would bridge the regrettable gap between worship and dogma.

272. Dulles, *The Craft of Theology*, 208.

4

Salvatore Marsili

Granting Priority to the Liturgy

Achille Maria Triacca suggests that "it would be worth writing a biography of Marsili to show its course parallel with the history of the liturgical movement in Italy, in a way that elevates the contribution to liturgical renewal of the meritorious Benedictine."[1] Though far from a biography, it is hoped that this chapter will make apparent some of the more important connections between the work of other theologians of the liturgical renewal and the particular contribution of Salvatore Marsili. Yet there are other interesting parallels to be drawn from the biography of Marsili that are perhaps more pertinent to this study.

---

1. "Varrebbe la spesa di scrivere una biographia di Marsili in modo parallelo con la storia del *movimento* liturgico in Italia, in modo che risalti l'apporto del benemerito benedettino al rinnovamento liturgico." A. Triacca, "Teologia della liturgia o teologia liturgica? Contributo di P. Salvatore Marsili per una chiarificazione," *Rivista Liturgica* 80 (1993): 267.

Letting the Principles Emerge:
I Segni del Mistero di Cristo

Marsili's personal history, his own formation and, the study and the scope of his teaching commitments situate him in a singular place of synthesis that undoubtedly gave rise to his unique perspective.[2] During the years crucial to the birth of *Sacrosanctum Concilium* and *Dei Verbum*, Salvatore Marsili was teaching both at the newly founded Pontifical Liturgical Institute at San Anselmo and at the Pontifical Gregorian University. Though, like René Latourelle,[3] Marsili played no direct part in the proceedings of the Council or in the formation of the documents, it could not be said that he took no active part.[4] Certainly it must be concluded that he was active in the extraordinary theological ferment that brought these unique documents forth. More particularly, his subsequent work benefited from his particular position.

Andrea Grillo detects in Casel, Vagaggini, and Marsili a recognition of the need to reformulate the general discourse of theology in a manner more suited to the times. For them, it is a matter of course that the liturgy is fundamental to this endeavor:

2. For a more detailed biographical analysis, see "Salvatore Marino Marsili," in AA.VV. *Mysterion, Nella celebrazione del Mistero di Cristo la vita della Chiesa, Miscellanea liturgica in occasione dei 70 anni dell'Abate Salvatore Marsili*, Quaderni di *Rivista Liturgica,* Nuova Serie n.5. (Turin: Leumann, 1981), ix–xvi; A. Chupungco, "Salvatore Marsili: Teologo Della Liturgia," in *Paschale Mysterium, Studi in memoria dell'Abate Prof. Salvatore Marsili (1910–1983)*, ed. G. Farnedi, Studia Anselmiana 91—Analecta Liturgica 10 (Rome: PIL, 1986), 15–24; M. Ballatori, "Abate Salvatore Marsili OSB, la figura e l'opera," *Il Letimbro* 49 (1983): 92; B. Neunheuser, "Don Salvatore Marsili: personalità e attività scientifica," in AA.VV., *Riforma liturgica tra passato e futuro. Atti della XIII Settimana dell'Associacione Professori di Liturgia*, Cassano Murge (Bari), 27–31 agosto 1984, *Studi di Liturgia*—Nuova Serie, 13 (Casale Monferrato, 1985), 139–53; B. Neunheuser, "Salvatore Marsili," *Ecclesia Orans* 1 (1984): 202–7.

3. For an evaluation of Latourelle's influence on the formation of *Dei Verbum* and the particular role of the Pontifical Gregorian University, see B. J. Cahill, *The Renewal of Revelation Theology (1960–1962): The Development and Responses to the Fourth Chapter of the Preparatory Schema De Deposito Fidei*, Tesi Gregoriana, Serie Teologica 51 (Rome: PUG, 1999), 222–31.

4. See H. Schmidt, *La Costituzione sulla Sacra Liturgia, Teso-Genesi-Commento, Documentazione* (Rome: Borla, 1966), 1137.

By thus uniting liturgy and fundamental theology in the one overall environment, these theologians of the liturgy appear the more efficacious for a deep study of the reflection on liturgy the more accurately they are analysed in their double value as thinkers and theologians of the "liturgy" and of "fundamental theology" without separating one area at the expense of the other.[5]

By examining some of the more substantial published works of Marsili, this chapter will seek to investigate his "double value" as a liturgical theologian. Happy biographical coincidences, the rich confluence of theological themes during the conciliar period, and Marsili's subsequent endeavors at interdisciplinary collaboration[6] will be seen to contribute to his belief that the liturgy is both "first theology" and the locus of synthesis.[7] Initially, however, we must begin with the liturgical movement and Marsili's engagement with it.

Schooled in an Atmosphere of Renewal

In the early part of the twentieth century, just as the liturgical movement[8] began to shift from an external renewal of ritual forms into a truly theological endeavor, Salvatore Marsili entered the lists.[9]

5. "Saldando così liturgia e teologia fondamentale in uno stesso ambito complessivo, questi teologi della liturgia si palesano tanto più efficaci per un approfondimento della riflessione sulla liturgia quanto più accuratamente vengono analizzati proprio nella loro duplice valenza di pensatori e teologi della 'liturgia' e della 'teologia fondamentale,' senza separare un ambito a scapito dell'altro." A. Grillo, *Teologia Fondamentale e Liturgia: Il rapporto tra immediatezza e mediazione nella riflessione teologica* (Padua: Edizioni Messaggero–Abbazia di Santa Giustina, 1995), 17-18.
6. See S. Maggiani, "La teologia liturgica di S. Marsili come 'opera aperta'" *Rivista Liturgica* 80 (1993): 341–57, especially 344–45, where Maggiani discusses Marsili's "openness" to the findings of the human sciences and his commitment to the study weeks of the Association of Professors and Scholars of Liturgy (APL).
7. In recent years interest in the notion of the liturgy as *theologia prima* has increased. See especially David W. Fagerberg, *Theologica Prima: What Is Liturgical Theology* (Chicago: Hillenbrand, 2004), for a discussion of the main theologians and themes but especially Dorothea Haspelmath-Finatti, *Theologia Prima: Liturgische Theologie für den evangelischen Gottesdienst* (Göttingen: Vandenhoeck & Ruprecht, 2014). Written from an evangelical and ecumenical perspective this usefully sets the work of Marsili in the wider context of this approach.

In 1920, at the age of only ten, he was accepted as an aspirant at the monastery of Finalpia, an abbey in Northern Italy responsible for the founding of the *Rivista Liturgica*. Singled out as a future collaborator on a journal that was to become the organ of the Italian liturgical renewal,[10] Marsili was dispatched to study at the Athenaeum Anselmiana. There, in an international atmosphere of prayer and study, Marsili flourished, and, with the help of experienced teachers, mastered the scientific skills required to communicate his growing knowledge and love of the liturgy.

Soon after ordination Marsili, returned to Finalpia, and, before beginning to teach, he accepted an invitation to holiday at the German abbey of Maria Laach. In fact, Marsili was to return for a whole year (1934–1935), and during this period, the life and teachings of the now-famous center of the liturgical movement exercised an inestimable influence on him.[11] Dom Ildefonso

8. Teresa Berger, "The Classical Liturgical Movement in Germany and Austria: Moved by Women?," *Worship* 66, no. 3 (1993), 231–51; Kathleen Hughes, ed., *How Firm a Foundation: Voices of the Early Liturgical Movement* (Chicago: Liturgy Training, 1990); T. Klauser, *A Short History of the Western Liturgy* 2nd ed. (Oxford: Oxford University Press, 1979); B. Neunheuser, "Introduzione, il movimento liturgico panorama storico e lineamenti teologici," in AA.VV., *La liturgia: momento nella storia della salvezza Anàmnesis 1*, 2nd ed. (Genoa: Marietti, 1979), 11–30; B. Neunheuser, "Movimento Liturgico," in *Nuovo Dizionario di Liturgia*, ed. D. Sartore and A. Triacca (Milan: Edizioni Paoline, 1983), 904–18; O. Rousseau, *Storia del movimento liturgico* (Milan: Edizioni Paoline, 1961); Sacerdotal Communities of St. Severin of Paris and St. Joseph of Nice, "The Liturgical Movement," in *The Twentieth Century Encyclopaedia of Catholicism*, vol. 115 (New York: Paulist, 1964), 31ff.

9. This is not an entirely inappropriate phrase, as Marsili later came to be known for his pugnacious academic spirit: "I monaci di Finalpia nelle note biografiche dell'Abate Marsili hanno rilevato un certo spirito battagliero in lui. . . . Nella lunga e difficile storia del Movimento liturgico c'è stato talvolta bisogno di uno spirito battagliero, coraggioso ed incisivo, simile nei suoi lineamenti a quello dei padri apologisti." A. Chupungco, "Salvatore Marsili: Teologo Della Liturgia," 16.

10. In 1947, Marsili was involved in the founding of the Centro di Azione Liturgica (CAL), a body committed to uniting the various liturgical forces in Italy. For details of the development of this organization and its relationship to the *Rivista Liturgica*, see S. Marsili and L. Adrianopoli, "Centro di Azione Liturgica," *Rivista Liturgica* 34 (1947): 203–4.

11. We can be sure that Marsili was speaking from personal experience when he spoke of the effect that Maria Laach had on his friend and colleague Burkhard Neunheuser. In a eulogy written in Neunheuser's honour, Marsili asserts, "Parliamo per il Neunheuser di una vita nella

Herwegen, abbot of Maria Laach, and the person and teaching of Dom Odo Casel[12] must be singled out as decisive influences in Marsili's formation. By 1948, his commitment to the mystery theology of Maria Laach was such that on the evidence of his writings in the *Rivista Liturgica*,[13] the Abbot General of the Subiaco Congregation, Emmanuelle Caronti, forbade Marsili to publish or speak on liturgical matters.[14] Only under the new Abbot General, Celestino Gusi, and after some ten years of silence, did Marsili return to San Anselmo to begin teaching and embark on what would be the most productive years of his life.

In 1961, with Dom Adrian Nocent and Dom Cipriano Vagaggini, Marsili founded the Pontifical Liturgical Institute[15] and within it the chair of liturgical theology, which he held until his death in 1983. Though elected abbot of Finalpia in 1972, the last twenty years of Marsili's life were primarily devoted to teaching. To be

liturgia, perché—come s'è già accennato—la sua formazione era avvenuta in un Maria Laach tutto polarizzato, come a un ideale vitale, verso la liturgia antica la quale, sopratutto per la riscoperta della sua carica 'misterica' mostrava un aggancio così esistenziale alla vita, che finiva per comunicare il proprio contenuto spirituale e per dare un suo stile di pensiero a chi, oltre che studiarla, la viveva." In *Eulogia, Miscellanea liturgica in onore di P. Burkhard Neunheuser OSB, Preside del Pontificio Instituto Liturgico*, Studia Anselmiana 68, Analecta Liturgica, 1 (Rome: PIL, 1979), v–vi.

12. The ways in which Marsili appropriated and developed Laachian mystery theology will become clearer as his writings are examined, but a broad overview of Casel's central theses can be found in E. Dekkers, "La liturgie, mystère chrétien," *La Maison Dieu* 14 (1948): 30–64; J. Hild, "L'Encyclique *Mediator Dei* et le mouvement liturgique de Maria Laach," *La Maison Dieu* 14 (1948): 15–29; B. Neunheuser, "Odo Casel in Retrospect and Prospect," *Worship* 50, no. 6 (1976): 489–504; H. Reinhold, "Timely Tracts: Dom Odo Casel," *Orate Fratres* 22 (1948): 366–72.

13. S. Marsili, "Partecipazione sacramentale al Sacrificio di Cristo," *Rivista Liturgica* 24, no. 6.12 (1937): 129–32; 273–79; S. Marsili, "Giubileo abbaziale [del P. Ildefonso Herwegen] e Venticinque anni di Apostolato Liturgico," *Rivista Liturgica* 25, nos. 7–8 (1938): 183–85; S. Marsili, "Il mistero di Cristo," *Rivista Liturgica* 26, no. 4 (1939): 73–78.

14. See A. Elberti, *Il sacerdozio regale dei fideli nei prodromi del Concilio Ecumenico Vaticano II (1903–1962)*, Analecta Gregoriana, 254 (Rome, 1989), 103–11.

15. For a brief history of the origins and development of the Institute, see A. Chupungco, "The Pontifical Liturgical Institute: A Benedictine Service to the Church," in *Sant'Anselmo: Saggi storici e di attualità*, Studia Anselmiana 98 (Rome, 1988), 193–221. See also A. Chupungco, *What, Then, Is Liturgy? Musings and Memoir* (Collegeville: Pueblo, 2010).

lecturing in the various pontifical universities in Rome[16] during the great theological ferment of the conciliar period meant that Marsili had to be constantly attentive to the work of his colleagues and the deliberations of the Council. But this unique situation also gave him the opportunity to develop his own voice. In the pedagogical context of the Lateran, the Gregorian, and his own Liturgical Institute, Marsili made the "concrete decisions and practical choices"[17] that honed his principles into a precisely articulated, mature position. Essentially, the works that will be examined derive from the class notes and *dispensae* of this period: either those that he perfected into the *Anàmnesis* series, or those that were published posthumously in the *Nuovo Dizionario Di Liturgia*, or as *I segni del mistero di Cristo* in the Liturgical Editions series of the Vincentian Liturgical Centre.

In order to appreciate development in the writings of a particular author it is normally best to proceed chronologically. In the case of Marsili, however, this approach is complicated by the fact that a number of works published posthumously are compilations of papers and notes that had been reworked over a considerable period. One such work, which will be examined later, is *I segni del mistero di Cristo*: a collection of class notes and articles produced over twenty years (1961–83) and subsequently shaped into a study on the sacraments.

16. Marsili began lecturing in liturgy and sacramental theology at the Gregorian University in the academic year 1963–1964 and carried on until 1968, though he continued teaching in the Institute for Religious Sciences until 1972. He also taught at the Lateran (1963–1964) and at the Regina Mundi Institute until his death. Cf. M. Alberta, "Nota Redazionale," in Marsili, *I segni del mistero di Cristo* (Rome: Edizioni Liturgiche, 1987), 7–8.

17. "The continuing research by fundamental theology about its own identity—this very book is a phase of it—is not just a theoretical problem about which to organise colloquia, congresses, and conferences. Teaching, which must continue in the meantime, requires concrete decisions and practical choices: choices that are bearers of responsibility. It concerns the formation of students, often inexpert and therefore easily influenced. More than specialized publications, read by a few, institutional teaching (and this is true for all disciplines) given to ever new generations of students, sometimes—as at the Gregorian—numerous, influences everyday life." M. Chappin, "Dalla Difesa al Dialogo: L'insegnamento della teologia fondamentale alla PUG, 1930–1988," in *Gesù Rivelatore: Teologia Fondamentale*, ed. R. Fisichella (Casale Monferrato: Edizione Piemme, 1988), 39.

The later, and posthumous, publication date of this work cannot be taken as an indication that the mature thought of Marsili is here represented. Though systematic editing has provided a unity to chronologically disparate material by structuring it around a single theme, as a whole the work is representative of his earlier reflections. Hence, though *La Liturgia: momento nella storia della salvezza* is styled as a general and introductory text, and though in places it is earlier than *I segni del mistero di Cristo*, as a whole the work is methodologically and thematically more mature. Therefore, the sequence followed here may not be called chronological in the strictest sense. Nevertheless, the procedure adopted should serve to clarify better the methodological development in Marsili's work, revealing an advance from the principles of a general stance to the consequences of a specific and systematically applied method. In order first to appreciate the methodological beginnings of Marsili's liturgical theology, an analysis of *I segni del mistero di Cristo* will be used to show how this nascent method gives a particular shape to a theology of the sacraments. Reflection on *La Liturgia: momento nella storia della salvezza*, the first volume in the *Anàmnesis* series, will subsequently afford insight into what had, by 1979 and in the light of Vatican II, become a more finely tuned and consistently applied methodology. Finally, two articles entitled "Liturgia" and "Teologia Liturgica," posthumously published in the *Nuovo Dizionario Di Liturgia*, will be analyzed as a means to both clarifying and extrapolating what Marsili had begun to see as the inevitable implications of his now-consolidated position for liturgical, and specifically sacramental, theology.

Fundamental Principles

Though compiled and edited after the death of Marsili, what we have in *I segni del mistero di Cristo* is in many ways similar to the enterprise of Latourelle in *Théologie de la Révélation*. The text is essentially a *dispensa*, the style and purpose of which centers around classroom teaching. In his "Preface,"[18] Dom Michele Alberta suggests that this work has its roots in an early decision of Marsili that the theology of the sacraments needed to be refounded.[19] Contrasting experiences of a liturgy that failed to give access and his own *caseliana*[20] experience at Maria Laach brought Marsili to the conviction that the only credible foundation for a theology of the sacraments was the mystery of Christ. Hence we are speaking not only of stylistic parallels between these two works. Near enough contemporary, both texts are part of the christocentric renewal of Catholic theology that the *ressourcement* had inspired.[21]

While adopting quite different perspectives of approach, Latourelle and Marsili were both seeking to establish a methodological discipline

18. Alberta, "Presentazione," in *I segni del mistero di Cristo*, 9–16.
19. "Dall'incoerenza, spesso constatata nei suoi 'excursus' storici, tra la realtà di Cristo, nella quale la celebrazione introduce, e l'inadeguatezza verbale o rituale di certe celebrazioni concrete, nasce nelle convinzioni del Marsili la necessità di una "rifondazione teologica" di ogni sacramento, di ogni discorso liturgico." Ibid., 10.
20. Ibid., 10.
21. See "The Christocentric Renewal" in Cahill, *The Renewal of Revelation Theology*, 211–54, as a contextualization for Marsili's own conviction that the *Rivista Liturgica* had its own part in this renewal: "La novità vera che non ha mai cessato di risuonare in *RL* e che si è andata gradualmente rafforzandosi in maniera sempre più evidente è l'aver posto il *tema cristologica* alla base e all'interno della Liturgia, per cui questa comincia già ad apparire in quella luce soteriologica o storico-salvifica, che in epoca a noi più recente non solo è diventata la chiave più autorizzata per la comprensione della Liturgia, ma ha ridato una nuova dimensione alla *ecclesiologia*, diventata così essa stessa un discorso sul mistero di salvezza il quale si va concretamente attuando negli uomini appunto attraverso la Liturgia. In altre parole, in *RL* si stringe sempre più il trinomio: Cristo-Chiesa-Liturgia, in quanto si va chiarendo sempre più l'idea secondo cui è dalla *Liturgia* che nasce la *Chiesa* come comunità salvifico-cultuale, ossia come communità di salvezza nella quale si attua concretamente il *mistero di Cristo* attraverso la celebrazione cultuale dello stesso mistero." S. Marsili, "*Rivista Liturgica* 1914–1973. Sessant'anni di servizio al movimento liturgico," *Rivista Liturgica* 61, no. 1 (1974): 27.

that would facilitate the theological and pastoral aspirations of the Council. The central content of their teaching remains remarkably similar, and, though allusion has already been made to the cross-fertilization of ideas that both geography and the remarkable opportunity of the Council made possible, it perhaps remains more likely that here are merely the overtures to a dialogue not yet properly begun.[22] Latourelle in any case would seem oblivious to a partner. Providing a rationale for the specific character of his teaching some twenty-five years after the Council, he made this claim: "The question that fundamental theology is *alone* in treating, that dogmatic theology does not deal with as such, and without which fundamental theology itself would lose its *raison d'être*, is one single block: the credibility-of-the-revelation-of-God-in-Jesus-Christ."[23]

That is to say, the question to be answered, which is in the competence of fundamental theology alone, is this: How is the reality of Christ "accessible, meaningful, identifiable, and thus believable"?[24] At the same time, it remains the conviction of Marsili that such a question can be answered properly only when one starts with the liturgy. Revelation happens in a "liturgical modality,"[25] which also means that liturgy is the only mode in which it can be accessed, understood, identified, or believed. Thus the mystery of Christ, the fullness of revelation, is definitively expressed when the sacraments are celebrated in the church. To appreciate better how Marsili begins to unravel this mystery, attention must be given to his developing

22. See J. Driscoll, *Theology at the Eucharistic Table* (Leominster, UK: Gracewing, 2003), ch. 6, especially 130–31.

23. R. Latourelle, "Absence and Presence of Fundamental Theology at Vatican II," in *Vatican II: Assessment and Perspectives Twenty-Five Years After (1962–1987)*, ed. R. Latourelle, 3 vols. (New York: Paulist, 1988), 3:394.

24. Ibid., 396.

25. "Infatti il mistero pasquale non è una certa determinazione temporale che indicherebbe solo un giorno speciale nel calendario religioso, ma è un fatto teologico il quale ha una modalità liturgica." S. Marsili, "Liturgia," in *Nuovo Dizionario di Liturgia*, ed. D. Sartore and A.-M. Triacca (Rome: Edizioni Paoline), 731.

method of liturgical theology and to the parallels that can be drawn with fundamentals. Marsili begins with signs.

An Economy of Signs

In his article on sign and symbol in the *Nuovo Dizionario di Liturgia*, Domenico Sartore points to the lack of consensus among scholars as to the precise definition and function of signs,[26] and this is something that has been seen in the two authors already studied. It should come as no surprise, then, that in the long years of Marsili's scholarly reflection, he moves continually to a more determined and defined position with regard to semiology. The decade surrounding the Second Vatican Council, at the end of which he published his first specific and sustained reflection on the theme, is crucial to the development of his understanding.[27]

From his teacher Odo Casel, Marsili knew how essential thinking symbolically was for a correct understanding of the liturgy.[28] Yet his

26. "Il compito di approfondire la dimensione simbolica della liturgia cristiana incontra una prima difficoltà nell'imprecisione e nell'equivocità con cui i termini 'segni–simbolo' vengono usati in vocabolari diversi attinenti il vasto campo del *simbolico*," D. Sartore, "Segno/Simbolo" in Sartore and Triacca, *Nuovo Dizionario di Liturgia*, 1370. A similar point is made by Rino Fisichella from the perspective of fundamental theology: "What immediately strikes one in defining a sign is the great number of answers that get given." See R. Fisichella, "Semiology," in *Dictionary of Fundamental Theology*, ed. R. Latourelle and R. Fisichella, (New York: Crossroad, 1995) 988.

27. S. Marsili, "I segni sacri: storia e presenza," in AA. VV. *Il segno nella liturgia*, CAL, Liturgia—Nuova Serie, 9 (Padua: Messaggero, 1970), 7–19. Also S. Marsili, "Terminologia segnale nella liturgia," in *Il segno nella liturgia*, 21–38.

28. "We live in an age which, after a long period of devotion to abstract intellectualism with its excessive evaluation of reasoning, is beginning once more to think in symbols, to make use of the ways in which divine truth has taken form in nature, art, and culture. For us it is doubly necessary to bring to memory those periods of history when symbolic thinking was in full flower. This is the peculiar worth of the history of religions, for it teaches us to understand and use the power and primitive strength of symbolic thinking, in contrast to the over-refinement of 'modern' methods. The first age of the Christian church had no need for this, for it lived in the midst of the mysteries and looked at everything as symbol of the divine. When we regard the ancient liturgy, the writing of the apostles and the fathers, we realize that for them everything is symbolical of Christ, and Christ is symbol of the Father: '*qui videt me, videt et patrem*: who hath seen me hath seen the Father' (Jn 14:9). Today we have to learn these things

earlier reflections show the ambiguity and lack of precision that many have claimed to be a feature of his master. In Marsili's earlier work signs may reveal an inner disposition[29] or be used for education and elevation,[30] and they are not always distinguished from symbols.[31] However, from the early 1960s onwards, reflecting on the Scriptures and studies in the phenomenology of religions, Marsili begins to elucidate a somewhat sharper definition. The fruit of these efforts forms the opening pages of I segni del mistero di Cristo. Natural signs, revealed prophetic signs, and real signs are distinguished[32] and, by means of a comparison of these categories, Marsili is able to clarify the place that the seven sacraments have within a sacramental economy of signs:

> Speaking also of the New Testament as a reality, it has to be said that it is presented to us as a whole series of signs that, exactly because they are signs of a reality, are not purely intentional, or designed to make us think of just one thing that perhaps does not exist in reality, but are signs that carry reality because they do not point to the future (i.e., to a thing that does not yet exist) but depend in themselves on a fact or event which has already happened. Furthermore, when the fact or event has already happened, it is not done and finished with, because if this were the case it would cease to be a fulfillment of the promise, but its 'ending', and as a result 'cessation' would indicate the end of the covenant, which is and is to be eternal in its realization, as it was in its promise.[33]

over again; we have to learn to think simply, in the most ancient way, and thus to become once more seers of the whole." O. Casel, *The Mystery of Christian Worship and Other Writings*, ed. B. Neunheuser (London: Darton, Longman and Todd, 1962), 172. This is a translation of O. Casel, *Das Christliche Kultmysterium* (Regensburg: Friedrich Pustet, 1932 and 1959).

29. Cf. S. Marsili, "La liturgia nel V Concilio Provinciale di Malines," *Rivista Liturgica* 26, no. 6 (1939): 171.

30. Cf. S. Marsili, "La Messa di Pasqua," *Rivista Liturgica* 29, no. 3 (1942): 23.

31. Cf. S. Marsili, "Il mistero liturgico: realtà e segno," *Rivista Liturgica*, 55, no. 5 (1968): 632–44. Marsili finally clarifies a distinction between the two terms in his much later "Teologia della celebrazione dell'eucharistia," in AA. VV., *La Liturgia Eucaristica: teologia e storia della celebrazione*, *Anàmnesis*, 3/2 (Genova: Marietti, 1983), 49.

32. Marsili, *I segni del mistero di Cristo*, 25–55.

33. "Tuttavia, anche parlando del NT su un piano di 'realtà,' si deve dire che questa stessa ci viene presentata *tutta in un regime di segni*, i quali però, appunto perché sono 'segni di una realtà,'

In this theologically dense passage, the central themes of Marsili's liturgical theology can be seen to begin to take shape. The history of salvation is a vast economy of signs that is brought to unity in Christ, the "fact or event which has already happened." Christ gives the content of reality that these signs carry, and, because Christ's "significance" is eternal, this covenant cannot pass away and forms the sacramental covenant of the church. It is under this increasingly clear category of sign that Marsili brings together three essential elements in his theology (and that of the Council):[34] the actual structure of the economy of revelation, the incarnational principle, and the absolute centrality of Christ in revelation and faith. Notice, however, the method by which Marsili effects this synthesis of ideas: the theological content of salvation is approached from the perspective of the liturgy precisely because that is the form under which it is revealed. The sacred signs of the Jewish religion, namely, circumcision, Passover, and temple, which Marsili analyzes carefully in this chapter, and the *semeia* of the Gospel of St. John, which he subsequently studies in a digression, are framed in liturgical feasts. It is this ritual framework that facilitates the believer's perception that the common thread within the sign economy is the paschal mystery of Christ.[35]

non sono segni puramente 'intenzionali,' ossia tali da far 'pensare' soltanto ad una cosa che forse non esiste realmerte; ma sono 'segni portanti della realtà,' perché non indicano un futuro (cioè una cosa non ancora esistente), ma dipendono nel loro *essere* da un *fatto o avvenimento* che si è *realizzato*. Inoltre, il fatto o avvenimento, una volta realizzato, non è 'passato e cessato'; perché se così fosse, non sarebbe già 'adempimento' della promessa, ma la sua 'cessazione,' e conseguentemente implicherebbe la cessazione dell' *alleanza,* che invece è e deve essere eterna nella sua *realizzazione* come lo fu nella sua *promessa*." Ibid., 41–42 (my translation).

34. See S. Marsili, "Liturgia," 733–37. Intentionally, and by way of comparison, I have taken these three fundamental aspects from a description by R. Latourelle in "Absence and Presence of Fundamental Theology at Vatican II," 402–5.

35. "Il filo conduttore di tutto questo cioè dei quadri e dello sfondo—è uno solo: il Mistero Pasquale di Cristo." S. Marsili, *I segni del mistero di Cristo*, 49.

The Transmission of Salvation

The liturgical-theological principles from which Marsili concludes that "signs carry reality" allow him, by means of the sacramental rite, to telescope into one living reality the shadows of the old law, the seven sacraments, and the paschal mystery of Christ that they carry.[36] Hence a relationship is established between the immediacy of revelation in Christ and the mediation of the sacraments.[37] It is this relationship, in all its aspects, that forms the basis of much of Marsili's teaching: a relationship that some would see to be the privileged focus of fundamental theology, for it is on exactly this relationship that the credibility of the gospel and the response of faith is founded. Thus, by means of a further examination of the concept of sign, Marsili proceeds to examine the "transmission" of this reality and the response it invokes:

> Signs, moreover, having meaning as they always do, indicate not only an instance of divine intervention taken, so to speak, in isolation, but are elements of the dialogue between God and man. Man responds to God's

36. This position is further clarified and its consonance with the Council made apparent in an article of 1963: "I 'segni sacri' non sono solo i gesti esteriori, ma l'insieme dell'azione liturgica concepita e realizzata come espressiva di realtà divina, se vista nella causa: Dio-Sacramento; e di realtà interiore, se vista nel soggetto; e dall'altra parte richiama al valore di segno esistente tanto nella creazione quanto nell'Incarnazione. Rilevato poi il valore *dinamico* del segno nella definizione della Liturgia data dal Concilio ('esercizio del Sacerdozio di Cristo in cui per mezzo di segni sensibili, viene significata e realizzata la santificazione dell'uomo e, nello stesso tempo, il Corpo mistico di Cristo esercita il culto pubblico integrale'), col mettere in rilievo l'uso della parola 'realizzata,' viene spiegato come il fine del segno non sia direttamente solo l'attuazione della realtà sacramentale, ma la comprensione di essa. Quindi più che ad una segnalità oggettiva, il rito liturgico tende ad una segnalità soggettiva, che è appunto la comprensione del rito da parte del soggetto. Questa segnalità oggettiva non mira però solo ad una comprensione intellettuale, ma ad un 'comprendere' che sia 'simul apprehendere,' in quanto suscitando l'atto di fede, che scopre la realtà interiore del rito, si ha *col segno e nel segno l'oggettiva* realtà della grazia e l'interiore adesione a Cristo e alla sua opera redentrice. Di qui la necessità della comprensibilità del segno liturgico." S. Marsili, "La liturgia nel Concilio Vaticano II," *Rivista Liturgica* 50, nos. 3–4 (1963): 263.
37. See the subtitle of A. Grillo's *Teologia Fondamentale e Liturgia: Il rapporto tra immediatezza e mediazione nella reflessione teologica.* His discussion of Marsili's theological contribution to this question can be found on 35–49.

sign. In fact, people create the sign in order to be able to remember the divine intervention and perpetuate the memory of it both for themselves and for those who come after them. Therefore, the sign is always a stage that should and does elicit a reaction on the part of people. In John's Gospel we see that this is the point upon which Christ himself and the evangelist, commenting upon the words of the Lord, insist upon: "You have seen the signs and yet you do not believe." To see the signs without believing means that the reaction that the sign is meant to produce is missing. If the sign does not speak, it is not a sign, but if it does speak it demands a response. It therefore serves to initiate a conversation.[38]

Interestingly, though speaking of a dialogue, Marsili does not envisage *word* as the primary category in the communication that exists between God and humanity. This might at once be contrasted with Latourelle, who, though latterly, amplifies the concept of word essentially describes speech as the principal mode of the self-revelation of God in its various forms of word, testimony, and encounter.[39] While he does admit a place for gesture, which is "to support and give depth"[40] to the revealing word, this understanding remains rooted in, and subservient to, the scholastic notion of *locutio Dei*. The significance of the concept of word, and remnants of the notion of divine legate, can be deduced when Latourelle summarizes

38. "I segni, d'altra parte, in quanto a significato—perché il segno ha sempre un significato—non indicano solo un intervento divino—per così dire, distaccato—ma sono elementi di *colloquio* tra Dio e l'uomo; l'uomo risponde al segno di Dio. Difatti *l'uomo crea il segno* per potersi ricordare dell'intervento divino, per poterne perpetuare la memoria, anché al di fuori di sé (per sé, per coloro che vengono dopo ecc.). Quindi il segno è sempre un *momento* che deve provocare—e provoca—una *reazione da parte dell'uomo.* Nel Vangelo di Giovanni vediamo che è sempre su questo punto che, ora Cristo direttamente, ora l'Evangelista commentando le parole del Signore, insistono: Voi avete *visto* I segni e non *credete.* Vedere i segni senza credere vuol dire che viene a mancare quella reazione che il segno deve produrre; il segno, se non parla, non è un segno, *ma se parla esige una risposta.* Quindi, serve a creare un colloquio." Marsili, *I segni del mistero di Cristo,* 55 (my translation).

39. R. Latourelle, *Théologie de la Révélation: Deuxième édition revue et augmentée* (Bruges: Desclée Brouwer, 1966), 387–402, [Eng. trans., Sr. Dominic Parker, *Theology of Revelation: Including a Commentary on the Constitution "Dei Verbum" of Vatican II* (New York: Alba House, 1966), 315–27].

40. Ibid., 317 [390].

the revelatory mission of the Son of God in the following way: "Christ, after having exercised his prophetic mission, that is after having made known the name of the Father (Jn 17:6, 26), the doctrine of the Father (Jn 7:16; 12:50), consummates, through the sacrifice of his life, the gift made by his word. Through his passion he accomplishes the charity that he came to signify."[41]

Here Latourelle recognizes the dynamic of what Marsili later calls the "works-signs"[42] synthesis—that is, the interplay of outer and inner significance that is the function of a sign. By means of an external sign, the addressee is invited to an inner significance—an invitation that demands a response. It is for this reason that Marsili constantly seeks to foreground the interactively complex dimensions of the sign category of communication, precisely because it is on this notion that he sees the whole economy of salvation to rest, and that in a liturgical mode of expression.

Quoting St. Paul's letter to the Ephesians and carefully amending the words of Vatican I, *Dei Verbum* stated, *Placuit Deo in sua bonitate et sapientia seipsum revelare et notum facere sacramentum voluntatis suae.* This might be translated literally as "It pleased God in his goodness and wisdom to reveal himself and to make for us a sacrament (or sacred sign) of his will."[43] It would seem that sign is a preferable category to word or symbol, and, though used loosely and in an underdeveloped way by Marsili, he has certainly resolved at this point to see sign as the basic category of God's self-communication. As yet, the primary reason may be that Marsili regards sign as a unit more consonant with an economy of salvation that as a whole is realized sacramentally—that is, "by deeds and words having an

---

41. Ibid., 392 [319].

42. "Opere-segni." Marsili, *I segni del mistero di Cristo*, 67.

43. For an analysis of *Dei Verbum* chapter 1, and a comparison with the corresponding texts of Vatican I's *Dei Filius*, see Latourelle, *Théologie de la Révélation*, 343–50, [457–63].

internal unity."[44] However, as we shall see, subsequently, Marsili's primary reason for selecting sign becomes the conviction that it is essentially a liturgical phenomenon.[45] While Latourelle had stretched his category of word to accommodate the paschal mystery, Marsili finds in that mystery the essential modality of the self-revelation of God. For, if the paschal mystery is the central and definitive act by which God makes himself known, and if this mystery is the Passover of the Lord, then the liturgical "framework" of this act cannot be insignificant. However, this is to give a coherence of expression at which Marsili has not yet arrived.

One indication of the ambiguity of Marsili here is the question of who makes the sign.[46] Though he insists that "the people make the sign in order to remember," he maintains also that the sign "*per se* is a sign of divine intervention." Psalm 111:4 says *[Domini] memoriam fecit mirabilium suorum misericors*—"The Lord has made a memorial of his marvellous deeds." This text makes a fitting parallel to that of *Dei Verbum*, which speaks of the Lord God making a sacrament of his will.[47] God, as Latourelle clearly insists, is always the first to act and invite his people to enter a dialogue. For Marsili, this is a sacramental relationship that goes beyond words. Here, human beings share not only in a momentary condescension of an otherwise inaccessible God, or even in a protracted dialogue with the transcendent, but in a personal communion of love ratified by sacramental signs.

---

44. *DV*, 3.

45. We shall see later the detailed interpretation that Marsili gives to this question in Marsili, "Liturgia," 735–36.

46. In the opening sections of his article "Liturgia," Marsili discusses clearly the question of the rightful subject of the liturgy. See "Liturgia," 726–29.

47. I am indebted to Jeremy Driscoll for this point that he made in a lecture course at the Gregorian. Cf. Ps. 110:4 *Biblia Sacra*, iuxta vulgatam versionem (Stuttgart: Deutsche Bibelgesellschaft, 1969).

The Christological Center

When we shift this argument into the christological key, we see that Christ is the sacramental sign through which the mystery of the Father's will is made known. It is Christ the Lord who had made a memorial of God's marvellous deeds—the eucharistic memorial of his Passover. This understanding of sign, expressed much more clearly at the end of Marsili's career, is what leads him now to a discussion of the unique nature and unity of salvation that is expressed in the mystery of Christ.

> Salvation, considered here as a unique and universal reality because "God wants all people to be saved," is historicized by signs. Although different at successive stages, signs form a single substantial unity among themselves, insofar as they are always in different ways the revelation and actuation of the one unique divine plan that is salvation. Therefore in the unity of salvation, signs in their temporal succession have a common denominator: the uniqueness of the divine plan. In fact, in another way signs are distinguished from each other by the fact that they are always the revelation and actuation of that unique reality. Therefore the sign presents two aspects: the aspect by which every sign is different from the next one, and the aspect by which in each and every sign, there is the revelation and the actuation of one and the same divine plan, realized in a different way.[48]

Here, Marsili reflects on the unity and singularity of redemption in Christ within the context of salvation history.[49] Originally, this pattern of theological thought had emerged within Protestant circles,

---

48. "La salvezza, presa qui sempre come realtà unica e universale—tale perché 'Dio vuole che tutti gli uomini siano salvi'—, viene storicizzata dai signi. Ora *i segni*, benché distinti in momenti successivi, formano una *unità sostanziale* tra di loro, in quanto sono sempre, in maniera diversa, *rivelazione e attuazione* di quell'unico disegno divino che è la salvezza. Quindi dall'unità della salvezza, i segni, pur nella loro successione temporale, traggono un comune denominatore: l'*unicità del disegno divino.* Infatti, in un modo diverso, nel quale appunto i segni si distinguono l'uno dall'altro, sono sempre *rivelazione attuazione* di quell' *unica realtà.* Quindi, il segno presenta due aspetti:—l'aspetto per cui *ogni segno è diverso da quello successivo;*—l'aspetto per cui, nell'uno e nell'altro segno, c'è in concreto *la rivelazione e l'attuazione dell'unico disegno divino,* realizzato però in maniera diversa." Marsili, *I segni del mistero di Cristo,* 57–58 (my translation).

in direct contradistinction to the metaphysical tradition that sought the truth in universal ideas and not in the unique facts of history. Jean Daniélou, Hans Urs von Balthasar, Karl Rahner[50] and others, however, had introduced historical themes into the Council to enliven stale scholastic categories, and, though well received, the critical question of the compatibility of a salvation-historical understanding and traditional Catholic metaphysics remained. Joseph Ratzinger recognizes two more related issues as being part of this longer inquiry: the extent to which scriptural mediation could exist together with ecclesial mediation, and the question of how the reactualization that links salvation and historical event can best be understood.[51] These issues become the center of Marsili's mature liturgical theology, and the event character of the biblical word, actualized when proclaimed in the liturgy of the church, becomes the focus of his inquiry. The mystery of Christ—the word who is actualized—is the key to a salvation that has been (and is being) expressed in a variety of forms and at various times.

The mystery of Christ provides the fundamental unity of content, which in turn establishes a singularity of form and a coincidence of time. Marsili describes this unity of the divine plan—founded on the mystery of Christ—as the "common denominator" of revelation.

---

49. For a thorough overview of salvation history and related themes, see the various entries under "History" in Latourelle and Fisichella, *Dictionary of Fundamental Theology*, 433–55. More specifically, see J. Daniélou, *L'entrée de l'histoire du salut* (Paris: Desclée, 1967), and also W. Kasper, "Linee fondamentali di una teologia della storia," in *Fede e Storia* (Brescia: Queriniana, 1975), 62–96.

50. For a commentary on the theology of Jean Daniélou and his particular role in influencing *Dei Verbum*, see B. Cahill, *The Renewal of Revelation Theology*, 240–54. A concise summary of Hans Urs von Balthasar's position can be found in his short book *A Theology of History* (New York: Ignatius, 1994); and the position of Karl Rahner is given in his "History of the World and Salvation History," in *Theological Investigations*, trans. K.-H. Kruger, vol. 5 (London: Darton, Longman and Todd, 1966), 97–114, and in "The Historicity of Theology," in *Theological Investigations*, trans. G. Harrison, vol. 9. (London: Darton, Longmann and Todd, 1972), 64–82.

51. See J. Ratzinger, *Principles of Catholic Theology* (San Francisco: Ignatius, 1989), 174–75. Particularly interesting is the comment that Ratzinger makes on Oscar Cullmann and Odo Casel, two of the most significant influences on Marsili with regard to this matter.

Interestingly, Latourelle uses a similar phrase when he discusses this same question of a unique but diverse aspect to revelation. For Latourelle, however, "the common element in Scripture and in the documents of the Church is *locutio* and *testimonium*."[52] Though, as already indicated, Latourelle considerably develops this category later, this was his position at the time of his classnotes in 1961. A profitable contrast can be made with the broader and less cerebral category that Marsili adopts. It is this concept of mystery (philologically prior to *sacramentum*) that allows Marsili, building on Casel, to make the liturgical link necessary for his later synthesis. While at this point he leaves "the question of the mystery understood in the sense of worship"[53] underdeveloped, the critical connections have already been made. It is not without significance that the same phrase of "common denominator" is used in a later text of Marsili, which examines this christological unity of revelation from a more explicitly liturgical dimension.[54]

A Unity of Time and Content

The structure of *I segni del mistero di Cristo* might be said to fall into three sections: the central section, which examines the seven sacraments individually, is flanked by an introductory and a concluding section that contextualize the particular celebrations. The introduction examines the fundamental themes of sacramentology

---

52. "Elementum igitur *commune* in scriptura, in documentis Ecclesiae, est locutio et testimonium." See R. Latourelle, *De Revelatione, Schemata lectionum ad usum alumnorum*, 2nd ed. (Rome: PUG, 1961), 164.

53. "Senza addentrarci nella questione del 'mistero' inteso nel senso di 'azione cultuale' chiariamo il concetto di 'Mistero di Cristo' che denomina la realtà della salvezza." Marsili, *I segni del mistero di Cristo*, 58.

54. "The common element of mystery is given definitive expression with regard to time, place, 'being' or content when the 'human body' of Christ, the 'church body' of Christ, and his 'sacramental body' are aligned on a level of common liturgical reality." See Marsili, *La liturgia: momento nella storia della salvezza*, 113 (my tanslation).

and the conclusion explores overarching themes of unity as expressed through the notion of the liturgical year. "Il Tempo Nella Storia Della Salvezza" falls into this concluding section, which would seem to be composed of relatively late work.[55] By this point Marsili asserts,

> The liturgy—we have seen—has a direct relationship with the "history" of salvation, inasmuch as this forms its content. But our liturgy is that of Christ, the structure and ritual form that renders present the mystery of Christ (salvation) at the level of "reality." And in the same way that Christ "synthesizes" the past and the future (the announcement and actualization of "reality"), also the liturgy resolves itself in a "synthesis" of the whole of salvation. In other words: that salvation that in Christ finds its highest realization does not cease to be "history" by the fact that Christ is "entered into glory."[56]

In this section, Marsili is beginning to structure his ideas on salvation history, inspired by Casel and Cullmann, according to the principles of his developing liturgical theology.[57] The questions of Ratzinger to which we have alluded are beginning to be answered here, and the point of synthesis is the liturgical actualization of the mystery of Christ:

> The derivation of all the "works-signs" from *the* major Sign-Work of

---

55. Comparison of the subjects covered here with those published in the *Rivista Liturgica* and elsewhere (for example, S. Marsili, "Il 'tempo liturgico' attuazione della storia della salvezza," *Rivista Liturgica* 57, no. 2 (1970): 207–35, and Marsili, "Il ciclo annuale dei misteri della salvezza: presentazione della liturgia di ogni domenica e festa," in *L'annuario del Parroco*, ed. G. Badini, Anno XIV (Rome: Edizioni INA, 1968), especially the indications contained in S. Marsili, *De Anno Liturgico. Quaestiones historicae et theologicae*, (Pro manuscripto) Pontificium Institutum Liturgicum Anselmianum, Athenaeum Sancti Anselmi de Urbe (Rome, 1968), would suggest that the latter articles of *I segni del mistero di Cristo* were written in the early 1970s.

56. "La Liturgia—abbiamo visto—ha un rapporto diretto con la 'storia' della salvezza, in quanto questa forma il suo contenuto. Ma la nostra liturgia è quella *di Cristo*, ossia è una forma rituale che rende presente il Mistero di Cristo (salvezza) a livello di 'realtà.' E siccome Cristo 'sintetizza' il passato e il futuro (annuncio e attuazione della 'realtà'), anche la liturgia si risolve in una 'sintesi' di tutta la salvezza. In altre parole: quella salvezza che in Cristo trova il suo culmine di realizzazione non finisce di essere 'storia' per il fatto che Cristo è 'entrato nella gloria.' Marsili, *I sengi del mistero di Cristo*, 439 (my translation).

57. See O. Cullmann, *Christ and Time* (Philadelphia: Westminster, 1964), and Casel, *The Mystery of Christian Worship*, especially 16–20.

salvation that is Christ must be understood in a concrete sense. The signs (the sacraments) are partial actuations of the one sole and unique reality that is the Father's will for our salvation realized in Christ, that is, God's infinite love for man. "God so loved the world that he gave his only Son" (John 3:16). It was for this reason that the author of the Letter to the Hebrews, who speaks in the New Testament in the text of Heb. 10:1, says that the Old Testament gives us "a reflection of the good things which were to come, whereas we (NT) have the image of the things which have been accomplished."[58]

In cultivating the notion of Christ as the primordial sacrament, Vatican II effected a "threefold innovation as regards the use and understanding of signs."[59] Until the Council, the signs of salvation were seen in an exclusively objectivist light, each sign serving its unique apologetic purpose as a factual contribution to the credibility of the gospel.[60] Once the Council welcomed a personalistic interpretation, signs ceased to be disassociated facts but cohered in the person of Christ. As Rino Fisichella points out, we have witnessed "a significant transition from signs to the sign."[61] It is to this transition that Marsili alludes here. His use of the term *Sign-Work* gives recognition to the fact that a personal sign is necessarily an historical sign—an event. If, then, all the "work-signs" of revelation come to unity in Christ, they are signs ultimately of the Christ event. This signification should be taken not lightly, however, but "in a

---

58. "La derivazione di tutte le opere-segni dal Segno-Opera massima della salvezza, che è Cristo, deve essere presa in senso concreto: I segni (ossia i sacramenti) sono attuazioni parziali della realtà essenziale, unica e unitaria che è la volontà di salvezza, esistente nel Padre e realizzatasi in Cristo, cioè l'Amore infinito di Dio per l'uomo. Dio ha tanto amato il mondo da dare il suo Figlio unigenito (Gv. 3.16). Per questo l'autore della Lettera agli Ebrei, il quale parla nel Nuovo Testamento, nel testo di Ebr. 10.1 dice que il VT ci dà l'ombra dei beni futuri, mentre noi (NT) abbiamo l'immagine delle cose fatte." Marsili, *I segni del mistero di Cristo*, 67 (my translation).

59. See R. Fisichella, "Semiology," in Latourelle and Fisichella, *Dictionary of Fundamental Theology*, 987.

60. See H. Fries, "The Grounding and Justification of the Claim of Revelation—The Problem of Credibility and Criteria," in *Fundamental Theology* (Washington, DC: Catholic University of America, 1996), 331–53.

61. Cf. Fisichella, "Semiology," 987.

concrete sense," and with this suggestion we return to the abiding question of the relationship between salvation and its actualization in history. Being founded on the salvific Christ event, the individual signs of salvation, though a partial expression, are nonetheless real. This is because Christ the primordial sign is situated at the climax of salvation, and there abides as the principle of intelligibility for all signs—those that preceded him are in his light only shadows, and those that follow bear the real image of his light.[62] This, essentially, is the purpose of the quotation from the Letter to the Hebrews that Marsili employs.

Gaining Insight from a New Perspective on Institution

As it is an idea that Marsili will return to, let us look rather more closely at this notion of partial yet concrete signs of salvation.[63] Karl Rahner, in a roughly contemporary essay, bases this notion of partiality on the teaching of the sevenfold nature of the sacraments by the Council of Trent. He asserts that the Council declares that "(1) the individual sacraments are not of the same dignity, (2) not equally necessary for salvation and (3) therefore (as we may add) among themselves need not necessarily be considered separate from one another."[64] This reasoning he then uses to explain the communication of the same Spirit in baptism and confirmation. Here, he suggests, "no difficulty really exists in speaking of the sacraments if one considers that the sevenfold articulation of the one word of grace on the part of the Church is irreversible and final. For the essence of the Church is the communication of the absolute and final word of salvation she

---

62. Ibid.
63. See Marsili, *I segni del mistero di Cristo*, 113–14.
64. K. Rahner, *A New Baptism in the Spirit: Confirmation Today* (Denville, NJ: Dimension, 1975), 15.

pledges as her commitment to the world."[65] There is an attempt to hold various points together here: Christ the primordial sacrament is the real meaning of all those signs that cohere in him. Though they may be a partial manifestation, they are nonetheless real, and perhaps their partiality conceals their specific function in the life of a believer—an invitation to participation. The other aspect of this argument is the light it sheds on notions of dominical institution. This is something that Marsili clearly recognizes when he states subsequently,

> The study of the way *apostolic catechesis* presents to us the sacraments of baptism and the Eucharist in the Holy Scriptures helps us to see that the institution of the sacraments on the part of Christ cannot and should not be seen along the lines of a "juridical pronouncement" of a "sacramental sign," that is, of the pronouncement that establishes by law what should be the exact nature of the sacramental sign *so that the grace* that Christ *wishes* to give can be attached to it. We do, however, see clearly that the institution of the sacraments can be seen along the lines of a reality, or that it can be seen simply in terms of *putting on the level of reality that which already existed in determined signs on the level of prophetic announcement.*[66]

As Rahner asserts in his seminal work *The Church and the Sacraments*,

> Because first of all and independently of the usual idea of sacrament, we envisage the Church and the fundamental or primal sacrament, and form the root idea of a sacrament in the ordinary sense as an instance of the fullest actualisation of the Church's essence as the saving presence

---

65. Ibid., 16.
66. "Lo studio sul modo come *la catechesi apostolica* ci presenta nella Scrittura i sacramenti del battesimo e dell'Eucaristica ci fa vedere che l'istituzione dei sacramenti da parte di Cristo non può e non deve essere vista sulla linea di una promulgazione giuridica di un segno sacramentale, cioè di una promulgazione che per legge stabilisce quale debba essere la composizione del segno sacramentale, affinché ad esso possa essere *annessa la grazia* che Cristo *vuole* dare. Risulta invece chiaramente che l'istituzione dei sacramenti deve essere vista sulla linea della realtà ossia che essa consiste semplicemente nel porre su un piano di *realizzazione quello che esisteva già in determinati segni sul piano dell'annunzio profetico.*" Marsili, *I segni del mistero di Cristo*, 86–87 (my translation).

of Christ's grace for the individual, we can in fact obtain from this an understanding of the sacraments in general.[67]

The particular understanding that Marsili obtains here concerns the question of institution. Prior to the Second Vatican Council, many theologians followed procedures that gave a false orientation to their work. Both Pius IX and later Pius XII advocated a method of approach that insisted that the theologian began with dogmatic truths, and in their light searched the obscure Scriptures for the implicit indications of these fully grown teachings. As Ratzinger says in his commentary on *Dei Verbum*, "This [method] is then developed to the point at which the task of theology is described as that of showing how what the teaching office has established is contained in the sources—and that precisely in the sense in which it has been defined."[68]

Until relatively recently, when looking to establish biblical warranty for seven sacramental rites, theologians simply combed the Scriptures for any such indication, no matter how implicit. One began with the seventh session of the Council of Trent, which decrees the dominical institution of the seven sacraments by Christ, and worked "backward." Yet such efforts, which mark sacramental theology even today, fail to take an holistic attitude to the Scriptures. Theologians generally apply themselves only to the New Testament; they excise texts from their *Sitz im Leben* and seek to make them bear a significance never intended. However, as we have seen, Marsili was ever conscious of retaining a sense of the overarching economy of God's revelation. In fact, his method was exactly that envisaged by *Dei Verbum* 12.[69] Basing his conclusions on scriptural analysis and

67. K. Rahner, *The Church and the Sacraments* (London: Burns and Oates, 1963), 24.
68. J. Ratzinger, "The Transmission of Divine Revelation," in *Commentary on the Documents of Vatican II*, ed. H. Vorgrimler, vol. 3. (London: Burns and Oates, 1968), 197.
69. "But since sacred Scripture must be read and interpreted with its divine authorship in mind, no less attention must be devoted to the content and unity of the whole Scripture, taking

apostolic catechesis, he declares that "the institution of the sacraments on the part of Christ cannot and should not be seen along the lines of a juridical pronouncement of a sacramental sign." How then do Scripture, tradition, and the analogy of faith contribute to a notion of institution?

According to Marsili, a synthesis can be made precisely because of the sacramental economy of salvation history. While the Scriptures largely frustrate any search for a juridical act on the part of Jesus, at the same time they require the theologian to relocate the search to a foundation where a firmer judgement can be made. Essentially, once the Scriptures have forced the theologian to take a larger perspective, the position of the sacraments becomes clearer. The Scriptures reveal that the divine economy of salvation has a sacramental shape. No matter at which point you splice into the self-revelation of God, it will take the form of a sacrament. This is true of creation, circumcision, temple, and Passover, of Christ himself and the church. Like those Russian dolls that fit one into another, God's mysterious plan reveals constantly a form that takes its shape, content, and meaning from Christ the Primordial Sacrament. Faced with this scriptural and patristic insight, Marsili revisits the notion of institution.

The seven sacraments were instituted when, by the presence of his person—the fulfilment of revelation's reality—Christ, by his words

into account the Tradition of the entire Church, and the analogy of faith, if we are to derive their true meaning from the sacred texts." (*DV* 12). We can get a further sense of this common hermeneutical search when we read Walter Kasper's definition of the analogy of faith mentioned here by the Council fathers: "The principle of the analogy of faith means, in broad terms, that each witness to the faith is true only in the context of all the other witnesses to the faith. This means not only that scripture must be interpreted in the light of dogma, but also that dogma must be interpreted in the light of scripture . . . every advance in exegetical knowledge is at the same time an advance in the interpretation of dogma. It is this dynamic and historical organization of the relations between dogma and exegesis that gives concrete form to the unity-in-tension which exists between gospel and dogma." W. Kasper, *Dogme et Évangile*, (Paris: Tournai, 1967), 109–12; translated in R. Latourelle and G. O'Collins, eds., *Problems and Perspectives in Fundamental Theology* (New York: Paulist, 1982), 80.

and actions, afforded to a series of signs that reality that meant they were now effective communications of himself.[70] The unity of revelation and salvation is again emphasized when Marsili explains further, "In giving the sacraments, Christ does not intend any more than giving to those who believe in him the means to insert themselves into the story of salvation on the level of realization or actualization."[71] In effect, that is to say that Christ seeks to share with humanity that real event that was the culmination of the mysteries of revelation and salvation. What Christ offers in the sacraments is insertion into the paschal mystery of his life, death, and resurrection.

Putting the Principles of Liturgical Theology in Place

Obviously, the door has been left open for a more explicitly liturgical interpretation of the mystery of salvation, but two related notions are beginning to take on particular significance within Marsili's developing argument. They are the notions of incarnation and participation.

> Christ actuating salvation in humanity (making the promise real) gives a real content to the signs of salvation, both to those affirming signs of the natural world as well as to the annunciatory signs of the Jewish world. His humanity is not just any kind of sign, but a sign that is "loaded" with the reality of salvation. The Word of salvation became the Incarnate Word, the "visible word," as Luther would say, but this is a

70. "Per congiungere tutte queste intuizioni in un insieme armonioso, questa parte cristologica si basa sul recente dialogo tra gli esegeti ed i dogmatici riguardo alla riscoperta della somiglianza tra gli ôt, o gesti simbolici, adoperati dai profeti d'Israele e quelli di Gesù. Diversi teologi sacramentali hanno trovato utile questo paragone per illuminare il nesso tra il comportamento rituale di Gesù e i riti liturgici della Chiesa." P. Rosato, *Introduzione alla Teologia dei Sacramenti* (Casale Monferrato: Piemme, 1992), 58. See also Rosato, "The Prophetic Acts of Jesus: The Sacraments and the Kingdom," in *Gottes Zukunft—Zukunft der Welt: Festschrift für Jürgen Moltmann zum 60. Geburtstag*, ed. H. Denser, et al. (Munich: Chr. Kaiser, 1986), 59–67.

71. "Spieghiamo: Cristo nel dare i sacramenti non intende e non può intendere altro che dare agli uomini, che crederanno in lui, il mezzo per inserirsi nella 'storia della salvezza,' a livello di 'realizzazione' o di 'attuazione.'" Marsili, *I segni del mistero di Cristo*, 87 (my translation).

loaded sign that has within itself the presence of salvation. Whoever, in the humanity of Christ (and wherever a Jew uses this name he does not just mean anyone but the Holy One of God, i.e., salvation incarnate) recognizes the sign of salvation as already made real, participates through this humanity, in the salvation that has already happened.[72]

In a later section than the one quoted above, Marsili comments that, in order to understand how the eternal plan of salvation is realised, an exact notion of the doctrine of the incarnation must be established.[73] The exactitude of the notion will not, however, depend on a theological or philosophical scrutiny of the hypostatic union, but on the concrete reality of the incarnation within the history of salvation. Karl Rahner insists that the connection between the doctrine of the incarnation and Christian belief as a whole is to be found not in creation, fundamental as it is, but in salvation history. This story shows that "the absolute, infinite and holy God wills in the freedom of his love to communicate *himself* by grace *ad extra* to what is not divine."[74] The humanity of Jesus is the definitive expression of this free communication and the fulfillment of the messianic promise.[75] It is the human nature of Christ that gives flesh

---

72. "Cristo, attuando nella sua umanità la salvezza (la promessa diventa reale, attuale), dà un contenuto reale ai segni della salvezza sia a quelli affermanti del mondo naturalistico, sia a quelli annunzianti del mondo ebraico; la sua umanità non è un segno qualsiasi, ma è un segno avente la carica della salvezza: la Parola di salvezza è diventata la Parola Incarnata—la Parola visibile direbbe Lutero—, ma è segno carico, che ha in sé stesso la presenza della salvezza. Chi nell'umanità di Cristo (quando l'ebreo dice questo nome non intende una persona qualunque, ma il Santo di Dio, cioé la salvezza incarnata) riconosce il segno della salvezza in quanto attuata, partecipa, per mezzo di questa umanità, alla salvezza in atto." Ibid., 106 (my translation). For an interesting discussion of Luther's notion of the sacramentality of the Word, to which Marsili alludes here and how it relates to Catholic sacramentology see: Rhodora E. Beaton, *Embodied Words, Spoken Signs* (Minneapolis: Fortress, 2014).

73. "Cristo, quindi, è il *Sacramento totale* della salvezza: tutta la salvezza per la totalità degli uomini (non soltanto geografica, ma anche temporale). Per intendere questa idea fondamentale, dobbiamo cercare di avere un concetto esatto dell' Incarnazione." Ibid., 110.

74. K. Rahner, "Incarnation," in *Sacramentum Mundi: An Encyclopaedia of Theology*, ed. K. Rahner, C. Ernst, and K. Smyth, vol. 3 (New York: Herder and Herder, 1969), 110.

75. Cf. E. Schillebeeckx, *Christ the Sacrament of the Encounter with God* (London: Sheed and Ward, 1963), 14.

and therefore full access to the promise of the preexistent Word spoken through the prophets. In this sense, as Marsili states, "Christ, actuating salvation in humanity (making the promise real, actual) gives a real content to the signs of salvation."

While we see in Christ one who provides meaning to creation (cf. Wis. 13:1-5; Rom. 1:18-32; 8:18-25) and the first covenant (Rom. 4:13—5:3), preeminently we see in him the fulfillment of humanity's hope of entering communion with God.[76] As Heinrich Fries insists, the fullness of time in which God sends his Son born of a woman (Gal. 4:4) "does not mean just that a certain stretch of time or a certain date has expired. Rather, the time has reached a certain measure—not ascending to extension but to content. In history, the specification intended by the God of Israel as Lord of history is realized."[77] The "specification" is that "all people should have access to the Father, through Christ the Word made flesh, in the Holy Spirit and thus become sharers in the divine nature."[78] According to content, the specified measure reached is flesh. The Word has become incarnate, and this economy has an effect on the very nature of revelation. Edward Schillebeeckx identifies the impact of this event when he says, "Now because the inward power of Jesus' will to redeem and of his human love is God's own saving power realized in human form, the human saving acts of Jesus are the divine bestowal of grace itself realized in visible form; that is to say they cause what they signify; they are sacraments."[79]

It is in this sense that Marsili speaks of the humanity of Jesus being "loaded with the reality of salvation."

---

76. See Fries, *Fundamental Theology*, 201–14.
77. Ibid., 304.
78. *DV*, 2.
79. Schillebeeckx, *Christ the Sacrament of the Encounter with God*, 16–17.

Participating in the Whole Christ

Allied to this point is the question of accessibility and participation. Evidently, the fact that God's plan of salvation is now being made manifest through an economy of the flesh means that human beings have a sort of connaturality with revelation that facilitates the recognition of the signs of salvation.[80] Not only that but, because in the act of his self-manifestation God makes known the mystery of his will, the means of responding to God's invitation are also disclosed in this fleshly economy. Hence Marsili concludes, "Whoever in the humanity of Christ recognizes the sign of salvation as already made real participates through this humanity in the salvation that has already happened." To recognize in Christ one who has achieved for humanity its highest possible goal—union and communion with God—is to participate in the sign of the incarnation.[81] It is to recognize in the reality of Christ's human presence a future that has, through his paschal mystery, been brought to its goal in the present moment. This is the incredible density of the sign of salvation that is Christ: a sign that, as St. Thomas says, causes what it signifies.

In his *Fundamental Theology*, Gerald O'Collins makes the pertinent point that

> the Second Vatican Council in its document on revelation noted the absolute nature of the revelation Christ brought but in doing so it did not invoke the Incarnation, the resurrection, or Christ's role as *the* Teacher. The Council turned rather to the theme of the new covenant (*Dei Verbum* n.4). Through Christ God has established a definite and eternal covenant with humanity so as to mediate revelation and salvation until the end of the world.[82]

---

80. Cf. St. Thomas Aquinas, *ST* 3a, q. 61, art. 1, in D. Bourke, ed., *The Sacraments, Summa Theologiae*, vol. 56 (Oxford: Blackfriars, 1975), 36–39.

81. Cf. Marsili, *I segni del mistero di Cristo*, 110. Underlying this point is the notion of *potentia obedientialis* that is clearly articulated in K. Rahner, "Christology within an Evolutionary View of the World," in *Theological Investigations*, vol. 5, 157–92, especially 181.

Why does the Council choose this particular way of expressing the definitive nature of the self-communication of God in Christ? Perhaps the term *incarnation* is too much associated with a single completed action of the past: one that may remain unrelated to the other mysteries of salvation, especially the paschal mystery. Maybe too the fathers were seeking to redress the dominance that an incarnational approach had held in classical Catholic systems for centuries. *New covenant*, on the other hand, while including the definitive incarnate promise made in Christ, at once relates it to the whole of salvation history. What happens in this covenant is definitively new and yet not unrelated to the promise made to chosen forebears. The term also effectively combines incarnation and paschal mystery in a single covenant event.[83] This is the new and everlasting covenant, and not an isolated event of salvation history. This covenant, like Christ's humanity, will never pass away, because it is the paschal covenant made in his blood. From Marsili's developing perspective, the ritual dimension provided by covenant is of particular pertinence. It is as liturgy that this covenant is celebrated in his memory, and it is there that we participate in Christ's saving action. Such an interpretation of the Council's maintenance of the connection between the incarnation and the whole of Christian faith should be no surprise, as Marsili always seeks in this work to set the seven sacraments within the mystery of salvation that is Christ. This point is clearly developed here:

> The realization of the sacrament that is the Mystery of Christ happens partially, in the individual sacraments:
>
> 1. Because the individual sacraments are particular projections of the

---

82. G. O'Collins, *Fundamental Theology* (New York: Paulist, 1981), 99.

83. Cf. Marsili's use of Leo the Great's Sermon 74, 1: "With Christ the sacrament of our salvation is complete from the day of the birth of the Lord up to the end of his passion (*exitus passionis*—the exit from his passion)." SMarsili, *I segni del mistero di Cristo*, 110.

whole sacrament of salvation. The sacrament is always a whole one, but is projected in particular under a certain sign. It is as if we put filters of various colors in front of something luminous such as the rays of the sun, letting only a certain type of rays pass through and not others. The source of light stays the same, but its projections take on different colors, according to the sign. As particular projections the sacraments [are] more than just realizations of the Mystery of Christ, they are also revelations of it. Each and every revelation only ever happens partially, by degrees (implied by the word itself, "an unveiling," which happens bit by bit).

2. Therefore they are to reproduce the stages in salvation history. This, precisely because it is "history," implies a gradual nature. The sacraments are to reproduce the essential stages of it.[84]

In a sense, our examination of *I segni del mistero di Cristo* has come full circle. It began by seeing how Marsili contextualized the sacraments in the history of salvation, within an economy of signs. Attention was given to the consistency of this economy—to the shape and content of the self-revelation of God. That shape and content, consistent from the beginning to its consummation, is founded on the mystery of Christ, who is the Primordial Sacrament. Hence the seven sacraments are signs of the mystery of Christ—but they are signs that retain that consistency of shape and content and therefore are real, with the power to reveal and save. Here Marsili elaborates on the nature

---

84. "La realizzazione del sacramento, che è il 'Mistero di Cristo,' avviene *parzialmente*, ossia nei singoli sacramenti: 1. *Perché i singoli sacramenti sono proiezioni particolari del sacramento totale della salvezza.* Il sacramento è sempre totale, ma si proietta particolarmente secondo un determinato segno. E come se davanti a un oggetto luminoso di luce a tipo solare ponessimo dei filtri di diversi colori, lasciando, volta a volta, passare soltanto una determinata categoria di raggi luminosi e non le altre: la fonte luminosa rimane sempre la stessa, ma le sue proiezioni assumono (secondo il segno) colori diversi. In quanto proiezioni particolari, i sacramenti. . . . Oltre che attuazioni sono anche rivelazioni del Mistero di Cristo: ogni rivelazione avviene sempre parzialmente, per gradi (lo dice la parola stessa: svelamento, che avviene a mano a mano), 2. Perché devono riprodurre le tappe della storia della salvezza. Questa, appunto in quanto storia implica una gradualità. I sacramenti devono riprodurne le tappe essenziali." Marsili, *I segni del mistero di Cristo*, 113–14 (my translation).

of the actualization of this revelation. Principally, he determines that each sacrament facilitates a partial (in the sense of particularly applied) revelation of the divine and his will. He uses the effective metaphor of the refraction of light by way of explanation, white light being the whole sacrament that is the mystery of Christ, and the seven sacraments being the refracted colors of the rainbow—each a partial expression of the whole.

In addressing this issue, Marsili opens up the crucial question of "the continuing presence and power of that saving revelation."[85] We have already seen that, while the Council insists on the complete and definitive nature of the revelation that has happened in Christ, it also insists that this revelation is still happening: "God who spoke in the past, continues to converse with the spouse of his beloved Son."[86] Various theologians have tried to systematize this unity in distinction.[87] Some speak of immediate and mediate revelation, and some of foundational and dependent revelation, to mention only a couple. However, it would seem that in this understanding of partial revelation, as yet, it must be said, undeveloped, Marsili offers an interpretation that avoids the weaknesses often found in other arguments. O'Collins points to the difficulties surrounding a description of the present experience of revelation as mediate rather than immediate. Mediate, he concludes, suggests a "second-handness" that is not proper to actual experience: "If we do not experience—and that means *immediately* experience—revelation and salvation, we simply do not receive either."[88] His point is a valid one, but the extent to which it is resolved by using the terms *foundational* and *dependent*

85. O'Collins, *Fundamental Theology*, 99.
86. *DV*, 8 [*974].
87. Cf. O'Collins, *Fundamental Theology*, 100–2, along with his article "Revelation Past and Present," in Latourelle, *Vatican II: Assessment and Perspectives,* 125–37; and Latourelle, "Revelation and its Transmission according to the Constitution *Dei Verbum*," in *Theology of Revelation*, 474.
88. O'Collins, *Fundamental Theology*, 101.

is less certain. These two terms suggest a difference in degree and perhaps an essential or qualitative difference also, presumably in the order of content or intensity. Maintaining as he does the unique nature of the experience of the apostles, this may be the conviction of O'Collins, though it does not seem to be that of Marsili. The real content of the sacraments, which does not permit of degree, is the mystery of Christ—a reality that is not diminished by partial possession. Speaking similarly of the relationship between his body and the world, and quoted by Gustave Martelet in a text to be studied later, Teilhard de Chardin asserts, "My matter, or my own body is not a part of the universe that I possess *totaliter*: it is the totality of the universe possessed by me *partialiter*."[89] Similarly, a sacrament is not a partial possession of the total mystery of Christ, which yet remains beyond reach, but the totality of that mystery (that subsists in the Church) possessed partially.

The sacraments then permit of the gradual revelation of the mystery of Christ that is known to humanity only through history and in history. Thus the liturgical celebration of the sacraments is charged with making actual the various events of salvation centred on Christ's paschal mystery, that is, of condensing into one moment the history of a vast economy. In placing this exact question at the thematic center of *La Liturgia: momento nella storia della salvezza*, Marsili sets himself the task of clarifying a theological–liturgical method that has the systematic resilience to answer better his emergent questions.

89. T. de Chardin, "What Exactly is the Human Body?" (1919), in T. de Chardin, *Science and Christ* (London: Collins, 1968), 13. Quoted in G. Martelet, *The Risen Christ and the Eucharistic World* (London: Collins, 1976), 42.

Arguing a Coherent Methodology:
La Liturgia: Momento Nella Storia della Salvezza

Raymond Brown begins his historical-critical study of the subapostolic period, *The Churches the Apostles Left Behind*, with a quotation from "A Death in the Desert" by Robert Browning:

> When my ashes scatter, says John, "there is left on earth
> No one alive who knew (consider this!)
> —Saw with his eyes and handled with his hands
> That which was from the first, the Word of Life.
> How will it be when none more saith, 'I saw?'"[90]

Brown sees in the poem an eloquent rendition of "an axiom" about revelation that has an abiding place in Catholic tradition.[91] The question concerns the ongoing transmission of revelation in the Christian community, the unfolding of God's ultimate manifestation of himself in Jesus Christ. For one concerned to show by analysis the living transmission of this revelation in the texts of the New Testament, this is an appropriate verse: Brown informs us "how it will be" by showing us that the churches become the witnesses who, speaking in the name of the apostles, can credibly say, "I saw." But perhaps Marsili would have chosen a later stanza from that same poem of Browning:

> To me, that story—ay, that Life and Death
> Of which I wrote "it was"—to me, it is;
> —Is, here and now: I apprehend nought else.
> Is not God now in the world his power first made?
> Is not his love at issue still with sin ?[92]

---

90. R. Browning, "A Death in the Desert," in *Browning: Poetical Works 1833–1864*, ed. I. Jack (Oxford: Oxford University Press, 1970), 818–36, 821. See R. Brown, *The Churches the Apostles Left Behind* (New York: Paulist, 1984), 13.

91. See Brown, *The Churches the Apostles Left Behind*, 14, and especially n2.

92. Browning, "A Death in the Desert," 823.

The meaning, accessibility, and credibility of revelation we saw to be a significant part of Marsili's efforts in *I segni del mistero di Cristo*. Appreciation of the concept of sign was central to the theology elucidated: signs are the means by which the mystery of God's eternal plan of salvation is made present and active in a particular moment. In many ways, Marsili's enterprise remains the same in *La Liturgia: momento nella storia della salvezza*—such is clear from the preface. Yet the title of the work, the intention of the series to offer solid, introductory theology for the post–Vatican II era, and refinements in his own theological understanding, show this work to be more consciously and radically determined by the liturgy. Themes already familiar to us from *I segni del mistero di Cristo* are here again examined, but this time the perspective is different. In speaking of the dynamic and essentially open aspect of Marsili's work, Silvano Maggiani declared,

> We are conscious of the remarkable contribution brought about by christological research to the comprehension of the liturgy. But we believe that with christological/liturgical clarification the walk might only be half finished: when the true content of the liturgy is revealed, it is then about seeing how this content is able to be effectively realized in the Church.[93]

Identifying an Approach

In *La Liturgia: momento nella storia della salvezza*, Marsili embarks on the second part of the journey. Here he seeks to deepen theological understanding of the divine economy of salvation, and the

---

93. "Siamo consapevoli del notevolissimo contributo apportato dalla ricerca cristologica alla comprensione della liturgia. Ma riteniamo che con la chiarificazione cristologia/liturgia il cammino sia compiuto solo a metà: quando si è scoperto il vero *contenuto* della liturgia, si tratta poi di vedere *come* questo contenuto si può effettivamente realizzare nella Chiesa." S. Maggiani, "La telogia liturgica di S. Marsili," 344 (my translation).

christological shape of its expression, by defining carefully the mode of that expression as liturgy.[94] In doing this Marsili begins to offer a plan for the effective realization of revelation in the church, a plan that he will go on to refine in his articles for the *Nuovo Dizionario di Liturgia*. The church expresses the history of salvation in her own time—and the moment of that history that the liturgy represents is the hour of Jesus that does not pass away. The story of "that Life and Death," the paschal mystery, is the time in which the worship of the church takes place. Let us turn, then, to see how Marsili redevelops his thought according to these principles.

The Liturgy—A Theological-Ecclesial Discourse

It was Marsili's conviction that the liturgical movement had failed to penetrate the life of the church more effectively because of the lack of a united effort by the different liturgical groups, particularly in Italy. More importantly, progress was dogged because the principles of liturgical theology, present at the movement's inception, were not assimilated by theologians who continued to regard the liturgy as, at best, a superior *locus theologicus*. It is surely no surprise, then, that on becoming editor of the *Rivista Liturgica* in 1964, Marsili should regard the journal as a means to overcoming these two difficulties. Indeed, their surmounting was at the heart of his own theological enterprise

---

94. "Siamo infatti di fronte a un'elevazione della Liturgia al rango di componente essenziale dell'opera di salvezza, e precisamente sulla linea 'cristologica.' Questo significa che una conoscenza vera della Liturgia non si può avere arrestandosi alla pura ricerca scientifica sul piano storico delle origini, delle fonti, dell'evoluzione o dell'involuzione delle formule e dei riti, ma che al contrario è necessario, al fine di una comprensione autentica della Liturgia in se stessa e in riferimento alla sua funzione nella Chiesa, inquadrarla e approfondirla nella sua dimensione 'teologico-economica' e cioè nella 'teologia del mistero di Cristo.' La Liturgia infatti dovrà rivelarsi come il momento attuatore della storia della salvezza, creando così il 'tempo della Chiesa' ossia l'estensione della salvezza nell'ambito della comunità umana, come l'Incarnazione era stata il momento attuatore della stessa storia di salvezza in Cristo." Marsili, "Presentazione," in *La Liturgia: momento nella storia della salvezza*, 5.

of "making the liturgy a theological-ecclesial discourse, so that it may become an insertion of life into the mystery of Christ."[95]

A survey of Marsili's own contributions as editor could only lead one to agree with the conclusions of Cristina Ghiretti: Marsili's particular perspective on the liturgy led him to pay close attention to the religious problem in general, and as it concerns the life of the modern person.[96] Marsili sought, by assiduous analysis of the nature of worship, to refocus the goal of the liturgical movement to be that of establishing the liturgy as the place where individuals have the reality of their lives as being in Christ revealed to them. The *Anàmnesis* series is part of this enterprise, and is the systematic presentation of the fruits of much reflection in the years 1964–1974.[97] In the opening chapter, "Towards a Theology of the Liturgy," we see that insertion into the life of Christ is the defining element of Christian worship from the outset:

> From the beginning, the Christian rites were the single perfect expression of "spiritual" worship, because they were the "sign-synthesis" of a salvific moment, that is, signs in which were condensed at the same time the *sanctifying presence* of the mystery of Christ and the *sanctified presence* of the faithful. The purpose of the Christian rite has always been to consecrate and sanctify people so that each in his own person would become—together with Christ and through Christ—and not through a substitute symbol, the "sacrifice-altar-temple" of God, in other words, the *reality* and *spiritual place* of the worship of God. The Christian *rites* were in fact true *sacraments* and *mysteries*. In other words: the Christian

---

95. See B. Neunheuser, "Salvatore Marino Marsili," in AA. VV. *Mysterion, Nella celebrazione del Mistero di Cristo*, xiii–xiv.

96. Cf. C. Ghiretti, "Il Movimento Liturgico in *Rivista Liturgica* tra il 1914 e il 1947," in *Ritorno alla liturgia, Saggi di studio sul Movimento Liturgico*, ed. F. Brovelli (Rome: Borla, 1989), 47–66.

97. That Marsili was constantly reflecting on the immediacy of actualized revelation that results from what he calls the "sign-synthesis," and on how this is expressed liturgically, can be seen by way of a selection of his articles published during this period: "La preghiera di Cristo nella Liturgia," *Rivista Liturgica* 55, no. 4, (1968): 471–89; Marsili, "Il mistero liturgico: realtà e segno," 632–44; Marsili, "Il 'tempo liturgico,'" 207–35; "Terminologia segnale nella liturgia," in AA.VV. *Il segno nella liturgia*, 21–38.

rites were really new when it came to worship, because worship was not the result of something organized alongside *life*, but constituted the reason for being Christian, that is, it created people who lived *in Christ*.[98]

In this opening chapter, Marsili traces the historical development of cultic worship, through pagan and Old Testament categories, he relates them to the new dispensation of Christianity, and begins an historical survey of liturgy in the life of the church.[99] In doing so, he reveals what is essentially new about the Christian dispensation. From the beginning, New Testament worship was a matter not of external rubrics and ritual, but of the relation of external actions and gestures to an inner reality, which is life in Christ. This is what Marsili terms *spiritual worship*—devotion that realizes a truly sacramental economy. The signs of Christian liturgy, being raised to the level of reality and reaching fulfillment in the paschal mystery of Christ, signify what they effect and effect what they signify. These signs manifest the inclusion of the believer in Christ and effect on the level of reality that incorporation into Christ's body.

The Continuing Mystery

So far, Marsili has simply described the reality of Christian liturgy, namely the way in which rites express spiritual relationship to God

---

98. "I riti cristiani erano fin dal principio l'espressione perfetta e unica del culto 'spirituale,' perché erano 'segni–sintesi,' di un momento salvifico, e cioè segni nei quali si condensava allo stesso tempo la *presenza santificatrice* del mistero di Cristo e la *presenza santificata* dei fedeli. Il rito cristiano ha infatti avuto sempre lo scopo diretto di consacrare e santificare l'uomo, affinché questi diventasse in tal modo nella sua stessa propria persona—insieme con Cristo e per Cristo—e non per un simbolo sostitutivo, 'sacrificio-altare-tempio' di Dio, ossia *realtà e luogo spirituale* del culto di Dio. I riti cristiani erano veramente una 'novità' in material di culto, perché questo non risultava un'azione organizzata a fianco della *vita*, ma costituiva la ragione stessa dell'essere cristiani, cioè creava uomini che vivevano *in Cristo*." Marsili, *La Liturgia: momento nella storia della salvezza*, 53 (my translation).

99. Cf. Triacca, "Teologia della liturgia o teologia liturgica?," 267–89, especially 272, when Triacca comments on Marsili's use of this historical overview.

because they represent a moment in salvation history when that relationship was established definitively. Hence these symbols effect a unity between the one who sanctifies and the ones who are sanctified. This synthesis is brought about in the believer who, in his or her own person, becomes the spiritual place of contact and worship. This is the mystery of worship. While it can be seen from this quotation that Marsili has the ingredients necessary to describe this sacramental encounter with Christ, he has not yet explained how the sign-synthesis of liturgical rites effects the believers' insertion into Christ. But this is the question at the heart of sacramental theology and central to Marsili's own enterprise of explaining how the liturgy actualizes the paschal mystery of Jesus.[100] It is at this point that the essential role that the thought of Odo Casel has in Marsili's liturgical theology can be discerned. Marsili reflects this clearly when he declares,

> The importance of Casel's position is enormous, even if it was not understood by everyone at first. By giving the salvific *event* of Christ priority over the *liturgy*, as its point of departure, the liturgy is seen not as an "institution" that has come to us from Christ, but as the *ritual continuation of the mystery of Christ*. In other words: *in the liturgy*, that is, in the ritual form (sign-reality), *the salvific event itself is made present and active* for people of every time and place, and consequently every liturgical action represents a succession of moments in the *history of salvation*. Here we have arrived at a "theology" of liturgy. Casel sees the liturgy as a "worship mystery" inserted into the same "mystery of Christ," which constitutes the point of arrival and reality of all

---

100. In his standard work on the sacraments, Bernard Leeming defines this as the central issue of sacramental theology, the one that has dogged the discipline from the beginning: "A basic difficulty about sacramental efficacy which demands an answer, is expressed in the question, "Is it credible that a material instrument should be used to produce a spiritual effect?. . . Sacraments are signs, symbols even, though they are instituted by God. How can they as signs do more than convey knowledge? How can they produce not merely in our minds, but an objective change in the condition and state of our souls?" B. Leeming, *Principles of Sacramental Theology* (London: Burns and Oates, 1956), 284. See also D. Tappeiner, "Sacramental Causality in Aquinas and Rahner: Some Critical Thoughts," *Scottish Journal of Theology* 28 (1975): 243–57.

revelation; thus liturgy is always for him a moment that makes that same revelation present, and therefore has a central place in theology.[101]

Conscious of Marsili's conviction that all theology is determined by the categories of the liturgy, it is easy to see why he regards Casel's teaching to be of such enormous consequence. Because the category of mystery allows equation between Christ and Christian worship, the liturgy becomes the privileged point of access to the realities of salvation, the point of arrival for revelation in the church. Here, then, is not only the nub of the sacramental principle but the essential reason why liturgy is *theologia prima*.

If interest in the liturgy was to remain on the level of the authority of canon law or be dependent on theological principles provided by scholasticism, then the liturgy was, in Casel's opinion, moribund.[102] However, the choosing of "new categories to apply to itself"[103] is an action of consequence larger than might be first imagined. To choose "mystery" was to choose "the supremacy of immediate knowledge against discursive reason,"[104] of experience over authority.[105] It was,

101. "L'importanza di questa posizione del Casel è enorme, anche se al primo momento non tutti la compresero. Mettendo infatti a monte della *Liturgia*, come suo punto di partenza, l'*avvenimento* salvifico di Cristo, la Liturgia non è soltanto una 'istituzione' venutaci da Cristo, ma è la *continuazione rituale del mistero di Cristo*. In alter parole: *nella Liturgia*—e cioè nella forma rituale (segno-realtà)—l'*avvenimento stesso della salvezza* viene *reso presente e attivo* per gli uomini di ogni tempo e luogo, e conseguentemente ogni azione liturgica rappresenta un succedersi di momenti nella *storia della salvezza*. Siamo finalmente arrivati alla 'teologia' della Liturgia. Inserendo questa come 'mistero cultuale' nello stesso 'mistero di Cristo,' che costituisce il punto di arrivo e la realtà stessa di tutta la rivelazione, il Casel fa della Liturgia un momento sempre attualizzatore della medesima rivelazione, e quindi le conferisce un posto centrale nella 'teologia.'" Marsili, *La Liturgia: momento nella storia della salvezza*, 78 (my translation).

102. Cf. S. Marsili, "*Prefazione*" to O. Casel, *Il mistero del culto cristiano* (Rome: Borla, 1985), 4.

103. See Grillo, *Teologia Fondamentale e Liturgia*, 26.

104. Ibid., 27.

105. It is not difficult to see why Casel's position should cause such misunderstanding and opposition: "The overturning of perspectives introduced by the formula that entitles this paragraph ["Theology as *Locus Liturgicus*: A Radical Perspective"] almost immediately evokes some ghosts: the irruption of 'experience' in the foundation and construction of theological science, the weakening of the principle of authority, the inversion of the relation between *lex credendi* and *lex supplicandi*; basically, behind the pressing request of space for the *liturgical* experience could be hidden (let it be clear in the conditional) the blind force of an

as Marsili recognises, to locate the origins of liturgy in the salvation revealed by Jesus Christ. And the particular consequence of this decision is to claim a priority for the liturgy that is fundamental to theology. Andrea Grillo reflects on such a decision:

> Liturgy as *ancilla theologiae* thus appears as a vision that is restricted and basically lacking in space, with respect to which it is necessary to gain an *immensely deeper and more extensive* perspective, able to understand the sense and source of the liturgy, its being *fons* not in a purely juridical and surreptitious sense, but rather founding and fundamental. To redefine the role of the liturgy as *locus* means also and above all to reconsider the entire *theological topology* in relation to the liturgical experience.[106]

If, as it would seem, the principle that allows such a Copernican revolution in the thought of Casel and Marsili is mystery, this category must be examined further. Casel pioneered the recovery of this concept and, while we will not examine the rich possibilities that his philological analysis of the Greek concept and its Latin translations might yield, we will attempt to describe the meaning of the term within Casel's enterprise.[107]

uncontrollable 'liturgical *experience.*' In one word, the line of advance and arrival of the same 'liturgical movement' could be just an aspect—slightly more moderate—of the phenomenon known as *modernism.*" Ibid., *Teologia Fondamentale e Liturgia,* 23 (my translation).

106. "La liturgia come *ancilla theologiae* appare dunque come una visione angusta e in fondo senza respiro, rispetto a cui occorre guadagnare una prospettiva *immensamente più profonda e più vasta,* capace di ricomprendere il senso fontale della liturgia, il suo essere *fons* non in senso puramente giuridico e surrettizio, ma piuttosto fondante e fondamentale. Ridefinire il ruolo della liturgia come *locus* significa anche e soprattutto riconsiderare l'intera *topologia teologica* in relazione alla esperienza liturgica." In ibid., 20 (my translation). For further reflection on the global significance of Casel's position, see A. Schilson, *Theologie als Sakramententheologie. Die Mysterientheologie Odo Casels* 2nd ed. (Tübingen: Matthias Grünewald, 1987); G. Lafont, "Permanence et transformation des intuitions de Dom Casel," *Ecclesia Orans* 4 (1987): 261–84.

107. To examine this concept by means of those writers who most influenced Marsili is a worthwhile venture and would comprise an examination of the following: I. H. Dalmais, "Mystery Theology," in *New Catholic Encyclopedia,* vol. 10 (Washington, DC: Catholic University of America Press, 1967), 164–66; B. Neunheuser, "Mistero," in Sartore and Triacca, *Nuovo Dizionario di Liturgia,* 863–83; L. Bouyer, *La vie de la liturgie* (Paris: Desclée, 1956); I. Herwegen, *Christliche Kunst und Mysterium* (Münster: Aschendorff, 1929); H. de Lubac, *Corpus Mysticum, L'Eucharistie et L'Église au Moyen Age, Etude Historique* 2nd ed. (Paris: Aubier, 1949);

The Mystery of Christian Worship

Mysterion indicates the realization and revelation of a divine plan or action. In the Christian sense, the goal of this mystery is the unity of all people in the life of the Blessed Trinity. *Mysterion*, simply defined, encompasses the sacramental economy of salvation as it draws into a single dispensation the mysteries of Christ and his church. Hence, by deduction, if the liturgy is the central act of the church, then it can be defined as "the mystery of Christ and of the church."[108] It is exactly this idea that Marsili radicalizes as the basis of his notion of liturgical theology:

> This "liturgical theology" is the theology of the presence and the action of God in the history of human salvation; it is the "theology of the mystery of Christ," or, as Casel has said, the "theology of the mysteries of Christ": that is to say, the theology of a concrete reality, made of presence and of divine action, and this in the anthropological dimension, because it is not an action and a presence like a sign from heaven *signum de caelo*, but is the presence of Christ in the incarnation, in humanity, in men.[109]

The question that we are brought back to constantly is that of the immediacy of the presence and action of the liturgy and the sense in which we can, as Marsili does, call it the "same revelation." In his notes to the fourth edition of Casel's *Das Christliche Kultmysterium*, Burkhard Neunheuser takes up this very issue and, commenting on Casel's assertion that the mystery of the liturgy is both symbolic and

---

C. Vagaggini, *Il senso teologico della Liturgia. Saggio di liturgia teologica generale* (Rome: Edizioni Paoline, 1957), especially 27.

108. Casel, *Il mistero del culto cristiano*, 58.

109. "Questa "teologia liturgica" è la teologia della presenza e dell'azione di Dio nella storia della salvezza umana; è la "Teologia dei misteri di Cristo": cioè la teologia di una realtà concreta, fatta di presenza e di azione divina, e questo in dimensione antropologica, perché non è un'azione e una presenza, come un *signum de caelo*, ma è la presenza di Cristo nell'incarnazione, nell'umanità, negli uomini." S. Marsili, "Liturgia e Teologia. Proposta teoretica," *Rivista Liturgica* 59 (1972): 469.

real, states, "To determine more precisely the degree of reality which this medial thing has is the thorny task of theology in our day."[110] Then he points to a subsequent elucidation of Casel himself as it appeared in the *Jahrbuch für Liturgiewissenschaft*: "In the knowledge born of faith we see in the sacramental image its original, the saving work of Christ. We see it in faith and *gnosis*, that is to say, we touch it, make it our own, are conformed to it by participation and reformed after the likeness of the crucified and risen Christ."[111]

Essentially, it is this notion that Marsili seeks to elaborate by analysing the "temporal" relationship of Christ and the church:

> *The Liturgy of the church is none other than the "uninterrupted continuation"* *of the worship already rendered by Christ* during his earthly life, precisely with the double dimension of "glorification of God and sanctification of men." This principle, which forms the basis of the theological nature of the liturgy, is in its turn founded on two complementary points: a) the worship nature of the church, and b) the presence of Christ, mediator and priest, in the church.[112]

Vatican II and the Double Dimension of the Liturgy

In thus asserting the ecclesial nature of the liturgy, Marsili makes explicit a relationship that Casel often presumes. In an effort to distance himself from an institutional conception of worship and to emphasize the immediacy of the believer's encounter with Christ

---

110. Casel, *The Mystery of Christian Worship*, 207.
111. O. Casel, *Jahrbuch für Liturgiewissenschaft*, vol. 15, *Glaube, Gnosis und Mysterium* (Münster: Aschendorff, 1941), 268 (translated in Casel, *The Mystery of Christian Worship*, 207).
112. "*La Liturgia della Chiesa non è altro che 'la continuazione ininterrotta' del culto già prestato da Cristo* durante la sua vita terrena, e precisamente nella duplice dimensione di 'glorificazione di Dio e sanctificazione degle uomini.' Questo principio, che forma l'elemento-base della natura teologica della Liturgia, si fonda a sua volta su due punti complementari tra loro: a) la natura cultuale della Chiesa, e b) la presenza di Cristo mediatore e sacerdote nella Chiesa." Marsili, *La Liturgia: momento nella storia della salvezza*, 81 (my translation).

in the liturgy, Casel can appear to overlook the role of the church in the sacramental transmission of revelation. In the context of his discussion of *Mediator Dei*, Marsili makes clear the fact that the ritual action of the liturgy is at one and the same time the salvific work of Christ and of the church. The reason why there is no interruption between the worship rendered by Christ and the liturgy of the church is because that liturgy is not the performance of a mere institution or social society, but the action of the body of Christ. "Only under this title is the 'presence' of Christ sacerdotally active in the church."[113] Liturgical celebrations cannot, then, be regarded as distinct symbols that are mere conduits of sacred realities. Christ and the church act as one, and in this way "the liturgy is truly the *united act of worship* of both head and body of the church in a total symbiosis-osmosis."[114] That the church as his body naturally takes on the various offices proper to Christ can be seen most clearly with regard to the Church's priestly action. This is because in the church, "as in Christ, all is ultimately drawn together in an orientation toward worship as a goal."[115] Indeed, it is exactly because of this fact that the Christian church has a liturgy, as only there can the church, by participation, enter Christ's worship and be accepted by the Father in the Holy Spirit. However, speaking of *Mediator Dei*, Marsili goes on to say, "As regards the strict *link made between Liturgy and the Mystical Body*, it must be recognized that this affirmation, authoritative though it may be, loses much of its value because it doesn't recognise the link that there is between *liturgy* and *salvation history*."[116]

---

113. Ibid., 82.
114. Ibid.
115. Ibid., 80.
116. "A proposito dello stretto *legame posto tra Liturgia e Corpo mistico*, bisogna riconoscere che la pur autorevole affermazione perde gran parte del suo valore per il mancato riconoscimento del nesso che intercorre tra *Liturgia e storia della salvezza*." Marsili, *La Liturgia: momento nella storia della salvezza*, 83 (my translation).

That is to say, Christ and the church can be properly related, while seen as distinct but unified realities, only when they are regarded as signs of salvation within a single sacramental economy of revelation.[117] Such a vision Marsili believes to be the particular contribution of the Second Vatican Council. Pius XII's restoration of the Easter Vigil in 1951, and his reform of the Holy Week rites in 1955, oriented and focused the Council toward the paschal mystery as the core of liturgical reality.[118] Such an endeavor, spurred by a desire to rethink the liturgy from a pastoral perspective, had a freshness about it, and this was certainly needed to reverse the great inertia that sought to limit liturgical reform to rubrical changes.[119] To achieve its true goal, the Council needed firstly to free the tradition, which affords living contact with Christ, from the traditions that obscure and distort that contact. Secondly, the reform must overcome a static and juridical view of the liturgy, whereby outward ceremonial swamped the spiritual content. The primary means of overcoming these tendencies was the reinsertion of the liturgy into the overarching context of salvation history, and that done with a consciousness that Christ is the central protagonist of that history and therefore acts and is always present in every celebration.[120] By way of these two major innovations, Vatican II renewed the liturgy in terms

---

117. Cf. P. Rocha, "The Principal Manifestation of the Church (SC41)," in Latourelle, *Vatican II: Assessment and Perspectives*, 2:3–26.

118. See Marsili, *La Liturgia: momento nella storia della salvezza*, 85–88.

119. This was prior to the time of which Aidan Kavanagh speaks in his introduction to a recent edition of Casel's *The Mystery of Christian Worship*: "The term 'mystery' has been so assimilated into the mindset and *patois* of ecclesiastical writers since the Second Vatican Council—which embraced Casel's teaching that it has become slick with use and barely one dimensional." Kavanagh, "Introduction," in Casel, *The Mystery of Christian Worship* (New York: Crossroad, 1999), xi–xii.

120. "When liturgy became again 'a moment in salvation history' it reassumed its position as true tradition, that is, the transmission of the mystery of Christ by means of a rite, which both *reveals* and *makes present* the same mystery in a manner which is always new and always adequate to variations in time and place." Marsili, *La Liturgia: momento nella storia della salvezza*, 88 (my translation).

of a sacramental economy, at the center of which is the mystery of Christ's worship of the Father. Hence Marsili can say of the liturgy that is born of this reform that

> here we have an expression not only of the intimate relationship that exists between Scripture and liturgy, but the liturgy appears clearly as a moment of revelation, of salvation history, inasmuch as it is the making present of the mystery of Christ, the object of all revelation. This making present concerns the mystery of Christ in himself (realization in time) as much as his proclamation. In other words: today the liturgy is, just as Christ himself, an *event* of salvation in which the *proclamation* that once promised the reality of Christ *continues* to be fulfilled. The liturgy is therefore the *moment of synthesis* of salvation history, because it encompasses "proclamation" and "event" (OT and NT); but it is at the same time the *final moment* of salvation history because, being "the continuation of the reality," which is Christ, its role is to gradually complete in each man and woman and in humanity as a whole the full image of Christ.[121]

An Hour That Does Not Pass Away

Once the Council has reasserted the place of the liturgy within salvation history, it is faced with the question of the "diversity of times" during which God's saving work is accomplished in Christ. While we might see in the Word made flesh the fulfillment or "condensation" of the whole mystery, the very fact of Christ's birth

---

121. "Qui abbiamo espressa non solo la intima relazione che passa tra Scrittura e Liturgia, ma la Liturgia chiaramente appare come momento della Rivelazione—storia della salvezza, in quanto *attuazione* del mistero di Cristo, oggetto di tutta la Rivelazione. Questa attuazione riguarda tanto il mistero di Cristo in se stesso—realizzazione nel tempo—quanto il suo annunzio. Oggi cioè la Liturgia è anch'essa—come Cristo stesso—un *avvenimento* di salvezza, nel quale *continua* a trovare compimento quell'*annunzio* che nel tempo antico prometteva la realtà di Cristo. La liturgia è quindi il *momento-sintesi* della storia della salvezza, perché congloba 'annunzio' e 'avvenimento' ossia AT e NT; ma allo stesso tempo é il *momento ultimo* della stessa storia, perché essendo la 'continuazione della realtà,' che è Cristo, suo compito è quello di ultimare gradualmente nei singoli uomini e nell'umanità la immagine piena di Cristo." Ibid., 92 (my translation).

in time gives that mystery an historical dimension. The mystery of salvation is, in Christ, an historical event. The eternal, salvific plan of God might thus be divided into a period of prophetic proclamation and a period of actualization. There is a moment in history when Christ completes his work of salvation—at that time, what the prophets had announced with longing is achieved and their expectation ended, but in that moment the expectation of the church for the salvation of Christ to be appropriated by all begins. So the church lives out in her liturgy the hour that does not pass away, the hour of the paschal mystery that is announcement, fulfillment, and consummation. This is the moment of synthesis, which makes of the liturgy an event in which the Word and work of God in revelation is actualized.

Evidently, then, the time of the church is the time of Christ's victory, but Marsili is keen to point to the purpose of the continuation of this mystery, which is the sanctification of men and women. The liturgy is the means by which we can adhere ontologically to Christ, appropriate his victory, and enjoy God's life. This process is brought about in the time of the church by effective signs: the sacraments. For, as Marsili maintains,

> In effect, when *Sacrosanctum Concilium* 6 speaks about the making present of the paschal mystery of Christ through ritual signs, it finally begins to speak about the *liturgy*. "Christ sent the apostles to *proclaim* the event of salvation to all men in his death-resurrection, and to *realize* the same salvation by means of the sacrifice and the sacrament, which form the central element of the liturgy." As one can see, the liturgy consists fundamentally in *making present the salvation* brought about by Christ. But since the same salvation, brought about in Christ, is none other than the real Passover, it is clear that the liturgy will be the making present of the Passover by means of the mystery, or by means of "real signs," that is, signs that are efficacious.[122]

122. "E in effetti la costituzione liturgia SC 6, proprio parlando dell'attuazione del mistero pasquale

In his commentary on the Constitution on the Sacred Liturgy, Josef Jungmann speaks of the Council fathers' choice of that phrase *paschal mystery* that, he says, they dared not translate as *Easter mystery* because of the theological overtones that may be lost. He regards the expression as a refinement of the expression "mystery of Christ," because it is

> the real kernel of the Christian order of salvation: the act with which Christ has redeemed us and which is continued in the activity of the Church. Like the *pascha* of the Old Testament, it is a remembrance of God's redeeming acts of salvation, the presence of salvation and the promise of the consummating future. It underlines at the same time the basic triumphant Easter character, which is of the essence of Christianity, of the work of the Church, its message and its sacraments.[123]

Article 6 of the Constitution on the Liturgy of which Marsili is speaking here seeks to show how the saving action of Christ is brought about in the mission of the church through word and sacrament. This, for Marsili, is true liturgy because it is fundamentally theological. Here again, one returns to the question of the continuation of the paschal mystery in the church through ritual signs, and to the necessity of overcoming any rupture that might be implied between the two. A tension is obviously present from the beginning of the New Testament church, and many have described it with the adage that Jesus proclaimed the kingdom of God and the church proclaimed Jesus. The difficulty arises from the interpretation

di Cristo attraverso segni rituali, entra finalmente a palare della *Liturgia*. 'Cristo mandò gli Apostoli ad *annunziare* l'avvenuta salvezza degli uomini nella sua morte-risurrezione, e ad *attuare* questa stessa salvezza per mezzo del sacrificio e dei sacramenti, che formano l'elemento centrale della *Liturgia*.' Come si vede, la *Liturgia* consiste fondamentalmente nella *attuazione della salvezza* realizzata da Cristo. Ma siccome questa stessa salvezza realizzata in Cristo altro non è che la Pasqua come fatto reale, è chiaro che la *Liturgia sarà l'attuazione della Pasqua per mezzo del mistero*, ossia per mezzo di 'segni reali,' cioè efficaci." Ibid., 99 (my translation).

123. J. Jungmann, "Constitution on the Sacred Liturgy," in *Commentary on the Documents of Vatican II*, ed. H. Vorgrimler, vol. 1 (London: Burns and Oates, 1967), 12.

that the church gives to the actions of Jesus; signs and miracles often being seen primarily as indications of his own identity.[124] However, in resituating Christ's actions within the whole, sacramental, divine economy, his prophetic signs and sacrifice are seen less as pointing to the truth about the identity of Jesus himself—and more as an integral part of the message he proclaimed. This message was announced by the Old Testament prophets, epitomised by the prophetic action of the Passover, fulfilled in the prophetic sign of his Last Supper, and actualized by his Passover from death to new life. The liturgy, then, is the word event that realizes the same salvation of Christ, because it effects the same signs that he raised to the level of reality by affording them the content of the paschal mystery.[125]

Experiencing the Event Character of the Word

Here we see Marsili moving toward an understanding of the actualization of the word of God in the liturgical assembly that suggests the density of an event. This notion, resting on the Hebrew concept of *dabar*, is seen to take definitive expression in the dynamic

124. "The tendency to interpret both miracles and prophetic actions as pointing us to the truth about the identity of Jesus himself, rather than seeing them as part of the message he proclaimed—the gospel about rather than the gospel of—is seen already in the Synoptic Gospels but increases in the Fourth Gospel. Jesus'actions are interpreted as 'signs' whose meaning is clear to believers, but is hidden from those without faith. For John, all these signs point forward to the Cross, where the true identity of the person who does them is finally revealed." See M. Hooker, *The Signs of a Prophet: The Prophetic Actions of Jesus* (Harrisburg, PA: Trinity, 1997), 78.

125. I find an explanation by Joseph Wong of the coincidence of diverse aspects in the one saving sign reality to be of help in this very complex area: "God's plan of putting everything under Christ as head is a realized fact though it will continue in the ages to come. Likewise, the revelation of the *mysterion* is connected with the reconciliation of Jews and gentiles already effected through the blood of Christ. Thus in Christ, God's 'immeasurable riches of grace' and his 'kindness towards us' are revealed precisely by becoming man's salvation. Consequently, the Christ event is at the same time instrument and aim, revelation and salvation in one. The idea of manifestation through realization in Christ constitutes the most specific element in Rahner's notion 'sacramental-symbolic causality.' The fundamental meaning of a 'sacrament-symbol' consists in that it signifies by effecting and effects by signifying. Hence Christ reveals God's saving attitude of love towards men by effectively channelling this love for their salvation." J. H. Wong, *Logos-Symbol in the Christology of Karl Rahner* (Rome: LAS, 1984), 259–60.

of the eucharistic liturgy, where word gradually becomes more and more flesh until it precipitates the effective sign of our salvation in the paschal sacrifice.[126] Hence Marsili comes to acknowledge that

> in the liturgy, the Scripture ceases to be a dead *written word* and assumes ever more the role of *annunciation-proclamation of a present event of salvation.* In other words: the event that one *reads about* in the Sacred Scripture is the same as that which is realized in the liturgy, and thus the Sacred Scripture finds its natural concrete interpretation in the liturgy, always on the level of salvation history and not that of an intellectual question to be solved. Christ is the "reality proclaimed" by Sacred Scripture, and Christ becomes the "reality realized and communicated" in the liturgy. In this way, it will be precisely the liturgy that, by means of the direct "experience" of the mystery of Christ (experience of inner salvation), will give us that "knowledge" and "revelation" of the same mystery, which can never remain purely intellectual, but will always, through the increase of "knowledge-revelation," bring us into a more intimate and existential "experience." Therefore Sacred Scripture, even as "revelation," finds its completion in the liturgy.[127]

126. Jeremy Driscoll, in discussing the dynamic relation of word and sacrament, points to this helpful insight of H. U. von Balthasar: " We can begin with a useful remark by H. U.von Balthasar who observes that as the life of Jesus progresses two things stand out: (1) The Word becomes more and more flesh and (2) the flesh becomes more and more Word. By the first he means that to the abstract nature of the words of the law and prophets Jesus imparts a divine, factual presence. By the second he is noting that Jesus increasingly unifies the scriptural words in himself, making his earthly life the perfect expression of all the earlier revelations of God. This idea can be extended in terms less immediately scriptural, i.e. ontologically: (1) the eternal Word, entirely in all that he is, becomes more and more flesh. (2) And all that is flesh is transformed more and more into all that the Word is. I want to suggest that this dynamic is the very dynamic that liturgy reveals, the very dynamic in which the liturgy consists." Driscoll, *Theology at the Eucharistic Table,* 132.

127. "Così si assiste ad un fatto importante: la Sacra Scrittura nella Liturgia cessa di essere una morta *parola scritta*, per assumere sempre più il ruolo di *annunzio-proclamazione di un avvenimento di salvezza presente.* In altre parole: l'avvenimento che *si legge* nella Sacra Scrittura, è quello stesso che *si attua* nella Liturgia, e così la Sacra Scrittura trova nella Liturgia la sua interpretazione naturalmente concreta e cioè sempre sul piano di storia della salvezza e non di elucubrazione intellettuale. Cristo è la 'realtà avverata-comunicata' dalla Sacra Scrittura, e Cristo diventa la 'realtà avverata-comunicata' dalla Liturgia. In questo modo sarà appunto la Liturgia, attraverso la diretta 'esperienza' del mistero di Cristo (esperienza di salvezza interiore), a darci quella 'conoscenza' e 'rivelazione' dello stesso mistero, che non potrà mai restare solo intellettuale, ma tendrà sempre a ripresentarsi, con l'aumento della 'conoscenza-rivelazione,' in una maggiore 'esperienza' intima ed esistenziale. La Sacra Scrittura quindi, anche come 'rivelazione' di salvezza, si completa nella Liturgia." Marsili, *La Liturgia: momento nella storia della salvezza*, 102 (my translation).

From the above passage, it becomes obvious why Marsili gave the title *Anàmnesis* to the series of which *La Liturgia momento nella storia della salvezza* is an introduction. In here exposing the relationship of word and sacrament, Marsili is in fact defining *anàmnesis* as the central liturgical "technique" that makes present the revelation of Christ. The Greek word defies succinct definition, as "memorial" or "remembrance" suggest too much of recollection and not enough of actualization.[128] There is a fine balance here, for the recalling of God's wonders that this notion implies is a call for him to act now as he has done in the past. Simply to narrate a memory without invocation or expectation of action is to frustrate the word's dynamic to sacramental fulfillment, and deny its impact on the present. The relationship of word to sign-sacrament within the economy of salvation is of crucial importance, as it forms the core of any reflection on how the message of Jesus Christ is manifested in the present through the ritual signs of the church.

Within the economy of salvation, the close, dynamic relationship between word and sacrament allows Marsili to locate the liturgy in that action that realizes the proclaimed word as present event. Once announced in the liturgical assembly, the word is interpreted by the sacramental signs, and gestures as the actual event that is presently celebrated.[129] Christ is the reality proclaimed, and Christ is the protagonist of the liturgy, so that, as *Dei Verbum* 2 says,

128. For a fuller exposition of this term, see L. Bouyer, *Eucharist* (Notre Dame: University of Notre Dame Press, 1968); Driscoll, *Theology at the Eucharistic Table*, ch. 7; J. Jeremias, *The Eucharistic Words of Jesus* (London: SCM, 1966), 237–55; D. Power, "The Anàmnesis: Remembering, We Offer," in *New Eucharistic Prayers*, ed. F. Senn (New York: Paulist, 1987), 146–68.

129. "When these *words* are proclaimed in the liturgy, they also proclaim the *event* of the *sacramental* celebration, which is that same event of salvation history actualised here and now. Put more simply perhaps: whatever it is that Scripture proclaims becomes sacrament." Driscoll, *Theology at the Eucharistic Table*, 133–34. And, for a fuller exposition of the relationship between word and sacrament, see D. Power, *Unsearchable Riches: The Symbolic Nature of Liturgy* (New York: Pueblo, 1984).

This economy of Revelation is realized by deeds and words, which are intrinsically bound up with one another. As a result the works performed by God in the history of salvation show forth and bear out the doctrine and realities signified by the words; the words for their part, proclaim the works, and bring to light the mystery they contain.

It is this dynamic that Marsili recognizes as part of the anamnetic function of the liturgy. The mutual interpretation of word and sign that takes place within the rite facilitates the realization that what is being proclaimed is being realized in the gathered assembly. The proclaimed word of God announces the events of salvation history, yet not *only* as history, because the word tells not merely of events but of "the mystery they contain." The proclaimed word, as it were, "contains" that mysterious, salvific plan of God that constantly seeks to express itself sacramentally. Within the liturgical assembly, the word seeks the fullness of sacramental expression in the gathered body of Christ. This is at the heart of what Marsili understands to be worship: the adhering of the assembly to the sacramental body of Christ in his paschal mystery. That is the communication and realization of the salvific will of the Father revealed in Jesus Christ, the Word made flesh. It is because this event comes about liturgically in "the sign-synthesis of a salvific moment" that Marsili feels free to call the liturgy an "experience" of the mystery of Christ, indeed that he dares to call Christian worship an "experience" of the revelation of God's Word.

The "astonishing similarity"[130] of function that binds word and sacrament in a single revelatory mission is also constitutive of the church. As Karl Rahner says,

This word of God (as inner moment of the salvific action of God on man and so with it and because of it) is the salutary word which brings with it

---

130. K. Rahner, "The Word and the Eucharist," *Theological Investigations*, trans. Kevin Smyth, vol. 4. (London: Darton, Longman and Todd, 1966), 253–86, 254.

318

what it affirms. It is itself, therefore, salvific event, which, in its outward, historical and social aspect, displays what happens in it and under it, and brings about what it displays. It renders the grace of God present.[131]

The word of God proclaimed in the assembly "brings with it" that salvific event, that rendering present of grace, which in its outward, historical, and social aspect we call the church. This is the direct consequence of the dynamic relationship existing between word and sacrament. Beginning with a quotation from *Lumen Gentium*, Marsili asserts that

> "As often as the sacrifice of the Cross by which 'Christ our Pasch is sacrificed' (1 Cor. 5:7) is celebrated on the altar, the work of our redemption is carried out. Likewise, in the sacrament of the eucharistic bread, the unity of believers, who form one body in Christ (cf. 1 Cor. 10:17), is both expressed and brought about (*LG* 3)." It is part of revelation that the church is the "body of Christ" and the "holy people of God." But, while the "body of Christ" is rather the *result* of the liturgical action, and the people of God is "holy," that is, consecrated to the *purpose* of rendering true and worthy worship to God, the "church" expresses above all the very moment at which the people of God are *in a position of worship around God*.[132]

Here is a reflection on the liturgical aspect of the church as expressed in *Sacrosanctum Concilium* 26. As Jungmann points out, this article lays down the principles for a liturgy that cannot be regarded as an isolated act of the clergy, but must be understood as an act of fellowship by the whole community.[133] Only in the liturgical

---

131. Ibid., 259–60.
132. "'Ogni volta che il sacrificio della croce, "nel quale Cristo, nostro agnello pasquale, è stato immolato" (1Cor 5, 7), viene celebrato all'altare, si attua l'opera della nostra redenzione; e insieme viene rappresentata e prodotta, nel segno sacramentale del pane eucaristico, l'unità dei fideli che costituiscono un solo corpo di Cristo (Cfr. 1 Cor 10, 17).' E' un punto di rivelazione che la Chiesa è 'Corpo di Cristo' e 'popolo santo di Dio.' Ma mentre il 'Corpo di Cristo' è piuttosto il *risultato* dell'azione liturgica; e il 'popolo di Dio' è 'santo' cioè consacrato al *fine* di dare un vero e degno culto a Dio, la 'Chiesa' esprime soprattutto il momento stesso in cui il popolo di Dio *si aduna in posizione cultuale* attorno a Dio." Marsili, *La Liturgia: momento nella storia della salvezza*, 110 (my translation).

celebration (of the Eucharist) is the nature of the church realized and expressed as a gathered, holy people, hierarchically ordered to a mission of revelation and unity. What becomes obvious from Marsili's analysis of ecclesial communities in the Old and New Testaments is that "the church is liturgical by its intrinsic constitution."[134] This is because, while the church might certainly be identified with the people of God gathered by the call of his word—they are gathered in the stance of worship. Moreover, from the perspective of the New Testament, the notion of the body of Christ as the church means that that body is the cultic expression of the worship offered by Christ to the Father. Here again, we might call to mind the interpenetration of the notions of word and sacrament: the word that calls people together is expressed and actualized in the church, which is the sign and sacrament of salvation.[135]

Achieving a Liturgical Theology

In *La Liturgia: momento nella storia della salvezza*, Marsili uses the historical approach thematically, interweaving various authors from the time of Beauduin to the Second Vatican Council in order to shape a theological notion of the liturgy. Grounding his whole enterprise on a basic intuition of the sacramental economy of salvation, Marsili shows by way of Vatican II that the liturgy, as the one action of Christ and the church, is the key component of the whole of God's

---

133. Jungmann, "Constitution on the Sacred Liturgy," 21.
134. Marsili, *La Liturgia: momento nella storia della salvezza*, 111.
135. Help with further reflection on the relationship of ecclesiology and liturgy can be gained from D. Doyle, *Communion Ecclesiology* (New York: Orbis, 2000); P. McPartlan, *Sacrament of Salvation: An Introduction to Eucharistic Ecclesiology* (Edinburgh: T. & T. Clark, 1995); McPartlan, *The Eucharist Makes the Church* (Edinburgh: T.& T. Clark, 1993); J. Zizioulas, *Being as Communion* (Crestwood, NY: St. Vladimir's, 1993).

mysterious plan. Hence a fitting conclusion to this particular text of Marsili can be drawn from his own words, which suitably integrate the themes constitutive of his understanding of liturgical theology at this stage:

> The common denominator that truly places the "human body" of Christ, the "church body" of Christ and his "sacramental body" on a level of *common reality* (i.e., beyond a merely external denomination) is found in the identity of *cultic destination* that is theirs in the light of revelation. It should suffice to note the *equation* of "*body time*" that is established within Jesus' human body both on the level of earthly existence ("Christ spoke of the *temple of his body*" John 2:21) and on that of sacramental existence ("Its temple is . . . the Lamb" Rev. 21:22), with the individual body of the Christian ("*Your body is a temple* of the Holy Spirit" 1 Cor. 6:19) and with the "body of the church"("*We are the temple* of the living God," 2 Cor. 6:16).[136]

This quotation summarizes the argument of *La Liturgia: momento nella storia della salvezza*, because it describes and integrates the major themes of the book according to its overarching premise: that liturgy is primary theology, as it is the fundamentally cohesive element of the aspects of the divine economy that occupy fundamental and dogmatic theologians. From this unique perspective, Marsili seeks consciously to integrate and interpret the values of sacramental renewal inaugurated by the Council.[137] Yet the quotation offers more than a general overview of the dominant themes of Marsili's work, by

---

136. "Il comune denominatore che pone veramente su un piano di *comune realtà*, e cioè al di là di una denominazione soltanto esterna, tanto il 'corpo umano' di Cristo, quanto il 'corpo-Chiesa' di Cristo e il suo 'corpo-sacramentale' si ritrova nell'identità di *destinazione cultuale*, che ad essi compete alla luce della rivelazione. Basterebbe per questo osservare anche solo l'*equazione* '*corpo-tempio*,' che viene stabilita con il 'corpo umano' di Gesù tanto a livello di esistenza terrena ('Cristo parlava del *tempio del suo corpo*': Gv 2:21) quanto a livello di esistenza sacramentale ('Suo tempio è . . . l'Agnello': Apoc 21:22), con il 'corpo individuale' del cristiano ('Il *vostro corpo è tempio* dello Sirito Santo': 1Cor 6:19) e con il 'corpo della Chiesa' ('*Noi siamo il tempio* del Dio vivo': 2Cor 6:16)." Marsili, *La Liturgia: momento nella storia della salvezza*, 113 (my translation).
137. Cf. R. Vaillancourt, *Toward a Renewal of Sacramental Theology* (Collegeville, MN: Liturgical Press, 1979).

drawing into summative focus the question that occupies this present study. For the liturgy is here presented as the event whereby the "equation" of Christ-church-believer is actualized and the mystery of salvation experienced. Christ fulfills revelation in his paschal mystery, and through his resurrected body offers access to that mystery in all times. Such access is experienced by adhering to Christ, the norm of salvation history, who manifests himself in these last days through the sacraments.[138] This experience Marsili would want to call revelation.

Reaping the Consequences:
Nuovo Dizionario di Liturgia

Study of *I segni del mistero di Cristo* and *La liturgia: momento nella storia della salvezza* inevitably identifies the major concern of Marsili, in the first postconciliar decade, to be the refinement of methodology. Such is evident, because his strongly held conviction that the liturgy formed the key to the theological reform that Vatican II desired is more than implicit in the two works that have been taken as exemplary of this period. Indeed, the constant refrain, throughout what is a theology of increasing specificity and clarity, is that the liturgy forms the necessary and most fundamental element in any process of theological *ressourcement* and *aggiornamento*.

138. An interesting gloss on what Marsili means by "the equation of body time" is given by von Balthasar in his *A Theology of History*: "In saying that as far as concerns the Lord himself, the sacramental form of existence does not differ from that of the forty days, we imply that he appears therein as interpreting, revealing and bestowing his earthly life, and in that sense bringing it with him, representing it, making it present. In this sense one may speak of a "mystery-presence"; and the main focus of interest in "mystery-theology" should perhaps be sought in the fact that Christ's presence in the sacraments, his gracious approach to man in the sacramental act, is qualitatively determined by himself personally, and is rooted in his earthly life." Von Balthasar, *A Theology of History*, 95.

A Determined Point of Departure

Approaching the posthumously published articles on liturgy and liturgical theology that Marsili wrote for the *Nuovo Dizionario di Liturgia*, one is immediately conscious of a sense of consolidation and progress. Decisions as to methodological procedure have been made, and what is evident in these two condensed pieces is the crystallization of a mature theology that has emerged naturally and necessarily from settled basic assumptions. Something of this "narrowing down" can be gleaned from the opening sections of the article "Liturgy":

> One could start from various points in an attempt to deepen one's understanding of liturgy: for example, from salvation history and its sacramental structure; from the sacramentality of the church in its concrete form; from the faith/sacrament problem; from our Christian experience; from an anthropological perspective, and so on. Our preferred method is to follow the very way in which the church has become progressively aware in recent decades of the mysterious and complex reality that we denote by the term *liturgy*—a reality that goes far beyond the etymological and historical meaning of the term.[139]

Though Marsili has begun from most of these individual points in past studies, and though each retains its status as a legitimate place of entry into the one complex reality, reflection on the relationship that conciliar theology had drawn between these elements allowed a prior and privileged point of departure to emerge. The question that Marsili had asked rhetorically at the beginning of each course

---

139. "Per approfondire il concetto di liturgia si potrebbero scegliere diversi punti di partenza: si potrebbe muovere ad es. dalla storia della salvezza e dalla sua struttura sacramentale; dalla sacramentalità della chiesa nella sua esplicitazione concreta; dalla problematica fede-sacramento; dalla nostra esperienza cristiana; da una prospettiva antropologica ecc. Noi preferiamo seguire la progressiva presa di coscienza da parte della chiesa negli ultimi decenni a riguardo di quella realtà misteriosa e complessa che indichiamo con il termine 'liturgia,' realtà che va ben oltre ciò che il termine può significare a livello etimologico e storico." S. Marsili, "Liturgia," 726 (my translation).

he taught, and that Anscar Chupungco recalls with affection from an October afternoon in the year the Council closed—"*Dunque, cos'è la Liturgia?*"—is one that occupied his own mind throughout the following decade, and to which, with scientific perseverance, he found a definitive answer.[140] Essential to this process was the publication of two articles in the early 1970s: "La Liturgia nella strutturazione della Teologia,"[141] and "Liturgia e Teologia. Proposta teoretica," both of which face squarely the methodological consequences that the theological insights of Vatican II have for liturgy.

Consequences for Methodology

Though frequently reduced to the level of formal and therefore superficial aesthetics, Trent at its best had given liturgy a status as part of the practical formation of priests. Whether intentionally or not, it remained clearly separate from the carefully structured order of the other theological disciplines.[142] The preoccupation with apologetics that marked every aspect of post-Tridentine theology meant that any attempt at a proper and full treatment of liturgical worship was going to be considerably hampered. Theology had limited study of the liturgical celebration of the sacraments in two major ways: by a determination of the scope of the discipline according to narrow constraints, and by the imposition of a stifling methodology. When not reduced to an *accessorio estetico*,[143] sacramentology was both

---

140. "Le sue prime parole, in quel pomeriggio di ottobre 1965, ai nuovi allievi del Pontificio Istituto Liturgico, rimangono impresse nella memoria: 'Dunque, disse, cos'è la Liturgia?'" Chupungco, "Salvatore Marsili: teologo della liturgia," 23. See also the more mature reflections of Chupungco on this question in his work A. Chupungco, *What, Then, Is Liturgy? Musings and Memoir* (Collegeville, MN: Liturgical Press, 2010).

141. S. Marsili, "La Liturgia nella strutturazione della teologica," *Rivista Liturgica*, 57 (1971) 153–162; Marsili, *Rivista Liturgica*, "Liturgia e Teologia. Proposta teoretica," 58 (1972) 455–73

142. Cf. Marsili, "La Liturgia nella strutturazione della teologica," 155.

confined to an historical retrospective that endeavored to demonstrate the veracity of already-fixed theological truths, and laden by the understanding that these truths could always be reduced to, and contained within, metaphysical categories. Hence the two main foci of preconciliar sacramental theology were the historical veracity of the Lord's institution of the seven sacraments, and the notion of sacramental causality, by which grace was transmitted to the individual.[144]

In the two texts already examined, Marsili has fruitfully amplified the scope, and, perhaps more importantly, the methodology of sacramental theology according to the principles of Vatican II. Taking the notion of biblical renewal seriously, Marsili has successfully utilized the christological and ecclesiological categories of the Council in order to set the sacraments within the coherent context of the sacramental economy of salvation history. However, for Marsili, the methodological conclusions of the renewal are fundamental and far-reaching for liturgy. If, as the Council suggested, the whole of theology is a reflection on the mystery of Christ and the story of salvation, then the position of the liturgy within the theological pursuit must be radically different from the place it had been consigned to since Trent. This is because the liturgy is the unique place that offers access to the mystery of Christ, and the unique place in which the history of salvation presently unfolds. The truths of salvation that can be revealed through the Scriptures as

---

143. "La liturgia era un po' per volta decaduta dalla sua natura di *fatto teologico* a quello di *accessorio estetico*." Ibid., 156.

144. "Ma la preoccupazione apologetica ha posto alla riflessione teologica sui sacramenti dei limiti anche più grandi, perché, oltre a determinarne il campo di ricerca, ne ha influenzato il metodo. Ora è noto quanto sia pericoloso, da un punto di vista strettamente scientifico, intraprendere delle ricerche storiche con la preoccupazione di dimostrare determinate verità già fissate, ed è altrettanto noto quanto sia facile cedere alla tentazione di ritenere che il dato Rivelato sia sempre e adeguatamente traducibile in termini e in categorie proprie di una determinata metafisica." E. Ruffini, "I grandi temi della teologia contemporanea dei Sacramenti," *Rivista Liturgica*, 54 (1967): 40.

promise and fact, that can be illustrated and expounded by dogmatics and ordered to a practical execution by morals, are, in the liturgy, actualized and realized sacramentally.[145] Thus Marsili responds to his own question,[146] and, in determining the nature of liturgical theology as present reflection on the presence and actualization of God in salvation history, establishes a point of departure for theology that has consequences for the whole doctrinal edifice.

The Liturgy in Relation to the Church

The fact that the liturgy is the action of Christ in the church, before being the action of the church towards God, is therefore of the utmost importance. The liturgy has both a natural and logical priority over the church, in that the church is first the passive subject of the liturgy, and then becomes its active subject. The opposite should be true if the "social" aspect were foremost in the liturgy, because that would imply that the church existed as a "society" *before* it was able to act as a society. Instead of this, the church has real existence only by reason of Christ's cultic action (baptism-Eucharist) that unites people in the church. Consequently, if the church is (in the first place) a passive subject of the liturgy, then liturgy is a constitutive element of the church.[147]

---

145. "Non si tratta quindi di portare la Liturgia né come intingolo preferenziale né come piatto di 'dessert' di chiusura sulla mensa della Teologia, ma si deve tener presente che l'unico 'Mistero di Cristo' e l'unica 'Storia della salvezza,' che la Scrittura ci *rivela* come promessa e come fatto, che la Dogmatica *illustra* ed *espone*, e la Morale *ordina* alla pratica esecuzione, è—a livello di *attuazione* e *realizzazione sacramentale*—operante nella Liturgia. In fondo si tratta—tenuto presente l'aspetto di 'economia' della rivelazione-salvezza." Marsili, "La Liturgia nella strutturazione della teologica," 162.

146. "Cos'è quindi la Teologia liturgica? Marsili risponde: 'è la teologia della presenza e dell'azione di Dio nella storia della salvezza umana. . . . E' la Teologia viva di un fatto, di un avvenimento, di qualcosa che è reale, che esiste, che si chiama Cristo, che si chiama Chiesa.'" Chupungco, "Salvatore Marsili: teologo della liturgia," 20.

147. "Di grandissima importanza dunque è il fatto che la liturgia, prima di essere l'azione della chiesa verso Dio, è l'azione di Cristo nella chiesa, così che la liturgia precede la chiesa con priorità e

What can be seen here is the inevitable consequence of Marsili's liturgical theology. As A. Triacca notes, "The mode of conceiving the liturgy influences also the conception of its relationship with the church."[148] Because the liturgy is understood by Marsili as the compact presentation of the action of Christ throughout salvation history, it is not in the first place a mode of the church's behavior; obviously not, because in Christ the liturgy is prior to the church. Instead, the liturgical mode of Christ's action—in its katabatic form—distinguishes the church as passive and receptive. This surely, is also the point of departure for *Lumen Gentium*, since the document asserts that "the church is in Christ as a sacrament or instrumental sign of intimate union with God,"[149] precisely because, as the church, she reflects Christ's light to the nations by pouring forth that word that she has received from the self-emptying Son of God.

Within such a vision, the Paschal Mystery can be seen as a "theological fact" in a "liturgical modality."[150] The will of God to protect, liberate, and save his people consists in the expression of a

di natura e di logica, in quanto la chiesa prima è soggetto passivo della liturgia, poi ne diventa soggetto attivo. Sarebbe vero il contrario se l'aspetto 'sociale' fosse principale nella liturgia, in quanto ciò implicherebbe che esistesse la chiesa come 'società' *prima* che essa possa agire come società. Invece la chiesa esiste realmente solo in forza dell'azione cultuale di Cristo (battesimo-eucaristia) che unisce gli uomini in chiesa. Conseguentemente: se la chiesa è soggetto in primo luogo passivo della liturgia, la liturgia è elemento costitutivo della (= che costituisce la) chiesa." Marsili, "Liturgia," 730 (my translation).

148. "Di fatto il modo di concepire la Liturgia influisce pure sulla concezione del suo rapporto con la Chiesa." Triacca, "Teologia della liturgia o teologia liturgica?," 274.

149. "Lumen gentium cum sit Christus. . . . Cum autem ecclesia sit in Christo veluti sacramentum seu signum et instrumentum intimae cum Deo." *LG* 1 [849]. For a brief history of the development of this phrase within the Constitution, see Ratzinger *Principles of Catholic Theology*, 44–48. A clear parallel can also be drawn between this text and *Dei Verbum* 4, which states: "Postquam vero multifariam multisque modis Deus locutus est in prophetis, 'novissime diebus istis locutus est nobis in Filio' (Heb 1, 1–2). Misit enim Filium suum, aeternum scilicet Verbum, qui omnes homines illuminat, ut inter homines habitaret iisque intima Dei enarraret (cf. Io 1, 1–18)." *DV*, 4 [972].

150. "Infatti il mistero pasquale non è una certa determinazione temporale che indicherebbe solo un giorno speciale nel calendario religioso ma è un *fatto teologico* il quale ha una *modalità liturgica*. Esso in realtà è quello stesso piano di salvezza; di redenzione, nascosto in Dio, il quale diventa 'mistero' nella rivelazione che esso trova in Christo." Marsili, "Liturgia," 731.

rite of Passover. Preaching at a celebratory Eucharist for his seventieth birthday at Finalpia, during which he was presented with the miscellany *Mysterion*, Marsili himself echoed *Dei Verbum* 4, as he declared of the liturgy,

> This therefore is the plan of God, flashed by the divine eyes in ancient days and distant years: a relationship of worship that isn't formed by exterior things, nor does it ever stop with them, but was molded by love, sourced by his voice, loyal in its allegiance. This is the plan that Jesus, our Lord, has come finally to realize in the world and for the world, but fulfilled first of all in himself: he embodies adoration of the Father, and he is simply listening in humility to his voice and remaining faithful. . . . In himself, in his resurrected body, he gave to the world the sign of a new religion, purified, that will be offered to God from all men in Christ.[151]

Liturgy as Invitation and Response

That, in the first place, liturgy is a salvific action "from above" is not in doubt. But, concurring with the other writers studied previously, Marsili is aware that the revelatory word, which has molded exterior things to the facilitation of its expression, demands a faith response from those whom it addresses. Essentially, Marsili is here giving a commentary on *Sacrosanctum Concilium* 5–7,[152] which centers on the priestly office of Jesus as being that instant in which the hypostatic union is brought into the sphere of action. The revelation of the

---

151. "Questo dunque il progetto di Dio, balenato allo sguardo divino nei giorni antichi e negli anni lontani: un rapporto di culto che non si formasse di cose esteriori né mai si fermasse comunque ad esse, ma fosse adesine d'amore, ricerca della sua voce, fedeltà di alleanza. È questo il progetto che Gesù, nostro Signore, è venuto finalmente a realizzare nel mondo e per il mondo, ma realizzandolo prima di tutto in se stesso: essere culto al Padre, ed esserlo semplicemente ascoltando in umiltà la sua voce e restando fedele. . . in se stesso, nel suo corpo risuscitato egli darà al mondo il segno del culto nuovo, purificato, che sarà offerto a Dio da tutti gli uomini in Cristo." S. Marsili, *Rivista Liturgica*, 68 (1981) 302–3; quoted in Maggiani, "La teologia liturgica di S. Marsili," 346–47 (my translation).

152. Cf. Marsili, "Liturgia," 731–32.

Father, which is made by the intimate and inseparable allegiance of the divine Word to humanity, receives its desired response in the liturgy of the body of Christ. Hence Marsili's understanding of liturgy reaches its mature synthesis:

> *Liturgy is worship on the level of revelation.* SC, without lingering over philosophical and anthropological considerations (which remain valid for liturgy on their own level), presents liturgy straightforwardly as a continuation and activation of the perfect worship that Christ offered to the Father in his humanity. This is defined as the "fullness of worship" (in Christo . . . divini cultus nobis est indita plenitudo; SC 5) and is that by which Christ revealed himself as the true and definitive activator of that perfect (i.e., interior and spiritual) "priesthood" that God asked of Israel in Exod. 19:5-6. Through his participation in, and assimilation to, Christ, the Christian continues this same worship in the liturgy, to the point where, in that worship, the rite no longer directly expresses in symbol that by which man seeks to enter into contact with God (as it does in natural worship). Rather, the rite is first of all a symbol of the action by which God transforms man in Christ. Indeed, as a consequence of this transformation, man will be to God what Christ was to the Father.[153]

What is achieved here is triumph over the "impasse"[154] that exists between a liturgy reduced to practico-aesthetics and the distant and unrelated theology of academia. By purifying liturgy to its most

153. "*La liturgia è culto a livello di rivelazione*—La SC, senza fermarsi su considerazioni di ordine filosofico e antropologico—considerazioni che rimangono valide sul loro piano anche a proposito della liturgia—presenta la liturgia immediatamente come continuazione/attuazione del culto perfetto che Cristo ha prestato, nella sua umanità, al Padre. Definito come 'culto dato in pienezza' (in Christo . . . divini cultus nobis est indita plenitudo: SC 5), esso è quello per il quale Cristo si è rivelato il vero e definitivo attuatore di quel 'sacerdozio' perfetto, cioè interiore e spirituale, che Dio in Es 19, 5-6 chiedeva da Israele. Di questo stesso culto il cristiano è, per la sua partecipazione e assimilazione a Cristo, il continuatore nella liturgia, al punto che in tale culto ormai il rito non è più direttamente—come avviene nel culto naturale—l'espressione simbolica del rapporto con cui l'uomo cerca di entrare in contatto con Dio, ma è prima di tutto simbolo dell'azione con la quale Dio opera la trasformazione dell'uomo in Cristo. È infatti a seguito di questa trasformazione che l'uomo sarà per Dio quel che Cristo era per il Padre." Ibid., 732 (my translation).

154. "Emergerebbe così quanto Egli ha operato per far superare l'impasse' dei vari tentativi di ridurre la 'liturgia' a rubricismo." Triacca, "Teologia della liturgia o teologia liturgica?," 268.

fundamental level, Marsili reveals it to be that which might have been embraced as the experience and principal resource of Christian life. To delineate liturgy as the primary locus of God's self-revelation and as the arena of human response is to establish its centrality and confer on it the status of fundamental theology. Such is achieved in the two articles of the *Nuovo Dizionario di Liturgia*, which, in elaborating the mature thought of Marsili on the liturgy, reveal the result of a process of study that has been both cumulative and a gradual refining.[155]

The Fundamental Implications of Liturgical Theology

Perhaps in this process the collaboration of *ressourcement* and *aggiornamento* can be detected. While a return to the sources purifies notions of the liturgy in the light of biblical and patristic sensibilities, *aggiornamento* makes sophisticated connections between the truths of faith in an effort to provide a coherent theology that is credible to the modern person. The coalescence of these two dynamics in the work of Marsili provides the fundamental theology of the liturgy, which he describes as follows:

> By this, its sacramental nature, the Christian liturgy is fundamentally and in origin a "theology" and thus the schism, noted in the OT,

155. "Senza dubbio i suoi sforzi, intesi a purificare il concetto di 'liturgia,' hanno dapprima cozzato contro i diffusi atteggiamenti di un dilettantismo pastorale, di una romantica sensibilità e di un radicato pragmatismo che—a titoli differenti—ostacolavano che la liturgia fosse compresa, e, di conseguenza, vissuta, come principale fonte di vita cristiana." Ibid., 268. The article "Teologia Liturgica" shows Marsili's mature position to be both an accumulation and a clarification of earlier positions when he states, "The word of God that announced salvation in Christ was condensed in as many mysteries that were real and concrete revelations of the salvation promised in that word, and that now in the liturgy, still and equally, forever constitute moments in which such a word is actuated in men, as if it is actuated in Christ." ("La parola di Dio che annunciava la salvezza, in Cristo si condensò in altrettanti misteri che furono rivelazioni reali e concrete della salvezza promessa in quella parola, e che ora nella liturgia costituiscono ancora e ugualmente sempre momenti nei quali tale parola si va attuando negli uomini, come si è attuata in Cristo.") Marsili, "Teologia liturgica," in Sartore and Triacca, *Nuovo Dizionario di Liturgia*, 1512 (my translation).

between priesthood and prophetism, which is the schism between liturgy and theology, between cult and life, is newly and definitively healed. The Christian liturgy is existentially theology, because it is always the word of God known in reality that is now acquired in the symbolic rite. This explains sufficiently why in the patristic age the liturgy was thought and lived as a particularly happy moment of true authentic theology.[156]

The refusal to consign liturgy to the realms of ritual and rubricism, and the determined pursuit of the consequences of that decision, ultimately expose the fundamental separation that affects all subsequent ones. The schism between priesthood and prophetism—between outward cultic expression and an inner movement of the heart—is the radical division between word and action that is the root cause of a crisis of authenticity and credibility.[157] For this reason, liturgical theology is not merely a methodological approach but is literally, and in fact, a way of life. This is what describing the liturgy as a primary and existential theology means.[158] And this fact brings the Marsilian understanding

156. "Per questa sua natura sacramentale la liturgia cristiana è fondamentalmente e per origine una 'teologia,' e così la scissione, notata nell'AT, tra sacerdozio e profetismo, che è poi scissione tra liturgia e teologia , tra culto e vita, viene nuovamente e definitivamente sanata. La liturgia cristiana è infatti essenzialmente ed esistenzialmente teologia, perché è sempre parola di Dio conosciuta nella realtà che ora acquista nel rito simbolico. Questo spiega a sufficienza perché nell'epoca patristica la liturgia fosse pensata e vissuta come un momento particolarmente felice di vera e autentica teologia." Ibid., 1513 (my translation).

157. "Cosi la 'Liturgia,' ossia l'azione esterna di culto esercitata dalla casta sacerdotale, diventa in parte il 'simbolo' ma, purtroppo, anche la 'sostituzione' del 'culto,' che il 'popolo' era stato chiamato a dare a Jahve con la santità della vita. Questa falsa concezione 'liturgico-sacerdotale,' che si era col tempo identificata con il Tempio di Gerusalemme, in parte era stata distrutta dal lungo periodo dell'esilio. Molti infatti avevano capito il richiamo dei profeti, sintetizzato da Os 6, 6: 'Voglio l'amore e non gli olocausti,' e nella obbligata mancanza del Tempio, di sacerdoti e di sacrifici, trovavano l'occasione di offrire a Dio 'la contrizione dell'anima e l'umiltà dello spirito come un sacrificio che fosse più gradito degli olocausi di tori e agnelli, perché impegnava a seguire Dio, a temerlo e a cercarne la faccia' (Dan 3, 39-41). Di questo nuovo atteggiamento, che attraverso i profeti ritrova il 'culto spirituale,' sono tra l'altro prova eloquente i *Salmi*. Di questi infatti alcuni affrontano direttamente il problema, come si può vedere in Sal 39, 7-9, Dio non gradisce né sacrifici e offerte, né olocausti e sacrifici d'espiazione, ma vuole che si faccia la sua volontà, perché in ciò si riassume il libro della Legge." Marsili, *La Liturgia: momento nella storia della salvezza*, 43.

to a point of new departure, exposing the liturgy to the inevitable consequences of a greater awareness of experience and pneumatology.[159]

Liturgical theology, as Marsili would have it, is theology in a concrete, existential mode because it represents the shaping of everyday realities by the inner word of God, so that his presence may be known and felt.[160] Symbol is essential to this process as the means by which the breach between inner and outer realities is reconciled. Theology as discourse on the Blessed Trinity is not in this way "bypassed"[161] by liturgy, but rendered immediate: the divine word given by the Father is actualized in the sacraments of Christ through the Holy Spirit. Thus divine presence and divine action are made concrete in the anthropological dimension, not as some extrinsic reality, but as the ultimate union of the prophetic heart of revelation with the mundane reality of human existence. In this sense, Christian experience must be an expression of the action of the Holy Spirit in the world.

---

158. "The liturgy justly came to be considered as 'first theology' inasmuch as it represented the first moment in which the profession of faith, transforming itself into lived practice, becomes the first concrete theological language." ("La liturgia veniva considerata come 'theologia prima,' in quanto essa rappresenta il primo momento nel quale la professione di fede, trasformandosi in prassi vissuta, diventa il primo concreto linguaggio teologico.") Marsili, "Teologia liturgica," in 1513 (my translation).

159. For a discussion of the particular relationship of cult and prophecy in the practical liturgy of the evangelical tradition and how this relates to Catholic understandings see: Dorothea Haspelmath – Finatti , *Theologia Prima*, 18–60

160. "Questa 'teologia liturgica' è la teologia della presenza e dell'azione di Dio nella storia della salvezza umana; è la 'Teologia del mistero di Cristo,' o, come diceva Casel, la 'Teologia dei misteri di Cristo': cioè la teologia di una realtà concreta, fatta di presenza e di azione divina, e questo in dimensione antropologica, perché non è un'azione e una presenza, come un *signum de caelo*, ma è la presenza di Cristo nell'incarnazione, nell'umanità, negli uomini." Marsili, "Liturgia e Teologia. Proposta teoretica," 469.

161. "Il discorso su Dio Uni-Trino (= Teologia) non può che passare, chiarirsi e rendersi concreto (dopo un primo momento qual è lo studio della Parola in fase di rivelazione, cioè il momento di attuazione in Cristo sacramento del Padre nello Spirito) nel secondo momento, dove la teologia non può che essere liturgica." Triacca, "Teologia della liturgia o teologia liturgica?," 275.

Opening Up New Opportunities

It is possible to return to the quotation that opened this section and understand better why Marsili insists upon a method of procedure that begins with the liturgy as a prior, mysterious, and complex whole, before particular perspectives can be fruitfully adopted on that one reality. Objectively, as *Dei Verbum* 2 points out, God has revealed his will in view of himself, so that human beings can come to a knowledge of the divine nature by experiencing the effects of his salvific purposes.[162] It is for this reason that priority must be given to the liturgy as objective revelation, though the subjective participation of believers in the very mode of its transmission is the means by which that revelation is appropriated.[163]

> In fact, to say the liturgy actuates the mystery of Christ in the sacramental dimension, that is through a symbol that is bearer of the salvific divine presence, means that it continually actuates in time—since it is done in time—the whole reality of which Christ is the sacrament. And Christ is the sacrament of the Father, of the Son, and of the Holy Spirit, the Trinity not static but operating through its personal being, which is not atemporal but historico-salvific; Christ is the sacrament of salvation at the direct operative level, in that the soteriological value of the divine design is actuated in him as eternally active priesthood and as universally valid mediation; Christ is the sacrament of the church, in that it is all and always present in him, body in the head; Christ is sacrament,

---

162. "Placuit Deo in sua bonitate et sapientia seipsum revelare et notum facere sacramentum voluntatis suae, quo homines per Christum, Verbum carnem factum, in Spiritu sancto accessum habent ad Patrem et divinae consortes efficiuntur." *DV*, 2 [972].

163. Marsili defines his unique understanding of liturgical theology as the discovery that the law of sacramentality is fundamental to the self-actuation of the word of God: "This in fact appears not as a proposition of truth that is abstractly quidditative (*quid sit deus*), but as salvific divine reality that is present and active in and through the humanity of Christ (*cur Deus homo*), who not only becomes the symbol-sacrament of salvation, but reveals how salvation, or the entire relation of God with man, cannot be realized except through sacramental symbolism." ("Questa infatti appare non come proposizione di verità astrattamente quidditativa (*quid sit Deus*), ma come realtà salvifica divina che è presente e attiva nella e per l'umanità di Cristo (*cur Deus homo*), che non solo diventa simbolo-sacramento di salvezza, ma rivela come la salvezza, ossia tutto il rapporto di Dio con l'uomo, non possa realizzarsi se non per via del simbolismo sacramentale.") Marsili, "Teologia liturgica," 1520–21 (my translation).

who in the individual "sacraments" actuates and communicates his own whole reality to men, through which men become in him—as he is—son of God in baptism, a person vivified by the Holy Spirit in confirmation, perfect adorers of the Father in spirit and in truth in the Eucharist.[164]

Salvatore Marsili died on 27 November 1983, before the *Nuovo Dizionario di Liturgia* went into circulation, and without the opportunity to respond to the reactions of the academic world to his singular conclusions. As Silvano Maggiani has emphasized, in seeking to distinguish and apprehend the liturgy in its most fundamental form and as a totality, Marsili left a work that is essentially "open." The final quotation from the article "Teologia Liturgica" above indicates at least implicitly what some of these possibilities may be.

Because the liturgy is not an abstract idea, but the revelation of the mystery of Christ in the sacramental dimension, then the fact that liturgy represents the convergence of a salvific event and a symbolic rite means that experience is a category that must be explored. Marsili's emphasis on the whole reality of the christological event taking place in time—the time of the church—is surely at the heart of this issue. And it is precisely there that another, and related, consequence of the Marsilian brand of *teologia liturgica* begins to emerge: the agent of this experience. Perhaps this new departure was the ultimate one explicitly indicated by Marsili, as into the study week of the *Associazione dei Professori e Cultori di Liturgia* that

164. "Dire infatti che la liturgia attua il mistero di Cristo in dimensione sacramentale, cioè attraverso un simbolo portatore di presenza salvifica divina, vuol dire che essa attua continuamente nel tempo—poiché nel tempo viene fatta—tutta la realtà della quale Cristo è sacramento del Padre, del Figlio e dello Spirito santo, Trinità non statica ma operante per il suo essere personale, non atemporale ma storico-salvifica; Cristo è sacramento della salvezza a livello operativo diretto, in quanto la valenza soteriologica del disegno divino si attua in lui come sacerdozio eternamente attivo e come mediazione universalmente valida; Cristo è sacramento della chiesa, in quanto la chiesa è tutta e sempre presente in lui, corpo nel capo; Cristo è sacramento, che nei singoli 'sacramenti' attua e comunica tutta la propria realtà agli uomini, per cui gli uomini diventano in lui—come lui—figli di Dio nel battesimo, persone vivificate dallo Spirito santo nella confermazione, adoratori perfetti del Padre in spirito e verità nell'eucaristia." Ibid., 1521 (my translation).

was to be his last, the great *Cristologo* of the liturgy introduced a pneumatological theme.[165] A method that is focused christologically, because it was a determined examination of the revelatory content of the liturgy, inevitably leads to questions surrounding the effective realization of this content in the life and members of the church. By way of unrelenting and diligent reflection, Marsili has opened up a window of research that sets a determined gaze on Christ as the paradigm of God's salvific work, performed in the human person by the Holy Spirit. That is to say, he has invited reflection that must exploit all the insights of Christian anthropology.

165. See Associazione dei Professori e Cultori di Liturgia, *Spirito Santo e liturgia: atti della XII Settimana di Studio dell'Associazione Professori di Liturgia, Valdragone: 22 agosto 1983* (Casale Monferrato: Marietti, 1984).

5

Gustave Martelet

Forming a Sacramental Anthropology

That the lives of the four theologians of our study are roughly contemporary, that their theological enterprises are not dissimilar, and their vocations as teachers and formators the same, means that by this stage the benefits of a cumulative and composite picture are beginning to be felt. Hopefully, with each chapter, further depth and a changed perspective are provided to the central question. Yet, while similarities in the broad outlines of the writers' lives allow for the establishment of certain coordinates, the unique response of each provides particularity and nuance.[1] Such parallels, intersections, similarities, and distinctions should become apparent from a brief synopsis of the theological career of Gustave Martelet.

---

1. "Come spiegare una simile visione teologica?," asks Rino Fisichella of René Latourelle, and he provides an answer valid for all: "Ognuno di noi, facendo teologia, traccia ugualmente parte della sua vita e della sua esperienza di fede." R. Fisichella, "Il Contributo di René Latourelle alla Teologia Fondamentale," in *Gesù Rivelatore: Teologia Fondamentale*, ed. R. Fisichella (Casale Monferrato: Edizione Piemme, 1988), 20.

Born in Lyons in 1916, he entered the Society of Jesus in 1935. Benefiting from protracted study in the literary and philosophical disciplines, he finally settled on theology. The France in which Martelet was formed as a theologian and priest was the France of two world wars, part of a Europe being "purged"[2] of the old order and seeking to rebuild. The same might be said of Catholic studies: the years of peace bringing a period of great theological activity and a surge of innovation. And, though these years were not without their tensions,[3] Martelet began his teaching career at a time of new departures and in the company of some of the greatest theological minds of the century. At Lyons-Fourvière, where he began to teach in 1952, and at Paris, there were Henri de Lubac and Jean Daniélou.[4] At Rome, where he presented his doctorate at the Gregorian in 1957, there were Stanislaus Lyonnet and William Van Roo, not to mention other faculty members and René Latourelle, who presented his own thesis a year later. Yet the most significant period in Martelet's theological career must be his involvement with the Second Vatican Council and his interaction there with other theologians and the Council fathers. Working as adviser for the French-speaking African bishops, Martelet was something of a conduit for the broad currents of contemporary Catholic theology, and more particularly of the central debates of the sessions. Though more a relator of information

2. E. Fouilloux, "The Antepreparatory Phase, the Slow Emergence from Inertia," in *History of Vatican II*, vol. 1: *Announcing and Preparing Vatican Council II, Toward a New Era in Catholicism*, ed. G. Alberigo and J. Komonchak (Louvain: Peeters, 1995), 55–166, 85.

3. "The general situation of society and the Church in the period between 1945 and 1959 was marked by two elements: first, a very strong and rapid evolution in various fields; and, second, within the Church itself, a clash between more open orientations and more conservative ones." G. Martina, "The Historical Context in which the Idea of a New Ecumenical Council was Born," in *Vatican II: Assessments and Perspectives, Twenty-Five Years After (1962-1987)*, ed. R. Latourelle, 3 vols. (New York: Paulist, 1988), 1:3.

4. See H. de Lubac, *Entretien autour de Vatican II* (Paris: Éditions du Cerf, 1985), especially the chapter "Prologue sur un temps lointain," 7–17; H. U. von Balthasar and G. Chantraine, *Le Cardinal de Lubac: l'homme et son œuvre* (Paris: Lethielleux, 1983); M.-J. Rondeau, ed., *Jean Daniélou 1905–1974* (Paris: Éditions du Cerf, 1975).

and guide, not an official *peritus*, Martelet worked closely with a team of theologians referred to as the "Conciliar Strategies Group," who had already been active in preparing opinions contrary to the prepared schemas before the Council debates began.[5] He enjoyed privileged and intense exposure to the theological debates of the various sessions, and experienced at firsthand the way in which the vision of certain individuals shaped the Council documents according to new theological categories and themes. After the Council, Martelet returned to teaching at Lyons-Fourvière, the Faculté de Philosophie et de Théologie des Jésuites de Paris, and in addition, worked as a visiting professor at the Gregorian University, Rome.

If the establishment of fundamental theology as a discipline of primary importance has been basic to the endeavor of each of the writers we have studied, then it is within this task that we can also determine their unique contribution. Contemporary with the *nouvelle théologie*, Martelet no doubt welcomed such an imaginative vision both to complement and break open the somewhat stale but sure foundation of scholasticism that he had received at Fourvière.[6]

5. Albert Melloni details the members of this group as "Volk, Musty, Guano, Garrone, Butler, Philips, Rahner, Féret, Häring, Liégé, Grillmeier, Martelet, Smulders, Martimort, Laurentin, Ratzinger, Semmelroth, Daniélou, and Congar." See A. Melloni, "The Beginning of the Second Period," in *History of Vatican II*, vol. 3: *The Mature Council, Second Period and Intersession, September 1963–September 1964*, ed. G. Alberigo and J. Komonchak (Louvain: Peeters, 2000), 62. See index for references to Martelet's membership on other committees, especially with Jean Daniélou and Yves Congar. Also G. Martelet, *Remarques sur la première série de schémas*, Léger Archive, 610. There are also Martelet's own comments in the introduction to his *Les idées maîtresses de Vatican II*: "Besides, what theologian, at the time, did not present some form of appraisal [of the Council]? Before suggesting my own personal method, I had already heard or collected from others reports drawn up hastily in Rome, by people like Abbé Laurentin, Père Schillebeeckx, Hans Küng, Père Wenger. They all started off from one central idea, *aggiornamento*, or openness, to assess the positive or inevitable weaknesses [of the Council]." ("Quel théologien d'ailleurs n'esquissait à l'époque l'ébauche d'un bilan? Avant de proposer ma façon de le faire, j'avais entendu moi-même ou recueilli par d'autres, l'écho d'autres bilans rapidement dressés à Rome même, par un Abbé Laurentin, un Père Schillebeeckx, un Hans Küng, un Père Wenger. Tous partaient de l'idée, bien centrale il est vrai, d'*aggiornamento* ou de celle d'ouverture, pour mesurer l'acquis et constater les inévitables lacunes.") G. Martelet, *Les idées maîtresses de Vatican II. Introduction à l'ésprit du Concile* (Paris: Desclée, 1966), 10 (my translation).

Like others, he was inspired by the return to the word of God and the writings of the Fathers that was so influencing Catholic theology, and his choice of thesis, *Figures et Parénèse Sacramentelles*, is expressive of this. From these sources came the inspiration for the *aggiornamento* of Vatican II, for there was a common—if hidden—theme. As the Fathers had sought to relate the scriptural tradition to the particular circumstances and experiences of the early church, so the bishops of the Council sought to relate that same tradition to the modern world. Preoccupied with this task, Martelet's concern is in the first place neither hermeneutic nor semiological, the primary and defining element of his fundamental theology being anthropology.[7] Such becomes quite clear at the time of the Council and with the publication of *Les idées maîtresses de Vatican II*.

Through a comparative examination of his doctoral thesis and the subsequent *Les idées maîtresses de Vatican II*, it should be possible to examine in detail common emerging themes. The central and prevailing conviction that the realities of faith are best understood from within the ambit of human life is enunciated clearly by both these texts and others to which we will make reference.[8] However, Martelet's most explicit and mature expression of that truth that Karl Rahner elsewhere simply states as the coincidence of anthropology and theology comes with his *Résurrection, eucharistie et genèse de*

6. Cf. A. Dulles, *The Craft of Theology*, 2nd ed. (New York: Crossroad, 1995), 44 and R. Latourelle, *L'Infini du sens: Jésus-Christ* (Québec: Éditions Bellarmin, 2000), 179–80.

7. "All'apriori costitutivo della centralità e basilarità della Rivelatione per ogni studio teologico, subentra una triplice suddivisione della Fondamentale che viene espresso come momento *ermeneutico, antropologico e semiologico*." R. Fisichella, "Il Contributo di René Latorelle alla Teologia Fondamentale," 12. According to this subdivision, and from a brief survey of Martelet's major works, we can say that his distinct contribution is certainly that of anthropological reflection.

8. G. Martelet, *L'au—dela retrouvé* (Paris: Desclée, 1975); G. Martelet, *Oser croire en l'Église* (Paris: Desclée, 1977); G. Martelet, *Vivre aujourd'hui la foi de toujours* (Paris: Desclée, 1979), G. Martelet, *Libre réponse à un scandale: La faute originelle, la souffrance et la mort* (Paris: Desclée, 1986).

l'homme.[9] In this work, the fundamentals of the Christian faith are examined through the liturgical expression of the simplicities of human life. Hence the themes of this study are treated explicitly. Yet let us begin with the sources of Martelet's mature convictions and with his doctoral thesis of 1957.

Ressourcement and the Word of God:
Figures et Parénèse Sacramentelles

Speaking of his theological formation in the early 1950s, Avery Dulles tells of the freshness that certain supplementary reading brought to the "arid manuals."[10] This was the work of *ressourcement*: an exposition of the tradition through the Scriptures and works of the Fathers that in itself revealed how narrow an aperture scholasticism had become. Patristic method and forms provided breadth of vision and new perspective to old questions that were becoming all the more insistent in the modern era. Perhaps this is why indications of the beginning of this new theology can be found at the end of the First World War.

---

9. G. Martelet, *Résurrection, eucharistie et genèse de l'homme, chemins théologiques d'un renouveau chrétien* (Paris: Desclée, 1972); English trans., T. Corbishley, *The Risen Christ and the Eucharistic World* (London: Collins, 1976). Page references given in square brackets refer to the English translation.

10. "Studying theology in the early 1950's, when the *nouvelle théologie* was beginning to become popular, I treasured the opportunity to read books and articles by authors such as Henri de Lubac, Yves Congar, Jean Daniélou, and Karl Rahner. It was a period of renewal of Catholic biblical studies, and my professors introduced me to the new developments in exegesis. The work of Roland de Vaux, Pierre Benoit, David Stanley, and John L. MacKenzie, to name but a few, was closely followed. I had the opportunity too to read distinguished Protestant biblical theologians such as Oscar Cullmann and Rudolf Bultmann, though of course such reading was in those days considered strictly extracurricular and even dangerous. Theological literature such as I have just mentioned formed a valuable supplement, and at some points a corrective, to the set theses of the manuals." So Dulles reflected on his own formation, yet how much more accessible and immediate were these studies to Martelet, who was working with the people who brought this new theology to birth. See A. Dulles, *The Craft of Theology*, 44.

As the century turned, fundamental theology had done little more than inherit the concerns of the First Vatican Council and likewise seek to protect the concept of revelation from attack. Yet, as Latourelle notes, with the publication of Ambroise Gardeil's *Le Donné révélé et la théologie*[11] in 1910, the suspicion arose that neither a comprehensive nor an adequate theology of revelation was being presented.[12] Thus begins a whole movement that, dissatisfied with the description of revelation as little more than a communication of intellectual ideas, positively seeks "a greater fidelity to the sources of Scripture and tradition."[13] While there were varied currents within the general stream of *ressourcement*, historical, patristic, kerygmatic, and homiletic,[14] and while the Dominicans of Le Saulchoir contributed much to the methodological debates that persisted until the Second World War,[15] a definitive moment within this whole movement was the founding of *Sources Chrétiennes* by de Lubac and Daniélou at Fourvière in 1943.[16] Here can be seen the practical

11. A. Gardeil, *Le Donné révélé et la théologie* (Paris: J. Gabalda, 1910).
12. R. Latourelle, *Théologie de la Révélation:* 225 [208].
13. Ibid., 231–32 [213].
14. Ibid., 238–57 [216–230].
15. See M.-D. Chenu, *Une école de théologie: Le Saulchoir,* 2nd ed. (Paris: Éditions du Cerf, 1985). This text, in which Chenu elaborates the historical method of what he called "le retour aux sources," was first published in 1937 and is here reprinted with a number of articles, by G. Alberigo and others, which usefully contextualize the whole debate.
16. "Le feu, qui couvait, fut soudain ranimé à la suite d'un article un peu journalistique du Père Jean Daniélou dans les *Etudes,* écrit rapidement en marge de ses propres travaux, qui vantait généreusement les efforts de renouveau accomplis par l'Église en France un peu dans tous les domaines. Il n'y avait point à y chercher malice; plusieurs cependant voulurent y voir un manifeste révolutionnaire! On s'inquiéta du même coup de la fondation des *Sources chrétiennes,* recueil de textes patristiques, qui en est aujourd'hui à son 320e volume. L'initiative en remontait, bien avant la guerre, au Père Victor Fontoynont. Dans l'atmosphère passionnelle du jour, elle fut soudain considérée par quelques polémistes comme une machine de guerre contre la théologie scolastique et même la foi de l'Église." H. de Lubac, *Entretien autour de Vatican II,* 10. For a full and useful description of the background to *Sources chrétiennes,* see also I. de la Potterie, "The Spiritual Sense of Scripture," *Communio: International Catholic Review* 23 (1996): 738–56.

application of the historical method and the purposeful initiation of the machinery of renewal.

Growing Toward a New Theology

Gustave Martelet became professor of fundamental theology at Lyon-Fourvière in 1952, and, in those early years of teaching, as his doctoral study began to take shape, the influence of colleagues, contemporaries, and associates must have been of great significance. And, although in later years de Lubac played down its somewhat mythical status,[17] the theological reflection, discussion, and output that this once infamous and now famous house engendered cannot be denied.[18]

Yet the scene was not all light. Two years prior to Martelet's taking up his teaching post, de Lubac had been deprived of the chair of theology, and for the next ten years he led an itinerant existence under the constant suspicion of the ecclesiastical authorities. Martelet could not be unaware that he was beneficiary to a legacy that held more significance than one might expect of a curious, provincial faculty. It was from his work on the Fathers that de Lubac provided a resource for what others called Fourvière's *nouvelle théologie*: an interest in humanity's natural desire for God, the mystery of the

---

17. "En cette grande maison de Fourvière, les générations se succédaient depuis le retour du scolasticat de Hastings à Lyon en 1926. Il ne faudrait pas s'imaginer que l'ardeur intellectuelle y fût toujours intense, ou qu'on y fût généralement épris de nouveautés. Jamais non plus il ne s'y forma quelque groupe compact, soudé par une visée commune." H. de Lubac, *Entretien autour de Vatican II*, 96.

18. From 1941, while at Fourvière, de Lubac was the inspirational force behind the clandestine journal of the Resistance, *Cahiers du témoinage chretién*, along with Pierre Chaillet and Gaston Fessard. From 1944 onward, he actively collaborated with the Jesuits of Lyon-Fourvière and with Jean Daniélou and Louis Bouyer in the collection *Théologie*. It was while at Fourvière during the period 1945–1950 that de Lubac was editor of *Recherches de science religieuse*. Cf. S. Wood, *Spiritual Exegesis and the Church in the Theology of Henri de Lubac* (Grand Rapids: Eerdmans, 1998), 2–5.

supernatural, the social aspects of dogma, and the true meaning of the sacramental body of Christ. It is not surprising that Martelet too should follow in the path of his illustrious teachers, and return to the sources in order to reorient his own theological endeavors,[19] but, before examining his own studies, a brief rehersal of the main lines in the thinking to which he was heir, and that he develops in his doctoral thesis, is in order.

The Insights of Spiritual Exegesis

What draws de Lubac, Daniélou, Louis Bouyer, Louis Charlier, et al.[20] to the Fathers' spiritual exegesis of the Scriptures is the "unique union of biblical, liturgical, and theological attitudes"[21] that they there express. In their works, the permanent foundation of Christian faith is elucidated, and the question that naturally arises for those who return to these sources is the extent to which the mode of their formulation is essential to their content. Integral to the teaching of the Fathers is the allegorical or typological use of the Old Testament. Indeed, this is the primary way in which the biblical, liturgical, and theological realities are resolved into a credible unity, and so of this nexus de Lubac asks,

> Whether the the beginning of revelation played a role, and perhaps a significant one, in the final formulation of revelation itself. Put in another way, may not the New Testament teaching be formulated and, in its literal meaning, become intelligible through some spiritual signification bestowed by Christ on the facts of the Old Law?[22]

19. It may be that Martelet was also affected by the prominent French *Annales* school of history, which specifically sought to incorporate social sciences into an understanding of the past, and was instrumental in developing interdisciplinary focus.
20. See I. de la Potterie, "The Spiritual Sense of Scripture," 746–47.
21. J. Ratzinger, *Principles of Catholic Theology* (San Francisco: Ignatius, 1989), 152.
22. H. de Lubac, *Scripture in the Tradition*, trans. L. O'Neill (New York: Crossroad, 2000), 8; French orig. *L'Ecriture dans la tradition* (Paris: Éditions Montaigne, 1967).

Such is the question to which Daniélou responds with a particular orientation in *Sacramentum Futuri: Études sur les Origines de la Typologie Biblique*,[23] and with which Martelet begins to grapple in *Figures et Parénèse Sacramentelles*:

> Should we have been looking at "baptism in Moses" and at "spiritual" food and drink in general, relating to the Rock that is Christ, as a simple prefigure of our present Eucharist? Or, on the contrary, should we be interpreting the "sacraments" in the Old Testament as happenings with a fixed purpose? . . . If there is truth in both views, what is the relationship between the two? . . . Should we look at the term *figures* or *types* in verse six as suiting both "sacraments" and "chastisements in the desert" . . . or should we look at "sacraments" without "chastisements" . . . or at "chastisements, omitting "sacraments"? If we accept the fact that Paul aims at using one term only for both realities, how then can a sacramental typology relate to a chastisement typology when, for the sake of unity, the two should never go together?[24]

We begin at the heart of the problem: the question of the nature and extent of the correspondence between the *qahal yahweh* of the Old Law and the New Testament *ekklesia*.[25] Martelet recognises in

---

23. J. Daniélou, *Sacramentum Futuri: études sur les origines de la typologie biblique* (Paris: Beauchesne et Ses Fils, 1950); English trans., W. Hibberd, *From Shadows to Reality: Studies in the Typology of the Fathers* (London: Burns & Oates, 1960). Interestingly, this whole work is a reflection on 1 Cor. 10:11, which is also fundamental to Martelet's study.

24. "Fallait-il, par exemple, chercher dans le baptême de Moïse, dans l'ensemble de la nourriture et de la boisson spirituelles, rapporté au rocher accompagnateur qui était le Christ, un pur diagramme de l'Eucharistie présente ou, en contraire, une détermination objective des "sacrements" passés? Et, s'il y a du vrai dans les deux tendances, quel rapport établir entre elles? Fallait-il chercher dans le mot "figures" ou "types" du verset sixième le terme presque technique qui convient aux "sacrements" et aux châtiments sans les "sacrements"? Si on accepte que Paul vise les deux à la fois par un seul terme, comment un typisme sacramentel déjà accompli peut-il être rapporté dans l'unité d'une seule fin parénétique à un typisme de châtiments qui, lui, ne devrait jamais s'accomplir?" G. Martelet, *Figures et Parénèse Sacramentelles* (Paris: Pontificia Universitas Gregoriana, 1957), 323–24 (my translation).

25. This is the enterprise of L. Cerfaux in *La Théologie de l'Église suivant saint Paul* 2nd ed. (Paris: Les Éditions du Cerf, 1948), on whom Martelet is dependent here. Cerfaux regards the figurative or symbolic connections that Paul makes between the cultic practices of both communities as essential to a correct understanding of their relationship: "Dans la I Cor, dès le dèbut du chapitre X, l'Apôtre, sans y être invité par le contexte, introduit l'idée d'unité. . . . Il n'y avait nul motif de relever ici l'unité du peuple, manifestée par l'identité d'une nouriture

1 Corinthians 1–11 both an indication of the complexity of the relationship and the principle according to which it might be unraveled. Indicative of the relative nature and status of these communities are the signs or *mirabilia* with which God visits the people and expresses his will. Noticing the obvious parallel that St. Paul draws between baptism and the spiritual food given by God through Moses to his people in the desert, Martelet wonders as to the relative status of the sacraments of the church. The question as to whether there is a simple correspondence between the signs of the old and new covenant, or whether they remain objectively distinct, is exacerbated by Paul's conviction that Christ is the common denominator. This makes it necessary for Martelet to examine in greater detail Paul's figurative or typological structures—what he calls "la loi de construction d'un ensemble figuratif."[26]

That typology is a principle of biblical theology, present in both testaments, is undeniable.[27] Daniélou points to its foundation in the old law, where the prophets announced future wonders of God, analagous to those of the past, by which they would know him.[28]

---

spirituelle. Ce n'était pas en cause; dans la ligne du développement, on devait simplement comprendre que les privilèges spirituels du peuple du désert ne l'ont pas préservé de l'idolâtrie. En réalité, la chose figurée (l'eucharistie chrétienne, à laquelle est liée la notion d'unité) a réagi sur l'antitype." 183. Cf. L. Cerfaux, *Le Christ dans la Théologie de S. Paul* (Paris: Éditions du Cerf, 1951).

26. G. Martelet, *Figures et Parénèse Sacramentelles*, 325.

27. "Thus it is that we are more likely to speak today of *typology*. The word is a neologism and has been barely a century in use. But it was very happily coined. Since the time of St. Paul, traditional exegesis has always been concerned with 'types,' figures, and we can occasionally find 'typical meaning' used synonymously with mystical or allegorical meaning, or even with figurative meaning, as in Pascal. 'Typology' also has the virtue of doing away, at least in intention, with all the straw in the grain of Christian exegesis, something which could not be accomplished by the word 'allegory' alone." H. de Lubac, *Scripture in the Tradition*, 16.

28. "Que les réalités de l'Ancien Testament soient des figures de celles du Nouveau, ceci est un principe de la théologie biblique. Cette science des correspondances entre les deux Testaments s'appelle la *typologie*. Il est bon d'en rappeler le fondement. Son point de départ se trouve dans l'Ancien Testament lui-même. Les Prophètes en effet ont annoncé au peuple d'Israël, au temps de sa captivité, que Dieu accomplirait pour lui dans l'avenir des œuvres analogues, et plus grandes encore, à celles qu'il avait accomplies dans le passé." J. Daniélou, *Bible et Liturgie, La*

Such types are clearly structured eschatologically. Yet, though these types meet their fulfillment in Christ, they are not the only ones within the scriptural economy. There is also the New Testament typology of the time of the church that aligns the actions of God in the lives of his Hebrew people and the life of his Son with the liturgical actions of gathered Christians. This is exactly what St. Paul does in the passage from 1 Corinthians 10, and Martelet sees this "unity of situation" as the foundation on which all figurative reflection rests.[29]

Problems Inherent to Typology

While the question of correspondence has perhaps been answered,[30] another question has appeared. For, as Martelet asks rhetorically in the above quotation from *Figures et Parénèse Sacramentelles*, if the "abiding structural figures"[31] of baptism and nourishment allow for the positing of a direct correspondence in Christ of the Old and New Testaments, then something also is being said as to their relative value. Perhaps here the inherent difficulty of typology has begun to emerge. This is a problem de Lubac describes as "the drawback of referring solely to a result, without alluding to the spirit or basic thrust of the process which produces that result."[32] Precisely because

théologie biblique des Sacrements et des fêtes d'après les Pères de l'Église (Paris: Éditions du Cerf, 1951), 8–9.

29. "Cette unité dans l'histoire du salut est importante. C'est elle qui fonde une unité de situations sur laquelle toute la réflexion figurative repose." G. Martelet, *Figures et Parénèse Sacramentelles*, 327.

30. "En tout cas, de même qu'en *Sag.* 12, 6 l'expression marque le rapport entre la génération de l'auteur et les premiers possédants de la terre promise, 'nos pères' insiste vigoureusement ici sur la continuité qui relie 'les appelés à être saints' de 'l'Église de Dieu qui est à Corinthe' et le peuple que Dieu a sauvé de l'Égypte. Par ce terme, Paul établit que l'axe historique des événements médités par le livre de la Sagesse passe par la communauté chrétienne." Ibid.

31. Ibid., 338–39.

32. H. de Lubac, *Scripture in the Tradition*, 16.

it is the means by which the sacramental signs came to be that interests the theologian, it is impossible for the typologies of the Old Testament to be dismissed as *mere* figures. It would be contrary to the unity of revelation and salvation so easily to empty these types of a lasting significance. As Martelet stresses,

> "Baptism into Moses," in the cloud, and in the sea is a structural figure of the baptism of Christ. It derives its hidden strength from the latter. There is, therefore, no actual presence of the "baptism of Christ" in the "baptism of Moses." The unity of both baptisms, of which the second in historical order is the *raison d'être* of the first, its form, in the true sense of the word. It is the union in Christ himself: two similar experiences of revelation in the history of salvation, but one is only the symbol of the other, and gives the first all its meaning.[33]

In denying a superficial participation in Christ of the Old Testament types, and by his insistence on a single "form" within the two moments of revelation, Martelet seeks to offset the inherent condescension in his further assertion that the sole reason for the existence of the type of Moses' baptism is the baptism of Christ. While Martelet is happy to describe the function of Old Testament types as preparatory, annunciatory, and indicative, he is not satisfied that this is their role in its entirety. For if the sole function of these "types" was annunciatory, then surely they are superfluous to the Christian dispensation in which the full and complete reality has been revealed. However, it is in fact the unity of form between type and antitype that allows for the conviction that the figures of the old law are not merely annunciatory but also illuminatory.

---

33. "Figure structurelle du baptême dans le Christ, le baptême à Moïse dans la nuée et dans la mer a déjà l'autre en lui comme sa vertu cachée. Nulle inclusion superficielle donc du baptême au Christ *dans* le baptême à Moïse. L'unité des deux baptêmes qui fait du second dans l'ordre historique; a seule raison d'être du premier, sa 'forme' au sens plénier du mot, c'est l'unité même du Christ en deux moments de la révélation d'un unique salut, mais dont l'un n'est que figure par rapport à la réalité de l'autre et lui doit tout son sens." G. Martelet, *Figures et Parénèse Sacramentelles*, 338–39 (my translation).

Horacio Simian-Yofre usefully amplifies Martelet's point by reflecting on a description of the role of the prophets in St. Irenaeus. There he discovers an insistence that the sign of a prophet is not simply an anticipatory word, but a fuller gesture that has a continuing participation in the announcement of salvation: "He [the prophet] makes efficient gestures under the guidance of the Spirit, although such gestures must be continued and repeated."[34] Irenaeus understands the role of the prophet as going beyond the verbal announcement of the word of God, augmenting his role to almost liturgical proportions. Yet here is the means by which Martelet can respond to the complexities of Paul's thought in 1 Corinthians 10, for the realization is that the *ensemble figuratif* is a sacramental reality.

Sacraments as *Ensembles Figuratifs*

If so far Martelet has established a linear continuity between the types of the Old Testament and the church and the antitype that is Christ, and if he has stressed the eschatological orientation of these signs and spoken of their real incluson in Christ, then he must conclude with Daniélou, "This means that the sacraments continue in our midst the mirabilia—the wonderful works of God, in the Old and New Testaments; the Deluge, the Passion, Baptism—God working in the

---

34. "By means of the prophets, the Spirit indicates the future. To indicate is to establish a system of signs that points toward the future. These signs are not only the words that the prophets utter, but also the visions, behavior, and gestures that they perform:quae quidem videnda erant visibiliter videntes, quae vero audienda erant, sermone praeconantes, quae vero agenda erant, operatione perficientesuniversa vero prophetice annuntiantes (IV, 20, 8). It is difficult to decide if the verbal forms should be translated simply as future ('that which will be seen,' as the edition of *Sources Chrétiennes* translate them) or rather with a sense of obligation ('they performed with acts what [also] was to be achieved in the future'). This interpretation insists on the continuity between the performance of the sign by the prophet, and that in which all participate." H. Simian-Yofre, "Old and New Testament: Participation and Analogy" in R. Latourelle, *Vatican II Assessment and Perspectives*, 1:277. In this context, cf. M. Hooker, *The Signs of a Prophet* (Harrisburg, PA: Trinity, 1997).

same way but at three different periods of Church history. . . . These are subject to judgement eschatologically."[35]

What is emerging is the depth and significance of typology. No longer can this reality be confined to a mere methodology. To borrow de Lubac's expression, what is becoming apparent is the fact that typology is not some pretty embroidery that has been tacked on to the fabric of salvation at a later date, but something that in itself furnishes the thread "from which is woven the Christian mystery in all its newness and transcendence."[36] The types of the Old Testament are signs of an inner significance that is Christ, and in their sacramentality they abide:

> That is why St. Paul uses the word *accompanist*. Do you see the wisdom of Paul when he points out that Christ is the Dispenser of all gifts, thus bringing the "figure" close to the reality? . . . He who provided them with such gifts, set the table, led *them* through the sea, and *you* through baptism. He gave *them* manna and water, and he gave *you* body and blood. In such an exegesis, "spiritual" is not equivalent to "miraculous," although the meaning is included. Neither can it be identified as "eucharistic," though it does point to that mystery. Between the "spiritual" and the "eucharistic," we have the mediation of Christ who establishes the relationship that Paul has in view, when he calls the food and drink of the desert "spiritual."[37]

---

35. "Par là est signifié que les sacrements continuent au milieu de nous les *mirabilia*, les grandes œuvres de Dieu, dans l'Ancien et le Nouveau Testaments: Déluge, Passion, Baptême nous montrent les mêmes mœurs divines à trois époques de l'histoire sainte et sont eux-mêmes ordonnés au Jugement eschatologique." J. Daniélou, *Bible et Liturgie*, 10.

36. H. de Lubac, *Scripture in the Tradition*, 8–10.

37. "C'est pourquoi il (Saint Paul) a dit 'accompagnateur.' Vois-tu la sagesse de Paul, comment il montre que le Christ est le dispensateur de l'ensemble et comment il conduit ainsi la figure tout roche de la réalité? Celui qui leur a procuré à eux ces choses-là, c'est celui qui a dressé cette table-ci et le même qui a conduit ceux-là par la mer et toi par le baptême, leur a procuré manne et eau, et, à toi, corps et sang. Dans une telle exégèse, 'spirituel' ne saurait équivaloir simplement à 'miraculeux,' encore qu'il enveloppe certainement cette signification, mais il ne peut pas davantage être identifié à 'eucharistique,' encore qu'il désigne à coup sûr ce mystère. Mais il y a entre le 'spirituel' et 'l'eucharistique' la médiation du Christ, donateur par lequel il faut passer pour trouver le rapport que saint Paul a en vue quand il appelle la nourriture et la boisson du désert 'spirituelles.'" G. Martelet, *Figures et Parénèse Sacramentelles*, 342 (my translation).

Martelet's use of the term *spiritual exegesis* here is pregnant with meaning. Throughout the 1940s, and again in the wake of *Humani Generis*, "impassioned debate developed in francophone spheres, around the problem of the sense of scripture."[38] De Lubac in particular was suggesting a profound link between spiritual exegesis and the supernatural realities of faith.[39] And, for this reason, von Balthasar was later to describe his spiritual exegesis as "an instrument permitting the discovery of the profound *interconnections* within the history of salvation."[40] This is the point that Martelet is making here about the exegesis of St. Paul in 1 Corinthians. There is a profundity about the interconnections that Paul makes between the Old and New Testament types of baptism and Eucharist which cannot be reduced to "simple equivalence." Because Christ is the means of interconnection or, as Martelet says, the "*accompagnateur*," the figures or types of Scripture function as sacraments that both reveal and conceal him.[41] Essentially, spiritual exegesis is a form of sacramental theology.[42]

38. "Let us recall the essential studies concerning the problem of the spiritual sense: L. Bouyer, *Liturgie et exégèse*, C. Charlier, *La lecture sapientielle de la Bible*; A. M. Dubarle, *Le sens spirituel de l'Ecriture*; J. Daniélou, *Revue des livres: autour de l'exégèse spirituelle*. By Fr. de Lubac himself there appeared at the end of this period four important studies: '*Typologie*' et '*Allégorisme*' in 1947; in 1948, the article from the *Mélanges Cavallera: Sur un vieux distique. La doctrine du quadruple sens*, which was in a sense an anticipation of a larger work on its way: *Exégèse médiévale. Les quatre sens de l'Ecriture* 1959–1964"; see I. de la Potterie, "The Spiritual Sense of Scripture," 746.
39. Some would trace this intuition back as far as *Catholicisme* (1938). See I. de la Potterie, "The Spiritual Sense of Scripture," 741–45; and P. Casarella, "Introduction," in H. de Lubac, *Scripture in the Tradition*, xviii–xix.
40. H. U. von Balthasar and Chantraine, *Le Cardinal de Lubac*, 100.
41. "Ainsi s'intègrent complètement en Saint Paul le contexte sacramentel et le sens du Christ: et le rapport d'ombres à réalités découvert entre le passé de nos pères et le présent de l'Église n'a d'autre center de perspective que le Christ lui-même. C'est ce rapport que saint Paul exprime, selon toute sa complexité, en l'appelant 'spirituel.'" G. Martelet, *Figures et Parénèse Sacramentelles*, 353 (my translation).
42. Cf. S. Wood, *Spiritual Exegesis and the Church*, 141.

The Liturgical Dimensions of Typological Exegesis

So another stage in unravelling this *construction d'un ensemble figuratif* has been reached. Once the parallelisms of the biblical figures have been given a simultaneity in Christ,[43] which reveals them as sacramental, the conviction that these same figures are expressive of a liturgical reality begins to arise. As Daniélou clearly notes in the introduction to his *Bible et Liturgie*: "This biblical symbolism, therefore, constitutes the primitive foundation which gives us the true significance of the sacraments in their original institution. . . . And so their [the Fathers'] sacramental theology must be considered as essentially biblical."[44] It is to this liturgical dimension of the mysterious realities of faith that Martelet turns when he says,

> But, inasmuch as they are "figures," the food and drink of the desert are simply "spiritual" and not specifically eucharistic. Really subject to Christ, they predict, as from the desert, his designs, though not yet within the historical gesture by which Christ will give the bread we break and the cup we bless—his body and blood. Nevertheless, because the food and drink of the desert, especially the manna, are "spiritually" a eucharistic figure, our Fathers marveled at the sight and collected it, in a, so to speak, liturgical manner. This explains the insatiable desire for meditation of Israel, in order to deepen their appreciation of this amazing food. And yet the Fathers who partook of the food and those who reflected on it, could not specify its contents, even after rendering homage and respect to the mystery of the manna. The mystery had to be proclaimed. Thus constant efforts of worship, some from within the rabbinic tradition, mainly concerning the Rock . . . but they went as far as aberration.[45]

43. "Pour en déterminer le sens exact, il nous faut donc voir comment jouent, en ce terme, à fois le rapport de la manne et de l'eau du désert au *Christ* et la rapport de cette manne et de cette eau du désert, au Christ *en fonction de l'Eucharistie*." G. Martelet, *Figures et Parénèse Sacramentelles*, 353–54.

44. "Cette symbolique biblique apparaît donc comme constituant le fond primitif, celui qui nous donne la vraie signification des sacrements dans leur institution originale. . . . Ainsi leur [patristic] théologie sacramentaire peut-elle être considérée comme essentiellement biblique." J. Daniélou, *Bible et Liturgie*, 12; English trans., *The Bible and the Liturgy*.

In his essay translated as "The Banquet of the Poor,"[46] Daniélou asserts that the earliest of typological correspondences to emerge proves to be eschatological, the prophetic books of the Old Testament being a clear example. And this is significant, for, as has already been noted, there is a direct relationship between prophecy and liturgy. An effective way in which Christianity distinguished itself from the religion of Israel was by a rejection of the outer trappings of the Levitical priesthood and an embracing of the purer prophetic "liturgy" of the desert.[47] Thus, in the first place, inner spiritual worship is the means by which continuity is established between the two testaments by the early church. It is because the patriarchs recognised the inner, spiritual significance of the manna that they gathered in a liturgical way to marvel at God's wonders. As it was, the prophetic proclamation itself had a sign value that often gave it a liturgical character. Therefore the "rites," gradually established to celebrate this spiritual worship, take their form from

45. "Mais en tant que 'figuratives,' nourriture et boissons du désert ne sont encore que "spirituelles" et non proprement 'eucharistiques'; réellement assujetties au Christ pour en prophétiser, dès le désert, les desseins, elles ne sont pas encore prises dans le geste historique par lequel le Christ donne désormais, par le pain que nous rompons et la coupe que nous bénissons, et son corps et son sang. Néanmoins c'est parce que la nourriture et la boisson du désert, et spécialement la manne, ont cette spiritualité d'une figure eucharistique, que nos pères s'étonnent en la voyant et la ramassent de façon pour ainsi dire liturgique; c'est pour cela que la méditation inapaisée d'Israël pousse toujours plus loin, toujours plus haut, la description de cette surprenante nourriture. Mais les pères qui mangèrent et ceux qui réfléchirent, tout en rendant hommage par leur respect liturgique et leur méditation incessante, au mystère pressenti de la manne, ne pouvaient en préciser le contenu." G. Martelet, *Figures et Parénèse Sacramentelles*, 357 (my translation).

46. J. Daniélou, "The Banquet of the Poor," in *The Lord of History: Reflections on the Inner Meanings of History* (London: Longmans, 1958), 214–40. This is an augmented English translation of "Les repas de la Bible et leur signification," *La Maison Dieu* 18 (1957): 28–30. This was later collected in J. Daniélou, *Essai sur le Mystère de l'Histoire* (Paris: Éditions du Seuil, 1958).

47. "Come si vede, la nuova *teologia del culto*, che il cristianesimo fonde tutta su una visione interamente "spirituale" del culto stesso, mentre ignora qualunque forma di ritualismo, implica tutta la vita in un clima cultuale, ridonando al fatto religioso un compito di coordinazione totale di tutta l'attività umana. Nel fare questo, la primitiva tradizione cristiana non cessa mai di richiamarsi all'interpretazione 'spirituale' che del culto avevano già dato i profeti, stabilendo così una continuità, sia pure differenziata, nelle rivelazione dei due Testamenti." S. Marsili, *La Liturgia: momento nella storia della salvezza*, 52.

the prophetic gestures by which Christ made himself known to the people of the first covenant. And these look to the forming of a "reciprocal interior tension"[48] with the rites of the new and everlasting covenant. Indeed, it is because the sacramental signs show a reciprocity with the old law that the covenant reveals itself as eternal. What Martelet recognises in St. Paul, then, is the extent to which the Christian present clarifies the biblical past and *vice versa*:[49]

> Hence, once more the necessity of specifying the movement that, in compensation to the movement that leads us by "figures" to our Fathers has, by the same "figures" brought the history of our Fathers to us. Hence also, the necessity to specify, over and over again, that our "present" has come from the "past," albeit in a hidden form. But their past was *real.*—This is particularly obvious in the case of the manna, but equally to some extent, in the water of the rock, in Moses, in the sea, and in the cloud. Hence, again, the role of continuous meditation, with the certitude that one day, things unnoticed will be part of our faith.[50]

Prophetic Signs as Resolution of the Interior Tension of Revelation

St. Augustine's proverbial phrase, "The New Testament is hidden in the Old Testament, and the Old is made manifest in the New,"[51] goes some way to elucidating the mutually enlightening transaction

---

48. "un rapporto di reciproca tensione interiore," Cf. S. Marsili, *La Liturgia: momento nella storia della salvezza*, 52.

49. "Saint Paul éclaire rétrospectivement le passé biblique qui donne ainsi à l'actualité sacramentaire chrétienne sa profondeur figurative passée." G. Martelet, *Figures et Parénèse Sacramentelles*, 358.

50. "De là encore la nécessité de préciser, en contrepartie du mouvement qui nous conduit par les 'figures' vers nos pères, le mouvement qui, par les mêmes 'figures,' a porté leur histoire vers nous. C'est pourquoi il nous a fallu constamment préciser comment notre présent était dans leur passé sous une forme encore cachée et comment cela faisait néanmoins pour eux un passé réel. De là—et la chose est particulièrement sensible dans le cas de la manne, mais vaut de quelque manière pour tout le reste: l'eau du rocher, Moïse, la mer et la nuée—de là, le rôle de la méditation incessante d'Israël qui repose sur la certitude qu'existe dans son histoire un sens encore inaperçu qui demande à venir au jour de la foi." G. Martelet, *Figures et Parénèse Sacramentelles*, 526 (my translation).

51. St. Augustine, *Quaest. In Hept.* 2, 73: PL34, 623.

that exists between the two Testaments. It would seem that Martelet wishes to go further, fighting shy of even the least suggestion of supersessionism. There is no sense in the above quotation from Martelet that the role of the Old Testament in the economy of salvation is merely propaedeutic, or that its narrative is in any way replaced by the proclamation of the gospel: the meditation of Israel is incessantly prophetic, and the memory of the church brings forward from it something totally new.[52] Old Testament types do not retain their significance as constant foils to the full reality, but because they contribute to that fullness constantly and in a cumulative way.[53] It is this successive construction of types that Daniélou describes toward the end of his essay "The Banquet of the Poor." Having carefully unwrapped the "manifold layers of significance" in the scriptural types of the Eucharist, he is struck simultaneously by the radical newness of the action of Christ at the Last Supper, and by a perfect unity between it and all that had gone before:

> And, more than all this, it was not merely a prefiguring but the actual institution of the sacrament of the Eucharist. From this point of view, it was altogether *sui generis*, belonging equally to the earthly life of Christ and to the sacramental life which it inaugurated. Thus it unified in the reality of one historical event all the various planes of our previous discussion: it is, as it were, the central mystery around which the whole biblical significance of the Meal is developed.[54]

52. De Lubac expresses this difficult point well when he says, "This is a '*concordiae consensus*' whose overall affirmation will never again cease, nor will its drive towards verifying, deciphering, or at least illustrating, signifying down to the smallest details, through a second degree of symbolism. To the *sed tunc* and the *nunc autem* of contrast will succeed the *iam tunc* and the *et nunc* of inclusion." H. de Lubac, *Scripture in the Tradition*, 116.

53. In this context it is interesting to note the sense of a cumulative process of significance that is present in the title of Daniélou's work of 1950, *Sacramentum Futuri*, and the loss of this sense in the English translation of 1960, *From Shadows to Reality*.

54. J. Daniélou, "The Banquet of the Poor," 240. Or, as de Lubac clearly describes the same experience, "This is something which makes us appreciate the *distantiam evidentissimam* between the Old Testament and the New. But at the very moment that the gift of the New Testament creates the contrast, it suppresses it. The distance is at once filled in. We find that

Here Daniélou is seeking to specify what Martelet calls the "movement" of "figures." The church moves toward the signs that were her origin, just as those figures move toward their future as sacraments.[55] This dual movement is the single action of revelation.

Sacramental Typology and the Dynamics of Conversion and Initiation

Typology plays a fundamental role within revelation, as it is a means of the transmission of the divine economy. And this "movement" by figures is, as has been seen, not limited to the two Testaments. Typology has a liturgical function also, a function that, as is to be expected of a symbolic reality, is both initiatory and participatory. So during baptismal initiation the *photizomenoi* move from shadows to reality by way of figures and types until the process is completed by the *redditio symboli*.[56] The person of faith stands between type and antitype, between the first Adam and the second, and is at once conscious of both the separation of sin and the unifying force of grace.[57] And so typology cannot remain an objective or extrinsic reality to the believer. For, as Martelet points out, the very fact that typology exposes a spiritual or inner sense mitigates against such distancing:

> Perè Guillet proposed to call the spiritual sense "interior," that dimension whereby the spiritual historical sense, identifiable in typology, becomes

the Old Testament itself has been unified, and the two Testaments together speak with a single voice." H. de Lubac, *Scripture in the Tradition*, 117.

55. For the people of the first covenant, that this "movement" is revelation is unclear. This is why Martelet quotes Dom Gribomont's idea of Israel's "spiritual subconscious." From representative signs, an implicit knowledge of a revelation in progress could be gained, but as Martelet says, this is "a yet unnoticed sense of that which will come on the day of faith." G. Martelet, *Sacrements et Parénèse Sacramentelles*, 526–7.

56. Cf. Ratzinger, *Principles of Catholic Theology*, 108–12; and J. Daniélou, *The Bible and the Liturgy*, 19–54.

57. Cf. J. Daniélou, "Adam and Christ in St. Irenaeus," in *From Shadows to Reality*, 30–47.

in us the principle of personal transformation. Basically, the vocabulary is not so important, provided we grasp, with the author, that the spiritual sense of Scripture implies both an objective consideration of revelation in itself and its transforming influence for holiness in ourselves. These two inseparable aspects of the spiritual sense express the whole *raison d'être* of "figures," regarding not only the future development of revelation but our own progress as well. We sometimes risk neglecting this second aspect and the parenetic intention of Paul. But 1 Corinthians 10 helps bring this issue back to light, showing that "figures" have no aim other than our own conversion.[58]

Because through typology the spiritual sense reveals the hidden mystery of the divine economy, it is by its nature interior.[59] Symbolic or sacramental in structure, typology invites participation and, through its dialogue of signs, leads us to the fullest reality of faith. Through the objective structures of revelation, a personal encounter with the fullness of God's self-expression, Christ, takes place, an encounter that transforms and sanctifies. And the transformation that the individual undergoes is also a typological one, because the process of revelation by which types become sacraments comes to its fullness in us, when, through the grace of conversion, we, like Christ, become sacraments of the Father.[60]

---

58. "Le P. Guillet a proposé d'appeler sens spirituel 'intérieur' cette dimension en vertu de laquelle le sens spirituel historique, qu'on peut identifier au typisme, devient en nous le principe d'une transformation subjective. Peu importe au fond le vocabulaire, pourvu que l'on voie bien avec l'auteur que le sens spirituel de l'Écriture implique à la fois la structure objective de la Révélation *en elle-même* et sa portée transformante de sanctification *en nous*. Ces deux aspects inséparables du sens spirituel expriment la totalité du devoir-être propre aux figures, qui concerne non seulement le devenir objectif de la Révélation pour nous, mais notre propre devenir à nous en elle et par elle. C'est ce second aspect qu'on risqué parfois de négliger et que l'intention parénétique de Saint Paul dans le chapitre X de la première épître aux Corinthiens, permet de remettre fortement en lumière, puisque les figures n'y ont pas d'autre but que notre propre conversion." G. Martelet, *Figures et Parénèse Sacramentelles*, 553 (my translation).

59. See L. Bouyer, "Liturgie et exégèse spirituelle," *La Maison Dieu* 7 (1946): 27–50, and de Lubac, *Scripture in the Tradition*, 17.

60. "The spiritual meaning, understood as figurative or mystical meaning, is the meaning which, objectively, leads us to the realities of the spiritual life and which, subjectively, can only be the fruit of a spiritual life. That is where it leads; for to the extent to which we have not arrived at it, we have not drawn a totally Christian interpretation from the Scriptures. It is certain that the

Embracing the New Theology of the Future

In conclusion, there are some things to be said of Martelet's doctoral study as a whole. Though scripturally based, the work is of an interdisciplinary nature,[61] and there is a sense in which liturgy might be seen as the interpreting element. Martelet's concerns are not theologically abstract, and the system or method of the schools is nowhere in evidence. Broadly, the thesis has an anthropological tone, showing interest in semiology and ritual, but within this, there is a clear christological focus. From the perspectives of both style and content, then, it is possible to say that this work was awake to the shifting sensibilities of preconciliar Catholic theology.[62]

That this work was "new" is evident not only from the particular interests of the supervisors and from a brief glace at the publishing dates of the bibliography, but preeminently because it was part of a contemporary discussion.[63] The second half of the 1940s witnessed a great debate, amongst francophile theologians in particular, on the nature of biblical exegesis in the church.[64] Martelet cites or quotes directly from most of the seminal articles of this debate. Though

Christian mystery is not something to be curiously contemplated like a pure object of science, but is something which must be interiorized and lived. It finds its own fulness in being fulfilled within souls." De Lubac, *Scripture in the Tradition*, 20–21.

61. Apart from the subject matter, this can be inferred from the first and second readers: S. Lyonnet, a Scripture scholar who taught the Pauline corpus, and W. Van Roo, a dogmatician specializing in the sacraments.

62. Cf. J. Komonchak, "Theology and Culture at Mid-Century: The Example of Henri de Lubac," *Theological Studies* 51 (1990): 579–602.

63. The "new" orientation of theology laid much emphasis on biblical renewal and particularly on an interpretation of the Old Testament as prophecy and figure [See J. Daniélou, "Les orientations présentes de la pensée religieuse," *Etudes* 249 (1946): 9]. And that the young directors of this thesis were associated with modern methodologies can be gleaned from the fact that in 1961, the Holy Office informed the Jesuit general that Stanislas Lyonnet was to be removed from the faculty of the Biblical Institute under suspicion of teaching erroneous doctrine. Though the general protested, in June of 1962 both Lyonnet and Maximilian Zerwick were suspended. Xavier Rynne points out that this was all part of a movement of resistance against the *aggiornamento* of biblical and theological studies by a reactionary curia. See X. Rynne, *Letters From Vatican City: Vatican Council II (First Session): Background and Debates* (London: Faber and Faber, 1963), 53.

1943 had witnessed the encouraging tones of *Divino Afflante Spiritu* with regard to Scripture studies, and had seen the formation of *Sources Chrétiennes*, the landscape had changed markedly by the time *Humani Generis* was promulgated in 1950. The "new theology" stood under suspicion, embarassed by the pope's teaching and dismissed by the curia. It was in this atmosphere that Martelet, alumnus of Lyon-Fourvière, began his studies in Rome. Like his former teacher, de Lubac, he could not be unaware that the search for the inner, spiritual meaning of historical realities according to the methods of *ressourcement* was part of a struggle that was not merely academic. The choice of a fresh, scripturally based thesis, free from scholastic technicalities and dry conceptualism, indicates that Martelet sought to be part of all that was new in theology. He, like de Lubac, wanted no part of a theology that, because of its supernatural emphasis, was showing itself to be unconnected to the life of modern humanity.[65] It is not too romantic to suggest that, with this study, Martelet's convictions about the need for theology to be credible to the world came of age.

Joseph Komonchak has described the controversy of the *nouvelle théologie* as "a dress rehearsal for the conciliar drama,"[66] and perhaps this was true for few more than for Martelet. Within five years of completing his doctorate and leaving the Gregorian to teach

---

64. Cf. I. de la Potterie, "The Spiritual Sense of Scripture," 745–48, and M. D'Ambrosio, "Henri de Lubac and the Critique of Scientific Exegesis," *Communio: International Catholic Review* 19 (1992): 365–88.

65. "What a shabby theology it is that treats the object of faith as an object of science, that does not know how to discern religion in its inner and universal reality and so sees it only as a system of truths and precepts, imposing themselves only on the basis of a certain number of facts! It confines dogma to the extremities of knowledge, in a distant province, out of touch with other provinces. It makes dogma a kind of 'superstructure,' believing that, if it is to remain 'supernatural' it must be 'superficial' and thinking that by cutting it off from all human roots, it is making dogma all the more divine. As if God were not the author of both nature and grace, and of nature in view of grace." H. de Lubac, "Apologetics and Theology," in *Theological Fragments* (San Francisco: Ignatius, 1989), 94–95.

66. J. Komonchak, "Theology and Culture at Mid-Century," 580.

fundamental theology in Lyons, he witnessed the opening of the Second Vatican Council. One can only wonder as to his thoughts as he listened to *Gaudet Mater Ecclesia*, the opening speech of John XXIII, which Giuseppe Alberigo later described as an unbroken reflection upon the historical conditioning of Christianity.[67] Still in France, he followed the debates of the first sessions and heard the Council's Message to the World, which had been drafted by Marie-Dominic Chenu:

> The decisions of the Council should be preceded by a broad declaration in which the plan of salvation is proclaimed in the language of the gospel and in the prophetic perspectives of the Old and New Testaments. . . . A declaration addressed to a human race whose greatness and misery, beneath the failures and errors, represent a longing for the light of the gospel.[68]

Surely, within these words by which the Council began to take direction, and as the initial schemata of the curia were rejected by the Fathers, Martelet began to see the realization of that "new theology" that he had tried to embrace in humble measure with *Figures et Parénèse Sacramentelles*. The Council's program of *aggiornamento* was beginning to be shaped by the fruits of the *ressourcement*.

With the pontificate of John XXIII and the lifting of the antimodernist campaign, fresh hope was brought to the new theology that was still feeling bruised by *Humani Generis*.[69] Many

---

67. G. Alberigo, "Cristianesimo e Storia nel Vaticano II," *Cristianesimo nella storia* 5 (1984): 584. Cf. also G. Ruggieri, "Faith and History," in *The Reception of Vatican II*, ed. G. Alberigo, J.-P. Jossua, and J. Komonchak (Washington, DC: Catholic University of America Press, 1987), 91–114, especially 95–98.

68. See A. Duval, "Le message au monde," in *Vatican II commence . . . Approches Francophones*, ed. É. Fouilloux (Leuven: Peeters, 1993), translated in *History of Vatican II*, vol. 2: *The Formation of The Council's Identity, First Period and Intercession, October 1962–September 1963*, ed. G. Alberigo and J. Komonchak (Leuven: Peeters, 1996), 54.

69. See G. Weigel, "The Historical Background of the Encyclical *Humani Generis*," *Theological Studies* 12 (1951): 208–30, especially 219–21.

regarded as its protagonists were brought to Rome as *periti*, and the pope announced that it was the duty of the church not only to guard the deposit of faith but "to leap forward toward a doctrinal penetration and a formation of consciences."[70] Freed from the rigid neo-scholasticism that those suspicious of all intercourse with modernity had imposed, the new theologians were willing collaborators with *aggiornamento*. As George Lindbeck, a Lutheran observer at Vatican II, remembers,

> The *ressourcement* and *aggiornamento* people at the Council thought of themselves as collaborators. *Ressourcement* and *aggiornamento* were understood to be two dimensions of the same reality. But the dimension labelled "*aggiornamento*" could be used in a programme of accommodation to the world, rather than one of an opening to the modern world; and when that happened, *aggiornamento* fell into opposition to *ressourcement*.[71]

In such a spirit were the dominant themes of the Council formed, and by means of such a spirit did Martelet make the leap from his doctoral studies to *Les idées maîtresses de Vatican II*.

Gaining Focus from the Council:
Les Idées Maîtresses de Vatican II

Gustave Martelet was called to Rome in 1963 to be the theological advisor of the recently named bishop of Fort Archambault (Chad). Gradually, his role was to expand to take in most of the French-speaking bishops of Equatorial Africa. But as the second session began, there was much uncerainty as to the future. This was a delicate

---

70. See John XXIII, *Gaudet Mater Ecclesia*, as quoted in Alberigo and Komonchak, *History of Vatican II*, 2:17.
71. G. Weigel, "Re-Viewing Vatican II: An Interview with George A. Lindbeck," *First Things* 48 (1994): 48.

period of transition, and many wondered how the Council would proceed under Paul VI, and whether the policy of *aggiornamento*, so dear to his predecessor, would be upheld by the new pope. Though many felt Montini to be John XXIII's favoured choice, and though he had himself voiced full acceptance of the pastoral aims of the Council, a change was inevitable. As Congar wrote in his Council Diary,

> During the last three weeks there has been much speculation as to whether the new pope would follow in the footsteps of John XXIII. Would he be of the same mind? Impossible to be exactly the same; John XXIII had a style, a manner which was the man himself, rather than a policy of ideas. No one else can be wholly John XXIII and have the same intuitions from the heart as he did, since he created them in harmony with the rhythm of his own life. Cardinal Montini, now Paul VI, is a man of quite superior intellect, with great personal authority and ability to work, remarkably well informed.[72]

Aggiornamento had been an intuition of the heart of John XXIII: a personal manner rather than an idea. In Paul VI, "whose name alone is indicative of a whole policy,"[73] that intuition was to be shaped by ideas—the ideas of *ressourcement* and the *nouvelle théologie*.[74] These, as Martelet was about to see, were to become *les idées maîtresses de Vatican II*.

---

72. Y.-M. Congar, *Report from Rome II: The Second Session of the Council* (London: Chapman, 1964), 21; French orig., *Vatican II, Le Concile au Jour le Jour, Deuxième Session* (Paris: Éditions du Cerf, 1964). See also Alberigo and Komonchak, *History of Vatican II*, 2:578–84.

73. Y.-M Congar, *Report from Rome*, 19.

74. R. Latourelle provides an interesting insight into the contrasting intuitions and ideas of the two popes: "Un texte concret, à savoir une lettre du 18 octobre 1962, adressée au Secrétaire d'État et reproduite dans la *Nouvelle Revue théologique* de juin 1985, illustre avec quelle lucidité le cardinal Montini envisageait la marche du Concile. Dans cette lettre, il observe que le Concile manqué d'efficacité parce qu'il manqué de 'structure organique.' Il disait: 'La matière qui a été préparée ne semble pas prendre une figure architecturale harmonieuse et unifiée, ni atteindre la hauteur d'un phare projetant sa lumière sur le temps et le monde.' . . . Cette lettre, d'une remarquable lucidité, assume les préoccupations essentielles de Jean XXIII, mais en même temps les structure. Effectivement, le Concile suivra cet ordre. Paul VI a donc reconnu l'opportunité et la grandeur de l'initiative de Jean XXIII." R. Latourelle, *L'Infini du sens*, 117–118.

The Spirit of *Aggiornamento*

That the feature that distinguished the two pontificates of the Council was their judgment of the meaning and value of the assembly in relation to an *aggiornamento* of the church goes largely without question.[75] Yet what is distinctive about the individual interpretations of the popes is more difficult to judge. Some have noted a marked change in the interpretation of *aggiornamento* in the later stages of the Council, and, linking this with remarks that Paul VI made at the final session and subsequently, have called into question his commitment to the vision of John XXIII.[76] Yet in essence, Paul VI merely echoes and restyles John XXIII's intentions,[77] indicating, as John had done, that *aggiornamento* is not the free and unruly task of modernization but one contained by the parameters of the content of the faith. The new pope, however, is more aware of the emerging consonance between *aggiornamento* and *ressourcement*, and for him the former has no meaning for the church outside the latter. So,

75. See G. Alberigo and J. Komonchak, *History of Vatican II*, 1: 72; D. Menozzi, "Opposition to the Council, 1966–84," in Alberigo, Jossua, and Komonchak, *The Reception of Vatican II*, 333; G. Ruggieri, "Faith and History," in Alberigo, Jossua, and Komonchak, *The Reception of Vatican II*, 91–114, especially 91–102. In *Les idées maîtresses de Vatican II*, Martelet quotes R. Laurentin as saying: "La différence est dans le style des deux papes successifs, l'un plus intuitif, et l'autre plus réflexif. L'un caractérisé par la bonhomie, l'optimisme, un don pour créer la confiance et l'euphorie, le goût de les susciter, et jusqu'à une certaine manière de 'jouer' avec les affaires sérieuses, qui décourageait toute tentation de critiquer. L'autre, caractérisé par une exigeante lucidité, par le mépris du camouflage et des satisfactions à bon marché, par la conscience aiguë des fardeaux et des difficultés." R. Laurentin, *Bilan de la 3e session* (Paris: Seuil, 1965), 296, in G. Martelet, *Les idées maîtresses de Vatican II*, 74.

76. See especially E. Schillebeeckx, *Vatican II: The Real Achievement* (London: Sheed and Ward, 1967), 83, English trans. of *Het tweede Vaticaans Concilie* (Bilthoven: Uitgeverij H. Nelissen, 1966); and also R. Laurentin, "Paul VI et l'après concile," in *Paul VI et la modernité dans l'Église* (Rome: Ecole Française de Rome–Palais Farnèse, 1984), 569–601.

77. Faithfulness to authentic doctrine newly expressed to meet the current needs of the world was exactly the message of *Gaudet Mater Ecclesia*, and yet it is correct to discern a change of emphasis in Paul VI's later speeches. Cf. *Gaudet Mater Ecclesia* in *The Documents of Vatican II*, ed. W. Abbot (London: Chapman, 1966), 710–19.

interpreting a speech of Cardinal Montini, made at the end of the first session, Bishop Christopher Butler says,

> The pastoral aim, the instinct of a charity that goes beyond all boundaries, the sense of mission not so much to human nature or the abstract human species, but to human persons and the actually existing human family, demanded that our *aggiornamento* be conceived in depth. The consequent need to discriminate between what the Church must always be, what the gospel for ever is, and the contingent elements in which, at any given moment, the Church presents herself in history, was driving the Council to some criterion. And this drive took her gaze ever backwards, behind the counter-revolutionary Church, behind the Counter-Reformation, behind the mediaeval synthesis, back to the Church before the estrangement of East and West, to the Church before the confrontation with Greek culture and philosophy, to the primal source: to Christ in Palestine.[78]

Looking back, after the Council had closed, and recalling the beginnings of his own involvement at the start of the second session, Martelet remembers how this "drive" toward purpose and definition took shape within his own thoughts and attitudes as he witnessed the unfolding debates. Gradually, *aggiornamento* took definition for him personally, and he began to appreciate the spirit of what people would later call the theology of Vatican II:

> All were left with the sense that *aggiornamento* or openness was a fundamental concept against which the hoped-for goals and unavoidable gaps of the Council could be evaluated. This method, while it was welcoming of deep views, did not exclude another procedure, without which the opening up of certain fresh ideas might have been neglected. These imposed themselves as three convergent aspects on my spirit, around which crowded many other elements that in a surer moment the Council would face. The object of these reflections was more precisely established, since my initial impressions were not refuted by the bishops to whom I expounded the first systematization of my

---

78. C. Butler, "The Aggiornamento of Vatican II," in *Vatican II: An Interfaith Appraisal*, ed. J. Miller (Notre Dame, IN: University of Notre Dame, 1966), 3–13, 10.

thoughts. The attention shown by the most diverse hearers, running from the most hardworking scholar to the Carmelites, confirmed in me the idea, at first fleeting, that the general public would also perhaps be interested in that which little by little came to be known as the main ideas of the Council.[79]

The three convergent elements of *aggiornamento* that Martelet is speaking of here have been detailed earlier as inner personal renewal, the spiritual reordering of ideas and conduct, and the active relation of the articles of faith with the needs of the world.[80] These come together and are expressed in a single drive that could be termed "the recovery of initial inspiration,"[81] and it is for this reason that, though the overriding approach may be retrospective, the thrust is undoubtedly forward. It is because of the unified impulse of these three convergent criteria that the work of the Council began to take shape, and it was against these that its progress could be judged. In the same way we might evaluate the shape of Martelet's own work, mapping as it does the development of the Council's theological approach. Divided into three major sections, "A Renewed Examination of the Sources," "The Paradoxical Union of Opposites,"

79. "Tous partaient de l'idée, bien centrale il est vrai, d'*aggiornamento* ou de celle d'ouverture, pour mesurer l'acquis et constater les inévitables lacunes. La méthode conduisait à quelques vues profondes. Elle n'était pas exclusive d'une autre, qui, sans négliger l'idée d'*aggiornamento* et d'ouverture, ne partirait pourtant pas d'elle. . . . Trois points de vue convergents s'imposèrent alors à mon esprit, autour desquels tant de choses se regroupèrent qu'il me sembla avoir, dans le Concile, discerné un visage. Cette impression n'ayant pas été dementie par les évêques à qui je communiquais le premier état de ces pensées, je me décidai à en préciser encore l'objet. L'intérêt rencontré auprès d'auditeurs aussi divers que le sont des étudiants et des carmélites, me confirma dans l'idée, d'abord fugitive, que le grand public lui aussi s'intéresserait peut-être à ce que j'ai décidé peu à peu d'appeler *les idées maîtresses de Vatican II*." G. Martelet, *Les idées maîtresses de Vatican II*, 10–11 (my translation).

80. "Mais ce qui est arrivé au Concile, cette decision de refonte de soi-même, ce réajustement spirituel de ses idées, de ses comportements, en fonction des données de la foi et des besoins du monde, bref cet *aggiornamento* ou cette conversion, cette fidélité et ce renouvellement, tout ceci doit devenir le bien commun de toute l'Église et trouver en chacun de nous son exacte et profonde réplique." G. Martelet, "Introduction," in ibid., 9. Cf. also J. Ratzinger, *The Principles of Catholic Theology*, 371.

81. C. Butler, "The Aggiornamento of Vatican II," 10.

and "The Spiritual Renewal of Signs," *Les idées maîtresses de Vatican II* echoes structurally the development of the three elements of *aggiornamento*; a return to the sources of revelation leads to a reordering of ideas and conduct, which in turn contributes to a renewal in the way these ideas are transmitted.[82] But, as Martelet says, these procedures should not be thought of as essentially concerned with the texts of the Council—what is happening here is a spiritual conversion of the whole church and of her members. A return to the sources of the Christian life seeks to resolve that which is paradoxical and contrary in life, and this in turn allows for a more effective witnessing to the gospel.[83] This spirit is what comes to inspire the written texts of the various constitutions and decrees.

Returning to the Sources of Renewal

In his preamble to the opening section, "A Return to the Sources," Martelet indicates something of the climate that gave rise to the "new theology." Highlighting the Counter-Reformation and the anti-Modernist campaign as major influences on the rigid and impoverished reading of St. Thomas that persisted in the schools, Martelet speaks of the fear and suspicion with which the sources of renewal were regarded.[84] But he speaks too of the enthusiastic openness of the Council toward the very ideas that had been so

82. It should be noted that *ressourcement* was also a key force in the Catholic reform of the fifteenth and sixteenth centuries: the great cry *ad fontes*, together with the notion of *ecclesia semper reformanda*—or in more current terms, *aggiornamento* were no recent innovation.

83. "Les *sources* dont il s'agit ici sont celles de la foi, les *contraires* représentent les points de vue apparemment contradictoires dont le Concile a opéré la synthèse, les *signes* sont le langage que l'Église de Vatican II entend tenir au monde pour être mieux compris de lui." G. Martelet, "Introduction," in *Les idées maîtresses de Vatican II*, 11.

84. For a fuller analysis of this period, see T. Denman, "Tentatives françaises pour un renouvellement de la théologie," *Revue de l'Université d'Ottawa*, Section Spéciale 20 (1950): 129–67; and T. Schoof, *A Survey of Catholic Theology 1800–1970* (New York: Paulist, 1970), 157–227.

recently condemned. This meant that the major ideas of Vatican II were in no way spontaneously generated at the discussion tables of the various commissions, but resulted from a theology that had been the long-suffering work of many before the Council began.

Comment has already been made about the ways in which Martelet's theological concerns in *Figures et Parénèse Sacramentelles* corresponded with the wider exegetical and theological interests of the *nouvelle théologie*. During the course of the second session of the Council, it is exactly these common perspectives and aims that start to give shape to the developing theology of Vatican II. The principles of spiritual exegesis, to which the new theologians had returned, provide an "intellectual framework"[85] for the current questions of theology. The orienting force of such a "framework" was brought home personally for Martelet the first time he saw the gospel enthroned and proclaimed in the Council Assembly, and that followed by the recitation of the creed. Here the *ensemble figuratif* that had occupied both himself and the early Fathers was actualized before him, and he saw a real unity of enterprise: "L'Évangile, la foi, le concile, tout ne forma alors qu'un tout à la gloire de Dieu et au service spirituel du monde: ce jour-là, à cette heure, j'eus vraiment l'impression d'avoir *vu* le concile."[86]

It is for this reason that Martelet sees the decision of the bishops to commence their discussions with the liturgy as providential. Indeed, he considers this choice to be consonant with the formation of the deposit of faith, and so in some senses to have been made a long time previously.[87] The liturgy is both the source of faith and the means

---

85. S. Wood, *Spiritual Exegesis and the Church*, 1.

86. "L'Évangile, la foi, le concile, tout ne forma alors qu'un tout à la gloire de Dieu et au service spirituel du monde: ce jour-là, à cette heure, j'eus vraiment l'impression d'avoir *vu* le concile." G. Martelet, *Les idées maîtresses de Vatican II*, 24.

87. "Le choix en fait allait plus loin. Pour un Concile, soucieux avant tout de vitalité spirituelle et de transmission pastorale de la foi, la liturgie était vraiment première et elle *devait* l'être." Ibid., 28–9.

of its pastoral transmission, therefore it is aptly discussed first. It is in the liturgy that the people of God hear the word and come into communion with the Lord sacramentally; hence, the liturgy may be regarded as the place of both catechetical initiation and encounter.[88]

> Together with Sacred Scripture, the liturgy was centered around the word and action of the Fathers of the church. Around their action, because they had no other objective save the sacramental initiation of people into Jesus Christ; around their word, insofar as they never initiated Christians to the sacramental life of the church without instructing them in the mysteries of faith and the meaning of the sacraments. The Fathers were ever the faithful servants of the table of the word and the table of the Eucharist—liturgy *par excellence*—which the Council recalls twice in *Dei verbum* (21 & 26). If we look through a volume of sermons by the great Pope St. Leo in *Sources Chrétiennes*, we will see that the liturgical season is a recurring theme of his preaching, continually repeated and updated. A hundred years earlier, in the fourth century, the main activity of Cyril of Jerusalem was catechesis. Throughout the paschal season, he instructed his catechumens, and through them all Christians, on the life-giving mysteries of the faith.[89]

What became clear to the Council fathers, as they worked on the Dogmatic Constitution *Dei Verbum* in the light of *Sacrosanctum Concilium*, was the fact that, essentially, theology is a reflection on the

---

88. "Cette double certitude, que la liturgie est le lieu par excellence où s'éduque la foi et que le mystère du Christ rendu plus accessible au-dedans devient par le fait même plus rayonnant au-dehors, cette double certitude est bien celle des Pères de l'Église, dont la pratique et dont l'esprit resurgirent au Concile, à propos de la Liturgie." Ibid., 29–30.

89. "Avec l'Écriture et inséparablement d'elle, la liturgie était le centre de la parole et de l'action des Pères de L'Église. De leur action, car ils n'avaient d'autre but que l'initiation sacramentelle des hommes à Jésus-Christ; de leur parole aussi, dans la mesure où ils n'initiaient jamais les chrétiens à la vie sacramentelle, sans les éclairer en même temps sur les mystères de foi que les sacraments signifient. Toujours les Pères se montrèrent serviteurs empressés de cette double table de la Parole et de l'Eucharistie—cette liturgie par excellence!—qu'évoque par deux fois le Concile (*DV* 21 et 26). Que l'on parcoure dans les *Sources Chrétiennes* un volume des sermons du Pape saint Léon et l'on verra que le temps liturgique fournit l'objet constant d'une predication sans cesse reprise et rénouvée. Cent ans plus tôt, au IVe siècle, un saint Cyrille de Jérusalem faisait de la catéchèse son activité principale. Au rythme du temps pascal il expliquait à ses catechumens et, à travers eux, à tous les chrétiens, les mystères vivifiants de l'institution de la foi." Ibid., 26–27 (my translation).

unifying role of Christ within the economy of salvation. The unity that Scripture reveals as promise and fact is operative in the liturgy as sacramental proclamation and actualization; hence the Council's insistence on the unity of the two tables of revelation, especially within the liturgical assembly. There is defined here an inextricable unity between Scripture and the liturgy, which the fathers of the church explained as the latter giving the form of a salvific and participatory event to the communicated word of God. In this sense, Martelet agrees with Marsili that liturgy is "first theology," because it represents the primary moment in which the faith is expressed in concrete theological language, and where it is transformed into a way of life that can be shared. So the reflections of the Fathers on the liturgy make clear its nature as a moment in the sacramental economy of salvation that is open to participation now.[90]

The Liturgy as Abiding and Immediate Source

By referring to the sermons of Pope St. Leo the Great, Martelet is careful to reject any sense of a timelessness in the liturgy. Liturgical time effects entry into a mysterious yet objectively real plain, into which has passed "all that was visible in our Redeemer."[91] The

90. Marsili's understanding of the status of the liturgy as primary theology, and of the way in which the liturgy effects humanity's participation in the salvific action of Christ, can be seen in the following: "Alla liturgia non basta una cristologia che sia un qualunque discorso su Cristo fatto *agli* uomini. Essendo la liturgia comunicazione della realtà di Cristo *negli* uomini, e cioè mistero di salvezza concreta per l'uomo concreto d'oggi, la nuova cristologia diventerà apporto vero per una liturgia viva e attuale se nello studio del Cristo approfondirà sempre più la conoscenza del suo 'essere per' secondo una dimensione di 'storicità' piena e totale per quanto riguarda il rapporto Cristo-uomo, in modo che Cristo sia visto sempre più inserito nella vicenda storica dell'uomo di oggi. Solo così contribuirà a che anche la celebrazione liturgica non si muova su un piano di 'atemporalità'; sarebbe un rito di salvezza oggettivamente valido, ma insieme incapace a trasmettere la medesima salvezza all'uomo, perché la salvezza non verrebbe inserita nel tempo reale dell'uomo." S. Marsili, "Cristologia e liturgia. Panorama storico liturgico," in AA. VV., *Cristologia e liturgia—Atti della VIII settimana di studio dell'associazione professori di liturgia: Costabissara (Vicenza) 27–31 agosto 1979*, Studi di liturgia, 8 (Bologna: EDB, 1980), 17–64, 62–63.

location of the sacraments within the economy of salvation, which had been the work of his doctoral thesis, allows certain conclusions to be made about the immediacy of God's self-manifestation in the liturgy. They are conclusions that derive from a cross-referencing of *Sacrosanctum Concilium* and *Dei Verbum*, the two constitutions that Martelet quotes from in this section. What the sacramental catechesis of the mystagogic Fathers teaches is that if "God chose to reveal himself and to make known the hidden purpose of his will" then that "work of our redemption" is best revealed and exercised in the liturgy. Yet such a conclusion invites the question of how Christ's saving activity is actualized in the present moment.

> The church, like Christ himself, can be understood only in function of its relationship to the Holy Spirit. The Council, in its Constitution, *Dei verbum*, noted that "Sacred Scripture must be read and interpreted with its divine authorship in mind" (*DV* 12), and it also mentions in its *Constitution on the Sacred Liturgy* that "the celebration of the Eucharist, where the victory and triumph of Christ over death are represented, is done through the operation of the Holy Spirit." We can therefore conclude that the Holy Spirit was present at the Council, just as he is in reality, as the one who initiates all the new *beginnings* of Christ, whether in the flesh, from his birth to his resurrection, or in the church at Pentecost; in Scripture through divine inspiration or in the sacraments,

---

91. Cf. Leo the Great, Sermon 74, 2: PL 54, 398. Hans Urs von Balthasar gives a very helpful explanation of this dynamic in his book *A Theology of History*: "The life of Christ, as was said, is the 'world of ideas' for the whole of history. He himself is the Ideal made concrete, personal, historical: *universale concretum et personale*. There is no moment at which he is a *universale ante rem*, an essence *preceding* existence, insofar as the *res* is his own historical and temporal existence. He is *universale in re*, the supra-temporal *in* time, the universally valid *in* the here and now, necessary being *in* concrete fact; in the thirty-three years of his life the accent is on the *res*, and during the Forty Days on the *universale*. And it is only as this *universale in re* that he becomes, in relation to the time of Promise, a kind of *universale post rem*, supplying the meaning after the event, and to the time of the Church and the individual Christian a kind of *universale ante rem*; both of these being inseparable from the *universale in re* of the Incarnation in its fulness. The *abstractio* involved is nothing other than the Holy Spirit [mentioned at the beginning of this chapter]. But he carries it out (since thus alone can it be the truth: cf. 1 Jn 2:22) in a continual '*conversio ad phantasma*' a continual reconversion to the sensible reality of the Gospel." H. U. von Balthasar, *A Theology of History* (San Francisco: Ignatius, 1994), 92–93.

particularly in the Eucharist, through his hidden action. The risen Christ communicates with the church and exists himself only through the power of the Holy Spirit.[92]

In the introductory section of *Les idées maîtresses de Vatican II*, Martelet noted that a consequence of *aggiornamento* would be the exposure of "inevitable lacunae"[93] in existing theological formulations. Therefore, when, toward the end of the first session, Bishop Emile Josef de Smedt of Bruges, gave in effect a charter of renewal as he criticized the schema *De Ecclesia*, he exposed the absence of a pneumatological element in the Council's ecclesiology.[94] The inspiration and sustaining force of renewal would be a new breath of the Spirit, or, as John XXIII was to say in the speech that closed this session, "a new Pentecost."[95] In seeking to overcome the besetting dangers of triumphalism, clericalism, and juridicism, the Council was to make an important contribution to the theology of the Spirit.

Appreciating the Work of the Spirit

Indicative of the approach of the Council is Martelet's statement, "The Church, like Christ, cannot be understood except in relation

---

92. "L'Église comme le Christ ne se comprend que par rapport à l'Esprit-Saint. Si l'on ajoute que le Concile dans la Constitution *Dei Verbum* a eu soin de noter que 'la Sainte Écriture doit être lue et interprétée à la lumière du même Esprit qui la fit rédiger' (*DV* 12), et qu'il n'avait pas manqué de dire non plus dans la *Constitution sur la Liturgie*, que 'la celebration de l'Eucharistie, où la victoire et le triomphe du Christ sur la mort sont représentés, se fait par la vertu du Saint-Esprit' (§ 6.), on pourra conclure que l'Esprit-Saint apparaît au Concile, ainsi qu'il l'est en réalité, comme l'initiateur de tous les *commencements* du Christ, soit en la chair, de la naissance à la Résurrection, soit en l'Église à la Pentecôte, soit en la Sainte Écriture par l'inspiration, soit dans les sacrements et notamment dans l'Eucharistie par le secret de sont action. Le Ressuscité ne se communiqué à l'Église, Il n'existe lui même que dans l'activité permanente de l'Esprit." G. Martelet, *Les idées maîtresses de Vatican II*, 53 (my translation).

93. "Les inévitables lacunes," ibid., 10.

94. Cf. Rynne, *Letters from Vatican City*, 217–19.

95. See ibid., 273–79, 276.

to the Holy Spirit." That is to say, interest in the Holy Spirit at Vatican II is relative to its christological, even ecclesiological focus.[96] The salvation history approach favored by the fathers is, in fact, an examination of the divine economy in terms of the Trinity. Though this is clearly shown by the much-quoted second paragraph of *Dei Verbum*,[97] it cannot be said that the role of the Holy Spirit receives extensive treatment at the Council. And so rejoicing at what is perhaps a more limited pneumatology than he would like, Martelet nevertheless emphasizes the particular role of the Spirit in the plan of salvation. Christ is the sole Savior, the Word of God who is the fullness of revelation, and yet the revealing of the "secret" hidden for all ages is accomplished in Christ and the church through the Spirit. "Hence ecclesiology is to be conceived in terms of the mission of the Son and the Holy Spirit (*Lumen Gentium* 14)."[98] The work of the Spirit in the economy is that of universalization and interiorization, and in that sense it is metahistorical. As John Zizioulas says, the role of the Spirit

is to liberate the Son and the economy from the bondage of history. If the Son dies on the cross, thus succumbing to the bondage of historical

96. For some explanation of the Council's christocentric agenda, see T. Citrini, "The Principle of 'Christocentrism' and its Role in Fundamental Theology," in *Problems and Perspectives of Fundamental Theology*, ed. R. Latourelle and G. O'Collins (New York: Press, 1982), 168–85. Since the Council, Y.-M. Congar in particular has pointed out the inherent problems in an ecclesiology that is predominantly or exclusively focused on Christ. In the postconciliar period, many of the pneumatological insights of Vatican II have been taken up more thoroughly. See Congar, "Pneumatologie et 'christomonisme' dans la tradition latine," *Ephemerides Theologicae Louvanienses* 45 (1969): 394–416; Y. M. Congar, *I Believe in the Holy Spirit*, 3 vols. (New York: Seabury, 1983); H. Küng, *The Church* (New York: Sheed and Ward, 1967), 150–202; W. Kasper and G. Sauter, *Kirche-Ort des Geistes* (Freiburg: Herder, 1976).

97. "Placuit Deo in sua bonitate et sapientia seipsum revelare et notum facere sacramentum voluntatis suae (cf. Eph 1:19), quo homines per Christum, Verbum carnem factum in Spiritu sancto accessum habent ad Paterem et divinae naturae consortes efficiuntur." ("In his goodness and wisdom, God chose to reveal Himself and to make known to us the hidden purpose of His will (cf. Eph 1:9) by which through Christ, the Word made flesh, man has access to the Father in the Holy Spirit and comes to share in the divine nature.") *DV* 2 [*972].

98. K. Rahner, "Church," in *Encyclopaedia of Theology: The Concise Sacramentum Mundi*, ed. K. Rahner (New York: Crossroad, 1991), 210.

existence, it is the Spirit that raises him from the dead (Rm 8:11). The Spirit is beyond history, and when he acts in history he does so in order to bring into history the last days, the *eschaton* (Acts 2:17).[99]

This liberation is a "dilation of history and time to the infinite dimensions of the *eschata*,"[100] which Martelet calls the "amplification" of the gospel in every age.[101] Thus the Spirit acts: from the words spoken through the prophets to the word proclaimed in the liturgical assembly, from the Word made flesh in a stable at Bethlehem to the Word made flesh on the altar at the Eucharist. Though the Holy Spirit is "the promoter of all these beginnings" in making the association between the inspiration of the Scriptures and the eucharistic epiclesis, thus reiterating the unity that exists between the two tables of the word, Martelet draws attention to the work of actualization that is particular to the Spirit. This work is apparent in the sacraments, particularly the Eucharist.

The Sacramental Unity That the Spirit Brings

In suggesting that the presence of sin in the church is related to a certain denial of the role of the Holy Spirit in the divine economy, Martelet opens up one of the more interesting ideas to have emerged from the Council. For if the work of the Third Person of the Trinity is to actualize in history the wonders of the kingdom, then it is the Spirit's function to symbolize or make incarnate that kingdom in the world.[102] To frustrate the work of the Spirit is to frustrate the

---

99. J. Zizioulas, *Being as Communion: Studies in Personhood and the Church,* 2nd. ed. (Crestwood, NY: St. Vladimir's Seminary Press, 1993), 130.
100. Ibid., 22.
101. "Une telle synthèse, montrant comment, de la Pentecôte à la Parousie, l'Esprit-Saint déploie l'ampleur évangélique et salutaire, sacramentelle et intérieure, eschatologique et trinitaire de ses dons, représente très bien ce que nous appelons la résurgence doctrinale de l'Esprit-Saint au Concile." G. Martelet, *Les idées maîtresses de Vatican II*, 54.

sacramental signification of God's glory in the church and the world. So Francesco Lambiasi shows how the prevailing sins of the church described by Bishop De Smedt (triumphalism, clericalism, juridicism) deny the role of the Holy Spirit and therefore impede the sign quality of the church.

> In identifying the Church with Christ and the kingdom of God, triumphalism overlooks the fact that, whereas at the redemption the Word acted through a human nature free from sin, now, in the era of the Church, he works with his Spirit through people marked by and subject to sin. Then, clericalism puts the person appointed to an office in the foreground as protagonist of salvation, and not Christ glorious and present in the Spirit. Lastly, legalism so stresses the ecclesiastical institution as to throw the interior working of the Spirit into the shade, who alone can make an act done by the Church a saving event.[103]

And yet to some extent, and paradoxically, it is between the poles of holiness and sin that the sign of the church is established with the dynamism of a sacrament. The Spirit, as source of holiness, is protagonist of the saving events of God, and his actions take shape sacramentally because of the sinful nature of humanity and the world. The paradigm of this economy is the incarnation, where Christ, in order to become the effective sacrament of our salvation, takes upon himself that which is sin.[104] As Martelet points out,

---

102. For a fuller explanation of the Holy Spirit's symbolizing role, see R. Haight, "The Case for Spirit Christology," *Theological Studies* 53 (1992): 257–87.

103. F. Lambiasi, "Holy Spirit," in *Dictionary of Fundamental Theology*, ed. R. Latourelle and R. Fisichella (New York: Crossroads, 1995), 455–62, 455.

104. "This sublime combination of 'opposites' by which the Incarnation is defined, is obviously paradoxical. That union depends solely on the power of God who, in his love for us makes the Son of God, a son of man, so that the sons of men can become sons of God. But if, forgetting that God is at work in Christ, man relates to the Lord in the sole light of reason, subject to sin, he is going to discover that a union which in itself is a divine, and adorable synthesis of 'opposites,' is contradictory, and therefore unacceptable." ("Cette sublime union des contraires qui définit l'Incarnation est évidemment paradoxale. Elle repose, en effet, sur la seule puissance de Dieu qui, dans son amour pour nous, fait du Fils de Dieu un fils de l'homme pour que les fils de l'homme deviennent Fils de Dieu. Mais si, oubliant que Dieu Lui-même est à l'œuvre dans le Christ, l'homme se met à regarder le Seigneur à la seule lumière d'une raison que les préjugés du péché enténèbrent, il va trouver *contradictoire* et donc inacceptable, une union qui n'est pourtant

Without abolishing our freedom, it always transcends a part of our misdeeds, to prove to the world that the church is the objective emergence of the universal sacrament of salvation. So it is that Christ in the sacramentality of the church is bound forever to the fragility of its contrary so as to communicate to some the life that must tansform all.. The sacramentality of the church expresses the inalienable character of holiness that sin yet always frustrates. For "if the Church on earth is endowed already with a sanctity that is real, it is still imperfect" (*LG* 48).[105]

In seeking a spiritual renewal of signs, such as we see in this interpretation of the sign of the holiness of the church the Second Vatican Council was keen to respond to a deep desire in the people of the modern age to be convinced of the reality of God's action in the world. A church that shows herself to be in continuity with the everlasting covenant of Christ by proclamation of the gospel and celebration of the sacraments is one such sign. And yet it is only a partially effective sign, because, as Martelet asks in *Sainteté de l'Église et vie religieuse*,

What point would there be in infallibly guaranteeing the gospel; in the sacraments, the pastoral conduct of God's people, if nothing resulted therefrom on the part of the Church? If no one ever lived the Christ-life, would we know that he had given himself? A gift attains its end only by arousing the loving response for which it was given.[106]

rien d'autre qu'une divine et adorable synthèse de *contraires*.") G. Martelet, *Les idées maîtresses de Vatican II*, (my translation) 72.

105. "Sans abolir nos libertés, il transcende toujours une part de leurs méfaits, en vue d'assurer dans le monde l'émergence objective du *signe* du salut. Le Christ, dans la sacramentalité de l'Église, se lie donc à tout jamais à la fragilité de ses contraires pour communiquer par quelques-uns, la Vie qui doit nous transfigurer tous. La sacramentalité de l'Église exprime donc le caractère *inaliénable* d'une sainteté que le péché pourtant toujours *altère*. Car si, dans l'Église de l'histoire, la sainteté, comme dit le Concile (cf. *LG*, 48, 3), est déjà *signifiée*, elle n'y est pas encore accomplie." Ibid., 101 (my translation). Cf. also G. Martelet, "De la sacramentalité propre à l'Église," *Nouvelle Revue Théologique* 95 (1973): 25–42.

106. G. Martelet, *The Church's Holiness and Religious Life* (Baltimore: Waverly, 1966), 15; French orig., *Sainteté de l'Église et vie religieuse* (Toulouse: Éditions Prière et Vie, 1964).

The Signs of the Spirit:
Credible Invitations to Faith

Thus the renewal of signs involves their amplification from monologue to dialogue for, if the gift of holiness that the Spirit communicates to the world in Christ and in the church is not seen as an invitation, it remains impotent. Effective signs establish a conversation between seemingly irreconcilable poles and effect a paradoxical synthesis: in this, they are effective motives for credibility.[107] Perhaps the most problematic paradox, and therefore potentially the most effective sign, is the coexistence of holiness and sin in the church.[108] It is out of this polarity that the dynamic sign of the church as sacrament of salvation is born. Taking shape from the primordial sacrament that is Christ, the church is the continuation of the incarnation, of the paradox that Christ became sin for our salvation. So it is that, in binding himself forever to the fragility of the human condition, Christ has invested our sinful nature with the power to symbolize and effect his holiness in the world.

The Holy Spirit sanctifies the church by making it more and more like Christ, by effecting that which integrates ever more perfectly the horizontal and vertical elements that make up the reality of the church: the community of believers and the resurrected body of Christ, respectively.[109] The force that so binds the members and symbolizes them as the true body is the love of the Spirit that binds Christ to the world. Speaking of this dynamic, *Lumen Gentium* 4 holds together three images, representative of different phases in the economy, which the Spirit binds as one.[110] As fountain, the Spirit is

---

107. F. Lambiasi sees this as a particular function of the Holy Spirit, and would here corroborate Martelet's own convictions. Cf. F. Lambiasi, "Holy Spirit," 455–62; and G. Martelet, *Les idées maîtresses de Vatican II*, 63, 73–76.

108. Cf. R. Latourelle, *Le Christ et l'Église: Signes du salut* 189–235, especially, 212 [211–64, especially 239].

109. Ibid., 219 [245].

the source of all life, human and divine; as indweller, he sustains the temple of the body and rebuilds it in death; and, as spouse, he is the future consummation of eternal life. Thus, throughout, the life of the Spirit keeps the church young by constantly leading her back to the sources, renewing her structures, and promising her future glory:

> The church becomes vividly aware of the "updated" duties toward the world that her ancient faith imposes on her. Having thus returned to its roots while maintaining the paradoxical union of "opposites," that is, her sincere commitment to the mystery of Christ, the Council inaugurates a spiritual renewal of signs. This can be identified today by a sincere, integral love for man and for the world.[111]

The Spirit Reveals the Essence of Humanity in Christ

Clearly, the work of the Spirit in the economy of salvation is echoed in the theology of the Council and in the structure of *Les idées maîtresses de Vatican II*. But these three aspects of *aggiornamento* have a single purpose: to demonstrate that the redeeming love of Christ and his church is not something opposed to the world, but something

---

110. "Opere autem consummato, quod Pater Filio commisit in terra faciendum (cf. Io 17, 4), missus est Spiritus sanctus die pentecostes, ut ecclesiam iugiter sanctificaret, atque ita credentes per Christum in uno Spiritu accessum haberent ad Patrem (cf. Eph 2, 18). Ipse est Spiritus vitae seu fons aquae salientis. . . . Spiritus in ecclesia et in cordibus fidelium tamquam in templo habitat. . . . Virtute evangelii iuvenescere facit ecclesiam eamque perpetuo renovat et ad consummatam cum sponso suo unionem perducit." ("The Holy Spirit was sent on the day of Pentecost in order that he might continually sanctify the Church, and that, consequently, those who believe might have access through Christ in one Spirit to the Father. He is the Spirit of life, the fountain. . . . The Spirit dwells in the Church and in the hearts of the faithful, as in a temple. . . . By the power of the Gospel he permits the Church to keep the freshness of youth. Constantly he renews her and leads her to perfect union with her Spouse.") *LG* 4 [*850]. See also R. Latourelle, *Le Christ et l'Église: Signes du salut*, 220 [246].

111. "Elle prend une conscience intrépide des devoirs nouveaux que son antique foi lui impose à l'égard de ce monde. Ayant donc assuré un vrai retour aux sources, sauvegardant cette paradoxale union des contraires qui signifie son adhésion sincère au mystère du Seigneur, le Concile inaugure un renouveau spirituel des signes, qui s'identifie de nos jours avec un amour *intégral* de l'homme et de son monde." G. Martelet, *Les idées maîtresses de Vatican II*, 136–7 (my translation).

integral to the world.[112] Teaching the paradoxical union of opposites, the sources of Christian dogma reveal a faith that seeks to effect the intimate union of Christ and the world by means of sacramental signs. Because of this, Christ cannot be considered first of all "in the dogmatic splendor of his glory,"[113] for, reading the signs of the times and seeking dialogue with them, the theology of the Second Vatican Council starts from another place: the world in which we live and the heart of humanity:

> The Christ of the Council was not the one whose triumph would overshadow the world or would miraculously circumvent it. The Christ of the Council is not, so to speak, the Christ on the road to Damascus who dazzles St. Paul and throws his chosen one momentarily into darkness. The Christ of the Council is rather the hidden Christ on the road to Emmaus. He is the discreet passerby who appears scandalously ignorant, who listens, questions, and joins his brothers on their journey. He is the one whose presence, demeanor and very soon, whose words kindle in those who meet him an irresistible desire not to lose him again. . . . It is to that Christ on the road to Emmaus that the Council wants to remain faithful, it is to him that it wants the Church to reassemble. In the Constitution *Lumen Gentium* we read, "The pilgrim Church . . . takes on the appearance of this passing world. She herself dwells among creatures who groan and travail in pain until now, and await the revelation of the sons of God" (*LG* 48). The community of Christians, declares *Gaudium et Spes*, realises that it is truly and intimately linked with mankind and its history (*GS* 1).[114]

112. Ibid., 9.
113. "Le Christ n'est donc pas *d'abord* considéré dans le rayonnement dogmatique de sa gloire." Ibid., 207.
114. "Le Christ n'est jamais au Concile Celui dont le triomphe éclipserait le monde ou dispenserait miraculeusement de lui. Le Christ du Concile n'est pas, si l'on peut dire, le Christ du chemin de Damas, qui éblouit saint Paul et jette son élu dans l'impossibilité momentanée de voir encore ce monde. Le Christ du Concile, ce serait bien plutôt Celui encore voilé du chemin d'Emmaüs. C'est le passant discret, qui nous paraît d'abord scandaleux d'ignorance, qui écoute, interroge et s'unit à ses frères sur la route qu'ils font. C'est Celui dont la présence, la marche et bientôt la parole éveillent en ceux qui le rencontrent ainsi, l'irrésistible envie de ne jamais Le perdre. . . . C'est donc à ce Christ d'Emmaüs que le Concile se veut surtout fidèle, c'est à Lui qu'il désire que l'Église ressemble: 'Pérégrinante, disait-il de l'Église dans la constitution dogmatique *Lumen gentium,* elle porte la figure de ce siècle qui passe, elle vit parmi les créatures qui gémissent et sont

This final quotation from *Les idées maîtresses de Vatican II* betrays the "pivotal point" of Martelet's total presentation: humanity itself.[115] Epitomizing the Christ of Vatican II as the one who meets his disciples on the Road to Emmaus, the pilgrim church is identified as that place where, conversing with the risen Christ, humanity learns the truth about itself and its destiny. Martelet rejects the miraculous and insistent Christ of the Damascus road, the man of signs and wonders, preferring the presence of a gentle, friendly, almost inconspicuous Lord. Such a one, who is intimately engaged in "all that has been happening" and in "the joys and hopes, griefs and anxieties of the men of his age,"[116] is the only one capable of a credible sign of salvation. Risen from the dead and Lord of history, the Christ of Emmaus is sacrament of the church in the modern world:

> In fact it is only in the mystery of the Word incarnate that light is shed on the mystery of humankind. For Adam, the first human being, was a representation of the future, namely, of Christ the Lord. It is Christ, the last Adam, who fully discloses humankind to itself and unfolds its noble calling by revealing the mystery of the Father and the Father's love. It is not therefore to be wondered at that it is in Christ that the truths stated here find their source and reach their fulfilment.[117]

encore maintenant en travail d'enfantement et attendent la révélation des fils de Dieu (48, 3).' La communauté des chrétiens, declare à son tour *Gaudium et spes,* se reconnaît ainsi, réellement et intimement solidaire du genre humain et de son histoire." Ibid., 207–8 (my translation).

115. "Hominis enim persona salvanda est humanaque societas instauranda. Homo igitur, et quidem unus ac totus, cum corpore et anima, corde et conscientia, mente et voluntate, totius nostrae explanationis cardo erit." ("For it is the human person that is to be saved, and human society to be restored. It is around humankind therefore, one and entire, body and soul, heart and conscience, mind and will, that our whole treatment will revolve.") Cf. *GS* 3 [*1070].

116. Cf. ibid., 1[*1069].

117. "Reapse nonnisi in mysterio Verbi incarnati mysterium hominis vere clarescit. Adam enim, primus homo, erat figura futuri, scilicet Christi domini. Christus, novissimus Adam, in ipsa revelatione mysterii Patris eiusque amoris, hominem ipsi homini plene manifestat eique altissimam eius vocationem patefacit. Nil igitur mirum in Eo praedictas veritates suum invenire fontem atque attingere fastigium." Ibid., 22 [*1081].

Beginning to Realize an Anthropological Aim

In this crucial passage of *Gaudium et Spes* are both echoes of the spiritual typology of Martelet's earlier work and anticipations of the perspectives that he will develop in *Résurrection, eucharistie et genèse de l'homme*. The mystery of the human person, the life of the individual believer, is lived out between type and antitype, between the figure and the fulfillment. This is the place of the genesis of humanity. In the passage quoted from *Lumen Gentium* 48 in *Les idées maîtresses de Vatican II*—indeed in the very line that Martelet omits—the Council fathers speak expressly of that time between the first Adam and the Last: the time of the pilgrim church.[118] In this time, in her liturgy and institutions, the Risen One takes on the appearances "of this passing world" and reveals himself to his journeying disciples in the breaking of bread.

Les idées maîtresses de Vatican II tells the story not only of how the spirit of *aggiornamento* shaped the theological notions of the Council, but also of how that period of reflection and debate brought clarity and orientation to Martelet's own ideas. As the title suggests, *Résurrection, eucharistie et genèse de l'homme* is an attempt to integrate

---

118. "Donec tamen fuerint novi coeli et nova terra, in quibus iustitia habitat (cf. 2 Pt 3, 13), ecclesia peregrinans, in suis sacramentis et institutionibus, quae ad hoc aevum pertinent, portat figuram huius saeculi quae praeterit et ipsa inter creaturas degit quae ingemiscunt et parturient usque adhuc et expectant revelationem filiorum Dei (cf. Rm 8, 19-22). Coniuncti ergo Christo in ecclesia et signati Spiritu sancto, 'qui est pignus hereditatis nostrae' (Eph 1, 14), vere filii Dei nominamur et sumus (cf. 1 Io 3, 1), sed nondum apparuimus cum Christo in Gloria (cf. Col 3, 4), in qua similes Deo erimus, quoniam videbimus eum sicut est (cf. 1 Io 3, 2)." ("However, until the arrival of the new heavens and the new earth in which justice dwells (cf. 2 Pet 3:13), the pilgrim Church, in its sacraments and institutions, which belong to this age, carries the figure of this world which is passing and it dwells among creatures who groan and till now are in the pains of childbirth and await the revelation of the children of God (cf. Rm 8:19-22). Joined, therefore, to Christ in the Church and sealed by the Holy Spirit "who is the guarantee of our inheritance" (Eph 1:14), we are called and really are children of God, (cf. 1 Jn 3:1), but we have not yet appeared with Christ in glory (cf. Col 3:4), in which we will be like God, for we shall see him as he is (cf. 1 Jn 3:2).") *LG* 48 [*888].

imaginatively and refine what, as the Council closed, were the broad but sure strokes of a sacramental anthropology.

Building on Renewal Themes:
Résurrection, Eucharistie et Genèse de L'Homme

If, at the time of the Council, there was an alliance between the spirit of *aggiornamento* and the methods of *ressourcement*, or if during that period their aims coincided with one another, in the years following such collaboration largely disappears.[119] It is now a well-documented fact, and one of their own admission, that certain theologians previously associated with the "new theology" became fearful of postconciliar interpretations of "updating."[120] The call for progress seemed to have become incessant and all-consuming, and in their opinion it was often indistinguishable from secularization. Those who had fought so hard for the Council to ratify the sources of renewal in Catholic theology now found themselves resisting further calls for *aggiornamento*. They were resisting what Ratzinger calls "an interpretation of the Council that understands its dogmatic texts as mere preludes to a still unattained conciliar spirit, that regards the

---

119. "This situation seems, in the meantime, to have ceased to exist. In the course of a few years a new awareness has arisen that is so filled with the burning importance of the present moment that it regards any recourse to the past as a kind of romanticism that might have been appropriate in less stirring times but has no meaning today. Instead of *ressourcement*, we have *aggiornamento*, a confrontation with today and tomorrow in which the content of theology is to be made current and effective. The Fathers have been pushed into the background; a vague impression of allegorical exegesis remains behind and leaves a bad taste and, indeed, a feeling of superiority that regards it as progress to keep yesterday as far as possible from today and so seems to promise an even better tomorrow." J. Ratzinger, *Principles of Catholic Theology*, 134.

120. See H. de Lubac, "The Church in Crisis," *Theology Digest* 17 (1969): 312–15; J. Daniélou, *Prayer as a Political Problem* (London: Burns and Oates, 1967), especially 105–20. Also the periodical *Communio*, in direct opposition to *Concilium*, and under the influence of Hans Urs von Balthasar, has styled itself as resistant to postconciliar theological innovation. For a general overview of these trends, see D. Menozzi, "Opposition to the Council (1966–84)," in Alberigo, Jossua, and Komonchak, *The Reception of Vatican II*, 325–48.

whole as just a preparation for *Gaudium et Spes* and that looks upon the latter text as just the beginning of an unswerving course towards an ever greater union with what is called progress."[121]

Yet if there were those who, with Paul VI, felt that "henceforth *aggiornamento* will mean to us: enlightened penetration into the Spirit of the Council and the faithful application of the directives so happily and firmly outlined,"[122] there were some who wanted to bind that spirit to the letter. Gustave Martelet was not one of these. He felt that a balance could be achieved between letter and spirit[123] and he still believed that at the source of the Christian Gospel was the answer to the problems of progress and change.

Founding an Argument on the Lord's Supper

In a wise retrospective reflection on the theology of the Council, Karl Rahner asserted that

if the meaning and nature of existentially important events in the life of an individual human being encompass more than this individual explicitly objectifies and aims at in his consciousness, this is even more

121. J. Ratzinger, *Principles of Catholic Theology*, 390.

122. Paul VI, Speech at the Eighth Public Session of the Council, 1965 in *Sacrosanctum Oecumenicum Concilium Vaticanum II. Constitutiones, Decreta, Declarationes* (Città del Vaticano, 1966), 1054.

123. "The same goes for Vatican II as for Scripture: if the letter (of the Law) should never dispense us from the spirit, in the same way, the spirit must never be separated from the letter. Likewise Vatican II must not be reduced to its documents—advertisers have already reminded us of that—but, nevertheless, we must not suit ourselves by neglecting the texts. Vatican II is inspiration, impetus and enthusiasm. True, Vatican II is Spirit—we have to surrender to it! But the inspiration is not without its poem, the impetus without its vector, the enthusiasm without its wings—thus allowing the 'threesome' to advance. The Spirit takes shape in the letter." ("Or il en va un peu de Vatican II comme il en va de l'Écriture: si la lettre ne doit jamais dispenser de l'esprit, jamais non plus l'esprit n'est vraiment séparable de la lettre. Pareillement, on ne saurait réduire Vatican II à ses seuls écrits—des publicistes l'ont déjà justement rappelé—mais on ne saurait pas davantage s'approprier son âme en négligeant ses textes. Vatican II, c'est une inspiration, un élan et un souffle, Vatican II, c'est un esprit et il faut s'y livrer! C'est vrai. Mais l'inspiration n'est pas sans son poème, l'élan sans son vecteur, le souffle sans la voilure qui permet au trois-mâts d'avancer, et l'esprit a pris corps dans la lettre.") G. Martelet, *Les idées maîtresses de Vatican II*, 9–10 (my translation).

true of important events in the history of the Church which to a specifically unique extent are under the direction of the Spirit of the Church.[124]

These sentiments would seem to sit more comfortably with Martelet's own experience and better express his positive appreciation of the Council's ongoing spirit in his own life and work. Yet we must also acknowledge that he could hardly be unaware of what many were calling a postconciliar crisis in theology. While he, no doubt, was happy to speak of *Gaudium et Spes*, others, seeing only grief and anguish, thought the document that best encapsulated the spirit of *aggiornamento* was better named "*Luctus et angor.*"[125] *Résurrection, eucharistie et genèse de l'homme*, taking direction from the anthropological perspective of the *Constitution on the Church in the Modern World*, seeks to address the problem of change and development. Returning to the ultimate source of all Christian truth, the Resurrected Lord, Martelet seeks to know whether at the heart of a seemingly chaotic history lies the genesis of the human person.[126] If, as the Council had assured, the New Adam fully reveals humankind to itself,[127] then where might the Risen One be encountered, where might his transforming love be experienced, and where his peace felt?

In response to the daunting exercise that such questions set, Martelet chooses to begin with the Eucharist:

There are many ways of showing that the Resurrection of Christ is

---

124. K. Rahner, "Towards a Fundamental Theological Interpretation of Vatican II," *Theological Studies* 40 (1979): 716.

125. J. Ratzinger, *Principles of Catholic Theology*, 389.

126. "Le monde change et il change vite: il mute. Où va-t-il en changeant? Son devenir, évident désormais pour tout homme, est-il une genèse ou simplement un chaos qui se meut? Sans augurer trop des ensembles, le chrétien répond que notre monde en son entier est un processus de croissance et de vie. Il dit encore, il dit surtout qu'une mutation sans pareille travaille notre monde: celle de la Résurrection à laquelle le Christ en Personne le livre et le promet déjà." G. Martelet, *Résurrection, eucharistie et genèse de l'homme*, 7 [11].

127. Cf. *GS* 22 [*1081].

the centre of gravity of world history. The starting point of our demonstration here will be the Eucharist itself, for the Eucharist is one of the most paradoxical forms in which the Lord is actualised. If Christ is not risen, then the Eucharist is in vain, and its supper is a hollow void. No emphasis on the community can, by itself, fill the gap; nor can any rethinking of the symbols of faith. You find young persons who suddenly give up the Eucharist after being told, for example, that Christ's walking on the waters is simply a myth. And they are quite right; for the truth is that if Christ is not he who in a real sense has mastery over the world and, in his resurrection, has conquered our death, then the Eucharist which depends upon him has no essential contribution to make. It is no more than the rite practised by a human group imprisoned to death, and it will disappear as that group disappears.[128]

The coalescence of some of the more dominant ideas in Martelet's thinking, and their focusing toward a particular theological enterprise, can be seen in this introductory passage. Faced with the "tragic ambivalence" of change in the life of modern humanity, and anxious as to its goal, the resurrection is invoked as a paradigm of meaning. And yet the method of approach is somewhat novel. That the resurrection is at the center of the theological task, the truth on which "Christianity stands or falls,"[129] is undisputed, but the procedure by which this truth is appreciated is not that of a traditional apologetic, but one which is centered on the Eucharist.[130]

---

128. "Il est bien des manières de montrer dans la Résurrection du Christ le centre de gravité de l'histoire du monde. Pour le faire, nous partirons ici de l'Eucharistie elle-même, parce qu'elle est une des formes les plus paradoxales de l'actualité du Seigneur. Si le Christ n'est pas ressuscité, l'Eucharistie est vaine, et 'vide' est son repas. Ni la seule insistance sur la communauté, ni les symboles repensés ne sauraient la remplir. Il existe des jeunes qui abandonnent subitement l'Eucharistie, après qu'on leur a dit, par exemple, que le Christ marchant sur les eaux ne serait plus qu'un mythe. Ils ont raison. De fait si le Christ n'est pas Celui qui maîtrise réellement le monde et qui domine notre mort dans sa Résurrection, l'Eucharistie qui se rapporte à lui, n'a plus rien d'essentiel à donner: elle n'est plus que le rite d'un groupe humain enclavé dans la mort et elle disparaîtra comme lui." G. Martelet, *Résurrection, eucharistie et genèse de l'homme*, 8 [12].

129. G. O'Collins, "Paschal Mystery II: The Resurrection of Jesus," in Latourelle and Fisichella, *Dictionary of Fundamental Theology*, 769.

130. For an appraisal of the classical apologetic presentation of the resurrection and its amplification within the fundamental theology of Vatican II, see R. Latourelle, "Fundamental Theology

The paradoxical shape and content of the Lord's Supper shows it to be the liturgical re-presentation of the mystery of the resurrection. Here, then, come together some themes already examined: the inseparability of word, liturgy, and creed in the communication of revelation, the centrality of symbol to this process, and the inevitably paradoxical form that such media give rise to. Hence the major idea groups of Vatican II, which have already been Martelet's concern, are focused on a particular and current issue.

The Symbol of the Body of Christ

The Scriptures give approbation to Martelet's method of bringing together the Eucharist and the resurrection. Yet the grounds of their compatability, and the focus of the emergent and mutually interpretive principle, is the phenomenon of symbol, more specifically the symbol of the body: "For what the Resurrection and the Eucharist are concerned with is the body of Christ."[131] In the intimate association of the Eucharist with the body of the faithful, the reality of the relationship of the resurrected Christ and the world is experienced. Hence the pivotal role of symbol. In the liturgy of the Eucharist, signs "capable of carrying the full weight of love, of glory, of life-through-resurrection"[132] are made, and through them the glory of the risen Lord is transmitted.[133]

I: History," in Latourelle and Fisichella, *Dictionary of Fundamental Theology*, 324–32; and G. O'Collins, *Jesus Risen* (London: Darton, Longman and Todd, 1987), 148–72.

131. "C'est du Corps du Christ qu'il s'agit dans la Résurrection et dans l'eucharistie," G. Martelet, *Résurrection, eucharistie et genèse de l'homme*, 8 [12]. On the relationship between the sacramental revelation of the church and the Eucharist, see G. Martelet, "De la sacramentalité propre à l'Église," *Nouvelle Revue Théologique* 95 (1973): 25–42, 29.

132. "Si ces affirmations ne sont pas irréelles, leur contenu doit faire surgir une anthropologie qui puisse porter le poids d'Amour, le poids de Gloire, le poids de Vie de la Résurrection en mettant au grand jour, dans l'homme et dans le Christ, l'importance suprême du corps." G. Martelet, *Résurrection, eucharistie et genèse de l'homme*, 8 [12].

In assessing the notion of symbol, Martelet makes two interesting observations that, in some ways, represent convictions he formed in *Figures et Parénèse Sacramentelles*. His study of the "symbol of the Apostles"[134] revives his interest in the conviction of the Fathers that the (baptismal) liturgy of the church is the place par excellence of the formulation and actualization of the deposit of faith. Indeed, it would seem that the eucharistic liturgy is the only place where the complex nexus of deposit-paradosis-symbol can be fully articulated. This is largely to do with the christological foundation of this symbolic reality: "We may even say that it is Christ himself who is the only great symbol . . . in the sense that he is in himself the only perfect *conjunction*."[135] The Word made flesh symbolizes simultaneously with "each of the terms of this supreme dissemblance,"[136] and being both God and man, he is the perfect mediator between the two. He is the *agape*—the absolute power of communion.[137] In his death and resurrection, there is the gathering together of God and humankind of the eternal and the finite, so that at once Christ reveals God definitively and inaugurates the fullness of time and the end of history. But if the resurrection is central to the symbol of faith, then this centrality is actualized by the symbols of the sacred synaxis, the *agape* supper. In communion, the absolute power of the risen Christ to show forth the self-manifestation of God and to inaugurate the end-time is experienced by believers. Paradoxically, however, this

---

133. For the broader outline of the relationship between the Eucharist and revelation, see T. Stanks, "The Eucharist: Christ's Self-Communication in a Revelatory Event," *Theological Studies* 28 (1967): 27–50.

134. G. Martelet, *Résurrection, eucharistie et genèse de l'homme*, 18–19 [22–23].

135. "C'est même Lui qui est le seul grand Symbole, non pas au sens où il se substituerait au mystère de Dieu mais au sens où Il est en lui même une *rencontre* pleinement réussie." Ibid., 19 [23].

136. "Symbolisant avec chacun des termes de cette suprême dissemblance que représente la créature dans sa distance d'avec Dieu." Ibid., [24].

137. Ibid., 19. Cf. also R. Latourelle, *Théologie de la Révélation*, 483 [400–1].

immediacy is mediated as much by distinction and separation as it is by conjunction and communion.

Consequences of the Separation That Symbols Presume

Initially, union would seem to be the primary function or task of symbol—a fact easily corroborated by etymology.[138] And yet the very fact that conjunction is necessary presupposes a division to be bridged. This gap between the subject and that which is other or beyond creates a longing, the "first repercussion"[139] of which is symbol. Separation, then, is both the source and the motivation for symbols. Humankind symbolizes God, the Absolute Other, but its efforts are partial and uncertain because, "without emerging from the empirical domain inhabited by our human possessions, powers, and knowledge,"[140] humanity cannot commune with God completely. Human beings cannot see God and live, because the symbols they possess are by nature finite and contingent and so, *sub speciae aeternitatis*, forever incomplete:

> Belief in God's personal entry into our world does not of itself entail enjoyment of the bliss communicated by his presence. "Even if we believe that Christ has overcome death, that he is living, present and active in this world, it yet remains true that, in some way, he *is still dead for us*. We shall not meet Christ in a relationship of the same sort as we find in simply human intercommunication. We are deluding ourselves if we claim to 'feel' the presence of Christ or his activity, and to place them on a plane other than that of faith, as though they could be included in the field of human experience in the same way as is the presence

---

138. G. Martelet, *Résurrection, eucharistie et genèse de l'homme*, 18 [22].
139. Drawing a parallel between symbol and language, Martelet states, "Le langage est en effet dans l'homme le premier contrecoup structurel d'un manque, un appel à ce qu'il n'est pas, la première sortie vers le différent de soi-même—choses et gens—et donc un aveu de l'absence qui nous prépare à rencontrer plus grand que nous." Ibid., 21 [25].
140. "Sans sortir du domaine empirique où règnent nos avoirs, nos pouvoirs et nos savoirs humains." Ibid.

and activity of someone of our own kind." It is true, as we shall see, that the risen Christ symbolizes only imperfectly with our universe. The absolute Living Being of Glory seems to us to be absent, not because he is really absent but because his life, which excludes all death, is not *empirically* apprehensible in a world where death still has the last word in reply to life.[141]

By virtue of this passage, in no way does Martelet enter the ranks of those modern theologians whose "writing has generally remained non-experiential."[142] Nor is his treatment of the category of experience indicative of the "rather sparing" apprehension that marked the Second Vatican Council, and which some saw as suspicion of a lingering modernism.[143] The question here concerns not the fact of human experience of God, or the suitability of such experience to the task of the theologian but the type and value of the experience itself.[144] While the liturgical movement sought to focus theology on the numinous encounter of the liturgy, fundamental theology appreciated the necessity of criteria to interpret this experience. Appreciation of the need to bring these two enterprises together has already been gained from an examination of the

141. "Qui croit d'ailleurs à la venue personnelle de Dieu dans notre monde ne sera pas pour autant livré aux félicités de la présence. 'Si nous croyons que le Christ a surmonté la mort, qu'il est vivant, présent et agissant en ce monde, il n'en subsiste pas moins que, d'une certaine façon, il est *encore mort pour nous*. Nous ne rencontrons plus le Christ dans une relation homogène à la simple communication des hommes entre eux. Illusion de prétendre 'sentir' la présence du Christ ou son action et que de les situer sur un autre plan que celui de la foi, comme si elles pouvaient tomber dans le champ de l'expérience humaine de la même façon que la présence ou l'action d'un semblable.' C'est vrai, nous le verrons, le Christ ressuscité ne symbolise qu'imparfaitement encore avec notre univers. Le Vivant absolu de la Gloire nous semble absent, non parce qu'il l'est en fait, mais parce que sa Vie, excluant toute mort, n'est pas *empiriquement* saisissable dans un monde où la mort a toujours le dernier mot contre la Vie." Ibid., 22–23 [28].

142. Cf. O'Collins, *Jesus Risen*, 201–9, 203.

143. Cf. G. O'Collins, "Experience," in Latourelle and Fisichella, *Dictionary of Fundamental Theology*, 307.

144. Cf. H. Bouillard, "Human Experience as the Starting Point of Fundamental Theology," *Concilium*, 6, no. 1 (1965): 79–91; T. O'Meara, "Towards a Subjective Theology of Revelation" *Theological Studies* 36 (1975): 401–27, G. O'Collins, "Theology and Experience," *Irish Theological Quarterly* 44 (1977): 279–90. See also F. Lawrence, "The Fragility of Consciousness: Lonergan and the Postmodern Concern for the Other," *Theological Studies* 54 (1993): 55–94.

liturgical theology of Salvatore Marsili, and particularly from his later intuitions concerning pneumatology and experience. Into what both writers recognize as a nascent area of theology, and one that demands sensitive and specific use of terminology Martelet introduces a fundamentally important principle—one frequently ignored or muted by theologians who seek to stress experiential categories. Symbolically mediated experience, while no less real, is qualitatively different from the empirically founded experience of everyday interaction. Such a distinction results from the fact that the Infinite will always elude the grasp of finite symbols.

Resurrection and the Struggle for a Symbol of Faith

It is necessary to be reminded of the overall method of *Résurrection, eucharistie et genèse de l'homme*. It is to move, by way of symbols, from the Eucharist to the resurrection and back again, in order to understand better the relationship between the transforming power of the resurrected Christ and the genesis of the human person.[145] Symbolization of a body is the common denominator. In the inherently ambiguous eucharistic gifts of bread and wine, humanity symbolizes itself, both its ingenuity and its hunger, its sufficiency and its need. Expressing itself as a product of the universe in these elements, humanity symbolizes with the whole of creation. Yet toward what objective reality do these symbols reach? To death and nothingness? Is this not the goal of the process of change that humanity experiences empirically in every moment of its finite existence? Or can the relationship with the world that conditions the historical existence of humanity "be redrawn in an entirely new way

---

145. G. Martelet, *Résurrection, eucharistie et genèse de l'homme*, 8–9 [12–13].

by him who in his own person establishes a universe from which death is excluded"?[146]

From the very beginning, Christianity could be characterized as a struggle for the symbols of faith, the battle for a credible representation of that which is other. And, although humanity is symbolic to its core, doubts emerge because each person is also conditioned by the empirical order. Humanity puts its trust more naturally in science and that which can be known by observation. Hence the historical method is an attractive hermeneutic, seeking as it does to explain all events within the continuity of a closed system of effects. So the symbol of the resurrection is dismissed as a construction of the faith of the disciples. The "event" is conceded no objective reality.[147] Yet, as Martelet points out, this is not really hermeneutics, because what is being denied is not an interpretation of the text, but the possibility of a personal experience of God or the credibility of any sign said to effect a divine self-communication. What is required is a positive hermenuetic that, free from presuppositions, will restore the possibility of the transcendent and approach the text in such a vein.[148] Then, in the description of the appearances and the empty tomb might be found the inspired struggle for a symbol of resurrection faith: witness of an event that

146. "Celle-ci ne le dispense pas d'une anthropologie de la grandeur de l'homme au sein de sa misère; elle lui donne l'assurance, devant le paradoxe effrayant de la mort, que le rapport au monde qui conditionne l'existence historique de l'homme peut être recréé d'une manière entièrement nouvelle, par Celui qui fonde en sa personne un univers dont la mort est exclue." Ibid., 57 [58–59].

147. For Martelet's discussion of Edward Le Roy's *Dogme et Critique*, and the particular contribution of Rudolf Bultmann, see G. Martelet, *Résurrection, eucharistie et genèse de l'homme*, 67–78 [67–80].

148. For a full discussion of this question, see G. Ghiberti, "Contemprary Discussion of the Resurrection of Jesus," in Latourelle and O'Collins, *Problems and Perspectives of Fundamental Theology*, 223–55. Also, O'Collins, *Jesus Risen*, 99–127; and for a useful survey of current Catholic thought on this topic, see J. Galvin, "The Resurrection of Jesus in Contemporary Catholic Systematics," *The Heythrop Journal* 20 (1979): 123–45.

symbolizes the "decisive absolute detachment from this mode of life."[149]

> In the Resurrection, *the relationship to this world* which defines Christ's body, as it defines man's, remains *the same in absolute value*, but it undergoes *a change of characteristic sign*. During his life it was ambivalent; inseparably both dominant and dominated; in death it became purely dominated and negative; then finally it becomes, and asserts itself as, entirely positive and purely dominant in his Resurrection. We then see the Resurrection as the *radical reverser* of direction at the level of death, and as the beginning of a completely new relationship which revolutionizes man's real development in his *world* and thereby in his *body*. Seen in this light, Christ risen from the dead can no longer be regarded as a second Lazarus. In his body, and therefore the universe, he becomes literally a "*mutant*," the *supreme* "*mutant*," or, more precisely still, history's only "Transfigured."'[150]

If, as Martelet has said, the body is "our point of insertion into matter,"[151] then a material union is established between Christ, humanity, and the world.[152] This means that, through the

---

149. "Elle est au contraire l'arrachement décisif, absolu, à ce mode de 'vie' où la mort règne sur nous par le moyen d'un corps, que saint Paul appelle un 'corps de mort' (Rm 7, 24)." G. Martelet, *Résurrection, eucharistie et genèse de l'homme*, 74 [74].

150. "Dans la Résurrection, *le rapport à ce monde* qui définit le corps du Christ, comme il 'définit' celui de l'homme, reste *le même en valeur absolue*, mais *il change de signe*. D'ambivalent qu'il fut durant la vie: inséparablement et dominant et dominé; de purement dominé et négatif qu'il se révéla dans la mort, il devient et s'affirme au contraire entièrement positif et purement dominant dans la Résurrection. La Résurrection nous apparaît alors comme l'*inverseur radical* de sens au niveau de la mort et comme le commencement d'un rapport tout nouveau qui bouleverse l'avenir réel de l'homme dans son *monde* et, par là, dans son *corps*. Sous une telle lumière, le Christ ressuscité des morts ne peut plus être pris pour un nouveau Lazare. En son corps et donc pour l'Univers, il devient à la lettre un '*Mutant*,' le *Suprême* '*Mutant*' ou, plus exactement encore le seul Transfiguré de l'histoire." Ibid., 86–87 [83–84].

151. "Assez proche en ceci des perspectives les plus modernes sur le *corps propre*, il définit le corps comme 'notre point d'insertion dans la matière.' Comme le dira Teilhard dans la formule que nous avons cité plus haut, mon corps n'est pas une partie d'univers que je posséderais totalement, mais la totalité de l'univers que je possède partiellement." Ibid., 78–79 [77].

152. This connection is fundamental to "the effort of Teilhard de Chardin to assuage modern man's anxiety by elaborating a guarantee of evolution's success as ultimately founded, as we have seen, upon the physical relationship between Christ, mankind, and the material world." See C. Mooney, *Teilhard de Chardin and the Mystery of Christ* (London: Collins, 1966), 104.

resurrection of Christ, the whole world order is transformed and transcended. Such an action cannot be attributed to the individual person who, in the face of death, is always defeated. The claim that, in the resurrection, death has been vanquished, "presupposes a dynamism, an energy or a love, which no longer derives from man's endemic finiteness."[153] Christ's resurrection is, then, the revelation of a spirit that is beyond and other than that belonging to humanity. The Holy Spirit is the "radical reverser" of that movement of history that ends in death. The Spirit reverses this movement by changing radically Christ's bodily relationship with the world. Yet this is not an absolute change; it is a mutation or transfiguration. Christ in his resurrected body is still bound to this world—matter is the point of his insertion—and yet he is not historically bound, as now he relates to the world in a deathless, eternal way.

This new character of Christ, and therefore the world, its glorious transformation, cannot be contained within history. If this were the case, what would be presented would be merely a second Lazarus. Here, however, is the first and absolute foundation of the Christian mysteries—*the* symbol of faith. It is this fact that fills the Eucharist with significance, as "what the Eucharist does is to actualize in signs the risen body of Christ, that is, of the Lord himself in his relationship, at once transfigured and transfiguring, with the world and with ourselves."[154]

---

153. "Suppose un dynamisme, une énergie ou un amour qui ne relève plus de la finitude endémique de l'homme et de sa défaillance insurmontable devant la mort." G. Martelet, *Résurrection, eucharistie et genèse de l'homme*, 90 [87].

154. "L'Eucharistie actualise en effet dans les signes le corps ressuscité du Christ, c'est-à-dire le Seigneur lui-même dans son rapport, tout à la fois transfiguré et transfigurant, avec le monde et avec nous." Ibid., 100 [95].

In the Liturgy the Spirit Creates a Credible Symbol

The second part of the study moves from the resurrection to the Lord's Supper. Yet while methodologically Martelet's focus remains anthropological, there is a shift from the realm of exegesis to that of liturgy. To understand dogmatically the relationship between the Eucharist and the body of Christ, Martelet examines the relationship between transubstantiation and epiclesis, because these are the liturgical expression of the transfigured body of Christ and of the transfiguring Spirit who raised him from death. In the liturgy of the Eucharist, the force of the resurrection is apprehended sacramentally. Unsurprising, then, is Martelet's decision to begin with the German liturgical movement and the idea of *presence* that emerged from the innovative writings of Romano Guardini, Odo Casel, and the "mystery school" of Maria Laach. The contribution of these ideas toward a "better theological answer to the fundamental demands of eucharistic realism"[155] is of particular interest to Martelet's objective in *Résurrection, eucharistie et genèse de l'homme*:

> Regarded, then, as *mystery* "in the old sense of the word" in which mystery is "more an action than a thing," the Eucharist is no longer only a, so to speak, instantaneous prodigy: it takes on a body in liturgy. The presence of Christ takes on also the dynamic character of a love which seeks to arouse a human *responder* as loving as Christ himself. No one, of course, has ever denied that the presence is a mystery of person in the Eucharist itself; but if this is not stated as clearly as the liturgy presupposes and demands, its full import may be overlooked. On the other hand, once so elementary a truth has been emphatically brought to our notice, we have a strong obligation to reread what the Council of Trent had to say; and in so doing not to confine ourselves to an academic theology which is not a true reflection of the Council.[156]

155. "Une meilleure réponse théologique aux exigencies fondamentales du réalisme eucharistique." Ibid., 105 [99].
156. "Ainsi saisie comme *mystère* 'au sens ancien du mot' où le mystère 'est plutôt une action qu'une chose,' l'Eucharistie n'est plus seulement un prodige pour ainsi dire instantané; elle prend corps

Within the systematic framework of neo-scholasticism, which shaped and controlled Catholic theology in the years before the Second Vatican Council, the work of Christ was interpreted primarily as his crucifixion.[157] Such a theology was in part inspired and in part confirmed by eucharistic celebrations preoccupied with sacrifice. The liturgy, or priestly work of Christ and his people, was seen predominantly as a re-presentation of Calvary that showed little awareness of the resurrection.[158] But then neither did Catholic dogmatics, which gave the resurrection only restricted coverage as a wonderful apologetic proof within fundamental theology show more balance. One of the most influential aspects of the liturgical movement, and one that helps to effect the christological reintegration of these disparate and disproportionate elements, is the conviction that the liturgy re-presents the supernatural reality of the entire work of salvation.[159] As already discovered, in the work of Odo Casel this takes the shape of what has come to be called a "mystery theology." The liturgy is a worship mystery that by way of sacramental signs is inserted into the saving mystery of Christ. As such, it is "the way in which Christ effects for us in worship his

---

en une liturgie. La présence du Christ revêt aussi le caractère dynamique d'un amour qui cherche a susciter un *répondant* humain aussi aimant que Lui. Qui donc avait jamais nié que la présence était un mystère de personne dans l'Eucharistie elle-même? Mais à ne pas le dire aussi clairement que la liturgie le suppose et l'exige, on risquait d'en méconnaître la portée. Par contre, une fois alerté sur une vérité aussi élémentaire, on devait, à tout prix, reprendre la lecture du Concile de Trente, par-delà une théologie scolaire avec laquelle on ne saurait l'identifier." Ibid., 111 [104–5].

157. Cf. Ludwig Ott, *Fundamentals of Catholic Dogma* (Cork: Mercier, 1962), 125–95.

158. "Per il *contenuto* basti pensare al *canone romano*, nel quale l'originale linea 'eucaristica' o di 'preghiera di ringraziamento,' ha ceduto il posto a quella direttamente 'sacrificiale' che è diventata dominante, e il contenuto 'anamnètico,' che prima comprendeva tutta la 'storia della salvezza' a cominciare dal momento 'cosmico' di essa fino all'adempimento del 'mistero di Cristo' nella sua totalità dall'Incarnazione alla Parusia, è stato ristretto al solo 'memoriale' della 'passione-risurrezione-ascensione,' nel quale appunto il momento 'sacrificiale' appare con maggiore evidenza." S. Marsili, *La Liturgia: momento nella storia della salvezza*, 54.

159. L. Beauduin, *Essai de manuel de Liturgie* (Louvain: "Mélanges liturgiques" de Mont-César, 1954), 76: See also Marsili, *La Liturgia: momento nella storia della salvezza*, 76–78.

permanent operation of grace,"[160] or, as Marsili put it, "that which constitutes the point of arrival and reality of all revelation."[161]

Humanity's Eschatological Goal Gives a New Density to Transubstantiation

This liturgical mystery that is communicated between Christ and his bride, the church, is an invitation, "since love resides in him only to pass into her and possess her entirely,"[162] and what passes in and is returned is the paschal mystery. This is why the Eucharist is no mere remembering, but the celebration and sharing of Christ's presence and action. Describing the movement of the work of salvation as it is celebrated in the Eucharist allows for the better understanding of the presence of Christ in the liturgy. It is for this reason that Martelet is led to a rereading of the Council of Trent. Once freed from the unintended strictures of any metaphysical system and approached as an actualized moment within the mystery of salvation, "transubstantiation" receives a greater density, amplified by its position in the economy to bodily and personal proportions. Indeed, in such a setting, the substantial conversion of the eucharistic elements takes on the inexplicable novelty of the resurrection.[163] And

160. "La manière dont le Christ actualise pour nous dans le culte son operation permanente de grâce." G. Martelet, *Résurrection, eucharistie et genèse de l'homme*, 108 [101].

161. "Che costituisce il punto di arrivo e la realtà stessa di tutta la rivelazione." Marsili, *La Liturgia: momento nella storia della salvezza*, 78.

162. "Puisque l'amour n'est en Lui que pour passer enelle et pour l'envahir tout entière." G. Martelet, *Résurrection, eucharistie et genèse de l'homme*, 109 [103].

163. "'Il ne s'agissait pas d'une explication rationelle du mystère, mais d'une affirmation catégorique de la réalité de la présence du Christ.' Le concile entend donc garantir l'existence de quelque chose d'ineffable et non pas l'épuiser; il n'accrédite en droit aucun système métaphysique qui lui serait associé. Il détermine seulement ce que nous devons affirmer pour ne compromettre, dans notre manière d'en parler, *l'originalité absolue* du mystère. Il ne désigne pas au coeur invisible des choses, je ne sais quelle plate-forme avancée, qui permettrait d'observer ce que fait le Seigneur ou moins encore ce qu'*Il doit métaphysiquement faire* pour être vraiment là. La *conversion* du pain et du vin au corps et au sang du Seigneur est tout aussi *originale* que le passage du corps mort de Jésus à son état de gloire." Ibid., 114–15 [107].

yet there is one paradoxical difference: once the bread and wine have been converted into the body of the risen Christ, *"they still remain elements that are immanent in this world."*[164] It is these elements that "become signs of a reality which still eludes us."[165]

Here, then, is a point of departure for theology. Basing his argument on Jean de Baciocchi and Franz-Jehan Leenhardt, Martelet asserts that this elusive "not yet" element of the Eucharist is in fact the ontological expression of a call to being.[166] For "the substance of things is not definable apart from the divine intention which is realized in them."[167] The will of Christ to give himself to us is so all-consuming "that it causes the things through which he gives himself to pass into the domain of his person."[168] In this sense, we can talk of a "purposive presence,"[169] and of the eschatological goal in us of the conversion of the elements.

> "As it is," says scripture, "we do not yet see everything in subjection to him" (cf. Heb 2:8) and in this, moreover, we are fortunate, for it is this obscurity surrounding the glorified identity of Christ that makes history possible. If the world were already seen here and now in conformity with the potential truth as very body of Christ, this would mean the conflagration of the world in the glory of God, and so the parousia too. But history must endure, and man must "become" in a world which he makes his own, by culture, as he does his body. We would therefore, seek in vain for the least real incompatability between the two phases of one single genesis: the cultural phase which makes the world man's *historical body*; and the *parousiac* fulfilment, founded upon the Resurrection, which makes from the world Christ's *glorified* body

164. "Demeurent cependant des elements immanents à ce monde." Ibid., 115 [107].
165. Ibid.
166. Ibid., 115–18 [108–10].
167. "La *substance* des choses n'est pas définissable en dehors de 'l'intention divine qui s'y réalise'." Ibid., 115–16 [108].
168. "L'acte qui nous les livre nous communique aussi Celui qui nous les donne, et l'amour du Christ donateur est si réel et si puissant qu'il fait passer en son *domaine de personne*, les *choses* à travers lesquelles Il *se* livre." Ibid., 117 [109].
169. "*Présence pour*," ibid.

and humanity rising again in Christ. Christ, as second and last Adam, in no way annihilates the first Adam.[170]

The Genesis of Humanity as the *Raison d'Etre* of the Church

In his essay "Christology and Anthropology: Toward a Christian Genealogy of the Human," Martelet suggests that the use of an excessive and abstract metaphysics in theology can easily be traced to the separation of faith and culture that began in earnest in the eighteenth century.[171] The gulf was set by the Enlightenment's rupture of symbolism. "Anti-patristic" culture challenged a christological interpretation of society, history, and the world. The "cure" lies in an openness "to the depths of him whom historical changes can only reveal more fully to the eyes of faith."[172] The obscurity that exists in the time between resurrection and Parousia—the time of the church—stems from the fact that "the risen Christ symbolizes only imperfectly with our universe."[173] This is not because he is in any way incomplete or incompatible with the world, but because creation has not achieved through the human person the culture of receptivity necessary for its recapitulation in Christ.

170. "Actuellement il est vrai, comme dit l'Écriture, 'nous ne voyons pas que tout lui soit soumis' (He 2, 8). Heureusement d'ailleurs, car cette obscurité sur l'identité glorieuse du Christ est la condition de l'histoire. Si le monde apparaissait d'ores et déjà selon sa vérité potentielle de corps même du Christ, ce serait l'embrasement du monde dans la gloire de Dieu et donc aussi la Parousie. Or l'histoire doit durer, l'homme doit 'devenir' dans un monde qu'il s'approprie, par la culture, comme son corps. Dès lors, on chercherait en vain la moindre incompatibilité réelle entre les deux moments d'une seule et unique genèse: le *moment culturel* qui fait du monde le *corps historique* de l'homme, et l'accomplissement *parousiaque*, fondé sur la Résurrection, qui fait du monde le corps *glorieux* du Christ et de l'humanité ressuscitant en lui. Le Christ comme second et comme dernier Adam, n'abolit nullement le premier." Ibid., 183 [163–64].

171. G. Martelet, "Christology and Anthropology: Toward a Christian Genealogy of the Human," in Latourelle and O'Collins, *Problems and Perspectives of Fundamental Theology*, 152.

172. Ibid., 152.

173. "Le Christ resuscité ne symbolise qu'imparfaitement encore avec notre univers." G. Martelet, *Résurrection, eucharistie et genèse de l'homme*, 23 [28].

History exists in this intermediate state of imperfection, constantly being called to the full stature of its perfection in Christ.

It is important to notice here that Martelet's thought has been guided by the patristic intuitions of spiritual exegesis. Apart from the explicit reference to Adam-Christ typologies,[174] the explanation of the two phases of a single genesis, namely, the cultural phase of preparation and the parousiac phase of fulfilment, which neither supersedes nor destroys the former phase, owes much of its clarity to the Old and New Testament typologies of the Fathers. In turn, these show themselves dependent on Pauline typologies and cosmologies.[175] Essentially, what is introduced by way of these methodologies is a sacramental system that, while elaborating the intentions of God in the economy of salvation, exposes the eschatological goal of humanity and its universe. That is to say, a methodology that holds together, in the one concept of mystery-sacrament, the different phases of a single economy in order to reveal and effect the future truth about Christ, humanity, and the world. Such is the *raison d'être* of the church, and the reason why her reality is most clearly displayed in the Eucharist.[176] As Martelet makes clear,

> This, in truth, is what the Eucharist is: the sacramental anticipation in history of the world's fundamental identity in the order of the Resurrection. The Eucharist makes manifest for faith, in signs, what still remains hidden from human experience in history; in a symbolic, and

174. Adam typology is examined in greater detail with regard to the resurrection and eschatology in "Christologie et Anthropologie la Symbolique des Deux Adam," the fourth chapter of G. Martelet, *L'au–Delà Retrouvé: Christologie des fins dernières* (Paris: Desclée, 1975), 99–117.

175. See L. Cerfaux, *The Church in the Theology of St. Paul*, 206–12; 254–59. See also S. Lyonnet, "La rédemption de l'univers," *Lumière et vie* 9 (1960): 41–62.

176. "The Church's destiny, therefore, is to be the true carrier of human evolution towards Christ-Omega between the resurrection and the Parousia; and it is this fact which is gradually responsible for Teilhard's referring to the evolutionary process not so much as cosmogenesis but rather as a Christogenesis." C. Mooney, *Teilhard de Chardin and the Mystery of Christ*, 167. Evidently, for Martelet the nature of the church's role of Christogenesis is most clearly expressed in the Eucharist.

so fragmentary and hidden way, it realizes the ultimate content of the Resurrection.[177]

Here, essentially, is a discussion of the sacramental nature of the church, and as ever, there is the difficulty of presenting credibly the paradox that the Eucharist makes "manifest" in a "hidden" way the "ultimate" realities that it "anticipates." In the effort to keep in tension the poles of this paradox, it is important to notice where the struggle lies. The risen Christ and the eucharistic world are incompatible not on the level of reality, but on the level of symbolization, and indeed that incompatibility is one of degree and not essence.[178] For the degree to which historically bound human beings can bear or apprehend the ultimate reality of the eschaton remains symbolic until Christogenesis is complete in us.[179] In no sense does this detract from the reality of Christ's presence to the world in the Eucharist:

> The Lord's Supper, therefore, is indeed a feast at which we eat the bread of absolute life and, by favour of the Spirit, drink from the well of glory. The Eucharist realizes *in us*, through the bread and wine, what the Incarnation effected *in Christ*; or, to put it even more precisely, through the Eucharist Christ introduces us into that for which he destines us by his Incarnation. In our eucharists is realized, according to the *mode of sacramental symbolism*, the mystery which Christ reveals and fulfils in his Incarnation, according to the *mode of historical manifestation*. Without the Eucharist, which makes available to us the fruits of the Incarnation itself, the mystery of the Lord would remain "*self contained*," if I may put

177. "Telle est en vérité l'Eucharistie: l'anticipation sacramentelle dans l'ordre de l'histoire de l'identité radicale du monde dans l'ordre de la Résurrection. L'Eucharistie fait apparaître pour la foi dans les signes ce qui demeure encore caché pour l'expérience humaine dans l'histoire; elle actualise de manière symbolique, et donc parcellaire et secrète, le contenu ultime de la Résurrection." G. Martelet, *Résurrection, eucharistie et genèse de l'homme*, 195 [175–76].

178. Cf. G. Martelet, "De la sacramentalité propre à l'Église," *Nouvelle Revue Théologique* 95 (1973): 30.

179. Partly this is also due to humanity's failure to appropriate the mystery into their whole life and to experience its fruits: "L'inachèvement que nous avons ici en vue est celui qui relève essentiellement de nos *misères*: nous trahissons l'eucharistie. L'inachevé concerne moins la forme même du Repas du Seigneur que la médiocrité des participants que nous sommes." G. Martelet, *Résurrection, eucharistie et genèse de l'homme*, 200 [181].

it so—something to which we could relate ourselves as though from a distance—but it would not be something fully *for us*, something which love can take to itself in a flesh, the flesh of Christ, transfigured by the free communication of the Spirit.[180]

As a result of our taking Christ's flesh in the Eucharist, the incarnation is realized in us, and we are introduced into the destiny that he became human to ensure. There is a reality to this symbolic action that is both joyous and awesome, for with consolation comes judgement. This is why the Holy Spirit is called down with pleading on the gifts and on the people: that they may become "one body, one Spirit in Christ." The transformation that the Spirit effects on the gifts is fulfilled in those who receive. The Spirit sets them in the sequence of the divine economy and orientes them toward their eschatological goal. Partaking of the sacramental food indicates the acceptance of a place in communion with both the history of salvation and its destiny, which is Christ. The Eucharist marks the completion of a believer's initiation into the paschal mystery of baptism, because the eucharistic bread realizes in us the life of the resurrection, which is the goal of our journey.

The Present Experience of Salvation

Having determined that the real content of the Eucharist remains unaffected by the mode of its symbolic communication, Martelet is

180. "Le Repas du Seigneur est donc bien un banquet où l'on mange le pain de la Vie absolue et où l'on boit grâce à l'Esprit aux sources de la Gloire. L'Eucharistie réalise *en nous*, par le pain et le vin, ce que l'Incarnation accomplit *dans le Christ*, ou plus exactement encore le Christ nous introduit par l'Eucharistie à ce à quoi Il nous destine par son Incarnation. Se réalise dans nos eucharisties, par *voie de symbolisation sacramentelle*, le mystère que le Christ révèle et accomplit dans son Incarnation, par *voie de manifestation historique*. Sans l'Eucharistie qui met à notre disposition les fruits de l'Incarnation elle-même, le mystère du Seigneur resterait un *en soi*, si j'ose ainsi parler, auquel nous pourrions adhérer comme à distance, mais il ne serait pas pleinement un *pour nous* que l'amour s'approprie dans une chair, celle du Christ, que transfigure la libre communication de l'Esprit." Ibid., 207 [188].

left with the question of how such "bodily" real yet sacramentally transmitted truths are apprehended by the believer. What is the nature of the experience of these divine realities? For enlightenment he turns to the liturgy, which is grounded in the affective core of the human person. Affectivity, intimately connected with the body as it is, Martelet understands as the *experience* in pleasure and pain of the way one affects, and is affected by, the world and other people. This reality has its center in the genetic roots of personality, and it yields to, and is shaped by, education, love, and friendship, or the lack of these. Such a center yields also to the liturgy, where experience of the divine persons is symbolized. The idiom of the liturgy's language indicates something of the nature of the experience it offers.[181] Symbolic penetration of the divine realities is expressed in the "most biological" terms, and this, Martelet interprets, as indicative of their "infra-conscious" nature.[182] They penetrate the nonrational elements of personality that constitute affectivity, and that the reason seeks to integrate and interpret. It is in these affective depths, the source from which we were individually drawn, that the love of Christ and the power of his resurrection is experienced: "What is more, when the Eucharist penetrates into our depths in the hope of transfiguring us, it is not lost in those depths. Working in the deepest abyss of man's being, it makes him ready to open himself to the immensity of the kingdom of the Resurrection."[183]

---

181. "Or, c'est sans doute une des merveilles de la liturgie de l'Église, qu'elle ait perçu d'instinct l'existence de ce centre qui reste trop souvent inexprimé dans l'homme. Elle l'a fait dans cette sorte de clair-obscur discret des oraisons eucharistiques où, inspirée par un mystère qui est 'esprit et vie,' la prière liturgique ouvre et consacre à l'investigation transformante du Christ, les fonds les plus secrets et les plus décisifs de notre personnalité. Son vocabulaire, difficile à traduire, de *penetralia*, de *viscera* et d'*affectus*, qui frôle de manière symbolique le réseau dérobé des racines subjectives de l'homme, nous paraît plein d'audace et de pressentiments." Ibid., 211 [192–93].

182. Ibid., 211 [193]. In terming this experience "infra-conscious," Martelet is nearer to fulfilling G. O'Collins's condition that "there is always at least a minimal cognitive dimension to experience," than if he had used the term *subconscious*. See O'Collins, "Theology and Experience," 281.

With this Martelet's methodological procedure is complete, and he has effected the interaction of the christological pole and the pneumatological pole[184] so that Eucharist and resurrection each become a sacrament of the other. So the Eucharist makes manifest "for the well-being of men and to assist what is most authentically their genesis, the emergence, the function, and the irresistable magnetism of Jesus Christ, Lord in the Holy Spirit of the Resurrection."[185]

Résurrection, eucharistie et genèse de l'homme shows forth the fruits of a properly oriented theology of *aggiornamento*. By returning to the sources of Scripture and tradition as they are primarily displayed in the liturgy of the church, and guided by the spirit of the Council, Martelet has revised the categories of theological reflection and reawakened a discussion between faith and the modern world. The dialogue has its starting point in the central mystery of the Christian faith, the resurrection, but, although sure that a firm foundation has been provided, Martelet is certain that the conversation is only beginning.[186]

---

183. "Au reste, en pénétrant dans la profondeur de nous-mêmes pour essayer de nous transfigurer, l'Eucharistie n'y est pas engloutie. Travaillant au plus secret abîme de l'homme, elle le prépare à s'ouvrir à l'immensité du Royaume de la Résurrection." Martelet, *Résurrection, eucharistie et genèse de l'homme*, 212 [193].

184. "Thus in the sacraments we have the interaction of the Christological pole—the particularity of the church-institution—and the pneumatological pole—the universality of the reign of God which knows no boundaries. Consequently, from another perspective, we see the interaction of the pole of God and the pole of humanity." L.-M. Chauvet, *The Sacraments: The Word of God at the Mercy of the Body* (Collegeville, MN: Liturgical Press, 2001), 169.

185. "Il manifeste et garantit, à sa manière irremplaçable, pour le profit des hommes et en vue de leur plus authentique genèse, l'émergence, le rôle et l'attrait sans pareil de Jésus-Christ Seigneur dans l'Esprit Saint de la Résurrection." G. Martelet, *Résurrection, eucharistie et genèse de l'homme*, 221 [201].

186. Ibid., 221 [202].

PART III

Evaluations and Prospectives

6

Moving Toward a Synthesis

The particular period in which the four writers of this study were contemporaries offered a unique opportunity for the employment and expression of their theological gifts. To look to their particular contribution is to look to the specific tasks that the moment set before them. Born within a decade that saw the burgeoning of progressive currents in Catholic theology, they witnessed both the suspicion and suppression of these themes in the last reaches of the Modernist crisis and their acceptance and legitimation at the Second Vatican Council. At the peak of production in the postconciliar period, each labored for the consolidation and systematization of the ideas that they had welcomed before the Council, and that they had seen it ratify. From this increasingly steady beacon, they gradually took orientation and began to develop the lines of enquiry that the bishops at the Council suggested. The task, then, to which their oeuvre responded was a threefold one, with themes roughly sequential yet always interrelated. For ease of procedure they will be analysed in turn.

A Threefold Task

Martelet, Latourelle, and Dulles represent a second generation of theologians—and although Marsili was chronologically somewhat nearer to the generation of masters who preceded him, his theology was also reliant on their insights. When these four began as writers and teachers, those themes suited to the rethinking and reformulation of Catholic theology had already been selected. Among others, M.-D. Chenu, H. de Lubac, Y.-M. Congar, and J. Daniélou had tried to renew the then-current theology by returning to the sources and appropriating certain insights from the nineteenth century.[1] Theology was being given a "new"[2] content and its methods revised. Yet, although much had been delineated,[3] these newly

1. The processes of *ressourcement* have been detailed previously, but some indication should be given of the appropriation of nineteenth-century theological themes by the new theologians. M.-D. Chenu, a pupil of A. Gardeil, received many insights from J. H. Newman and from the Tübingen School, especially J. E. Kuhn. In fact, M.-D. Chenu was responsible for the topic of Y.-M. Congar's 1928 lectoral thesis on J. A. Möhler. Subsequently, Y.-M. Congar combined the intellectual argument of the Tübingen School with the philosophical insights of M. Blondel and the biblical ones of P. Garrigou-Lagrange. H. de Lubac, too, was close to M. Blondel and also to P. Rousselot, and although not nineteenth-century, É. Mersch was the other major influence on de Lubac's work. Much of the work of J. Daniélou is comparative study of the church fathers and modern philosophers such as Marx, Kierkegaard, and Bergson. For a fuller analysis of these themes, see T. Schoof, *A Survey of Catholic Theology 1800–1970* (New York: Paulist Newman, 1970); A. Dulles, *Revelation Theology* (London: Burns and Oates, 1969); A. Nichols, *Yves Congar* (London: Geoffrey Chapman, 1989); H. Boersma, Nouvelle Théologie *and Sacramental Ontology. A Return to Mystery* (Oxford: Oxford University Press, 2009); G. Flynn and P. D. Murray, eds., *Ressourcement: A Movement for Renewal in Twentieth-Century Catholic Theology* (Oxford: Oxford University Press, 2012).
2. Speaking of H. de Lubac's theology, C. Chantraine says, "His theology was not new except inasmuch as it was less recent than a certain so-called commonly held theology or than certain of his critics. It simply returned to the sources. . . . Thus it was not new except inasmuch as it was traditional and dialogical." C. Chantraine, *Le Cardinal de Lubac: L'homme et son oeuvre* (Paris: Éditions du Cerf, 1983), 21. See also G. Martina, "The Historical Context in Which the Idea of a New Ecumenical Council Was Born," in *Vatican II: Assessment and Perspectives, Twenty-Five Years After (1962-1987)*, ed. R. Latourelle, 3 vols. (New York: Paulist, 1988), 1:36–37.
3. Some idea of the content and method deemed appropriate for theology can be gleaned from Y.-M. Congar, "Tendances actuelles de la pensée religieuse," *Cahiers du Monde Nouveau* 4 (1948): 33–50; J. Daniélou, "Les orientations présentes de la pensée religieuse," *Etudes* 249 (1946): 5–21, H. de Lubac, "Bulletin de théologie fondamentale: le problème du devéloppement du dogme," *Recherches de Science Religieuse* 355 (1948): 130–59. An overview of emergent themes can be

developing themes needed to be welcomed and tested more widely for such a significant shift to be effected.

Thematization and Legitimation

Martelet and Latourelle presented their doctoral theses at the Gregorian University within a year of one another. And, although their areas of research were somewhat dissimilar, what is clear from both is a confluence of prioritized themes that had marked and were further to mark the Catholic theology of the twentieth century. Latourelle gave this new thematization its clearest expression. In the introduction to his doctoral thesis, *La révélation chrétienne*, he detailed the theological themes that were to give shape to a Catholic study of revelation. They were the following: a consciousness of the Protestant contribution; biblical renewal; the relationship between revelation and dogmatic development; and recent modern currents that made clear the personal, historical, and essentially christological nature of the economy of salvation.[4] Martelet does not make his intentions quite so explicit in *Figures et parénèse sacramentelles*, yet the biblical, historical, and christological renewal themes closely associated with the *nouvelle théologie* of Fourvière obviously shape his enterprise. A slightly later arrival to the Jesuit theologate, and separated geographically from the intellectual ferment of Europe,

gained from T. Citrini, *Gesù Cristo, rivelazione di Dio: il tema negli ultimi decenni della teologia cattolica*, Dissertatio ad Lauream in Facultate Theologiae Pontificiae Universitatis Gregorianae (Rome: PUG, 1969).

4. R. Latourelle, *La Révélation Chrétienne: notion biblique, notion theologique*, Excerpta ex dissertatione ad Lauream in Facultate Theologiae Pontificiae Universitatis Gregorianae (Montreal, 1957), 8. For the influence of De Lubac's "Bulletin de théologie fondamentale" on Latourelle, see B. Cahill, *The Renewal of Revelation Theology (1960-1962): The Development and Responses to the Fourth Chapter of the Preparatory Schema De Deposito Fidei*, Tesi Gregoriana, Serie Teologia, 51 (Rome: Editrice Pontificia Università Gregoriana, 1999), chapter 5: "The Christocentric Renewal of Theology," 216. See also Latourelle's own comments in R. Latourelle, *L'Infini du sens: Jésus-Christ* (Québec: Bellarmin, 2000), 25–26.

Dulles's contact with the new theology was vicarious but none the less intense.[5] The very title of one of his earliest publications, *Apologetics and the Biblical Christ* (1963) is enough to indicate a thematic consonance with his European confrères.

Meanwhile Marsili, working in a very different context and tradition, serves to prove the consistency with which Catholic theology endeavored to appropriate these new categories in which to execute its task. The (Italian) liturgical movement,[6] in which Marsili came to maturity as a monk and scholar, was shaped by the same themes of renewal as the new theology.[7] A parallel can be drawn: just as *la nouvelle théologie*, fortified by the credible stature that a Christology of biblical and historical proportions had generated, attempted to rescue Catholic theology from the stale inertia of the scholastic manualists, the similarly strengthened liturgical movement tried to retrieve Christian worship from the grasp of ritualists and canon lawyers.

The first action of these writers was to make the ideas and categories of renewal central to their own work, and in this way advance their acceptance and credibility. However, though Latourelle, Martelet, and Marsili worked to establish these thematic changes before the Council,[8] Vatican II was an essential element in

---

5. Cf. A. Dulles, *The Craft of Theology*, 2nd. ed. (New York: Crossroad, 1995), 44–45.

6. "Basato su un punto di partenza spiccatamente teologico, il movimento liturgico italiano volle indicare *la via del ritorno a Cristo per mezzo della Liturgia nella Chiesa*, concepita non come organizzazione esterna, ma come organismo vivo di trasmissione di grazia in forza della sua funzione sacerdotale." S. Marsili, "Liturgia-Vita della Chiesa," *Sacra Doctrina* 7, no. 28 (1962): 560.

7. Kevin Irwin summarises the characteristic elements of the work of Marsili, saying, "For Marsili liturgy *is* theology par excellence with two basic components. First it is biblical theology in the sense that the word is revealed in every act of liturgy. Second it is fundamentally a liturgical theology because the revealed word is enacted and operative among the faith community at worship. Marsili's work is Christologically rich and ecclesiologically grounded, in so far as he profoundly articulates the uniqueness of Christ's saving paschal mystery while stressing that Christ's followers experience this divine work again and again in worship." K. Irwin, *Liturgical Theology: A Primer* (Collegeville, MN: Liturgical Press, 1990), 26.

this process of thematization and legitimation. Three of the writers studied here were involved in the Council's acceptance of renewal themes, yet it is difficult to know the extent to which these men had influence on that process. None addressed the Council, neither were they official *periti*, and perhaps only Latourelle had input that could be directly traced to a text.[9] And yet maybe their type of involvement opened spheres of influence that while implicit and incalculable, were nonetheless significant and far-reaching.[10] Speaking of the role of theologians at the Council, Karl-Heinz Neufeld situates their major field of activity outside the discussion hall. It was when invited by the bishops or the press to give talks that would contextualize the various debates theologically, or when asked on a particular point, that the theologians gained their sway. He clarifies further the significance of this role by stating that

> we can take as certain that it was not limited to helping the bishops to formulate their awareness of their faith. They themselves had animated, deepened, and strengthened this awareness of faith, so that the Church represented at the Council could go out toward the world without fear and with a new confidence of the Lord living within her. She needed first to be reminded once more of many things that had long since been forgotten or had been left inactive in the background. The theologians helped with these discoveries.[11]

8. See the changes that Latourelle made to his courses at the Gregorian in the years before the Council charted in M. Chappin, "Dalla difesa al dialogo. L'insegnamento della teologia fondamentale alla PUG, 1930–1988" in *Gesù Rivelatore: Teologia Fondamentale*, ed. R. Fisichella (Casale Monferrato: Piemme, 1988), 31–45. See also the recurrent themes in Marsili's articles in the *Rivista Liturgica*—an overview can be gained from M. Ballatori and M. Alberta, "Bibliografia dell'Abate Salvatore Marsili" *Rivista Liturgica* 80 (1993): 373–88.

9. See R. Latourelle, *L'Infini du sens*, 99–100; 107–10. Cf. Cahill, *The Renewal of Revelation Theology*, 215–231.

10. See R. Latourelle, *L'Infini du sens*, especially chapter 4, entitled "Vatican II: événement et expérience," 99–112.

11. K.-H. Neufeld, "In the Service of the Council: Bishops and Theologians at the Second Vatican Council," in Latourelle, *Vatican II: Assessment and Perspectives*, 1:74–105, 98.

It was the role of the theologian at the Council to remind the fathers of the sources of renewal. That is to say, they were to provide the core themes around which the various discussions could take place and the documents could be drafted. Largely, this took place in more or less formal meetings between the bishops and their theologians. Latourelle's absence from the public arena of conciliar discussion is perhaps best explained by the tacit decision of the Gregorian to remain somewhat neutral in what could be an often dangerously polarized climate.[12] The same cannot be said of Martelet. Described as "among the most active"[13] theologians at the Council, he gave frequent conferences to various groups of bishops.[14] He was a member of the Conciliar Strategies Group, which met to prepare opinions contrary to the curial schemas;[15] he was consulted by the subcommissions of *Lumen Gentium* and *Gaudium et Spes*; and was a member of other significant working parties.[16] In all this he worked

12. "The Gregorian held itself aloof from the controversy, ensuring its students a solid and 'safe' education, at the cost of keeping them relatively isolated from contemporary discussions and problems." Martina, "The Historical Context," 48. As Latourelle himself stated, "J'ai participé au concile, non comme expert, mais comme conseiller d'évêques ou de théologiens eux-mêmes au service du concile, tels Daniélou et de Lubac. Ma contribution la plus importante se situe au niveau des écrits: articles et ouvrages." Latourelle, "L'Université Grégorienne et le *De Revelatione*," in *L'Église canadienne et Vatican II*, ed. G. Routhier (Montréal: Éditions Paulines, 1997), 319–33, 319.

13. G. Ruggieri, "The First Doctrinal Clash," in *History of Vatican II*, vol. 2: *The Formation of The Council's Identity, First Period and Intercession, October 1962–September 1963*, ed. G. Alberigo and J. Komonchak (Leuven: Peeters, 1996), 236.

14. Hilari Raguer describes the growing influence of the "Central European Bloc" or "World Alliance" of bishops and theologians on the conciliar debates, and something of the extent of Martelet's influence can be gained from the following: "A further reason for this group's growing influence was that the lack of famous experts from which some third-world episcopates suffered led them to seek the opinions of the Europeans. Thus Father Gustave Martelet gave a lecture to the bishops of French-speaking Africa on November 5; this was followed by another by Congar on November 7, and a third by Martelet again, on November 10. Some bishops of Asian Dioceses with historical and cultural ties with France (Indochina for example) also approached this group." H. Raguer, "An Initial Profile of the Assembly," in Alberigo and Komonchak, *History of Vatican II*, vol. 2, 167–232, 205.

15. Cf. A. Melloni, "The Beginning of the Second Period: The Great Debate on the Church," in *History of Vatican II*, vol. 3: *The Mature Council, Second Period and Intersession, September 1963–September 1964*, ed. G. Alberigo and J. Komonchak (Louvain: Peeters, 2000), 1–115, 62.

16. Cf. Alberigo and Komonchak, *History of Vatican II*, vol. 3, 79, 286, 404, 413.

closely with the other French-speaking theologians, De Lubac, Daniélou, and Congar, and hence an impression can be gained of how the themes of theological and pastoral renewal came to permeate the consciousness of the Council.

Marsili was, like Latourelle, somewhat peripheral to the inner workings of the Council, and what contribution to the debate on the liturgy he may have made through his colleagues at San Anselmo by way of their submissions, can only be imagined. Nevertheless, Marsili was involved in the dissemination of the Council's discussions and decisions, and frequently, by means of public addresses and articles in *L'Osservatore Romano*, he gave clarity and solidity to the politically and emotionally charged machinations of the liturgy debate.[17] Repeatedly, in his work of this time, he brings the debate back to its central focus: a christological renewal of the liturgy based upon the word of God.[18]

Even if the uncovering of the theological categories that were to dominate Catholic theology in the conciliar period was the task of a previous generation, the establishment of these themes and their ratification by Vatican II was to some extent the work of the authors studied. And here is where thematization overlaps with consolidation. For, when speaking of the involvement of theologians at the Council

17. "The Fathers were able to study the schema in depth with the aid of many liturgists gathered in Rome from various parts of the world. These experts held conferences, lectures and dialogues. For example, Herman Schmidt, S. J. (October 25), Salvatore Marsili, O. S. B. (November 3), and Pierre-Marie Gy, O. P. (November 15) spoke in the pressroom of the Holy See to the journalists accredited to the Council." A. Bugnini, *The Reform of the Liturgy 1948–1975* (Collegeville, MN: Liturgical Press, 1990), 31. See also, for example, "Lingua viva e liturgia," *L'Osservatore Romano* CII/256 (1962, 8 novembre) 6 [signed: S. M.]; "I primi passi della riforma liturgica," *L'Osservatore Romano*, CIV/24 (1964, 30 gennaio) 2, [signed: S. M.]. Some comment is also made by R. Wiltgen, *The Rhine Flows into the Tiber* (New York: Hawthorn, 1967), 139, and in Alberigo and Komonchak, *History of Vatican II*, vol. 3, 253.

18. See S. Marsili, "Riforma liturgica dall'alto. Note preliminari ad una attuazione practica della Costituzione Conciliare," *Rivista Liturgica* 51, no. 1 (1964): 76–91; Marsili, "Note esplicative alla *Istruzione per l'applicazione della Costituzione conciliare sulla sacra liturgia*," *Rivista Liturgica* 51, no. 4 (1964): 526–69; Marsili, "Commenti alla Costituzione Liturgica," *Rivista Liturgica* 51, no. 4 (1964): 587–92.

in the passage already quoted, K.-H. Neufeld goes on to say, "This produced a new awareness of themselves [the theologians], that is to say, a knowledge of their own strengths and limits, a mutual association that bore the seal of openness and responsibility. Naturally, it is difficult to produce evidence of this development, but the numerous isolated pointers should convey a certain corporate impression."[19]

That the documents of Vatican II had incorporated many of the themes of renewal which the Council theologians had enunciated instilled a certain confidence in them, and so began a period of consolidation.

Consolidation and Systematization

While the adoption by the Council of progressive themes and the methodology of *ressourcement* was a victory for the "new" theologians, in some senses their work was only beginning when the documents were promulgated. For it would be wrong to overestimate the achievements of the Council fathers. Vatican II offered only a broad outline or a blueprint, and did not provide a systematic theology of *aggiornamento*.[20] This was the task before our writers: the consolidation of renewal themes and their systematic expression. And, if Aidan Nichols defines consolidation as the "marriage of affirmation and nuance,"[21] then when these

---

19. Neufeld, "In the Service of the Council," 98.

20. "Nor did the Council provide any systematic theoretical foundation for its pervasive theme *aggiornamento*. The Council's decrees were committee compositions, born of compromise, marked by ambiguity, and often reluctantly acceptable to all and passionately loved by few. Technical theological language was avoided at the price of precision or coherence. Moved by pastoral concerns, the documents are characterized more by the desire to appeal to the affective priorities of all persons of good will than by the intention of responding to a need for theory." S. Duffy, "Catholicism's Search For A New Self-Understanding," in *Vatican II: Open Questions and New Horizons*, ed. G. Fagin (Dublin: Dominican, 1984), 9–37, 10.

21. Nichols, *Yves Congar*, ix.

characteristics come together in the postconciliar writings of these men, the concrete renewal of theology can be seen to be taking place.

Avery Dulles asserts that the publication of *Théologie de la Révélation* was "especially propitious" before Vatican II resumed its deliberations on the schema *De revelatione*.[22] Perhaps he too felt the work to be one that would both invigorate the Council with its insights and provide a systematic framework for the study of its findings. The ease with which the Constitution on Revelation and a commentary were later appended to Latourelle's text would suggest this to be the case.[23] For this is the first dogmatic synthesis of revelation structured around the principles of theological renewal that were to be ratified by *Dei Verbum*.[24] As R. Fisichella says, "*Théologie de la Révélation* effects a shift from manualist theology, so that for the first time we encounter an organic, christocentric, and historical-salvific notion of revelation."[25]

Latourelle consolidates the notion of revelation as a dynamic interpersonal encounter by providing a particularly nuanced analysis

---

22. A. Dulles, "The Theology of Revelation," *Theological Studies* 25 (1964): 45.

23. This is not to suggest that *Théologie de la Révélation* simply presents that theology that the Council ratified with *DV* (certain differences will be noted later), but it *is* to claim that the work provides both a thematic framework for discussion and a systematic structure for the consolidation of these ideas.

24. The reviews welcome the work for two main reasons: the shift it effects from apologetics to dogmatics, and its comprehensive, systematic nature. See, for example the following: "Our age certainly can do with a book which treats this 'first of all Christian realities' dogmatically rather than apologetically as has been the fashion up till now. This is the need which Latourelle has attempted to fill. He describes his book as an 'approach to a dogmatic treatise on revelation.' The description is too modest. This is such a treatise and it is a good one." F. McCool, review of R. Latourelle, *Théologie de la Révélation*, *Biblica* 45 (1964): 278. "En réalité, l'étude qu'il nous offre, sans être pleinement exhaustive, est extraordinairement documentée et trouve son couronnement dans une explication systématique équilibrée, claire et pénétrante." J. Alfaro, "Une Dogmatique de la Révélation," *Sciences Ecclesiastiques* 16 (1964): 352.

25. "Per chi era abituato ad avere della Rivelazione cristiana una visione intellettuale, concettualistica, frutto della produzione della teologia del manuale, si incontra per la prima volta qui con una visione organica, cristocentrica e storico-salvifica della Rivelazione." R. Fisichella, "Il contributo di René Latourelle alla teologia fondamentale," in Fisichella, *Gesù Rivelatore*, 11–22, 13.

of the category of word within this communication. Amplifying dry scholastic conceptions of revelation as the transmission of a body of information by an analysis of speech according to the categories of word, witness, and encounter, Latourelle highlights a human dimension that rescues the inquiry from the realms of the supernatural. Skillfully, the way to such a conclusion is prepared by the historical overview of the first four sections. Here Latourelle charts the gradual favouring of personal and existential aspects before a concept of revelation as an immutable, divinely guaranteed body of evidence.[26] Retrieval of the core elements of revelation is rooted in the paradigm of Christ, and in essence it is this focus that allows for a fresh theology of revelation to be articulated outside the categories of a scholastic apologetic.

The move from apologetic[27] to dogmatic applauded in *Théologie de la Révélation* is essentially what takes place in Dulles's *Models of the Church*.[28] Here is a methodological reinterpretation of the

26. "An interesting result of this survey is the impression that the personal, historical and existential aspects of revelation were thrust into the background earlier than we had thought so that for quite a long time the concept of revelation as an immutable, divinely guaranteed body of doctrine held the field in Christian thought. This overconcentration on an undoubtedly valid but partial concept explains the *malaise* of Christian thinkers in the last two centuries and underscores the importance of Latourelle's final section." McCool, review of *Théologie de la Révélation*, 278.

27. In some ways, *Revelation Theology* (1969) and *A History of Apologetics* (1971) allowed Dulles to clarify somewhat the nature and task of fundamental theology in the postconciliar period. As he says in the preface to the second of these books: "If the theologians of the coming generation are to take full responsibility for the truth-claims that seem to be inseparable from Christianity itself, the apologetical task will have to be carried on. In view of all that has been learned from depth psychology about the unconscious, from sociology about ideologies and plausibility structures, from comparative religion about the faiths of other people, and from linguistic analysis about the hazards of metaphysical discourse, the contemporary believer can scarcely stave off the real difficulties by an easy appeal to blind faith." Dulles, preface to *A History of Apologetics* (London: Hutchinson, 1971), xviii.

28. Though somewhat nervous of it, J. Sheets recognises this shift in his review of *Models of the Church*: "In general, the book reflects a move away from anything that can be considered objectively normative, whether it is revelation seen as articulated in propositions or an institutional Church that can mediate in an authoritative way the whole of Christ to the world." Sheets, review of A. Dulles, *Models of the Church*, *America* 144 (March 23, 1974): 224.

classic treatise *De Ecclesia* from the standpoint of Vatican II, indeed, one might say, according to the perspectives by which Latourelle preempted the Council in the introduction to his doctoral thesis. For the guiding principles of Dulles are the same: ecumenical awareness, biblical renewal, and an attention to organic change and christological focus. This imaginative synthesis of ecclesiology according to contemporary perspectives of renewal is made possible by an innovative methodology. Definition is "bypassed"[29] in favor of symbolic images that appeal to the subjective dimensions of human apprehension. With Latourelle, Dulles is helping to redress the repression of the personal and existential dimensions of revelation so that a fuller, more dynamic understanding may emerge. This is the work of consolidation.

Separated by a period of ten years, these two works are evidence of the theological development of the postconciliar church. *A* theology of revelation has given way to theological model*s* of the church, and with the increased pluralism comes the need to hold a still center in the content and method of theology. To some extent, theologians turn to the Council's category of sign in order to satisfy this need. So, reviewing *Christ and the Church: Signs of Salvation*, Thomas Potvin asserts, "Latourelle's main approach is phenomenological, i.e., how the Church appears to the eyes of the beholder. Thus the emphasis placed on the need for authentic witnessing on the part of the members of the Church in order to touch contemporary man with his personalistic mentality."[30]

29. Cf. Dulles's quotation from G. Weigel: "The most significant result of the debate was the profound realization that the Church has been described, in its two thousand years, not so much by verbal definitions as in the light of images. Most of the images are, of course, strictly biblical. The theological value of the images has been stoutly affirmed by the Council. The notion that you must begin with an Aristotelian definition was simply by-passed. In its place, a biblical analysis of the significance of the images was proposed." Dulles, *Models of the Church*, 2nd ed. (London: Doubleday, 1987), 19.

If Dulles's *Models of the Church* attempted a reworking of ecclesiology according to the themes of Vatican II, then Latourelle's *Le Christ et l'Église* is committed to a similar endeavor. Building on *A Jésus par les Évangiles*, which examines the credibility of Gospel data in the search for the historical Jesus, this work seeks to expose the semiological depths of such evidence. Christ is here described as the "founding moment"[31] in a theology of signs, and Latourelle establishes him as the unique and central sign within the divine economy, the hermeneutical key to all the signs of revelation. Thus Latourelle makes clear that an essential aspect of emergent fundamental theology is a recognition of divine manifestations beyond that of apologetic proof. By relating all signs back to the person of Christ, revelation is given both an internal coherence and a deeply personal dimension. From such a stance, renewed significance can be given to the role of the church within the overall economy of signs. The traditional apologetic notes of ecclesiology are reworked by Latourelle, their dimensions benefiting from the personal depth and coherence afforded by a christological reinterpretation. It is according to such a framework that the witness of the personal holiness of the baptized takes on such increased significance as a testimony of authenticity. No longer can the credibility of the church remain dependent on objective realities unrelated to the personal existence of the members of Christ's body. Within this renewed vision, Christology, ecclesiology, and semiology are aligned in the fresh way that the Council's notion of salvation history would suggest, and the significance of the church as a credible sign and motive for faith is worked out with new vigor.

---

30. T. Potvin, review of R. Latourelle, *Christ and the Church: Signs of Salvation*, The American *Ecclesiastical Review* 168 (1974): 359.
31. Fisichella, "Il contributo di René Latourelle," 16.

Similarly, the symbols of Christ and the church are at the thematic center of the series *Anàmnesis*, which gives a rereading of the liturgy in the light of Vatican II.[32] In volume one, Marsili seeks to deepen awareness of the liturgy beyond a scientific study of the history of ritual. Again, it is the category of symbol that allows him to envisage ritual celebrations as both personal and profound gateways into the mystery of Christ.[33] As the title of the series suggests, the liturgical symbols of word and gesture are the means by which the mysteries of salvation are re-presented now. The word of God, once given in the incarnation, is actualized in the liturgy, and there it becomes a source of salvation and theology. Just as with Latourelle the very dynamism of signs involves an inevitable return to Christ, so too with Marsili. Yet, in Marsili's *La liturgia momento nella storia della salvezza*, he adds a penetrating methodological insight: as sign, the liturgy is fundamental to any inquiry into the truths of faith, and it must be interpreted as a theology of revelation precisely because its shape and content make manifest God's presence and action in the world.[34] Marsili endorses this position by reference to the insistence of *Sacrosanctum Concilium* that the liturgy be ranked as one of the

---

32. "Il Vaticano II ha riportato in modo veramente nuovo la Liturgia alla coscienza della Chiesa, riscoprendola come 'il termine più alto (*culmen*) cui tende tutta l'azione della Chiesa e insieme come la sorgente (*fons*) donde a questa derivano tutte le sue energie' (SC 10). Con questa affermazione, che supera d'un colpo ogni visione tanto di ordine puramente esterno-rubricale, quanto di valore prevalentemente giuridico-giurisdizionale, la Liturgia viene situata, insieme con Cristo e—com'è chiaro—dipendentemente da lui, come 'l'alfa e l'omega, il principio e la fine' di tutta la vita della Chiesa." S. Marsili, "Presentazione," in *La liturgia: momento nella storia della salvezza Anàmnesis 1*, 2nd ed. (Genoa: Marietti, 1979), 5.

33. "The first volume sets out the basic premises and the theological framework for understanding liturgical phenomena not only as historical facts but also as vital symbols offering Christian persons and communities an invitation to participate in the paschal mystery of Jesus Christ." K. Seasoltz, review of S. Marsili *La Liturgia momento nella storia della salvezza*, *Worship* 60 (1986): 84.

34. "Marsili is more inductive than deductive and understands liturgical theology to address the nature of God's presence and action in the world, the mystery of Christ, and the liturgical event that signifies and actualizes Christ's presence in the incarnation and in all humanity." Irwin, *Liturgical Theology*, 26.

principal subjects, and that it be taught in theological faculties under its various aspects.

Reflection on Martelet's *Les idées maîtresses de Vatican II*, perhaps the text most indicative of this stage of transition in theology, should serve as a useful summary and revision of the elements that have emerged so far. Explicit from the very title onwards is Martelet's desire to give a systematic synthesis to the major themes of the Council; that is to say, a fundamental theology of Vatican II.[35] As such, the work seeks to offer the principal lines of a theological framework, which can be exploited later to support more speculative suggestions and for the purposes of development. One might say that in the major subdivisions of this book, there is an echo of the pattern of thematization, consolidation, and development that has been chosen to guide this analysis. In the first part, the author concentrates on how the Council's program of renewal has affected the parameters of theology; that is, on an appreciation of the new dimensions that a return to the sources has provided for the content of revelation. The second part identifies the methodological implications for such a rereading of the mysteries of faith. The third and longest part begins to grapple with the consequences of the Council's stance for certain questions such as the relationship of the church and the world, and religious liberty. So the reader moves through a threefold study: from the sources of revelation as expressed through the Scriptures, the Fathers, the liturgy, and the magisterium; to a way of understanding this gift as the paradoxical union or resolution of opposites; and on to the practical consequences that this faith has for life. A short section, which is central to the work

---

35. "Son titre suggère un désir de synthèse, toujours chimérique et pourtant nécessaire s'il se sait inaccompli; son sous-titre indique l'élan qui a soutenu le concile et qui demeure le nôtre. En donnant ce sous-titre, j'ai toujours hésité sur un mot. *Initiation*, ai-je écrit, mais aussi *Introduction* à l'esprit du Concile." See G. Martelet, "Préface de la deuxième édition," in *Les idées maîtresses de Vatican II* (Paris: Les Éditions du Cerf, 1985), iv.

as a whole, opens part 3 and addresses the question of the spiritual renewal of signs. It is as a result of this structure that *Les idées maîtresses de Vatican II* can be seen as paradigmatic of the works already mentioned.

These postconciliar texts made a considerable contribution to the consolidation of renewal themes. In the first place, they make clear the central role of the Scriptures in the expression of a renewed theological vision. The dynamic, anthropologically centered images of the Bible not only afford to the truths of the faith a new vitality and credibility, but also help effect the shift away from the static, noetic categories of scholasticism. The conscious scriptural dimension of these works must be noticed and applauded.

Secondly, within this biblical perspective, the centrality of the person of Christ to the theological endeavor is made absolutely plain. Whereas the older apologetics, capitulating somewhat to the demands of sceptical rationalism, tended to concentrate on proofs isolated from the fiduciary context, and separated signs from their subject so as to give a certain scientific detachment, fundamental theology comes to see this personal center as that which provides coherence and credibility to the whole of revelation and the faith response. The first consequence of this stance is the affirmation of a certain consistency of shape and content in the signs of salvation based on their origin and center, Christ.

Thirdly, and perhaps most significantly, within a dynamic, personal, and historically contingent understanding of revelation, the category of sign-symbol takes on an increased significance. This is why the section on the spiritual renewal of signs is pivotal to *Les idées maîtresses de Vatican II*—lying as it does between the chapters on theological theory and those on its practical expression. Clearly, this is due to the fact that the category of sign-symbol is the means by which revelation is both communicated and interpreted. God manifests himself to humanity in signs, and through them humanity participates in the life of God. At once, signs constitute the content of revelation and are the means of its transmission. Hence, the key consequence of the consolidation and systematization of Vatican II themes is the emergent centrality of a notion of sign–symbol. The final chapters of *Les idées maîtresses de Vatican II* begin to show how the category of sign becomes a principle by which the truths of the faith can be renewed and re-presented. In this sense, the beginnings of orientation and development can already be seen.

Centered as they are on the major ideas of Vatican II, the five texts mentioned above have a predominantly retrospective point of reference. Inspiration is drawn from the renewal agenda that a return to the sources of revelation had yielded, and the various works consolidate and further the systematic structure into which the Council documents had attempted to shape often diverse and interrelated ideas. Of great significance here is the nature of these works as teaching material.[36] Each of the books was intended as an introduction to a particular discipline, and gave the writer the opportunity to lay out a clear method and content. As some of the first textbooks since the Council and the demise of the manuals, the works are innovative, serving to establish the new shape of postconciliar theology. Using the major notions of Vatican II, Latourelle works to launch a restructured fundamental theology,[37]

36. "Siamo personalmente convinti che la ricchezza di presentazione, la scelta delle tematiche, l'organicità della struttura, insomma la vera sistematicità dell'opera di Latourelle, provenga appunto da questo impatto positivo con la vita accademica." See Fisichella, "Il Contributo di René Latourelle," 21. See also Latourelle's autobiographical reflections on the interrelationship between theology and pedagogy in Latourelle, *L'Infini du sens*, especially 48–61.

37. "Avec une belle régularité dans la publication, le Père Latourelle poursuit l'exécution de son programme de renouvellement de la théologie fondamentale, ou tout au moins de l'aspect apologétique de cette discipline." J.-P. Torrell, review of R. Latourelle, *Théologie de la Révélation*, *Revue Thomiste* 86 (1986): 654. See also R. Latourelle, "A New Image of Fundamental Theology," in *Problems and Perspectives of Fundamental Theology*, ed. R. Latourelle and G. O'Collins (New York: Paulist, 1982), 37–58, 51–56.

Marsili endeavors to set in place the contours of liturgical theology,[38] Dulles provides the methodological basis for a postconciliar ecclesiology,[39] and Martelet sketches the outlines of a new dogmatic[40]. The works are foundational in every sense, and their pedagogical style and intention is not insignificant to the task of consolidation and systematization with which the authors were faced at the close of Vatican II.

Good introductory works always contain within them the suggestions of future development. Initiating the reader into the main currents of twentieth-century theological renewal necessarily involves an orientation toward their future development. Through an analysis of the major themes in the texts remaining, it is possible to see how the writers begin to reorient themselves. Retrospection yields to the forward movement of future development, and the writers look less for the approbation of the Council and more toward the expansion and deepening of its themes within contemporary

38. "Di fatto, se Casel ha riscoperto la categoria misterica, a Marsili si deve il primo tentativo "sistematico" (e per questo anti-sistematico!) di costruzione di una 'teologia liturgica,' nel senso non di una liturgia interpretata teologicamente ma di una teologia compresa in ottica liturgica, dove non c'è fede senza atto cultuale (a livello di prassi) e non c'è scienza teologica senza scienza liturgica (a livello di teoria)." A. Grillo, *Teologia Fondamentale e Liturgia: Il rapporto tra immediatezza e mediazione nella riflessione teologica* (Padova: Edizioni Messaggero-Abbazia di Santa Giustina, 1995), 35–36. "Il lavoro di Marsili si configura come tentativo di costruire una *teologia liturgica*, ossia una teologia strutturata in ottica liturgica, e precisamente secondo la 'forma' sacramentale." G. Bonaccorso, *Introduzione allo studio della liturgia* (Padova: Edizioni Messaggero-Abbazia di S. Giustina, 1990), 64.

39. "Though it is not a systematic treatise *de ecclesia*, it is an indispensable commentary on all treatises, as on the documents of Vatican II which must be the basis for any contemporary synthesis of theology." R. Murray, review of A. Dulles, *Models of the Church, The Heythrop Journal* 19 (1978): 79.

40. It is interesting to see how R. Latourelle's description of a new dogmatic describes Martelet's efforts in *Les idées maîtresses de Vatican II* : "A theology which takes the history of salvation as its axis is therefore called upon to renew its life both in its source and in its implications; in its source, through biblical, patristic and liturgical theology, in its implications through pastoral and spiritual theology. The way in which each mystery of faith impinges upon spiritual and pastoral life—rather an *hors d'oeuvre* in the eyes of theologians in the past—is from now on an essential part of their task." Latourelle, *Theology: Science of Salvation* (New York: Paulist, 1969), 121–22.

philosophy and culture. Gradually, foundational themes are developed according to their own methods and interests, and it is possible to notice particular insights and emerging similarities. To some extent, the category of sign-symbol has already been isolated as a "major idea" within conciliar theology, so as an exploration of the orientation and development of major themes is undertaken, it is perhaps not unreasonable to begin there.

Orientation and Development

In the preface to *Models of Revelation*, Dulles asserts that "theological method generally presupposes a doctrine of revelation and uses revelation as a norm."[41] This is certainly true of Latourelle's *Le Christ et l'Église*, and the doctrine of revelation it presupposes is that of *La Théologie de la Révélation*. Though invested with a biblical sensitivity, a new dynamism and a dialogical character, the concept of revelation described in this work nevertheless remains noetic and strangely monolithic. With such a notion of revelation as the guiding norm for an analysis of Christ's status as a sign, according to the teachings of Vatican II, it should not be surprising that *Le Christ et l'Église* follows a largely deductive method. As previously noted, Latourelle intended in these texts to give an exposition of the Council's teachings that would facilitate a systematic framework for the development of fundamental theology. The fact that the arguments were largely internal meant that standard theological methods seemed appropriate.[42] Such is not the case for Dulles, because he seeks to

---

41. A. Dulles, "Preface," in *Models of Revelation* (New York: Doubleday, 1983), vii.
42. Any appreciation of the enormous consequences for fundamental theology of the Council's definitive abandoning of scholastic apologetic will assure the reader that this remark is not meant pejoratively: "We can be thankful to Latourelle for pointing out that a good Christology, ecclesiology and semiology are prerequisites both for a presentation of Christ and the Church as signs of salvation and for their discernment as such. Within such a context, the author can

develop the elements of the argument along more speculative lines. The point of departure is neither Scripture nor magisterial teaching, but the nontheological locus of a philosophical theory of tacit knowing. His basis is somewhat more experiential, and therefore a method such as models was maybe to be expected.

Free from the strictures of the deductive method and having gained an external perspective on the truths of revelation, Dulles is able to establish his central thesis: revelation is realized, transmitted, given, and received through symbolic communication. And such is the contribution of Michael Polanyi's theory of tacit knowing that Dulles can conclude that symbolic knowledge is participatory and not speculative. Hence it has a transforming effect that influences praxis and the moral life. Symbolic communication therefore amplifies notions of revelation beyond the comprehension of defined truths and strictly linguistic categories, and, by appealing to a broader base, begins to hold together orthodoxy and orthopraxis.

The particular notion of symbol that Dulles weds to Polanyi's theory is that of Karl Rahner's *Realsymbol*. Bearing within them what they signify, these symbols are at once both subjective and objective. From the context of everyday life, by means of a tacit awareness of what O'Donovan calls "informal modes of inference and our personal framework of commitment,"[43] an objective symbol of revelation is fashioned.[44] Adopting this theological context, Dulles

---

enumerate calmly the historical deviations which took place in the Church, while inviting us to recognise the signs of Christ's fidelity to his Bride, thus avoiding both triumphalism and defeatism." Potvin, review of *Christ and the Church*, 359.

43. L. O'Donovan, review of A. Dulles, *Models of Revelation*, *America* 153 (May 28, 1983): 424.

44. "This concept of the intrinsic symbol, though developed so briefly here, must now be employed if we are to grasp what characterizes sacramental causation, and if we are to do this on the basis of the ecclesiological origin of the sacraments. The Church in her visible historical form is herself an intrinsic symbol of the eschatologically triumphant grace of God; in that spatio-temporal visible form, this grace is made present. And because the sacraments are the actual fulfilment, the actualization of the Church's very nature, in regard to individual men, precisely in as much as the Church's whole reality is to be the real presence of God's grace, as the new covenant, these sacramental signs are efficacious. Their efficacy is that of the intrinsic symbol."

broaches the question of revelation *in nobis* and begins to resolve some of the difficulties he had outlined in his chapter on revelation as inner experience. While Dulles asserts that revelation never occurs as a purely inner experience, Rahner's category of *Realsymbol* helps him to overcome the impasse between the objective manifestation of salvation and its subjective realization that had so preoccupied the *nouvelle théologie*.

Dulles regards his work in *Models of Revelation* as "a contribution to fundamental theology" that is "predogmatic."[45] In opening up the question of revelation according to the methods of this "boundary discipline,"[46] it is his intention to be both systematic and speculative. The later function of dogmatics will be to contextualize and interrelate these findings with the superstructure of defined truths. This is why O'Donovan is correct to assert that "it is the language, as much as the mode of thought, that seems to me this book's greatest contribution."[47] Dulles offers an accurately defined vocabulary that provides "a living way to speak of what revelation is and how it occurs."[48] That this language should be living is of crucial importance, because that indicates the completion of a paradigm shift from the stance of technical and critical theology to the context of lived faith. As a result, Dulles reaches beyond theological models so as to further the reinvigoration of revelation categories: a process that was begun with the preconciliar return to the sources.

Perhaps the predogmatic nature of this text gives the best explanation of Dulles's reluctance to make explicit the relationship between the sacraments and revelatory symbols.[49] Yet language

---

K. Rahner, *The Church and the Sacraments*, trans. W. J. O'Hara (London: Burns and Oates, 1963), 39.

45. Dulles, "Preface," in *Models of Revelation*, x.

46. See Latourelle, "A New Image of Fundamental Theology," 37.

47. O'Donovan, review of *Models of Revelation*, 424.

48. Ibid.

choice betrays an implicit theological preference which to some extent distinguishes sacraments of salvation from symbols of revelation. The unique contribution of Marsili's *I segni del mistero di Cristo* is the insistence that, because the sacramental dimension of revelation emerges within every moment of the history of salvation, the two realities cannot be separated. This fact is defined and elaborated by the celebration of the sacraments, because the liturgy is the place where the continuing story of salvation is realized. That is to say, the symbolic communication of the sacraments renders visible and actual the words and actions of Christ, who is the unique revelation of the Father. If Dulles chose a more secular rendering of Rahner's *Realsymbol*, one more compatible with his fundamental enterprise, then Marsili labors to establish a more consciously dogmatic rendering of Rahner's concept.[50] With the liturgy as the locus of this endeavor, and with the help of biblical, patristic, and anthropological insights, he revitalizes sacramentology in the light of a theology of symbol.

An element fundamental to the thesis of Marsili is the sacramental consistency of the divine economy. Hence, the opening chapter of *I segni del mistero di Cristo* distinguishes the anthropological basis of primitive signs, the sacred signs of the Hebrew people, and the signs

49. Something of the confusion of Dulles's implicit suggestions can be gained from Bishop Christopher Butler's review: "If I have not misunderstood Fr. Dulles, and despite the fact that he concedes that the word 'sacrament' usually refers not so much to revelation as to the 'communication of grace and sanctification,' it appears that a symbol which contains, expresses and conveys what it symbolises can well be called a sacrament. In this connection he appears to accept the modern usage whereby Jesus Christ is, as a realised and realising symbol, described as a 'sacrament of God,' while the Church, in its turn, is 'the sacrament of Christ' (Fr. Dulles empathises with Vatican II). In their turn, the seven sacraments both symbolise and contain and convey that of which they are symbols." B. C. Butler, review of A. Dulles, *Models of Revelation*, *New Blackfriars* 65 (1984): 235.

50. For an analysis of the influence of Casel and Rahner on the development of liturgical notions of symbol, see D. Power, R. Duffy, and K. Irwin, "Sacramental Theology: A Review of Literature," in *Theological Studies* 55 (1994): 661–63. Also A. Schilson, "Erneuerung der Sakramententheologie im 20. Jahrhundert," *Liturgisches Jahrbuch* 37 (1987): 18–41.

sacred to Christians. With the help of the church fathers, Marsili then relates these signs to one another by demonstrating that their definitive reality is Christ: invisible in natural religion, promised and anticipated by Judaism, and fully revealed in the incarnation. In such a context, it becomes apparent that this theology of the sacraments is a further specification of liturgical theology. The symbols used in the celebration of the seven sacraments gather into one interpretive moment the whole history of salvation—and they reveal the words and gestures of Christ to be at its center. Hence the reality of the paschal mystery is defined as that which the liturgical symbols make present.

Though these "punti di teologia sacramentale" present neither a complete nor a systematic reflection, they do offer a richly integrated synthesis of biblical, patristic, and liturgical perspectives. If Dulles provided a living vocabulary by which theologians could speak of revelation and its occurrence, then Marsili provides a context for these words so that their full meaning and significance can be realized.[51] Understood within the liturgical perspectives of *I segni del mistero di Cristo*, the significant elements of symbolic mediation take on the theological clarity and practical relevance that Dulles would probably have wished for his predogmatic propositions. Yet the subtitle *From Symbol to System* given to his later work, *The Craft of Theology*, suggests that he also saw the need to develop a structured context for the theology of symbol that he had introduced in *Models of Revelation*.[52] Interestingly, in the later work he addresses, among

51. This Marsili later elaborates as part of a two-fold process. See S. Marsili, "Teologia liturgica," in *Nuovo Dizionario di Liturgia*, ed. D. Sartore and A.-M. Triacca (Milan: Edizioni Paoline, 1983), 1524 also S. Marsili, "La liturgia nel discorso teologico odierno. Per una fondazione della liturgia pastorale: individuazione delle prospettive e degli ambiti specifici," in *Una liturgia per l'uomo. La liturgia pastorale e i suoi compiti*, ed. P. Visentin, A. Terrin, and R. Cecolin (Padova: Messaggero-Abbazia di S. Giustina, 1986), 17–47.

52. "The subtitle leads us to expect a unified treatment of how applying the category of symbol to theology provides both a clue into Dulles's theological method and how it might enrich the

other things, the biblical, patristic, and liturgical aspects of theology, out of which Marsili had shaped his own theology of the sacraments.

The postcritical stance of *Models of Revelation* and its eclectic, recollective style suggest that a theological system adequate to the depth and nuance of the Christian symbols can never be found.[53] Yet Dulles is convinced that context is all-important for theological reflection on the content of Christian faith. An ecclesial character is essential to this study, as only within the faith-setting of a worshiping community do theologians participate in that truth that they seek to understand.[54] Part of the reason for this assertion is Dulles's view of the role of method in fundamental theology. He is convinced of the practical impossibility of demonstrating the credibility of the Christian faith on the grounds of reason alone. Despite the fact that reason always works under grace, the object of faith is such that knowledge must be participatory and therefore involves more than cognitive faculties.[55] Fundamental theology should, then, concern itself with the processes of conversion if it is to communicate with any credibility the mode and reality of revelation. Thus the category

way theology is practiced today." J. Burkhard, review of A. Dulles, *The Craft of Theology*, *New Theology Review* 7 (1994): 106–7.

53. "The sub-title of the book 'from symbol to system' gives an idea of the general *leitmotiv* of Dulles's approach to theology. For our author, 'The Christian religion is a set of relationships with God mediated by Christian symbols.'. . . Since symbols are richer than concepts, no concept can ever exhaust the symbol. Christian theology has the task of thinking in symbols, of contemplating them from ever-new perspectives. But theology can never do full justice to the reality it contemplates. Hence no final system will ever be possible in theology." J. O'Donnell, review of A. Dulles, *The Craft of Theology*, *Gregorianum* 74 (1993) 373–74.

54. "In line with this general approach Dulles insists that Christian theology always has an ecclesial character. It can be done only within the community of faith and is intimately linked to prayer, preaching and liturgical worship. Detached from this context, it loses its *raison d'être*." Ibid.

55. To some extent, Dulles here responds to criticisms made of *Models of Revelation*; for example, "While the typology and the comments are helpful, the book assumes that revelation is primarily a cognition of realities. Therefore it overlooks the non-cognitive (or more than cognitive) aspects of much biblical language—promise, command, forgiveness, invitation to commitment—as well as liberation theology's emphasis on praxis." E. TeSelle, review of A. Dulles, *Models of Revelation*, *Religious Studies Review* 10, no. 3 (July 1984): 38.

of experience enters the focus of theological reflection as a privileged and indispensable source.[56]

Dulles has alerted theology to the significance of the category of symbol in the communication of revelation. He has stressed particularly the participatory dimensions of symbolic realities within the process of initiation, and later he allies to this reflection the category of experience so as to appreciate more fully the human apprehension of God's self-manifestation. Yet though these links have been made, to a large extent they remain notional, and the context for their proper integration missing. Nevertheless, as Bernard Cooke points out, if theology has come to the point where it recognizes the gap between theological systems and the felt symbols of salvation, then "one must recognize that it is Avery Dulles himself who has done so much to sensitize us to the very issue."[57] The existential realization of the symbols of faith within the individual and the community of believers is a question that Dulles leaves to the craft of future theology.

Martelet's *Résurrection, eucharistie et genèse de l'homme* locates the means of an individual's self-realization in the realm of the symbolic: the relationship a person has with the entire universe being expressed in that life-giving integration of elements that is the symbol of the human body. Bringing all together in themselves, each symbolizes

---

56. "The chapter [Fundamental Theology and the Dynamics of Conversion] makes it clear that Dulles is fully aware of the current emphasis on religious experience—as a privileged source of theological research and reflection; and if he himself leans towards a more 'rational' type of theology, that is the result of a carefully chosen professional decision." B. Cooke, review of A. Dulles, *The Craft of Theology*, *America* 168 (January 23 1993): 21.

57. "Symbols are certainly basic to the process of shaping and expressing our human awareness; they are key to our communication with one another and, therefore, foundational forces in our culture—all this Dulles has clarified for us; but we not only communicate symbolically, as individuals and communities we exist symbolically. It seems to me that this is a critical issue for Christian theologians who deal with the mystery of God's Word incarnated. Unless I misread him, Dulles understands theology as a movement beyond symbol to method, as the title of the book suggests. To be honest and fair, however, one must recognize that it is Avery Dulles himself who has done much to sensitize us to the very issue I have mentioned." Ibid.

the victory of life over death's forces of dissolution. In this fact, Martelet sees a certain congruity with the resurrection and the Eucharist. There, the elements of a corruptible cosmos are caught up into a symbolic reality from which death is excluded. In his risen body, Christ has entered into a new relationship with the matter of the universe through the action of the Spirit. The eucharistic symbols become the particular locus of that which "has embraced the whole universe,"[58] and they give a present appreciation of the risen presence of the Parousia. Hence he can conclude that the Eucharist actualizes symbolically the risen body of Christ, so that participation in this symbol involves transformation of self and of the universe.

Certain elements of Martelet's method become immediately apparent.[59] Foremost is the anthropological dimension of the work. If fundamental theology is to establish the credibility of the Christian revelation by recovering a stance of faith for the modern person then Martelet asserts that this task must begin with the human reality. In the light of the gospel, the human is not scorned but understood as part of a progression of which Christ is the culmination. The Pauline typologies of the two Adams show "that adherence to Christ by faith and the discovery of the full reality of the human person should be one and the same process."[60] If Dulles attested that the truths of revelation emerge most clearly within the dynamic of conversion, then Martelet's particular contribution is to expose the roots of this symbolic process. In a sense he provides what Bernard Cooke felt to be missing from Dulles's theological vision, namely, an existential

---

58. J. Sheets, review of G. Martelet, *The Risen Christ and the Eucharistic World*, *Worship* 51 (1977): 466.

59. "This book can well serve as a model of theological method. The focus is clear, namely, the nature of Christ's presence in the Eucharist; the thesis is also clearly set forth, the need to understand presence through bodily presence, in particular through the mode of Christ's risen-bodily-presence." Ibid.

60. G. Martelet, "Christology and Anthropology: Toward a Christian Genealogy of the Human," in Latourelle and O'Collins, *Problems and Perspectives of Fundamental Theology*, 152.

grounding for the symbols of faith within the human reality.[61] This anthropology in turn supports a Christology that is itself dynamic, personal, and historically based, and effects a unity between the object of revelation and subjective participation in it.

Marsili placed great significance on the consistently sacramental structure of revelation, so much so that he gave the impression that a certain interchangeability existed between the different symbolic moments of the economy. Yet, while Martelet sees the sacramental economy as the locus of humanity's encounter with Christ, the honesty with which he applies the anthropological method means he is always aware of the particular mode of sacramental symbolism. The symbol of the Eucharist does express a real unity between finite human bodies and the risen body of Christ, but at the same time it stimulates that unity by making plain the separation that exists between the Risen One and those who live by faith. That Martelet should so clearly express the "not yet" element of the sacramental symbols perhaps results from his differing theological perspective.

The future is the coordinating perspective of *Résurrection, eucharistie et genèse de l'homme,* looking as it does to the epicletic realization of the Parousia in the sacraments rather than the anamnetic representation of the past. Fundamental to the thesis of Martelet is the conviction that without the resurrection, there can be no real Eucharist, for the presence encountered there is that of the risen Christ. Thus he expresses an alternative approach to the actualization of revelation in the sacraments. The ritual remembering of the future (an aspect of anamnesis that Marsili does recognise) is as important as representing the past, because to actualize the risen Christ is to reveal the past and present recapitulated in future glory. A consequence of this perspective is a greater sensitivity to the work

61. Cf. B. Cooke, review of *The Craft of Theology,*" 21.

of the Holy Spirit in the economy of revelation and salvation. And this, combined with the privileged status that Martelet gives to the liturgy in his methodology, means that the immediate experience of revelation within the sacramental encounter is a question implicit to the research of the book.

The questions that emerge from the theological method of *Résurrection eucharistie et genèse de l'homme* are echoed in Latourelle's *Miracles de Jésus et théologie du miracle*. This is the second part of Latourelle's reflection on the signs of revelation, having already examined the fundamental signs of Christ and the church in the book of that name. The object now is to "better situate"[62] these signs that were such a focus for classical apologetics, but this relocation also shows a progression in method from the first part of the enterprise in *Le Christ et l'Église*. Dividing the work into three main sections, Latourelle discusses problems of approach, the historicity of the miracles, and emergent theological questions. In this way, he builds not only on *Le Christ et l'Église*, but also on *L'homme et ses problèmes dans la lumière du Christ* and *L'accès à Jésus par les Évangiles*, bringing together the hermeneutic, semiological, and anthropological aspects of the fundamental theologian's task. It is the mature synthesis of these principal elements that causes the more searching questions about the relationship of the believer to the revealer to emerge.

In the opening chapter, Latourelle describes an approach to the theology of signs close to the one followed by Martelet. The theological starting point must be anthropological. It must be

---

62. "Une théologie des signes doit donc commencer par une étude du signe premier et fondamental qu'est le Christ, puis du signe qui lui est inséparable, l'Église. C'est l'approche proposée par l'A. dans *Le Christ et l'Église: Signes du salut.* Cette étude des signes fondamentaux du christianisme ne dispense pas pour autant du traitement des signes particuliers. C'est ici que la théologie fondamentale actuelle se relie aux préoccupations de l'apologétique traditionnelle, mieux situées toutefois et analysées avec des techniques et une méthode renouvelées." A. Charbonneau, review of R. Latourelle, *Miracles de Jésus et théologie du miracle, Science et Esprit* 38, no. 2 (1986): 257.

centered on Christ, historically rooted, and liturgically elaborated. Not surprisingly, many similarities emerge between miracles and sacraments—both symbols of the sacramental economy—and this allows for interesting comparisons to be made. Miracles manifest on a sensible level the invisible wonders of the kingdom, and in that they allow a glimpse of the glorious order that has been introduced by Christ's bodily resurrection. Initiation into this new order is dependent upon the complex sign function of communication, revelation, attestation, and liberation that miracles display. Reflecting on the power of miracles to liberate individuals to live the gospel, Latourelle introduces a significant element of praxis—revelation acts not only on the perception but also on the will. To apprehend the truths of salvation renders one free to act. The questions of the recognition of miracles and of their impact on the Christian life thus become the two important questions of the final section.

In discussing the recognition of miracles, Latourelle details a dialectical process by which a person faced with an exceptional event in the order of creation comes to knowledge of its theological significance. He insists that the sign of the miracle cannot be judged in isolation from its religious finality. That is to say, an absolute distinction between the sign that expresses a transcendent reality and that reality itself is impossible. An unbroken correspondence must be established between the signifier and the signified, so that one illumines the other. There is obvious import here for a theology of the sacraments that must address the issue of the subjective apprehension of God's objective revelation. Indeed, here too is the beginning of a reflection on the relationship between immediacy and mediation within the symbolic transmission of revelation.

Orientating the work toward these questions, Latourelle has shifted noticeably toward the postcritical agenda that Dulles outlines in *The Craft of Theology*. Starting with a presupposition of faith, Latourelle seeks to articulate the Christian symbols not in strictly scientific terms, but by participating in them.[63] This is why there is a clear turn toward praxis and mention of the liturgical expression of the signs of salvation in this work. The "tacit" elements of faith have become increasingly important in Latourelle's elaboration of a theology of revelation. The closer the synthesis of the anthropological, hermeneutic, and semiological elements has become, the sharper the focus on the reception of revelation.[64]

Despite their postcritical sensibilities, their interest in tacit awareness, and the individual's recognition of and response to the signs of revelation, neither Dulles nor Latourelle speaks much of experience. The topic is still treated suspiciously within an article that Latourelle wrote for the relatively recent *Dictionary of Fundamental Theology*. Clearly, he points out the dangerous ambiguity of this concept when used in conjunction with revelation. His reluctance to accept experiential terminology centers on the essential subjectivity of the category and the fact that experience is apparently bound by no objective norm. Yet, at the core of his suspicions is the scant recognition that theologies of experience give to the foundational revelation of Christ and the apostles "something by means of which" the gift of God's self-communication can be accepted in faith.[65] Such

---

63. "Cela paraît bizarre à dire, mais on sent que l'A. a fait du miracle son affaire personnelle. Ce n'est plus ici le savant pur et simple qui parle, mais l'homme de foi qui veut faire partager sa conviction à ses contemporains. Après tant d'essais récents dont le caractère cérébral apporte si peu à la vie théologale, il est réconfortant de lire celui-ci dont la solide documentation a su ne pas se faire aux dépens de ce qui est premier et qui doit le rester." J.-P. Torrell, review of R. Latourelle, *Miracles de Jésus et théologie du miracle*, *Revue Thomiste* 86 (1986): 659.

64. One might compare here Latourelle's reflection on "Theology and the Interior Life" and part 5 of *Theology: Science of Salvation*, which sets out the main "axes of contemporary theology" and their orientations at the close of Vatican II, with the first and last chapters of *Miracles de Jésus et théologie du miracle*. The better integrated the themes of development, the more acute the problem of the nature of participation becomes. Cf. Latourelle, *Theology: Science of Salvation* (New York: St. Paul's, 1969), 232–70.

65. See R. Latourelle, "Revelation" in *Dictionary of Fundamental Theology*, ed. R. Latourelle and R. Fisichella (New York: Crossroad, 1995), 943–45, for Latourelle's most developed reflection on this concept. Though Jean Mouroux's *L'Expérience chrétienne* (Paris: Aubier, 1952) is a work

is not the case when we come to the later articles of Marsili published posthumously in the *Nuovo Dizionario di Liturgia*. Here there is more talk of actuation and actualization, of spiritual incidence and experience.[66] Seen by some as the product of a gradual radicalization of the mystery theology of Odo Casel, these articles present the final turn in a long development.[67] For Casel, "mystery" enjoyed an ambiguity that kept all but nuanced notions of experience at a distance. Once Marsili had identified the truths of faith with the liturgy, and once he has asserted that liturgical theology was the only appropriate mode of reflection on that deposit, he made his most radical conclusion: theology is born from the liturgy as experience of faith. That is to say, when the contours of liturgical theology had been clearly defined and contradistinguished, Marsili began to examine and repeatedly point out the role that experience plays within the liturgy, and hence within the transmission of revelation.

While to some extent the liturgical movement had always sought a via media between the existential and transcendent realities of faith,[68] Marsili's assertion about the role of experience in the symbolic communication of the liturgy remains a brave one.[69] The shadows

cited by Latourelle in earlier works, this is not in direct connection with its major theme of Christian experience. Such terminology is consciously avoided, and though the theme is alluded to occasionally, nowhere is it treated systematically or at length. See A. Sierra, *La Revelación Según René Latourelle*, Tesi Gregoriana, Serie Teologia, 60 (Rome: PUG, 2000), 52–60; 372. For an example of the diffidence with which Dulles approaches this subject, see his introduction to D. Edwards, *The Human Experience of God* (Dublin: Gill and Macmillan, 1984).

66. Cf. Marsili, "Teologia Liturgica," 1514; 1517, 1524.
67. "Sulla scia di Casel ha riscoperto la categoria misterica, a Marsili si deve il primo tentativo sistematico (e per questo antisistematico!) di costruzione di una 'teologia liturgica,' nel senso non di una liturgia interpretata teologicamente ma di una teologia compresa in ottica liturgica, dove non c'è fede senza atto cultuale (a livello di prassi) e non c'è scienza teologica senza scienza liturgica (a livello di teoria). Tuttavia una delle caratteristiche più importanti di questo autore sta nella *radicalizzazione di questa intuizione caseliana*, per arrivare ad una concezione in cui, come la fede finisce con l'identificarsi con il culto, così la teologia finisce per identificarsi con la teologia liturgica. In questa linea anche la sua interpretazione di Casel e della sua comprensione del culto si dimostra estremizzata." Grillo, *Teologia Fondamentale e Liturgia*, 35–36.
68. Cf. R. Franklin, "Humanism and Transcendence in the Nineteenth Century Liturgical Movement," *Worship* 59 (1985): 342–53.

cast by the Modernist crisis were long ones, and perhaps this explains why experience is the last category to be exploited by the children of the *aggiornamento*. Nevertheless, the stringent application of the methods of liturgical theology taught Marsili that the viewpoint of the experiencing subject emerged naturally from a dynamic and anthropologically sound theology of revelation, and could not be ignored. What can be seen clearly in the late Marsili is a conviction, perhaps implicit in each of the chosen writers, that the duty of this generation is to retrieve whatever was of value in the subjective approach of the Modernists, and with it complete the task of renewal.[70] For now, more than ever, it is the task of the church to read the signs of these rapidly changing and complex times and interpret them in the light of the gospel.

In this brief and historically structured reflection, it is possible to see what the overarching contributions of these writers were to the restructuring and development of Catholic theology in the post-Council period. To a large extent, the focus has been on major emergent methodologies and themes. It is necessary now to draw these conclusions into a further synthesis built more clearly around points of convergence and divergence, so as to establish more clearly the core contribution of these writers.

---

69. In "Experience and Symbols," the ninth chapter of his *Retrieving Fundamental Theology*, G. O'Collins charts the slow recovery of a theology of experience from the prescriptions of *Dei Filius* and *Pascendi*. Despite the approbation given by *DV* to experience as a source for theology, the response of theologians has been sparse, with the notable exception of Pope John Paul II. See O'Collins, *Retrieving Fundamental Theology* (New York: Paulist, 1993), 108–19.

70. On the occasion of the sixtieth anniversary of the death of George Tyrrell, a retrospective on post–Vatican II impressions of the Modernists was released and is of value here. Cf. *The Heythrop Journal* 10, no. 3 (1969).

Points of Theological Convergence and Divergence

To a large extent, the authors of this study were recipients of a static and compartmentalized theological heritage with which they show a common dissatisfaction. They believed their task of renewal to involve embracing theological categories that were dynamic and existentially grounded. Decadent scholasticism thrived on abstraction and deduction, a combination of which had made the truths of revelation appear notional and remote. Christology gave acute expression of this, being structured as it was around the almost complete separation of Christ from the work of salvation. But it was this discipline that was recognized as central to a successful restructuring of theology. In effecting the reunion of Christology and soteriology, these authors had three aims: to reclaim for Christ his rightful place in the history of salvation, to provide theology with its interpretative center and means of synthesis, and to bring out more clearly the *pro nobis* element of the divine economy. Methodologically, this demanded an approach that was biblical, historical, and anthropocentric, and according to these principles a dynamic Christology became the foundation of theological reform.

Points of Theological Convergence

The embracing of these themes, and their systematization into coherent working theologies, essentially involved elaborating the consequences of the christological renewal for other areas of theology. Aloys Grillmeier notes in his *Sacramentum Mundi* article the effect of this renewal on Trinitarian theology, sacramental theology, and ecclesiology.[71] The christological remolding of these tracts

---

71. A. Grillmeier, "Jesus Christ," in *Encyclopaedia of Theology: The Concise Sacramentum Mundi*, ed. K. Rahner (New York: Crossroad, 1991), 744–51.

provides a certain unity from which a coherent theology of revelation emerges. By treating it as a whole and by interrelating various aspects of the economy, the writers are in part responsible for the dynamic and more coherent theology that distinguishes itself from pre-Council scholasticism. As "schoolmen" of this new theology, they took care to ensure a full and balanced curriculum by establishing distinct disciplines, but also by having an eye to synthetic unity.[72] The earlier of these works, especially, might be said to converge stylistically as well as theologically, not only in the sense of their clear and structured pedagogy, but also in their clear shift away from the apologetic and interrogative style of the manuals. These authors sought a more holistic and integrated rendering that allowed for the pluralism and nuance required of modern theology.[73]

When christological studies looked to the biblical narratives to invigorate predominantly conceptual notions of the person of Christ, New Testament and patristic sources yielded many symbolic descriptions. Hence theologians gradually developed the idea of Christ the primordial symbol. This category became increasingly significant in the theology of the conciliar period, and recognition of its centrality to theological renewal is a point of substantial convergence between these authors. Contemporary research of a philosophical, sociological, and psychological nature has revealed the multivalent depth of this concept, and therefore its supreme value within theological language. Basic to the psyche, symbols are the primary mode of human expression and constitutive of social structures. A fundamental turning point for modern Catholic

72. Cf. J. Alfaro, H. Bouillard, H. Carrier, G. Dejaifve, R. Latourelle, G. Martelet, "La théologie fondamentale à la recherche de son identité: Un carrefour," *Gregorianum* 50 (1969): 757–76. Also S. Marsili, "La Liturgia nella strutturazione della teologia," *Rivista Liturgica* 58, no. 2 (1971): 153–62, and Latourelle, *L'Infini du sens*, 155–77.

73. Cf. R. Latourelle, "Apologétique et fondamentale: problèmes de nature et de méthode," *Salesianum* 27 (1965): 255–74.

theology was full recognition of its christological content, but perhaps of equal significance was the discovery of symbol as the interpretive key to the different modes of revelation in Christ. If Christology unified theology according to content, then the notion of symbol provided a unity of expression. Thus, when *Lumen Gentium* compared the church to a sacramental symbol, the concept was firmly established in the theological vocabulary, even if its full depths had not been plumbed.[74]

Each of the authors made a significant contribution to the development of a theology of revelation based on their particular elaboration of the concept of symbol. One effect of these various studies of symbol as word, communication, sacrament, or model is that there is a point of common contact within quite different perspectives that should offer the framework for further reflection and synthesis. This is what E. Cassirer refers to as a "symbolic grammar," and, although R. Fisichella sees its establishment as one of the first tasks to be taken in hand by fundamental theology, the potential of an interdisciplinary study needs also to be recognized.[75]

Lastly, within the work of these four theologians it is possible to detect an increasing common resonance with the postcritical agenda, especially if the criteria of Dulles are taken as indicative of this somewhat nebulous classification. Though these writers retain their critical edge and seek to give a credible account of Christian faith, they remain unabashed by their fiduciary context and happily rely on convictions born from belief. This in itself allows for an interesting interplay between the demands of critical objectivism and the subjectivism of personal encounter. These writers, among others, are responsible for widening and strengthening the categories by

---

74. See G. Martelet, *N'oublions pas Vatican II* (Paris: Éditions du Cerf, 1995), 61–67.
75. R. Fisichella, "Semiology II: Symbol," in Latourelle and Fisichella, *Dictionary of Fundamental Theology*, 990.

which a deeper understanding of revelation can be gained. They draw on modern personalist philosophies, psychology, and sociology that serve to amplify theological notions from a pastoral perspective. If part of the postcritical agenda is a creative reworking of aspects of the tradition in the light of more tacit truths, then it should not be surprising if these authors grow in reference to the liturgy and Christian praxis and arrive at the threshold of a theology of experience.

Even such a brief analysis of the theological convergence of these writers gives sufficient indication of the major trends shaping and being shaped by their work. However, it is perhaps areas of notable divergence that indicate the deeper questions pertinent to this book. This section on the positive contributions of the writers will conclude with a study of contrasting and more individual perspectives.

Points of Theological Divergence

It may seem strange to include the concept of symbol as a point of theological divergence as well as a source of unity among these writers, but this results from the inherent complexity of the category itself. Within it, there is a scope of interpretation that allows for considerable difference while affirming general agreement. Though these distinctions might be said to be predominantly methodological, they nevertheless betray something of the fundamental position of the writer. This is certainly true of the choice between "sign" and "symbol," which as L.-M. Chauvet points out, can indicate the characteristic stance of a writer:

> In the concrete world, sign and symbol are always mixed together. It is impossible to say unilaterally that "this object is a sign" and "that object is a symbol." As with concepts like "metaphysics" and "the symbolic," the value of these two concepts of "sign" and "symbol" is first of all

methodological; their distinction plays a *heuristic* role in allowing us to discriminate between complex empirical realities.[76]

Such an observation needs to be understood in the context of the four authors, since while Latourelle and initially Marsili make a preferred option for the concept "sign," Dulles and Martelet retain "symbol" throughout.[77] Hence it is necessary to examine the methodological distinction that these writers were making, and to note the influence that their position has on their overall depiction of the relationship between the sacraments and revelation.

Symbols, it would seem, are not merely complex signs that draw on every aspect of a situation for their signification. They differ fundamentally from signs in the method of their communication. A sign functions by reference to something other than itself by means of certain sensible signifiers, while a symbol introduces a person into an order of relationships to which it already belongs. It is because symbols make identification between subjects that they draw on all the elements of human culture and not merely on the cognitive dimension, which remains the principal medium of signs.[78] Already one begins to see how particular terminology is indicative of wider assumptions about the theology of revelation.

Though Latourelle does not enter into an epistemological discussion of the differences between sign and symbol, his preference

76. L.-M. Chauvet, *Symbol and Sacrament* (Collegeville, MN: Liturgical Press, 1995), 111.

77. Though Martelet uses the term *sign* frequently in his earlier work, even then the concept described is hard to distinguish from his later and more developed notion of *symbol*.

78. "If the symbol has necessarily a distinctive, formal 'value,' if, even from this formal point of view, one must consider it as the interior witness which renders possible any culture as a coherent system of values, still its function is not, like that of a sign, to refer to a 'something else' (*aliud aliquid*) that always stands on the plane of value, measure, calculation: a cognitive value of representations with regard to the real, an economic value of possessions with regard to what the group might have at its disposal, a technical value of objects with regard to the work to carry out, an ethical value of behavior with regard to the norms of society, and so forth. The primary function of the symbol is to *join* the persons who produce or receive it with their cultural world and so to *identify* them as subjects in their relations with other subjects." Chauvet, *Symbol and Sacrament*, 120–121.

for sign, made most clearly in *Le Christ et l'Église: Signes du salut*, perhaps has more than terminological significance. Concerned with Christian hermeneutics, the work as a whole recognizes meaning as the central question facing contemporary theology. The gospel gains its credibility from certain signs that reveal its divine origin and authenticity—hence the careful articulation of the signs of salvation is one the central tasks of fundamental theologians. Although Latourelle places the Council's christological renewal of signs, and particularly their personalization, at the heart of this work, his primary focus remains the objective meaning that these signs convey, rather than the interrelation of subjects that they inspire. The evocation of a concrete causal relationship between realities, which is the inherent function of a sign, appeals to Latourelle's enterprise, and seems to him to have the warranty of both the Scriptures and the Council fathers. However, while the literal, cognitive aspects of sign are important to Latourelle, it cannot be said that he is using the term in the simple scholastic sense.[79] Indeed, what is perhaps happening within the complete span of Latourelle's work is a bridging of older apologetic notions of sign with the newer theological notions of symbol, while the former biblically sensitive terminology is retained.[80] This said, it cannot be without significance that the author least interested in the subjective experience of revelation, and whose

79. That is to say in the purely noetic sense of Aquinas, who claims "Signum est per quod aliquis divenit in cognitionem alterius." Thomas Aquinas, *S. Th.* III, 60, 4. Cf. also Chauvet's comparative reading of the metaphysical and the symbolic in *Symbol and Sacrament*, 7–44.

80. Cf. Fisichella, "Semiology II: Symbol," 990. There is a sense in which Latourelle's thinking becomes more obviously "symbolic" in his mature reflections on the miracles of Jesus. This can be understood from his full discussion of the renewal of the theology of signs in the opening chapter of *Miracles de Jésus et théologie du miracle*. Indication of a change of terminology might also be implied in *Du prodige au miracle*, where he states, "Le symbole survient alors pour évoquer l'Absolu qui fait irruption dans notre monde sans être de notre monde. Le symbole est une réalité présente en expansion indéfinie vers l'infini." Latourelle, *Du prodige au miracle* (Montréal: Les Éditions Bellarmin, 1995), 121.

notion of revelation is predominantly cognitive, prefers the term *sign* to that of *symbol*.

Again, what is an implicit development within the writings of Latourelle takes explicit expression in the work of Marsili. Immediately, one would recognise a certain congruence between the notion of sign elaborated in *Le Christ et l'Église: Signes du salut* and that set forth in *I Segni del mistero di Cristo*. But while for most of his career, Marsili seems unconcerned to distinguish sign from symbol, toward the end of his life he works out clear definitions and shows an obvious preference for the concept of symbol in the elaboration of his liturgical theology.[81] Significantly, it was in 1983, the year of his death and the same year in which the articles on "Liturgia" and "Teologia liturgica" were later posthumously published in the *Nuovo Dizionario di Liturgia*, thus indicating a shift toward experience, that Marsili began to develop a theology of symbolization. At his final *Congresso Internazionale di Liturgia*, he stated a double intention: to show how liturgical symbols have been downgraded in their role and are often identified and confused with signs, and to retrieve for symbols their sacramental significance within liturgy as the means by which the signifier and the signified are related.[82]

What is happening in the late writings of Marsili is a synthesis of liturgy, theology, and anthropology—the inevitable consequence of the fundamental premises of liturgical theology. For if the liturgy is the discourse on God actualized in ritual form, then the anthropology

---

81. See A. Grillo, "L'esperienza rituale come 'dato' della teologia fondamentale: ermeneutica di una rimozione e prospettive teoriche di reintegrazione," in *Liturgia e incarnazione*, ed. A. Terrin (Padova: Edizioni Messaggero, 1997), 175.

82. "1) Illustrare come il 'simbolo' liturgico sia stato declassificato, nell'importanza e nel ruolo che aveva nella liturgia, dal fatto di essere stato identificato e confuso con il segno; 2) ricuperare al 'simbolo' la sua vera natura che è quella di dare—per il rapporto che passa tra 'significante' e 'significato'—la vera ragione della 'sacramentalità' del rito liturgico." S. Marsili, "Il simbolismo della iniziazione cristiana alla luce della teologia liturgica," in *I simboli dell'iniziazione cristiana. Atti del I Congresso Internazionale di Liturgia: P. I. L., 25–28 maggio 1983*, ed. G. Farnedi, Studia Anselmiana 87, Analecta Liturgica 7 (Rome, 1983), 260.

of its communication and appropriation must be studied. According to Marsili, a theology of symbol is the means to a correct interpretation. Because the signified is present in the signifier, symbols mediate all the moments of the history of salvation in one moment.[83] Hence the main themes of the liturgical renewal, synthesized according to the principles of liturgical theology, are oriented toward the more contemporary question of experience and the liturgy.[84]

Among these four writers, Marsili offers the best example of the increasing centrality that an understanding of symbol has gained in contemporary theology and of the potential for the synthesis of interdisciplinary reflection which the concept offers. Yet these realizations are present in the works of Martelet and Dulles also, both of whom successfully synthesize the Council's spiritual renewal of signs with recent symbol theologies. Obviously dependent on Rahner's *Realsymbol*, Dulles carefully examines the correspondence between revelation and realizing symbols, and provides a worthy predogmatic or fundamental study that remains inspirational. By way of models, Dulles bridges the gap between the reflections of the

---

83. "La celebrazione liturgica è dunque propriamente il momento nel quale l'uomo esprime tanto la propria presa di coscienza di Dio e dell'azione benefica di lui nei suoi confronti, quando la propria riposta a queste realtà. Ma se il rito religioso, fondamentalmente e nel suo insieme, è costituito da questo duplice processo di presa di coscienza e di risposta, queste due componenti in esso presenti non procedono per linee parallele, ma si compenetrano a vicenda come azione divina che postula una riposta umana e come riposta umana data all'azione divina, e fondano il contenuto di quella esperienza globale umano–divina che è appunto la liturgia." S. Marsili, "Editoriale," *Rivista Liturgica* 67, no. 3 (1980): 283–84.

84. "In tutto ciò è facile vedere rappresentata, forse al suo livello ancor oggi più alto, una *prima linea di tendenza della riflessione liturgica contemporanea*, animata da una particolare forma di *passione per il fondamento* e che rielaborando i dati della tradizione del Movimento liturgico cerca di istituire faticosamente un rapporto convincente tra liturgia, teologia e antropologia." Grillo, "L'esperienza rituale," 175. "Negli ultimi scritti, inoltre, affiora quasi come metodo il segnalare vie e strumenti da percorrere e da utilizzare perché il mistero cristiano celebrato sia sempre più approfondito per essere vissuto. Come ogni vero maestro, ci sembra che sia scomparso troppo presto verso una liturgia celeste, anche se la sua memoria è così viva." S. Maggiani, "La teologia liturgica di S. Marsili come 'opera aperta,'" *Rivista Liturgica* 80 (1993): 357.

Council and the increasingly pluralistic atmosphere of the revelation debate.

Martelet's reflections, too, are given clear orientation by the work of the Council. *Les idées maîtresses de Vatican II* and the article "Horizon théologique de la deuxième session du Concile" make it clear that a renewal of signs was at the heart of the Council's work and is indicative of the way forward for theology. Even at this stage, Martelet sought to amplify the two-dimensional notions of the scholastics into a reality that held together inseparably the *signum* and the *res*, so that the sign can never be regarded as a distinct reality.[85] And this is the central idea of *Résurrection, eucharistie et genèse de l'homme*: "The risen Christ comes to us not through what is alien to him, but through what belongs to him in his risen body, which becomes the here-and-now realization of his risen presence, reaching its final epiphany only in the parousia."[86] The symbolizing elements of the Eucharist contain or, perhaps more correctly, are contained by, the risen body of Christ. In the Eucharist, the created order is introduced into an order of relationship to which the bread and wine, as the body and blood of Christ, already belong. Martelet draws on the concept of symbol in its fullest sense as that which facilitates a dynamic and real participation in the reality it signifies. Hence, he can establish the somatic unity between the risen body of Christ, his earthly body, and the body of the church, which is fundamental to this study. Of great significance here, however, is the role that the resurrection has in giving a completely different perspective to the sacramental symbols.

---

85. "En effet, la relation du signe à la réalité ne va pas sans réciprocité. . . . La *res* n'est pas plus séparable du *signe* qui la conditionne, que le *signe* n'est séparable de la *res* qui le finalise." G. Martelet, "Horizon théologique de la deuxième session du Concile," *Nouvelle Revue Theologique* 86 (1964): 457.
86. Sheets, review of *The Risen Christ and the Eucharistic World*, 466.

Apart from Martelet and the later Marsili, these writers employ a predominantly hermeneutic theological method. Access to revelation is focused on a retrospective approach that is centered on the historical Jesus, whether that be by means of liturgical *anàmnesis*, symbolic mediation, or by interpreting the signs of salvation as the effective continuation of the incarnation. Perhaps a symptom of the christological renewal, such a perspective is considerably widened when Martelet insists that access to Jesus is only by way of the resurrection. Thus the gaze of the believer is directed toward a future that only the Holy Spirit can actualize now in the body of Christ. Hence the beginning of a realization, shared by Marsili,[87] that pneumatology is an essential ingredient of the Council's desire for a reinvigorated and renewed Christology. Showing also a great sensitivity to the liturgy, these two theologians begin to focus the themes of renewal according to the question of the ritual experience of revelation.

Assessing Some Limitations

In so plotting one or two of the particular contributions of these writers in the light of cumulative and more general shifts, one inevitably becomes aware of certain shortcomings or omissions in their work—limitations sometimes made more significant by comparison. In trying to identify areas of possible development that

---

87. As Marsili said months before his death, "L'intento del nostro studio è un altro. È quello di ricercare se e come la liturgia sia, in profondità, un fatto pneumatico, cioè un fatto intrinsecamente dipendente, nel suo essere, dallo Spirito santo, che perciò risulti esserne elemento costitutivo essenziale. Si tratta di vedere se e in che senso sia lo Spirito santo a fare della liturgia la celebrazione autentica del mistero di Cristo nella Chiesa. . . . Siamo consapevoli del notevolissimo contributo apportato dalla ricerca cristologica alla comprensione della liturgia. Ma riteniamo che con la chiarificazione cristologia/liturgia il cammino sia compiuto solo a metà: quando si è scoperto il vero *contenuto* della liturgia, si tratta poi di vedere *come* questo contenuto si può effettivamente realizzare nella Chiesa." S. Marsili, "Presentazione," in AA. VV., *Spirito Santo e Liturgia* (Casale Monferrato: Marietti, 1984), 5–6.

might contribute to a better understanding of the topic of this book, it is important that these issues be examined.

Using criticisms of *Théologie de la Révélation* as a basis for outlining current areas of weakness that require redress, Dulles points to three lacunae in Latourelle's study:[88] the absence of a notion of revelation developed beyond the cognitive or doctrinal, a lack of reflection on the continuation of God's self-manifestation in the present, and the failure to give to the interior illumination of grace a constitutive role in the process of transmission.[89] When related, these three points focus on the central question of our theme—the present actualization of revelation in the life of the believer by the liturgy. Though Latourelle successfully foregrounds the personal, historical, and existential elements in a christological renewal of revelation, any sense of subjective encounter and appropriation is muted or even lost in the effort to assert the objective credibility of the signs of salvation. But to expect such a reflection would perhaps be asking for something beyond the scope of his enterprise, which was to assert the credibility of revelation while establishing the framework of fundamental theology. Such a task meant that, in some ways, Latourelle's sensibilities never became truly postcritical. Perhaps because he remained ever conscious of detractors[90] and of the need to justify the act of faith in the modern world, he fought shy of source

---

88. Dulles, "The Theology of Revelation," 43–58.

89. These criticisms, especially the last one, are echoed by P. Benoît, review of R. Latourelle, *Théologie de la Révélation*, *Revue Biblique* 71 (1964): 93–97.

90. One wonders if the pugnacious way in which Latourelle asserts the historical credibility of the miracles is indicative of his critical stance. Perhaps his failure to become "postmodern" explains Wendy Cotter's reaction to *Miracles de Jésus et théologie du miracle*: "But ultimately one wonders why he was so moved about the historicity question that he engaged disciplines outside his competence. Who are the components against whom he crusades? The biblical experts in miracle narrative today (e.g. Achtemeier, Theissen, Kee) are received favourably. And it is not the case that responsible biblical critics are denouncing the historicity of Jesus' miracles—for the most part they recognize that no scholar can make such categorical statements one way or the other based on what little evidence exists." Wendy Cotter, review of R. Latourelle, *Miracles de Jésus et théologie du miracle*, *Toronto Journal of Theology* 6, no. 1 (Spring 1990): 118.

categories he deemed subjective or vague, such as the liturgy or experience. This, combined with his desire to establish a scientific and synthesized theology of revelation, consonant with the teachings of the magisterium,[91] means that his assertions can seem overly rational and distant from the lived expression of the gospel. Certainly, Latourelle's earlier works can be excused somewhat in the light of these points. However, it must be said that relatively more recent studies, such as his *Miracles de Jésus et théologie du miracle,* do not take full cognizance of the sensitivity to Christian praxis and experience to which such phenomena as the charismatic movement and theologies of liberation had alerted the church. A comparison of the length of the three sections of this later book shows that Latourelle's main concern remains the hermeneutical credibility of faith. The final section, which includes a discussion of the recognition and impact of miracles, offers far more scope to further a subjective analysis of human response to God's loving disclosure of himself.

Dulles certainly addresses some of these weaknesses in his own works. Paying particular attention to the concept of symbol in the transmission of revelation, he has contributed much to our understanding of its inner workings and present realization, especially through his analysis of conversion. However, his preference for rational-cognitive models has meant that his description of revelation is clear and accurate but, despite his best efforts, somewhat cold.[92] Methodologically, Dulles remains cut off

---

91. Cf. P. Misner, review of R. Latourelle, *Christ and the Church: Signs of Salvation, Theological Studies* 34 (1973): 185–86.

92. "Though it must be conceded that the third of Dulles's models of revelation is that of inner experience, he finds little of merit but that this approach provided a foil to an arid scholasticism and encouraged devotion. His assessment of this model seems to be based largely on a narrow view of the Modernists and their rejection of any rational content within revelation. His comments on Schillebeeckx are fleeting." Hence E. TeSelle can still maintain that "the book assumes that revelation is primarily a cognition of realities. Therefore it overlooks the non-cognitive (or more than cognitive)." See TeSelle, review of *Models of Revelation,* 38.

from the sources of a subjective analysis of revelation that would serve to balance his predominantly objective stance.[93] An example of this identified by some reviewers is his failure to use the liturgy as a source for his reflections.[94] Although in *The Craft of Theology* Dulles does make more reference to the liturgy, it would seem to remain just that: reference that avoids active participation with symbols that transmit revelation presently and on the level of experience. The failure of Dulles to discuss symbolic mediation in terms of the liturgy or Christian experience seems to sever God's self-communication from the praxis of faith response.[95] Given the care with which Dulles discusses the participatory nature of symbols, it is strange that he leaves these aspects undeveloped. Yet something holds these limitations in content and method together. Perhaps behind Francis Gerald Downing's criticism that Dulles draws very little on "Orthodox or charismatic-experiential"[96] categories in the elaboration of his ideas is the recognition that the fundamental weakness of Dulles's work is an absence of pneumatology. And the same may be said of Latourelle.

Though Dulles is less concerned with the historicity of revelation, and his method is not one of classical hermeneutics, the sense conveyed by both these authors is that the core of revelation subsists in the historical Jesus rather than in the Christ who has been raised

---

93. Cf. B. Cooke, review of A. Dulles, *Models of Revelation*, *America* 168 (January 23, 1993): 21–22.

94. For example, G. O'Collins, review of A. Dulles, *Models of Revelation*, *Gregorianum* 65 (1984): 181.

95. "Dulles' approach is too 'armchairish,' too removed from the drama of human existence. Secondly Dulles lacks a fully satisfying theory of how the Divine and the human co-participate in the drama of experience, and of how this co-participation engenders varying kinds of symbolism." W. Thompson, review of A. Dulles, *Models of Revelation*, *Theological Studies* 45 (1984): 358. "Some will question whether the author has fully completed his move towards a consciously social and historical theology. And I wonder whether, beyond the difficulties he himself acknowledges for the acceptance of revelation, there are not still deeper questions posed by the massive injustice and suffering in our world and the wave of historical relativism that has swept over western society." O'Donovan, review of *Models of Revelation*, 424.

96. F. Downing, review of A. Dulles, *The Craft of Theology*, *Theology* 87 (1984): 295.

by the Spirit. That the resurrection should play such an insignificant role in the work of both these writers is puzzling and worthy of note.[97] Yet, in some senses, scant reflection on the resurrection is a consequence of poor pneumatology, which is in itself a symptom of the sustained christological focus of conciliar theology. However, this point cannot avert all criticism, as many recognized at the time of the Council that a vibrant theology of the Holy Spirit was the key to christological renewal.[98] Hence, in subsequent years theologians began to focus on the collaboration of Christ and the Spirit in the economy of salvation. Latourelle and Dulles show little openness to these developments.

As Silvano Maggiani points out, there are those works that, though completed, remain open to "a continual germination of internal relationships."[99] Such could be claimed of the two writers who remain. Writing in the spirit of Casel and De Chardin, the work of Marsili and Martelet possesses an unrelenting dynamism. As a result, weaknesses are identified and developed within an overall vision, and this in itself affords a sort of "openness." In Marsili, a threefold development might be described. First, a predominantly rubrical and liturgical-historical thesis gives way to a subsequent conception of liturgy as the essential component in Christ's work of salvation.

---

97. *Théologie de la Révélation* focuses on the categories of creation, history, and incarnation to help elaborate an understanding of revelation. Though the absence of a chapter devoted to the resurrection might be explained in terms of methodology, that the climax of God's self-manifestation is not discussed in the chapter on miracles or eschatological vision constitutes a serious omission. Nor is the resurrection discussed in *Miracles de Jésus et théologie du miracle* because, claims Latourelle, the topic is receiving generous coverage elsewhere and demands special treatment. Nowhere in the books chosen from Dulles is there a developed reflection on the resurrection.

98. See Mary Cecily Boulding, "The Doctrine of the Holy Spirit in the Documents of Vatican II," *Irish Theological Quarterly* 51, no. 4 (1985): 253–67; Y.-M. Congar, *I Believe in the Holy Spirit*, 3 vols. (London: Geoffrey Chapman, 1983), 1:167–172; P. Corcoran, "Some Recent Writing on the Holy Spirit," parts 1–3, *Irish Theological Quarterly* 39 (1972): 276–87; 365–82, and 40 (1973): 50–62.

99. Maggiani, "La teologia liturgica di S. Marsili," 342.

Finally, there is a focus shift to liturgy as the sacramental actualization of this word-phase of revelation—a stage that is necessarily pneumatological. In some ways, this development is self-correcting, but it must be said that, although an overemphasis on christological *anàmnesis* is eventually resolved in a more future-oriented vision of revelation, the former remained the predominant model in most of Marsili's work. That is to say, in earlier writings and particularly in his theology of the sacraments, the incarnation is the interpreting principle of revelation. To a large extent, the church and the sacraments are for Marsili the present extensions of Christ's saving work in history. This was in spite of a more than implicit pneumatology in the teaching of Vatican II. *Lumen Gentium* made it quite clear that, though Christ achieved his redemptive work once and for all on Calvary, this plan of God to save creation, founded as it is on the incarnation of the Son, is made operative only through a church vivified by the Holy Spirit.[100] The interpreting principle here is the collaboration of Christ and the Spirit in the work of salvation, the definitive expression of which is the resurrection of Jesus.[101] Thus although Michele Alberta submits that the title of *I segni del mistero di Cristo* indicates a reflection on the presence and action of the living and glorified Christ in the church, this is not the principal focus of the book.[102] *Liturgia: momento nella storia della salvezza* and

---

100. *LG* 7 [852]: "Communicando enim Spiritum suum, fratres suos, ex omnibus gentibus convocatos, tamquam corpus suum mystice constituit. . . . Dedit nobis de Spiritu suo, qui unus et idem in capite et in membris existens, totum corpus ita vivificat, unificat et movet, ut Eius officium a sanctis Patribus comparari potuerit cum munere quod principium vitae seu anima in corpore humano adimplet." *LG* 8: "Ideo ob non mediocrem analogiam incarnati Verbi mysterio assimilatur. Sicut enim natura assumpta Verbo divino ut vivum organum salutis, Ei indissolubiliter unitum, inservit, non dissimili modo socialis compago Ecclesiae Spiritui Christo, eam vivificanti, ad augmentum corporis inservit." Cf. also *LG* 52 [891–92].
101. See Boulding, "The Doctrine of the Holy Spirit," 255–56.
102. "Dicendo 'Mistero di Cristo' si intende la presenza e l'azione di Cristo vivo e glorioso che comunica agli uomini le realtà salvifiche divine." M. Alberta, "Presentazione," in S. Marsili, *I segni del mistero di Cristo* (Rome: Edizioni Liturgiche, 1987), 14.

I segni del mistero di Cristo are both concerned with the liturgy as the hermeneutical source of the mystery of Christ, but the approach is clearly predominantly one of *memoria*.

Hence it may be said that, in the main, Marsili shares weaknesses similar to those of Latourelle and Dulles, as neither of these works display what might be called a pneumatology, or reflect systematically on the significance of the resurrection within salvation history. Indeed, it could be claimed that within the orbit of liturgical theology such lacunae have a further gravity, especially when one considers that liturgical reflection on *epiclesis* was the spur for a greater inclusion of the Spirit at Vatican II.[103] Nevertheless, Marsili must be credited with more than the beginnings of a remedy in his last writings. There, as has been seen, he turns simultaneously to the question of the Holy Spirit and experience.

This reassessment also awakened other issues, such as the pastoral nature of the liturgy and its relationship to Christian praxis.[104] Yet, if it is true to say that as a whole the work of Marsili tended to focus on the *lex orandi, lex credendi* axis to the detriment of any notion of *lex vivendi*, it must be said also that, for him, a correct notion of the latter could be born only out of the former relationship.[105] A refusal

---

103. "Latin Ecclesiology has evolved merely in its Christic dimension, but is still adolescent in its pneumatic dimension. . . . It is the action of the glorified Christ which the Spirit represents. Eastern tradition lives the sacred liturgy under the sign of the *epiclesis*. The faith that the Holy Spirit reveals represents the Incarnate Word in the economy of salvation." Ignatius Ziadé (Archbishop of Beirut), "Conciliar Speech, 15 September 1964," in *Third Session Council Speeches of Vatican II*, ed. W. K. Leahy and A. T. Massimini (Glen Rock, NJ: Paulist, 1966), 9.

104. See Maggiani, "La teologia liturgica di S. Marsili," 341–57, especially 355–56.

105. "Chi parte ammettendo una dicotomia tra teologia e liturgia, crerebbe implicitamente un controsenso già in partenza qual è quello di chiedere a una 'non teologia' di dare riposta a questi teologici, e viceversa. Sia 'teologia' che 'liturgia' pur essendo in teoria autonome, secondo una determinata concezione che si può avere di loro, ed ammettendo anche che ciascuna delle due sia fornita di un metodo proprio, si deve addivenire che gravitano attorno ad un comune interesse: la fede 'creduta—professata—celebrata.' Di fatto la teologia, che è anche ripensamento della fede, è portata alla sua pienezza solo sul piano dell'attuazione celebrativa." A. Triacca, "Teologia della liturgia o teologia liturgica? Contributo di P. Salvatore Marsili per una chiarificazione," *Rivista Liturgica* 80 (1993): 267–89, 282.

to compromise the foundational principles of his liturgical theology meant that it was always the aperture through which all else had to be understood.[106] And, though this assures a consistent synthesis, it can mean that the theory appears remote from the lived realities of faith communities.[107] While this may be true, it cannot be forgotten that the openness of Marsili's fundamental structures and the orientations he gave to research made much of the later study possible.

In *Jesus Risen*, G. O'Collins makes the "broad claim" that "much recent Christology has not been adequately symbolic, experiential and liturgical."[108] *Résurrection, eucharistie et genèse de l'homme* does not prove this thesis wrong but shows Martelet to be an exception. Drawing on liturgical data, he faces squarely the symbolism of the resurrection, seeing it as the interpreting principle of Christ's eucharistic presence and the means of creation's glorification. The locus of the drama of salvation is found in the experience of a human body that is determined by nature, expressed in culture, and troubled by death, and this is the focus of the book. Published some fifteen years before O'Collins made his assessment, Martelet's work certainly offered *chemins théologiques d'un renouveau chrétien*.[109] These paths had their origin in Vatican II, and to a large extent this work is a speculative response to the charter set by *Les idées maîtresses de Vatican II*. Perhaps it was the coincidence of his personal intuitions with the objective teachings of the Council that led Martelet to an early recognition of the crucial role of the Holy Spirit in the renewal of

---

106. See Maggiani, "La teologia liturgica di S. Marsili," 356.

107. Speaking of the *Anàmnesis* series, K. Seasoltz asserts, "The weakness of the volumes, however, lies in the absence of a sound pastoral dimension and their failure to deal theologically with liturgical questions that are being urgently raised by social scientists in general and by specialists in ritual behavior and communication theory in particular." Seasoltz, review of S. Marsili, *Anàmnesis* series, *Worship* 60 (1986): 86.

108. G. O'Collins, *Jesus Risen* (New York: Paulist, 1987), 202–3.

109. This is the subtitle of the original French edition: G. Martelet, *Résurrection, eucharistie et genèse de l'homme: chemins théologiques d'un renouveau chrétien* (Paris: Desclée, 1972).

the symbols of faith. Certainly, by his attention to pneumatology, particularly to the liturgical *epiclesis*,[110] and through an analysis of the resurrection, Martelet begins to explore the interface of human experience with divine revelation—an encounter shaped and expressed in symbol.

For some, emphasis on the resurrection and the genesis of creation by means of its liturgical actualization in the *epiclesis* detracts from the singular action of Christ's saving death.[111] The glorification of humanity is not merely a process—a coming-to-be through the action of the Spirit. The genesis of the human is dependent absolutely on the unique sacrifice of Christ. Such a criticism is easily exaggerated, but whether it is valid or not it highlights the fact that the saving action of God is revealed only in the story of salvation narrated by Christ the Word. The Spirit actualizes this narrative exactly because he is the Spirit of Christ—a fact verified by the liturgical coalescence of *anàmnesis* and *epiclesis*.[112] Maybe in his eagerness to redress the imbalance, which many more authors than O'Collins had recognized, Martelet has not sufficiently stressed the

110. "Fr. Martelet surveys usefully some recent writing on the Real Presence, contending that this has suffered from neglect of the doctrine of the Resurrection, and in two further chapters traces briefly the stages by which an unsatisfactory position was reached, and the contribution which can be drawn for a better understanding from Eastern Orthodox teaching about the epiclesis." C. Hichling, review of G. Martelet, *The Risen Christ and the Eucharistic World*, *The Heythrop Journal* 18 (1977): 466.

111. "Teilhard admitted difficulty fitting into his system the idea of an historical event such as the fall of man. He should have realized that he has similar difficulties admitting an historical event that is not only *uniting*, but *re-uniting*, namely the paschal mystery. It seems to me, then, that Martelet's treatment of eucharistic presence has the same weakness. The fact that union is brought about through sacrifice seems to be practically left out." Sheets, review of *The Risen Christ and the Eucharistic World*, 466.

112. Noteworthy here is that, although G. O'Collins is rightly insistent on a theology formed in the key of the liturgy he emphasises the anamnetic role to the exclusion of the epicletic: "Through *anamnesis* the liturgical actions, above all the Eucharist, bring to mind certain historical events which conveyed the revealing and saving interventions of God. The faithful assembled for worship are invited to recall and appropriate for themselves God's salvific manifestation which Christ brought to a definitive climax for all and once and for all. For every new generation the liturgy re-presents *the* redemptive revelation that was the paschal mystery." O'Collins, *Retrieving Fundamental Theology*, 46.

collaboration of Word and Spirit in the work of salvation. This point is related to a final criticism of Martelet's work. In the light of renewal themes, *Résurrection, eucharistie et genèse de l'homme* works through a clearly structured thesis, yet the conclusions are not focused toward Christian praxis or mission.[113] This may be symptomatic of the fact that Christology and pneumatology need to be better integrated in this work, a point that will be further developed later with specific reference to the contribution of Yves Congar.

Holding the unique contributions of these writers in tension with areas that require further development should provide a fair assessment and also allow possible ways forward to emerge. Therefore it is necessary to begin to marshal these findings toward a resolution of the proposed thesis.

Paths Toward Further Development

The central problem of the book is the relationship between the mysteries of salvation uniquely and historically revealed in Christ, and their liturgical articulation in the life of the believer. The four writers studied have indicated various avenues of response to this question, but, to focus and advance the book, four areas have been isolated for development. They are the role of the Holy Spirit, the resurrection of Christ, the method of liturgical theology, and experience as a source for Christian reflection. Two of these points are concerned with the content of theology and two with its method, and the intention of this section is to see how a study of their interrelation may reveal new perspectives on the question in hand.

---

113. "Those to whom the book as a whole, in its Teilhardian inspiration, is too distant from precisely attainable meaning to have much value will nevertheless find some material of interest." C. Hichling, review of *The Risen Christ and the Eucharistic World*, 466.

In his poem *The Dry Salvages*, T. S. Eliot declares,

We had the experience but missed the meaning,
And approach to the meaning restores the experience
In a different form, beyond any meaning
We can assign to happiness. I have said before
That the past experience revived in the meaning
Is not the experience of one life only
But of many generations—not forgetting
Something that is probably quite ineffable.[114]

To try to capture the experience of the paschal mystery in meaningful language is the task of Christian theology. And yet meaning and experience, or method and content, are so closely connected that discerning the best approach to take can be difficult. As Eliot recognizes, though the experience is necessarily prior, its full significance may be appreciated or "restored" only by a meaningful method of approach. Hence the following section will focus first on aspects of the content of Christian faith, and then on methodological ways of approach that might restore the ineffable faith experience of many generations to the present.

Developing a Pneumatology

Ever since *Divinum illud munus*, the church's forgetfulness of the Holy Spirit has been a theme of increasing importance in theology. The documents of Vatican II charter a growing awareness of pneumatology,[115] and the remarks of Paul VI in the years after the Council redoubled the efforts of many theologians in this sphere.[116]

---

114. T. S. Eliot, "The Dry Salvages," in *Collected Poems 1909–1962* (London: Faber and Faber, 1963), 208.
115. "In his essay 'L'Esprit-Saint dans Lumen Gentium,' Mgr. Charue traces the history of the increasing prominence given to the Holy Spirit in *Lumen Gentium*, as it developed from the initial drafts to the final version. He speaks of the pre-pneumatical stage of the Vatican Council. . . . There is a point in Vatican II when the Holy Spirit is hardly mentioned at all. There is also

Undeniably, the immediate theological heritage was christological, the fruit of a renewal that sought to center the whole of theology on the figure of Jesus Christ. This personal focus was to loosen the abstract categories of a decadent scholasticism and offer a fresh dynamism to the study of the faith. Yet there is a point at which pneumatology must be recognized as essential to this task and not distinct from it. To suggest that its development is an alternative in some ways opposed to christological renewal would be to designate study of the Spirit as a distinct and separate tract.[117] However, recognition of a compatibility of aim is indicative of the fact that attention to the Spirit does not furnish theology with a distinct content, but with a new interpretive perspective.[118]

The primary effect of the enhanced pneumatology of the conciliar period was a shift away from the incarnation as the sole interpreting principle of revelation.[119] To a large extent, this perspective had

a point when one may almost say that the Holy Spirit is all over the place." Corcoran, "Some Recent Writing on the Holy Spirit III," 51.

116. "The Christology and especially the ecclesiology of the Second Vatican Council should be followed by a new study and a new cult of the Holy Spirit, as an indispensable complement of the conciliar teaching." General Audience on 6th June 1973, in *La documentation catholique*, 1635 (July 1, 1973) 601.

117. The Protestant theologian J. Bosc is quoted by Y.-M. Congar as saying, "It could be that in demanding an isolated doctrine of the Holy Spirit we go counter to what we are seeking. There is in fact no separate doctrine of the Holy Spirit for this always refers us to the truth of the Lord." See Congar, "Pneumatologie' ou 'christomonisme' dans la tradition latine?" in *Ecclesia a Spiritu Sancto edocta, Lumen Gentium, 53; Mélanges théologiques Hommage à Msgr. Gerard Philips*, Bibliotheca Ephemeridium Theologicarum Lovaniensium 27 (Gembloux: Duculot, 1970), 65.

118. The Orthodox theologian P. Evdokimov recognises that the pneumatology of the East and the "new theology" of the West have a similar impact on Christology: "On the plane of ecumenical meetings, the Eastern contribution is to be found in an emphatic sense of the Mystery. It is less sensitive to the juridical and rational aspects of theological problems; it is deeply influenced by the liturgy. The East has no difficulty in reverencing the Mystery even in the strong technical sense of our time. The Eastern reaction to 'new theology' is positive in so far as this theology is an appeal to go beyond an abstract and archaic theology in which modern man finds himself switched off." Evdokimov, *L'Esprit-saint dans la tradition orthodoxe* (Paris: Éditions du Cerf, 1969), 12, quoted by Corcoran, "Some Recent Writing on the Holy Spirit I," 278.

119. "From the second century on the incarnation has often served to focus beliefs about the person and saving work of Christ, creation (understood as reaching its highpoint in his created humanity), the Church (as the extension of the incarnation) and so forth. Nevertheless, Christianity began with the disciples proclaiming not the incarnation, but the resurrection

been responsible for much of the stasis in Christology, as it focused theological attention on a fixed and finished historical event. As Kevin McNamara pointed out just after the close of Vatican II,

> The danger lies in the image of the human body in the background. It is not that the image is invalid: it has the authority of St. Paul behind it. The mistake lies in forgetting that the human body as we know it is a limiting, restricting and isolating factor in our lives. It is, it is true, a medium of communication with the world and our fellow-man, but it is a limited one. And this is true even of the earthly body of Jesus, of Jesus in his historical, human condition, such as we have in mind when we speak of a continuation of the Incarnation. It is not true, however, of the risen Jesus.[120]

The shift in focus from incarnation to resurrection that results from a pneumatological perspective engenders a sense of vibrancy and dynamism within the economy of revelation. Moreover, in allowing for a point of synthesis that is metahistorical, the Spirit collates the individual mysteries of salvation into the one paschal mystery of Christ. In doing so, the Spirit bridges the gulf between the objective realization of these events and their subjective fulfilment in the hearts of believers.

---

of the crucified Jesus." O'Collins, *Jesus Risen* 149. Recognising this imbalance with particular reference to sacramental theology, L.-M. Chauvet states, "The concrete fabric of Christ's historical life is not taken into consideration as a concrete place for understanding the significance of his death as a 'death for us.' Because of this, everything is already over, theologically speaking, in the first part of . . . Christology, that is in the hypostatic union. The redemption, the major weight of which is essentially borne by the passion and cross, is nothing more than a consistent, and certainly costly, development of what was already inscribed in the incarnation. As for the *resurrection*, it draws attention for a short while." Chauvet, *Symbol and Sacrament*, 455.

120. K. McNamara, "The Holy Spirit in the Church," *Irish Theological Quarterly* 32 (1965): 289–90.

Focusing on the Resurrection

In recent years there has been a growing awareness of the central significance of the resurrection for fundamental theology.[121] *Dei Verbum* asserts that, above all, it was the glorious resurrection of Christ from the dead that revealed God to us.[122] The reason for this is given in an earlier section, where the Constitution makes clear that, in revelation, God manifests himself and his will.[123] Indeed, he reveals himself in the accomplishment of his will. The resurrection is the "definitive high point of divine self-revelation,"[124] because it is the perfect fulfillment of the will of God for creation and hence the clearest manifestation of God himself. In response to such a centering of the theological task on the origin of Christian faith, O'Collins points out four main questions for fundamental theologians to tackle.[125] The final three are concerned with what a theology of the resurrection can offer for an understanding of the transmission, content, and present continuation of revelation. In elucidating a response to these questions, it should become clear why any analysis

---

121. See J. Galvin, "The Resurrection of Jesus in Contemporary Catholic Systematics," *The Heythrop Journal* 20 (1979): 123–45; "Focus of Revelation," chapter 6 of O'Collins, *Jesus Risen*; and F. Schüssler Fiorenza, "The Resurrection of Jesus and Roman Catholic Fundamental Theology," in *The Resurrection: An Interdisciplinary Symposium on the Resurrection of Jesus*, ed. S. Davis, D. Kendall and G. O'Collins (New York: Oxford University Press, 1997), 211–48.

122. "For this reason Jesus perfected revelation by fulfilling it through his whole work of making himself present and manifesting himself: through his words and deeds, his signs and wonders, but especially through his death and glorious resurrection from the dead and final sending of the Spirit of truth." ("Tota suiipsius praesentia ac manifestatione, verbis et operibus, signis et miraculis, praesertim autem morte sua gloriosa ex mortuis resurrectione, misso tandem Spiritu veritatis revelationem complendo perficit ac testimonio divino confirmat") *DV*, 4 [972–73].

123. "Placuit Deo in sua bonitate et sapientia seipsum revelare et notum facere sacramentum voluntatis suae." *DV*, 2 [*972].

124. See G. O'Collins, "Paschal Mystery II: The Resurrection of Jesus," in Latourelle and Fisichella, *Dictionary of Fundamental Theology*, 769.

125. "What did the first Christians mean by their claim about Jesus' resurrection? How did they come to know about and believe in Jesus as risen from the dead? How did the resurrection of the crucified Jesus bring the definitive self-revelation of the tripersonal God? In what way can we legitimate Easter faith today?" Ibid.

of the liturgical actualization of divine revelation must focus on the resurrection.

Two catalysts for Easter faith can be identified in the tradition: encounter with the risen Lord, and the sign of the empty tomb.[126] While nobody witnessed the actual event of resurrection, points crucial to an understanding of revelation can be deduced from the subsequent experience of the disciples. The defining elements of these events might be summed up as follows: in their encounters with the risen Jesus, the Easter witnesses were made aware of his eschatological and christological significance. Such awareness stemmed from an apprehension that was not merely interior but involved an external visual perception. As a result of this unique meeting, the disciple received a specific, personal mission.[127]

Using this definition as the basis for a comparison between the *sacramental* experience of the risen Christ, in say baptism or confirmation, with that of the Easter witnesses, it seems difficult to draw any distinction between the two. That is, until one realizes the unique nature of those first encounters. O'Collins maintains that the singular and unrepeatable nature of the Easter appearances involves the founding of the church and the inauguration of its mission. "That unique function," he insists, "rests upon some difference in their respective experiences . . . expressed by John's classic distinction between those who have seen and believed and those who are 'blessed' because they 'have not seen and yet believe' (John 20:29)."[128] While O'Collins is right to insist on the theological importance of

---

126. See ibid., 771.
127. This is based on R. H. Fuller's definition: "They [the postresurrection appearances] were not in their innermost essence open to neutral observation or verification, but revelatory events in which the eschatological and Christological significance of Jesus was disclosed, and in which the recipient was called to a particular function in salvation history." Quoted in D. Kendall and G. O'Collins, "The Uniqueness of the Easter Appearances," *The Catholic Biblical Quarterly* 54 (1992): 288.
128. O'Collins, *Jesus Risen*, 116.

this experiential difference in order to maintain both the normativity of the apostolic witnesses and their status as founders of the church, it remains necessary to clarify the nature of the distinction.

If an immediate, first-hand, and concrete experience[129] of the risen Christ is to be attributed to believers in the present,[130] the uniqueness of the apostles' experiences and those of the women cannot be explained by a difference or superiority of content. Nor can the difference be explained by their access to an encounter of greater immediacy.[131] Rather, the factor that made the experiences of the first witnesses unique was the interpretive context that they enjoyed. Having been intimates of the historical Jesus in every aspect of his life and ministry, and having seen his designs collapse in failure, they possessed that prior knowledge[132] and interpretive element[133] that facilitates full apprehension of the objective phenomenon. Exemplary in this is the disciple "whom Jesus loved," who had reclined next to him at the supper and stood at the foot of the cross; he is the first to reach the tomb, "and he saw and believed" (John 20:8). While

129. See G. O'Collins, *Fundamental Theology,* 2nd ed. (New York: Paulist, 1986), 33–41.

130. "To deny present revelation is to doubt the active power here and now of the Holy Spirit as guiding the Tradition and mediating the presence of the risen Christ. In effect, this also means reducing faith to the acceptance of some revealed truths coming from the past rather than taking faith in its integral sense—as the full obedience given to God revealed here and now through the living voice of the gospel." G. O'Collins, "Revelation Past and Present," in Latourelle, *Vatican II: Assessment and Perspectives,* 1:129.

131. "As far as we are concerned that Easter experience of the disciples can never be merely an external transmission of information (as though they acted as a telephone wire or a telescope) which is, as it were, discarded the moment we have made contact with the event itself." K. Rahner, "Experiencing Easter," in *Theological Investigations,* trans. D. Burke, vol. 7 (London: Darton, Longman and Todd, 1971), 164.

132. "Is all experience somehow conscious? Without taking time off here to prove this assertion in detail, I want to maintain that there is *no experience truly prior to knowledge.* We can experience innumerable things, without being either fully aware of them and their implications or capable of properly verbalizing their significance." O'Collins, *Fundamental Theology,* 35.

133. "Experience is always *interpreted* experience. 'Experience' without interpretation would be a mere sensation. . . . In reality there never was a non-interpreted Jesus. Right from and in their earliest encounters the twelve and other disciples began to interpret him." O'Collins, *Retrieving Fundamental Theology,* 114–15; see also E. Schillebeeckx, *Christ: The Christian Experience in the Modern World* (London: SCM, 1980), 49.

this essentially personal correlation of events might account for the differing reactions to the risen Christ among the disciples, to some extent the problem of St. Paul, the last to whom the risen Christ appeared, remains. And yet it might be said that, by the *via negativa*, even he was intimate with the Lord and the justification he brings.[134]

This is not to say, as Schillebeeckx has done, that the only advantage the first witnesses have over present believers is "that they were there at the time."[135] It is to suggest that experience is a dialogical phenomenon, and that the interpretive context of the historical Jesus forms an integral part of what the apostles apprehend in the appearances.[136] Moreover, it is because the unique encounters of the first disciples are born out of their knowledge of the incarnate Jesus that they can bridge the gap between Christ and the church.[137] In the upper room, at the lakeside, or on the road to Emmaus, Christ opened up a perspective within the horizon of the disciples'

---

134. One could base such a claim for St. Paul also on O'Collins's statement that "Paul misunderstood the righteousness given through faith in Christ and persecuted the early Church. Yet this faultless rectitude in keeping the law (Phil 3:6) also served as a kind of preparation for his seeing the risen Christ, a preparation which evidently was not verified in the case of Caiaphas, Pilate, Herod Antipas and the members of the Roman Senate." O'Collins, *Jesus Risen*, 120.

135. E. Schillebeeckx, *Interim Report on the Books "Jesus" and "Christ"* (London: SCM, 1982), 7. Quoted as part of a discussion of Schillebeeckx's position in O'Collins, *Jesus Risen*, 115–18.

136. As Schillebeeckx says, "The element of 'revelation' can thus be known 'in' the experiential encounter with the reality of the world, *in* the interpretation of this experience as an intrinsic element of that encounter, and *in* the religious language of faith." Schillebeeckx, *Christ: The Christian Experience in the Modern World*, 54.

137. See C. K. Barrett: "The disciples of the first generation had the unique distinction of standing as a link between Jesus and the Church; John indicates this in saying that their successors equally may believe, and their faith places them on the same level of blessedness with the eyewitnesses or maybe above it." Also R. Brown: "The whole community does share an eschatological existential encounter with the Word become flesh. But this is possible only because there was a group who encountered Jesus historically." Both are quoted in an excellent survey of scholarly literature on this question: Kendall and O'Collins, "The Uniqueness of the Easter Appearances," 304–5. Such a distinction is made also in the later writings of K. Rahner. See K. Rahner, "Hope and Easter," in *Christianity at the Crossroads* (London: Darton, Longman and Todd, 1975), 90–91, cf. a discussion of this point in J. Galvin, "The Resurrection of Jesus in Contemporary Systematics," *The Heythrop Journal* 20 (1979): 128.

experience of him that revealed to them his risen glory, so that with the gift of his Spirit they could found the church.[138]

To focus on the resurrection appearances and to establish their unique significance within salvation history has also served to clarify common ground between the experience of the first disciples and that of present believers. If intimate intercourse with the life and mission of the historical Jesus was the necessary context for unique experiences of the first witnesses, it is time now to turn to an examination of the settings that interpret the contemporary experiences of Christians as revelations of the risen Christ. In this, the importance of an experiential starting point and a liturgical methodology will come to light.

Returning to the Source of the Liturgy

The liturgical movement and certain twentieth-century theologians[139] sought to rehabilitate the notion of *lex orandi* in the wake of the isolation and rubricization of liturgical studies that had come about in the wake of the Council of Trent.[140] And, with the statement of *The Constitution on the Sacred Liturgy* concerning the priority to be given to liturgical studies, there was further stimulus to the development of a doxological theology.[141] Yet when, in 1963,

---

138. Cf. Schillebeeckx, *Christ: The Christian Experience in the Modern World*, 30–64, especially 48.

139. See I. Dalmais, "La liturgie comme lieu théologique," *La Maison Dieu* 78 (1964): 99; G. Wainwright, *Doxology. The Praise of God in Worship Doctrine and Life; A Systematic Theology* (New York: Oxford University Press, 1980), 219–24.

140. See Irwin, *Liturgical Theology*, 13.

141. *Sacrosanctum Concilium* 16 states that "the study of the sacred liturgy should be ranked among the major courses . . . in theological faculties . . . [and] be taught under its theological, historical, spiritual, pastoral and juridical aspects . . . [and] other professors, while striving to expound the mystery of Christ and the history of salvation from the angle proper to each of their own subjects, must nevertheless do so in a way which will clearly bring out the connection between their subjects and the liturgy." Translation from *The Documents of Vatican II*, ed. W. Abbott, (New York: Guild, 1966), 144–45 [*824–*25].

the Orthodox theologian, Alexander Schmemann, stated that the problem of the relationship between liturgy and theology "was on the theological agenda of our time,"[142] he had in mind a task deeper than the mutual glossing that some regarded as the aim of *lex orandi, lex credendi*.[143] Rather, liturgical theology was to become the method of breaching the gap between "nature and grace, reason and faith, scholarship and piety, theology and doxology, historical past and existential present."[144] To do this, liturgical theologians would have to show how the liturgical–sacramental celebrations of the church are sourced and shaped by the self-communication of the Triune God definitively revealed in the resurrection of the Son.[145] By virtue of its anamnetic and epicletic dimensions, liturgical theology will therefore be the method that not only amplifies the christological focus of the Council by unfolding the implications of pneumatology, but also sets forth Trinitarian principles that will open up a new future for study of the sacraments. Jean Corbon's meditative work *The Wellspring of Worship* is one of the first of these examples, and adequate demonstration requires a substantial quotation:

> The tomb remains the sign of the extremity of the love with which the Word wed himself to our flesh, but it is no longer the place of his body: "he is not here" is the insistent message of all three Synoptic Gospels. He has become the beginning of the wholly new covenant struck by the resurrection. Now the ebb and flow of Passover merge into one; in the risen Christ the incarnate Word is a living human being, and the

---

142. A Schmemann, "Theology and Liturgical Tradition," in *Worship In Scripture and Tradition*, ed. M. Shepherd (New York: Oxford University Press, 1963), 165.

143. To gain a better and general sense of Schmemann's understanding of this task within its historical setting see a useful collections of his essays: Thomas Fisch, ed., *Liturgy and Tradition: Theological Reflections of Alexander Schmemann*, (Crestwood, NY., St Vladimir's Press, 2003). Also useful is David W. Fagerberg's discussion of Schmemann's contribution to liturgical theology in David. W. Fagerberg, *Theologia Prima*, 189–213.

144. See D. Ritschl, *Memory and Hope* (New York: Macmillan, 1966), xiii, quoted in Irwin, *Liturgical Theology*, 8.

145. See E. Kilmartin, "Foreword," to J. Corbon, *The Wellspring of Worship* (New York: Paulist, 1988), v.

living human being becomes child of God. In him the suffering of the Father for humankind is brought to its fulfilment: "You are my son, today I have fathered you" (Ps 2:7). On this day of birth the river of life becomes LITURGY as it spreads out from the tomb and reaches us in the incorruptible body of Christ. Its wellspring is no longer the Father alone but also the body of his Son, since this is henceforth wholly permeated by his glory. If it be true that the drama of history is the interplay of God's gift and human acceptance of it, then the drama reaches its climax, and its eternal beginning, on this day, because these two energies are now joined together forever. The consent of the Son to his eternal birth from the Father completely permeates the body of his humanity. As a result of this anointing with superabundant life Jesus rises and becomes "Christ" to the fullest possible extent.[146]

Though single in aim, the movement for renewal, launched in the nineteenth century and confirmed by the Second Vatican Council, was twofold: it was liturgical and theological. To a large extent, and even lately, these have remained distinct pursuits. Recently, Anne Hunt has reaffirmed the paradox of such a separation:

Is it not also somewhat paradoxical that we make the prayer "In the name of the Father and of the Son and of the Holy Spirit" while at the same time tracing on ourselves the sign of the cross? In our prayer, *lex orandi*, the cross and the Trinity are in this very concrete way intimately and inextricably connected and yet, when we turn to study the classical expressions of Trinitarian theology, the *credenda*, as expressed in the Augustinian-Thomistic synthesis at the apogee of Latin Trinitarian theology, we find no direct or explicit connection at all between the Trinity and the Easter events of Jesus' death and resurrection, even though it was through precisely those events that Jesus' disciples came to proclaim that Jesus is Lord and that God is Father, Son, and Holy Spirit. The *redemptive* significance of Jesus' death and resurrection was clearly recognized, but not its *revelatory* significance.[147]

---

146. Corbon, *The Wellspring of Worship*, 32.

147. Anne Hunt, *The Trinity and the Paschal Mystery: A Development in Recent Catholic Theology* (Collegeville, MN: Liturgical Press, 1997), vii–viii.

However, though she expresses the problem so eloquently in the foreword of *The Trinity and the Paschal Mystery*, nowhere in her study does she draw on the liturgy as source, or recognize the liturgical method in theology as the means of reinvigoration and integration. Yet what has emerged from an analysis of the four authors of this study is that further advance can come about only when the liturgical and theological movements merge into a synergy[148] of action and reflection, as only then will sacramental theology have a method appropriate to its object.

Starting with Experience

In a sense, it may have been better to begin this discussion of methodology with experience rather than liturgy. But somehow it seemed more appropriate to treat the summit expression before describing the source—the constant, existential experience of God that the liturgy actualizes symbolically. Having insisted that the resurrection must be the central focus of this study, let us turn again to an insight of J. Corbon. Speaking of the appearances of the risen Christ, he says,

> From this point forward, and in his integral humanity, Jesus IS; any element of phenomenality would be a sign of continuing subjection to death. That is why he does not "appear" to his disciples as though he were someone absent who put in occasional appearances; rather, as the

148. "Literally, [synergy means] 'joint activity,' combined energies. This classical term of the Fathers attempts to express what is novel in the union of God and human being in Christ, and more specifically, what is novel in the energy of the Holy Spirit that permeates the energy of human beings and conforms them to Christ. The full realism of the liturgy and of our divinization has its sources in this synergy." Corbon, *The Wellspring of Worship*, 7. This is increasingly more evident as research and discussion of the liturgy as *theologia prima* seems to be occupying a wider number of experts. See Dwight W. Vogel, ed., *Primary Sources of Liturgical Theology* (Collegeville, MN: The Liturgical Press, 2000) also the recent studies of David. W. Fagerberg and Dorothea Haspelmath-Finatti both entitled *Theologia Prima* and cited elsewhere are evidence of this.

vocabulary of the Gospels makes clear, he "lets himself be seen" by them. He does not change form but IS; it is they who, in the measure of their faith recognize him.[149]

To borrow the terms of others, the symbol of the risen Christ presents the disciples with a transcendental or boundary situation that is tangible.[150] His manifestation forms the pinnacle and symbolic expression of their resurrection experience. Yet, by implication, these encounters must be sourced from a passive, nonthematic experience that results from the Risen One's constant relationship with the world.[151] Rahner extends this point into the context of sacramental theology, describing the sacraments not as momentary revelations *ad extra*, but as summits within a permanent subconscious or more-than-conscious experience:

> There is a salvation history as history of divine and human freedom, but the latter is precisely the history of the ever present deification of the world by God's self-communication, through which alone salvation history can be conceived at all and hence the history of the world must be understood even in a true and radical sense as history of God. The sacraments accordingly are not really to be understood as successive individual incursions of God into a secular world, but as "outbursts" (if we can express it in this way) of the innermost, ever present gracious endowment of the world with God himself into history.[152]

It is this nonthematic substratum that conditions all people with an existential experience of the supernatural, and this forms the starting point for theology.[153] The act of faith in the resurrection of Jesus

149. Ibid., 31.
150. Cf. O'Collins, *Fundamental Theology*, 32–33.
151. See K. Rahner, "Experience of Self and Experience of God," in *Theological Investigations*, trans. D. Bourke, vol. 13 (London: Darton, Longman and Todd, 1975), 123.
152. K. Rahner, "On the Theology of Worship," in *Theological Investigations*, trans. E. Quinn, vol. 19 (London: Darton, Longman and Todd, 1984), 143.
153. Opening his article on the resurrection in *Sacramentum Mundi*, K. Rahner states, "If the resurrection of Jesus is to be proclaimed credibly at the present day as a fundamental dogma of Christianity, then (logically) we must first establish the *a priori* horizon within which it

ultimately emerges from an "experiential correlate."[154] The personal experiences of the everyday, which are partial, sometimes sorrowful and often seemingly absurd, are thematized by the gospel witness and meaningfully interpreted in faith. The Holy Spirit is at the heart of this correlation. "Marked by a certain lack of conceptual mediation,"[155] the third person of the Trinity reveals himself as he is poured into the hearts of generations of believers, manifesting himself in their words and actions as he did in Christ, making us the same yesterday, today, and forever.[156] Thus, in the Spirit, the words and actions of mundane existence secretly become a point of entry into Trinitarian life. This is why theology must start with experience, for, as Kilian McDonnell states with admirable simplicity, "When one builds a theology, one does not start with a consideration of God, nor with humankind in itself. One starts at that point where the one 'touches' the other."[157]

Before moving on to develop the implications for sacramentology of the four points detailed above, it might be helpful to draw together the insights that have emerged into some sort of interim conclusion. An experiential and liturgical methodology assures theology of a content of particular relevance to the question in hand, one that takes account of the indispensable role of the Spirit and is focused on the

---

can 'dawn' intelligibly and credibly." K. Rahner, "Resurrection," in Rahner, *Encyclopaedia of Theology*, 1430.

154. "God's self-manifestation either meets us in our experience or it does not meet us at all. Given the essentially personal and interpersonal character of revelation, non experienced revelation would be a simple contradiction in terms." O'Collins, *Retrieving Fundamental Theology*, 108. See also G. O'Collins, *The Easter Jesus,* 2nd ed. (London: Darton, Longman and Todd, 1980), 69–72.

155. See Congar, *I Believe in the Holy Spirit*, 1:vii.

156. "In this context it has been suggested that the Holy Spirit empties himself, in a kind of kenosis, of his own personality in order to be in a relationship, on the one hand, with 'God' and Christ and, on the other, with men, who are called to realize the image of God and his Son. 'In order to reveal himself, he did not, like Yahweh in the Old Testament and Jesus in the New, use the personal pronoun 'I.' The Holy Spirit is revealed to us and known to us not in himself, or at least not directly in himself, but through what he brings about in us." Ibid., vii–viii.

157. K. McDonnell, "A Trinitarian Theology of the Holy Spirit?" *Theological Studies* 46 (1985): 208.

resurrection of Christ. Within the context of their own lives, the Holy Spirit makes believers attentive to the signs of the times and helps them to recognise there the presence of the Risen One. God's self-manifestation reaches its height and the fullness of its expression when believers can say that the Risen Christ is present and acting. Thus the Spirit elaborates the depths of human experience in the light of the Word of God made actual in the symbols of the liturgy, and leads believers into the presence of the risen Christ:

> these things God has revealed to us through the Spirit; for the Spirit searches everything, even the depths of God. 11 For what human being knows what is truly human except the human spirit that is within? So also no one comprehends what is truly God's except the Spirit of God. 12 Now we have received not the spirit of the world, but the Spirit that is from God, so that we may understand the gifts bestowed on us by God. (1 Cor. 2:10-13. NRSV).[158]

With the help of the work of other eminent theologians an attempt will be made to further these insights so as better to understand the revelation of God bestowed in the gift of his sacraments.

Joining the Objective and Subjective Poles of Revelation: Inspirations from Yves Congar and Karl Rahner

The subtitles alone of the three books that make up Congar's major work on the Holy Spirit, *Je crois en l'Esprit Saint*, indicate his fundamental concern to expound the Holy Spirit as the divine link between the objective eternal content of revelation and its subjective application in the present.[159] Successive volumes bind individual experience to ecclesial life and Eastern themes to Western ones. The

---

158. See also W. Kasper, *Der Gott Jesu Christi* (Mainz: Grünewald, 1982); English trans. M. O'Connell, *The God of Jesus Christ* (London: SCM, 1983), 223.

159. They are, in order, *The Holy Spirit in the Economy, Revelation and Experience of the Spirit; Lord and Giver of Life*, and *The River of Life Flows in the East and West*.

pneumatology that emerges from these texts and others has great import for the development of a liturgical-sacramental theology.

For Congar, the point of departure for theology was a study of the human person who, according to biblical testimony, is made in the divine image. But what he regarded as the essential truth of this doctrine was the profoundly relational character it implied to existence. To be *imago Dei* means to be determined by a tendency to communion, a desire to live through, with, and in the life of another. Of course, this image has been obscured and the free, selfless search for unity distorted by the alienating force of sin. The mutual mission of the Word and the Breath of God is to heal this breached communion and restore the divine image to humanity. It is the unique task of the Spirit to create in us "the filial life of Jesus, that life which Jesus led, in a humanity that is similar to our own, as a perfect human expression of orientation towards the Father."[160] The Spirit, present in the hearts of believers as prayer, supplication, and praise,[161] prepares, initiates, sustains, and completes this new creation in us—just as he did in Christ. So shaping us into the body of Christ and drawing us into communion with one another, the Spirit makes the church. This is the reason why the third article of the Creed, which concentrates on the works of the Holy Spirit—one baptism, the remission of sins, resurrection, and eternal life—shifts to a confession of the church, namely, because an account of the Spirit's action is an account of ecclesial life.[162] Here then is the converging of two themes that had dominated Congar's work for some time, and that were termed in his "own jargon"[163] as pneumatological anthropology and pneumatological ecclesiology.[164]

---

160. Y.-M. Congar, *La Parole et le Souffle* (Paris: Desclée, 1984), English trans., D. Smith, *The Word and the Spirit* (London: Geoffrey Chapman, 1986), 123.
161. Congar, *I Believe in the Holy Spirit*, 2:17.
162. Ibid., 2:5–7; also Congar, *The Word and the Spirit*, 123.
163. Congar, *The Word and the Spirit*, 122.

Evidently, most interesting to this study is the point and cause by which subjective experience of the Spirit emerges into an objectively recognizable ecclesial form.[165] According to Congar, the cause is the intimate collaboration of the Holy Spirit with the paschal sacrifice of Christ,[166] and the point of emergence is the word and the sacraments.[167] Thus, within the theological system, the sacraments can be located as that point at which the work of the Blessed Trinity is revealed in human experience, and where the ecclesial community is born symbolically out of anthropology. Concentrating on the creative aspect of the Holy Spirit in the final chapter of *La Parole et le Souffle*, Congar makes clear that the liturgical celebration of the sacraments is the coalescent point of the subjective and objective poles of revelation. He states quite simply, "In the liturgy, we see him [the *creator Spiritus*] in the perspective of our inner, spiritual life."[168] That is to say, in the liturgy the creator Spirit objectifies and

---

164. "There is no separation of the activity of the Spirit from the work of Christ in a full pneumatology. Everything that I have said so far points to the impossibility of making such a division. A pneumatology of this kind, however goes beyond simply making present the structures set up by Christ; it is the actuality of what the glorified Lord and his Spirit do in the Church." Congar, *I Believe in the Holy Spirit*, 1:157. See also Elizabeth Groppe, "The Contribution of Yves Congar's Theology of the Holy Spirit," *Theological Studies* 62 (2001): 457–65.

165. See P. Rosato, *Introduzione alla Teologia dei Sacramenti* (Casale Monferrato: Piemme, 1992), 34–51.

166. "A pneumatological ecclesiology presupposes a pneumatological Christology, that is to say an appreciation of the role of the Spirit in the messianic life of Jesus, in the resurrection and glorification that have made him Lord and have caused the humanity hypostatically united to the eternal Son to pass from the *forma servi* to the *forma Dei*." Y.-M. Congar, "Pneumatologie dogmatique," in *Initiation à la pratique de la théologie*, ed. B. Lauret and F. Refoulé, vol. 2 (Paris: Éditions du Cerf, 1982), 485–516, 495–96, quoted in Groppe, "The Contribution of Yves Congar's Theology of the Holy Spirit," 461. Two years later, Congar returns to the complexity of this relationship when he asserts, "The problem is always how to separate the work of the Word who reveals the Father from that of the Spirit. They co-institute the Church. The Spirit is not autonomous in the substantial aspect of the work to which the Word of God, the incarnate Son, has to give form." Congar, *The Word and the Spirit*, 79.

167. "The Church appears therefore to come both from the Word in his incarnation and from the Spirit—or the glorified Lord—who is unceasingly active both in men and women and in sacramental or juridical structures. Truly, God works with his two hands conjointly." Ibid., 83.

168. Ibid., 122.

completes the salvific work of God once manifest in Christ. Lest it be thought that Congar is interested merely in a rarefied theology of ritual that bears no impact on the world, in this same work—*La Parole et le Souffle*—he welcomes a preference for the word *evangelization* rather than *mission*. He does this "since it provides us with a real link that unites the Word and the Breath."[169] Christian praxis flows from an orthodoxy that bears witness to the Trinitarian structure of revelation, because discipleship itself demands witness to a God revealed by Christ in the Holy Spirit. Hence a theology of Christian praxis must be rooted in, and flow from, the collaboration of Word and Spirit that the liturgy demonstrates. Congar expresses this point beautifully as he concludes the third and final volume of *Je crois en l'Esprit Saint*:

> The Church is, after all, an institution of a very special kind. It acts in the present on the basis of past events and in the prospect of a future which is nothing less than the kingdom of God, the eschatological City and eternal life in communion with God himself. This is undoubtedly a sacramental structure, containing the memory of the event of foundation, a prophetic sign of an absolute future, and present grace coming from the first and preparing the way to the latter. It is however the Holy Spirit who ensures the unity of these three aspects. There is a sacramental presence where the Holy Spirit enables, by means of "earthly" elements, men to live here and now from the past, present and future work of Christ, and where he makes them live from salvation.[170]

What emerges from this very brief overview is that one major consequence of Congar's insistence on the inseparable collaboration of Spirit and Word in the coinstitution of the sacrament of the church is a focus on the present. The believer is to look for credible signs of salvation in the here and now, because the glorified Lord reveals himself still in the transformation of earthly elements and

169. Ibid., 131.
170. Congar, *I Believe in the Holy Spirit*, 3:271.

the continuing "creation" of the church. The "sacred mysteries" of revelation are for Congar both noetic and liturgical.[171] The ritual celebration of the sacraments mirrors and manifests the self revelation of the hidden God, who discloses himself in word and deed for the salvation of humanity. Thus, like all good Thomists, Congar shows a keen awareness of the demonstrative element within the sacramental reality.

The Present Actuality of the Glorified Lord— The Work of His Spirit in the Church

The Thomistic foundation of the sacramentology developed and enhanced by Congar's pneumatology is quite clear.[172] Aquinas, unlike his predecessors,[173] is not primarily concerned with the sacraments as remedy for sin, but places them in a cultic setting, the commerce of God's glory and human sanctification.[174] They are

171. "[Divine revelation] is not confined to knowledge alone; in actual fact, a new life–relation is in question, which requires on God's part a sharing with us of vitality and energy with a view to our achieving fellowship with him a fellowship which will be at once personal and collective. The new and definitive order brings, in this gesture of bestowal, wholly new gifts which render effectively possible the divinizing possession of God by his creatures. Revelation is a disclosure of his mystery which God makes to men; not the total disclosure of himself by himself which would freeze us for ever in our chosen state and put a stop to history, but a disclosure through created signs, guaranteed by God not to mislead us." Y.-M. Congar, *Tradition and Traditions* (London: Burns and Oates, 1966), 237–38.

172. One must stress foundation here, as the pneumatological and ecclesiological perspectives that Congar gives to sacramentology are corrective of weaknesses in Thomas's vision. As Chauvet says, "If statistics have any interest, one cannot help noticing that Christ (the Incarnate Word, the passion of Christ, the priesthood of Christ, the power of the excellence of Christ, and so on) is mentioned in almost every one of the thirty-eight articles of the '*Treatise on the Sacraments*'—and often several times in the course of one article, a number which altogether easily exceeds a hundred—while the Holy Spirit, outside the few quotations of the baptismal formula, which are not commented upon, is mentioned only five times." Chauvet, *Symbol and Sacrament*, 461. For an overview of the pneumatological and ecclesiological weaknesses of the *Summa Theologica* in general, see *Symbol and Sacrament*, 456–74.

173. See H.-F. Dondaine, "La définition des sacrements dans la 'Somme Théologique,' *Revue des sciences philosophiques et théologiques* 31 (1947): 213–28.

174. *ST.* III, Q. 60. a. 5: "In usu sacramentorum duo possunt considerari, scilicet cultus divinus et sanctificatio hominis."

sacred signs that bear a threefold function: "At once commemorative of that which has gone before, namely, the passion of Christ; and demonstrative of that which is brought about in us through the passion of Christ, namely grace; and prognostic, that is to say, a foretelling of glory."[175] With regard to the Eucharist, Saint Thomas expresses this theology in a poetic antiphon composed for the newly instituted feast of Corpus Christi:

> O sacrum convivium
> in quo Christus sumitur,
> memoria passionis eius recolitur
> mens impletur gratia
> et futurae gloriae nobis pignus datur.

Thomas is careful to keep the commemorative, demonstrative, and prognostic elements of the sacramental event in balance. However, it is important to notice that these three aspects are inherent to a reality that, in itself and as a unified whole, is significatory:

> The term *sacrament* is properly applied to that which is designed to signify our sanctification. In this, three factors may be taken into consideration: namely, the actual cause of our sanctification, which is the passion of Christ; the form of our sanctification, which consists in grace and virtues; and the ultimate end that our sanctification is destined to achieve, which is eternal life. Now as signs, the sacraments stand for all of these.[176]

Fragmentation, or differentiation according to importance of the triple dimension of the sacrament, would be a misreading of Thomas

---

175. *ST.* III, Q. 60, a. 3: "Unde sacramentum est et signum rememorativum ejus quod præcessit, scilicet passionis Christi; et demonstrativum ejus quod in nobis efficitur per Christum passionem, scilicet gratiae; et prognosticum, id est prænuntiativum, futurae gloriae."

176. *ST.* III, Q. 60, a. 3: "Sacramentum proprie dicitur quod ordinatur ad significandam nostram sanctificationem. In qua tria possunt considerari: videlicet ipsa causa sanctificationis nostrae, quae est passio Christi; et forma nostrae sanctificationis, quae consistit in gratia et virtutibus; et ultimus finis nostrae sanctificationis, qui est vita aeterna. Et haec omnia per sacramenta significantur."

and detrimental to a balanced and coherent theology of the sacraments.[177] Nevertheless, it would seem that a certain priority must necessarily be granted to the *signum demonstrativum*, as that dimension is fundamental to the sign function of the sacrament as a whole.[178] Having made such an assertion, distance must be taken immediately from writers such as A.-M. Roguet and J. Pohle, who base their preferential assessment of the demonstrative element on the fact that it alone can produce what it signifies.[179] Moreover, to counter any suggestion that priority given to the *signum demonstrativum* is born out of a "minimalism which focuses on the essential formula and the precise material"[180] it is necessary to reiterate that the central element of the triple structure takes priority solely because of its fundamental qualities. It is precisely by participating in the symbolic demonstration of the present sign that access is gained to "the broader context of salvation history,"[181] that Christ's passion is recalled and future glory expected. Indeed, neither of these equally important aspects could be adequately apprehended without being existentially grounded in the grace given now.

The fundamental significance of the demonstrative aspect of sacramental life is plainly apparent from even the most cursory of liturgical histories. Though from the time of the early Christians until the dawn of the great scholastics, claim could not be made to a precise

177. See L. Bergin, *O Propheticum Lavacrum: Baptism as Symbolic Act of Eschatological Salvation* (Rome: Analecta Gregoriana, Editrice Pontificia Università Gregoriana, 1999), 18–26.

178. Cf. *SC*, 59.

179. See A.-M. Roguet, *Les Sacrements* [*Somme théologique* 3ᵃ. 60–65] (Paris: Aubier, 1945), 312 and J. Pohle, *The Sacraments in General. Baptism. Confirmation. A Dogmatic Treatise I*, adapted by A. Preuss (London: B. Herder, 1931), 15. Both are quoted in Bergin, *O Propheticum Lavacrum*, 24–25.

180. Ibid., 25.

181. See J. M. R. Tillard, "La triple dimension du signe sacramentel," *Nouvelle Revue théologique* 83 (1961): 249; and also J. Daniélou, "The Sacraments and the History of Salvation" in *The Liturgy and the Word of God* (Collegeville, MN: Liturgical Press, 1959), 31.

theology of sacrament, within a developing awareness, the *signum demonstrativum* was crucial. As Raymond Vaillancourt points out,

> The first Christian communities sought to experience more fully the major events that occurred in the midst of ordinary life by relating them to the paschal mystery of Christ. They gradually discovered that a number of human situations could be privileged occasions for proclaiming and revealing to all, Christian or non-Christian, the profound meaning of certain events in human life.[182]

From the third century onwards, the great period of *Katecheseis Mystagogikai* is in full flow, as attested by the procatecheses and catecheses of Fathers such as Cyril of Jerusalem, Theodore of Mopsuestia, Ambrose, and Augustine.[183] Now the obscure connection that exists between the Pauline Greek *mysterion* and the Latin *sacramentum* is somewhat clarified, as the rites demonstrate the connection between sacramental life and the eternal plan of God revealed in his Son Jesus Christ. The ecclesial expression of the sign element of sacramental theology was certainly at its high point during this period, and, though the conceptualization and privatization of the sacramental rites that comes about in the Middle Ages to some extent detracts from the demonstrative element, David Bourke can still claim, "If there is one key idea which lies at the very roots of St. Thomas' treatise as a whole it is the idea that the new life of the redemption wrought by God in the incarnate Word is

---

182. R. Vaillancourt, *Toward a Renewal of Sacramental Theology* (Collegeville, MN: Liturgical Press, 1979), 11–12.

183. "The postbaptismal catecheses are rarely didactic. Their content, tenor and style is marked by a rhetorical ornamentation and theological splendour that is unparalleled by contemporary standards. The patristic mystagogues are given to images, metaphors and stories that reveal the significance and deeper meanings of the baptismal symbols. It is owing to the theological incisiveness of the fathers that they are able to discern in the complex of baptismal symbols, gestures, and signs the economy of salvation that is offered to the neophyte." J. Baerwald, "Mystagogy," in *The New Dictionary of Sacramental Worship*, ed. P. Fink (Collegeville, MN: Liturgical Press, 1990), 881–83, 883. See also Anne Field, *From Darkness to Light* (Ann Arbor, MI: Servant, 1978).

communicated to man through created media, physical things, or acts combined with words."[184]

Despite its many achievements, later scholastic theology of the sacraments labored under some severe limitations. Though the specific scientific methodology employed was appropriate to the questions the scholastics sought to resolve, a consequence was that the sacraments remained objective realities, scrutinized from without and cut off from the life of the believer.[185] One might say that it was the neglect of the combined elements of proclamation and revelation proper to the *signum demonstrativum* of the sacraments that elicited the negative reaction of the Reformers.[186] The legacy of the church's guarded reaction at the Council of Trent,[187] along with the polemical bias of the schools in subsequent years, meant that for a long time sacramental theology remained docile to an overbearing canonical minimalism. As has been seen throughout this study, the converging factors that contributed to its reawakening center on the demonstrative element.[188] To claim that a central theme of Congar's work is the assertion that the "Church is an earthly

---

184. D. Bourke, "Introduction," vol. 56 of the Blackfriars Edition of the *Summa Theologiae*, xx, quoted in B. Davis, *The Thought of Thomas Aquinas* (Oxford: Clarendon, 1992), 350.

185. "Appropriately it asked questions of sacraments that were fitting to scientific objects: who made it? Where did it come from? What constitutes it to be what it is? When does it cease to be itself? Who may use it? When? And for what purpose? This question set allowed theologians to weave together a well-wrought network of understanding which rooted the understanding of the sacraments directly, or at least indirectly, in the life of Christ." P. Fink, "Sacramental Theology After Vatican II," in Fink, *The New Dictionary of Sacramental Worship*, 1107–14, 1108.

186. "Liturgical forms were frozen to protect doctrine; they were neither seen as, nor given free reign to be, living expressions of the Church's living faith." Ibid., 1108. In the face of Luther's protest that justification comes through faith alone, such casuistic and seemingly mechanical rites remained an affront (see M. Luther, "The Babylonian Captivity of the Church," in *Luther's Works*, ed. H. Lehmann, vol. 36 (Philadelphia: Fortress Press, 1970), 66).

187. Unfortunately, in responding to the teachings of the Reformers, Trent completely ignores the liturgical context that Aquinas had established by describing the sacraments as "acts of worship," and founded its defense squarely on the performance of the rite *ex opere operato* (see *DS* 1600 and 1608).

188. Peter Fink identifies the liturgical movement, biblical scholarship, the demise of scholastic conceptualism, a return to patristic symbolism, and growth in mystery theology. See Fink, "Sacramental Theology After Vatican II," 1107–14, 1108–9.

and historical revelation, by the communication of the grace of the Trinitarian mystery,"[189] is to reveal a protagonist in the postconciliar spiritual renewal of signs.[190] It is to identify one who recognises the fundamental significance of the Thomistic dictum: *sacramenta significando efficiunt gratiam*.

The Sacramental Bond between the Supernatural and the Existential in the Theology of Karl Rahner

Early in the *Quaestio disputata, The Church and the Sacraments*, Rahner points to the problematic axis that has bedevilled sacramental theology from the beginning: the relationship between the *signum demonstrativum* and the resultant existential encounter with grace:

> In all these theories it is noteworthy that the fact that sacraments are signs plays no part in explaining their causality. Their function as signs and their function as causes are juxtaposed without connection. The axiom everywhere quoted, *sacramenta significando efficiunt gratiam*, is not in fact taken seriously. Nor do these theories take into account the fundamentally human element in the sacraments as sacred rites which have a past and a background in the whole history of man's religious activity.[191]

189. This is Congar's own phrase. See *Fifty Years of Catholic Theology: Conversations with Yves Congar*, ed. B. Lauret (London: SCM, 1988), 59.

190. Congar's involvement with the production of both *Lumen Gentium* and *Ad Gentes*, and his extensive work in pneumatology, ecclesiology, and ecumenism since the Council, have had a significant effect on the development of sacramental theology. For an insight into his conciliar contribution, see Y.-M, Congar, "Principes Doctrinaux (nos. 2. à 9.)" *L'Activité missionnaire de l'Église, Décret "Ad Gentes,"* Unam Sanctam 67 (1967): 185–221; Y.-M. Congar, "The Council as an Assembly and the Church as Essentially Conciliar," in *One, Holy, Catholic and Apostolic: Studies on the Nature of the Church in the Modern World*, ed. H. Vorgrimler (London: Sheed and Ward, 1968), 44–88; and D. Doyle, "Journet, Congar, and the Roots of Communion Ecclesiology," *Theological Studies* 58 (1997): 461–79. To begin to estimate some effects on sacramental theology, see I. Kizhakkeparampil, *The Invocation of the Holy Spirit as Constitutive of the Sacraments according to Cardinal Yves Congar* (Rome: PUG, 1995); and J. Anderson, *A Vatican II Pneumatology of the Paschal Mystery: The Historical-Doctrinal Genesis of Ad Gentes I, 2–5* (Rome: PUG, 1988).

191. Rahner, *The Church and the Sacraments*, 36.

Rahner's effort to "connect" everyday human existence and the gracious self-manifestation of God was a project more far-reaching than a theology of the sacraments, though there, perhaps, it finds its clearest expression. In 1966, Rahner made explicit his belief that, for dogmatic theology to be fruitful and relevant to the modern age, it must adopt an anthropocentric perspective and starting point.[192] Yet previous to this, in his two works *Spirit in the World* and *Hearers of the Word*, Rahner was already working out a theory of human transcendence that was to give "something of a systematic character"[193] to his whole theology.

In *Spirit in the World*, Rahner develops a theory of cognition that describes the human mind as being able to understand the whole realm of being as finite and, in doing so, as gaining a sense of infinity. Through the finite, the infinite is grasped against what Rahner calls an "horizon," "field," or "background" of infinity.[194] In *Hearers of the Word*, he adds to this understanding by describing human existence as fundamentally oriented toward God: a God who is encountered only in the world and through history.[195] From the

---

192. K. Rahner, "Theology and Anthropology," *Theological Investigations*, trans. G. Harrison, vol. 9 (London: Darton, Longman and Todd, 1972), 29.

193. W. Dych, *Karl Rahner* (London: Geoffrey Chapman, 1991), 32.

194. "What we mean by the pre-concept must be further clarified. It is a *capacity* of dynamic self-movement of the spirit, given *a priori* with human nature, directed towards all possible objects. It is a movement in which the particular object is, as it were, grasped as an individual factor of this movement towards a goal, and so consciously grasped in a pre-view of this absolute breadth of the knowable. Through this preconcept the particular is always, as it were recognised under the absolute ideal of knowledge. Hence it has already been set within the conscious sphere of the totality of knowable things. Hence too it is always already known as not completely filling up this sphere, that is, as limited. Insofar as it is seen to be limited, the essential definition will be understood in itself as wider, as relatively unlimited—that is, it is abstracted." K. Rahner, *Spirit in the World* (New York: Sheed and Ward, 1968), 59–60.

195. "This basic constitution of man which he affirms implicitly in each of his cognitions and actions we designate as his spirituality. Man is spirit, that is, he lives his life in a perpetual reaching out towards the Absolute, in openness to God. This openness to God is not a contingency which can emerge here or there at will in man, but is the condition for the possibility of that which man is and has to be, even in the most forlorn and mundane life." K. Rahner, *Hearers of the Word* (London: Sheed and Ward 1969), 66.

perspective of these fundamental principles, Rahner is able to identify the action of grace as something intrinsic to human existence, while it remains radically distinct. This understanding was developed further when these principles were reworked in the light of the universal salvific will of God. In this way, Rahner refined and sharpened his teaching on grace into the notion of the supernatural existential.[196] Thus the difficulty posed by the gulf between humanity and the self-communication of God is overcome.[197] As Eugene TeSelle points out,

> The crucial point of the distinction between nature and grace is that grace opens up a possibility which does not lie within the scope of man's natural powers and is not implied by his being a man. This distinction becomes necessary when grace is understood as not implied by man's humanity as such. This last point is the contribution of the thirteenth century theology as it is presented in Aquinas. The validity of this supernaturalist language of grace, however, is dependent on the naturalism it presupposes. Once a closed system of nature with imminent, proportioned goals gives way to one in which nature and human existence are seen as radically open to an indefinite future and even an infinite goal, the concept of the supernatural may be disregarded even as the notion of utter gratuity must be retained.[198]

196. In his *Theological Dictionary*, Rahner describes the supernatural existential as the dogmatic fact that our concrete, actual historical state is one of being called to grace which means that "antecedently to justification by grace, received sacramentally or extra-sacramentally, man is already subject to the universal salvific will of God, he is already redeemed and absolutely obliged to tend to his supernatural end. This 'situation' is not merely an external one; it is an objective, ontological qualification of man, added indeed to his nature by God's grace and therefore supernatural, but in fact never lacking in the real order." K. Rahner and H. Vorgrimler, *Theological Dictionary* (New York: Herder and Herder, 1965), 161.

197. "This difficulty is resolved when we transfer to uncreated grace the concepts of formal ontology which appear in the *visio beatifica*: God communicates himself to the man to whom grace has been shown in the mode of formal causality, so that this communication is not merely the consequence of an efficient causation of created grace." K. Rahner, "Some Implications of the Scholastic Concept of Uncreated Grace," in *Theological Investigations*, trans. C. Ernst, vol. 1 (London: Darton, Longman and Todd, 1965), 334. See also Rahner, "Concerning the Relationship between Nature and Grace," in *Theological Investigations,* vol. 1, 297–317; and Rahner, "Nature and Grace," in *Theological Investigations*, trans. K. Smyth, vol. 4 (London: Darton, Longman and Todd), 36–73.

198. E. TeSelle, "The Problem of Nature and Grace," *The Journal of Religion* 45 (July 1965): 238–41, quoted in R. Haight, *The Experience and Language of Grace* (New York: Paulist, 1979), 74–75.

What TeSelle recognises in Rahner's system is the potential for grace to be a personal, existential encounter rather than an extrinsic, ontological fact.[199]

It is Rahner's assertion of a fundamental possibility of transcendence,[200] coupled with his theology of symbol, that causes "something of a Copernican revolution"[201] in the realm of sacramental theology. Although his theory of *Realsymbol* has already been examined in this study, in order to give a comprehensive sense of his contribution here, and hopefully trace a degree of development within it, it may prove helpful to quote a review summary of Van Roo:

> Thus briefly elaborated, this concept of the inner (real) symbol must be exploited now, if the proper character of sacramental causality is to be grasped, and understood in turn from the point of view of the ecclesiological origin of the sacraments. The Church in her historical perceptibility is herself the inner symbol of God's eschatologically victorious grace. In this spatio-temporal perceptibility, this grace renders itself present. Since the sacraments are the self-fulfilments of the Church, actualizations of the Church in relation to the individual man, insofar as the Church in her whole reality is the presence [*Da-sein*] of God's grace (as the "New Covenant"): these signs become efficacious. Theirs is the efficacy of the inner symbol: Christ deals with man through the Church precisely by making his action corporeal in space and time, by letting the offer of his grace become perceptible in the sacrament.[202]

---

199. For a fuller exposition of Rahner's theology of grace, see S. Duffy, *The Graced Horizon: Nature and Grace in Modern Catholic Thought* (Collegeville, MN: Liturgical Press, 1992), 85–114; L. O'Donovan, ed., *A World of Grace: An Introduction to the Themes and Foundations of Karl Rahner's Theology* (New York: Crossroad, 1987), 64–75.

200. "Human beings say their yes or no to their graced condition (their orientation towards the immediacy of God) over some worldly reality because they have this orientation consciously and freely only in a relationship to someone or something in this world. This is why their history is the history of their free relationship to their graced transcendentality, why it is salvation history." K. Rahner, *Meditations on the Sacraments* (London: Burns and Oates, 1979), 282.

201. Ibid.

202. W. Van Roo, "Reflections on Karl Rahner's *Kirche und Sakramente*," *Gregorianum* 44 (1963): 472.

Immediately apparent from this short reflection on the sacramentology that emerges from Rahner's system, and that he elaborates in *The Church and the Sacraments*, is the fact that it is derived completely from Christology. This not only sets the work in sharp contrast to the contribution of Yves Congar, just examined, but also gives some sense of why he expanded and refined this understanding in later essays. J. J. Buckley criticises Rahner's symbolic system on the grounds of its vertical imbalance, implying that in so explaining the existential bond of God's self-communication, it is difficult to preserve the unique nature of its manifestation in Jesus Christ. Hence, while a contemporaneity of past events with those of today is clear, according to a symbolization that comes via Christ as the objective correlative of all revelation, it is not clear how this contemporaneity is maintained "on the horizontal plane of historical continuity."[203] This point is crucial to an understanding of the possible simultaneity of foundational and dependent revelation in the liturgy, and, although Rahner looks to notions of tradition to supplement this thesis,[204] it would seem that a complete answer to the problem cannot be gained from a notion of symbol alone.

Perhaps as a consequence of this predominant "verticality" within Rahner's symbolic system come criticisms that his notion of church and sacrament promote a certain quietism with regard to social and political change.[205] In subsequent articles, Rahner took this criticism very seriously, and in a number of essays he argues keenly for an ecumenical, democratized, and socio-critical church. What can be

203. See J. J. Buckley, "On Being a Symbol: Appraisal of Rahner," *Theological Studies* 40 (1979): 464.
204. See K. Rahner, "Theology of the New Testament," in *Theological Investigations*, trans. K.-H. Kruger, vol. 5 (London: Darton, Longman and Todd, 1978), 23–41; K. Rahner, "The Eternal Significance of the Humanity of Jesus for Our Relationship with God," in *Theological Investigations*, trans. K.-H. Kruger and B. Kruger, vol. 3 (London: Darton, Longman and Todd, 1974), 35–46.
205. See particularly J.-B. Metz, *Faith in History and Society: Toward a Practical Fundamental Theology* (New York: Seabury, 1980), 158–61.

seen, then, is a gradual deepening of understanding in the years following the Second Vatican Council, during which Rahner's *The Church and the Sacraments* was first published.[206] The development follows avenues already examined in reference to the four authors of this study, and pertains particularly to liturgy,[207] pneumatology[208] and orthopraxis.[209] The purpose of detailing the christological emphasis of *The Church and the Sacraments* and its concomitant deficiencies is, as Van Roo has said, in order to "accentuate the positive contribution made by Father Rahner."[210] Credit must be given to the singular contribution that he made to the development of sacramentology. His influence, to varying degrees, can be seen in the work of all four writers studied in this thesis, and undoubtedly, his theologies of grace and symbol provided fundamental synthetic principles that opened up new possibilities for understanding revelation and its communication. In summary, what can be said of Rahner can be said also of Latourelle, Dulles, Marsili, and Martelet: the aspect of their work that remains incomplete is a discussion of the phenomenological processes by which believers participate in the profound mystery of revelation.[211] However, shifts toward the disciplines of liturgy, pneumatology, pastoral and political theology,

---

206. See L. O'Donovan, ed., "A Changing Ecclesiology in a Changing Church: A Symposium on Development in the Ecclesiology of Karl Rahner," *Theological Studies* 38 (1977): 736–62.

207. See M. Skelley, *The Liturgy of the World: Karl Rahner's Theology of Worship* (Collegeville, MN: Liturgical Press, 1991).

208. See K. Rahner, "Experience of Self and Experience of God," 122–32; Rahner, "Experience of the Spirit and Existential Commitment," in *Theological Investiagtions*, trans. D. Morland, vol. 16 (London: Darton, Longman and Todd, 1979), 24–34.

209. See K. Rahner, "The Function of the Church as Critic of Society," in *Theological Investigations*, trans. D. Bourke, vol. 12 (London: Darton, Longman and Todd, 1974), 229–49; Rahner, "The Church's Commission to Bring Salvation and the Humanization of the World," in *Theological Investigations*, trans. D. Bourke, vol. 14 (London: Darton, Longman and Todd, 1976), 295–313.

210. W. Van Roo, "Reflections on Karl Rahner's *Kirche und Sakramente*," 484.

211. With specific reference to *The Church and the Sacraments*. See D. Tappeiner, "Sacramental Causality in Aquinas and Rahner: Some Critical Thoughts," *The Scottish Journal of Theology* 28 (1975): 243–57.

and the social sciences that are present to varying degrees in their later writings express an intuition of where the answers lie.

Schillebeeckx:
A Further Step to Synthesis

It is appropriate that our attempts to present a conclusion to this book, which is at once corrective and synthetic, should lead, at last, to Edward Schillebeeckx, not only because he has offered a perhaps more sustained reflection on the sacramental economy, but because, in some ways, he integrates the theological perspectives and intuitions of Yves Congar and Karl Rahner in this regard. Biographically speaking, Schillebeeckx enjoyed a rich confluence of Jesuit and Dominican insights both from the distinct but complementary schools of Le Saulchoir and Lyon-Fourvière, but also in the Dominican philosopher Dominic-Marie de Petter (1905–1971), who, under the influence of the Belgian Jesuit Joseph Maréchal, sought to wed Thomistic philosophy with phenomenology.[212] Imbued with the spirit of *aggiornamento* that this intellectual ferment had inspired in many of his contemporaries, Schillebeeckx wanted to understand why Christian revelation in its traditional form had ceased to provide credible answers to contemporary questions about God. He concluded that "it is partly because we are blind to the 'signs of the times,' that God's word, in all that we say of him, is returning to him void—just the opposite of what the Old Testament prophet assured us would happen."[213]

---

212. For a concise and comprehensive discussion of the major influences on Schillebeeckx's philosophical and theological formation, see P. Kennedy, Schillebeeckx (London: Geoffrey Chapman, 1993), 13–53.
213. E. Schillebeeckx, *God the Future of Man* (New York: Sheed and Ward, 1968), 53.

In this short assertion, surface the major elements of Schillebeeckx's theological enterprise. Within the grand *exitus-reditus* schema of Aquinas, he sets the contemporary world and the human mind as the point from which the eschatologically oriented word of God departs. With Rahner, Schillebeeckx recognises human experience, specifically understood,[214] as the place in which the revealing word is active. In earlier writings,[215] condensed and republished in English during Vatican II under the title *Christ, the Sacrament of Encounter with God,*[216] Schillebeeckx brings the philosophy of phenomenology to bear on his understanding of the believer's experience of God in the sacraments of the church. Like Rahner, what he is struggling with here is the fact that

> so far no balanced solution has in fact been found in contemporary theology for the problem involved in reconciling the concepts of "revelation" and "man's understanding of himself." The reason for this seems to me to be the fundamental ambivalence of the source from which modern theology has found refreshment, "existential phenomenology." . . . Phenomenological thought bears witness, on the one hand, to the "crisis of objectivity" and, on the other, to the "insufficiency of subjectivity." The fact that the distinctive manner in which existential phenomenology has tried to resolve the problem of object and subject is unsatisfactory is clearly echoed in present-day Protestant thinking and, stemming from this, in modern Catholic thought as well. An attempt is being made to solve the problem of discussing God without reverting, on the one hand, to the "objectivizing orthodoxy" and, on the other, to the nineteenth-century

214. "As the absolute reality, God by definition eludes direct experience. Because of this, a humanly meaningful faith in God is only possible within a rational sphere of understanding if our human reality *itself* contains a real reference to God, which is therefore part of our experience." Ibid., 71.

215. E. Schillebeeckx, *De Sacramentele Heilseconomie: Theologische bezinning op S. Thomas' sacramentenleer in het licht van de traditie en van de hedendaagse sacramentsproblematiek* (Antwerp: H. Nelissen, 1952).

216. E. Schillebeeckx, *Christ the Sacrament of the Encounter with God* (London: Sheed and Ward, 1963).

"liberalism of subjectivity." But it has not yet been possible to find a satisfactory balance between these two extremes.[217]

However successful one regards Schillebeeckx's efforts in the search for a "balanced solution,"[218] the effect of his introduction of overtly phenomenological language into sacramentology cannot be underestimated. Use of the word *encounter* provides a simple but telling example, the significance of which Cornelius Ernst recognises in his foreword to Schillebeeckx's book. Such a term typifies the way in which phenomenology sees meaning and truth to be clarified; that is, in terms of the subject-object structures of consciousness. Hence, Ernst declares,

> Now, "encounter" is a fundamental mode of existence of the human existent, a structural possibility inherent in it. We may treat each other as physical objects or mechanisms, but that is to choose to mistreat each other; the misuse, the deficiency, throws light on that preordained openness to our fellows which releases our being into the fellowship of a *we*. It may be noted further that our *bodily* presence to each other is essential to encounter; we may smile at each other or make our faces into masks, give ourselves to each other or withhold ourselves. Again, just as there are conventions in any given culture which shape the styles of this bodily encounter, so there is a ritual idiom, continuous with the ceremonial of secular life, which shapes the styles of our liturgical encounter with God.[219]

---

217. Schillebeeckx, *God the Future of Man*, 84–85.

218. Kenan B. Osborne maintains, "In sacramental theology one finds this transcendental Thomistic approach in Rahner's *The Church and the Sacraments*, and in Schillebeeckx's *Christ the Sacrament of Encounter with God*. In both of these volumes the sections the respective authors devote to Jesus as sacrament and the church as sacrament echo with Heideggerian and phenomenological overtones. However, when Rahner discusses individual sacraments, and when Schillebeeckx considers such themes as sacramental character, *ex opere operato* and *ex opere operantis*, the revival of the sacrament, matter and form, both authors revert to a neo-Thomistic, onto-theological framework. In sacramental theology neither author satisfactorily unites the Heideggerian and phenomenological side with the scholastic side." K Osborne, *Christian Sacraments in a Postmodern World* (New York: Paulist, 1999), 53.

219. C. Ernst, "Foreword," in Schillebeeckx, *Christ the Sacrament of the Encounter with God*, xv–xvi.

In the search for a credible language with which to speak of God, the language of the liturgy, if continuous with the "ceremonial of secular life," provides the context for God's word, so that all we say of him may not return to him void.

Such may be said of Schillebeeckx's position in the mid-1960s, but this would not take into account the "momentous philosophical turnabout"[220] that he experienced around the close of that decade. Largely, it would seem, as a result of a number of lecture tours in the United States of America, Schillebeeckx had to face a crisis of pluralism and rapidity of change that meant that he sustained something of a "paradigm shock." The amalgam of Thomism, *ressourcement* theology, and phenomenology through which he had interpreted the question of faith, no longer seemed an even remotely adequate response to the vast and changing presuppositions of the modern world. The only categories that would seem to approach the universality required for the accessibility and credibility that modern culture demanded seemed to be the experience of suffering and the reality of Christian praxis.[221]

Schillebeeckx's confrontation with secularization, and his recognition that the gospel tradition must be reinterpreted in the light of contemporary models of thought if faith is to remain alive, coincides with his appointment as a teacher of hermeneutics at the University of Nijmegen. In the tradition of Le Saulchoir, Schillebeeckx returns to the sources again, but this time his interest is in how biblical texts can be interpreted in the light of contemporary experience. The work that emanates from this sustained hermeneutical refelction is his three-volumed Christology, the original Dutch titles of which better reveal the motive of Schillebeeckx's enterprise. *Jesus, the Story of One Alive*, is followed

---

220. Kennedy, *Schillebeeckx*, 42–45.
221. Ibid., 44.

by *Christ, Justice and Love: Grace and Liberation*, and completed by *Church, Human Beings as God's Story*.[222] Common to each part of the trilogy is a search for a credible point of encounter with the living God as he is actualized through the word of God, in Christian praxis, and in the reality of *communio* or church. Two aspects of these long and intricately argued texts could be profitably highlighted within the present study. Schillebeeckx always maintains that the life, the death, and the resurrection of Jesus cannot be understood in isolation from each other, because the moments of the paschal mystery are mutually interpretive. In some senses, the second aspect to be noted follows from this, which is the assertion that the objective truth of each aspect of the paschal mystery has an inseparable, distinct, and yet complementary subjective element through which it is interpreted and accessed. Thus, Schillebeeckx can assert that "the resurrection effected in the person of Jesus is at the same time the gift of God's Spirit for us."[223] Necessarily, then, the anamnetic and epicletic elements of the community's consciousness are fundamental to the present actualization of salvation. For as Schillebeeckx asserts, "Without the Christian experience of faith we have no organ which can give us a view of Jesus's resurrection. But conversely: without the personal resurrection of Jesus there can be no Christian experience of Easter."[224]

Both Rahner and Schillebeeckx indicate experience as a category crucial to a correct appreciation of how God's salvation is revealed; Schillebeeckx locates its manifestation primarily in Christian praxis and the upbuilding of the kingdom, while Rahner tends toward a

---

222. See ibid., 67–68 for the more accurate titles of the Dutch editions. The English editions are respectively, E. Schillebeeckx, *Jesus: An Experiment in Christology* (London: Collins, 1979); Schillebeeckx, *Christ: The Christian Experience in the Modern World* (London: SCM, 1980); Schillebeeckx, *Church: the Human Story of God* (London: SCM, 1990).
223. Schillebeeckx, *Interim Report on the Books "Jesus" and "Christ,"* 135.
224. Ibid., 79.

worship setting for its actualization.[225] An ecclesial context and a pneumatological dimension remains essential to both their studies. Like Rahner, Schillebeeckx points to possible avenues of development that would be fruitful for our own study—the most obvious being a reinterpretation of his earlier reflections on the sacraments in the light of his later hermeneutic of christological experience.[226]

By Way of Conclusion

Van Roo makes a telling, if slightly petulant, criticism of *The Church and the Sacraments* at the beginning of his "Reflections on Karl Rahner's *Kirche und Sakramente*." He maintains that "Father Rahner is not engaged in dialogue with representative contemporary theologians."[227] That was in 1963, and since then, dialogue between the particular theological disciplines shaped at the time of the Council has been an ever-increasing phenomenon. In the years directly after the Council, liberation theologians such as Juan-Luis Segundo and Leonardo Boff lifted an insistent voice pointing out that any developing theology of the sacraments must retrieve the prophetic and transforming elements of these rites, as without such a dimension the church's sacramental system could be seen to support social exploitation. In such a light some have interpreted the second volume of Schillebeeckx's study in Christology as "liberation theology for the West." There was then, and is still, an urgency about the conversation that must take place between liturgical orthodoxy and Christian orthopraxis. In recent years, Jeremy Driscoll, Andrea Grillo, and others have made the lack of dialogue between liturgists and

---

225. See Schillebeeckx's essay "Secular Worship and Church Liturgy," in *God the Future of Man*, 93–116.
226. Cf. Kennedy, *Schillebeeckx*, 63.
227. Van Roo, "Reflections on Karl Rahner's *Kirche und Sakramente*," 465.

fundamental theologians abundantly clear, and have taken significant steps to rectify it. The series *Alternative Futures For Worship*, edited by B. Lee, is founded on the ambition to understand the sacraments in the light of the human sciences, and the last twenty-five years in particular have seen a growing number of works on the sacraments that are solidly interdisciplinary.[228] As Regis Duffy points out in a recent survey of sacramental theology, "There is a growing rigor in the methodologies employed and wider familiarity with subspecialties within the human sciences. This has revitalized the areas of sacramental thinking that had become rather abstract and analytical and gives promise of further creative insight."[229]

"Promise of further creative insight" was the reason why the conclusions drawn from the quadrilogue of chosen authors were set within the critical context of Congar and Rahner. At this point, the multifaceted nature of the discussion necessary to resolve the question under discussion was undoubtedly confirmed. Yet emerging from the juxtaposition of the writers' particular insights and blind spots are certain definite conclusions that will give shape and direction to any further reflection. By way of summary, the present task before sacramental theologians will be outlined in particular reference to the central aim of this book.

Drawing the Principles of Sacramental Theology from the Renewed Liturgy

Salvatore Marsili took very seriously the injunction of *Sacrosanctum Concilium* 16 concerning the teaching of the liturgy in seminaries and theological faculties. There it is made quite clear that the liturgy

---

228. For an excellent overview of the growing interdisciplinarity in sacramental studies, see Power, Duffy, and Irwin, "Sacramental Theology: A Review of Literature," 657–705.
229. R. Duffy, "The Post-Rahnerian Formulation," in ibid., 675.

is to be a source of unity for the theological enterprise because of its *fundamental* characteristics. The liturgy is the self-manifestation of God in a unique mode, and until fundamental and dogmatic theology fully grasp that fact, they will be impoverished in their understanding of both the phenomenology and the content of revelation, and of its shape and modes of transmission. One thing that the *hodie* of the liturgy will not let dogmatics deny is that the fullness of that reality, of which Christ is the eternal sacrament, is revealed and saves in the present moment. Therefore, any effort that seeks to understand the convergence of the event of salvation and its current actualization must *begin* with the liturgy that represents it. One might say that, had this been the case from the beginning, the "particular ritual shapes"[230] of *anàmnesis* and *epiclesis* would have given a balanced foundation to the theological inquiry that seeks to understand how the believing community encounters the God who reveals himself. From the first, cognizance would have been taken of the necessary integration of christological and pneumatological dimensions within this inquiry—an equilibrium that sacramental theology is still in the process of appropriating.

One might look to recent developments in the debate on apostolic succession to see how the liturgy functions not only as *teologia prima*, but also as a force for integration within theological debate. The liturgy at once reveals the complexity of the issue and offers the methodological means of synthesis.[231] In the case of apostolic succession, the eucharistic liturgy, in its anamnetic and epicletic dimensions, has revealed the complex nexus of *communio, successio, traditio* to be at the heart of the question concerning the content

---

230. J. Driscoll, *Theology at the Liturgical Table* (Leominster, UK: Gracewing, 2003), 159.
231. Cf. J. Zizioulas, *Being as Communion: Studies in Personhood and the Church* (Crestwood, NY: St. Vladimir's Seminary, 1993); D. Fagberberg, *Theologia Prima: What is Liturgical Theology?* (Chicago: Hillenbrand, 2007).

and transmission of the apostolic *paradosis*. Reflection on the liturgy would seem to have raised the debate from the tired antithesis of Western historical notions and Eastern pneumatological ones.[232] Perhaps headway could be made in similar fashion with regard to the integration of what O'Collins has helpfully termed "foundational" and "dependent" revelation.[233] So far, dependent revelation seems to be characterised christologically and historically, yet attention to the liturgy would give a resurrection focus that indicates that present revelation is equally dependent on the Holy Spirit and the future. Just as within apostolic succession the figure of "the twelve" has a historical and an eschatological role, so notions of present revelation see the sacraments of the church as being dependent on both the historical Jesus and the risen Christ. Through the complex nexus of *commemoratio*, *demonstratio*, and *praefiguratio*, the liturgy reveals the sacraments to be at the heart of questions surrounding the present actualization of divine revelation.

Harmonizing Sacramental Theology with the Language of the Christian People

Necessarily, the liturgy makes theology begin with experience. Detailing his intentions in the preface of *Spirit and Sacrament: The Humanizing Experience*, Joseph Powers makes the following reflection:

> It is beyond triteness to say that we live in a time of change, a time when the problem of meaning is particularly critical. We hear the question asked from every side, addressed to almost every symbol system. In some instances, the question implies the meaninglessness of the symbols which

---

232. See W. Kasper, "Apostolic Succession in the Office of Bishop as an Ecumenical Problem," *Theology Digest* 47, no. 3 (Fall, 2000): 203–10.

233. See again G. O'Collins, "Revelation Past and Present," in Latourelle, *Vatican II: Assessment and Perspectives*, 1:125–37.

structure our life, our experience and the urge to tear the whole thing down. These reflections are not made in that spirit. Rather, they are an attempt to discover what experience—human experience—these symbols should contain and produce. They are written in an attempt to find how we might reload these symbols with the power they should have for our lives.[234]

This study has made clear the enormous theological advances that took place at the time of the Second Vatican Council. Perhaps most noteworthy were the christological renewal of theology and the establishment of credible motives for faith in the incarnate and risen Christ. What requires further exploration is the phenomenology of the symbolic exchange that exists between Christ and the believer by virtue of their common humanity. As Rahner and others have shown, the symbolization of the seemingly mundane elements of life is at the heart of this question, and, until sacramental theology expresses itself in harmony with the language of Christian experience, sacramental signs will be increasingly emptied of their significance. Further credibility must be given to experience as a source of reflection on the mysteries of salvation, and it is perhaps no accident that Congar, who has concerned himself with experience of the Holy Spirit, should offer a pointer in this endeavor. As Aidan Nichols points out, speaking of Congar's early theological career,

> The idea came to him that his own generation should rescue for the Church whatever was of value in the approach of the Modernists. In his judgement this meant two things. First, it meant the application of the historical method to Christian data—though not a restrictively "historical-critical" method where the dimension of faith was epistemologically blotted out. Secondly, it meant greater attention to the viewpoint of the experiencing subject, whose needs and concerns shift with the contours of history itself.[235]

---

234. J. Powers, *Spirit and Sacrament: The Humanizing Experience* (New York: Seabury, 1973), x.
235. Nichols, *Yves Congar*, 4–5.

This ambition was not fully accomplished in the lifetime of Congar, and it is only recent years that have seen the rehabilitation of a significant amount of "Modernist" thought.[236] As sacramental theology is the subject of a new coherence emerging from the anthropological, christological, pneumatological, and ecclesiological renewal of the Council, the time is right for a reappropriation of Modernist insights, as a more balanced context now exists for their interpretation. In this way, new vigor may be given to further the dialogue between the categories of revelation and experience.

As indicated previously, a liturgico-experiential methodology should ensure balance within the content of the theological pursuit. That is to say, it should encourage attention to the pneumatological dimensions of the debate, and secure the paschal mystery as the central focus of theological reflection. However, a danger of this methodology can be a tendency to avoid the classical formulations of sacramental theology within the tradition. Care must be taken to use any new insights as a means to penetrate and reexpress the basic intuitions at work in these tracts, so that they may be incorporated effectively into the new synthesis begun by the conciliar renewal.[237]

Reflecting on the human being's knowledge of God in the *Prima Pars* of the *Summa Theologiae*, St. Thomas explains that the creature comes to know the Creator through his works: "Although in this life,

---

236. "Modernism is not reducible to the deviations that *Pascendi* isolated as alien to perennial Catholic thought. On the contrary, modernism derives its meaning and reality from the never-ending effort of Christian thought to explain the foundational events of Christianity. Modernism attempted to situate the Christian faith against a much broader backdrop than simply the traditional teaching of the Church, and to find for this faith, a language adapted to those transformations of the human mind of which the development of the modern sciences was both a symptom and an agent. Inasmuch as we have been hearing for thirty years about the renewal of exegesis and theology, it seems that the modernist project was not *a priori* unacceptable." N. Provencher, "Modernism" in Latourelle and Fisichella, *Dictionary of Fundamental Theology*, 722. In this spirit, see N. Provencher, *La révélation et son développement dans l'Église selon Alfred Loisy* (Ottawa: PUG, 1972); G. Daly, *Transcendence and Immanence: A Study in Catholic Modernism and Integralism* (Oxford: Clarendon, 1980).
237. See Vaillancourt, *Toward a Renewal of Sacramental Theology*, 67–119.

revelation does not tell us what God is, and thus joins us to him as to an unknown, nevertheless it helps us to know him better in that we are shown more and greater works of his and are taught certain things about him that we could never have known through natural reason, as for instance that he is both three and one."[238]

Recent theology has criticized the separation that the *Summa* seemingly implies between the Blessed Trinity and the paschal mystery.[239] The inner life of the Godhead is discussed in metaphysical detail in the opening part, yet the singular merit of Christ's passion is not treated until the *Tertia Pars*[240] (one must look elsewhere for comment on the resurrection[241]). And yet, while the theological benefits of identifying the immanent and economic Trinities were opened up by the *Grundaxiom* of Karl Rahner, the precise systematization of Aquinas yields an abiding insight.[242] The great works of God in the death and resurrection of his Son are situated within that part of his system that deals with the return of human beings to God. In the work of the paschal mystery, God reveals himself in the achievement of his will and so "joins us to him." Though St. Thomas was clear about the cultic nature of this movement, it was some years before his rational approach, eagerly adopted by the schoolmen, was tempered by an experiential component. It was at the beginning of the twentieth century that someone, struck by the spirit of the liturgy, who was not "always immediately asking 'why?' and 'wherefore?'"[243] began to bridge the gap:

---

238. *ST* 1a. 12, 13 ad. 1.
239. See Hunt, *The Trinity and the Paschal Mystery*, 1–7.
240. *ST* 3a. 48, 1 ad. 3.
241. In epist. 2 ad Tim. 2 lect. 2. R. Cal, ed., *Super Epistolas S. Pauli Lectura* 2 (Rome: Marietti, 1953). Quoted in Hunt, *The Trinity and the Paschal Mystery*, 5.
242. See K. Rahner, *The Trinity* (London: Burns and Oates, 1970), 21–24.
243. R. Guardini, *The Spirit of the Liturgy* 2nd ed. (New York: Crossroad, 1998), 71.

The liturgy has laid down the serious rules of the sacred game which the soul plays before God. And, if we are desirous of touching bottom in this mystery, it is the Spirit of fire and holy discipline "Who has knowledge of the world"—the Holy Ghost—Who has ordained the game which the Eternal Wisdom plays before the heavenly Father in the Church, Its kingdom on earth. And "Its delight" is in this way "to be with the children of men."[244]

The spirit of the liturgy is the Spirit of wisdom, who knows the world. Guardini had an insight that has been unfolding slowly in twentieth-century theology and is developing still. The Holy Spirit plumbs the paschal life of God in the sacred mysteries of the liturgy, and there unites confession and expression of the death and resurrection of Jesus to "the experience of life that it signifies for us."[245] Mysteriously, in this symbolic correlation, the God who in this life remains an unknown is revealed and united to us as Father, Son, and Spirit. Perhaps it was in the temple that Jesus proclaimed: "My Father is still working, and I also am working." (John 5:17. NRSV),[246] for it is in the sacraments of the church that revelation is constantly actualized, and we are taught things about him that we could never have known.

---

244. Ibid., 71.
245. See G. Lafont, *God, Time, and Being* (Petersham, MA: St. Bede's, 1992), 282. The third part of this book, entitled "Ancient and New Revelations of Being," is very interesting on this subject; see 257–324.
246. See reflections on this text and the "now" of faith in G. Aulén, *The Drama and the Symbols: A Book on Images of God and the Problems They Raise* (London: SPCK, 1970), 49–54.

Conclusion

It was always the advice of my teachers never to introduce new material into the conclusion of an essay. On this occasion I will risk ignoring what I recognize is generally sound advice for two reasons. To have offered a study that has reflected at length on the relationship between revelation and the liturgy in the period of Vatican II without significant mention of Joseph Ratzinger seems clumsy, if not foolhardy.[1] Moreover, perhaps the questions and tensions that can be found in Ratzinger's work in regard to our subject both identify the key issue clearly and also indicate avenues of possible resolution in such a way as to offer us a suitable conclusion.

---

1. "Perhaps no single figure besides Pope John Paul II has dominated the ecclesiastic consciousness over the past twenty years as much as Joseph Cardinal Ratzinger." John F. Baldovin obviously made this assessment before Ratzinger was elected pope in 2005, and without reference to his influence on the Second Vatican Council and as a theologian and prolific writer. With justification, our estimation of his influence may be increased both in length and extent. See J. F. Baldovin, "Cardinal Ratzinger as Liturgical Critic," in *Studia Liturgica Diversa: Essays in Honour of Paul F Bradshaw*, ed. M. E. Johnson and L. E. Phillips (Portland, OR: Pastoral, 2004), 227. Some estimation of his theological work and its significance can be usefully gained from E. De Gaál, *The Theology of Pope Benedict XVI: The Christocentric Shift* (New York: Palgrave Macmillan, 2010); A. Nichols, *The Theology of Joseph Ratzinger* (London: T. & T. Clark, 1988); T. Rowland, *Ratzinger's Faith: The Theology of Pope Benedict XVI* (Oxford: Oxford University Press, 2008). Interestingly, each of these works has discrete chapters on Ratzinger's fundamental theology and his liturgy, and while Aidan Nichols is the only one who tries to integrate these theological disciplines, the title of his chapter at least seems to suggest that Joseph Ratzinger "the liturgist" is distinct from him as theologian.

Given the area of Ratzinger's expertise as a theologian, and also the questions to which he has returned with particular frequency as university teacher, bishop, cardinal-prefect, and pope, it is perhaps no surprise that in deciding not to discuss the theological and ecclesial drama of the conciliar period, he allows himself two exceptions: the liturgy and revelation.[2] In his memoirs, Ratzinger speaks of his work as professor of fundamental theology and dogma at the College of Philosophy and Theology in Freising (1956–1958), his work as ordinary professor of fundamental theology at the University of Bonn (1959–1963), Münster (1963–1966), Tübingen (1966–69) and his moving to help set up the new Bavarian University of Regensburg in 1969. Many have commented on his exceptional abilities as a teacher—for expressing the complex in a lucid and accessible way—qualities evident especially in his popular and much-reprinted classic texts *Introduction to Christianity*[3] and *Principles of Catholic Theology: Building Stones for a Fundamental Theology*.[4] Likewise, Ratzinger's *Milestones* frequently returns to the liturgy as the memory central to his experience of the Christian faith. Such a sense of his deep love for the liturgy and a recognition of its essential importance in the life and mission of the church and every believer can be seen in his more popular publications: *The Feast of Faith: Approaches to a Theology of the Liturgy*,[5] *A New Song for the Lord: Faith in Christ and Liturgy Today*,[6] and *The Spirit of the Liturgy*.[7] The question,

---

2. See J. Ratzinger, *Milestones: Memoirs: 1927–1977* (San Francisco: Ignatius, 1998), 121–31, and for an interesting commentary on this fact, see A. Marchetto, *The Second Vatican Ecumenical Council: A Counterpoint for the History of the Council* (Chicago: University of Scranton Press, 2010), 549–56.

3. J. Ratzinger, *Introduction to Christianity* (London: Burns and Oates, 1969).

4. J. Ratzinger, *Principles of Catholic Theology: Building Stones for a Fundamental Theology* (San Francisco: Ignatius, 1987).

5. J. Ratzinger, *The Feast of Faith: Approaches to a Theology of the Liturgy* (San Francisco: Ignatius, 1986).

6. J. Ratzinger, *A New Song for the Lord: Faith in Christ and Liturgy Today* (San Francisco: Ignatius, 1996).

perhaps tension, that remains, however, is the extent or way in which Ratzinger and others see these two essential elements of his oeuvre to be related. In a sense, he is a test case or barometer for the recognition of liturgical theology[8] as the necessary means to address some of the questions and dichotomies this book has served to highlight.

In what one senses is a very restrained discussion of Ratzinger as liturgical critic, John F. Baldovin rehearses the various and often polemicized aspects of the liturgical debate that form a significant part of the later pope's work. However, during an interesting discussion of what he sees to be Ratzinger's approach to the Eucharist, Baldovin makes a telling remark:

> What is important for Ratzinger is the dogmatic content of this meal, and not its structure. In other words, the meal sacramentalizes Jesus' sacrifice by means of a *eucharistia*, the thanksgiving-sacrifice of the lips. Thus the early Church needed to develop a liturgy on the basis of this content, rather than as an imitation of the Last Supper itself, which if it were a Passover meal could only be repeated once a year. He is certainly onto something here.[9]

Is he? Certainly, here we arrive at a significant question for liturgical theology—whether the liturgy is indeed *theologia prima* or merely the secondary expression of a primary content.[10] It is true that in his

---

7. J. Ratzinger, *The Spirit of the Liturgy* (San Francisco: Ignatius, 2000).

8. It is not without significance that the very meaning of "liturgical theology"—that is, the way in which liturgy and fundamental theology relate—remains a nuanced and contested question until today. As well as the classic texts of A. Kavanagh, *On Liturgical Theology* (Collegeville, MN: Liturgical Press, 1992) and A. Schmemann, *Introduction to Liturgical Theology* (Crestwood, NY: St. Vladimir's Seminary, 1966), and those given in D. W. Vogel, ed., *Primary Sources of Liturgical Theology: A Reader* (Collegeville, MN: Liturgical Press, 2000), see the more recent and lively debate presented in D. W. Fagerberg, *Theologia Prima: What Is Liturgical Theology?* (Chicago: Liturgy Training, 2004). That the particularly clear approach of the work of Salvatore Marsili is conspicuously absent from recent discussions is a significant disappointment.

9. Baldovin, "Cardinal Ratzinger as Liturgical Critic," 220.

10. See Ratzinger, *Introduction to Christianity*, 15–64, *Principles of Catholic Theology*, 15–55. The sparcity of Ratzinger's use of the word *liturgy* is noticeable. In *Principles of Catholic Theology*, explicit discussion of the liturgy is only consequent to elaboration of the notions of *memoria* and

discussion of the structure and content of Catholic faith, which can be found in the works of fundamental theology mentioned above, Ratzinger seems to give the impression that he regards content as primary. For instance, he distinguishes the acclamatory form in which nominal faith (Jesus is Lord!) was expressed from the doctrinal content of faith (belief in what God has done in Christ) that "stands alongside" it.[11] What he does not seem to make explicit is the fact that it is the liturgy that integrates these two elements—nominal word and verbal deed—into an event moment that realizes the content of revelation now.[12] That is to say, while Ratzinger admits that it is within a "cultic and eschatological manifestation" that "who Christ is" is revealed "in what he is for us,"[13] he does not explicitly identify the liturgy as this privileged place of encounter. While it would be unfair to claim that Ratzinger sees the expressive form of the faith as secondary and subservient to the primary dogmatic content, one must acknowledge that he does not develop the notion that the liturgy is the form in which the words and gestures of revelation take shape and are actualized through the response of faith that worship makes possible. Further, though he recognizes that the faith deteriorates into a disintegrated catalog of content when it is separated from the Trinitarian form that the living ecclesial expression of the community provides, the liturgy is not explicitly identified as this privileged locus.[14] However, as we have consistently seen, liturgy is the locus of the intimate personal dialogue between

---

communio. Also, where explicit discussion of the liturgy begins with reflection on the meaning and structure of the sacraments, Ratzinger makes an explicit distinction between "a liturgical and theological awareness." See *Principles of Catholic Theology*, 27.

11. Ratzinger, *Principles of Catholic Theology*, 18.

12. This, as we saw in chapter 4, is the unique contribution of Salvatore Marsili.

13. Ratzinger, *Principles of Catholic Theology*, 19. See also Ratzinger's classic exposition of the opening articles of *DV* in *Commentary on the Documents of Vatican II*, ed. H. Vorgrimler, vol. 3 (London: Burns & Oates, 1968), 170–72.

14. Ratzinger, *Principles of Catholic Theology*, 21.

God and humanity, and as such needs to be seen as a "constitutive characteristic of revelation."[15]

While we might say the primary status of the liturgical form is not explicitly clear in Ratzinger, it is nevertheless strongly implicit. Primarily, this is because of the explicit relationship that Ratzinger establishes between the communal act of faith and the life of the Blessed Trinity. To clarify this, we must ask what Ratzinger means by identifying *communio* as "the structural precondition of the testimony" of faith.[16] Here he follows de Lubac in paralleling the *ec-stasy* of the one trinitarian God with the *ec-stasy* of the one church, the communion of the body of Christ, and that with the *ec-stacy* of the distinct believer who must lose individuality in order to gain the communion of trinitarian life. Ratzinger describes this as follows, in what we might say is a singularly theological key:

> In other words the "I" of the credo embraces the transition from the individual "I" to the ecclesial "I." In the case of the subject, the "I" of the Church is a structural precondition of the creed: this "I" utters itself only in the *communio* of the Church; the oneness of the believing subject is the necessary counterpart and consequence of the known "object," of that "Other" who is known by faith and who thereby ceases to be merely the "Other."[17]

This same reality is described by Jeremy Driscoll in a clearly liturgical key. Reflecting on the profession of faith within the celebration of the Eucharist, he states,

> The invitation to believe which is addressed to me by the proclamation of this life of Jesus is an invitation to participate in this community of divine giving-all-and-receiving-all, an invitation to become a person after the image of the divine Persons. I am equipped for this act whereby

15. J. Driscoll, *Theology at the Eucharistic Table* (Leominster, UK: Gracewing, 2003), 107.
16. Ratzinger, *Principles of Catholic Theology*, 22.
17. Ibid., 23. See also Ratzinger, *Introduction to Christianity*, 23. See also Jeremy Driscoll's discussion of this point within the writing of Rino Fisichella in *Theology at the Eucharistic Table*, 109–10.

I become person because I have a personal freedom (also in this am I in the image of God) in which I am genuinely free to give all of myself and receive all of my being . . . or not. If I keep all that I am for myself, I stand alone; I am a part of no community, no communion. When I give myself away, I become able to receive the other and be received by another. This is to be a person, and it coincides with an act that is essentially communal.

Ratzinger claims that it is the *communio Ecclesiae* that "is the mediator between being and time"[18]—between God and history—and he uses Augustine's theology of memory to assist in the explanation of this. Again, however, this can be given an explicitly liturgical foundation. As Ratzinger says, "Christian faith, by its very nature, includes the act of remembering; in this way, it brings about the unity of history and the unity of man before God, or rather: it can bring about the unity of history because God has given it memory."[19]

Surely, it must be acknowledged that the act of remembering by which Christian faith brings about the unity of history, of humanity, and God is a liturgical memory elaborated par excellence in the Eucharist?[20] Hence Ratzinger can say that "formulas live by the logic that supports them"[21]—the content of the word of faith only releases its meaning when it is supported by the communion that actualizes its truth in the present through memory. Hence the church does not

---

18. Ratzinger, *Principles of Catholic Theology*, 23.

19. Ibid.

20. "The Christian understanding of anamnesis is rooted in the Old testament notion of a memorial, captured in the verse from the psalm (Ps 111:4) 'The Lord has made a memorial of his wonders.' The great events of Israel's history, when narrated in a feast, become contemporary to the hearers, to those celebrating the feast. If other cultures believed that by the festive narration of the primordial origins of the cosmos, they could thereby be brought gain within the realm of cosmic purity and power, it was Israel's unique position that something similar could happen regarding actual events from history. This position is a logical consequence . . . of the fact that Israel understood the very events of history to be a word of God to her, and as such could not grow old or stale or grow weaker or lose its effects. 'The Word of the Lord remains forever.' Thus, it was enough to repeat the words which narrated the events to bring each new generation of Israelites into participation with the originating events of the community." Driscoll, *Theology at the Eucharistic Table*, 161.

21. Ratzinger, *Principles of Catholic Theology*, 26.

develop a liturgy based around the content of faith—this is one of Ratzinger's strongest fears—but faithful elaboration of the liturgical memory of the community actualizes the living truth of faith: encounter with God.

This conviction, understated and more muted in Ratzinger's works of fundamental theology, is given clearer expression in his reflections on the liturgy, especially in *The Spirit of the Liturgy*. Here Ratzinger asks, "What *is* the liturgy? What happens during the liturgy? What kind of reality do we encounter here?"[22] The response he gives here is surprisingly clear: "It [the liturgy] contains its measure within itself, that is, it can only be ordered by the measure of revelation, in dependency upon God."[23]

Through an analysis of certain texts in Exodus, Ratzinger shows that in liturgy God makes known his self and his will,[24] that he does this through a mediator who concretizes this event in worship. This liturgy—which Ratzinger characterizes as life oriented or looking on God—transmits to human beings the true form of life. Through word and symbol, God reveals a covenant with humanity that transmits life in every respect and makes a people.[25] Ratzinger goes so far as to say that the whole of creation exists to be a space for the covenant, the space where God and humanity meet, the space for worship.[26] Indeed he goes further in suggesting that the transubstantiated Host is the anticipation of the transformation of this whole space into the fullness of the risen Christ.[27]

Yet though we might hear echoes of the four writers we have examined and trace the contours of an implicit liturgical theology

---

22. Ratzinger, *The Spirit of the Liturgy*, 13.
23. Ibid., 16.
24. Ibid. One wonders if the echoes of *DV* §2 here could be unconscious.
25. Ratzinger, *The Spirit of the Liturgy*, 18.
26. Ibid., 26.
27. Ibid., 29.

in the work of Joseph Ratzinger, we must also acknowledge that lack of an explicit dialogue between revelation and the liturgy that has impoverished the theology of the last sixty years in general. Within his oeuvre, it is fair to say that fundamental theology and liturgy remain essentially distinct disciplines, and in particular that the theological categories he carefully elaborates for the better understanding of revelation are transferred to the liturgy in only a limited way. Certainly, Ratzinger has developed some of the themes that the authors of our previous chapters have discussed: a theology of word and dialogue so central to the work of Latourelle,[28] a theology of symbol and a concern for the church's role in the transmission of revelation that is also prominent in the thought of Dulles,[29] and a sense of the Eucharist as the effective communication of the transforming work of the resurrection clearly apparent in Martelet.[30] However, with Ratzinger what is most noticeable is not that as a fundamental theologian or dogmatician he does not focus on the liturgy, but exactly that the liturgy is not developed as first theology—as what Marsili would call the actualization of divine revelation. Certainly, Ratzinger understands prayer as the most transparent moment of the dialogue between God and humanity, a moment that allows him to present dogmatic truths in an imaginative and captivating way. Such is true of his refreshing approach to Christology, ecclesiology, and eschatology.[31] Yet this is still the

28. In addition to Ratzinger's Commentary on *DV*, where proximity and similarity to Latourelle is clear, see especially J. Ratzinger, *God's Word: Scripture, Tradition, Office* (San Francisco: Ignatius, 2008).

29. See J. Ratzinger, *Theologie der Liturgie. Die sakramentale Begründung christlicher Existenz*, in *Joseph Ratzinger Gesammelte Schriften*, ed. G. Müller, vol. 11 (Freiburg: Herder, 2008).

30. See especially J. Ratzinger, *The Feast of Faith: Approaches to a Theology of the Liturgy* (San Francisco: Ignatius, 1986), 45.

31. See J. Ratzinger, *Behold the Pierced One: An Approach to a Spiritual Christology* (San Francisco: Ignatius, 1986); Ratzinger, *Eschatology: Death and Eternal Life*, vol. 9 in *Dogmatic Theology*, ed. Johann Auer and Joseph Ratzinger (Washington, D. C.: Catholic University of America, 1988); Joseph Ratzinger, *Pilgrim Fellowship of Faith: The Church as Communion* (San Francisco: Ignatius, 2002).

content of faith being illumined from a liturgical angle—it is not the full recognition of the liturgy as the privileged mode of transmission: the constitutive sign and effective instrument of revelation. It is not liturgical theology in its most profound sense.

In *The Spirit of the Liturgy*, Ratzinger sets out to search for the foundations of the liturgy, for the inner structure of the rite that, unchanging though living, is maintained from generation to generation. He acknowledges that only engaging this form with integrity allows the participants access to the living content of faith, and itself is the means of both preserving and animating this deposit as the *mysterium fidei*. By carefully elaborating the theological categories of liturgy and divine revelation according to four different writers, this study effectively shows that the foundation, inner structure, and mode of transmission are the same for liturgy and revelation. Essentially, then, there can only be a single search for foundations in which common categories are mutually enlightening: for the fundamental truths of revelation, faith, and worship are one.

> one Lord, one faith, one baptism, one God and Father of all, who is above all and through all and in all. . . (NRSV)

Bibliography

Magisterial Documents

Leo XIII, *Aeterni Patris*. ASS 12 (1879): 97–115. English translation in Carlen, *The Papal Encyclicals 1878–1903*, 17–26.

———. *Divinum Illud Munus*. ASS 29 (1897): 644–58. English translation in Carlen, *The Papal Encyclicals 1878–1903*, 409–17.

———. *Mirae Caritatis*. ASS 34 (1902): 645. English trans. in Carlen, *The Papal Encyclicals 1878–1903*, 502.

———. *Providentissimus Deus*. ASS 26 (1893): 269–92. English trans. in Carlen, *The Papal Encyclicals 1878–1903*, 325–38.

Pius IX. *Divino Afflante Spiritu*. AAS 35 (1943): 297–325. English translation, G. Smith, *Biblical Studies and Opportune Means of Promoting Them*. London: CTS, 1943.

———. *Humani Generis*. AAS 42 (1950): 561–78. English translation, R. Knox, *False Trends in Modern Teaching*. London: CTS, 1959.

———. *Inter Multiplices*. Acta Pii IX 1 (1853): 439–48.

———. *Mediator Dei*. AAS 39 (1947): 521–600. English translation, G. Smith, *Christian Worship*. London: CTS, 1954.

———. *Mystici Corporis Christi*. AAS 35 (1943): 193–248. English translation, G. Smith, *On The Mystical Body of Jesus Christ and Our Union with Christ Therein*. London: CTS, 1943.

———. *Pascendi Dominici Gregis*. *ASS* 40 (1907): 593–650. English translation, in B. Reardon, *Roman Catholic Modernism*, 237–242. London: Adam and Charles Black, 1970.

———. *Syllabus Errorum*. *Acta Pii IX* 3, (1864): 687–700 (*Quanta cura*), 701–11 (*Syllabus errorum*).

Second Vatican Council. *Dei Verbum*. *AAS* 58 (1966): 817–35.

———. *Gaudium et Spes*. *AAS* 58 (1966): 1025–1120.

———. *Lumen Gentium*. *AAS* 57 (1965): 5–71.

———. *Sacrosanctum Concilium*. *AAS* 56 (1964): 97–138.

Abbott, W. M., and J. Gallagher, eds. *The Documents of Vatican II.* London: Geoffrey Chapman, 1966.

Catechism of the Catholic Church. English translation. London: Geoffrey Chapman, 1994.

Denzinger, H. and A. Schönmetzer, eds. *Enchiridion symbolorum definitionum et declarationum de rebus fidei et morum*. Freiburg: Herder, 1976.

Flannery, A., ed. *Vatican Council II: The Conciliar and Post-Conciliar Documents*. Vol. 1. Leominster, UK: Fowler Wright, 1988.

Neuner, J. and J. Dupuis, eds. *The Christian Faith in the Doctrinal Documents of the Catholic Church*. London: Collins, 1983.

Tanner, N. P., ed. *Decrees of the Ecumenical Church*. Vol. 2: *Trent—Vatican II.* London: Sheed and Ward, 1990.

Primary Texts

Works by René Latourelle (in Chronological Order)

Latourelle, R. *La Révélation Chrétienne: notion biblique, notion théologique*. Excerpta ex Dissertatione ad Lauream in Facultate Theologiae Pontificiae Gregorianae. Montréal: PUG, 1957.

———. *De Revelatione*. Rome: Pontificia Universitas Gregoriana, 1959.

———. *De Revelatione, Pars dogmatica*. Schemata lectionum ad usum privatum auditorum. Rome: Pontificia Universitas Gregoriana, 1961.

———. *De signis divinis, Pars apologetica*. Schemata lectionum ad usum privatum auditorum. Rome: Pontificia Universitas Gregoriana, 1961.

———. Église et parole." *Sciences ecclésiastiques* 15 (1962): 195–211.

———. "Faith: personal encounter with God." *Theology Digest* 10 (1962): 233–238.

———. "Miracle et Révélation." *Gregorianum* 43 (1962): 492–509.

———. "Révélation, histoire et Incarnation." *Gregorianum* 44 (1963): 225–62.

———. *Theologia Revelationis, Pars prima: De ipsa Revelatione*. Schemata lectionum ad usum privatum auditorum. Rome: Pontificia Universitas Gregoriana, 1963.

———. *Theologia Revelationis, Pars altera: De signis Revelationis*. Schemata lectionum ad usum privatum auditorum. Rome: Pontificia Universitas Gregoriana, 1964.

———. "Apologétique et fondamentale: problèmes de nature et de méthode." *Salesianum* 27 (1965): 255–74.

———. "Revelation, history and the Incarnation." *Theology Digest* 13 (1965): 29–34.

———. "La Sainteté signe de la Révélation." *Gregorianum* 46 (1965): 36–65.

———. "Le Christ, Signe de la Révélation selon la Constitution *Dei Verbum*." *Gregorianum* 47 (1966): 685–709.

———. "La testimonianza della vita, segno di salvezza." in *Laici sulle vie del Concilio*, 377–395. Assisi: Cittadella Editrice, 1966.

———. *Théologie de la Révélation: Deuxième édition revue et augmentée*. Bruges: Desclée Brouwer, 1966. English translation, Dominic Parker, *Theology of Revelation: Including a Commentary on the Constitution "Dei Verbum" of Vatican II*. New York: Alba House, 1966.

———. "L'économie des signes de la Révélation." *Sciences ecclésiastiques* 19 (1967): 7–31.

———. "Sanctity, a sign of revelation." *Theology Digest* 15 (1967): 41–46.

———. "The Internal Coherence of the Signs of Revelation." *Theology Digest* 16 (1968): 221–26.

———. "Vatican II et les signes de la Révélation." *Gregorianum* 49 (1968): 225–52.

———. *Théologie, Science du salut.* Montréal: Éditions Bellarmin, 1968. English translation, Mary Dominic, *Theology: Science of Salvation.* New York: Paulist, 1969.

———. *Le temoignage chrétien.* Montreal: Éditions Bellarmin, 1971.

———. *Le Christ et l'Église: Signes du salut.* Tournai: Desclée et Cie; Montréal: Éditions Bellarmin, 1971. English translation, Dominic Parker, *Christ and the Church: Signs of Salvation.* New York: Alba House, 1972.

———. "Authenticité historique des miracles de Jésus: Essai de critériologie." *Gregorianum* 54 (1973): 225–62.

———. *Nuova immagine della Facoltà di teologia.* Roma: Editionis Universitatis Gregorianae, 1974.

———. *L'accès à Jésus par les Évangiles. Histoire et herméneutique.* Tournai: Desclée et Cie; Montréal: Éditions Bellarmin, 1978. English translation, A. Owen, *Finding Jesus Through the Gospels: History and Hermeneutics.* New York: Alba House, 1983.

———. "L'uomo 'decifrato' da Cristo." In *Annunciare Cristo ai Giovani,* ed. A. Amato and G. Zevini, 265–80. Rome: LAS, 1980,

———. *L'homme et ses problèmes dans la lumière du Christ.* Tournai: Desclée et Cie; Montréal: Éditions Bellarmin, 1981. English translation, M. O'Connell, *Man and His Problems in the Light of Jesus Christ.* New York: Alba House, 1983.

———. "A New Image of Fundamental Theology." In Latourelle and O'Collins, *Problems and Perspectives of Fundamental Theology,* 37–58.

———. "Originalité et Fonctions des Miracles de Jésus." *Gregorianum* 66 (1985): 641–53.

———. *Miracles de Jésus et théologie du miracle*. Paris: Éditions du Cerf, 1986; English translation, M. O'Connell, *The Miracles of Jesus and the Theology of Miracles*. New York: Paulist, 1988.

———. "Assenza e presenza della Fondamentale al Vaticano II." In *Vaticano II: Bilancio e Prospettive. Venticinque anni dopo (1962–1987)*, ed. R. Latourelle. Vol. 2, 1331–1415. Assisi: Cittadella Editrice, 1987. English translation, "Absence and Presence of Fundamental Theology at Vatican II." In Latourelle, *Vatican II: Assessment and Perspectives*, 3:378–415.

———. "General Introduction." In Latourelle, *Vatican II: Assessment and Perspectives*, 1:9–19.

———, ed. *Vatican II: Assessment and Perspectives, Twenty-Five Years After (1962–1987)*. 3 vols. New York: Paulist, 1988.

———. "Blondel." In Latourelle and Fisichella, *Dictionary of Fundamental Theology*, 78–84.

———. "Dei Verbum." In Latourelle and Fisichella, *Dictionary of Fundamental Theology*, 218–24.

———. *Du prodige au miracle*. Montréal: Éditions Bellarmin, 1995.

———. "Fundamental Theology I: History." In Latourelle and Fisichella, *Dictionary of Fundamental Theology*, 324–32.

———. "Maurice Blondel." In Latourelle and Fisichella, *Dictionary of Fundamental Theology*, 78–84.

———. "Testimony." In Latourelle and Fisichella, *Dictionary of Fundamental Theology*, 1044–60.

———. "L'Université Grégorienne et le *De Revelatione*." In *L'Église canadienne et Vatican II*, ed. G. Routhier, 319–33. Montréal: Éditions Bellarmin, 1997,

———. *Comment Dieu se révèle au monde: Lecture commentée de la Constitution de Vatican II sur la Parole de Dieu*. Québec: Éditions Fides, 1998.

———. *L'Infini du sens: Jésus-Christ*. Québec: Éditions Bellarmin, 2000.

———. *Seigneur Jésus, montre-nous ton visage*. Québec: Éditions Bellarmin, 2001.

Latourelle, R., and R. Fisichella, eds. *Dictionary of Fundamental Theology.* New York: Crossroad, 1995.

Latourelle, R., and G. O'Collins, eds. *Problems and Perspectives of Fundamental Theology.* New York: Paulist, 1982.

Works by Avery Dulles (in Chronological Order)

Dulles, A. *A Testimonial to Grace.* New York: Sheed and Ward, 1946.

———. "The Theology of Revelation." *Theological Studies* 25 (1964): 43–58.

———. *Revelation Theology: A History.* New York: Seabury, 1965.

———. "Dogma as an Ecumenical Problem." *Theological Studies* 29 (1968): 397–416.

———. *Revelation Theology.* London: Burns and Oates, 1969.

———. *A History of Apologetics.* London: Hutchinson, 1971.

———. "Method in Fundamental Theology: Reflections on David Tracy's *Blessed Rage for Order.*" *Theological Studies* 37 (1976): 304–16.

———. *A Church to Believe In.* New York: Crossroads, 1982.

———. "The Church: Sacrament and Ground of Faith." In Latourelle and O'Collins, *Problems and Perspectives in Fundamental Theology,* 259–74.

———. *Models of Revelation.* Maryknoll, NY: Orbis, 2013.

———. "Introduction." In D. Edwards, *The Human Experience of God.* Dublin: Gill and Macmillan, 1984.

———. "Vatican II and the Church's Purpose." *Theology Digest* 32, no. 4 (1985): 341–52.

———. "Paths to Doctrinal Agreement: Ten Theses." *Theological Studies* 47 (1986): 32–47.

———. *Models of the Church.* 2nd ed. London: Doubleday, 1987.

———. "Vatican II and the Recovery of Tradition." In *The Reshaping of Catholicism.* San Francisco: Harper and Row, 1988.

———. "A Half Century of Ecclesiology." *Theological Studies* 50 (1989): 419–42.

———. *The Assurance of Things Hoped For: A Theology of Christian Faith.* Oxford: Oxford University Press, 1994.

———. "Apologetics I: History." In Latourelle and Fisichella, *Dictionary of Fundamental Theology,* 28–35.

———. *The Craft of Theology,* 2nd ed. New York: Crossroad, 1995.

———. "Conversion." In Latourelle and Fisichella, *Dictionary of Fundamental Theology,* 191–93.

———. *John Henry Newman.* London: Continuum, 2002.

Works by Salvatore Marsili (in Chronological Order)

Marsili, S. "Partecipazione sacramentale al Sacrificio di Cristo." *Rivista Liturgica* 24, no. 6.12 (1937): 129–32; 273–79.

———. "Giubileo abbaziale [del P. Ildefonso Herwegen] e Venticinque anni di Apostolato Liturgico." *Rivista Liturgica* 25, no. 7–8 (1938): 183–85.

———. "La liturgia nel V Concilio Provinciale di Malines." *Rivista Liturgica* 26, no. 6 (1939): 121–26; 145–49; 169–76; 211–12.

———. "Il mistero di Cristo." *Rivista Liturgica* 26, no. 4 (1939): 73–78.

———. "La Messa di Pasqua." *Rivista Liturgica* 29, no. 3 (1942): 21–23.

———. "Lingua viva e liturgia." In *L'Osservatore Romano* 102, no. 256 (November 8, 1962): 6.

———. "Liturgia—Vita della Chiesa." *Sacra Doctrina* 7, no. 28 (1962): 549–76.

———. "La liturgia nel Concilio Vaticano II." *Rivista Liturgica* 50, no. 3–4 (1963): 259–72.

———. "Commenti alla Costituzione Liturgica." *Rivista Liturgica* 51, no. 4 (1964): 587–92.

———. "I primi passi della riforma liturgica." In *L'Osservatore Romano* 104, no. 24 (January 30, 1964): 2.

———. "Note esplicative alla *Istruzione per l'applicazione della Costituzione conciliare sulla sacra liturgia*." *Rivista Liturgica* 51, no. 4 (1964): 526–69.

———. "Riforma liturgica dall'alto. Note preliminari ad una attuazione practica della Costituzione Conciliare." *Rivista Liturgica* 51, no. 1 (1964): 76–91.

———. *De Anno Liturgico. Quaestiones historicae et theologicae.* (Pro manuscripto) Pontificium Institutum Liturgicum Anselmianum, Athenaeum Sancti Anselmi de Urbe. Rome: 1968.

———. "Il ciclo annuale dei misteri della salvezza: presentazione della liturgia di ogni domenica e festa." In *L'annuario del Parroco, Anno XIV*, ed. G. Badini. Rome: Edizioni INA, 1968.

———: "Il mistero liturgico: realtà e segno." *Rivista Liturgica* 55, no. 5 (1968): 632–44.

———. "La preghiera di Cristo nella Liturgia." *Rivista Liturgica* 55, no. 4 (1968): 471–89.

———. "I segni sacri: storia e presenza." In *Il segno nella liturgia*, AA.VV., 7–19. CAL, Liturgia—Nuova Serie, 9. Padova: Messaggero, 1970.

———. "Il "tempo liturgico" attuazione della storia della salvezza." *Rivista Liturgica* 57, no. 2 (1970): 207–35.

———. "Terminologia segnale nella liturgia." In *Il segno nella liturgia*, AA.VV., 21–38. Liturgica—Nuova Serie 9. Padova: CAL, 1970.

———. "La Liturgia nella strutturazione della teologia." *Rivista Liturgica* 57, no. 2 (1971): 153–62.

———. "Liturgia e Teologia. Proposta teoretica." *Rivista Liturgica* 58 (1972): 455–73.

———. "*Rivista Liturgica* 1914–1973. Sessant'anni di servizio al movimento liturgico." *Rivista Liturgica* 61, no. 1 (1974): 22–34.

———. *Anàmnesis 1: La Liturgia: momento nella storia della salvezza.* 2nd ed. Genova: Marietti, 1979.

———. *Eulogia, Miscellanea liturgica in onore di P. Burkhard Neunheuser OSB, Preside del Pontificio Instituto Liturgico.* Studia Anselmiana 68, Analecta Liturgica, 1. Rome: 1979.

———. "Cristologia e liturgia. Panorama storico liturgico." In *Cristologia e liturgia—Atti della VIII settimana di studio dell'associazione professori di liturgia: Costabissara (Vicenza) 27–31 agosto 1979*, AA.VV., 17–64. Studi di liturgia, 8. Bologna: EDB, 1980,

———. "Editoriale." *Rivista Liturgica* 67, no. 3 (1980): 283–84.

———. "Editoriale." *Rivista Liturgica* 68 (1981): 307–8.

———. "Liturgia." In Sartore and Triacca, *Nuovo Dizionario di Liturgia*, 725–42.

———. "Teologia della celebrazione dell'eucharistia." In *La Liturgia Eucaristica: teologia e storia della celebrazione*, AA.VV. Anàmnesis, 3/2. Genova, Marietti, 1983.

———. "Teologia Liturgica." In Sartore and Triacca, *Nuovo Dizionario di Liturgia*, 1508–25.

———. "Presentazione." In *Spirito Santo e Liturgia*, AA.VV., 5–6. Casale Monferrato: Marietti, 1984,

———. "*Prefazione.*" In O. Casel, *Il mistero del culto cristiano*, 1–11. Rome: Borla, 1985.

———. "La liturgia nel discorso teologico odierno. Per una fondazione della liturgia pastorale: individuazione delle prospettive e degli ambiti specifici." In *Una liturgia per l'uomo. La liturgia pastorale e i suoi compiti*, ed. P. Visentin, and A. Terrin—R. Cecolin, ed., 17–47. Padova: Edizioni Messaggero— Abbazia di S. Giustina, 1986.

———. *I segni del mistero di Cristo, teologia liturgica dei sacramenti.* Rome: Edizioni Liturgiche, 1987.

Marsili, S., and Adrrianopoli, L. "Centro di Azione Liturgia." *Rivista Liturgica* 34 (1947): 203–4.

Works by Gustave Martelet (in Chronological Order)

Martelet, G. *Figures et Parénèse Sacramentelles.* Paris: Pontificia Università Gregoriana, 1957.

———. "Horizon théologique de la deuxième session du Concile." *Nouvelle Revue Théologique* 86 (1964): 449–68.

———. *Sainteté de l'Église et vie religieuse.* Toulouse: Éditions Prière et Vie, 1964; English translation, R. Sullivant, *The Church's Holiness and Religious Life.* Baltimore: Waverly, 1966.

———. *Résurrection, eucharistie et genèse de l'homme: chemins théologiques d'un renouveau chrétien.* Paris: Desclée, 1972. English translation, R. Hague, *The Risen Christ and the Eucharistic World.* London: Collins, 1976.

———. "De la sacramentalité propre à l'Église." *Nouvelle Revue Théologique* 95 (1973): 25–42.

———. *L'au-Delà Retrouvé: Christologie des fins dernières.* Paris: Desclée, 1975.

———. *Oser croire en l'Église.* Paris: Desclée, 1977.

———. *Vivre aujourd'hui la foi de toujours.* Paris: Desclée, 1979.

———. "Christology and Anthropology: Toward a Christian Genealogy of the Human." In Latourelle and O'Collins, *Problems and Perspectives of Fundamental Theology,* 151–67.

———. *Les idées maîtresses de Vatican II, Introduction à l'ésprit du Concile.* 2nd ed. Paris: Éditions du Cerf, 1985.

———. *Libre reponse à un scandale: La faute originelle, la souffrance et la mort.* Paris: Desclée, 1986.

———. *N'oublions pas Vatican II.* Paris: Éditions du Cerf, 1995.

———. *Remarques sur la première série de schémas.* Léger Archive.

Secondary Texts

AA.VV. *Mysterion, Nella celebrazione del Mistero di Cristo la vita della Chiesa, Miscellanea liturgica in occasione dei 70 anni dell'Abate Salvatore Marsili.* Quaderni di *Rivista Liturgica*, Nuova Serie n. 5. Torino: Leumann, 1981.

AA.VV. *Spirito Santo e Liturgia.* Casale Monferrato: Marietti, 1984.

Acerbi, A. *Due ecclesiologie: Ecclesiologia giuridica e ecclesiologia di communione nella "Lumen Gentium."* Bologna: Dehoniane, 1975.

Alberigo, G. "The Authority of the Church in the Documents of Vatican I and Vatican II." In *Authority in the Church and the Schillebeeckx Case*, ed. L. Swidler and P. Fransen, 119–45. New York: Crossroad, 1982.

———. "Cristianesimo e Storia nel Vaticano II." *Cristianesimo nella storia* 5 (1984): 577–92.

Alberigo, G., and J. Komonchak. *History of Vatican II.* 3 vols. Louvain: Peeters, 1995–2000.

Alberta, M. "Presentazione." In S. Marsili, *I segni del mistero di Cristo*, 9–16. Rome: Edizioni Liturgiche, 1987.

Alexander, A. "Thomas Aquinas and the Encyclical Letter." *The Princeton Review* 5 (1880): 245–61.

Alfaro, J. "Une Dogmatique de la Révélation." *Sciences Ecclesiastiques* 16 (1964): 351–57.

Alfaro, J, H. Bouillard, H. Carrier, G. Dejaifve, R. Latourelle, and G. Martelet. "La théologie fondamentale à la recherche de son identité: Un carrefour." *Gregorianum* 50 (1969): 757–76.

Alting von Geusau, L. G. M. *Liturgy in Development.* London: Sheed and Ward, 1965.

Amato, A. "Dall'uomo al Cristo, Salvatore assoluto, nella teologia di K. Rahner." *Salesianum* 41 (1979): 3–35.

Anderson, J. *A Vatican II Pneumatology of the Paschal Mystery: The Historical-Doctrinal Genesis of Ad Gentes I, 2–5.* Rome: Editrice Pontificia Università Gregoriana, 1988.

Anton, A. "Lo sviluppo della dottrina sulla Chiesa nella teologia dal Vaticano I al Vaticano II." In *L'ecclesiologia dal Vaticano I al Vaticano II*, 27–98. Milano: Editrice La Scuola, 1973.

Aubert, R. "Aspects divers du néo-thomisme sous le pontificat de Léon XIII." In *Aspetti della cultura cattolica nell'età di Leone XIII*, 133–227. Rome: Edizioni 5 Lune, 1961.

———. *The Christian Centuries*. Vol. 5: *The Church in a Secularised Society*. London: Darton, Longman and Todd, 1978.

———. "L'enciclica *Aeterni Patris* e le altre prese di peozione della Santa Sede sulla filosofia cristiana." In *La filosofia cristiana nei secoli XIX e XX*. Vol. 2: *Ritorno all'eredità scolastica*, ed. E. Coreth, W. Neidl, and G. Pligersdorffer. Rome: Città Nuova Editrice, 1994.

———. *Le Pontificat de Pie IX, (1846–1878)*. Paris: Bloud et Gay, 1952.

———. *Le Problème de l'acte de foi*. Louvain: Warny, 1950.

Aulén, G. *The Drama and the Symbols: A Book on Images of God and the Problems They Raise*. London: SPCK, 1970.

Baerwald, J. "Mystagogy." In *The New Dictionary of Sacramental Worship*, ed. P. Fink, 881–83. Collegeville, MN: Liturgical Press, 1990.

Ballatori, M. "Abate Salvatore Marsili OSB, la figura e l'opera." *Il Letimbro* 49 (December 24, 1983), 92.

Ballatori, M., and M. Alberta. "Bibliografia dell'Abate Salvatore Marsili." *Rivista Liturgica* 80 (1993): 373–88.

Ballinger, P. *The Poem as Sacrament: The Theological Aesthetic of Gerard Manley Hopkins*. Louvain: Peeters, 2000.

Balthasar, H. U. von. "Current Trends in Catholic Theology and the Responsibility of the Christian." *Communio* 5 (1978): 79.

———. *Verbum Caro, Skizzen zur Theologie, 1*. Einsiedeln: Johannes, 1960; English translation, *Word and Revelation: Essays in Theology 1*. New York: Herder and Herder, 1964.

———. *The Theology of Henri de Lubac*. San Francisco: Ignatius, 1991.

———. *A Theology of History*. San Francisco: Ignatius, 1994.

Balthasar, H. U. von, and Chantraine, G. *Le Cardinal de Lubac: l'homme et son œuvre*. Paris: Lethielleux, 1983.

Barrett, C. K. *The Gospel According to John*. London: SPCK, 1958.

Baum, G., ed. *The Twentieth Century: A Theological Overview*. New York: Orbis, 1999.

Beauduin, L. *La Piété de L'Église: Principes et Faits*. Louvain: Abbaye du Mont-César, 1914; English translation, V. Michel, *Liturgy the Life of the Church*, 3rd ed. Farnborough: St. Michael's Abbey, 2002.

———. *Essai de manuel de Liturgie*. Louvain: "Mélanges liturgiques" de Mont-César, 1954.

Benoit, P. Review of R. Latourelle, *Théologie de la Révélation*. *Revue Biblique* 71 (1964): 93–97.

Berger, T. "The Classical Liturgical Movement in Germany and Austria: Moved by Women?" *Worship* 66, no. 3 (1993): 231–51.

Bergin, L. *O Propheticum Lavacrum: Baptism as Symbolic Act of Eschatological Salvation*. Rome: Analecta Gregoriana, Editrice Pontificia Università Gregoriana, 1999.

Bernard, A. "Panorama des ètudes symboliques." *Gregorianum* 55 (1974): 379–92.

Blondel, M. "Lettre sur les exigences de la pensée contemporaine en matière de la philosophie dans l'étude du problème religieux." In *Les Premièrs Écrits de Maurice Blondel*. Vol. 2. Paris: Presses Universitaires de France, 1956.

———. *Lettres philosophiques*. Paris: Aubier, 1961.

Boardman, B. *Between Heaven and Charing Cross: The Life of Francis Thompson*. London: Yale University Press, 1988.

Boersma, H. Nouvelle Théologie *and Sacramantal Ontology. A Return to Mystery*. Oxford: Oxford University Press, 2009.

Baldovin, J. P. "Cardinal Ratzinger as Liturgical Critic." In *Studia Liturgica Diversa: Essays in Honour of Paul F Bradshaw*, ed. M. E. Johnson and L. E. Phillips, 211–28. Portland, OR: Pastoral, 2004.

Bonaccorso, G. *Introduzione allo studio della liturgia*. Padova: Messaggero—Abbazia di S. Giustina, 1990.

Botte, B. *Le mouvement liturgique: Témoignage et souvenirs*. Paris: Desclée et Cie, 1973; English translation, J. Sullivan, "Birth of the Movement." In *From Silence to Participation: An Insider's View of Liturgical Renewal*, 9–19. Washington, D. C.: Pastoral, 1988.

Bouillard, H. "Human Experience as the Starting Point of Fundamental Theology." *Concilium* 6, no. 1 (1965): 79–91.

Boulding, M. C. "The Doctrine of the Holy Spirit in the Documents of Vatican II." *Irish Theological Quarterly* 51, no. 4 (1985): 253–67.

Bourke, D. "Introduction." In T. Aquinas, *Summa Theologiae*. Vol. 56: *(3a. 60–65) The Sacraments*, xiii–xxiii. Oxford: Blackfriars, 1975.

Bouyer, L. *Eucharist*. Notre Dame: University of Notre Dame Press, 1968.

———. *Liturgical Piety*. Notre Dame: University of Notre Dame Press, 1966.

———."Liturgie et exégèse spirituelle." *La Maison Dieu* 7 (1946): 27–50.

———. *La vie de la liturgie*. Paris: Desclée, 1956.

Boyer de Sainte Suzanne, R de., *Alfred Loisy, entre la foi et l'incroyance*. Paris: Éditions du Centurion, 1968.

Bremond, H. "Father Tyrrell as an Apologist." *New York Review* 1 (June–July 1905): 762–70.

Brown, D. *Continental Philosophy and Modern Theology*. Oxford: Blackwell, 1987.

Brown, R. *The Churches the Apostles Left Behind*. New York: Paulist, 1984.

Browning, R. "A Death in the Desert." In *Browning: Poetical Works 1833–1864*, ed. I. Jack, 818–36. Oxford: Oxford University Press, 1970.

Brunsmann, J. *A Handbook of Fundamental Theology*. Vol. 2: *Revealed Religion*. Adapted and edited by A. Preuss. London: Herder, 1929.

Buckley, J. J. "On Being a Symbol: Appraisal of Rahner." *Theological Studies* 40 (1979): 453–73.

Buehrle, M. C. *Rafael Cardinal Merry Del Val*. Milwaukee: Bruce, 1957.

Bugnini, A. *The Reform of the Liturgy 1948–1975*. Collegeville, MN: Liturgical Press, 1990.

Burke, R. "Loisy's Faith: Landshift in Catholic Thought." *Journal of Religion* 60 (1980): 138–64.

———. "Was Loisy Newman's Modern Disciple?" In *Newman and the Modernists*, ed. M. J. Weaver, 139–157. Lanham, MD: University Press of America, 1985.

Burkhard, J. Review of A. Dulles, *The Craft of Theology*. *New Theology Review* 7 (1994): 106–7.

Butler, B. C. Review of A. Dulles, *Models of Revelation*. *New Blackfriars* 65 (1984): 235.

Butler, C. "The Aggiornamento of Vatican II." In *Vatican II: An Interfaith Appraisal*, ed. J. Miller, 3–13. Notre Dame: University of Notre Dame, 1966.

Cahill, B. *The Renewal of Revelation Theology (1960–1962): The Development and Responses to the Fourth Chapter of the Preparatory Schema De deposito Fidei*. Tesi Gregoriana, Serie Teologia, 51. Rome: Editrice Pontificia Università Gregoriana, 1999.

Cal, R., ed. *Super Epistolas S. Pauli, Lectura* 2. Rome: Marietti, 1953.

Carlen, Claudia. *The Papal Encyclicals 1878–1903*. Raleigh: McGrath, 1981.

Casarella, P. "Introduction." In H. de Lubac, *Scripture in Tradition*, translated by L. O'Neill, xi–xxii. New York: Crossroad, 2000.

Casel, O. *Das Christliche Kultmysterium*. 4th ed. Regensburg: Friedrich Pustet, 1960; English translation, B. Neunheuser, *The Mystery of Christian Worship and Other Writings*. London: Darton, Longman and Todd, 1962.

———. *Jahrbuch für Liturgiewissenschaft*. Vol. 15, Glaube, Gnosis und Mysterium. Münster: Aschendorff, 1941.

———. *Il mistero del culto cristiano*. Rome: Borla, 1985.

Cassirer, E. *An Essay on Man*. New Haven: Yale University Press, 1944.

Caussade, J.-P. de. *Lettres Spirituelles*. Vol. 2. Edited by M. Olphe-Galliard. Paris: Desclée de Brouwer, 1962.

Cerfaux, L. *Le Christ dans la Théologie de S. Paul*. Paris: Éditions du Cerf, 1951.

———. *The Church in the Theology of St. Paul*. New York: Herder and Herder, 1959.

———. *La Théologie de l'Église suivant saint Paul*. 2nd ed. Paris: Éditions du Cerf, 1948.

Chadwick, O. *The Secularization of the European Mind in the Nineteenth Century*. Cambridge: Cambridge University Press, 1975.

Chantraine, C. *Le Cardinal de Lubac: L'homme et son oeuvre*. Paris: Éditions du Cerf, 1983.

Chappin, M. "Dalla difesa al dialogo. L'insegnamento dellla teologia fondamentale alla PUG, 1930–1988." In *Gesù Rivelatore: Teologia Fondamentale*, ed. R. Fisichella, 31–45. Casale Monferrato: Piemme, 1988.

Charbonneau, A. Review of R. Latourelle, *Miracles de Jésus et théologie du miracle*. In *Science et Esprit* 38, no. 2 (1986): 257–60.

Chardin, T. de. "What Exactly is the Human Body?" In *Science and Christ*, 5–26. London: Collins, 1968.

Chauvet, L.-M. *Symbole et sacrement. Une relecture sacramentelle de l'existence chrétienne*. Paris: Éditions du Cerf, 1987; English translation, Patrick Madigan and Madeleine Beaumont, *Symbol and Sacrament*. Collegeville, MN: Liturgical Press, 1995.

———. *The Sacraments: The Word of God at the Mercy of the Body*. Collegeville, MN: Liturgical Press, 2001.

Chenu, M.-D. *Une école de théologie: Le Saulchoir*. 2nd ed. Paris: Éditions du Cerf, 1985.

Chupungco, A. "The Pontifical Liturgical Institute: A Benedictine Service to the Church." In *Sant'Anselmo: Saggi storici e di attualità*, ed. A. Chupungco, 193–221. Studia Anselmiana 98. Rome: 1988.

———. "Salvatore Marsili: Teologo Della Liturgia." In *Paschale Mysterium, Studi in memoria dell'Abate Prof. Salvatore Marsili, (1910–1983)*, ed. G. Farnedi, 15–24. *Studia Anselmiana* 91—Analecta Liturgica 10. Rome: 1986.

———. *What, Then, Is Liturgy? Musings and Memoir.* Collegeville, MN: Liturgical Press, 2010.

Citrini, T. *Gesù Cristo, rivelazione di Dio: il tema negli ultimi decenni della teologia cattolica.* Dissertatio ad Lauream in Facultate Theologiae Pontificiae Universitatis Gregorianae. Rome: Editrice Pontificia Università Gregoriana, 1969.

———. "The Principle of 'Christocentrism' and Its Role in Fundamental Theology." In Latourelle and O'Collins, *Problems and Perspectives of Fundamental Theology*, 168–85.

Clements, K. W. *Friedrich Schleiermacher, Pioneer of Modern Theology.* London: Collins, 1987.

Collins, J. "Leo XIII and the Philosophical Approach to Modernity." In *Leo XIII and the Modern World*, ed. E. T. Gargan, 181–209. New York: Sheed and Ward, 1961.

Congar, Y.-M. "The Council as an Assembly and the Church as Essentially Conciliar." In *One, Holy, Catholic and Apostolic: Studies on the Nature of the Church in the Modern World*, ed. H. Vorgrimler, 44–88. London: Sheed and Ward, 1968.

———. *L'Église de saint Augustin à l'époque moderne* Paris: Éditions du Cerf, 1970.

———. *A History of Theology.* New York: Doubleday, 1968.

———. *Jalons pour une théologie du laicat*. Paris: Éditions du Cerf, 1953; English translation, *Lay People in the Church*. London: Geoffrey Chapman, 1957.

———. *Je crois en l'Esprit Saint*. Vol. 1: *L'Esprit Saint dans l'Economie, révélation et experience de l'Esprit*. Paris: Éditions du Cerf, 1979; English translation, *I Believe in the Holy Spirit*. Vol. 1: *The Experience of the Spirit*. London: Geoffrey Chapman, 1983.

———. *Je crois en l'Esprit Saint*. Vol. 2: *Il est Seigneur et Il donne la vie*. Paris: Éditions du Cerf, 1979; English translation, *I Believe in the Holy Spirit*. Vol. 2: *Lord and Giver of Life*. London: Geoffrey Chapman, 1983.

———. *Je crois en l'Esprit Saint*. Vol. 3: *Le Fleuve de Vie (Ap 22, 1) coule en Orient et en Occident*. Paris: Éditions du Cerf, 1980; English translation, *I Believe in the Holy Spirit*. Vol. 3: *The River of Life Flows in the East and the West*. London: Geoffrey Chapman, 1983.

———. *La Parole et le Souffle*. Paris: Desclée, 1984; English translation, D. Smith, *The Word and the Spirit*. London: Geoffrey Chapman, 1986.

Cook, M. L. "Revelation as Metaphoric Process." *Theological Studies* 47 (1986): 388–11.

———. *Un peuple messianique: L'Église sacrement du salut et liberation*. Paris: Éditions du Cerf, 1975.

———. "Pneumatologie et 'christomonisme' dans la tradition latine." *Ephemerides Theologicae Louvanienses* 45 (1969): 394–416. Reprinted in *Ecclesia a Spiritu Sancto edocta, Lumen Gentium, 53; Mélanges théologiques Hommage à Msgr. Gerard Philips*. Bibliotheca Ephemeridium Theologicarum Lovaniensium, 27. Gembloux: J. Duculot, 1970.

———. "Pneumatologie dogmatique." In *Initiation à la pratique de la théologie*, ed. B. Lauret and F. Refoulé. Vol. 2, 485–516. Paris: Éditions du Cerf, 1982.

———. "Principes Doctrinaux (nos. 2. à 9.) in *L'Activité missionnaire de l'Église, Décret "Ad Gentes."* Unam Sanctam 67 (1967): 185–221.

———. "Tendanes actuelles de la pensée religieuse." *Cahiers du Monde Nouveau* 4 (1948): 33–50.

———. *La Tradition et les traditions.* 2 vols. Paris: Librairie Artheme Fayard, 1960, 1963; English translation, *Tradition and Traditions.* London: Burns and Oates, 1966.

———. *Vatican II, Le Concile au Jour le Jour, Deuxième Session.* Paris: Éditions du Cerf, 1964; English translation, *Report from Rome II: The Second Session of the Council.* London: Chapman, 1964.

Cooke, B. Review of A. Dulles, *The Craft of Theology. America* 168 (January 23, 1993): 19–23.

Corbon, J. *Liturgie de Source.* Paris: Éditions du Cerf, 1980; English translation, M. O'Connell, *The Wellspring of Worship.* New York: Paulist, 1988.

Corcoran, P. "Some Recent Writing on the Holy Spirit I." *Irish Theological Quarterly* 39 (1972): 276–87.

———. "Some Recent Writing on the Holy Spirit II." *Irish Theological Quarterly* 39 (1972): 365–82.

———. "Some Recent Writing on the Holy Spirit III." *Irish Theological Quarterly* 40 (1973): 50–62.

Cotter, W. Review of R. Latourelle, *The Miracles of Jesus and the Theology of Miracles." Toronto Journal of Theology* 6, no. 1 (Spring 1990): 118–19.

Coulson, J. "Hans Urs von Balthasar: Bringing Beauty back to Faith." In *The Critical Spirit and the Will to Believe: Essays in Nineteenth Century Literature and Religion,* ed. D. Jasper and T. R. Wright, 218–32. London: Macmillan, 1989.

———. *Newman and the Common Tradition.* Oxford: Clarendon, 1970.

Cousins, E. "Models and the Future of Theology." *Continuum* 7 (1969): 78–91.

Crichton, J.D. *Lights in the Darkness: Forerunners of the Liturgical Movement.* Dublin: Columba, 1996.

Cullmann, O. *Christ and Time*. Philadelphia: Westminster, 1964.

D'Ambrosio, M. "Henri de Lubac and the Critique of Scientific Exegesis." *Communio: International Catholic Review* 19 (1992): 365–88.

Dalmais, I. H. *Introduction to the Liturgy*. Translated by Roger Capel. Baltimore: Helicon, 1961.

———. "La liturgie comme lieu théologique." *La Maison Dieu* 78 (1964): 97–106.

———. "Mystery Theology." In *New Catholic Encyclopedia*. Vol. 10, 164–166. Washington, D. C.: Catholic University of America Press, 1967.

Daly, G. "Newman and Modernism: A Theological Reflection." In *Newman and the Modernists*, ed. M. J. Weaver, 185–204. Lanham, MD: University Press of America, 1985.

———. "Some Reflections on the Character of George Tyrrell." *The Heythrop Journal* 10, no. 3 (1969): 256–75.

———. *Transcendence and Immanence: A Study in Catholic Modernism and Integralism*. Oxford: Clarendon, 1980.

Daniélou, J. *Bible et Liturgie, La théologie biblique des Sacrements et des fêtes d'après les Pères de l'Église*. Paris: Éditions du Cerf, 1951; English translation, *The Bible and The Liturgy*. Notre Dame: University of Notre Dame Press, 1956.

———. *L'entrée de l'histoire du salut*. Paris: Desclée, 1967.

———. *Essai sur le Mystère de l'Histoire*. Paris: Éditions du Seuil, 1958.

———. *The Liturgy and the Word of God*. Collegeville, MN: Liturgical Press, 1959.

———. "Les orientations présentes de la pensée religieuse." *Études* 249 (1946): 5–21.

———. *Prayer as a Political Problem*. London: Burns and Oates, 1967.

———. "Les repas de la Bible et leur signification." *La Maison Dieu* 18 (1957): 28–30; English translation, "The Banquet of the Poor." In *The Lord of*

History: Reflections on the Inner Meanings of History, 214–40. Augmented ed. London: Longmans, 1958.

———. *Sacramentum Futuri: Études sur les Origines de la Typologie Biblique*. Paris: Beauchesne et Ses Fils, 1950; English translation, W. Hibberd, *From Shadows to Reality: Studies in the Typology of the Fathers*. London: Burns & Oates, 1960.

Davis, B. *The Thought of Thomas Aquinas*. Oxford: Clarendon, 1992.

De Gaál, E. *The Theology of Pope Benedict XVI: The Christocentric Shift*. New York: Palgrave Macmillan, 2010.

Dekkers, E. "La liturgie, mystère chrétien." *La Maison Dieu* 14 (1948): 22–35.

Denman, T. "Tentatives françaises pour un renouvellement de la théologie." *Revue de l'Université d'Ottawa*, Section Spéciale 20 (1950): 129–67.

Dessain, S., et al., eds. *The Letters and Diaries of John Henry Newman*. Vol. 11. Oxford: Clarendon, 1961.

Dewailly, L.-M. *Jésus-Christ, Parole de Dieu*. Paris: Desclée, 1945.

Dezza, P. *Alle origini del neotomismo italiano*. Milan: Fratelli Bocca, 1940.

Dieckmann, H. *De Revelatione Christiana*. Freibourg: Herder & Co., 1930.

Dillistone, F. W. *The Power of Symbols*. London: SCM, 1986.

Dodd, C. H. *The Interpretation of the Fourth Gospel*. Cambridge: Cambridge University Press, 1955.

Dondaine, H.-F. "La définition des sacrements dans la 'Somme Théologique.'" *Revue des sciences philosophiques et théologiques* 31 (1947): 213–28.

Donnelly, P. "The Gratuity of the Beatific Vision and The Possibility of a Natural Destiny." *Theological Studies* 11 (1950): 374–404.

———. "On the Development of Dogma and the Supernatural." *Theological Studies* 8 (1947): 471–91.

———. "The Surnaturel of Henri de Lubac." *Theological Studies* 9 (1948): 554–60.

Downing, F. Review of A. Dulles, *Models of Revelation*. *Theology* 87 (1984): 295–97.

Doyle, D. "Journet, Congar, and the Roots of Communion Ecclesiology." *Theological Studies* 58 (1997): 461–79.

———. *Communion Ecclesiology*. New York: Orbis, 2000.

Driscoll, J. *Theology at the Eucharistic Table*. Leominster: Gracewing, 2003.

Dru, A. *The Church in the Nineteenth Century: Germany 1800–1918*. London: Burns and Oates, 1963.

Dru, A. and I. Trethowan. *Maurice Blondel: The Letter on Apologetics and History and Dogma*. London: Burns and Oates, 1964.

Duffy, R. "The Post-Rahnerian Formulation." In D. Power, R. Duffy, and K. Irwin, "Sacramental Theology: A Review of Literature." *Theological Studies* 55 (1994): 665–75.

Duffy, S. "Catholicism's Search For A New Self-Understanding." In *Vatican II: Open Questions and New Horizons*, ed. G. Fagin, 9–37. Dublin: Dominican, 1984.

———. *The Graced Horizon: Nature and Grace in Modern Catholic Thought*. Collegeville, MN: Liturgical Press, 1992.

Dupuis, J. *Christianity and the Religions: From Confrontation to Dialogue*. Maryknoll, NY: Orbis, 2002.

Duval, A. "Le message au monde." In *Vatican II commence . . . Approches Francophones*, ed. É. Fouilloux, 105–18. Leuven: Peeters, 1993.

Dych, W. *Karl Rahner*. London: Geoffrey Chapman, 1991.

Edwards, D. *The Human Experience of God*. Dublin: Gill and Macmillan, 1984.

Ehrle, F. *Zur Enzyklika "Aeterni Patris"; Text und Kommentar*. Rome: Editioni di storia e letteratura, 1954.

Elberti, A. *Il sacerdozio regale dei fideli nei prodromi del Concilio Ecumenico Vaticano II (1903–1962)*. Analecta Gregoriana, 254. Rome: PUG, 1989.

Eliot, T. S. "The Dry Salvages." In *Collected Poems, 1909–1962*, 205–13. London: Faber and Faber, 1963.

Evdokimov, P. *L'Esprit-saint dans la tradition orthodoxe*. Paris: Éditions du Cerf, 1969.

Fabro, C. *La svolta antropologica di Karl Rahner*. Milan: Rusconi, 1974.

Fagerberg, D. W. *What Is Liturgical Theology: A Study in Methodology*, Collegeville, MN: Liturgical Press, 1992.

———.*Theologia Prima*: What Is Liturgical Theology 2nd ed. Chicago: Hillenbrand, 2004.

Falconi, C. *I papi del ventesimo secolo*. Milan: Rusconi, 1967; English translation, M. Grindrod, *The Popes in the Twentieth Century from Pius X to John XXIII*. Boston: Little, Brown and Co., 1967.

Farnedi, G., ed. *I simboli dell'iniziazione cristiana. Atti del I Congresso Internazionale di Liturgia: P. I. L., 25–28 maggio 1983*. Studia Anselmiana 87, Analecta Liturgica 7. Rome: 1983.

Farrer, A. *The Glass of Vision*. Westminster: Dacre, 1948.

Fenwick, J., and B. Spinks, *Worship in Transition: The Twentieth Century Liturgical Movement*. Edinburgh: T. & T. Clark, 1995.

Field, A. *From Darkness to Light*. Ann Arbor: Servant, 1978.

Fink, P. "Sacramental Theology After Vatican II." In *The New Dictionary of Sacramental Worship*, ed. P. Fink, 1107–14. Collegeville, MN: Liturgical Press, 1990.

Fisichella, R., ed. "Il contributo di René Latourelle alla teologia fondamentale." In *Gesù Rivelatore*, ed. R. Fisichella, 11–22. Casale Monferrato: Edizione Piemme, 1988.

———. "Dei Verbum." In Latourelle and Fisichella, *Dictionary of Fundamental Theology*, 214–18.

———. *Gesù Rivelatore: Teologia Fondamentale*. Casale Monferrato: Piemme, 1988.

———. *Introduction to Fundamental Theology*. Translated by J. Driscoll. Casale Monferrato: Edizioni Piemme, 1996.

———. "John Henry Newman." In Latourelle and Fisichella, *Dictionary of Fundamental Theology*, 734–38.

———. "Semiology." In Latourelle and Fisichella, *Dictionary of Fundamental Theology*, 987–92.

Fisch, T. ed. *Liturgy and Tradition: Theological Reflections of Alexander Schmemann*. Crestwood, NY: St. Vladimir's, 2003.

Fitzmyer, J. *The Biblical Commission's Document "The Interpretation of the Bible in the Church": Text and Commentary*. Rome: Editrice Pontificio Istituto Biblico, 1995.

Flynn, G., and P. D. Murray, eds. *Ressourcement: A Movement for Renewal in Twentieth-Century Catholic Theology*. Oxford: Oxford University Press, 2012.

Forbes, F. A. *Rafael Cardinal Merry Del Val: A Character Sketch*. London: Longmans, Green and Co., 1932.

Foudy, T. "George Tyrrell and Modernism." *Irish Theological Quarterly* 49, no. 1 (1982): 1–18.

Fouilloux, E. "The Antepreparatory Phase, the Slow Emergence from Inertia." In *History of Vatican II*. Vol. 1: *Announcing and Preparing Vatican Council II, Toward a New Era in Catholicism*, ed. G. Alberigo and J. Komonchak, 55–166. Louvain: Peeters, 1995.

Franklin, R. "Humanism and Transcendence in the Nineteenth Century Liturgical Movement." *Worship* 59 (1985): 342–53.

Fries, H. *Fundamental Theology*. Washington, D. C.: Catholic University of America, 1996.

Gallagher, M. P. *Dive Deeper: The Human Poetry of Faith*. London: Darton, Longman and Todd, 2001.

Galot, J. *Who is Christ?* Rome: Gregorian University Press, 1980.

Galvin, J. "The Resurrection of Jesus in Contemporary Catholic Systematics." *The Heythrop Journal* 20 (1979): 123–45.

Gardeil, A. *Le Donné révélé et la théologie.* Paris: J. Gabalda, 1910.

Garrigou-Lagrange, R. *De Revelatione.* 2nd ed. Rome: Libreria Editrice Religiosa, 1932.

Geiselmann, J. R. *Die Katholische Tübinger Schule.* Freiburg: Herder, 1964.

Gellner, E. *Postmodernism, Reason, and Religion.* London: Routledge, 1992.

Ghiberti, G. "Contemporary Discussion of the Resurrection of Jesus." In Latourelle and O'Collins, *Problems and Perspectives of Fundamental Theology,* 223–55.

Ghiretti, C. "Il Movimento Liturgico in *Rivista Liturgica* tra il 1914 e il 1947." In *Ritorno alla liturgia, Saggi di studio sul Movimento Liturgico,* ed. F. Brovelli, 47–66. Rome: Borla, 1989.

Golinas, J.-P. *La restoration du Thomisme sous Léon XIII et les philiosophies nouvelles, Étude de la pensée de M. Blondel et du Père Laberthonnière.* Washington, D. C.: Catholic University of America, 1959.

Gössmann, E. "Scholasticism." In *Sacramentum Mundi: An Encyclopedia of Theology,* ed. K. Rahner, C. Ernst, and K. Smyth, vol. 6, 27–34. New York: Herder and Herder, 1969.

Grillmeier, A. "Jesus Christ." In Rahner, *Encyclopaedia of Theology: The Concise Sacramentum Mundi,* 744–51.

———, "The Mystery of the Church." In Vorgrimler, *Commentary on the Documents of Vatican II,* 1:138–52.

Grillo, A. "L'esperienza rituale come "dato" della teologia fondamentale: ermeneutica di una rimozione e prospettive teoriche di reintegrazione." In *Liturgia e incarnazione,* ed. A. Terrin, 167–224. Padova: Edizioni Messaggero— Abbazia di Santa Giustina, 1997.

———. *Teologia Fondamentale e Liturgia: Il rapporto tra immediatezza e mediazione nella riflessione teologica.* Padova: Edizioni Messaggero— Abbazia di Santa Giustina, 1995.

Groppe, E. "The Contribution of Yves Congar's Theology of the Holy Spirit." *Theological Studies* 62 (2001): 457–65.

Guardini, R. *Vom Geist der Liturgie*, 20th ed. Mainz: Matthias-Grünewald, 1997; English translation, *The Spirit of the Liturgy*, 2nd ed. New York: Crossroad, 1998.

Guarinos, T. "Postmodernity and Five Fundamental Theological Issues." *Theological Studies* 57 (1996): 654–89.

Haight, R. "The Case for Spirit Christology." *Theological Studies* 53 (1992) 257–87.

———. *The Experience and Language of Grace*. New York: Paulist, 1979.

———. "Unfolding of Modernism in France: Blondel, Laberthonnière, Le Roy." *Theological Studies* 35 (1974): 632–66.

Hardon, J. "Robert Bellarmine's Concept of the Church." In *Studies in Medieval Culture*, ed. J. Sommerfeldt, vol. 2, 120–127. Kalamazoo, MI: Western Mitchigan Press, 1966.

Harper, T. "The Encyclical." *The Month* 18, no. 37 (1879): 356–84.

Haspelmath-Finatti. D. *Theologia Prima: Liturgische Theologie für den evangelischen Gottesdienst.* Göttingen: Vandenhoeck & Ruprecht, 2014.

Hedley, J. C. "Pope Leo XIII and Modern Studies." *The Dublin Review* 34, no. 1, 3rd series (1880): 190–210.

Hellwig, M. "Twenty Five Years of an Awakening Church: Liturgy and Ecclesiology." In *The Awakening Church: 25 Years of Liturgical Renewal*, ed. L. J. Madden. Collegeville, MN: Liturgical Press, 1992.

Hennesey, J. "Leo XIII's Thomistic Revival: A Political and Philosophical Event." *The Journal of Religion* 58 Supplement (1978): S185–97.

Herwegen, I. *Christliche Kunst und Mysterium*. Münster: Aschendorff, 1929.

Hichling, C. Review of G. Martelet, *The Risen Christ and the Eucharistic World*. *The Heythrop Journal* 18 (1977): 465–66.

Hild, J. "L'Encyclique *Mediator Dei* et le mouvement liturgique de Maria Laach." *La Maison Dieu* 14 (1948): 1–20.

Hillis Miller, J. *The Disappearance of God: Four Nineteenth-Century Writers.* London: Oxford University Press, 1963.

Himes, M. "Introduction." In J. Möhler, *Symbolism,* xi–xxi. New York: Crossroad, 1997.

Hocedez, E. *Histoire de la théologie au xixe siècle.* 3 vols. Paris: Desclée, 1948.

Holmes, J. D. "Some English Reactions to the Publication of *Aeterni Patris.*" *The Downside Review* 93 (1975): 269–80.

———. *The Triumph of the Holy See: A Short History of the Papacy in the Nineteenth Century.* London: Burns and Oates, 1978.

Hooker, M. *The Signs of a Prophet: The Prophetic Actions of Jesus.* Harrisburg, PA: Trinity, 1997.

Huerga, A. "La enciclica de Leon XIII sobre el Espiritu Santo." In *Credo in Spiritum Sanctum.* Vol. 1: *Atti del congresso teologico Internazionale di pneumatologia,* 507–16. Vatican City: Libreria Editrice Vaticana, 1983.

Hughes, J. J. *Absolutely Null and Utterly Void.* London: Sheed and Ward, 1968.

Hughes, K., ed. *How Firm a Foundation: Voices of the Early Liturgical Movement.* Chicago: Liturgy Training, 1990.

Hunt, A. *The Trinity and the Paschal Mystery: A Development in Recent Catholic Theology.* Collegeville, MN: Liturgical Press, 1997.

Hurley, M. "George Tyrrell: Some Post-Vatican II Impressions." *The Heythrop Journal* 10, no. 3 (1969): 243–55.

Irwin, K. "Liturgical Actio: Sacramentology, Eschatology and Ecology." *Questions Liturgiques/Studies in Liturgy* 81, nos. 3–4 (2000): 171–83.

———. *Liturgical Theology: A Primer.* Collegeville, MN: Liturgical Press, 1990.

Jedin, H., ed. *History of the Church.* Vol. 7: *The Church between Revolution and Restoration.* London: Burns and Oates, 1981.

Jeremias, J. *The Eucharistic Words of Jesus.* London: SCM, 1966.

Jodock, D, ed. *Catholicism Contending with Modernity: Roman Catholic Modernism and Anti-Modernism in Historical Context.* Cambridge, Cambridge University Press, 2000

———. "Introduction I: The Modernist Crisis." In Jodock, *Catholicism Contending with Modernity*, 1–19.

———. "Introduction II: The Modernists and the Anti-Modernists." In Jodock, *Catholicism Contending with Modernity*, 20–29.

John Paul II. "Address on "The Interpretation of the Bible in the Church." In *The Biblical Commission's Document "The Interpretation of the Bible in the Church": Text and Commentary*, ed. J. Fitzmyer. Roma, Editrice Pontificio Istituto Biblico, 1995.

———. *L'Osservatore Romano.* English edition. September 16, 1991, 12.

Jounel, P. "From the Council of Trent to Vatican II." In *The Church at Prayer.* Vol. 1: *Introduction to the Liturgy*, ed. A. G. Martimort, 41–50. Shannon: Irish University Press, 1968.

Jungmann, J. "Constitution on the Sacred Liturgy." In Vorgrimler, *Commentary on the Documents of Vatican II*, 1:1–104.

———. *The Mass of the Roman Rite: Its Origins and Development.* Vol. 2. New York: Benziger Brothers, 1955.

Kasper, W. "Apostolic Succession in the Office of Bishop as an Ecumenical Problem." *Theology Digest* 47, no. 3 (Fall 2000): 203–10.

———. *Dogme et Évangile.* Paris: Tournai, 1967.

———. *Der Gott Jesu Christi.* Mainz: Grünewald, 1982; English translation, M. O'Connell, *The God of Jesus Christ.* London: SCM, 1983.

———. *Jesus, The Christ.* London: Burns and Oates, 1976.

———. "Linee fondamentali di una teologia della storia." In *Fede e Storia*, 62–96. Brescia: Queriniana, 1975.

———. "Neuansatze gegenwartiger Christologie." In *Christologische Schwerpunkte*, ed. W. Kasper. Dusseldorf: Patmos, 1980.

Kasper, W., G. Sauter. *Kirche—Ort des Geistes.* Frieburg: Herder, 1976.

Kavanagh, A. "Introduction." In O. Casel, *The Mystery of Christian Worship*, vii–xii. New York: Crossroad, 1999.

———. *On Liturgical Theology*. Collegeville, MN: Liturgical Press, 1992.

Kelly, G. B., ed. *Karl Rahner: Theologian of the Graced Search for Meaning*. Minneapolis: Augsburg Fortress, 1992.

Kendall, D., and G. O'Collins. "The Uniqueness of the Easter Appearances." *The Catholic Biblical Quarterly* 54 (1992): 287–307.

Kennedy, P. *Schillebeeckx*. London: Geoffrey Chapman, 1993.

Ker, I. "Newman's Theory—Development or Continuing Revelation." In *Newman and Gladstone: Centennial Essays*, J. D. Bastable, 145–59. Dublin: Veritas, 1978.

Kerr, F. *After Aquinas: Versions of Thomism*. Oxford: Blackwell, 2002.

———. "Did Newman Answer Gladstone?" In *John Henry Newman: Reason, Rhetoric and Romanticism*, ed. D. Nicholls and F. Kerr, 135–52. Bristol: Bristol, 1991.

Kilmartin, E. *Christian Liturgy: Theology and Practice I; Systematic Theology of Liturgy*. Kansas City: Sheed and Ward, 1988.

———. "Foreword." In J. Corbon, *The Wellspring of Worship*. New York: Paulist, 1988.

Kizhakkeparampil, I. *The Invocation of the Holy Spirit as Constitutive of the Sacraments According to Cardinal Yves Congar*. Rome: Editrice Pontificia Università Gregoriana, 1995.

Klauser, T. *A Short History of the Western Liturgy*. 2nd ed. Oxford: Oxford University Press, 1979.

Knauer, P. *Der Glaube kommt vom Hören*. Frankfurt am Main: Styria, 1982.

Komonchak, J. "Theology and Culture at Mid-Century: The Example of Henri de Lubac." *Theological Studies* 51 (1990): 579–602.

———. "Returning From Exile: Catholic Theology in the 1930s." In *The Twentieth Century A Theological Overview*, ed. G. Baum, 35–48. New York: Orbis, 1999.

Küng, H. *The Church*. New York: Sheed and Ward, 1967.

Kuykendall Thomson, P. van. *Francis Thompson: A Critical Biography*. Edinburgh: Thomas Nelson & Sons, 1961.

Labbé, Y. "Réceptions Théologiques de la "Postmodernité." *Revue des sciences philosophiques et théologiques* 72 (1988): 397–426.

Lacroix, J. *Maurice Blondel: An Introduction to the Man and His Philosophy*. New York: Seabury, 1968.

Lafont, G. *Dieu, le Temps et l'Être*. Paris: Éditions du Cerf, 1986; English translation, *God, Time, and Being*. Petersham, MA: St. Bede's, 1992.

———. "Permanence et transformation des intuitions de Dom Casel." *Ecclesia Orans* 4 (1987): 261–84.

Lambiasi, F. "Holy Spirit." In Latourelle and Fisichella, *Dictionary of Fundamental Theology*, 455–62.

Lamennais, F. de. *Essai sur l'indifference en matière de religion*. 2nd ed. Paris: Tournachon-Molin et Seguin, 1818.

Latourette, K. S. "The Church and the World in the Nineteenth Century." In *Leo XIII and the Modern World*, ed. E. T. Gargan, 51–62. New York: Sheed and Ward, 1961.

Laurentin, R. *Bilan de la 3e session*. Paris: Seuil, 1965.

———. "Paul VI et l'après concile." In *Paul VI et la modernité dans l'Église, actes du colloque organise par l'Ecole française de Rome*, 569–601. Rome: École Française de Rome—Palais Farnèse, 1984.

Lauret, B., ed. *Fifty Years of Catholic Theology: Conversations with Yves Congar*. London: SCM, 1988.

Lawrence, F. "The Fragility of Consciousness: Lonergan and the Postmodern Concern for the Other." *Theological Studies* 54 (1993): 55–94.

Le Guillon, M.-J. "Church." In Rahner, *Encyclopaedia of Theology: The Concise Sacramentum Mundi*, 205–21.

Lease, G. "Merry Del Val and Tyrrell: A Modernist Struggle." *The Downside Review* 102 (1984): 133–56.

————. "Vatican Foreign Policy and the Origins of Modernism." In Jodock, *Catholicism Contending with Modernity*, 31–55.

Lecanuet, R. P. *La Vie de l'Église sons Léon XIII*. Paris: Aubier, 1930.

Leclerq, J. "Le renouveau solesmien et le renouveau religieux du XIX siécle." *Studia monastica* 18 (1976): 157–98.

Leeming, B. *Principles of Sacramental Theology*. London: Burns and Oates, 1956.

Leroquais, V. *Les sacramentaires et les missels manuscripts des bibliothèques publiques de France*. Vol. 1. Paris: Letouzey et Ané, 1924.

Loisy, A. *Autour d'un petit livre*. Paris: Alphonse Picard et Fils, 1903.

————. *Choses passées*. Paris: Nourry, 1913; English translation, R. Wilson Boynton, *My Duel with the Vatican*. 2nd ed. New York: Greenwood, 1968.

————. *L'Évangile et L'Église*. Paris: Alphonse Picard et Fils, 1902; English translation, C. Home, *The Gospel and the Church*. London: Pitman and Sons, 1908.

————. *Mémoires pour servir à l'histoire religieuse de notre temps*. 3 vols. Paris: Nourry, 1930–31.

Lonergan, B. *Method in Theology*. London: Darton, Longman and Todd, 1972.

————. "Theology and Understanding." In *Collection*, 121–41. New York: Herder and Herder, 1967.

Loome, T. M. "George Tyrrell: Revelation as Experience." *The Heythrop Journal* 12, no. 2 (1971): 117–49.

————. *Liberal Catholicism, Reform Catholicism, Modernism: A Contribution to a New Orientation in Modernist Research*. Mainz: Grünewald, 1979.

Lubac, H. de. "Apologetics and Theology." In *Theological Fragments*. San Francisco: Ignatius, 1989.

————. "Bulletin de théologie fondamentale: le problème du devéloppement du dogme." *Recherches de Science Religieuse* 355 (1948): 130–59.

———. *Catholicisme: Les aspects sociaux du dogme.* Paris: Éditions du Cerf, 1938; English translation, *Catholicism: A Study of Dogma in Relation to the Corporate Destiny of Mankind.* New York: Sheed and Ward, 1958.

———. "The Church in Crisis." *Theology Digest* 17 (1969): 312–15.

———. *Corpus Mysticum, L'Eucharistie et L'Église au Moyen Age, Étude Historique.* 2nd ed. Paris: Aubier, 1949.

———. *L'Écriture dans la tradition.* Paris: Éditions Montaigne, 1967; English translation, L. O'Neill, *Scripture in the Tradition.* New York: Crossroad, 2000.

———. *Entretien autour de Vatican II.* Paris: Éditions du Cerf, 1985.

———. *Méditation sur L'Église.* 3rd ed. Aubier, Paris: 1954.

———. *Surnaturel: Études historiques.* Paris: Aubier, 1946.

———. *Theology in History.* San Francisco: Ignatius, 1996.

Luther, M. "The Babylonian Captivity of the Church." In *Luther's Works,* ed. H. Lehmann, vol. 36. Philadelphia: Fortress Press, 1970.

Lyonnet, S. "La rédemption de l'univers." *Lumière et vie* 9 (1960): 41–62.

Maggiani, S. "La teologia liturgica di S. Marsili come 'opera aperta.'" *Rivista Liturgica* 80 (1993): 341–57.

Maréchal, J. *Le Point de départ de la métaphysique: Leçons sur le developpement historique et théorique du problème de la connaissance.* 5 vols. Paris: Aclan, 1922–26.

Marlé, R. *Au coeur de la crise moderniste: le dossier inédit d'une controverse.* Paris: Aubier, 1960.

Martina, G. "The Historical Context in Which the Idea of a New Ecumenical Council Was Born." In Latourelle, *Vatican II: Assessment and Perspectives* 1:3–73.

May, J. L. *Father Tyrrell and the Modernist Movement.* London: Burns, Oates and Washbourne, 1938.

McCool, F. Review of R. Latourelle, *Théologie de la Révélation. Biblica* 45 (1964): 278.

McCool, G. *Catholic Theology in the Nineteenth Century: The Quest for a Unitary Method*. New York: Seabury, 1977.

———. *From Unity to Pluralism: The Internal Evolution of Thomism*. New York: Fordham University Press, 1989.

———. "Karl Rahner and the Christian Philosophy of St. Thomas Aquinas." In *Theology and Discovery: Essays in Honour of Karl Rahner, SJ*, ed. W. J. Kelly, 63–93. Milwaukee: Marquette University Press, 1980.

———. *Theologie als Glaubensverständnis*. Würzburg: Echter, 1953.

———, "Twentieth Century Scholasticism." *The Journal of Religion* 58 Supplement (1978): S198–21.

McDonnell, K. "A Trinitarian Theology of the Holy Spirit?", *Theological Studies* 46 (1985): 191–227.

McFague, S. *Metaphorical Theology*. Philadelphia: Fortress Press, 1982.

McNabb, V. *Francis Thompson and Other Essays*. London: Blackfriars, 1955.

McNamara, K. "The Holy Spirit in the Church." *Irish Theological Quarterly* 32 (1965): 281–94.

McPartlan, P. *The Eucharist Makes the Church: Henri de Lubac and John Zizioulas in Dialogue*. Edinburgh: T. & T. Clark, 1993.

———. *Sacrament of Salvation: An Introduction to Eucharistic Ecclesiology*. Edinburgh: T. & T. Clark, 1995.

Mehok, C. J. "Hans Küng and George Tyrrell on the Church." *Homiletic and Pastoral Review* 72 (1972): 57–66.

Melloni, A. "The Beginning of the Second Period: The Great Debate on the Church." In *History of Vatican II*. Vol. 3: *The Mature Council, Second Period and Intersession, September 1963—September 1964*, ed. G. Alberigo and J. Komonchak, 1–115. Louvain: Peeters, 2000.

Menozzi, D. "Opposition to the Council (1966–84)." In *The Reception of Vatican II*, ed. G. Alberigo, J.-P. Jossua, and J. Komonchak, 325–48. Washington, D. C.: Catholic University of America Press, 1987.

Mersch, E. *Le Corps Mystique du Christ*. Louvain: Museum Lessianum, 1936; English translation, J. R. Kelly, *The Whole Christ*. London: Dennis Dobson, 1938.

———. *La Théologie du Corps Mystique*. Louvain: Museum Lessianum, 1944; English translation, C. Vollert, *The Theology of the Mystical Body*. New York: Herder, 1952.

Metz, J.-B. *Faith in History and Society: Toward a Practical Fundamental Theology*. New York: Seabury, 1980.

Meynell, E. *The Life of Francis Thompson*, 2nd ed. London: Burns Oates & Washbourne, 1925.

Meynell, W., ed. *The Works of Francis Thompson, Poems*. Vol. 1. London: Burns Oates & Washbourne, 1913.

Milburn, D. *A History of Ushaw College*. Durham: Northumberland, 1964.

Milton, J. "Paradise Lost, Book I." In *Milton Poetical Works*, ed. D. Bush. 2nd ed. Oxford: Oxford University Press, 1973.

Misner, P. Review of R. Latourelle, *Christ and the Church: Signs of Salvation*. *Theological Studies* 34 (1973): 185–86.

———. "Catholic Anti-Modernism: The Ecclesial Setting." In Jodock, *Catholicism Contending with Modernity*, 56–87.

Mitchell, N. "Symbols are Actions, not Objects." *Living Worship* 13, no. 2 (1977): 1–19.

Mooney, C. *Teilhard de Chardin and the Mystery of Christ*. London: Collins, 1966.

Moore, S. "The Desire of God." *Downside Review* 45 (1947): 246–59.

Mouroux, J. *L'Expérience chrétienne*. Paris: Aubier, 1952; English translation, *The Christian Experience: An Introduction to a Theology*. London: Sheed and Ward, 1955.

Murray, R. Review of A. Dulles, *Models of the Church*. *The Heythrop Journal* 19 (1978): 79.

Neufeld, H.-K. "In the Service of the Council: Bishops and Theologians at the Second Vatican Council." In Latourelle, *Vatican II: Assessment and Perspectives*, 1:74–105.

Neunheuser, B. "Don Salvatore Marsili: personalità e attività scientifica." In *Riforma liturgica tra passato e futuro. Atti della XIII Settimana dell'Associacione Professori di Litugia*, Cassano Murge (Bari), 27–31 agosto 1984, AA.VV., 139–153. *Studi di Liturgia*—Nuova Serie, 13. Casale Monferrato: Marietti, 1985.

———. "Introduzione, il movimento liturgico panorama storico e lineamenti teologici." In *Anàmnesis 1: La liturgia: momento nella storia della salvezza*, AA.VV., 11–30. 2nd ed. Genova: Marietti, 1979.

———. "Mistero." In Sartore and Triacca, *Nuovo Dizionario di Liturgia*, 863–83.

———. "Movimento Liturgico." In Sartore and Triacca, *Nuovo Dizionario di Liturgia*, 904–18.

———. "Odo Casel in Retrospect and Prospect." *Worship* 50, no. 6 (1976): 489–504.

———. "Salvatore Marino Marsili." In *Mysterion, Nella celebrazione del Mistero di Cristo la vita della Chiesa, Miscellanea liturgica in occasione dei 70 anni dell'Abate Salvatore Marsili*, AA.VV., xiii–xiv. Quaderni di Rivista Liturgica, Nuova Serie n. 5. Torino: Leumann, 1981.

———. "Salvatore Marsili." *Ecclesia Orans* 1 (1984): 202–7.

Newman, J. H. *A Letter addressed to His Grace the Duke of Norfolk, on occasion of Mr Gladstone's Recent Expostulation, by John Henry Newman D.D., of the Oratory*. London: 1875. Reprinted in Newman, *Certain Difficulties Felt by Anglicans in Catholic Teaching Considered*, vol. 2, 171–378. London: Longmans, Green and Co., 1879.

———. *Essay on the Development of Christian Doctrine*. 3rd ed. London: 1878; reprinted, Notre Dame: University of Notre Dame Press, 1989.

———. *An Essay in Aid of a Grammar of Assent.* Edited by I. Ker. Oxford: Oxford University Press, 1985.

Nichols, A. *From Newman to Congar: The Idea of Doctrinal Development from the Victorians to the Second Vatican Council.* Edinburgh: T. & T. Clark, 1995.

———. *A Grammar of Consent: The Existence of God in Christian Tradition.* Edinburgh: T. & T. Clark, 1991.

———. *A Pope and a Council on the Sacred Liturgy.* Farnborough: St Michael's Abbey, 2002.

———. "Rahner and Balthasar: The Anonymous Christianity Debate Revisited." In *Beyond the Blue Glass*, 107–128. London: Saint Austin, 2002.

———. *The Theology of Joseph Ratzinger.* London: T. & T. Clark, 1988.

———. "Thomism and the *Nouvelle Théologie*." *The Thomist* 64 (2000): 1–19.

———. *Yves Congar.* London: Geoffrey Chapman, 1989.

O'Collins, G. *The Easter Jesus.* 2nd ed. London: Darton, Longman and Todd, 1980.

———. "Experince." In Latourelle and Fisichella, *Dictionary of Fundamental Theology*, 306–8.

———. *Fundamental Theology.* 2nd ed. New York: Paulist, 1986.

———. "Jacques Dupuis's Contribution to Interreligious Dialogue." In *Theological Studies* 64 (2003), 388-397.

———. *Jesus Risen.* New York: Paulist, 1987.

———. "Paschal Mystery II: The Resurrection of Jesus." In Latourelle and Fisichella, *Dictionary of Fundamental Theology*, 769–76.

———. *Retrieving Fundamental Theology.* New York: Paulist, 1993.

———. "Revelation Past and Present." In Latourelle, *Vatican II: Assessment and Perspectives*, 1:125–137.

———. Review of A. Dulles, *Models of Revelation. Gregorianum* 65 (1984): 181.

———. "Theology and Experience." *Irish Theological Quarterly* 44 (1977): 279–90.

O'Connell, M. R. *Critics on Trial: An Introduction to the Catholic Modernist Crisis.* Washington, D. C.: Catholic University of America, 1994.

O'Connor, F. M. "Notes and Comments: Tyrrell's Cross-Roads." *The Heythrop Journal* 5, no. 2 (1964): 188–91.

O'Donnell, J. *The Mystery of the Triune God.* London: Sheed and Ward, 1988.

———. Review of A. Dulles, *The Craft of Theology. Gregorianum* 74 (1993): 373–74.

O'Donovan, L., ed. "A Changing Ecclesiology in a Changing Church: A Symposium on Development in the Ecclesiology of Karl Rahner." *Theological Studies* 38 (1977): 736–62.

———. Review of A. Dulles, *Models of Revelation. America* 153 (May 28, 1983): 423–24.

———, ed. *A World of Grace: An Introduction to the Themes and Foundations of Karl Rahner's Theology.* New York: Crossroad, 1987.

———. "For the Salvation of All Who Believe." In *Faithful Witness: Foundations of Theology for Today's Church*, ed. L. O'Donovan and T. Howland Sanks, 27–46. London: Geoffrey Chapman, 1989.

O'Meara, T. F. "The Origins of the Liturgical Movement and German Romanticism." *Worship* 59 (1985): 326–42.

———. "Toward a Subjective Theology of Revelation." *Theological Studies* 36 (1975): 401–27.

O'Neill, C. E. *Meeting Christ in the Sacraments.* Cork: Mercier, 1964.

Osborne, K. B. *Christian Sacraments in a Postmodern World.* New York: Paulist, 1999.

Ott, L. *Grundriss der Katholischen Dogmatik* Freiburg: Herder, 1952; English translation, P. Lynch, *Fundamentals of Catholic Dogma.* Cork: Paulist, 1962.

Oury, G.-M. "Le romanticisme de Dom Guéranger: un faux probléme?" *Collectanea Cisterciensia* 48 (1986): 311–23.

Paul VI. Speech at the Eighth Public Session of the Council, *Sacrosanctum Oecumenicum Vaticanum II. Constitutiones, Decreta, Declarationes.* Città del Vaticano: 1966, 1054.

———. General Audience on June 6th, 1973, in *La documentation catholique,* 1635 (July 1st, 1973): 601.

Perrier, J. *Revival of Scholastic Philosophy in the Nineteenth Century.* New York: AMS, 1967.

Perrone, J. *Praelectiones theologicae.* 4 vols. Paris: Gaume Fratres Bibliopolae, 1883.

Petre, M. *Autobiography and Life.* Vol. 2. London: Arnold, 1912.

———, ed. *Essays on Faith and Immortality.* London: Arnold, 1914.

———. *Von Hügel and Tyrrell: The Story of a Friendship.* New York: E. P. Dutton and Co., 1937.

Philips, G. "Dogmatic Constitution on the Church: History of the Constitution." In Vorgrimler, *Commentary on the Documents of Vatican II,* 1:105–37.

———. *L'Église et son Mystère au IIe Concile du Vatican.* Paris: Desclée, 1967.

Pieper, J. *The Silence of St. Thomas.* South Bend, IN: St. Augustine's, 1999.

Pohle, J. *The Sacraments in General. Baptism. Confirmation. A Dogmatic Treatise I.* Adapted by A. Preuss. London: B. Herder, 1931.

Polanyi, M., and H. Prosch. *Meaning.* Chicago: University of Chicago Press, 1975.

Post, P. "Life Cycle Rituals: A Ritual-Liturgical Perspective." *Questions Liturgiques/ Studies in Liturgy* 83, no. 1 (2002): 10–29.

Potterie, I. de la. "History and Truth." In Latourelle and O'Collins, *Problems and Perspectives of Fundamental Theology,* 87–104.

———. "The Spiritual Sense of Scripture." *Communio: International Catholic Review* 23 (1996): 738–56.

Potvin, T. Review of R. Latourelle, *Christ and the Church: Signs of Salvation.* *The American Ecclesiastical Review* 168 (1974): 358–60.

Potworowski, C. "Dechristianization, Socialization and Incarnation in Marie-Dominique Chenu." *Science et Esprit* 43 (1991): 17–54.

Poulat, E. *Église contre bourgeoisie.* Tournai: Casterman, 1977.

Power, D. *Unsearchable Riches: The Symbolic Nature of Liturgy.* New York: Pueblo, 1984.

———. "The Anamnesis: Remembering, We Offer." In *New Eucharistic Prayers*, ed. F. Senn, 146–68. New York: Paulist, 1987.

Power, D., R. Duffy, and K. Irwin. "Sacramental Theology: A Review of Literature." *Theological Studies* 55 (1994): 657–705.

Powers, J. *Spirit and Sacrament: The Humanizing Experience.* New York: Seabury, 1973.

Pozzo, G. "Method I: Systematic Theology." In Latourelle and Fisichella, *Dictionary of Fundamental Theology*, 670–84.

Provencher, N. "Modernism." In Latourelle and Fisichella, *Dictionary of Fundamental Theology*, 719–23.

———. *La révélation et son développment dans l'Église selon Alfred Loisy.* Ottawa: Dissertatione ad Lauream in Facultate Theologiae Pontificiae Gregorianae, 1972.

Puntel, L. B. "Participation." In Rahner, *Encyclopedia of Theology: The Concise Sacramentum Mundi*, 1160–63.

Raguer, H. "An Initial Profile of the Assembly." In *History of Vatican II.* Vol. 2: *The Formation of the Council's Identity, First Period and Intersession, October 1962—September 1963*, ed. G. Alberigo and J. Komonchak, 167–232. Louvain: Peeters, 1997.

Rahner, K. *Christian at the Crossroads.* London: Darton, Longman and Todd, 1975.

———. "Christianity and the Non-Christian Religions." In *Theological Investigations*, trans. K-H. Kruger, vol. 5, 115–34. London: Darton, Longman and Todd, 1966.

———. "Christology within an Evolutionary View of the World." In *Theological Investigations*, trans. K-H. Kruger, vol. 5., 157–92. London: Darton, Longman and Todd, 1966.

———. "The Church's Commission to Bring Salvation and the Humanization of the World." In *Theological Investigations*, trans. D. Bourke, vol. 14, 295–313. London: Darton, Longman and Todd, 1976.

———. "Concerning the Relationship Between Nature and Grace." In *Theological Investigations*, trans. C. Ernst, vol. 1, 297–317. London: Darton, Longman and Todd, 1961.

———. "Considerations on the Active Role of the Person in the Sacramental Event." In *Theological Investigations*, trans. D. Bourke, vol. 14, 161–84. London: Darton, Longman and Todd, 1976.

———. "Current Problems in Christology." In *Theological Investigations*, trans. C. Ernst, vol. 1, 149–200. London: Darton, Longman and Todd, 1961.

———. "The Death of Jesus and the Closure of Revelation." In *Theological Investigations*, trans. E. Quinn, vol. 18, 132–42. London: Darton, Longman and Todd, 1975.

———. "The Development of Dogma." In *Theological Investigations*, trans. C. Ernst, vol. 1, 39–77. London: Darton, Longman and Todd, 1974.

———. "Der dreifaltige Gott als transzendenter Urgrund der Heilsgeschichte." In *Mysterium Salutis*, ed. J. Feiner and M. Löhrer, vol. 2, 317–410. Einsiedeln: Benziger, 1965; English translation, J. Donceel, *The Trinity*. London: Burns and Oates, 1970.

———. *Encyclopaedia of Theology: The Concise Sacramentum Mundi*. New York: Crossroad, 1991.

———. "The Eternal Significance of the Humanity of Jesus for Our Relationship with God." In *Theological Investigations*, trans. K-H Kruger and B. Kruger, vol. 3, 35–46. London: Darton, Longman and Todd, 1967.

———. "Experience of Self and Experience of God." In *Theological Investigations*, trans. D. Bourke, vol. 13, 122–32. London: Darton, Longman and Todd, 1975.

———. "Experience of the Spirit and Existential Commitment." In *Theological Investigations*, trans. D. Morland, vol. 16, 24–34. London: Darton, Longman and Todd, 1979.

———. "Experiencing Easter." In *Theological Investigations*, trans. D. Burke, vol. 7, 159–68. London: Darton, Longman and Todd, 1971.

———. "The Function of the Church as Critic of Society." In *Theological Investigations*, trans. D. Bourke, vol. 12, 229–249. London: Darton, Longman and Todd, 1974.

———. *Geist in Welt*. Innsbruck: Felizian Rauch, 1939; English translation, W. V. Dych, *Spirit in the World*. New York: Sheed and Ward, 1968.

———. *Grundkurs des Glaubens: Einführung in den Begriff des Christentums*. Freiburg: Herder, 1976; English translation, W. V. Dych, *Foundations of Christian Faith*. London: Darton, Longman and Todd, 1978.

———. "The Historicity of Theology." In *Theological Investigations*, trans. G. Harrison, vol. 9, 64–82. London: Darton, Longman and Todd, 1972.

———. "History of the World and Salvation History." In *Theological Investigations*, trans. K.-H. Kruger, vol. 5, 97–114. London: Darton, Longman and Todd, 1966.

———. *Hörer des Wortes: Zur Grundlegung einer Religionsphilosophie*. Munich: Kösel-Puset, 1941; English translation, R. Walls, *Hearers of the Word*. London: Sheed and Ward, 1969.

———. "Incarnation." In *Sacramentum Mundi: An Encyclopaedia of Theology*, ed. K. Rahner, C. Ernst, and K. Smyth, vol. 3, 110–18. New York: Herder and Herder, 1969.

———. *Kirche und Sakramente.* Freiburg: Herder, 1961; English translation, W. J. O'Hara, *The Church and the Sacraments.* London: Burns and Oates, 1963.

———. "Nature and Grace." In *Theological Investigations,* trans. K. Smyth, vol. 4, 36–73. London: Darton, Longman and Todd, 1966.

———. *A New Baptism in the Spirit: Confirmation Today.* Denville: Dimension, 1975.

———. "On the Theology of Worship." In *Theological Investigations,* trans. E. Quinn, vol. 19, 141–49. London: Darton, Longman and Todd, 1984.

———. "Priest and Poet." In *Theological Investigations,* trans. K.-H. Kruger and B. Kruger, vol. 3, 294–318. London: Darton, Longman and Todd, 1967.

———. "Reflections on Methodology in Theology." In *Theological Investigations,* trans. D. Bourke, vol. 11, 68–114. London: Darton, Longman and Todd, 1974.

———. "Resurrection." In Rahner, *Encyclopaedia of Theology: The Concise Sacramentum Mundi,* 1430–31.

———. *Die Siebenfältige Gabe.* Munich: Ars Sacra, 1974; English translation, *Meditations on the Sacraments.* London: Burns and Oates, 1979.

———. "Some Implications of the Scholastic Concept of Uncreated Grace." In *Theological Investigations,* trans. C. Ernst, vol. 1, 319–346. London: Darton, Longman and Todd, 1961.

———. "Theology and Anthropology." In *Theological Investigations,* trans. G. Harrison, vol. 9, 28–45. London: Darton, Longman and Todd, 1972.

———. "The Theology of Symbol." In *Theological Investigations,* trans. K. Smyth, vol. 4, 221–52. London: Darton, Longman and Todd, 1966.

———. "Theology of the New Testament." In *Theological Investigations,* trans. K.-H. Kruger, vol. 5, 23–41. London: Darton, Longman and Todd, 1966.

———. "Towards a Fundamental Theological Interpretation of Vatican II." *Theological Studies* 40 (1979): 716–27.

———. "The Word and the Eucharist." In *Theological Investigations*, trans. K. Smyth, vol. 4, 253–86. London: Darton, Longman and Todd, 1966.

Rahner, K., and H. Vorgrimler. *Theological Dictionary*. New York: Herder and Herder, 1965.

Ratté, J. *Three Modernists*. London: Sheed and Ward, 1968.

Ratzinger, J. *Behold the Pierced One: An Approach to a Spiritual Christology*. San Francisco: Ignatius, 1986.

———. "Dogmatic Constitution on Divine Revelation: Origin and Background." In Vorgrimler, *Commentary on the Documents of Vatican II*, 3:155–66.

———. *Eschatology: Death and Eternal Life*. In *Dogmatic Theology*, ed. Johann Auer and Joseph Ratzinger, vol. 9. Washington D. C.: Catholic University of America, 1988.

———. *The Feast of Faith: Approaches to a Theology of the Liturgy*. San Francisco: Ignatius, 1986.

———. *Introduction to Christianity*. London: Burns and Oates, 1969.

———. *Milestones: Memoirs: 1927–1977*. San Francisco: Ignatius, 1998.

———. *A New Song for the Lord: Faith in Christ and Liturgy Today*. San Francisco: Ignatius, 1996.

———. *Pilgrim Fellowship of Faith: The Church as Communion*. San Francisco: Ignatius, 2002.

———. *Principles of Catholic Theology*. San Francisco: Ignatius, 1989.

———. *The Spirit of the Liturgy*. San Francisco: Ignatius, 2000.

———. *Theologie der Liturgie. Die sakramentale Begründung christlicher Existenz*. In *Joseph Ratzinger Gesammelte Schriften*, ed. G. Müller, vol. 11. Freiburg: Herder, 2008.

———. "The Transmission of Divine Revelation." In Vorgrimler, *Commentary on the Documents of Vatican II*, 3:181–98.

Reardon, B. *Roman Catholic Modernism*. London: Adam and Charles Black, 1970.

———. "Roman Catholic Modernism." In *Nineteenth Century Religious Thought in the West*, ed. N. Smart, J. Clayton, S. Katz, and P. Sherry, vol. 2, 141–77. Cambridge: Cambridge University Press, 1985.

Reed, J. C. *Francis Thompson: Man and Poet*. London: Routledge & Kegan Paul, 1959.

Reinhold, H. "Timely Tracts: Dom Odo Casel." *Orate Fratres* 22 (1948): 366–72.

Ricoeur, P. *The Conflict of Interpretations*. Evanston: Northwestern University Press, 1974.

———. *Interpretation Theory*. Fort Worth: Texas Christian University, 1976.

Ritschl, D. *Memory and Hope*. New York: Macmillan, 1966.

Rocha, P. "The Principal Manifestation of the Church (SC41)." In Latourelle, *Vatican II: Assessment and Perspectives*, 2:3–26.

Rode, F. *Le miracle dans la controverse moderniste*. Paris: Desclée, 1965.

Roguet, A.-M. *Les Sacrements* [*Somme théologique* 3ª. 60–65]. Paris: Aubier, 1945.

———. *The Sacraments: Signs of Life*. London: Blackfriars, 1954.

Rondeau, M.-J., ed. *Jean Daniélou 1905–1974*. Paris: Éditions du Cerf, 1975.

Roo, W. van. "Reflections on Karl Rahner's *Kirche und Sakramente*." *Gregorianum* 44 (1963): 465–500.

Rosato, P. J. *Introduzione alla Teologia dei Sacramenti*. Casale Monferrato: Piemme, 1992.

———. "The Prophetic Acts of Jesus, the Sacraments and the Kingdom." In *Gottes Zukunft—Zukunft der Welt, Festschrift für Jürgen Moltmann zum 60. Geburtstag*, ed. H. Deuser et al., 59–67. Munich: Chr. Kaiser, 1986.

Rousseau, O. *Histoire du mouvement liturgique, Esquisse historique depuis le début du XIX siècle jusqu'au pontificat de Pie X*. Paris: Éditions du Cerf, 1945; English translation, *The Progress of the Liturgy: An Historical Sketch from the Beginning of the Nineteenth Century to the Pontificate of Pius X*. Westminster: Newman, 1951.

———."The Liturgical Movement from Dom Guéranger to Pius XII." In *The Church at Prayer*. Vol. 1: *Introduction to the Liturgy,* ed. A. G. Martimort, 51–57. Shannon: Irish University Press, 1968.

———. *Storia del movimento liturgico*. Milano: Edizioni Paoline, 1961.

Rousselot, P. *The Eyes of Faith,* English translation J. Donceel. New York: Fordham University Press, 1990.

Routhier, G., ed. *L'Église canadienne et vatican II*. Montréal: Éditions Paulines, 1997.

Rowland, T. *Ratzinger's Faith: The Theology of Pope Benedict XVI*. Oxford: Oxford University Press, 2008.

Ruffini, E. "I grandi temi della teologia contemporanea dei Sacramenti." *Rivista Liturgica* 54 (1967): 39–52.

Ruggieri, G. "Faith and History." In *The Reception of Vatican II*, ed. G. Alberigo, J.-P. Jossua, and J. Komonchak, 91–114. Washington, D. C.: Catholic University of America Press, 1987.

———. "The First Doctrinal Clash." In *History of Vatican II*. Vol. 2: *The Formation of the Council's Identity, First Period and Intersession, October 1962—September 1963*, ed. G. Alberigo and J. Komonchak, 233–49. Louvain: Peeters, 1997.

Rynne, X. *Letters From Vatican City: Vatican Council II (First Session): Background and Debates*. London: Faber and Faber, 1963.

Sacerdotal Communities of St. Severin of Paris and St. Joseph of Nice. "The Liturgical Movement." In *The Twentieth Century Encyclopaedia of Catholicism*, vol. 115, 31–38. New York: McGraw-Hill, 1967.

Sagovsky, N. *"On God's Side": A Life of George Tyrrell*. Oxford: Clarendon, 1990.

Sales, M. *Surnaturel: Études historiques*. Paris: Desclée de Brouwer, 1991.

Sartore, D. "Alcuni recenti trattati di sacramentaria fondamentale, considerazioni di un liturgista." *Rivista Liturgica* 75 (1988): 321–39.

———. "Segno/Simbolo." In Sartore and Triacca, *Nuovo Dizionario di Liturgia*, 1279–89.

Sartore, D., and A. M. Triacca, eds. *Nuovo Dizionario di Liturgia*. Milan: Edizioni Paoline, 1983.

Sarup, M. *Post-Structuralism and Postmodernism*. London: Harvester Wheatsheaf, 1993.

Schillebeeckx, E. *Christ: The Christian Experience in the Modern World*. London: SCM, 1980.

———. *Christ the Sacrament of the Encounter with God*. London: Sheed and Ward, 1963.

———. *God the Future of Man*. New York: Sheed and Ward, 1968.

———. *Interim Report on the Books "Jesus" and "Christ."* London: SCM, 1980.

———. *Jesus: An Experiment in Christology*. New York: Seabury, 1979.

———. *De Sacramentele Heilseconomie: Theologische bezinning op S. Thomas' sacramentenleer in het licht van de traditie en van de hedendaagse sacramentsproblematiek*. Antwerp: H. Nelissen, 1952.

———. *Het tweede Vaticaans Concilie*. Bilthoven: Uitgeverij H. Nelissen, 1966; English translation, *Vatican II: The Real Acievement*. London: Sheed and Ward, 1967.

Schilson, A. "Erneuerung des Sakramententheologie im 20. Jahrhundert." *Liturgisches Jahrbuch* 37 (1987): 18–41.

———. *Theologie als Sakramententheologie. Die Mysterientheologie Odo Casels*, 2nd ed. Tübingen: Matthias Grünewald, 1987.

Schleiermacher, F. *Der christliche Glaube nach den Grundsätzen der evangelischen Kirche un Zusammenhange dargestellt*. 2 vols. 2nd ed. Berlin: G. Reimer, 1830–31; English translation, *The Christian Faith*. New York: Harper and Row, 1963.

Schmemann, A. *Introduction to Liturgical Theology*. Crestwood, NY: St. Vladimir's Seminary, 1966.

———. "Theology and Liturgical Tradition." In *Worship In Scripture and Tradition*, ed. M. Shepherd, 165–78. New York: Oxford University Press, 1963.

Schmidt, H. *La Constituzione sulla Sacra Liturgica, Teso-Genesi-Commento, Documentazione*. Rome: Borla, 1966.

Schnackenburg, R. *New Testament Theology Today*. London: Geoffrey Chapman, 1963.

———. *Die Sakramente im Johannesevangelium, Sacra Pagina. Miscellanea biblica congressus internationalis catholici de re biblica*. Vol. 2. Gembloux: J. Duculot, 1959.

Schoof, T. *Aggiornamento*. Baarn: Het Wereldvenster, 1970; English translation, *A Survey of Catholic Theology 1800–1970*. New York: Paulist Newman, 1970.

Schultenover, D. "George Tyrrell: Devout Disciple of Newman." *The Heythrop Journal* 33, no. 1 (1992): 20–44.

Schüssler-Fiorenza, F. "The Resurrection of Jesus and Roman Catholic Fundamental Theology." In *The Resurrection: An Interdisciplinary Symposium on the Resurrection of Jesus*, ed. S. Davis, D. Kendall, and G. O'Collins, 211–48. New York: Oxford University Press, 1997.

Seasoltz, K. Review of S. Marsili, *Anàmnesis* series. *Worship* 60 (1986): 84–86.

Sheets, J. Review of A. Dulles, *Models of the Church. America* 144 (March 23, 1974): 224.

———. Review of G. Martelet, *The Risen Christ and the Eucharistic World. Worship* 51 (1977): 465–67.

Sierra, A. *La Revelación Según René Latourelle*. Tesi Gregoriana, Serie Teologia, 60. Rome: Editrice Pontificia Università Gregoriana, 2000.

Simian-Yofre, H. "Old and New Testament: Participation and Analogy." In Latourelle, *Vatican II: Assessment and Perspectives*, 1:267–98.

Skelley, M. *The Liturgy of the World: Karl Rahner's Theology of Worship*. Collegeville, MN: Liturgical Press, 1991.

Soderini, E. *Il pontificato di Leone XIII.* 3 vols. Milan: A. Mondadori, 1932–33; English translation, B. Carter, *The Pontificate of Leo XIII*, vol.1, and *Leo XIII, Italy and France*, vol. 2. London: Burns, Oates and Washbourne, 1934.

Stanks, T. "The Eucharist: Christ's Self-Communication in a Revelatory Event." *Theological Studies* 28 (1967): 27–50.

Talar, C. J. T. "Innovation and Biblical Interpretation," in Jodock, *Catholicism Contending with Modernity*, 191–211.

Tappeiner, D. "Sacramental Causality in Aquinas and Rahner: Some Critical Thoughts." *The Scottish Journal of Theology* 28 (1975): 243–57.

Terrin, A., ed. *Liturgia e incarnazione.* Padova: Edizioni Messaggero—Abbazia di Santa Giustinia, 1997.

TeSelle, E. "The Problem of Nature and Grace." *The Journal of Religion* 45 (July 1965): 238–41.

———. "Review of A. Dulles, *Models of Revelation.*" *Religious Studies Review* 10, no. 3 (1984): 38.

Thibault, P. *Savoir et pouvoir: Philosophie thomiste et politique cléricale au XIX siècle.* Québec: Les Presses de l'Université Laval, 1972.

Thomas, R. S. *Collected Poems.* London: Phoenix, 1996.

Thompson, W. Review of A. Dulles, *Models of Revelation. Theological Studies* 45 (1984): 357–59.

Thompson, W. M. *The Jesus Debate.* New York: Paulist, 1985.

Tillard, J. M. R. "La triple dimension du signe sacramentel." in *Nouvelle Revue Théologique* 83 (1961): 225–54.

Torrell, J.-P. Review of R. Latourelle, *Miracles de Jésus et théologie du miracle. Revue Thomiste* 86 (1986): 654–59.

Tracy, D. *Blessed Rage for Order.* New York: Seabury, 1975.

———. "*Models of God*: Three Observations." In *Readings in Modern Theology*, ed. R. Gill, 82–86. London: SPCK, 1995.

———. "The Necessity and Insufficiency of Fundamental Theology." In Latourelle and O'Collins, *Problems and Perspectives in Fundamental Theology*, 23–36.

———. "Theology and the Many Faces of Postmodernity." In *Readings in Modern Theology*, ed. R. Gill, 225–35. London: SPCK, 1995.

Tresmontant, C., ed. *Maurice Blondel—Lucien Laberthonnière: Correspondance philosophique*. Paris: Seuil, 1961.

Triacca, A.-M. "Teologia della liturgia o teologia liturgica? Contributo di P. Salvatore Marsili per una chiarificazione." *Rivista Liturgica* 80 (1993): 267–89.

Tugwell, S. *Ways of Imperfection*. Springfield: Templegate, 1985.

Tyrrell, G. *Christianity at the Cross-Roads*. London: Longmans, Green and Co., 1909; London: George Allen and Unwin Ltd., 1963.

———. *Lex Credendi: A Sequel to Lex Orandi*. London: Longmans, Green and Co., 1906.

———. "A Perverted Devotion." *Weekly Register* 100 (1899): 797–800.

———. "The Relation of Theology to Devotion." *The Month* 94 (1899): 461–73.

———. *Through Scylla and Charybdis or The Old Theology and the New*. London: Longmans, Green and Co., 1907.

Vagaggini, C. *Il senso teologico della Liturgia. Saggio di liturgia teologica generale*. Rome: Edizioni Paoline, 1957.

Vaillancourt, R. *Vers un Renouveau de la Théologie Sacramentaire*. Montreal: La Corporation des Éditions Fides, 1977; English translation, M. J. O'Connell, *Toward a Renewal of Sacramental Theology*. Collegeville, MN: Liturgical Press, 1979.

Vandervelde, G. "The Grammar of Grace: Karl Rahner as a Watershed in Contemporary Theology." *Theological Studies* 49 (1988): 445–59.

Vidler, A. "Foreword." In Tyrrell, *Christianity at the Cross-Roads*.

Vogel, D. W. ed. *Primary Sources of Liturgical Theology: A Reader.* Collegeville, MN: Liturgical Press, 2000.

Vorgrimler, H., ed. *Commentary on the Documents of Vatican II.* 3 vols. London: Burns and Oates, 1967–69.

———. *Understanding Karl Rahner: An Introduction to His Life and Thought.* London: SCM, 1986.

Wainwright, G. *Doxology: The Praise of God in Worship Doctrine and Life. A Systematic Theology.* New York: Oxford University Press, 1980.

———. "Tradition as a Liturgical Act." In *The Quadrilog: Tradition and the Future of Ecumenism. Essays in Honour of George H. Tavard*, ed. K. Hagen, 129–46. Collegeville, MN: Liturgical Press, 1994.

Walgrave, J. *Unfolding Revelation.* Philadelphia: Westminster, 1972.

Ward, W. "Leo XIII." *The Fortnightly Review* 80 (1903): 252–65.

Weaver, M. J., ed. *Letters from a "Modernist": The Letters of George Tyrrell to Wilfred Ward 1893–1908.* Shepherdstown, WV: Patmos, 1981.

———. *Newman and the Modernists.* Lanham, MD: University Press of America, 1985.

Weigel, G. "The Historical Background of the Encyclical *Humani Generis.*" *Theological Studies* 12 (1951): 208–30.

———. "Leo XIII and Contemporary Theology." In *Leo XIII and the Modern World*, ed. E. T. Gargan, 213–26. New York: Sheed and Ward, 1961.

———. "Re-Viewing Vatican II: An Interview with George A. Lindbeck." *First Things* 48 (1994): 44–50.

Wheelwright, P. H. *Metaphor and Reality.* Bloomington: Indiana University Press, 1962.

White, J. F. *Roman Catholic Worship: Trent to Today.* New York: Paulist, 1995.

Wicks, J. *Introduction to Theological Method.* Casale Monferrato: Piemme, 1994.

Wiles, M. Review of A. Dulles, *The Craft of Theology. Theology* 96 (1993): 402–4.

Wiltgen, R. *The Rhine Flows into the Tiber: The Unknown Council*. New York: Hawthorn, 1967.

Wong, J. H. P. *Logos-Symbol in the Christology of Karl Rahner*. Rome: LAS, 1984.

Wood, S. *Spiritual Exegesis and the Church in the Theology of Henri de Lubac*. Grand Rapids: Eerdmans, 1998.

———. *Sacramental Orders*. Collegeville, MN: Liturgical Press, 2000.

Zapelena, T. *De Ecclesia Christi—Pars Apologetica*. Rome: Typis Pontificiae Universitatis Gregorianae, 1946.

Ziadé, I. "Conciliar Speech, 15 September 1964." In *Third Session Council Speeches of Vatican II*, ed. W. K. Leahy and A. T. Massimini, 9. Glen Rock: Paulist, 1966, 9.

Zizioulas, J. *Being as Communion: Studies in Personhood and the Church*. 2nd ed. Crestwood, NY: St. Vladimir's Seminary, 1993.

Index of Names

Achtemeier, Paul, J., 171, 446n90

Adam, Karl, 379, 380, 397

Alberigo, Giuseppe, 360

Alberta, Michele, 274, 450

Alexander, Archibald, 32n51

Ambrose, St., 475

Aquinas, *see* Thomas, St.

Aristotle, 28, 29, 51

Arnold, Matthew, 5

Aubert, Roger, 21n18

Augustine, St. (of Hippo), 36, 58, 202n44, 354, 475, 502

Baldovin, John F., 497n1, 499

Bautain, Louis, 45-7, 50

Beauduin, Lambert, 78-81

Bellarmine, Robert, St., 201

Benoit, Pierre, 341n10

Bergson, Henri, 406n1

Beumer, Johannes, 34n58

Billot, Louis, 3, 5n15, 6, 55-7, 62

Blondel, Maurice, 28, 58, 59-62, 65, 67, 68, 94, 95, 123n25, 262, 406n1

Boff, Leonardo, 488

Bonaventure, St., 35

Bosc, Jean, 456n117

Bouillard, Henri, 44n83

Bourke, David, 475

Bouyer, Louis, 344

Bremond, Henri, 64

Brown, Raymond, 206, 207n63, 300

Browning, Robert, 300

Brunsmann, Johannes, 56n118

Bouyer, Louis, 343n18

Buckley, J. J., 481

Bultmann, Rudolf, 172, 341n10

Butler, Christopher, 339n5, 364, 425n49

Cajetan, Thomas (Cardinal), 35

Caronti, Emmanuelle, 271